Listen to This

Fourth Edition

To Bob

Listen to This

Fourth Edition

MARK EVAN BONDS

Department of Music
University of North Carolina at Chapel Hill

with contributions by Jocelyn Neal (popular music), Joseph Kaminski and
N. Scott Robinson (world music), and William Gibbons (video game music)

 Pearson

Senior Publisher: Roth Wilkofsky
Editorial Assistant: Laura Hernandez
Field Marketing Manager: Kelly Ross
Field Marketing Assistant: Andrea Giaimis
Senior Managing Editor: Melissa Feimer
Content Producer: Barbara Marttine Cappuccio
Cover Design: Kathryn Foot

Cover Images: Barn owl flight landing sequence #BHN27H / Andy Harmer/ ©Andy Harmer / Alamy Stock. photo. Earbuds / Adobe Stock file# 79644667 author: ipopba
Senior Producer: Rich Barnes
Full-Service Project Management: SPi Global/Julie Kidd
Composition: SPi Global

Acknowledgements of third party content appear in the credits section, which constitutes an extension of this copyright page.

Library of Congress Cataloging-in-Publication Data
Names: Bonds, Mark Evan, author. | Neal, Jocelyn R., 1973-, author | Kaminski, Joseph, author. | Robinson, N. Scott, author. | Gibbons, William, author.
Title: Listen to this / Mark Evan Bonds, with contributions by Jocelyn Neal, Joseph Kaminski, N. Scott Robinson, and William Gibbons.
Description: Fourth edition. | NY NY : Pearson, 2017. | Includes index.
Identifiers: LCCN 2016027412 (print) | LCCN 2016027939 (ebook) | ISBN 9780134419510 | ISBN 9780134475172
Subjects: LCSH: Music appreciation. | Music—History and criticism.
Classification: LCC MT90 .B63 2017 (print) | LCC MT90 (ebook) | DDC 780—dc23
LC record available at https://lccn.loc.gov/2016027412

1 16

Student Edition
ISBN-10: 0-13-441951-0
ISBN-13: 978-0-13-441951-0

Books a la Carte
ISBN-10: 0-13-441980-4
ISBN-13: 978-0-13-441980-0

Contents

Listen to This: Listening Guides and Recordings

The audio examples for *Listen to This* are available through these sources:

- **Revel**, where audio streams at the click of a button within each chapter in two places—"Listen to This First" and "Listening Guide." The former streams through a simple audio player and the latter streams through an interactive player that synchronizes music with guided narration or text.
- **MyMusicLab**, where audio streams from playlists organized by chapter. Again, it is possible to listen to the music with or without a companion listening guide.
- **Mp3 download** to any computer or portable device, available by purchase of a download card with a unique code. Timings in the print listening guide correspond to the timings within these audio files. Note however that digital files play at slightly different speeds on different devices, and timings may vary.

Chapter	Composer, Title	Listen to This First Page Number	Listening Guide Page Number	Download Track
Introduction	Examples illustrating the Elements of Music			1–16
Introduction	Benjamin Britten, *Young Person's Guide to the Orchestra*		18	17
1	Hildegard von Bingen, *Play of Virtues* (excerpt)	25	30	18
2	San Ildefonso Indians of New Mexico, *Eagle Dance*	33	36	19
3	Plainchant Alleluia, "Caro mea"	38	40	20
4	Francesco Landini, "Behold, Spring"	42	45	21
5	Guillaume de Machaut, "No More than One Man Could Count the Stars"	48	50	22
6	Alfonso el Sabio, *Songs to the Virgin Mary*, no. 147, "The Talking Sheep"	52	55	23
7	Josquin des Prez, "The Cricket"	64	67	24
8	Thomas Weelkes, "Since Robin Hood"	70	73	25
9	William Byrd, "Sing Joyfully"	76	79	26
10	Giovanni Pierluigi da Palestrina, *Pope Marcellus Mass*, "Gloria"	82	86	27
11	Rhyming Singers of the Bahamas, "My Lord Help Me to Pray"	89	92	28
12	Tielman Susato, *Moorish Dance*	94	97	29
13	Claudio Monteverdi, *Orpheus*, selection from Act II	108	111	30
14	Henry Purcell, *Dido and Aeneas*, selections	114	118	31–32
15	Mbuti Pygmies, "Marriage Celebration Song"	121	124	33
16	Barbara Strozzi, "Revenge"	127	130	34
17	Antonio Vivaldi, *The Four Seasons*, "Winter," first movement	134	138	35

Chapter	Composer, Title	Listen to This First Page Number	Listening Guide Page Number	Download Track
18	Johann Sebastian Bach, Fugue in G Minor, BWV 578 ("Little")	141	145	36–37
19	Johann Sebastian Bach, Brandenburg Concerto no. 2 in F Major, BWV 1047, finale	149	152	38
20	Johann Sebastian Bach, Cantata 140: *Awake, a Voice Calls to Us*, selections	155	160	39–40
21	George Frideric Handel, *Messiah*, selections	162	167	41–42
22	Joseph Haydn, String Quartet in C Major, op. 76, no. 3, second movement	178	184	43
23	Master Musicians of the Ikuta-ryu, *Cherry Blossom*	187	190	44
24	Joseph Haydn, Symphony no. 102 in B-flat Major, third and fourth movements	193	200	45–46
25	Wolfgang Amadeus Mozart, Symphony no. 40 in G Minor, K. 550, first movement	203	208	47
26	Wolfgang Amadeus Mozart, Piano Concerto in A Major, K. 488, first movement	213	218	48
27	Wolfgang Amadeus Mozart, *The Marriage of Figaro*, Act I, "Cosa sento"	221	224	49
28	Jingju, "The Reunion"	229	232	50
29	William Billings, "Chester"	234	238	51
30	Ludwig van Beethoven, Symphony no. 5 in C Minor, op. 67	248	252	52–55
31	Franz Schubert, "Erlkönig," D. 328	258	260	56
32	Felix Mendelssohn, *Overture to a Midsummer Night's Dream*	265	268	57
33	Hector Berlioz, *Symphonie fantastique*, fourth movement ("March to the Scaffold")	271	274	58
34	Fanny Mendelssohn Hensel, Piano Trio in D Minor, op. 11, third movement ("Song")	277	279	59
35	Robert Schumann, "Dedication"	282	286	60
36	Clara Wieck Schumann, "Forward!"	290	292	61
37	Frédéric Chopin, Mazurka in B-flat, op. 7, no. 1	296	300	62
38	Louis Moreau Gottschalk, *Union: Concert Paraphrase on National Airs*	303	306	63
39	Ravi Shankar, *Raga Sindhi-Bhairavi*	310	314	64
40	Giuseppe Verdi, *La Traviata*, Act I, selection ("Follie!")	317	320	65

Chapter	Composer, Title	Listen to This First Page Number	Listening Guide Page Number	Download Track
41	Richard Wagner, *The Valkyrie*, Act III, selection ("Wotan's Farewell")	325	330	66
42	Peter Ilyich Tchaikovsky, *Swan Lake*, Act IV, finale	335	338	67
43	Johannes Brahms, Symphony no. 4 in E Minor, op. 98, finale	341	344	68
44	Antonín Dvořák, String Quartet in F Major, op. 96 ("American"), third movement	350	354	69
45	Claude Debussy, *Voiles*	365	371	70
46	Charles Ives, *The Unanswered Question*	374	378	71
47	Arnold Schoenberg, "Columbine" from *Pierrot lunaire*	380	383	72
48	Igor Stravinsky, *The Rite of Spring*, Part One	386	394	73
49	Scott Joplin, *Maple Leaf Rag*	398	403	74
50	Robert Johnson, "Terraplane Blues"	406	410	75
51	Duke Ellington, "Cotton Tail"	414	418	76
52	Charlie Parker, "Ornithology"	425	428	77
53	Ruth Crawford, *Piano Study in Mixed Accents*	432	436	78
54	Germaine Tailleferre, Concertino for Harp and Orchestra, finale	439	442	79
55	William Grant Still, "A Black Pierrot" from *Songs of Separation*	445	448	80
56	Aaron Copland, "Hoe-Down" from *Rodeo*	451	454	81
57	Béla Bartók, *Concerto for Orchestra*, second movement ("Game of Pairs")	457	460	82
58	Leonard Bernstein, "Tonight" from *West Side Story*	463	466	83
59	John Cage, Sonata II from *Sonatas and Interludes*	472	476	84
60	Gamelan Gong Kebyar of Belaluan, Bali, Kebyar Ding III, "Oncang-oncangan"	479	482	85
61	Philip Glass, "Knee Play 1" from *Einstein on the Beach*	487	490	86
62	Mahalia Jackson (performer), "It Don't Cost Very Much"	494	498	87
63	Tania León, *A la Par*, second movement ("Guaguancó")	502	505	88
64	Corey Dargel, "On This Date Every Year"	508	512	89
65	Austin Wintory, "Nascence," from *Journey*	515	518	90

Dear Reader,

Why study music? Isn't it enough just to enjoy it? It's certainly my hope that you *will* enjoy the music in this book, but I firmly believe that the more we understand things, the greater the pleasure we can take from them. Think about food: we can certainly enjoy a good dish without the foggiest notion of how it was made. But if we know what goes into it and how it was prepared, we're likely to enjoy it that much more. It even *tastes* different.

Music works the same way: if we know what goes into it—how it's put together—it will *sound* different. Music can also tell us a lot about ourselves, not only as individuals, but as members of a larger community and culture. The music we love is a big part of who we are. People often say that music is a universal language, but the fact is that every culture has its own particular way of "speaking," and some of these languages can seem very foreign to us, especially if we go back in time. The challenge for me in writing this book was to connect our passion for the music we already love with the immense varieties of music from throughout history and from all over the world.

When I started thinking about how to do this, I stumbled onto a very basic fact that others had discovered long before: that all music, no matter where or when it comes from, is built on some combination of only a few basic elements—melody, rhythm, harmony, texture, timbre, dynamics, and form—and that if we listen for those elements we can better understand how a piece of music actually works, no matter how unfamiliar it may seem to us at first. The elements of music *are* universal. They can give us a good foundation for learning—and enjoying—many new musical languages.

Listen to This encourages you to listen actively, and the new Revel digital learning environment that is part of this edition helps you do just that. The interactive listening guides available for each chapter allow you to focus on as many or as few elements as you wish: you can decide exactly how much detail you want every time you listen. Animated notations and graphical scores help take some of the mystery out of musical notation and let you "see" the music as it unfolds through time. Revel also engages you by asking you questions, creating writing environments, and providing for self-testing so that you can monitor your progress throughout the semester.

Listen to This will change the way you hear music— all kinds of music, from many different times and places, including what's already on your own personal playlist. It will give you the tools that will help you listen to the music, hear the elements, and ultimately expand your own musical horizons. There is some great music in this book, from plainchant to Gospel, from Beethoven to Broadway, and my hope is that you'll make connections here with the music you already know and love. Happy listening!

Evan Bonds

Mark Evan Bonds
Evan.Bonds@gmail.com

What's New to This Edition?

*L*isten to This introduces the study of music with an emphasis on developing listening skills within a chronologically-organized, broad range of repertoire. The unique organization—one work per chapter, examined with a focus on the elements of music—is modular, so that instructors can construct their ideal music appreciation course. This new fourth edition offers additional works to choose from as well as an enhanced digital learning environment in Revel, where text, audio, and video are seamlessly integrated.

New Narrated Listening Guides, written and spoken by Evan Bonds, offer another way for students to recognize key musical events as they listen to the chapter examples. Ideal for auditory learners, students studying on a mobile device, or even for use in the classroom, these narrated guides make judicious use of voiceovers and include brief introductions to each work.

New and expanded topic coverage includes new text and videos in the Elements section, introducing the instruments of the orchestra; a new listening guide to Britten's *Young Person's Guide to the Orchestra*; a new chapter on Palestrina's "Gloria" from the *Pope Marcellus Mass* as an example of Renaissance polyphony for the Catholic service; a new chapter on Tchaikovsky's *Swan Lake* as an example of Russian Romanticism and ballet music; "Dido's Lament" from *Dido and Aeneas* as an additional example of Purcell's expressive use of ostinato bass; and new selections for Machaut and Alfonso el Sabio based on new recording options. In addition, a number of chapters that had previously been "ebook only" are now available in print: the medieval plainchant alleluia "Caro mea," Tielman Susato's *Moorish Dance*, Robert Schumann's "Dedication," Mahalia Jackson's rendition of "It Don't Cost Very Much," and the Beijing opera "The Reunion." In every chapter, the text has been carefully revised to make sure that it is as clear and accessible as it is lively and engaging.

Expanded recordings package, including 90 tracks for 6½ hours of music, chosen by the author. The music is available in three options: streaming through Revel, streaming through My-MusicLab, and downloaded to your music library.

Revel[TM]: Educational Technology Designed for the Way Today's Students Read, Think and Learn

When students are engaged deeply, they learn more effectively and perform better in their courses. This simple fact inspired the creation of Revel: an immersive learning experience designed for the way today's students read, think, and learn. Built in collaboration with educators and students nationwide, Revel is the newest, fully digital way to deliver respected Pearson content.

In Revel for *Listen to This*, media interactives and assessments are integrated directly within the written narrative, providing opportunities for students to read about, listen to, and practice course material in one place.

- In every chapter, musical selections stream in two ways: in a simple audio player, located at the start of each discussion of the elements ("Listen to This First"), and in the Listening Guide player, after students have learned the key vocabulary and concepts.

- Within each Listening Guide player, there are multiple options for guided listening, so that students can pick the options that best fit their learning style and listening environment.

◊ **Interactive Listening Guides** scroll descriptions as the music is playing. Each key element in a piece is represented by a distinctly colored line, allowing students to track changes in melody, harmony, rhythm, texture, timbre, and/or dynamics as well as form. Students can move around in the piece using these lines, and then can hide lines if they want a tighter focus.

◊ **Narrated Listening Guides** combine music audio with a spoken description of what to listen for in each selection. As an alternative to reading while listening, the narrated guides—designated "Mobile Guides" when used in mobile devices—re ideal for students on-the-go as well as in the classroom.

◊ For readers who prefer a guide that scrolls from top to bottom, the vertical **Scrolling Listening Guide** is available.

◊ Animated visualizations for selected works allow users to "see" the way the music sounds. These animations were developed by the composer and educator Stephen Malinowski.

• The extensive video program includes animated notations that illustrate musical concepts even for students who do not read music. In addition, a series of brief instrument videos, featuring performances by college music students, provides a lively and informative introduction to the timbre and methods of playing orchestral instruments.

• Students have the option of listening to a spoken version of the text in which the narrator demonstrates simple musical concepts as he reads.

• Auto-graded listening quizzes and concept review quizzes in every chapter offer students the chance to apply and test their understanding of chapter content.

• Writing prompts help foster critical thinking about musical ideas. In every chapter, "Journaling" questions are geared toward developing basic skills in musical analysis, while "Shared Writing" prompts that students answer in an online discussion space ask them to apply musical concepts to their own playlists. A third type of writing assignment, the short essay, is available at the discretion of the instructor; this assignment resides in Writing Space, a site that includes resources to help students with drafting and editing and to help teachers with grading and responding.

Additional Resources & Listening Choices

Pearson recognizes that a strong set of recordings is essential to the music appreciation course. Every selection in this book is available in the recording package created in partnership with Sony Music. (See page xv for a list of recordings.) The audio examples for *Listen to This* are available through these sources:

• Revel, where audio streams at the click of a button within each chapter in two places—"Listen to This First" and "Listening Guide." The former streams through a simple audio player and the latter streams through an interactive player that synchs music with guided narration or text.

• MyMusicLab, where audio streams from playlists organized by chapter. Again, it is possible to listen to the music with or without a companion listening guide.

• Mp3 download to any computer or portable device with an audio player, available by purchase of a download card with a unique code. Timings in the print listening guide correspond to the timings within these audio files. Note however that digital files play at slightly different speeds on different devices, and timings may vary.

In addition to the paperbound textbook and the Revel digital version, *Listen to This* is available in the following formats to give you and your students more choices—and more ways to save.

- **The Books a la Carte edition** offers a convenient, three-hole-punched, loose-leaf version of the traditional text at a discounted price—allowing students to take only what they need to class. Books a la Carte editions are available both with and without access to Revel.

- **Build your own Pearson Custom course material:** for enrollments of at least 25, the Pearson Custom Library allows you to create your own textbook by (1) combining chapters from best-selling Pearson textbooks in the sequence you want and (2) adding your own content, such as a guide to a local music venue, your syllabus, or a study guide you've created. A Pearson Custom Library book is priced according to the number of chapters and may even save your students money. To begin building your custom text, visit www.pearsoncustomlibrary.com or contact your Pearson representative.

- **My Music Lab:** For students using a print text, MyMusicLab offers students access to the listening selections, listening guides, videos, and listening quizzes.

- **MediaShare** is a learning application for sharing, discussing, and assessing multimedia. Instructors easily can assign instructional videos to students, create quiz questions, and ask students to comment and reflect on the videos to facilitate collaborative discussion. MediaShare also allows students to record or upload their own videos and other multimedia projects, which they can submit to an instructor and peers for both evaluation via rubrics and review via comments at time-stamped intervals. Additionally, MediaShare allows students working in a group to submit a single artifact for evaluation on behalf of the group.

For instructors, Pearson offers the following supplements:

- **Instructor's Manual**

  Completely revised and updated for the fourth edition, this robust Instructor's Manual provides you with detailed teaching strategies and in-depth information about each chapter of Listen to This. Sections include Chapter Overview, Key Terms, Lecture and Discussion Topics, Resources, and Writing Assignments. Available as a free download at https://www.pearsonhighered.com/educator/profile/ircHomeTab.page.

- **Test Item File**

  Build your own exams and quizzes using this downloadable set of questions, including multiple choice, short answer, and essay questions. Available as a free download at https://www.pearsonhighered.com/educator/profile/ircHomeTab.page.

- **MyTest**

  Create customized tests quickly and easily using this flexible, online test-generating software that includes all questions found in the Test Item File. Available at www.pearsonmytest.com.

- **PowerPoints**

  Use this Microsoft PowerPoint® program to enhance your lecture presentations on *Listen to This*. Available as a free download at https://www.pearsonhighered.com/educator/profile/ircHomeTab.page.

*For further information on Teaching and Learning Resources, please contact your local Pearson sales representative. To find the name of your Pearson representative, go to http://www.pearsonhighered.com/educator/replocator/.

Acknowledgments

From the very start, this book has been a collaborative effort. I am particularly grateful to my co-contributors, Jocelyn Neal, University of North Carolina at Chapel Hill; William Gibbons, Texas Christian University; Joe Kaminski, Queens College; and Scott Robinson, Towson University, for their outstanding work on chapters dealing with popular, video game, and world musics. Ryan Ebright of Bowling Green State University was tremendously helpful in developing the self-tests and journal questions. Shelley Axelson and the talented students at Montclair State University did an excellent job with the new instruments of the orchestra videos created for the fourth edition. At Pearson, I am grateful to Roth Wilkofsky, senior publisher, and Barbara Cappuccio, content producer. With her keen eye for both detail and the big picture, Cynthia Ward, my development editor, has helped shaped virtually every aspect of this new fourth edition in countless ways. For their work on the listening guides, thanks to David Alick, technical product manager, and Rich Barnes, senior producer. On the permissions front, Tom Laskey (Sony) made the extraordinary routine.

Developing *Listen to This, Fourth Edition*

The fourth edition reflects the advice of the following reviewers, who provided valuable feedback on how to improve *Listen to This* for course use:

John Anderson, Polk Community College
Alison Bjorkedal, Pasadena City College
Noe Dinnerstein, John Jay College
Matthew Herman, Southcentral Kentucky Community and Technical College
Anne Kilstofte, Glendale Community College
Kevin Lambert, Angelo State University
Linsey Leach-Sparks, The University of North Carolina at Pembroke
Brenda Luchsinger, Alabama State University

Andrew Maz, Cerritos College
Matthew Mihalka, University of Arkansas
Mary Ann Nilsson, Durham Technical Community College
Peggy Lupton, Cape Fear Community College
Elizabeth Pauly, Minneapolis Community and Technical College
Robert Ross, Community College of Philadelphia
Don Saginario, The University of Tampa
Robert Starner, Antelope Valley College
James Urbanski, Pasco Hernando Community College

We are grateful to all who have provided feedback on the manuscript, design, and resource package over the course of the previous editions, including the following:

Alabama
Howard Goldstein, Auburn University
Katrina Phillips, Alabama State University
Aleesa J. Naish, University of Alabama at Birmingham
Carolyn Sanders, University of Alabama in Huntsville
Alan Flowers, University of North Alabama
Nancy Kudlawiec, University of West Alabama

Arkansas
Cynthia Thompson, Carrell Harding University
Patricia Cox, Harding University
Cliff Ganus, Harding University
Steve Cooper, Northwest Arkansas Community College
Andrew Bishko, Ozarks Technical Community College
Betsy Wahl, Ozarks Technical Community College
Larisa Hart, Ozarks Technical Community College
Milton Lites, Pulaski Technical College
Barry McVinney, Pulaski Technical College

Arizona
John T. Brobeck, University of Arizona
Patricia Cox, Harding University
Cliff Ganus, Harding University

California
Thomas W. Acord, California State University Eastbay, Hayward Campus
William Toutant, California State University, Northridge
Richard Scott Kravchak, California State University, Dominguez Hills
Timothy Howard, California State University, Northridge
Gigi Rabe, California State University, Northridge
Shulamit Hoffman, College of San Mateo
Gary McRoberts, Fullerton College
Bill Alves, Harvey Mudd College
Nedra Wheeler, Los Angeles Southwest College

David Chapman, Modesto Junior College
Gary Fair, Modesto Junior College
Laura Basini, Sacramento State
Maurice Poe, Sacramento State
Stephanie Robinson, San Diego City College
Scott Fogelsong, San Francisco Conservatory
Robert Busan, San Francisco State University
Ray Ashton, Sierra College
Cynthia McGregor, Southwestern College
Barbara Bennett, University of California, Riverside
Eric Wood, University of the Pacific
Scott Walton, Palomar College

Colorado
Tyson Alishie, Front Range Community College
Betsy Glesner, Metropolitan State College
Peter Schimpf, Metropolitan State University

Connecticut
Laura Nash, Fairfield University

District of Columbia
Emily Green, American University

Delaware .
Paul K. Fessler, Wilmington University

Florida
Josh Martin, Chipola College
Matthew Shaftel, Florida State University
John Anderson, Polk Community College
Mary Macklem, University of Central Florida
Scott Warfield, University of Central Florida
Nick Curry, University of North Florida
William P. Hayden, University of South Florida
Zoe Lang, University of South Florida

Georgia
Robert L. Harris, Armstrong Atlantic State College
Sharyn Battersby, Clayton State University
Michelle Debruyn, Columbus State University
Greg McLean, Georgia Perimete College
Francisco Albo, Georgia State University
Marva Carter, Georgia State University
Gayle Melton, Gwinnett Technical College
Edward Eanes, Kennesaw State University
Tom Rule, Macon State
Andrew Kosciesza, Montgomery County Community College
Melvin Foster, Morehouse College
Robert Tanner, Morehouse College
Beth Farber, Southern Polytechnic State University
David Haas, University of Georgia
Linda C. Ferguson, Valparaiso University

Iowa
Jeanette Hinkeldey, Buena Vista University
Carol Ayres, Iowa Lakes Community College
Jonathan Sturm, Iowa State University
Elizabeth Aubrey, University of Iowa
Jonathan Chenoweth, University of Northern Iowa

Idaho
Eric Schneller, Idaho State University
Paul Moulton, the College of Idaho

Illinois
Chris Woods, Greenville College
Rudolf Zuiderveld, Illinois College
Norman Engstrom, Illinois Valley Community College
Nora Beck, Lewis & Clark Community College
Elinor Olin, National-Louis University
Rebecca Bennett, Northwestern University
Megan McFadden, Northwestern University
Peter Webster, Northwestern University
Michael Barta, Southern Illinois University
Tim Pitchford, Southern Illinois University
Meng Chun-Chi, Southern Illinois University, Carbondale
Jeanine Wagner, Southern Illinois University, Carbondale
Gail Fleming, Southwestern Illinois College

Ed Jacobs, Southwestern Illinois College
Joseph Jones, University of Illinois at Urbana-Champaign
Maria M. Chow, DePauw University

Indiana
Heather Platt, Ball State University
Linda Pohly, Ball State University
Cathy Ann Elias, DePaul University
Matthew Balensuela, DePauw University
Constance Cook Glen, Indiana University
Carole Miklos, Indiana University Northwest
Todd Guy, Indiana Wesleyan University
Valerie Meidinger, Marian College
Sr. Mary Karita Ivancic, Notre Dame College
Patricia Hales, Purdue University Calumet
William Briegel, Indiana Tech

Kansas
Steven Maxwell, Kansas State University
Bradford Blackburn, Truman State University

Kentucky
Dr. Pamela Hopton-Jones, Appalachian State University
John Day, Elizabethtown Community College
Diane Earle, Kentucky Wesleyan College
Robert Reynolds, Lindsey Wilson College
Tom Jordan, Northern Kentucky University
Seow-Chin Ong, University of Louisville

Louisiana
La Wanda J. Blakeney, Louisiana State University
Ann Sorensen, Louisiana Tech University
Carol Britt, Nichols State University
David Johansen, Southeastern Louisiana University
Gene Ditch, St. Charles Community College
John Walker, St. Charles Community College
Jonathan Kulp, University of Louisiana at Lafayette

Massachusetts
Janice Salvucci, Curry College
Marjorie Ness, Fitchburg State College
Vincent Cee, University of Massachusetts, Amherst
Miriam Jenkins, University of Massachusetts, Amherst
Lance Lehmberg, University of Massachusetts, Amherst
David Patterson, University of Massachusetts, Boston
Mary Brown-Bonacci, Westfield State College
Sonya Lawson, Westfield State College
Matt Rippere, Westfield State College

Maine
Dennis Harrington, Thomas College

Michigan
Keith Clifton, Central Michigan University
Margaret Skidmore, Eastern Michigan University
Richard Scott Cohen, Ferris State University
Marlen Vavrikova, Grand Valley State University
Christina Hornbach, Hope College
Beth May, Hope College
Tom Donahue, Muskegon Community College
Linda Christensen, Wayne State University
Christian Matijas-Mecca, University of Michigan

Christopher Heidenreich, University of Michigan–Flint

Minnesota
Gerard Aloisio, Minnesota State University

Mississippi
Jeremy Owens, Blue Mountain College
Teri Herron, Delta State University
Darcie Bishop, Jackson State University
Sandra Cox, Northwest Mississippi Community College

Missouri
Kierstin Bible, Crowder College
Robert Ensor, Crowder College
Leigh Graf, Mineral Area College
Tom Schneideer, Missouri Western State University
Karen Werner, Moberly Area Community College
Pamela Shannon, Northwest Missouri Community College
James Sifferman, Southeast Missouri State University

Montana
Fern Glass, University of Montana
James Randall, University of Montana
Jeri Bonnin, University of Montana, Western

Nebraska
Ting-Lan Chen, University of Nebraska at Kearney
Melissa Derechailo, Wayne State College

New Hampshire
Theresa Arsenault, Nashua Community College

New Jersey
Kim Hunter, Burlington Community College
James Ieraci, Burlington Community College
Michael Billingsley, Camden County Community College
Allen Cohen, Fairleigh Dickinson University
Karen Goodman, Montclair State University
James Stepleton, Stevens Institute of Technology
Peter Coll, William Paterson University
Darren Gage, William Paterson University

New Mexico
James Leger, New Mexico Highlands University

New York
Anne Swartz, Baruch College of the City University of New York
Andrew Tomasello, Baruch College of the City University of New York
Elizabeth Wollman, Baruch College of the City University of New York
Giuseppe Gerbino, Columbia University
Laura Silverberg, Columbia University
Carmelo Comberieti, Manhattanville College
Laura Peterson, St. Bonaventure University
Brian Campbell, St. John's University
Max Lifchitz, State University of New York at Albany

North Carolina
Stephanie Lawrence-White, Bennett College for Women
Ran Whitley, Campbell University

Jocelyn Nelson, East Carolina University
Lori Wacker, East Carolina University
Glendora Powell, Louisburg College
Michael Day, North Carolina A&T State
Candace Bailey, North Carolina Central University
Alison Arnold, North Carolina State University
Katharine Boyes, Saint Augustine's College
Anne Harley, University of North Carolina, Charlotte
James A. Grymes, University of North Carolina, Charlotte
Soo Goh, University of North Carolina, Pembroke
Emily Orr, University of North Carolina, Pembroke
Barry Salwen, University of North Carolina, Wilmington
Donna Gwyn Wiggins, Winston-Salem State University

North Dakota
Dorothy Keyser, University of North Dakota

Ohio
Karen McCall Dale, Cleveland State Community College
Will Benson, Cleveland State University
Eric Ziolek, Cleveland State University
Ron Emoff, Ohio State University at Newark

Oklahoma
Mary Susan Whaley, Northeastern Oklahoma A&M College
Kristen Todd, Oklahoma Baptist University
Celeste Johnson, Oklahoma State University

Oregon
Hugh Foley, Rogers State University
Judy Cepetto Hedberg, Portland Community College
Reeves Shulstad, Salem College

Pennsylvania
Mark Jelinek, Bloomsburg University
Ann Stokes, Bloomsburg University
Barry Long, Bucknell University
Michael Boyd, Chatham University
Arlene Caney, Community College of Philadelphia
Bruce Kaminsky, Drexel University
Lynn Riley, Drexel University
Thomas Kittinger, Harrisburg Area Community College
Victor Vallo Jr., Immaculata University
Dr. Matthew Baumer, Indiana University of Pennsylvania

Ronald Horner, Indiana University of Pennsylvania
R. Todd Rober, Kutztown University of Pennsylvania
Mahlon Grass, Lock Haven University
Glen Hosterman, Lock Haven University
Dr. Daniel M. Heslink, Millersville University
Stephen Hopkins, Penn State University
John Packard, Penn State University
Charles Youman, Penn State University
Fred Dade, Shippensburg University
Margaret Lucia, Shippensburg University

South Carolina
Audrey L. Barksdale, Morris College
Fabio Parrini, North Greenville University

South Dakota
Christopher Hahn, Black Hills State University

Tennessee
Stephen Clark, Austin Peay State University
Francis Massinon, Austin Peay State University
Gail Robinson Oturu, Austin Peay State University
Ann L. Silverburg, Austin Peay State University
Ken Cardillo, Chattanooga State University
Amanda Hyberger, Chattanooga State University
Mark Lee, Columbia State Community College
David Bubsey, East Tennessee State University
Lee Weimer, Lambuth University
Eric Fisher, Middle Tennessee State University
Steve Shearon, Middle Tennessee State University
Laura Feo-Fernandez, University of Memphis
Julie Hill, University of Tennessee at Martin

Texas
Kevin Lambert, Angelo State University
Sharon Davis, Austin Community College
Kimberly Harris, Collin College
Kurt Gilman, Lamar University
Charlotte Mueller, Lee College
Charles Carson, Lone Star College–Montgomery
Mandy Morrison, McLennan Community College
Norval Crews, Midwestern State University
Gary Lewis, Midwestern State University
Beth May, Northwest Vista College
Ryan Gilchrist, Sam Houston State University
Sheryl Murphy-Manley, Sam Houston State University
Karen Marston, San Jacinto College Central

Cecilia Smith, South Texas College
James Weaver, Stephen F. Austin State University
Vicky Johnson, Tarleton State University
Marianne Henry, Texas A&M University
Prudence McDaniel, Texas A&M University
Michael Berry, Texas Tech University
Eric Fried, Texas Tech University
Lynn Lamkin, University of Houston
Josef Butts, University of Texas
Ronald Noble, University of Texas at San Antonio
Drew Stephen, University of Texas at San Antonio
James Syler, University of Texas at San Antonio
Dr. Jeffrey Emge, University of Texas at Tyler
Melissa Colgin-Abeln, University of Texas, El Paso

Utah
Luke Howard, Brigham Young University
Thomas Priest, Webster State University

Virginia
Gary Evans, Ferrum College
Mary Kay Adams, James Madison University
Vicki Curry, James Madison University
Jonathan Gibson, James Madison University
Brenda Witmer, James Madison University
Lise Keiter-Brotzman, Mary Baldwin College
Louise Billaud, New River Community College
Wendy Matthews, Northern Virginia Community College
Robert C. Ford, Tidewater Community College
John Husser, Virginia Tech

Virgin Islands
Vanessa Cornett-Murtada, University of St. Thomas

Washington
Keith Ward, University of Puget Sound
Bertil van Boer, Western Washington University
Laura Stambaugh, Western Washington University

West Virginia
Lloyd Bone, Glenville State College

Wisconsin
Daniel Fairchild, University of Wisconsin–Platteville

Wyoming
Katrina Zook, University of Wyoming

No matter what the period or style, all music grows out of some combination of these basic elements:

Melody

Melody: The Tune. Melody is a single line of notes heard in succession as a coherent unit. A melody has shape, moving up or down in ways that capture and hold our attention over a span of time. A melody is like a story: it has a beginning, a middle, and an end.

Dynamics

Dynamics: Loud to Soft. The same music can be performed at many degrees of volume, from very soft to very loud. Dynamics determine the volume of a given work or passage in a work of music.

Rhythm

Rhythm: The Time. Rhythm is the ordering of music through time. Not all music has a melody, but all music has rhythm. A drum solo, for example, makes its effect primarily through rhythm. Rhythm can operate at many levels, from a repetitive, underlying pulse or beat to rapidly changing patterns of longer and shorter sounds.

Harmony

Harmony: Supporting the Melody. Harmony is the sound created by multiple voices playing or singing together. Harmony enriches the melody by creating a fuller sound than can be produced by a single voice.

Texture

Texture: Thick and Thin. Texture is based on the number and general relationship of musical lines or voices. Every work of music has a texture from thick (many voices) to thin (a single voice). Sometimes one line or voice is more important; at other times, all the lines or voices are of equal importance.

Timbre

Timbre: The Color of Music. Timbre is the character of a sound. The same melody sounds very different when performed by a violin, a clarinet, a guitar, or a human voice. These sources can all produce the same pitch, but what makes the same melody sound different is the timbre of each one.

Form

Form: The Architecture of Music. A single melody is usually too short to constitute a complete work of music. Typically, a melody is repeated, varied, or contrasted with a different melody. The way in which all these subunits are put together—the structure of the whole—is musical form. Form is based on repetition (**A A**), variation (**A A'**), contrast (**A B**), or some combination of these three possibilities.

Word–Music Relationships

Word–Music Relationships: How Words Shape What We Hear. If there is a text to be sung, we must consider the relationship of the words to the music. How does the music capture the meaning and spirit of its text? And even if there is not a text to be sung, many works have titles that suggest how we might hear them. Titles like *Winter*, *Rodeo*, and *The Rite of Spring* strongly influence the way in which we hear these works. Some composers have even written detailed descriptions of what a particular work is about in what we call "program music."

In any given piece of music these elements work together quite closely. By isolating and examining the nature and function of each separately, we can better appreciate their specific contributions to the music we hear.

We can best hear how each of these elements works by considering how each one can change the nature of a single, well-known piece of music. We all know "The Star-Spangled Banner" from having heard it countless times, but how often have we actually *listened* to it? We can hear and recognize the tune easily enough, but listening demands that we focus on its various elements and the ways they work together. Let's look at each of the basic elements of music to see how it functions in this song.

Melody

Melody is a single line of notes heard in succession as a coherent unit. A **note** is the smallest unit of music, the building block out of which larger structures are created. So what makes the notes of a melody hang together? How is the melody of "The Star-Spangled Banner" organized? What are its individual units, and how do we know it's over, other than by having heard it so often? Think about how we sing this melody and where we draw a breath:

> O, say can you see (*breath*) by the dawn's early light (*breath*)
> What so proudly we hailed (*breath*) at the twilight's last gleaming? (*breath*)

These breaths correspond to the ends of **phrases** in both the poetry and the music. The first line of the text breaks down into two phrases (O, say can you see / by the dawn's early light), which together make a larger phrase (the entire line). This larger phrase constitutes a complete unit of thought, which happens to be a question. But do we feel a sense of closure when we sing "dawn's early light"? Not really. The phrase sounds as if it hasn't quite finished yet, which indeed it has not. Only when we get to the end of the second line ("twilight's last gleaming") do we feel a sense of arrival, a sense of completion. The second line is organized on the same principle as the first (two subphrases), but by the time we sing "at the twilight's last gleaming," we feel as if we have reached a goal of sorts. This is the end of a still larger phrase, a complete musical statement that covers the first two lines of text. When we hear a point of arrival like this, we are hearing what is called a **cadence**. A cadence is like a comma or period in a sentence: It signals the end of a unit. We sense a point of resolution, of closure. And just as commas and periods indicate different levels of completion (phrase vs. sentence), music has weaker and stronger cadences.

The melody of "The Star-Spangled Banner" is typical of the way melodies in general are constructed: Smaller units (subphrases) combine into larger units (phrases), which in turn combine into still larger units (complete statements), which end with a cadence. A series of these complete statements—musical sentences, in effect—combine to create an entire musical work. Sometimes it is helpful to listen to the structure of the smallest units; at other times, it is helpful to listen to the medium- and large-scale units. In the end, we can listen to how all these units operate together to form a complete and satisfying whole.

Another important component of melody is the nature of the **melodic motion**. Do the notes move smoothly in stepwise fashion (as in "land of the free")? Or do they make big leaps (as in "O, say can you see")? Smooth, stepwise motion with notes very close to each other is called **conjunct motion**; motion by leaps, especially large leaps, is called **disjunct motion**. Most melodies, including "The Star-Spangled Banner," consist of a combination of both kinds of motion. "The Star-Spangled Banner" alternates between the two, opening with disjunct motion ("O, say can you see") followed by a brief passage of conjunct motion ("by the dawn's"), followed in turn by a large leap downward (between "dawn's" and "early"), followed by more conjunct motion. Graphically, this variety of motion can be represented in such a way that even if you cannot read music, you can see the relationship between the downward or upward movement of the notes and the distances between them.

Disjunct motion   Conjunct motion

▶ **Graphical Score:** Melodic Motion

Very few melodies are entirely conjunct or disjunct. "The Star-Spangled Banner" is typical in combining both kinds of motion, and in balancing downward and upward contours.

The notes of any given melody typically derive from the notes of a **scale**. The familiar "do-re-mi-fa-so-la-ti-do" is a scale, a series of notes that moves stepwise and covers a complete span called an **octave** (so called because it covers eight notes).

W = Whole step   H = Half step

The distance between each note is called an **interval**. The intervals in the standard scale are mostly whole steps, with two strategically placed half steps. Every adjacent note on the keyboard, whether it is a white key or a black key, is a half step apart.

A scale by itself is not as particularly interesting as a melody, but a scale provides the notes—the essential building blocks—of a melody.

Audio:
The C Major Scale

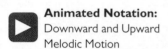

Animated Notation:
Downward and Upward Melodic Motion

The opening of "The Star-Spangled Banner" in the key of C major.

The upward or downward movement of notes is conveyed graphically in music notation. A melody that moves downward also moves downward on the staff (the system of parallel horizontal lines). Even if you cannot read music, you can see that higher notes appear higher on the staff than lower notes. This kind of visual aid can help reinforce what we hear.

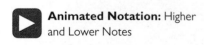

Animated Notation: Higher and Lower Notes

A higher note is on a higher line or space

A lower note is on a lower line or space

Scales can begin and end on any pair of notes. The diagrams above show a scale that begins and ends on the note "C," and a melody that centers on this same note (on "O, *say* can you *see*"). Because C is the central note of the scale on which this melody is based, we would say that this melody is in the **key** of C. But the same melody can be played in any key. Thus "The Star-Spangled Banner" can also be performed in the key of D, the key of A-flat, or in any other key.

In the standard system in use in Western music since about 1600, there are 12 keys, one on each of the 12 half steps in any octave. An octave is an interval between two notes with the same name (a lower "C" to a higher "C," or a lower "do" to a higher "do": see the earlier scale diagram). In notation, the sharp sign (#) indicates that a note is raised a half step, while a flat sign (♭) indicates that a note is lowered a half step. For each of these keys, whether it is E-flat or F-sharp or A, there are two modes: major and minor. The **major mode** corresponds to the scale produced by singing "do-re-mi-fa-so-la-ti-do." Melodies using these notes tend to sound brighter. "The Star-Spangled Banner" is in the major mode. Because it seeks to convey a mood of optimism and joy, it uses a melody derived from a major-mode scale.

The **minor mode**, by contrast, strikes most listeners as darker, more somber, and less optimistic. Most of the notes in the minor mode are also in the major. But two of the seven notes—the third ("mi") and sixth ("la")—are slightly lower, and this creates a very different kind of sound. Listen to what "The Star-Spangled Banner" would sound like in the minor mode; all the notes are the same as in the original except for "mi" and "la."

Very few national anthems begin and end in the minor mode (Israel's *Hatikva*—"The Hope"—is one notable exception). Many national anthems (and many melodies of all kinds), however, mix minor-mode phrases into the middle of melodies that begin and end in major. This creates a sense of contrasting moods that can be very effective in creating a sense of triumph over adversity, for the minor mode is especially well suited for settings of texts that express grief or anguish or (as in the case of Israel's *Hatikva*) longing. (In fact, "mode" and "mood" come from the same root word in Latin.)

Audio: Minor Mode

Dynamics

Dynamics is a term used to indicate the volume of sound, ranging from very soft to very loud. We have all heard "The Star-Spangled Banner" played at a single (loud) volume by a military band. We have also heard it performed at a level only slightly above a whisper, often by an ensemble of unaccompanied voices. And we have heard performances that move from one extreme to the other. Dynamics can change suddenly, or they can change gradually.

Volume is a relative quality: What seems loud to one listener might be barely audible to another, and vice versa. In music, it is common to use Italian terms to refer to volume:

pianissimo (pp)—very soft

piano (p)—soft

mezzo piano (mp)—medium soft

mezzo forte (mf)—medium loud

forte (f)—loud

fortissimo (ff)—very loud

Rhythm

Rhythm is the movement of music in time. The most basic framework of this temporal ordering is **meter**. In music, as in poetry, meter is an underlying pattern of beats that maintains itself consistently throughout a work. If we slowly read aloud the first line of "The Star-Spangled Banner," we can hear that it falls into a regular pattern of three-beat units: LONG-short-short, LONG-short-short, etc., with the long syllables accented (emphasized) and the short ones unaccented (′ = long; ˘ = short):

O, | say can you | see, by the | dawn's early | light?

In poetry, this meter is known as *dactylic* (LONG-short-short). In music, this meter corresponds to what is known as **triple meter**: one accented (strong) beat followed by two unaccented (weak) beats. The rhythm of the music to "The Star-Spangled Banner" is thus organized within the framework of triple meter (**1**-2-3, **1**-2-3, **1**-2-3, etc.), following the meter of its poetry. (The "O" at the very beginning of the text stands outside the first unit: Both rhythmically and textually, its function is to get us started without actually saying much of anything.)

3	**1** 2 3	**1** 2 3	**1** 2 3	**1** 2 3	**1** 2 3	**1** etc.
O,	*say* can you	*see* by the	*dawn's* early	*light* What so	*proud*-ly we	*hailed* . . . etc.

In music, each of these rhythmic units is known as a **measure**. Ordinarily, the first note of each measure receives a relatively strong accent, called the **downbeat**, which helps project the pattern of the meter, just as you would emphasize certain words (*say*, *see*, *dawn's*, *light*) if you were reading the text out loud without singing it. But meter is only one aspect of rhythm. Not every note of "The Star-Spangled Banner" is simply accented or unaccented, strong or weak. Some notes are noticeably longer in duration than others ("say can you SEE," "the rockets' red GLARE"), whereas others are extremely brief (the word *the* in "and the rockets' red glare," for example). The duration of a note—its rhythmic value—is indicated through the note's head (the oval part), its stem (the line going straight up or down from the note head), its flags (the curvy lines coming out of the stems), and other marks. In general, the simpler a note (an empty note head, no stem, no flag), the longer its rhythmic value; the more elaborate a note (a back note head and stem with many flags), the shorter its rhythmic value.

Graphical Score:
Rhythmic Values

These longer and shorter notes function flexibly within the broader framework of the underlying meter. So long as the basic pattern of the rhythmic unit is maintained (**1**-2-3), the actual number and duration of the notes within each unit can vary considerably. A melody in which all the notes were exactly the same length would be quite monotonous. Here is what the beginning of "The Star-Spangled Banner" would sound like if all the notes were of equal value:

Animated Notation: Same
Rhythmic Value

The opening of "The Star-Spangled Banner," with notes in all the same rhythmic values.

The meter is still triple (**1**-2-3), but the individual notes have lost all rhythmic differentiation.

What would "The Star-Spangled Banner" sound like in a different meter? An American composer named E. E. Bagley (1857–1922) actually worked the opening of the melody into a march he called *National Emblem*. Here, the music moves in **duple meter**, with only two beats to each measure (**1**-2, **1**-2, **1**-2, etc.). This corresponds to the function of the music, to help soldiers or band members march in step (**Left**-right, **Left**-right, **Left**-right, etc.).

Notice how the pitches (the notes) are the same as the tune we know as "The Star-Spangled Banner." But the meter—the framework of the rhythm—is fundamentally different: LONG-short, LONG-short instead of LONG-short-short, LONG-short-short. Could we march to the standard version of "The Star-Spangled Banner"? Not really, because it's in triple meter, and with two legs, it's much easier to march to duple meter.

Another important aspect of rhythm is **tempo**, the speed at which a work of music is performed. We've all heard versions of "The Star-Spangled Banner" that are very slow (often sung by an unaccompanied vocalist) and others that are quite brisk (typically as performed by a military band). Faster or slower tempos can change the mood of a work dramatically.

Audio: E. E. Bagley, *National Emblem*

Harmony

Harmony is the sound created by multiple notes played or sung simultaneously. Whether we realize it or not, we've all heard "The Star-Spangled Banner" performed in many different harmonizations. The melody stays the same, but the notes underneath the tune are different. The resulting harmony can change the character of the work, sometimes subtly, sometimes radically. There is no official version of the harmony of "The Star-Spangled Banner." (Indeed, there is not even an official version of the melody itself.)

If we think of music in terms of space, then melody can be said to function horizontally, harmony vertically. Just as melodies can outline selected notes of a scale through time, harmony presents notes drawn from a scale simultaneously, sounding together. When we hear three or more notes played at the same moment, we often speak of these as a **chord**. A melodic line can be accompanied by a series of chords that change as the melody progresses. A melody as rich as "The Star-Spangled Banner" would sound monotonous—and downright wrong—if it were harmonized with a single chord from beginning to end. The most common harmonization of the tune supports the melody with a variety of different chords, each built upward from a specific note like C (the chord C-E-G) or A (A-C-E) and so on.

We all know what a melody without harmony sounds like (just think of the many times "The Star-Spangled Banner" is sung by a soloist with no accompaniment at all). But what about harmony without melody? Here is one harmonization of "The Star-Spangled Banner" without the melody.

Audio: "The Star-Spangled Banner," Harmony without the Melody

A single melody can always be harmonized in more than one way, and "The Star-Spangled Banner" is no exception. Some harmonizations are more unconventional than others. Consider, for example, the following harmonization of the melody by the American composer Louis Moreau Gottschalk (see Chapter 38), from a piece for piano titled *Union*, written shortly after the beginning of the Civil War. Even today, almost 150 years later, musicians are still coming up with new ways of harmonizing this same melody. South City Voices, an Atlanta-based vocal jazz ensemble, recently recorded their own version of the tune. The melody is the same as the one we hear all the time, but the harmonies are not.

Audio: Louis Moreau Gottschalk, *Union,* and "The Star-Spangled Banner," performed by South City Voices

Graphical Score: "The Star-Spangled Banner," Harmonized Version

Melody

O, say can you see, by the dawn's ear - ly light? what so

Harmony: C Major   A Minor   A Minor   D Major   G Major

proud - ly we   hailed   at the   twi - light's last   gleam - ing?

C Major   G Major   D Minor   C Major   G Major   C Major

A harmonized version of "The Star-Spangled Banner," with the melody in the upper staff and the chords of the harmony in the lower staff, in red.

Harmony works on a larger scale as well. If a melody is in the key of C major, its primary harmony also centers on C major, establishing this key at the beginning as a kind of home base and returning to it at the end to create a sense of closure. We call this primary key area the **tonic**. A piece that began in one key but ended in another would sound somehow open-ended and incomplete. "The Star-Spangled Banner" begins and ends in the same key, no matter what key is used in performance. If it begins in the key of C major, it ends in C major; if it begins in G major, it ends in G major; and so on.

Texture

Texture is a function of the number and general relationship of musical lines to one another. Textures can range from thick (many voices or instrumental lines) to thin (a single voice or a single instrumental line).

When "The Star-Spangled Banner" is performed as a single melodic line, with no accompaniment at all, the texture is **monophonic** (*mono* = "single"; *phonic* = "sounding"). This may be a single soloist, or it may be a group of performers all playing or singing the same melody. When multiple performers are singing or playing a single melody together, we call this kind of monophonic texture **unison**.

When the melody is performed with a supporting accompaniment, the texture is **homophonic** (*homo* = "same," as in "sounding at the same time"). This is the most common form of performance of this particular song whenever there is a soloist. The soloist sings the melody, while an instrumental ensemble or backup chorus provides musical

Marvin Gaye sings a homophonic arrangement of "The Star-Spangled Banner."

support. Marvin Gaye's performance of "The Star-Spangled Banner" is decidedly homophonic: The focus is entirely on the melody, while the accompaniment (a drum set) stays very much in the background.

When the melody is performed against another line of equal importance, the texture is **polyphonic** (*poly* = "many"). In polyphonic texture, every line is, in effect, a melody. Think about the children's song "Row, Row, Row Your Boat," for example: When performed by several people, every voice is singing the same music, so we can't say that one voice has the melody and others don't. And yet all the voices work together to create a satisfying sound.

Polyphonic realizations of "The Star-Spangled Banner" in its entirety are rare, but they do exist. John Knowles Paine's *Concert Variations on "The Star-Spangled Banner"* for organ, which he wrote at the height of the Civil War, features an extended passage in which the principal melody is played against other lines that are melodic in their own right and not mere accompaniment. Listen to the melody at the beginning in a single voice, all by itself. Then notice how the same melody enters later, in a second voice (at 0:11), later again in a third voice (at 0:34), and so on. In the end, no one voice is subordinate to any other. Polyphonic texture can also consist of melodies that are different but sound good when played or sung together.

 Audio: "The Star-Spangled Banner," performed by Marvin Gaye

 Graphical Score: John Knowles Paine, *Concert Variations on "The Star-Spangled Banner"* (excerpt)

Timbre

Timbre is the color of music, the character of sound. The same melody can sound very different depending on who is singing or what instruments are playing. At one time or another, "The Star-Spangled Banner" has been performed by probably just about every instrument, voice, or combination of the two imaginable. Listen to the audio clips and compare, for example, the different timbres produced by a solo tenor, an ensemble of mixed voices (men and women), a trumpet in a small jazz ensemble, and a large orchestra.

What makes different instruments sound different? The answer to this question goes to the heart of what timbre is—the quality of a sound, apart from its pitch or volume. A **pitch** is a specific frequency of sound (measured as cycles per second), and many instruments can play the same pitch. The pitch "A," for example, is a sound wave of 440 cps (cycles per second), but the same pitch sounds very different on an oboe than on a violin, a guitar, or a saxophone. The basic wavelength of the sound produced by these instruments on this one pitch—the distance between each "peak" of the sound wave—will always be the same, but the shape of these wavelengths can vary considerably.

Just as individual colors blend different light waves, any naturally produced sound is the product of a mixture of many different sound waves. The basic sound wave is known as a *fundamental*. When produced by a machine (as in the case of a midi file), we hear *only* the fundamental: The sound is pure, but for that very reason it is unnatural. This is what makes midi files sound so mechanical. When produced by a musical instrument such as a violin, guitar, or piano, the sound wave of the fundamental is enhanced by the addition of many *partials*, frequencies that blend with the fundamental to create a richer and more distinctive quality of sound.

Instruments and voices vary widely in the range of pitches they can produce. Each voice or instrument has its own distinctive **register**, the span of pitches it

 Audio: "The Star-Spangled Banner," performed by Marvin Gaye, South City Voices, Louis Armstrong, and London Symphony Orchestra (Stravinsky arrangement)

Louis Armstrong playing the trumpet, 1964.

(a) flute   (b) trumpet   (c) soprano saxophone   (d) violin   (e) bassoon

The look of different sounds: oscilloscope readings of the same pitch (A = 440 cps) played by (a) a flute, (b) a trumpet, (c) a soprano saxophone, (d) a violin, and (e) a bassoon. Notice that the wavelengths—the distance between each peak—are the same (producing the same pitch), but the shape of the vibrating air column is different in each instrument (producing contrasting timbres).

can create, from high to low. Some voices or instruments—like the soprano or violin—operate in a relatively high register, whereas others, like the tenor or viola, move in a middle register. Still others occupy the lower end of things, like the bass voice or the tuba. By combining voices and instruments of different registers, musicians can create a wide variety of sounds that differ not only in their quality but also in their range.

Voices: The Human Sound

The human voice is conventionally divided into four basic registers: **soprano** (highest), **alto** (next-highest), **tenor** (second lowest), and **bass** (lowest). The first two are normally sung by women, the last two by men. Two additional "in-between" registers are sometimes also used: A **mezzo-soprano** has a register between soprano and alto, and a **baritone** sings in a range between tenor and bass.

Voice	Register
Soprano	Highest
Mezzo-Soprano	↓
Alto	↓
Tenor	↓
Baritone	↓
Bass	Lowest

Instruments of the Orchestra

Voices and instruments can play by themselves—solo—or join forces with other voices and instruments to create many different kinds of ensembles, from vocal choruses to jazz combos, from solo saxophone to a marching band. In the chapters that follow, we examine a number of different ensembles, along with keyboard instruments such as the organ (Chapter 18) and piano (Chapter 37). As an introduction to timbre, the modern orchestra provides a good sampling of some of the instruments used in many of the works discussed in this text.

The **orchestra** is a large ensemble that consists of several different kinds of instruments, usually of different families. There is no standard size or makeup of the orchestra; the one presented here is that used for Benjamin Britten's *The Young Person's Guide to the Orchestra*, a work discussed in

Tambourine   Xylophone   Triangle   Bass drum   Timpani (4)   Snare drum   Whip   Cymbals   Wood block

Castanets   Trombones (3)   Tuba   Gong

Horns (4)   Trumpets (2)

Clarinets (2)   Bassoons (2)

Flutes (2)   Oboes (2)

Piccolo   Harp

Second violins (16)   Violas (12)

First violins (18)   Conductor   Cellos (10)   Double basses (8)

| Strings | Woodwinds | Brass | Percussion |

Orchestra seating plan used in Benjamin Britten's *Young Person's Guide to the Orchestra*

more detail at the end of this chapter. "Closer Looks" of some other orchestral configurations can be found in Chapter 24 ("The Chamber Orchestra") and Chapter 48 ("The Mega-Orchestra").

The String Family.   Stringed instruments are made of wood that are plucked (such as the harp, guitar, ukulele, or mandolin) or played with a bow (such as the violin, viola, cello, or double bass). The strings themselves are made of finely wound metal of different thicknesses: the thinner the

Instruments of the Orchestra: Violin, Viola, Cello, Double Bass

string, the higher the sound. The bow consists of wood on top and hair from a horse's tail on the bottom. A knob at the end of the bow allows the player to tighten or loosen the hairs. Watch as the players draw the bow across the strings: this causes the body of each instrument to vibrate, and these vibrations are what we hear. The videos in MyMusicLab demonstrate each of the orchestra's principal stringed instruments in action.

- **Violin:**   The violin is the smallest—and therefore the highest-sounding—of the stringed instruments. It is small enough to be held under the chin by the performer as it's played. The violin is one of the most versatile instruments of the orchestra. Watch the video to hear how a single violin sounds.

- **Viola:**   The viola is a slightly larger version of the violin and therefore deeper in its range and mellower in sound. The viola usually plays in the middle range of the orchestra, filling in harmonies and enriching the sound. Listen for its darker tone quality.

- **Cello:**   The cello is an even larger and deeper-sounding version of the violin. It is so large, in fact, that it is held between the knees rather than under the chin. The rich, low sound of the cello often supports melodies in higher-sounding instruments, but can also project lyrical melodies of its own to great effect.

- **Double Bass:**   The largest and deepest member of the string family is the double bass. Although the double bass cannot be played with as much agility as the cello, it provides a firm harmonic foundation for the string section and for the entire orchestra. Listen for the extremely low range of this instrument.

- **Harp:**   The harp is a plucked-stringed instrument that comes in many shapes and sizes. The standard harp has a wide range, with a set of seven pedals that control the length—and thus the pitch—of all the strings as a unit. This gives the instrument even greater versatility. While the harp is perfectly capable of playing a melody, its most characteristic sound is the sweeping glissando, a "blur" of notes moving gracefully up or down.

The Woodwind Family.   Woodwind instruments produce sound when a player blows across a hole (as with the flute or piccolo) or into a reed or double reed (as with an oboe, clarinet, bassoon, contrabassoon, English horn, or saxophone). The vibrations of the air cause the instrument to vibrate, which in turn produces the sound we hear. The size and shape of each instrument gives each instrument its register and distinctive sound. The videos in MyMusicLab demonstrate each of the principal woodwind instruments of the orchestra in action.

Instruments of the Orchestra: Flute, Piccolo, Oboe, Clarinet, Bassoon

- **Flute:**   The flute was originally made of wood and is therefore classified as a woodwind instrument. Nowadays, however, it is usually metal. The instrument is held sideways, and sounds are produced by blowing across a hole in the mouthpiece according to the same principle used in blowing across the top of a bottle. Different pitches are produced by moving the fingers on holes and keys.

- **Piccolo:**   The piccolo is a smaller variety of flute. As with all instruments, the smaller the size, the higher the sound, and the piccolo is both very small and very high. Indeed, *piccolo* is the Italian word for "small." A single piccolo, because of its high, penetrating sound, can project quite clearly above the sound of an entire orchestra.

- **Oboe:**   The oboe is played by blowing through a double reed made of cane. Two small pieces of thin cane ("reed") are tied together and vibrate against each other. The suave quality of the oboe's sound is often compared to that of the human voice. Because the oboe varies little in pitch, the other instruments usually tune to it. Before a classical concert, when the concert master gives the signal for tuning, you can listen carefully and hear the pitch being given first by the principal oboist.

- **Clarinet:**   The clarinet is the most agile of all the woodwinds. It is played with a single reed, also made of cane, which is attached to the top of a solid mouthpiece. The clarinet has a very wide range of nearly four octaves and three distinct registers. In the low register, it sounds deep and melancholy. In the middle register, it's singing and warm. In the high register, it can be piercing and shrill.

- **Bassoon:**   The bassoon is the largest and therefore lowest-sounding of all the woodwind instruments. Its length is disguised because it is made of a tube doubled back on itself. If it were straight, it would be more than nine feet long. Like the oboe, the bassoon uses a double reed. The instrument has a full, rounded, vibrant sound in its low register and a somewhat muted, rather haunting sound in its high register.

The Brass Family.   Brass instrumentalists produce sound by vibrating their lips into a cup-like metal mouthpiece. They control pitch in two ways: by altering the way they blow into the mouthpiece, and by altering the length of the tube into which the vibrating air passes. The keys and valves on their instruments—or in the case of the trombone, the flexible slide—shorten or lengthen the column of air, which in turn creates higher or lower pitches. The principal instruments of the brass family are the horn (sometimes called the "French horn"), trumpet, trombone, and tuba. The videos in MyMusicLab demonstrate each of the principal brass instruments of the orchestra in action.

Instruments of the Orchestra: Trumpet, Horn, Trombone, Tuba

- **Trumpet:**   The trumpet is the highest-pitched brass instrument. Composers often take advantage of its bold, strident quality in fanfare-like passages, though a trumpet playing quietly can sound delicate and mysterious.

- **Horn:**   The horn, also known as the "French" horn, is often associated with outdoor sounds like hunting calls, though it also has a round, mellow quality. It has a wide range and adds a quality of richness to the sound of the orchestra as a whole.

- **Trombone:**   The trombone sounds very powerful and grand, sometimes even frightening. As with the horn, however, it has the potential to produce a rich, smooth, and mellow sound. A trombonist changes the length of the valve by moving the instrument's "slide" up and down, thereby changing the pitch. There are three sizes of trombone: the smallest and highest is the alto trombone, the middle one is the tenor trombone, and the largest and lowest is the bass trombone. The video demonstrates what they sound like in an ensemble.

- **Tuba:**   The tuba is the largest and lowest-sounding of the brass instruments. With its round, deep tone, it gives added weight and richness to the sound of the orchestra. If it were uncoiled in a straight line, the tuba would be sixteen feet long.

The Percussion Family.   Percussion instruments produce sound when they are shaken or struck, either with the hand or with a stick or mallet of some kind. Again, the basic principle of all instruments holds: The larger the area in which air vibrates, the deeper the sound. There are two main categories of percussion instruments, tuned and untuned. Tuned percussion instruments can produce specific pitches (such as the xylophone or timpani), while untuned percussion instruments (such as the snare drum, bass drum, or tambourine) cannot. The piano, also a percussion instrument (its keys are "struck"), is examined in Chapter 37 ("Closer Look: The Grand Piano"). The videos demonstrate some of the many orchestral percussion instruments in action.

- **Timpani:**   The timpani are also known as kettle drums because the base is made of copper and resembles a large kettle. The surface is covered with animal skin or plastic and can be tuned by tightening or loosening the handles around the edge of the instrument. Two, three, or sometimes four of these large drums are arranged in a semicircle around the player, who uses either hard wooden sticks or soft padded ones. Timpani instruments can sound like distant thunder. Often, however, they are used simply to reinforce the beat and the bass.

- **Xylophone:**   The xylophone has two sets of bars made of wood and is played with two hard sticks. Each key produces a single pitch, very much like the piano. The sound of the xylophone is bright and penetrating and can be heard clearly even when the entire orchestra is playing.

- **Snare Drum, Bass Drum, Cymbals:**   Untuned percussion instruments produce a rhythm but no specific pitch. The snare drum has metal wires attached to its underside that vibrate when the drum is struck, creating a rattling sound. These wires can also be disengaged to create a sound that is dry and crisp. The enormous bass drum gives a deep thump. Cymbals come in many shapes and sizes and are often used to emphasize climactic moments in orchestral music. Their crashing sound can reverberate for several seconds.

- **Triangle, Gong, Castanets, Tambourine, Whip (Clapper):**   Many untuned percussion instruments are used for special effects. Some are made of metal: these include the triangle and gong. The gong has a particularly long reverberation and is used only sparingly. Untuned percussion instruments made of wood include the castanets, the tambourine, and the whip (or clapper). These are also used to emphasize particular rhythms or special moments in a piece.

Instruments of the Orchestra: Timpani, Xylophone, Snare Drum, Bass Drum, Cymbals, Triangle, Gong, Castanets, Tambourine, Whip

 # Form

Form is the structure of a musical work, the way in which its individual units are put together. Form is based on three and only three possible strategies: repetition, variation, and contrast. When we say something, we can then do only one of three things: say once again exactly what we have just said, word-for-word (repetition); repeat what we have just said in a slightly different manner (variation); or say something altogether different (contrast).

- Repetition: Hello, hello.
- Variation: Hello, hi.
- Contrast: Hello. Goodbye.

These three strategies apply to music as well. In "The Star-Spangled Banner," the opening phrase of the music is repeated literally for the second phrase:

- Phrase 1: O, say can you see by the dawn's early light what so proudly we hailed at the twilight's last gleaming?

- Phrase 2 (same melody, repeated): Whose broad stripes and bright stars through the perilous fight, o'er the ramparts we watched were so gallantly streaming?

If we label the music of phrase 1 as **A**, then phrase 2 would also be labeled as **A**. The form of the first half of "The Star-Spangled Banner"—the music, independent of the text—can therefore be diagrammed as **A A**.

What happens next? "And the rockets' red glare . . . " is, of course, completely different from what we have heard before. For that reason, we can call this phrase "B." And the concluding phrase of "The Star-Spangled Banner" ("Oh, say does that star-spangled banner yet wave . . . ") is different yet again ("C"). So the form of the song as a whole can be represented as **A A B C**.

This form happens to be extremely common in songs from many different times and places (Martin Luther's famous hymn "A Mighty Fortress Is Our God," Stephen Foster's "Oh, Susanna," and Radiohead's "Black Star"). Forms can also be expanded (**AABCA**) or contracted (**ABA**) in an almost infinite variety of combinations.

Audio: "The Star-Spangled Banner," performed by Marvin Gaye

While the notated music of "The Star-Spangled Banner" opens with repetition (**A A**), performers often take liberties and alter the second statement of **A** to create **variation**. Listen again to Marvin Gaye's performance and you will hear that the way he performs the second **A** ("Whose broad stripes and bright stars . . . ") is different from the first one and yet recognizably an embellished version of the phrase we had heard before. Gaye varies this initial statement with added notes, changed notes, and new leaps (up to "stars") we had not heard before. Yet this phrase is still recognizable as a varied statement of the one we had heard at the beginning. We would diagram this kind of form as **A A' B C**. Variation is a basic technique of musical form: It allows us to hear any given musical idea repeatedly, but in a new guise each time.

Word–Music Relationships

Words and music often seem made for each other. But exactly how do notes relate to words? So far, we have examined only the music of "The Star-Spangled Banner," not its text. Let's look now at the **word–music relationships**: how the music fits the text and vice versa.

Structurally, the text (or at least its first stanza) consists of three questions, interrupted by a statement. (The second, third, and fourth stanzas of the text provide answers to all these questions, but no one ever sings them, and for purposes of brevity, we focus here on the first stanza.)

First Question

O, say can you see by the dawn's early light
What so proudly we hailed at the twilight's last gleaming?

Second Question

Whose broad stripes and bright stars through the perilous fight,
O'er the ramparts we watched were so gallantly streaming?

Statement

And the rockets' red glare, the bombs bursting in air,
Gave proof through the night that our flag was still there.

Third Question

Oh, say does that star-spangled banner yet wave
O'er the land of the free and the home of the brave?

If we consider the overall structure of the melody—the tune—we can see how well it fits the words:

Music	A	A	B	C
Text	Question 1	Question 2	Statement	Question 3

The opening two questions are sung to the identical music (**A**), but the statement presents a very different melodic idea in a very different range. With the words "And the rockets' red glare . . . ," the music moves into a different theme (**B**) and a higher range, which helps set the stage for a return to the opening range of the song (and one last question) in the concluding section (**C**).

Notice, too, how the range of the melody corresponds to the content of the text. The voice moves into a very high register at the words "And the rockets' red glare," appropriately enough. And it hits this same high note—the highest one in the entire melody—again just before the end, on "free" in "o'er the land of the free."

A Framework for Listening: Genre

Music is more than the sum of its elements: It is an experience. We always hear music in some sort of context, and that context shapes the way we hear the music. We have definite expectations of the kinds of music we will hear from a marching band during a halftime performance at a football game, and a very different set of expectations from what we will hear when we buy a ticket to the opera or when we go into a dance club. Each of these kinds of music serves a different function, and throughout this text, we give particular attention to the function of each work studied.

One of the most important factors that shapes our expectations of any given work of music is its **genre**. Genre is the category of a given work (symphony, sonata, song), determined by a combination of its performance medium and its social function. Knowing the genre of a work we are about to hear tells us a great deal about what to expect. It gives us a framework for listening. Let's suppose you're at the Olympics, witnessing a medals ceremony. The athlete who has won the gold medal has just received her medal, but you've never heard of the country she represents, and you certainly have never heard its national anthem, which is about to play. Yet based on your knowledge of the genre of national anthems, you can actually anticipate a fair amount about this piece of music you've never heard before. You can reasonably expect a work of fairly short duration—probably between one and two minutes—that is lively in tone and has a bright sound, and that will probably be performed by a wind band (trumpets, trombones, clarinets, and the like), possibly with a drum. These expectations are based on the principal function of a national anthem: to arouse in citizens a sense of national pride. There are exceptions to this rule, of course, just as there are exceptions to generic expectations in all kinds of music, but knowing the typical nature and function of the work we are about to hear can help us relate the unknown (the new work) to its archetype (the genre, or works we know from that genre).

"The Star-Spangled Banner" certainly fits the pattern of the genre of national anthem. It is short (about a minute-and-a-half to two minutes, depending on how slowly or quickly it is performed), in major mode, and is performed in its "standard" version—the one played at the Olympics, for example—by a wind band with drums.

Some of the many genres to be discussed in this book include opera, oratorio, concerto, string quartet, symphony, song, and ballet. Each of these provides a set of expectations for what you, the listener, will hear.

Hearing the Elements Together: Britten's *The Young Person's Guide to the Orchestra*

When we listen, we normally do not think about all the elements of music individually. This is because they typically work together to create a satisfying whole. But if we make a special effort to isolate them when we listen, we can better understand the role that each of these individual elements can play. For this reason we have a separate column for each significant element in the listening guides that accompany the music in this text. Do we need to be conscious of all these elements as we listen? No. Do we need to know a work's genre or form or texture or timbre in order to enjoy it? No. But the more we know, the better we can listen. And the better we listen, the more we can enjoy the experience.

Benjamin Britten's *The Young Person's Guide to the Orchestra* (1945) offers an excellent example of how a composer can coordinate the various elements of music in a single work and how we as listeners can develop an appreciation for the complexity and beauty of the work that results. *The Young Person's Guide to the Orchestra* showcases the principal instruments of the orchestra and presents them in systematic fashion, first as the four major families of instruments (woodwinds, brass, strings, percussion) and then individually, so that each one (oboe, clarinet, violin, viola, trombone, etc.) gets the chance to display its own distinctive sound. In this way, Britten creates an enormous variety of timbre because the "lead" instrument or family of instruments is constantly changing.

The melody, rhythm, harmony, texture, and dynamics also change throughout and are closely coordinated with the work's overall form. Indeed, the subtitle of this piece—*Variations and Fugue on a Theme of Purcell*—tells us even before we hear a single note that this will be a series of variations on a single theme, and that the one on which this piece is based was originally written by the great seventeenth-century English composer Henry Purcell (whose opera *Dido and Aeneas* we examine in Chapter 14). The fugue that comes at the end of the work is a dazzling display of a particular type of polyphony in which different instruments play the same melody but enter in quick succession one after the other (think: "Row, Row, Row Your Boat"). The theme of this fugue is yet another variation on Purcell's original theme.

The Listening Guide below will help direct your attention to the most important elements at work in Britten's *The Young Person's Guide to the Orchestra*. Here as in other Listening Guides throughout this book, the focus is on the most important elements within any given work. In this instance, the focus is on the elements of Form, Timbre, and Rhythm. Other elements are in play here as well, but these are the most significant.

Audio: Benjamin Britten, *The Young Person's Guide to the Orchestra*

Listening Guide))

Benjamin Britten Composed 1946

The Young Person's Guide to the Orchestra (17:23)

Time	▥ Form (Melody)	〜 Timbre	▦ Rhythm (Tempo)
0:00	Theme	Full orchestra	Moderately fast, majestic, with breadth
0:41	Variation 1	Woodwinds	
1:11	Variation 2	Brass	
1:42	Variation 3	Strings	
2:07	Variation 4	Percussion	
2:26	Theme repeated	Full orchestra again	
3:00	Variation 5	Flutes (2) & Piccolo	Presto (very fast)
3:29	Variation 6	Oboes (2)	Lento (very slow)
4:32	Variation 7	Clarinets (2)	Moderato (moderately)
5:15	Variation 8	Bassoons (2)	Allegro, march-like
6:11	Variation 9	Violins	Brilliantly, like a polacca (a type of dance)
6:58	Variation 10	Violas	Meno mosso (with less motion)
7:46	Variation 11	Cellos	
8:43	Variation 12	Double Basses	Starting slowly and then accelerating
9:40	Variation 13	Harp	Majestically

Time	Form (Melody)	Timbre	Rhythm (Tempo)
10:31	Variation 14	Horns (4)	
11:12	Variation 15	Trumpets (2)	Vivace (lively)
11:47	Variation 16	Trombones (3) & Tuba	Fast and pompously
12:48	Variation 17a	Timpani	Moderately
13:06	17b	Bass Drum & Cymbals	
13:16	17c	Tambourine & Triangle	
13:27	17d	Snare Drum & Wood Block	
13:38	17e	Xylophone	
13:49	17f	Castanets & Gong	
14:02	17g	Whip (Clapper)	
14:08	17h	All percussion instruments together	
14:44	Fugue	Full orchestra again, with the instruments entering one by one. The brass present Purcell's original theme in its majestic tempo simultaneously, with the much faster fugue at 16:31.	Very fast

PART 1

476 CE – Early Fifteenth Century

The Middle Ages

What we now think of as the **Middle Ages**, or the medieval era, covered almost a thousand years in European history between the fall of the Western Roman Empire in 476 CE and the beginning of the Renaissance in the early fifteenth century. The people of this time did not think of themselves as being in the "middle" or "between" anything at all, of course. Only later did historians see this span of time as a period lying between antiquity and the Renaissance. Very little notated music has survived from antiquity—the period before the Middle Ages—whereas the preserved repertory of medieval music is enormous.

The music of the Middle Ages reflects its many and varied social functions, both sacred and secular. The church dominated intellectual and cultural life during this period. Music, along with all the other arts, was perceived as a means of serving God. Over the course of several hundred years, generations of anonymous composers—most of them monks or priests—developed an enormous repertory of plainchant (also known as Gregorian chant), which consisted of monophonic, unaccompanied melodies sung by a single voice or by a choir in unison. Plainchant projected the words of the sacred liturgy in a manner that was at once clear and moving. Secular courts also needed music for their ceremonies and entertainments, and composers provided a steady stream of songs, settings of poems that tell of love, pain, heroism, and all the other emotions that make up the human

The Middle Ages

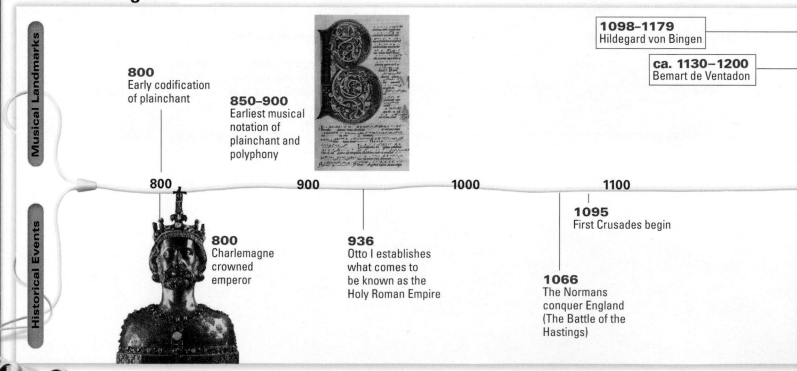

Musical Landmarks

800
Early codification of plainchant

850–900
Earliest musical notation of plainchant and polyphony

1098–1179
Hildegard von Bingen

ca. 1130–1200
Bemart de Ventadon

800   900   1000   1100

Historical Events

800
Charlemagne crowned emperor

936
Otto I establishes what comes to be known as the Holy Roman Empire

1066
The Normans conquer England (The Battle of the Hastings)

1095
First Crusades begin

condition. Polyphony—multiple independent voices sung or played together—became increasingly important for both sacred and secular music from the tenth century onward.

The sounds of medieval music, both sacred and secular, may at first seem unfamiliar to us today: The scales on which they based their melodies differ from ours, and most of their instruments are no longer in common use. But the more we listen to this music, the more we can hear in it the same basic elements we still use today. Above all, we can recognize in this music the effort of medieval composers to heighten the expressivity of the texts they set and to elevate music beyond language. This basic urge connects us with music that is a thousand years old.

Music for Sacred Spaces

By far the largest and most imposing structures of the Middle Ages were its churches, monuments to God, and physical testimonies to the power of the church itself. This was the era of the great Gothic cathedrals, buildings of unprecedented size, grace, and light. These structures did more than provide a space for worship, they were meant to inspire, to lift the eye heavenward, to instruct mortals about their relationship to the divine. The stained glass windows in these churches were similarly instructive, depicting biblical scenes in ways that could be understood even by those who could not read or write.

Sacred music fulfilled a similar function. Its purpose was to enhance the texts being sung and inspire worshippers with the beauty of their sound.

According to legend, Pope Gregory (ca. 540–604) received the melodies of plainchant from the Holy Spirit, which appeared to him in the form of a dove. This repertory of music would later come to be known as Gregorian chant.

1221–1284 Alfonso el Sabio

ca. 1300–1377 Guillaume de Machaut

ca. 1325–1397 Francesco Landini

ca. 1376–1445 Oswald von Wolkenstein

ca. 1180–early 1200s Pérotin

ca. 1201 Léonin dies

ca. 1213 Beatriz de Dia dies

1360 Jacopo da Bologna

ca. 1372 Lorenzo da Firenze dies

1200   **1250**   **1300**   **1350**   **1400**

1163 Cornerstone of Notre Dame Cathedral laid in Paris

1213 King John of England signs the Magna Carta

1337 Hundred Years' War begins

1348–1350 The Black Death ravages Europe

1387 Geoffrey Chaucer begins work on *The Canterbury Tales*

Plainchant was the perfect vehicle for projecting sacred texts with great clarity across enormous spaces. All the services of the church were provided with their appropriate melodies. And there were many services: The typical monk or nun attended church nine times a day. Eight of these services were devoted to the reading and singing of prayers, psalms, and hymns. The most important service of each day was Mass, a ritual reenactment of Christ's Last Supper with his disciples. The anonymous composers of the early Middle Ages

> **Chapter 3**
> Plainchant Alleluia "Caro mea"

devoted special efforts to the many chants of the Mass. Morality plays like Hildegard von Bingen's *Play of Virtues* (*Ordo virtutum*) combined plainchant with newly composed poetry to convey the teachings of the church and help the faithful learn the differences between good and evil.

> **Chapter 1**
> Hildegard von Bingen: *Play of Virtues*

Music for Entertainment

As the great cathedrals were symbols of divine power, medieval castles were symbols of secular, worldly power. Their stone walls and watery moats reflected the constant threat of attack from the outside. Medieval Europe was divided into a series of kingdoms, duchies, and fiefdoms of widely varying sizes, each ruled by a lord to whom subjects paid their allegiance—and taxes. Medieval courts used the arts as a means of projecting their cultural power and impressing subjects and visitors alike. Rulers competed for the services of the best poets, singers, and dancers.

Courtly life demanded courtly entertainments. Wandering minstrels passed from town to town and castle to castle providing poetry, song, acrobatics, and juggling—sometimes combining all at once. Poet-composers known variously as *troubadours* (in the south of present-day France), *trouvères* (in the north), and *minnesingers* (in what is now Germany) sang and played songs about love, heroism, and the pastoral life. Other courts employed their own full-time musicians and composers. Music featured prominently at nearly every courtly gathering. Medieval listeners, like listeners of today, enjoyed music that captured the simple pains and pleasures of being human. "Behold, Spring" ("Ecco la Primavera"), by the prolific blind composer Francesco Landini, welcomes spring as a season of lightheartedness, beauty, and love. Its flowing melody and resonant harmonies still speak to us today.

> **Chapter 4**
> Landini: "Behold, Spring"

Literary works like Giovanni Boccaccio's *Decameron* and Geoffrey Chaucer's *Canterbury Tales*, both from the fourteenth century, remind us that medieval song texts could be as bawdy and explicit as any today. In each, travelers must take turns entertaining their companions, and song plays an important role throughout. Significantly, Boccaccio (1313–1375) and Chaucer (ca. 1342–1400) both wrote in the vernacular languages of their respective regions (present-day Italy and England), rather than in Latin—the language of the church. Similarly, a good deal of medieval secular music,

Reims Cathedral (France), where composer Guillaume de Machaut's "Messe de Nostre Dame" ("Mass of Our Lady") was first performed. By the 13th century, builders could construct high, vaulted ceilings to draw both the eye and the spirit upward toward the heavens. Plainchant was crafted to fill these immense spaces.

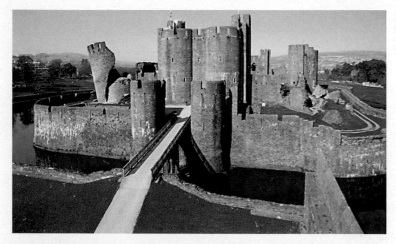

Caerphilly Castle, Wales, dates from the 13th century. Its daunting exterior was a defense against invaders.

including Guillaume de Machaut's "No More than One Man Could Count the Stars," was sung to texts in the language of the people.

Chapter 5
Machaut: "No More than One Man Could Count the Stars"

Music for Dancing

In an era when relationships with the opposite sex outside of marriage were closely regulated, dance was a highly significant social activity. We have no detailed descriptions of medieval dance, but we do have images of dancing as well as actual works of dance music that have survived from this time. Most dances appear to have been group activities, somewhat similar to present-day line dancing. And almost every image of dancing comes with a drummer providing the basic beat.

When thinking about medieval art and life today, we should consider not only what it looked like, but what it sounded like. The instruments of the Middle Ages were for the most part quite different from those of today. The shawm used in Alfonso el Sabio's "The Talking Sheep," for example, was an early wind instrument that would eventually be replaced by the modern oboe. Yet this work would sound very different if played on an oboe, for the shawm's more open and raspy sound belongs as much to the medieval world as the era's great churches and castles.

Chapter 6
Alfonso el Sabio: "The Talking Sheep"

An acrobat balances on a pair of swords, accompanied by two musicians. The one on the left plays the pipe and tabor (a small drum), while the one on the right plays a double flute.

Five couples in a line dance, accompanied by a drummer (left) and a bagpipe player (right). This image is from a medieval manuscript of the *Romance of the Rose*, a long story-poem written in France in the 13th century. The gold paint actually contains a high percentage of finely ground gold.

Information Technology 1.0

The earliest medieval music was not notated: Until about the tenth century, music was transmitted orally, not in written form. (The image on page 21 of the scribe writing music was created long after the time of Pope Gregory I, who reigned in the sixth century.) The earliest chant manuscripts show simple symbols above the texts, indicating motion of the pitch up or down (see "Closer Look: A Twelfth-Century Plainchant Manuscript").

Written music remained hard to come by, even after the development of notation. Printing did not emerge until the middle of the fifteenth century, and so music (like all other texts) had to be written out by hand, one copy at a time. Making a manuscript was a time-consuming and costly process: Ink and parchment were expensive (paper did not become widely available until the Renaissance), and scribes had to work slowly and carefully. Manuscripts, moreover, are not always entirely accurate. Scribes were only human, and anyone who has ever hand-copied a text of any complexity will know how easy it is to leave out, repeat, or garble words or even whole passages of text. Even in the hands of the most-skilled medieval scribes, these manuscripts were not always entirely faithful to the original.

CLOSER LOOK   **A Twelfth-Century Plainchant Manuscript**

This twelfth-century plainchant manuscript, prepared in what is now northern Germany, is a work of art in its own right. The scribes who produced documents like this were often monks of great artistic talent. Every large church or monastery had its own workshop that produced manuscripts, reminding us once again of the church's control over what could—and could not—be reproduced and distributed.

The initial letter "B," the first letter in the first word of one of the chants on this page, is oversized and elaborately illustrated with workers making wine. The images may illustrate Jesus's parable of the laborers in the vineyard (Matthew 20: 1-15).

To start the process, the worker at the top **harvests the grapes**.

To protect the harvest, this **archer** takes aim at a wild beast eating the grapes.

At the end of the **wine-making process,** this laborer mashes the grapes.

Some portions of **plainchant** are melodically simple and syllabic, with only one note per syllable and not very much rise or fall in the melody.

These early forms of **notes** are called **neumes**. The musical notation shows how the notes of the melody rise or fall, but it does not indicate specific pitches. The monks or nuns knew these chant melodies more or less by heart and so did not need precise notation. Newer chant melodies, such as those composed by Hildegard, called for more precise pitch-notation.
By the time Landini was writing in the later fourteenth century, an even more precise system of notation was in place.

The words were written onto the parchment first, the notes added later, probably by a different scribe. Here, the **text scribe** clearly did not leave enough room for the **music scribe!**

The red lines indicate that a single syllable of text is sung to many notes. These are elaborate **melismas**. Here, the beauty of the music takes precedence over the intelligibility of the text.

The J. Paul Getty Museum, Los Angeles. "Inhabited Initial B" by Unknown (Illuminator). about 1170s. From the Stammheim Missal (97.MG.21, Folio 58). Tempera colors, gold leaf silver leaf, and ink on parchment bound between wood boards covered with alum tawed pigskin. Leaf: 28.2 x 18.9 cm (11 1/8" x 8 7/16").

Hildegard von Bingen

Play of Virtues (excerpt)

Composed: ca. 1150

Plainchant consists of a single melodic line sung without accompaniment of any kind. Hildegard von Bingen's *Play of Virtues* uses plainchant to enhance the emotional impact of a morality play that pits the forces of good (the Virtues) against evil (Satan). Each of the 16 Virtues—Charity, Obedience, Chastity, Humility, Victory, and so on—is sung by a different singer.

Listen to This First

🌐 Texture	🎵 Melody	🎧 Word–Music Relationships	🥁 Rhythm
Listen for the sound of a single voice, or multiple voices singing the same music in unison: this is monophonic texture. ∎	Listen for occasional leaps in the otherwise smooth and flowing melodies. Listen, too, for the cadences—brief resting points—throughout. ∎	Note that most characters sing their lines, but one speaks (or shouts) his. Notice how clearly the singers project the Latin words, mostly with one note per syllable, but occasionally with many notes drawn out over a single syllable. Listen also for the climax of the drama, when the pitches move into a very high range. ∎	Listen to the way the rhythm is free for the most part, reflecting the irregular rhythms of the words being sung. ∎

Music exerts a powerful pull on the human spirit, and medieval composers put this power to good use. Hildegard von Bingen recognized that the words of her *Play of Virtues* (*Ordo virtutum*), while moving in their own right, could be made even more expressive when set to music.

Hildegard was the abbess—director—of an abbey of nuns in what is now western Germany. Her *Play of Virtues* consists of a series of confrontations between Satan and 16 Virtues. Each of the Virtues is personified by a different singer, with Humility portrayed as the "Queen of Virtues." When the Virtues sing together as a single chorus, they all sing exactly the same melody. Satan, however, never sings at all; he simply shouts his lines. In the medieval period, music was widely perceived as a divine gift of heaven, and it seems only fitting that the devil should have no music at all. The contrast between the spoken part of Satan and the sung part of the Virtues is immediate and striking.

In setting this morality play to music, Hildegard was building on a long tradition of liturgical **plainchant**, the music used in the daily services of the church. This repertory of chant had developed slowly over many centuries. It grew out of the chants of Jewish services of worship, particularly the melodic recitation of the Psalms. Over time, many of the texts of the Christian liturgy were set to music by a series of anonymous composers, most of whom were presumably monks and priests. The melodies were transmitted orally and not put in writing until they already

LEARNING OBJECTIVES

1.1 Discuss the origins and uses of plainchant.

1.2 Compare Hildegard's *Play of Virtues* with the morality plays of today.

1.3 Listen for the monophonic texture of chant.

1.4 Characterize the melodic contour of chant.

1.5 Explain how syllabic and melismatic passages function.

1.6 Listen for the relatively free rhythms of the melodies in *Play of Virtues*.

1.7 Describe Hildegard's life as a composer and explain how she defended the use of music in the church.

had been circulating for many centuries. Hildegard's style of chant is similar to the more florid kinds of plainchant found in the services of worship. The most important service of worship—the Mass—was itself a ritual reenactment of Christ's Last Supper with his disciples, with the celebrant priest (a representative of Christ) distributing bread and wine to his followers (see "Historical Context: The Mass," Chapter 10, page 83). The idea of a bodily reenactment of past events gradually extended to readings from scripture as well: Dramatized performances of such events as the two Marys finding the empty tomb of Christ on Easter morning became increasingly common from the eleventh century onward. Hildegard's setting of a play about the struggle for an innocent soul extends this practice.

The Clarity of Monophonic Texture

The **monophonic texture** of this music—whether sung by one singer or by a group of singers in **unison**—allows the performers to project the text with great clarity.

The earliest preserved music from the Middle Ages was monophonic. In the church, this repertory came to be known as plainchant because of the simplicity of its texture. (Later, it would also be called **Gregorian chant** on the grounds that Pope Gregory I was said to have written the bulk of it in the late sixth century.) Plainchant fulfilled its function perfectly: It projected its text—the main focus of attention for worshippers—with wonderful clarity and a melodic beauty that enhanced the meaning of the words. It was particularly well suited for performance in the large, resonant spaces of medieval churches. The beauty of the melodies and words together, echoing off the stone walls, must have made an enormous impact on worshippers.

HISTORICAL CONTEXT   **The Morality Play**

In a scene from *Empire Strikes Back*, Luke Skywalker (Mark Hamill) and Darth Vader (David Prowse) carry out the battle between good and evil.

How do we learn the difference between good and evil, and how do we learn to choose between them? In the Middle Ages, morality plays like Hildegard von Bingen's *Play of Virtues* offered a way of dramatizing such questions literally. But morality plays did not end with the Middle Ages. Popular works today like the *Star Wars*, *Harry Potter*, and *Lord of the Rings* series are built on the same basic plot outline: An innocent figure struggles between the forces of good and evil.

Work	Evil	Innocent Soul	Good
Hildegard, *Play of Virtues*	Satan	The Soul, Penitent	The Virtues
Tolkien, *Lord of the Rings*	Sauron	Frodo	Gandalf
Lucas, *Star Wars*	Darth Vader	Luke Skywalker	Jedi knights
Rowling, *Harry Potter*	Voldemort	Harry Potter	Dumbledore

In each case, the embodiment of evil was once good: Sauron began as a good spirit, Darth Vader was once a Jedi knight, Voldemort was originally an innocent boy named Tom Marvolo Riddle, and Satan himself was a fallen angel.

Music plays a powerful role in all of these more recent dramas, and especially in their film adaptations. Think, for example, of the difference in sound between the darkness of Darth Vader's music and the stirring march that symbolizes the Jedi knights. These aural cues reinforce the essence of the good and evil characters.

🎵 Medieval Melody

Hildegard's flowing melodies move primarily by step (**conjunct motion**), but the occasional leaps (**disjunct motion**) provide variety and give each phrase of text a clear profile. Many of the melodic phrases begin with a leap upward and then descend gradually through a series of steps, ending on the same note with which the phrase began. This kind of melodic contour is typical of plainchant in general and is always related to the structure of the text being sung: a sentence of text almost invariably ends with a musical resting point known as a **cadence**.

Melodic contour: rising, then falling

73. The Soul, Penitent

E - go om - nes vi - as me-as ma-las es-se co-gno - - vi, et i - de-o fu - gi a te;
I recognised that all my ways were wicked,   so I   fled you.

D   D   D   D   D D D   D   D D
                                        (brief   (brief
                                        cadence)   cadence)

mo - do au - tem, o   il - lu - sor,   pu - gno con - tra   te.
But   now,   you trickster,   I'll fight   you   face to face.

D   D D   D   D
                                                                   (cadence)

The opening of the present excerpt, represented in modern notation. Each melodic phrase starts and ends on D, rising and then falling to a cadence.

Text and translation from *Nine Medieval Latin Plays*, translated and edited by Peter Dronke. Copyright © 1994 Cambridge University Press.

A 13th-century plainchant manuscript. The elaborate initial for the letter "A" at the beginning shows Saint Gregory transcribing the melodies whispered into his ear by the dove, who represents the Holy Spirit.

What has sometimes been described as the "otherworldly" sound of plainchant—the quality that makes plainchant sound different from other kinds of music—is due in part to the scales on which these melodies are based. Whereas today we have only two basic kinds of scales (corresponding to the major and minor modes), medieval composers had four additional **modes**, each of which uses a sequence of whole steps and half steps different from the pattern found in the standard scales of today. The easiest way to imagine (and hear) the full range of medieval modes is to play a series of notes upward on the piano using only the white keys starting and ending on D, then another series on E, then another on F, and finally another on G. Each of these scales—modes—sounds slightly different from the others, and each also sounds different from the standard major and minor modes of today. (The major mode can be heard on the white keys from C to C, and the minor mode on the white keys from A to A.) In the Middle Ages, each of these scales (modes) was given its own Greek name, based on the mistaken belief that these corresponded to the modes of ancient Greek music. The medieval modes are Dorian (on D), Phrygian (on E), Lydian (on F), Mixolydian (on G), Aeolian (on A), and Ionian (on C). The opening of this particular excerpt from Hildegard's *Play of Virtues* is based on the Dorian mode, beginning and cadencing on the note D.

Projecting Words through Music

A composer has two basic choices in setting words to music: he or she can set each syllable to a single note or the composer can set each syllable to multiple notes. The first style—one note per syllable—is called **syllabic**, and it ensures that the words will be heard with special clarity. The second style—more than one note per syllable—is called **melismatic**. A **melisma** is a syllable sung to many notes. This kind of setting provides variety and emphasizes key words in a text, such as the word *regina* ("queen") after 0:54 or the word *curre* ("hasten" or "run") after 1:26. An entirely melismatic setting might make it difficult for listeners to understand every word, whereas an entirely syllabic setting might not provide sufficient musical variety. By mixing syllabic and melismatic settings, Hildegard provides musical variety, even while providing for a clear projection of the text.

Note, too, how certain passages are sung in a very high **register**, or range. When Satan has been bound—the climactic moment of the drama (3:24 in the Listening Guide)—Victory sings in an extremely high register. The effect is thrilling.

Free Rhythm

No one is absolutely certain exactly how plainchant was performed. There are two general approaches, free or measured. The performance here presents the music in a relatively free rhythm, with the individual notes lengthened or shortened according to the length of the syllables in the words being sung. A measured performance would adhere to a consistent meter, such as **duple meter** (**1**-2-**3**-4 | **1**-2-**3**-4 | etc.).

Now listen to this excerpt again, using the Listening Guide.

CONNECT YOUR PLAYLIST

Monophony

Find a piece that contains monophonic texture.

Example: Ed Sheeran, "I See Fire" (2015)
This song begins with a monophonic verse before adding additional voices and instruments later.

PROFILE   Hildegard von Bingen (1098–1179)

Visions through Music

We can securely attribute more compositions to Hildegard von Bingen than to any other musician, male or female, who worked before the early fourteenth century. In spite of her impressive output, Hildegard did not consider herself a professional composer or musician. Born into a noble family in what is now western Germany, she entered a Benedictine convent at the age of 7 and committed herself to a life in the church when she was 16. In her early 30s, she began to experience visions and revelations, which she recorded in a series of books. She considered herself a channel through which the Holy Spirit transmitted its message to humankind, sometimes in the form of prose, sometimes in the form of poetry, sometimes in the form of poetry with music. Hildegard was the first woman to receive explicit permission from a pope to write on theology. She also wrote on such diverse subjects as medicine, plants, and the lives of the saints, all while directing the life of a thriving convent near Bingen, a city on the Rhine in present-day Germany. Like many medieval persons, she took her name ("of Bingen") from her place of residence.

Hildegard von Bingen, shown in a contemporary manuscript. She looks heavenward for inspiration as she records what she called her "visions," which included both words and music.

EXPAND YOUR PLAYLIST: HILDEGARD VON BINGEN

Nuns and monks in Hildegard's time attended church services not just once a week, or even once a day, but usually nine times a day. Hildegard wrote many chants for these services of worship. Here are some examples:

- **"Lord, Have Mercy"** (*Kyrie eleison*) is one of five sections of the Mass, the ritual reenactment of Christ's Last Supper with his disciples. *Hildegard von Bingen: Heavenly Revelations.* Oxford Camerata, Naxos.

- **"O Blessed Infancy"** (*O beata infantia*) is an antiphon, a short piece sung before and after a psalm is sung in church. *The Complete Hildegard von Bingen, Volume Three: O Nobilissima Viriditas.* Celestial Harmonies B00005.

- **"Honor Be to the Holy Spirit"** (*Spiritui sancto honor sit*) is a responsory, a type of chant sung after the reading of scriptures in church. This type of chant takes its name from the fact that a chorus of singers responds to the singing of a soloist. *Hildegard von Bingen: 11,000 Virgins.* Anonymous 4. Harmonia Mundi Fr. B0000B003O.

- **"Hail, Generous One"** (*Ave generosa*) is a hymn, a devotional chant to a freely composed text, often with many strophes or stanzas. *Hildegard von Bingen: Heavenly Revelations.* Oxford Camerata, Naxos.

Listening Guide

Hildegard von Bingen Composed: ca. 1150

Play of Virtues (excerpt) (3:58)

Time	Character	Latin Text	English Translation
0:00	The Devil (speaks, does not sing)	Que es, aut unde venis?	Who are you? Where are you coming from?
		Tu amplexata es me, et ego foras eduxi te. Sed nunc in reversione tua confundis me; Ego autem pugna mea diciam te!	You were in my embrace, I led you out. Yet you now are going back, defying me—but I shall fight you and bring you down!
0:19	The Soul, Penitent	Ego omnes vias meas malas esse cognovi et ideo fugi a te; modo autem, o illusor pugno contra te. Inde tu, o regina Humilitas, tuo medicamine adiuva me.	I recognized that all my ways were wicked, so I fled you. But now, you trickster, I'll fight you face to face. Queen Humility, come with your medicine, give me aid!
1:13	Humility (to Victory)	O Victoria, que istum in celo superasti, curre cum militibus tuis, et omnes ligate diabolum hunc.	Victory, you who once conquered this creature in the heavens, run now, with all your soldiery, and all of you bind this Fiend!
1:45	Victory (to the Virtues)	O fortissimi et gloriosissimi milites, venite, et adiuvate me istum fallacem vincere.	Bravest and most glorious warriors, come, help me to vanquish this deceitful one!
2:14	The Virtues	O dulcissime bellatrix, in torrente fonte qui absorbuit, lupum rapacem!	Oh sweetest warrior, in the scorching fountain that swallowed up the voracious wolf—
		O gloriosa coronata, nos libenter militamus tecum contra illusorem hunc.	Glorious, crowned one, how gladly we'll fight against the trickster, at your side!
2:48	Humility	Ligate ergo istrum, o virtutes preclare!	Bind him then, you shining Virtues!
3:05	The Virtues (binding Satan here)	O regina nostra, tibi parebimus et precepta tua in omnibus adimplebimus.	Queen of us all, we obey—we'll carry out your orders totally.
3:24	Victory	Gaudete, o socii, quia antiquus serpens ligatus est.	Comrades, rejoice: the age-old snake is bound!
3:47	The Virtues	Laus tibi Christe, rex angelorum!	Praise be to you, Christ, King of the angels!

Text and translation from *Nine Medieval Latin Plays*, translated and edited by Peter Dronke. Copyright © 1994 Cambridge University Press.

Rhythm	Word–Music Relationships	Texture
Free, corresponding to length of syllables	The devil's shouting reflects the medieval belief that hell is a place with no music.	(Spoken)
	Melisma on *regina* ("queen") suggests her importance	Monophonic (solo)
	Melisma on *curre* ("run")	
		Monophonic (unison chorus)
		Monophonic (solo)
		Monophonic (unison chorus)
	Notes in extremely high register—climax of the drama	Monophonic (solo)
		Monophonic (unison chorus)

Q Student FAQs

Why are there only women singing?

Two reasons: (1) During the Middle Ages, the Virtues personified in this work—Humility, Victory, Chastity, Love, Obedience, Mercy, Discretion, Patience, and so on—were almost all associated with the female gender. (2) Hildegard wrote this work to be performed in her own convent—that is, by her fellow nuns.

If it was performed by nuns, who spoke the part of the devil?

Only priests—thus only males—could celebrate the Mass, and so each convent had assigned to it a priest to administer the sacraments. In all likelihood, this priest would have played the role of the devil.

Is plainchant still used in churches?

In some churches on some occasions, yes. But chant is no longer the principal vehicle for singing texts in the Roman Catholic Church. It is still possible to hear special plainchant services from time to time, however.

THE COMPOSER SPEAKS Hildegard Defends the Practice of Music

Over 850 years ago, Hildegard von Bingen was embroiled in a debate that continues today: What is the impact of music on the human mind and spirit? Does it support the religious experience, or does it serve as a sensual distraction from religion? To the present day, some religions embrace music, while some limit or even shun it.

Hildegard landed in the center of this controversy when church authorities forbade her nuns from singing in church; they were only allowed to speak the words of the services. The authorities wanted to punish Hildegard because she was alleged to have allowed excommunicated individuals—barred from receiving Communion because of a grave offense against the church—to be buried on the consecrated ground of her convent's cemetery. In a lengthy letter to the church authorities, Hildegard eloquently defended the practice of music. Church officials eventually relented and allowed Hildegard's convent to resume its singing.

◆

"In obedience to you we have until now given up the singing of the Divine Office, celebrating it only by quiet reading—and I heard a voice coming from the living light, telling of those various kinds of praise concerning which David speaks in the Psalms: "Praise him with the sound of the trumpet, praise him with the psaltery and the cithara [plucked string instruments], praise him with the tympanum and the chorus, praise him with strings and the organ, praise him with the well-sounding cymbals, praise him with the cymbals of jubilation. Let every spirit praise the Lord" [Psalm 150: 3–6]. In these words we are taught about inward concerns by external objects, how according to the makeup of material things (the properties of musical instruments) we ought best to convert and to refashion the workings of our interior man to the praise of the Creator. . . .

Thus it is just that God be praised in everything. And since man sighs and moans with considerable frequency upon hearing some song, as he recalls in his soul the quality of celestial harmony, the prophet David, considering with understanding the nature of what is spiritual (because the soul is harmonious) exhorts us in the psalm, "Let us confess the Lord on the cithara, let us play to him on the psaltery of ten strings" [Psalm 32:1], intending that the cithara, which sounds from below, pertains to the discipline of the body; that the psaltery, which sounds from above, pertains to the striving of the spirit; and that the ten strings refer to the contemplation of the Law. Thus they who without the weight of sure reason impose silence upon a church in the matter of songs in praise of God, and thereby unjustly deprive God of the honor of his praise on earth, will be deprived themselves of the participation in the angelic praises heard in Heaven, unless they make amends by true regret and humble penitence. "

Source: Epistle 47: To the Prelate of Mainz. From Strunk's *Source Readings in Music History*, Leo Treitler, General Editor. Reprinted by permission of Leo Treitler.

  EXPAND YOUR PLAYLIST

Chant

Christianity is only one of many faiths that use monophonic chants in sacred rituals. Jewish, Buddhist, Hindu, Islamic, Native American (see Chapter 2), and other traditions employ some form of chanting.

Buddhist chant
• *Tibetan Mantras and Chants.* Buddhist Monks of Maitri Vihar. Sounds of the World B00000IXHK. A selection of Buddhist chants from a contemporary Tibetan monastery.

Christian chant
• *Chant.* The Benedictine Monks of Santo Domingo de Silos. Angel B000002. A selection of different types of plainchant sung in the Catholic Church. This recording became a triple-platinum album when it was released on CD in the mid-1990s, selling more than 3 million copies in the United States alone.

Hindu chant
• *Sacred Hindu Chants and Mantras.* Retro Music B000BS6XYS. A wide range of meditative Hindu chants.

Islamic chant
• *Music of Islam, Vol. 10: Qur'an Recitation.* Celestial Harmonies B0000007Z5. Selections from the *Qur'an*.

Jewish chant
• *Chants Mystique: Hidden Treasures of a Living Tradition.* Musical Heritage Society 514284Y. A wide range of chants from various branches of Judaism.

San Ildefonso Indians of New Mexico

Eagle Dance

Traditional; recorded: ca. 1951

Monophonic chant is an almost universal phenomenon. It appears in a great many cultures throughout the world and across historical epochs, and not only in the Middle Ages. The *Eagle Dance*, part of an ancient Native American rain ceremony, is always accompanied by chant. This chapter's recording captures the sounds of the dance as performed by the San Ildefonso Indians of New Mexico.

Listen to This First))

🌐 Texture	🥁 Rhythm	🎵 Melody	🏛 Form
Notice that all voices sing in unison, singing one melodic line together throughout. ■	Listen for the change from free rhythm at the beginning to duple meter later on. ■	Listen for the consistently downward contour of each melodic unit. ■	Listen for the repetition of large-scale sections of the chant. ■

Monophonic chant has long been—and remains—essential to sacred rituals throughout the world. Many Christians and Jews still incorporate chant in their religious services. The Hindu Vedas, Tibetan chants, Thai and Vietnamese Buddhist chants, as well as Confucian, Buddhist, Taoist, and shamanic chants in China, Korea, and Japan still play an important role in worship.

Chant is the predominant form of music in Native North American Indian culture. Where it has not died out from the effects of the nineteenth-century wars with Euro-American settlers, it survives on reservations. Native American chanting can be heard today primarily at **powwows**, intertribal gatherings where Native Americans of mixed tribes express their mutual bond and identity.

Each powwow begins with a "Grand Entry," a procession of all the participants into the arena where the event is to be held. After all have entered, flags are brought into the arena, including various tribal flags and the U.S. flag, carried by military veterans. Next to enter are the tribal elders and honored guests, followed by the dancers, men first, then women. A round dance usually ends the opening ceremonies. Various groups then perform dances that range from war dances to religious and ceremonial dances. Each group competes for the best performance. Singers perform the traditional songs to accompany these dances, along with other musicians, primarily drummers. Some of the traditional dances performed include the gourd dance, grass dance, and jingle dance, and the fancy feather or eagle dance.

The *Eagle Dance* portrays the life cycle of the eagle, a creature regarded as the connecting link between heaven and earth. Two men in eagle feathers dance movements that imitate eagles turning, flapping, and swaying in the air. The eagle's feathers bear prayers and are not allowed to touch the ground.

LEARNING OBJECTIVES

2.1 Discuss the universality of chant in world cultures.

2.2 Describe the use of monophony in Native American chant.

2.3 Describe patterning in North American Indian chant melodies.

2.4 Define vocables.

2.5 Explain what a powwow is and how it uses music.

2.6 Listen for the ABA form of the *Eagle Dance*.

2.7 Listen for the terraced downward contour of each melodic phrase in San Ildefonso Indians of New Mexico: *Eagle Dance*.

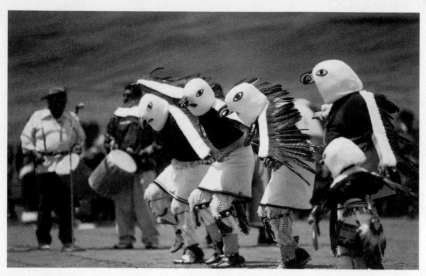

Eagle Dancers from the San Juan Pueblo, New Mexico.

 ## Texture: Monophony

Like the other forms of chant we have heard, the *Eagle Dance* consists of a single melodic line. It is sung by male voices in **unison**. Even the percussion instruments are conceived as "singing" the chant: Their sounds punctuate the rhythm of the chant rather than furnish a contrasting and independent rhythmic line. Nearly all Native American music is **monophonic**, and most often it is accompanied by percussion. In this performance, the drumming is done with a single drumstick. If a larger drum is used, several players strike the rhythm together.

 ## Free versus Metered Rhythm

The opening section of this chant is in free rhythm: The voices move fluidly over a rapid pulsation of even drumbeats, and we hear no pattern of strong or weak beats. The bulk of the chant, however, is in **duple meter**, with a strong accent on the first beat of two- or four-beat units (**1**-2 | **1**-2 | **1**-2 or **1**-2-3-4 | **1**-2-3-4). The occasional change in **tempo**—the speed of the music—does not alter the underlying rhythm.

 ## Melodic Contour

The melodic units of this chant move consistently downward. Each phrase begins on a relatively high note and moves to lower and lower pitches and eventually cadence on a low note. This pattern is typical of North American Indian chant melodies.

There are no "words" to this melody. In Native American culture, songs are believed to come from the spirit world. A song is transmitted through a person who hears it in a dream or revelation and then teaches it to others. Because songs are not about worldly matters, the words of humans have no place. Native American chant thus makes use of **vocables**—meaningless sung syllables, the sound of which is like a melodic instrument. Some syllables are more accented than others, and all syllables are sung as prescribed, for they are part of the song. This requires careful memorization.

 ## Form: ABA

The chant for the *Eagle Dance* is in three sections, **ABA**, with a brief introduction. Each section has its own melody, built of smaller, repeating units. Varied vocable order at the end of each melody group creates contrast within each section.

The **A** melody consists of two phrases with identical vocables:

A

(Ya hey ya ha ye ya hey ye) (ya hey ya ha ye ya hey ye)

This melody occurs three times, on slightly different pitches, but with the same downward **terraced contour**. This means that the same basic melodic unit begins on a slightly lower note each time it is repeated. After the third time, vocables are sung in a varied order, creating a tapered ending for the **A** section.

The essential **B** melody consists of the shorter vocable set "*Hey le ya,*" likewise sung twice:

B

(Hey le ya) (hey le ya)

CONNECT YOUR PLAYLIST

Vocables

Find a song that uses vocables to imitate a melodic instrument.

Example: Bobby McFerrin, "Don't Worry, Be Happy" (1988) Pop/jazz vocalist Bobby McFerrin has made a career out of his amazing vocal abilities. In this song, a number-one pop hit, McFerrin uses vocables to imitate the sound of a funky bass and a synthesizer, among other instruments.

This melodic phrase is repeated. The third time, it varies slightly at the end and concludes with different vocables (*hey ya ay*):

(Hey le ya) (hey ya ay)

This is followed by a compressed version of what has been sung so far:

(Hey le ya)   (hey le ya)   (hey le ya)

Varied syllables bring this set of phrases to a close, and the music slows briefly. Then the entire pattern repeats, once again tapering off with a succession of varied syllables that bring the entire **B** section to a close.

Now listen to this chant again, following the Listening Guide.

Listening Guide

San Ildefonso Indians of New Mexico Recorded: ca. 1951
Eagle Dance (2:56)

Time	🏛 Form	Text (vocables)	🥁 Rhythm	🎵 Melody
0:00	Free introduction	*Hyo hey ya* *hyo hey ya hey ya* *hwey ye ya* *hya hey ya* *hey hey hey he* *hya hey ya* *hey hey ya*	Free	Nonmetered chant with rapid drum pulsations.
0:21	Metered part of the introduction	*Hey ye hey ya* *hey ye hey ye* *hey ya hey ye ye ye*	Duple	The chant becomes metered: slow groups of four beats.
0:31	A	*Ya hey ya ha ye ya hey ye ya hey ya ha ye ya hey ye* (three times, followed by vocables in varied order, tailing off the section)		The **A** melody is sung three times with slightly different pitches, but with the same terraced downward contour. After the third time, the vocables and melodic fragments are sung in a varied order.
1:02	B	*Hey le ya, hey le ya* (twice) *Hey le ya, hey le ya, hey ya ay*		Contrasting terraced melody. Faster meter of four beats, more than double the speed of **A**.
1:16	The first half of **B** concludes	(Varied vocables)		Varied vocables and melodic fragments. The chant slows to a halt.
1:18	Resumed tempo of **B**	*Hey le ya, hey le ya* (twice) *Hey le ya, hey ya ay* *Hey le ya, hey le ya, hey ya ay*		The **B** melodic pattern repeats.
1:30	Slowing down	(Varied vocables)		The chant slows to a halt again.
1:33	A	*Ya hey ya ha ye ya hey ye ya hey ya ha ye ya hey ye* (three times, followed by vocables in varied order, tailing off the section)		The slow meter of the **A** unit returns with the first terraced melody.

🔍 Student FAQs ⚙

Why do traditional Native American chants often move from a higher to a lower tone?

Descending melodies are typical of many forms of traditional vocal music. The descending tone mirrors the exhalation of breath.

Why is this dance performed by men only?

Traditionally, only males were allowed to participate in the ceremonial songs and dances of Native Americans. At today's powwows, the *Eagle Dance* is still usually performed by men. The eagle is a strong symbol of virility to Native Americans, and in this dance it is associated with maintaining the fertility of the land and thus the survival of the tribe.

EXPAND YOUR PLAYLIST

Native American Music

Creation's Journey: Native American Music
- Smithsonian Folkways Recordings SFW40410.

Anthology of North American Indian and Eskimo Music
- Folkways Records FW04541.

Cry from the Earth: Music of the North American Indians
- Folkways Records FW37777.
  These are all good anthologies that give an overview of Native American musical styles.

Hopi Sunshield Singers
- *Pow-Wow Songs Live!* Canyon CR-6180.
  Intertribal powwow songs recorded live.

An Historical Album of Blackfoot Indian Music
- Folkways Records FW34001.
  These historic recordings are from cylinder recordings made in the 1920s and 1930s; while the sound quality is not the best, the performances are rare and interesting.

Blackfire
- *One Nation Under.* Canyon CR-7049.
  Blackfire is a group of Native American siblings who play what they describe as "fire-ball alternative punk." Joey Ramone makes a guest appearance on this disc. Political lyrics comment on the plight of Native Americans.

3

Plainchant Alleluia
"Caro mea"
Composed: ca. 1275

This brief chant is from the Mass for the Feast of Corpus Christi. It is a responsorial chant in which a chorus "responds" to a solo singer. As is so often the case with medieval plainchant, we do not know the identity of the composer, though it was probably written by a monk or priest. This chapter's recording, by an all-male ensemble, reflects the way this chant would have been sung in a medieval monastery.

Listen to This First))

ᴎ Timbre
Listen for the contrast between the soloist (a single voice) and the chorus (many voices, all singing in unison). ■

⊕ Texture
Listen for the monophonic texture throughout. No matter how many voices are singing, there is never more than one melodic line. ■

♫ Melody
Listen for sections of the melody that repeat or return over the course of the entire chant. ■

↻ Word–Music Relationships
Listen for the difference between syllables that are sung to a single note and those that are sung to many notes. ■

LEARNING OBJECTIVES

3.1 Describe how the Alleluia functioned in the context of the Mass.

3.2 Define "responsorial chant."

3.3 Identify the unison texture of plainchant as it is heard In "Caro mea" from the Mass for the Feast of Corpus Christi.

3.4 Explain the use of contrast in the performance of "Caro mea."

3.5 Define "melisma" and identify melismas in "Caro mea."

3.6 Describe how plainchant assists in promoting calm and well-being.

Plainchant was an integral part of every service of worship in the Medieval church. The Alleluia "Caro mea" is one of many **plainchants** used during the Mass for the Feast of Corpus Christi (Latin for "Body of Christ"), which celebrates the Holy Sacrament, the body (bread) and blood (wine) of Christ. Like all Masses, the Mass for the Feast of Corpus Christi consists of a combination of elements that are unchanging (the "Ordinary"—the Kyrie, Gloria, Credo, Sanctus, and Agnus Dei) and elements that change according to the specific Sunday or feast day (the "Propers"—Introit, Gradual, Alleluia, Offertory, Communion). The texts for the Propers of the Mass for the Feast of Corpus Christi all deal in some way with the ritual of the Holy Sacrament.

The text for the Alleluia for this feast day is taken from the Gospel of John, 6:55–56. These are the words Jesus spoke to his disciples and others at the synagogue at Caprenaum, and they foreshadow the words he would say at the Last Supper the night before his crucifixion, when he distributed bread and wine to his disciples as part of the traditional Passover meal.

Timbre: Soloist and Chorus

This Alleluia is a **responsorial chant**, one that alternates between a soloist and chorus. The soloist intones the opening word ("Alleluia"), and the chorus "responds" by repeating both the words and music of what the soloist has just sung. The soloist then sings the two biblical verses, and when he has finished, the chorus closes the chant by repeating the word "Alleluia" to the original music once again. This kind of call-and-response format is found in the music of many religions throughout the world.

 ## Texture: Monophony

Listen for the **monophonic texture** throughout. No matter how many voices are singing, there is never more than one melodic line. The chorus of men's voices sings in unison—exactly the same notes—throughout.

 ## Melody

The melody throughout has a "floating" quality that projects well across the large spaces of a church. The music to the opening word, "Alleluia" (labeled "**A**" in the Listening Guide), is sung four times: first by the soloist, then immediately after by the chorus, then toward the end by the soloist (to different words), and finally (once again on the word "Alleluia") by the chorus. The middle portion of this chant is given to the two biblical verses that transmit Christ's words. This is a melodically contrasting section (labeled "**B**" in the Listening Guide).

A priest (center) leads the celebration of Mass with the assistance of monks (left), who are singing from a notated manuscript.

 ## Word–Music Relationships: Singing Syllables

Even though the words may be the same, reciting a text and singing it are two very different things. Singing lengthens and extends each syllable and allows the singer to project the words over a much larger space. By singing many notes to one syllable—a **melisma**—a singer can further embellish and emphasize the words to heighten their expression. The word "Alleluia," for example, when spoken, lasts only a second or two. When sung with extended melismas, as it is here, it can run to almost half a minute.

The **register** of the melody can also set into relief key words of the text. Listen to how the melody reaches its highest point at the words *sanguis meus vere est potus* ("and my blood is drink indeed"). The long descent to *meam carnem* ("my flesh") helps these key words stand out as well.

While the text and music of the Alleluia section of the Mass change throughout the year, they always begin and end with the word "Alleluia," and the melodies on the final syllable "-a" are often quite elaborate, reflecting the joyous and even ecstatic nature of the word. (The same word would inspire Handel many centuries later when he wrote the "Halleluiah Chorus" for *Messiah*—see Chapter 21).

With these elements in mind, listen again to this chant, using the Listening Guide.

CONNECT YOUR PLAYLIST

Call-and-Response

Find a piece in which a solo singer or instrumentalist "calls" and then receives a "response" from a larger group.

Example: The Isley Brothers, "(You Make Me Wanna) Shout" (1959) This song features a lead singer who commands the chorus and/or audience.

Plainchant Alleluia "Caro mea" Composed: ca. 1275

(3:13)

Time	Latin Text	English Translation	Timbre	Melody	Word–Music Relationship	Texture
0:00	Alleluia.	Alleluia.	Soloist	A	Long melisma on final "a"	Monophonic
0:30	Alleluia.	Alleluia.	Chorus	A	Long melisma on final "a"	
1:02	Caro mea vere est cibus,	For my flesh is food indeed,	Soloist	B	Melisma on "cibus" ("food")	
1:14	et sanguis meus vere est potus:	and my blood is drink indeed:	Soloist		Melismas on "sanguis" ("blood") and "potus" ("drink")	
1:34	qui manducat meam carnem,	He who eats my flesh	Soloist		Melismas on "manducat" ("eats") and "meam" ("my")	
1:52	et bibit meum sanguinem,	and drinks my blood	Soloist		Melismas on "meum" ("my") and "sanguinem" ("blood")	
2:08	in me manet, et ego in eo.	abides in me, and I in him.	Soloist	A	Melisma on "me" ("me") and long melisma on "eo" ("him")	
2:37	Alleluia.	Alleluia.	Chorus	A	Long melisma on final "a"	

Q Student FAQs ⚙

Who sings the solo passages in the service?

This can be sung by the priest, one of his assistants, by the leader of the chorus, or by a member of the chorus.

Is plainchant still used in churches?

In some churches on some occasions, yes. The Vatican choir has recently begun using plainchant once again on a regular basis. But chant is no longer the principal vehicle for singing texts in the Roman Catholic Church. It is still possible to hear special plainchant services from time to time, however.

PERFORMANCE **Chilling to Chant**

Plainchant has long been recognized as an element that enhances meditation, prayer, and devotion: It figures prominently in many of the world's religions (see Expand Your Playlist: Chant, Chapter 1). The gentle flow of the melodies, the absence of repetitive rhythms, and the relatively narrow range of timbre all help create a sense of calm and well-being. Scientists are gradually discovering that there is a physiological factor at work here as well. Dr. Alan Watkins, a senior lecturer in neuroscience at Imperial College London, has noted that "the musical structure of chanting can have a significant and positive physiological impact . . . studies also demonstrate that such practices have been shown to lower blood pressure, increase levels of the performance hormone DHEA as well as reducing anxiety and depression."

© Dr. Alan Watkins, Senior Lecturer in Neuroscience at Imperial College London.

The monks of the Stift Heiligenkreuz, near Vienna, Austria, are among those who have made recent recordings of Gregorian chant.

 Expand Your Playlist

The Plainchant Mass

As you listen to more recordings of plainchant, you will begin to hear a tremendous variety in the performances. The size of the ensemble, tempo, phrasing, and the quality of the singing can all vary widely. Here are some examples of various plainchant Masses available on CD and/or mp3.

Mass for Christmas Day
• *Christmas Chants* (Jade 35668). Choir of The Monks of Montserrat Abbey. The monks of this Benedictine Abbey, near Barcelona, Spain, have made many chant recordings.

Mass for Easter
• *Easter* (Paraclete S822). Saint Pierre de Solesmes Monks' Choir. Solesmes, in northern France, has long been a center for the study and practice of plainchant.

Mass for the Dedication of a Church
• *Heavenly Voices* (DG 000289 477 7526 3). Monks of the Benedictine Abbey of Münsterschwarzach. In the Middle Ages, the choir of each church would sing this Mass not only at the dedication of the sanctuary, but on the anniversary of that date every year as well.

Selections from Various Masses
• *Chant* (EMI Classics 55138). The Benedictine Monks of Santo Domingo de Silos. The best-selling recording of plainchant ever issued: the CD version (1994) went triple-platinum in the United States and sold six million copies worldwide.

4

Francesco Landini
"Behold, Spring"
Composed: ca. 1350–1397

This brief song illustrates an important feature in the development of medieval music: polyphony. We hear in Landini's "Behold, Spring" not one voice or group of voices singing the same melodic line, but two voices singing independent and equally important lines.

Listen to This First

🌐 Texture
Listen to the contrast between the melodies of the two voices, one high, one low. ■

🎛 Rhythm
Feel the regular pulse of three beats, with the first accented (**1**-2-3 | **1**-2-3 |). ■

🎵 Melody
Listen for the stepwise motion in both voices, and notice the brief stopping points that break the melody into smaller units. ■

🎼 Form
Listen for the repetition of large-scale units. ■

🎧 Word–Music Relationships
Notice the largely syllabic text setting—one note per syllable, and listen for the occasional melismatic setting—multiple notes sung to a single syllable. ■

LEARNING OBJECTIVES

4.1 Explain the role of song in the courtly love tradition.

4.2 Listen for the polyphonic texture in two voices in Francesco Landini's "Behold, Spring."

4.3 Listen for the cadences within "Behold, Spring."

4.4 Listen for the use of triple meter in "Behold, Spring."

4.5 Listen for the contrasts of syllabic and melismatic settings of text.

4.6 Discuss aspects of Francesco Landini's life.

4.7 Discuss the significance of the Squarcialupi manuscript as a source of medieval music.

Music was already the food of love in the Middle Ages long before Shakespeare coined the phrase. Poets were inspired to write love poetry, and composers were inspired to set those poems to music to make them even more moving. "Behold, Spring" ("Ecco la primavera") by the Italian composer Francesco Landini is a setting of one such poem. It is a ballata for two voices. The ballata was one of many genres of secular song in the Middle Ages, and in the patterned rhythms of "Behold, Spring" we can hear the origins of the genre in dance (in Italian, *ballata* means "danced"). Landini's setting captures the feeling of bodies in motion.

The repertory of secular (worldly, nonsacred) song from the Middle Ages is enormous. This was the age of **courtly love**, a highly stylized form of love in which a knight declares himself as the servant of the lady he is wooing. All his heroic deeds are done in her honor, and his love for her ennobles him, even if—especially if—she rejects his advances. Some songs describe the lady's beauty, others the knight's suffering (caused by her rejection of him), and still others the pleasures of love. In the *Decameron*, poet Giovanni Boccaccio—who lived in Florence at the same time as Landini and undoubtedly knew him—describes how a small group of lords and ladies, fleeing the plague (the "Black Death") in a group, sings "Behold, Spring" and songs like it "in amorous tones" to "divert their minds with music."

Florence was—and remains—an important center of culture on the Italian peninsula. In Landini's time, it was also an important center of political power.

The Richness of Polyphonic Texture

This brief work uses a new kind of musical texture that had been emerging slowly for several centuries: **polyphony**. In polyphony, two or more voices of equal importance combine in such a way that each voice retains its own identity (*poly* = "many"; *phon* = "sound"). Here, the upper and lower voices are of equal importance, and while our ear is drawn to the upper line for acoustical reasons (higher pitches always tend to stand out more), the lower line is every bit as melodious.

Composers created the earliest polyphonic works sometime around the eighth or ninth century by adding new lines above or below existing plainchant melodies. These new melodic lines were crafted in such a way as to embellish what was already present, and church authorities sanctioned this new kind of music on the grounds that it provided, in effect, a gloss or commentary on a well-known passage of text and music (the chant). Some of the earliest works of polyphony were based on an existing plainchant melody. A twelfth-century cleric named Perotin, who worked at the Cathedral of Notre Dame in Paris, wrote immensely long and intricate works known as organum (see Expand Your Playlist). These used plainchant melodies in long note values in the lowest voice, with faster-moving voices layered above the plainchant. These polyphonic works thus preserved the plainchant (in the lowest voice) even while enhancing it with new melodies (in the upper voices). Gradually, composers began writing polyphony against new, original melodies, extending the technique beyond sacred music to include secular music as well. Landini's "Behold, Spring" is one of these entirely new secular compositions.

Rhythm: The Pulse of Meter

If you are a composer writing for two or more voices, you need to consider how to make the parts mesh properly and stay together: The rhythmic freedom of monophony, as in plainchant, is no longer an option. Landini organizes "Behold, Spring" around a steady pattern of **triple meter** (**1**-2-3 I **1**-2-3 I etc.). The lengths of the individual notes vary, but the music falls into consistent units of three beats.

Units of Melody

The mostly **conjunct** (stepwise) melodic lines are subdivided into smaller units, each of which ends with a **cadence**, a brief stopping point at which the music pauses (or, in the case of the final cadence, ends). Cadences are to music as punctuation is to verbal expression: When we are writing, we indicate the end of individual units of thought with a comma, semicolon, period, or other end mark, and when we speak, we make correspondingly briefer or longer pauses. By breaking our speech into units (clauses and sentences), we make it easier for listeners to understand what we are saying. Music operates on the same principle. Here, Landini inserts a brief cadence at the end of the second and fourth lines in each four-line unit of the poetry. In this particular work, Landini always cadences on the **unison**—that is, both voices sing exactly the same note. The rhythms of the two voices also emphasize the arrival on each cadence. At times the two voices move in the same rhythmic pattern, whereas at other times their rhythms diverge, but the rhythms always coincide just before each cadence.

Form: Turning Poetry into Music

In most vocal music, the form of the text shapes the form of the work. "Behold, Spring" is no exception. The poetry consists of three verses, known as **strophes** (or **stanzas**—the terms are interchangeable), with the first repeated at the end. The music of the second strophe contrasts with the others. Landini thus uses both repetition and contrast to create a musical form that can be diagrammed as **ABAA**:

Strophe	1	2	3	4 (=1, repeated)
Music	**A**	**B**	**A**	**A**

This combination of repetition, variation, and contrast is basic to all musical forms. Once an idea is presented (in this case, the text and music of the first strophe, "1/**A**"), only one of three things can happen:

1. It can be repeated.
2. It can be varied.
3. It can be contrasted through the introduction of a new idea.

Landini uses all three of these devices:

1. He contrasts 1/**A** by presenting both a new text and new music in 2/**B**.
2. He varies 1/**A** by presenting the same music with a new text in 3/**A**.
3. He repeats both the text and music of 1/**A** in strophe 4/**A**.

Word–Music Relationships: Syllabic versus Melismatic

Landini sets the text in a manner that is largely **syllabic**, with one note per syllable. He uses **melismas**—multiple notes per syllable—only occasionally, as on "temp'è" (line 3 of the first strophe) and again on "tempo" in the third line of the second strophe. This creates a welcome degree of variety: Listening to an entirely syllabic setting might be a bit monotonous. But the syllabic setting allows the text to be projected quite clearly, even though the two voices are not always singing together in exactly the same rhythm.

Now listen to this ballata again, using the Listening Guide.

CONNECT YOUR PLAYLIST

Melismas

Find a piece that makes prominent use of melismas.

Example: The Righteous Brothers, "Unchained Melody" (1965)
The Righteous Brothers's version of this 1955 song features melismas on nearly every note.

Listening Guide

Francesco Landini Composed: ca. 1350–1397

"Behold, Spring" (1:13)

Time	Strophe	Italian Text	English Translation	Form	Melody
0:00	1	Ecco la primavera che 'l cor fa rallegrare; temp'è da 'nnamorare e star con lieta cera.	Behold, Spring, which makes the heart rejoice; it's the time to fall in love and to be of good cheer.	Music can be labeled as **A**.	Melisma on *primavera* Cadence on *rallegare* Melisma on *temp'è* Cadence on *cera*
0:15	2	No' vegiam l'aria e 'l tempo che pur chiama allegreza; in questo vago tempo ogni cosa ha vagheza.	We see the air and weather bringing about gladness; in this lovely time every thing has loveliness.	Contrasting music (**B**)	Melisma on *tempo* Cadence on *allegreza* Melisma on *tempo* Cadence on *vagheza*
0:37	3	L'erbe con gran frescheza e fiori copron prati; e gli alberi adornati sono in simil maniera.	The meadows are covered with fresh grass and with flowers; and the trees are adorned in a similar manner.	Same music as strophe 1, (**A**), different words	Melisma on *frescheza* Cadence on *prati* Melisma on *e* Cadence on *maniera*
0:54	4	Ecco la primavera che 'l cor far allegrare; temp'è da 'nnamorare e star con lieta cera.	Behold, Spring, which makes the heart rejoice; it's the time to fall in love and to be of good cheer.	Text and music (**A**) of strophe 1 repeated	[Same as Strophe 1]

Q Student FAQs ⚙

The words are about spring and flowers and falling in love. Why doesn't the music sound happier?

What makes music sound "happy" differs widely according to place and time. Our notions of what makes music sound lively or optimistic today (major mode, a "bright" sound, fast rhythmic motion) are culturally conditioned and did not emerge in Western music until the sixteenth century.

Was this written for women's voices?

This recording features women's voices. Women often performed together, as they do in this painting. Still, the piece could be performed just as easily by men's voices, or by men's and women's voices together.

PROFILE   FRANCESCO LANDINI (ca. 1325–1397)

The Composer as Poet

Blinded by smallpox at an early age, Landini was the most famous and prolific Italian composer of the fourteenth century. He served as organist at a church in Florence for many years and also won renown as a poet. The phenomenon of the poet-composer was not unusual in the Middle Ages: Many of the songs from this era feature poetry and music by the same individual. Landini is believed to have written more than 150 secular songs, which together represent about one-third of all Italian music that has survived from the fourteenth century.

One of Landini's contemporaries praised him so lavishly as a composer, performer, and poet that he acknowledged that readers might think he was exaggerating about the abilities of any one individual in so many diverse fields. But this contemporary seemed certain that everyone would agree that "[no one] ever played the organ so well. For this reason, in a public ceremony in Venice, he was recently [i.e., in 1364] crowned with laurel by His Illustrious and Noble Majesty the King of Cyprus, in the same way that poets were once crowned by the Emperors of Rome."

Source: *The Works of Francesco Landini, second edition.* Ed. Leonard Ellinwood. Cambridge, MA: The Mediaeval Academy of America, 1945, p. 302. Quotation from *De Ioanne Bartholo et Francisco Musicis* (1847), translated from the Latin by Mark Evan Bonds.

This image of Francesco Landini is from the Squarcialupi Codex, a richly illuminated manuscript of polyphonic music from the 14th century (see page 47). Landini is shown playing a small portative (or portable) organ.

 EXPAND YOUR PLAYLIST: LANDINI

- **"I feel the flame of love"** (*Sento d'amor la fiamma*): Another ballata

- **"My dear lady"** (*Cara mia donna*): A ballata for three voices

- **"Farewell, farewell sweet lady"** (*Adieu, Adieu, dous dame*): A virelais (a genre of French song) that exists in two versions—one for two voices, one for three

- **"Thus thoughtful"** (*Così pensoso*): A caccia or hunting song for three voices

HISTORICAL CONTEXT   Producing a Manuscript

Unlike today, in the Middle Ages every musical document had to be written by hand. "Manuscript" means literally "handwritten" (*manu* = "hand"; *scriptus* = "that which is written"), so each manuscript was by its very nature unique.

These manuscripts could be extraordinarily expensive to produce. The one known today as the Squarcialupi Codex (a *codex* is a manuscript of many pages bound together) is an unusually elaborate example. Its material alone represented an enormous investment:

- **Parchment.** This codex consists of more than 216 leaves of parchment, the prepared skin of a sheep or goat, cleaned, dried, and stretched to form a smooth surface for writing.
- **Gold leaf.** Many of the painted miniatures within the codex are decorated with gold leaf, actual pieces of gold beaten very thin.
- **Miniature portraits.** All 146 of Landini's works in the Squarcialupi Codex appear in one continuous section, with his portrait at the beginning.

We know where the Squarcialupi Codex was made—the monastery of Santa Maria degli Angeli in Florence (present-day Italy)—but we do not know who commissioned it or paid for it. The music of the Squarcialupi Codex is largely secular (worldly), not sacred, and thus it was probably commissioned by an affluent individual. At some later point in the fifteenth century, this manuscript came into the possession of the Florentine organist Antonio Squarcialupi (1416–1480), after whom it is now named. There was no commercial market for a manuscript like this: It was created for, funded, and enjoyed by a single individual.

The Squarcialupi Codex, showing a portrait of the composer and organist Francesco Landini.

 EXPAND YOUR PLAYLIST

Medieval Polyphony

Perotin
- "All the Ends of the Earth Have Seen" ("Viderunt omnes"). The three upper voices weave in and around each other over a slow-moving fourth voice, derived from plainchant. The effect is mesmerizing.

Anonymous
- "In Paris/It Is Said/Fresh Strawberries" ("À Paris/On parole/Fraise nouvele"). One of many thirteenth-century polyphonic works with multiple texts: Each of the three voices sings its own text, the upper two about the virtues of life in Paris, the third a street vendor's cry selling fresh fruit.

Anonymous
- "Summer is a-comin' in" ("Sumer is icumen in"). A round for two voices that is sung over a repeating phrase for two additional voices in the bass. This song about the arrival of summer was composed in England around 1250.

Lorenzo da Firenze
- "All in Their Places" ("A poste messe"). A fourteenth-century Italian caccia, a stylized hunting song that imitates the sounds of horns and dogs.

5

Guillaume de Machaut
"No More than One Man Could Count the Stars"
Composed: ca. 1350

This song by Guillaume de Machaut illustrates the expansion of polyphonic texture from two to three voices. It gives voice to the medieval art of courtly love, in which the knight praises the beauty and virtue of a noblewoman who is (or at least pretends to be) indifferent to him.

Listen to This First

Texture

This is a polyphonic work for three equally important voices. Listen to the contrast in speed between the faster uppermost voice and the slightly slower two voices below. ▪

🎵 Melody

Listen for the cadences—points of rest in the music—within the melody. ▪

🎹 Form

Listen for the repetition of large units of music. The music of the opening section is repeated to new words, and the closing section presents a contrasting melodic idea. ▪

LEARNING OBJECTIVES

5.1 Listen for the three-part polyphonic texture of this work.

5.2 Listen for the structural cadences within this work.

5.3 Discuss how the text of Guillaume de Machaut's "No More than One Man Could Count the Stars" reflects the medieval ideal of courtly love.

5.4 Listen for the difference in melodic motion between the upper voice and the two lower voices in "No More than One Man Could Count the Stars."

5.5 Listen for the **AAB** form of the work.

5.6 Outline Guillaume de Machaut's career as a composer.

Love songs are as old as songs themselves. In the Middle Ages, many of these songs adopted the perspective of **courtly love**, in which a nobleman admires and literally sings the praises of a noblewoman, even if—or rather, *especially* if—she takes no interest in him. By forging ahead in spite of the woman's indifference, the singer could demonstrate his zeal and devotion. This particular song plays on the age-old idea that the poet cannot express his love any more than he could count the stars in the sky, drops of rain, waves in the sea, or the grains of sand on the shore.

Three-Voice Texture

This work is for three voices, each of which presents a melodic line completely different from the two others. Medieval composers like Machaut were constantly exploring the possibilities of combining two, three, four, and even five independent voices to create **polyphonic textures**.

The uppermost voice is the easiest to hear. Not only is it the highest voice, it is also the one that is most rhythmically active and fluid. The two lower voices move at a slightly slower speed and sing slightly longer (and fewer) notes. Because these two lower voices move in the same range and at a similar speed, it can be difficult to distinguish clearly between them, but together they create an underpinning for the lead voice on top.

A Melody Punctuated by Cadences

Listen for the **cadences**—points of arrival, coupled with a brief pause in the forward motion—within the course of the upper voice's melody. These cadences occur at the end of each important phrase in the poetry, and of course at the very end of this first verse. This entire verse consists of a single sentence and in performance runs a little over two-and-a-half minutes, so it is essential that its phrases stand out clearly from one another. Think of these cadences as the musical equivalent of commas that mark off divisions within the sentence of the text: each unit of the melody between the cadences presents a more or less self-contained poetic idea, and the cadences help articulate the end and beginning of each melodic section.

AAB Form

Machaut's text consists of seven lines (see the Listening Guide). The music of the opening two lines (**A**) is repeated for the second set of two lines as well. In other words, we hear the same music twice, but with new words the second time. A contrasting melodic idea (**B**) appears for the closing three lines of the text and is not repeated. The overall form of the music can thus be represented as **AAB**. This is the same form as "The Star-Spangled Banner." As in "The Star-Spangled Banner," the "**B**" section is considerably longer than the "**A**" section. This is, as noted earlier, a common form in music of many times and places.

Now listen to the piece again, using the Listening Guide.

CONNECT YOUR PLAYLIST

Three-Voice Texture

Find any work or extended passage for three voices.

Example: Kingston Trio, "M.T.A." (1957)
This song, made popular by the Kingston Trio's recording, features three-part texture throughout.

Guillaume de Machaut Composed: ca. 1350

"No More than One Man Could Count the Stars" (2:32)

Time	French Text	English Translation	Texture	Form	Melody
0:00	Ne qu'on porroit les estoiles nombrer, Quant on les voit luire plus clerement,	No more than one man could count the stars when one sees them shining at their brightest,	Three-voice polyphony throughout	A	Cadence on *nombrer* (0:24) Cadence on *clerement* (0:53)
0:55	Et les goutes de pluie et de la mer, Et la greve seur quoy elle s'estent,	nor drops of rain and the waves of the sea, nor the sands of the shore along which it stretches,		A	Cadence on *mer* (1:14) Cadence on *s'estent* (1:43)
1:45	Et compasser le tour dou firmament, Ne porroit on penser ne concevoir Le grant desir que j'ay de vous veoir.	nor measure out the circle of the firmament, No more could one imagine or conceive the great desire I have of seeing you.		B	Cadence on *concevoir* (2:13) Cadence on *veoir* (2:32)

🔍 Student FAQs ⚙

This music sounds almost modern. Why is that?

Medieval melodies and harmonies are based on a different system of scales (modes) than the ones we use today; many of the conventional turns of phrase we expect to hear in melodies simply did not exist at the time, which creates a feeling that the music sounds somehow strange and different today, and to some ears, "modern."

Are those men's or women's voices on the recording or both?

These are all men (three of them). The bottom two are singing in the range of a tenor, the upper end of the male register. The top voice is singing in the range of an alto, which is the lower end of the female register. The singer accomplishes this by singing in a manner known as falsetto, in which only a small portion of the singer's vocal cords vibrate; the effect is a higher-than-normal register. The Beach Boys, the Bee Gees, Michael Jackson, and Prince have all frequently used this technique.

PROFILE   Guillaume de Machaut (ca. 1300–1377)

Poet and Composer

Machaut was both a poet and composer, writing the words as well as music to his secular (worldly, nonsacred) songs. He spent much of his life in the service of various monarchs and traveled widely throughout northern Europe. A member of the clergy, he was appointed a canon at the Cathedral of Reims in 1335. Machaut's "Messe de Nostre Dame" ("Mass of Our Lady") is the first known polyphonic setting of all the sung movements of the Mass Ordinary (Mass for every day) by one composer. The Mass had been sung as plainchant for centuries before (see Chapter 3), but Machaut was the first to write a complete set of multivoiced movements to be sung in a service.

Toward the end of his life, Machaut supervised the copying of what amounts to his complete works in a series of six large manuscripts called the "Machaut Manuscripts." They total more than 2,100 leaves and are richly illustrated. The image of Machaut here comes from one of those manuscripts and shows the composer still being inspired by the goddess of love, even in his old age.

Nature introduces her children Emotion, Rhetoric, and Music to Guillaume de Machaut, who is at work in his study.

 EXPAND YOUR PLAYLIST: MACHAUT

- **"Messe de Nostre Dame"** ("Mass of Our Lady"). The first complete polyphonic setting of the Mass Ordinary.

- **"Rose, liz, printemps verdure"** ("Rose, lily, spring, greenery"). A love song for five voices.

- **"Ma fin est mon commencement"** ("My Beginning Is My End"). A song for three voices in which the two upper voices are the same melody, one sung forward, the other sung backward at the same time. The words match the structure of the music.

 EXPAND YOUR PLAYLIST

The Art of Courtly Love

Jacopo da Bologna
- "Never Did Diana Please Her Lover More" ("Non al suo amante"). A song for two voices by a fourteenth-century Italian composer. It ends with the words "My whole body trembled with the cold chill of love."

Bernart de Ventadorn
- "The Fool on the Bridge" ("Le fou sur le pont"). A song from the twelfth century by one of the most famous of all troubadours.

Oswald von Wolkenstein
- "Ah, Suffering and Longing" ("Ach senliches Leiden"). A song from the early fifteenth century by one of the leading *Minnesinger*, the German-language counterpart of the troubadours.

6

Alfonso el Sabio

Songs to the Virgin Mary, no. 147, "The Talking Sheep"
Composed: Late Thirteenth Century

The penetrating sound of the shawm, a double-reed instrument featured on this chapter's recording of "The Talking Sheep" ("A Madre do que a bestia de Balaam"), offers a good example of just how vivid and intense medieval timbres could be. The recording recreates how drums and two wind instruments might have brought to life a work originally notated for only one voice.

Listen to This First

〰 Timbre

Listen for the contrast between the wind instruments (three shawms) and the percussion instruments (drums and small bells). ■

▥ Form

Listen for the two contrasting melodies. Notice the way these melodies are repeated and varied. ■

🌐 Texture

Listen for three distinct textures on the shawms:

1. All instruments play the same notes together in unison (monophony).
2. Two instruments play the melody in unison while the third holds a long, single note (homophony).
3. Two instruments play the same melody but not in unison, weaving around each other and moving independently (polyphony). ■

LEARNING OBJECTIVES

6.1 Listen for the contrasting timbres of percussion and woodwind instruments in Alfonso el Sabio's "The Talking Sheep."

6.2 Describe the use of repetition and contrast to create a large-scale form.

6.3 Listen for the three different kinds of texture featured in "The Talking Sheep": monophonic, homophonic, and polyphonic.

6.4 Discuss the use of instruments in music of the Middle Ages.

6.5 Describe the difference between single- and double-reed wind instruments.

6.6 Explain why the identity of so many composers of medieval music remains unknown.

6.7 Name other instruments used in the Middle Ages.

Relatively little music written specifically for instruments survives from the Middle Ages. But we know from numerous accounts that composers and musicians rarely made sharp distinctions between vocal and instrumental music, and that they often performed vocal lines on instruments if not enough singers happened to be available for a performance. So while the original version of "The Talking Sheep" is for voices, with a text to be sung, the performance for this chapter reflects the common medieval practice of performing music with whatever resources happened to be at hand. Jazz musicians still commonly arrange songs with words for instruments alone. When the great jazz saxophonist John Coltrane performed "My Favorite Things" (from *The Sound of Music*) on his saxophone in 1961, he was carrying on a tradition that had begun in the Middle Ages.

"The Talking Sheep" is one of the *Songs to the Virgin Mary* (*Cantigas de Santa Maria*) attributed to Alfonso el Sabio ("Alfonso the Wise"), who ruled the Kingdom of Castile and León on the Iberian Peninsula between 1252 and 1284. The *Cantigas* is a collection of more than 400 songs preserved in several different manuscripts. One of these sources, now housed in the library of the monastery in Escorial, Spain, is full of miniatures showing a great variety of medieval instruments, lending further support to the idea that this music was not meant exclusively for

The Iberian Peninsula in the Middle Ages.

voices. The original text of this particular song tells the story of a devout old woman who entrusts one of her sheep to a shepherd who later claims that it has been eaten by a wolf. But like the donkey in the Biblical story of Balaam, the sheep can talk and says to the woman: "Here I am."

Timbre: The Sound of Double Reeds

The **shawm** is a double-reed instrument because the player blows through the tiny space between a pair of cane strips. The vibrating air resonates down a long, open-ended tubular base made of wood and produces a reedy, slightly nasal sound. Although the shawm is still widely used in northern Africa and the Middle East, it had largely disappeared from western Europe by the end of the Renaissance. The closest relative of this **woodwind instrument** in the modern-day orchestra is the oboe, but the oboe's sound is more refined and not as delightfully raucous.

The large drum and the small bells heard in this chapter's recording are **percussion instruments** that resonate when struck. The drum here is played with the hands. (For more on instruments of this era, see "Closer Look: Musical Instruments of the Middle Ages.")

Form: Repetition and Contrast

This performance begins with an extended introduction in which the players give the impression of "warming up." There is no clear melody here; instead, the shawm players seem to be loosening their fingers and getting their lungs ready for the performance to follow. One of the musicians holds a steady note underneath that creates a **drone bass** to the freer material above. When the percussion instruments enter, the shawms launch into the first of two fairly short melodic units, which we can label as **A** and **B**. The form of this piece arises out of the repetition and contrast of these two melodic ideas. Toward the end, the players extend the **A** theme several times to close out the work.

A modern performer in medieval garb plays the shawm, the wind instrument heard in this performance of "The Talking Sheep." Today's musicians have revived medieval instruments like the shawm, which had fallen out of use over time.

CONNECT YOUR PLAYLIST

Drone Bass

Find a piece that uses a single bass note for an extended time.

Example: Civil Wars, "Devil's Backbone" (2013)
The first verse of this song is sung over a two-note drone in the bass, creating a sparse, melancholy sound.

 # Three Kinds of Texture

In this piece, we hear three different textures:

1. **Monophony:** All the instruments play the same notes together, in unison.
2. **Homophony:** One or two instruments play the melody, the other a drone bass—that is, a long note held underneath the melodic line. The effect is very much like that of a bagpipe, another instrument widely used in medieval times.
3. **Polyphony:** Toward the end of the introduction (0:30–0:40), the two shawms playing above the drone bass stop playing in unison, and each pursues its own independent melodic line.

Now listen to this work again, using the Listening Guide.

PERFORMANCE   Reed Instruments

If you've ever created a sound by blowing on a blade of grass, you've applied the basic principle common to all reed instruments. These range from the medieval shawm (heard here) to the modern-day saxophone. By blowing into a reed instrument's mouthpiece, the player sets in motion either one or two thin strips of cane that have been specially shaped and dried. This vibrating cane, known as a *reed*, creates a resonance that produces the instrument's distinctive sound.

There are two subfamilies of reed instruments:

A close-up of the mouthpiece of a shawm with its double reed, next to the "bell" of the instrument.

- **Double-reed instruments:** The mouthpiece consists of two reeds opposed to one another. One reed thus vibrates initially against the other reed, which tends to produce the slightly "buzzy" sound heard here on the shawm. The two main double-reed instruments in use today are the oboe and the bassoon.

- **Single-reed instruments:** The mouthpiece consists of a single reed secured to a hard surface. The principal single-reed instruments today are the clarinet and the saxophone. Finding good reeds is a challenge for musicians. More advanced players often make their own reeds, buying the raw material—strips of thin cane, specially grown and processed—and then shaving them down to just the right degree of thickness. A reed that is too thick will produce a "wooly" sound, but if it is too thin, it will break after only a short time.

A clarinet mouthpiece with its single reed.

Listening Guide))

Alfonso el Sabio Composed: Late Thirteenth Century

Songs to the Virgin Mary, no. 147, "The Talking Sheep" (3:03)

Time	Form	Timbre	Texture
0:00	Introduction: free, improvisatory	3 shawms	Largely homophonic: drone bass underneath the faster-moving voices (0:03, 0:15, 0:25, etc.)
0:30			Polyphonic: above the continuing drone bass, the upper voices move independently of each other.
0:40	A	3 shawms, drum, small bells	Monophonic (unison)
0:48	A		
0:56	A		
1:03	A		
1:10	B		Homophonic: drone bass underneath the melody
1:24	A		
1:32	A		Monophonic
1:39	B		Monophonic
1:46	B		
1:54	A		
2:02	A		
2:08	A extended		Homophonic: drone bass
2:28	A extended		
2:50	A extended		

Q Student FAQs ✿

Why shawms?

Why not? The performers in this recording could have used almost any instrument and still been in keeping with medieval attitudes toward performing vocal music without singing.

Were the drum parts really that lively in the Middle Ages?

Drum parts were never notated in the Middle Ages, but we know from paintings that they were central to many instrumental ensembles, so we can assume that musicians used the notated music as a starting point, adding and embellishing as they saw fit. In this respect, medieval instrumental music was probably very much like today's jazz: A melody provides the basis of a more elaborate performance that takes liberties with the original tune.

PROFILE   Alfonso el Sabio (1221–1284)

The King Gets All the Credit

The manuscripts preserving the music and poetry known as the *Songs to the Virgin Mary* (*Cantigas de Santa Maria*) ascribe these works to Alfonso el Sabio ("Alfonso the Wise"), who ruled the Kingdom of Castile and León. Scholars now believe that if Alfonso wrote any of the words or music at all, he probably wrote only a relatively small number of them. We can be certain, however, that Alfonso was the moving force behind the creation and compilation of these songs; he commissioned many works in a variety of fields, including literature, philosophy, theology, and even chess.

The real composer of this particular song is in all likelihood anonymous, as is the case with so many medieval artists. After all, we often do not even know the names of the architects who designed the great Gothic cathedrals and churches being built around this same time in the thirteenth century. Many of these composers were monks, priests, or nuns; others were employed as musicians at courts; still others were troubadours, trouvères, and minnesingers who traveled widely.

Alfonso el Sabio (center) listens to musicians performing a song in praise of the Virgin Mary (right). This image is from one of the several 13th-century manuscripts that preserve the *Songs to the Virgin Mary*.

CLOSER L👓K   Musical Instruments of the Middle Ages

This illustration from a fourteenth-century Italian treatise shows a variety of musical instruments. The placement of the figures is strategic, with King David, the author of the Psalms, at the top and Saint Cecilia, the patron saint of music, in the middle. The Psalms of David were meant to be sung, making frequent references to musical instruments.

The **vielle** was a forerunner of today's violin, with a wider and flatter body. Like the violin, the vielle had a penetrating sound and could be used to accompany both song and dance.

The **tambourine** is a percussion instrument. It combines the sound of a drum—the taut membrane of an animal skin—and small rattling cymbals around the edges. The tambourine, also known as the timbrel, is one of the instruments specifically mentioned in Psalm 150.

Bagpipe (left) and **shawm** (right). The bagpipe is an ancient instrument: the "bladder," which supplies the air squeezed through the pipes, was often made from an animal's stomach. The woman plays a short and therefore high-pitched shawm.

Drums, like the tambourine, are percussion instruments. They come in all shapes and sizes and can be played with the hands or (as shown here) with drumsticks. This drummer seems distracted by the volume of sound coming from the trumpets.

King David enjoys pride of place in his own special frame. Here, he plays the **psaltery**, a forerunner of today's dulcimer, a plucked stringed instrument. Many of the instruments in this image are mentioned in David's Psalm 150: 3-4: "Praise him with the sound of the trumpet: praise him with the psaltery and harp. Praise him with the timbrel and dance: praise him with stringed instruments and organs."

The **lute** was one of the most popular instruments in Medieval and Renaissance times. The player here uses a plectrum or "pick" to pluck the strings.

Castanets or **"clappers."** This small percussion instrument, held in the hands, creates a very sharp sound and was used in dance music. The musician here in fact seems to be dancing.

Saint Cecilia plays the organ, one of the instruments with which she is often depicted. This type of organ is called a **portative** ("portable") **organ**. While the organ rests on the left side of her lap, she plays the keys with her right hand. With her left hand, she pumps air through the pipes with a kind of bellows mechanism not visible from this angle.

Two **straight trumpets**. These are brass instruments consisting of a single long tube, without the coiling and keys found on modern trumpets.

EXPAND YOUR PLAYLIST

Instrumental Music of the Middle Ages

Kyrie cunctipotens genitor

- An arrangement, for organ, of a liturgical vocal composition from the Mass, with a chant melody in the slow-moving lower voice and a free embellishment in the upper voice. Ensemble Unicorn, *Codex Faenza: Instrumental Music of the Early 15th Century*. Naxos 8.553618, Track 16.

Palästinalied

- An arrangement of a German song from the time of the Crusades ("Palestine Song"), performed here on a recorder (a flute-like instrument) and a small drum. *The World of Early Music*. Naxos 8.554770, Track 5.

La quinte estampie real

- The *estampie* was an energetic type of dance that involved stamping of the feet, as its name suggests. This performance is by an ensemble of wind and percussion instruments. Dufay Collective, *A Dance in the Garden of Mirth*. Chandos CHAN 9320, Track 9.

Saltarello

- Another type of dance, this one involving leaping (*saltare* in Italian means "to jump"). This recording is for hurdy-gurdy, vielle, and drum. St. George's Canzona, *A Medieval Banquet*. ASV Living Era, Track 1.

PART 1 Summary

Texture	Both monophonic and polyphonic		**Harmony**	A by-product of counterpoint
Melody	Flowing, largely conjunct, divided into sections by cadences; melodies based on scales of the medieval modes		**Form**	Based on repetition, variation, and contrast
Rhythm	Free (plainchant) and metrically structured		**Word–Music Relationships**	Syllabic settings to project texts clearly; melismatic settings to emphasize key words

IN REVIEW: Medieval Style

Monophony A single melodic line, whether sung by a solo voice or by a choir in unison. This was the essential texture of plainchant, the earliest music of Christian worship.

- Hildegard von Bingen, *Play of Virtues* (Chapter 1)
- Plainchant Alleluia "Caro mea" (Chapter 3)

Polyphony Two or more different melodic lines performed simultaneously. This texture was used in both sacred and secular music.

- Francesco Landini, "Behold, Spring" (Chapter 4)
- Guillaume de Machaut "No More than One Man Could Count the Stars" (Chapter 5)

Heterophony Two voices singing the same melody simultaneously, but with different embellishments.

- Alfonso el Sabio, *Songs to the Virgin Mary*, no. 147, "The Talking Sheep" (Chapter 6)

Syllabic and melismatic text-setting Text set to one note per syllable or multiple notes per syllable.

- Hildegard von Bingen, *Play of Virtues* (Chapter 1)
- Franceso Landini, "Behold, Spring" (Chapter 4)

Metered rhythm Rhythm structured around a fixed metrical pattern, allowing polyphonic voices to coordinate.

- Francesco Landini, "Behold, Spring" (Chapter 4)
- Guillaume de Machaut "No More than One Man Could Count the Stars" (Chapter 5)

Instrumental music Medieval performers could and did play vocal music on a variety of different instruments, such as the shawm.

- Alfonso el Sabio, *Songs to the Virgin Mary*, no. 147, "The Talking Sheep" (Chapter 6)

PART 2 ca. 1425–1600
The Renaissance

During the **Renaissance** many of the arts and sciences from antiquity that had been lost or forgotten during the Middle Ages were recovered. *Renaissance* is the French word for "rebirth," and what was reborn in this era was the spirit of **humanism**, an intellectual and cultural movement that explored human interests and values through the pursuit of science, philosophy, literature, painting, sculpture, and music—particularly vocal music.

Renaissance composers brought the spirit of humanism to their art by setting both sacred and secular texts in ways that united words and music more directly than ever before. Composers devoted special attention to both the rhythm of the poetry and the meanings of individual words. They created a sound based on the ideal of equal-voiced parts in three, four, five, and eventually even six voices. The typical Renaissance vocal composition features a full, rich sound, intricate in both its texture and rhythm, yet always attentive to the text being sung.

Music for Catholics, Music for Protestants

As a Catholic, composer William Byrd had to watch his step in an England ruled by a Protestant monarch. While maintaining his own faith, he cultivated favor with Queen Elizabeth I in part by writing large quantities of music for Protestant church services, including the brilliant choral anthem *Sing Joyfully*.

Chapter 9
Byrd, *Sing Joyfully*

The Renaissance

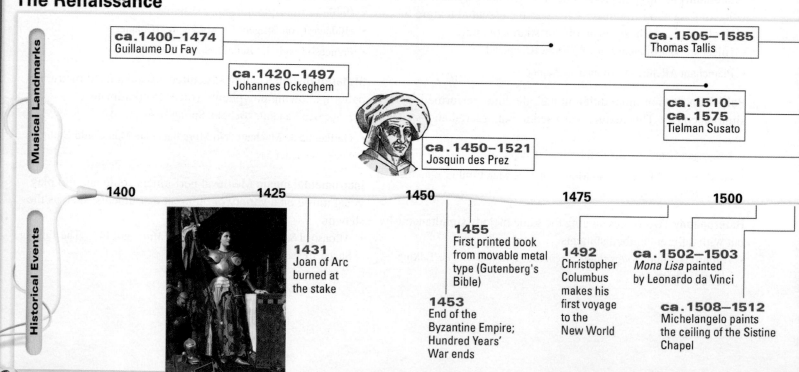

Musical Landmarks

ca.1400–1474
Guillaume Du Fay

ca.1420–1497
Johannes Ockeghem

ca.1450–1521
Josquin des Prez

ca.1505–1585
Thomas Tallis

ca.1510–
ca.1575
Tielman Susato

1400　　1425　　1450　　1475　　1500

Historical Events

1431
Joan of Arc
burned at
the stake

1453
End of the
Byzantine Empire;
Hundred Years'
War ends

1455
First printed book
from movable metal
type (Gutenberg's
Bible)

1492
Christopher
Columbus
makes his
first voyage
to the
New World

ca.1502–1503
Mona Lisa painted
by Leonardo da Vinci

ca.1508–1512
Michelangelo paints
the ceiling of the Sistine
Chapel

The rift among Christians had begun in 1517, when an obscure German monk named Martin Luther nailed a list of complaints on the doors of a church in Wittenberg. Luther was responding to what a number of people saw as growing corruption and a weakening spirituality in the church. He set in motion a revolution, known as the Reformation, that would establish Protestantism as a new branch of Christianity. From that point onward, the Western church would be divided into two main branches, Protestant and Catholic. The faith of any European monarch—Catholic or Protestant—would determine the faith and the politics of his or her realm. Composers responded to these changes by writing new music for the Protestant liturgy in languages other than Latin. Catholic composers, in turn, responded in their own way. In what became known as the Counter-Reformation, composers like Giovanni Pierluigi da Palestrina redoubled their efforts to write music that would move the souls of the faithful.

Chapter 10
Palestrina, *Pope Marcellus Mass*, "Gloria"

Music for Growing Markets

Renaissance composers and musicians benefited from the enormous economic growth throughout Europe that began in the fifteenth century. The Italian peninsula and the area known as the Low Countries (present-day Belgium and the Netherlands) led the way in this new era of economic expansion. First contact with the "New World"—Christopher Columbus lived his entire life (1451–1506) in the Renaissance—swelled royal and private coffers still more. As kingdoms, duchies, and city-states expanded both in population and in wealth, the demand for music and the arts in general became greater and greater. The best composers and musicians could command high salaries.

Martin Luther, 1529. Luther was a composer as well as a theologian: He wrote both the words and the music to the Protestant hymn "A Mighty Fortress Is Our God" ("Ein' feste Burg ist unser Gott"). This portrait is by the famed German artist Lucas Cranach the Elder.

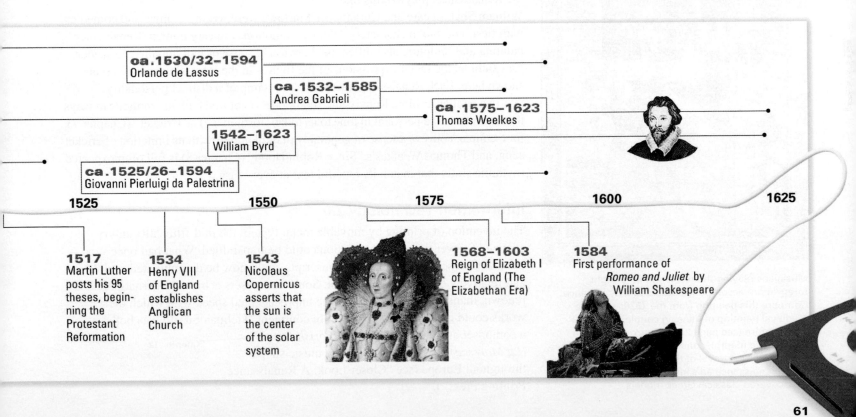

ca.1530/32–1594
Orlande de Lassus

ca.1532–1585
Andrea Gabrieli

ca.1575–1623
Thomas Weelkes

1542–1623
William Byrd

ca.1525/26–1594
Giovanni Pierluigi da Palestrina

1525   **1550**   **1575**   **1600**   **1625**

1517
Martin Luther posts his 95 theses, beginning the Protestant Reformation

1534
Henry VIII of England establishes Anglican Church

1543
Nicolaus Copernicus asserts that the sun is the center of the solar system

1568–1603
Reign of Elizabeth I of England (The Elizabethan Era)

1584
First performance of *Romeo and Juliet* by William Shakespeare

The ideal "Renaissance man" was someone who cultivated knowledge and experience in the full range of arts and sciences. In his famous handbook of behavior, *The Book of the Courtier*, Italian nobleman and writer Baldassare Castiglione recommended that every would-be gentleman learn the basic arts of singing and playing an instrument such as the lute. Music lovers entertained themselves and their listeners with such whimsical songs as Josquin des Prez's "The Cricket" ("El grillo") or with madrigals such as Thomas Weelkes's "Since Robin Hood," using whatever instruments or voices were on hand.

Chapter 7
Josquin des Prez, "The Cricket"

Chapter 8
Thomas Weelkes, "Since Robin Hood"

Hans Holbein the Younger's *The Ambassadors* (1533) shows two courtly gentlemen with the symbols of their status: a globe and navigational instruments, and (on the bottom shelf of the table behind them) a lute, a set of four flutes, and an open hymnal. (The odd object in the foreground is a distorted rendering of a skull, a reminder of human mortality.)

A New Sense of Individuality

The Renaissance was an age of growing confidence in the powers of human reason and the distinctiveness of every individual. Art became more personal. The contrasts between drama in the Middle Ages and in the Renaissance provide a revealing example of this new sense of individuality. Medieval drama had tended toward allegory: the Innocent Soul in Hildegard von Bingen's *Play of Virtues (Ordo Virtutum)* (Chapter 1) is a symbolic figure torn between other symbolic figures, the Virtues and the Devil. By the end of the Renaissance, playwrights like William Shakespeare and Christopher Marlowe were writing dramas and comedies with flesh-and-blood characters. Hamlet's emotions are very human. Renaissance painting and sculpture also reflect this newfound sense of individuality. Consider, for example, the facial expressions of the figures in the Renaissance dance scene shown here. Each Renaissance face bears the stamp of a distinct personality.

In a similar fashion, Renaissance composers captured human emotions in ways that seem far more personal in tone to us today. Josquin's "The Cricket" (Chapter 7), for example, conveys a sense of genuinely playful humor with its imitation of cricket song, and Thomas Weelkes's "Since Robin Hood" (Chapter 8) is full of unexpected rhythmic shifts that match its fanciful text at every turn.

Information Technology 2.0

The invention of printing by movable metal type in the mid-fifteenth century changed forever the way information could be transmitted. What had once circulated in scarce, expensive manuscripts could now be disseminated rapidly and relatively cheaply through print. Some composers achieved international renown, thanks in no small part to the unprecedented speed with which their works could circulate across the entire continent. Tielman Susato was both a composer and a publisher. His *Moorish Dance (La Moresca)* could be purchased in music shops throughout Europe (see "Closer Look: A Renaissance Printing Press").

Chapter 12
Susato, *Moorish Dance*

Musicians playing the drum and flute (right foreground) accompany a lord and lady in dance. Compare this painting from the 1520s with the medieval painting of dancing couples from 100 years before (see page 23). The strong sense of perspective (depth), considerable detail in the faces, and realistic portrayal of the individual figures show Renaissance art's inspiration from newly rediscovered classical Greek models.

CLOSER LK   A Renaissance Printing Press

Before the invention of the printing press, the only way to reproduce a text was to copy it by hand. The end result of this laborious process was a single copy. The printing press made it possible to create hundreds and even thousands of copies of a text in a single process. Individuals could now buy music for their own use at a reasonable price. By 1500, printing had become a major enterprise, and countless presses, big and small, began to spring up across Europe.

A delivery man brings fresh paper to the shop. **Paper mills** made large sheets of paper by straining fibers, usually derived from old rags. This process was much cheaper and faster than working with animal skin to make parchment.

A workman applies ink to the set type, using two sponge-like applicators called **"ink balls."** He will then lay a sheet of clean paper over the inked type and slide both into the wooden press.

The **pressman** pulls the press: The screw mechanism (adopted from wine-making technology) exerts the enormous pressure needed to affix the ink to the paper. Printed sheets are then hung up to dry on a line nearby.

The **manuscript** of the text to be set is clipped to the wall.

Two **typesetters** set the type, pulling individual metal-cast letters one by one out of the cases before them. Each case is divided into an upper half and a lower half: The one above stores the capital letters, hence the term "upper case" for capital letters, even today.

The **owner** of the print shop supervises the operation. He pays the workers, negotiates contracts with authors, and invests the capital needed to run his small business.

This worker is one of two carrying out the **proofreading** process. His colleague, standing to his side, reads aloud the original text that has been typeset while the seated worker corrects any errors by rearranging type. The corrected typeface will go back to the press to be run off in multiple copies.

A young boy (known as the **"printer's devil"**) assists with miscellaneous tasks around the shop. If he proves himself trustworthy, he will eventually be given one of the more responsible jobs in the shop.

7

Josquin des Prez
"The Cricket"
Composed: ca. 1500

"The Cricket" is a good example of Renaissance polyphony. It is for four voices, all equally important, and the music projects with special clarity the subject of its text: a cricket.

Listen to This First

Texture

Listen for the polyphony of four distinct voices, all of equal importance. Listen for the difference between those passages in which the voices sing together in the same rhythm and those in which they go their own separate ways. ■

Word–Music Relationships

Listen for the examples of word painting, in which the music imitates the sounds of a cricket. ■

Form

Listen for the return of the opening section toward the end, and notice the contrast between the song's middle and outer sections. ■

LEARNING OBJECTIVES

7.1 Discuss the whimsical nature of the text of "The Cricket" and how Josquin's setting reflects this nature.

7.2 Listen for the four equal voices characteristic of Renaissance style.

7.3 Recognize how Josquin's music depicts specific words in the text of "The Cricket."

7.4 Listen for the contrasting sections of the **ABA** structure.

7.5 Describe various performance options for "The Cricket."

7.6 Discuss highlights of Josquin's life.

Why do composers write songs? Why set poetry to music? The answer is really quite simple: The right music makes any text more vivid and memorable. The poem inspires the composer, and the composer's melding of words and music inspires us as listeners. Think how much easier it is to remember verses that have been set to melody than it is to remember a poem all by itself. The challenge for composers has always been to find music that matches a text in just the right way.

When Josquin decided to compose "The Cricket" ("El grillo"), he accepted the challenge of writing music that would be as humorous as the poem itself. The text praises the singing of crickets over that of birds. It lauds the insect's versatility as a singer: He can sing long notes and stay in one place for long periods of time, unlike birds, who flit from place to place. The cricket can sing drinking songs, and when the weather turns warm in May, he sings of love. Josquin uses catchy, clever rhythms to imitate the sound of the cricket. His melodic lines enhance the spirit of the poem, and his textures bring out the meaning of key words.

Josquin's setting is typical of Renaissance song in general, in that it speaks a musical language that seems almost contemporary to us today. Its melodies, rhythms, and textures certainly strike us as more familiar than those of the Middle Ages. Hildegard von Bingen (Chapter 1), Francesco Landini (Chapter 4), and Guillaume de Machaut (Chapter 5) were equally inspired by the texts they set, yet their musical language is somehow less direct, more hauntingly austere. Medieval and Renaissance musical styles might be said to differ in the way that Old English differs from modern English. It is a not a matter of one language being better than the other.

Medieval and Renaissance songs create their own distinct kinds of beauty by using the same basic elements of music in different ways.

Medieval and Renaissance scribes often inserted humorous vignettes into otherwise very serious manuscripts. Here, the scribe seems to be commenting on the parallels between human musicians and the noises animals make.

Texture: Polyphony in Four Voices

The four voice parts of "The Cricket" correspond to the four registers of the human voice:

- **Soprano** (highest range)
- **Alto** (second-highest range)
- **Tenor** (second-lowest range)
- **Bass** (lowest range)

In Josquin's setting, these four voices are essentially equal, and they move together in step for most of the work. Only occasionally does Josquin differentiate among the voices rhythmically, and the words we hear at those moments stand out from the rest of the song. The most striking of these moments occurs at the words *longo verso* ("long verse") at 0:07–0:13, and at *amore* ("love") at 0:50–0:54, when each voice momentarily goes its own way, setting these key words apart from all others in the text.

Equal-voice texture—**polyphony**—is the norm for Renaissance music in general, as opposed to **monophony** (a single melodic line) or **homophony** (a melodic line accompanied by other voices of lesser importance). Renaissance composers took great pride in their skill at **counterpoint**, a system of rules and procedures governing the composition of multiple melodies that are satisfying when played alone and that also sound good when played together. "Counterpoint" takes its name from the Latin word *contrapunctum*, or "note-against-note" (the Latin word for "note" is *punctum*). Counterpoint is a demanding art and one that aspiring composers still learn today in almost exactly the same manner as in the Renaissance, by writing a new melody against an existing one and then adding a third melody, a fourth, and so on.

Word Painting: Music Imitates the Text

When the text speaks of the cricket's ability to "hold a long line" of music (*longo verso*, at 0:07), the top and bottom voices sing very long notes, while the inner voices weave around each other in the middle. Josquin is also playing on a pun in the text here: In Italian, *verso* can mean a line of verse, or it can also mean the noise an animal makes. So what we hear at this point is both a long-held note and the sound of the cricket.

When the text tells us that the cricket also sings about drinking (*dalle beve*, at 0:14), we hear a cricket-like chirping sound a little like the hiccups of someone who has had a bit too much to drink. The music then repeats these same words to a series of rapid-fire notes with all four voices singing together in exactly the same rhythm, repeating each word nonsensically ("Of of drinking drinking cricket cricket sings," at 0:21). Finally, when the cricket sings of love (*amore*, at 0:50), we hear all four voices break into an extended melisma. Here, on this one word, the music is at its most passionate and intense, in keeping with the spirit of the text. All of these passages are examples of **word painting**, a technique by which a composer "illustrates" a word or phrase through music that in some way reflects its meaning.

CONNECT YOUR PLAYLIST

Word Painting

Find a piece that uses word painting.

Example: Taylor Swift, "Blank Space" (2014)
Each time the lyrics mention the "blank space" for the lover's name, the music inserts a surprising moment of "empty" silence.

Ternary Form: ABA

As is almost always the case in vocal music, the form of the text shapes the form of the music. The text of "The Cricket" falls into two broad sections:

1. How the cricket can hold a long note and can sing of drinking
2. How the cricket is different from birds, who also sing

Josquin gives distinctive music to each of these two sections (labeled **A** and **B** in the Listening Guide). By repeating the opening section of the text and music (**A**) at the end, however, he creates what is known as **ternary form**, which consists of three parts, **ABA**. Ternary form uses the basic principles of contrast (**B** contrasts with **A**) and return (**A** comes back at the end).

Now listen to this piece again, using the Listening Guide.

Listening Guide

Josquin des Prez Composed: ca. 1500

"The Cricket" (1:33)

Time	Form (Musical Section)	Original Italian Text	English Translation	Word–Music Relationship	Texture
0:00	A	El grillo è buon cantore Che tienne longo verso.	The cricket is a good singer Who can hold a long line.	Word painting with long notes on *longo verso* ("long line" or "long noise").	Polyphonic (four equal voices)
0:14		Dalle beve grillo canta El grillo è buon cantore.	Of drinking the cricket sings The cricket is a good singer.	Back-and-forth between upper and lower voices imitates the chirping of the cricket.	
0:29	B	Ma non fa come gli altri uccelli, Come li han cantato un poco, Van' de fatto in altro loco Sempre el grillo sta pur saldo.	But he doesn't do what birds do: After they've sung a bit, They go somewhere else; The cricket always stays put.	Contrasting section, slightly lower in register, slightly darker in sound.	
0:43		Quando la maggior è 'l caldo Al'hor canta sol per amore.	And when the weather is hottest He sings solely for love.	Elaborate melismas make the word *amore* ("love") stand out.	
0:55	A	El grillo è buon cantore Che tienne longo verso. Dalle beve grillo canta El grillo è buon cantore.	The cricket is a good singer Who can hold a long line. Of drinking the cricket sings The cricket is a good singer.	Work ends as it began, with text and music repeated, suggesting that the cricket goes on singing just as before.	

Student FAQs

I hear only one melody here, in the top voice. How can there be more than one melody going on at the same time?

For acoustical reasons, our ear tends to be drawn to the highest-sounding voice within a group of voices. But if you listen to the lower voices—isolate them, in effect—you will hear three other well-shaped melodic lines as well.

Are the two higher voices here sung by men or women?

Normally, the soprano and alto parts are sung by women, for these ranges lie naturally within the range of the female voice. But in this recording, as in many recent recordings of earlier music (pre-1700), the two upper parts are sung by men, reflecting the performing practice of earlier times. The higher of these—the soprano part—is sung by a man singing **falsetto**, a technique by which the voice bypasses the larynx, which is the part of the throat that otherwise gives men's voices a deeper register. Many modern male groups or singers have used this technique (such as the Beach Boys, Marvin Gaye, and Coldplay). For more on this style of singing, see Chapter 9.

At the very end, it doesn't sound as if the music is quite finished. Why is that?

Like most music written before 1600, the melodic lines are derived from one of the medieval modes—in this case, the mode on D (Dorian), and the conventions for final cadences were different from what we might expect today. So to Josquin's contemporaries, the final cadence of this work would have sounded quite normal and not incomplete at all.

PROFILE Josquin des Prez (ca. 1450–1521)

"Master of the Notes"

Josquin was an international celebrity in his time. Even nonmusicians knew who he was: Famed theologian Martin Luther declared that "Josquin is the master of the notes, which must follow his wishes, while other composers must follow what the notes demand." And music publishers were eager to put Josquin's name on the music they wanted to sell, regardless of whether he had actually written it or not. Josquin knew his own worth, too. An agent of the Duke of Ferrara, who was seeking to hire a new composer for his court, reported to his master that the two best available composers were Josquin and Heinrich Isaac. "Josquin composes better," the agent wrote, "but he works when he wants to, not when one wants him to, and he demands 200 ducats for his salary while Isaac will accept the position for only 120." To the duke's credit, he hired Josquin anyway.

Though Josquin is generally considered the greatest composer of the early Renaissance, much of his life is shrouded in mystery. He was born and died somewhere in an area on the border between what is now France and Belgium, but he spent much of his life working in Italy, including St. Peter's in Rome. Scholars have recently discovered that there were several composers going by the name of "Josquin" in the late fifteenth and early sixteenth centuries, and it may be one of these "other" Josquins who wrote "The Cricket." For the moment though, no one can be absolutely certain.

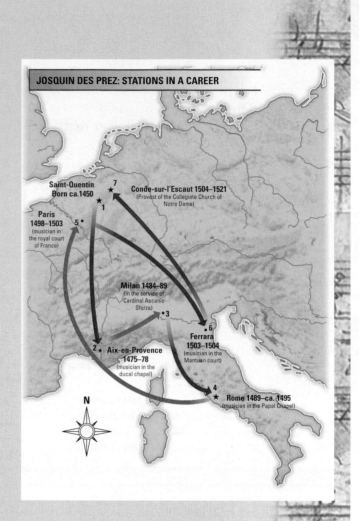

JOSQUIN DES PREZ: STATIONS IN A CAREER

Saint-Quentin Born ca. 1450

Conde-sur-l'Escaut 1504–1521
(Provost of the Collegiate Church of Notre Dame)

Paris 1498–1503
(musician in the royal court of France)

Milan 1484–89
(in the service of Cardinal Ascanio Sforza)

Ferrara 1503–1504
(musician in the Mantuan court)

Aix-en-Provence 1475–78
(musician in the ducal chapel)

Rome 1489–ca. 1495
(musician in the Papal Chapel)

N

 EXPAND YOUR PLAYLIST: JOSQUIN DES PREZ

- **Missa Pange Lingua.** A setting of the Ordinary of the Mass (those portions said or sung at every Mass, regardless of the occasion). The work takes its name from the medieval plainchant hymn melody that provides the basis for many of Josquin's themes.

- **Missa La Sol Fa Re Mi.** Another setting of the Mass Ordinary, this one based on a series of notes that corresponds to a scale descending from "La" (A) to "Mi" (E). Josquin challenged

himself to give variety to such a basic and simple idea repeated over and over.

- **"Hail Mary . . . Serene Virgin"** (*Ave Maria . . . virgo serena*). A motet (sacred song) for four voices, one of Josquin's most famous compositions.

- **"Virgin Nurse of God, Undefiled"** (*Illibata Dei virgo nutrix*). Another motet in praise of the Virgin Mary, for five voices. The first letter of each line spells out "Josquin des Prez."

PERFORMANCE Playing and Singing

Today's songwriters know that any big hit is likely to be performed in many different ways: with words, without words, and arranged for all kinds of instruments and instrumental ensembles. Josquin almost certainly felt the same way. Like many Renaissance composers, he wrote music in such a way that it could be either sung (with a text) or played (without a text), and played on different kinds of instruments. Indeed, a great deal of the vocal repertory from this time has come down to us in manuscripts that have no vocal texts at all. We know what words to sing only because the texts have survived in other manuscripts. Renaissance musicians were resourceful, and they used whatever combination of voices or instruments were available at any given moment. In the case of "The Cricket," listeners might lose the witty connections between the text and the music (the chirping sounds, for one), but this did not prevent them from enjoying vocal music on instruments, or allowing instruments to fill in one or more of the vocal lines.

A mixed group of instrumentalists and a vocalist perform a piece that was written as a vocal composition. The woman on the left sings; another, on the right, plays the lute; and the one in the center plays the flute. Presumably, the lutenist is also singing.

 EXPAND YOUR PLAYLIST

The Music of Sounds

All music may be sound, but are all sounds music? There are no easy answers, but sounds from the outside world have found their way into the music of almost every culture, time, and place.

Birds
- Clément Janequin's "The Song of the Birds" ("Le chant des oiseaux," early sixteenth century), imitates the songs of thrushes, robins, nightingales, and cuckoos.

- The music of the Kaluli of Papua New Guinea is modeled on the sounds of the rainforest, including frogs, insects, and birds. *Voices of the Rainforest: A Day in the Life of the Kaluli People* (Rykodisc 10173).

- The French composer Olivier Messiaen incorporated birdsong into many of his works. His "Awakening of the Birds" ("Réveil des oiseaux," 1953) consists almost entirely of imitated bird songs.

Monkeys
- The *Cecak* or *Ketjak*, also known as the "Ramayana Monkey Chant," from Bali (Indonesia) features a group of 100 or more men who imitate, through gesture and song, a group of legendary fighting monkeys. *Audio:* Nonesuch H-72028. *Video:* Video excerpts of this chant are widely available on the Internet.

Trains
- Arthur Honegger named his orchestral work *Pacific 231* (1923) after a type of steam locomotive. The piece builds slowly in momentum before reaching full speed.

- Billy Strayhorn's *Take the "A" Train* (1941), made famous by Duke Ellington's big-band recording, imitates the driving rhythms of the New York City subway line running from Manhattan to Harlem.

Battle
- Clément Janequin's *La bataille* (early sixteenth century) imitates battle noises, trumpet calls, cannon fire, and the cries of the wounded.

- Ludwig van Beethoven's *Wellington's Victory* (1813) imitates the firing of cannon, using bass drums.

- Pyotr Ilich Tchaikovsky's *1812 Overture* (1882) imitates cannon fire through the use of bass drums. Some orchestras, including the Boston Pops in their outdoor performances on the Fourth of July, use fireworks. Now and then, performances even use the real cannons Tchaikovsky called for in the score.

8

Thomas Weelkes
"Since Robin Hood"
Composed: 1608

The madrigal, usually written for three to six voices, was the most important type of secular song in the Renaissance. The genre emerged in Italy and then found its way to England in the closing decades of the sixteenth century. This three-voice madrigal features extensive word painting, and the shifting meters of the music reflect the shifting meters of the poetry.

Listen to This First

🌐 Texture	📖 Rhythm	💿 Word–Music Relationships
Listen to the three distinct voices, each of equal weight. This texture is polyphonic. ■	Listen for the shift in rhythm in the middle of the piece from duple to triple meter. ■	Listen to the descriptive nature of the music with certain words, such as "to skip" and "trip it." ■

LEARNING OBJECTIVES

8.1 Define madrigal.

8.2 Situate the Morris dance and its music in Renaissance culture.

8.3 Listen for the relationship between the shifting meters of the poetry and the shifting meters of the music.

8.4 Listen for instances of word painting in Thomas Weelkes's "Since Robin Hood."

8.5 Discuss the social role of musicians in private households in Elizabethan England.

8.6 Discuss Thomas Weelkes as a Shakespearean composer.

What seems simple on the surface can often be quite intricate. On first listening, this song strikes most people as a fairly straightforward setting of a lightweight, almost nonsensical text. But with careful listening, we can begin to hear the many remarkable ways in which Weelkes has captured the spirit of this text.

"Since Robin Hood" is a **madrigal**, a musical setting of a text in a single strophe (stanza), and the text of this madrigal is a poem about dancing. "Kemp" is English actor William Kemp, who was a friend of Shakespeare and an original shareholder in London's Globe Theatre. (Among his many roles, Kemp played the role of the nurse in *Romeo and Juliet* in an age when women were not allowed onstage.) What Kemp later called his "Nine-Day Wonder" was a feat of shameless self-promotion. Like any good promoter, Kemp wrote a book about his exploits.

The dance that Kemp performed over these nine days was the Morris dance, a traditional English dance of obscure origins whose name is probably a corruption of "Moorish dance." Tielman Susato's *Moorish Dance (La Moresca)* belongs to this same tradition (see Chapter 12). It is a group dance, with stock characters that include a hobby horse (a dancer wearing the costume of a horse's body from his waist down) and Maid Marian (a male dressed in women's clothing). The dancers—all male in Kemp's time—wore small bells on their calves. The group nature of the dance made Kemp's feat all the more unusual, for as the lyrics of the song tell us, he

A 16th-century portrayal of Kemp on his nine-day Morris dance tour, accompanied by a pipe-and-tabor player.

"did dance alone," with the other figures (Robin Hood, Maid Marian, Little John, and the hobby horse) all absent ("forgot").

Texture: Polyphony in Three Voices

The texture is **polyphonic** throughout, which is typical of the Renaissance madrigal. No one voice predominates, and all three contribute equally to the whole. The three voices move together in more or less the same rhythm, making the text easier to understand, for it is as if all the voices are reciting the text together—in song.

The melody in the uppermost voice of Weelkes's setting would have been familiar to Shakespeare's contemporaries, for this was a tune already well known by the end of the sixteenth century and one closely associated with Morris dancing. (It is even called "The Morris Tune" in various sources of the time.) But the lines in the two lower voices have their own distinctive melodic profiles as well.

Poetic Rhythm in Music

To understand the rhythm of the music, we must first consider the rhythm of the poetry. The **meter** of a poem is its basic rhythmic unit. Most metrical poems stick to a single meter from beginning to end. But "Since Robin Hood" is unusual because it keeps shifting from one meter to another.

Read the text out loud and exaggerate the rhythmic patterns of the accented (long) syllables. The pattern that emerges at the beginning is iambic: short-LONG, short-LONG, short-LONG, short-LONG, which can be represented by the symbols ˘ (= short) and ´ (= LONG):

> Since **Rŏbĭn Hŏod**, Mǎid **Mărĭan**,
>
> And **Lĭttlĕ Jŏhn** are **gŏne**,
>
> The **hŏbbў hŏrse** was **quĭte** fŏr**gŏt**,
>
> Whĕn **Kĕmp** dĭd **dance ălŏne**.

But in the second section of the poem, the meter changes. Read this part out loud, again emphasizing the natural stresses within the words:

> **Hĕ** dĭd **lăbŏur áftĕr** the **tăbŏr**.
>
> **Fŏr** tŏ **dănce** thĕn **ĭntŏ Frănce**.

If you try to read these lines in the iambic meter of the opening (short-LONG), you'll realize at once that it just doesn't work: The accents are all wrong because these lines are in trochaic meter (LONG-short, LONG-short, etc.).

In the third and final section of the poem, the meter becomes quite jumbled, moving briefly back to iambic (short-LONG) for one line:

Ĭn **hópe** ŏf **gáins**

before shifting to yet another kind of meter, anapestic (short-short-LONG):

Hĕ dĭd **tríp** ĭt ŏn thĕ **tóe,**

Diddle **did**dle diddle **doe.**

Now that you've read the text with an eye (and ear) to its meter, listen to how these shifts in the meter of the poetry are reflected in the shifting meters of the music.

1. The opening lines (iambic) are in **duple meter,** and the note lengths are fairly even:

Since | **Rób**-ĭn **Hóod**, Măid | **Már**-ĭ-**án**, ănd | **Lít**-tlĕ **Jóhn** ărĕ | **góne**

(4) | **1** 2 3 4 | **1** 2 3 4 | **1** 2 3 4 | **1**

With four beats to each musical measure, beats **1** and **3** and especially **1** are the beats that are normally emphasized, and the poetry fits this scheme quite nicely.

2. The second section (trochaic) shifts to **triple meter** to accommodate the new trochaic meter of the poetry (LONG-short):

Hé dĭd | **lá**-bŏur | **áf**- tĕr thĕ | **tá**- bŏr

1-2 3   1-2 3   1-2 3   1-2 3

The accented syllables on "1" are longer: They get two beats, whereas the unaccented syllables (or groups of syllables) get only one beat.

3. Even though the text remains in trochaic meter ("He took pains to skip it . . . "), Weelkes returns to duple meter, as at the beginning. But here, the notes are **syncopated**—that is, they run against the regular pulse of the musical meter, with accents on beats other than "1" and "3." This allows Weelkes to present the words "to skip" in almost graphic fashion, with the voices tossing these two words back and forth among themselves. In this way, we lose any strong sense of metrical pulse, just at that moment when the text talks about skipping.

CONNECT YOUR PLAYLIST

Songs about Dancing

Find a piece that deals with the subject of dancing.

Example: Chubby Checker, "The Twist" (1960)
This is one of many popular songs to inspire a craze by describing a particular dance.

Word Painting in the Renaissance Madrigal

As noted previously, certain words ("to skip," "did trip it") are set quite graphically, instances of **word painting**. These are among the few passages in the entire madrigal in which the voices are not singing in rhythm together. Instead of declaiming these words in a clear fashion, the voices in effect "skip" ahead of themselves. Word painting is a device that is well suited to the Renaissance madrigal. Composers used whatever musical elements they could to enhance the meaning and pleasure of the poetry, and word painting is so common in this repertory that it is sometimes called a *madrigalism*.

Now listen to this piece again, using the Listening Guide.

Listening Guide

Thomas Weelkes Composed: ca. 1575–1623

"Since Robin Hood" (1:10)

Time	Text	Poetic Meter	Musical Meter	Word–Music Relationships	Texture
0:00 (repeats at 0:09)	Since Robin Hood, Maid Marian, And Little John are gone, The hobby horse was quite forgot, When Kemp did dance alone.	Iambic (short-LONG)	Duple (1-2-3-4)		Polyphonic (three equal voices)
0:19 (repeats at 0:43)	He did labour after the tabor. For to dance then into France.	Trochaic (LONG-short)	Triple (1-2-3)	Music changes meter when the text changes meter, following— "laboring after"—the rhythm of the imaginary drum to which Kemp is dancing	
0:29 (repeats at 0:53)	He took pains to skip it	Trochaic (LONG-short)	Duple (with syncopation, that is, accents off the normally accented beats)	Syncopation reflects "skipping"	
0:33 (repeats at 0:57)	In hope of gains.	Iambic (short-LONG)	Duple (with syncopation, that is, accents off the normally accented beats)	Syncopation (in a different meter now) reflects striving, the "hope of gains"	
0:36 (repeats at 1:00)	He did trip it on the toe, Diddle diddle diddle doe.	Anapestic (short-short-LONG)	Duple (no syncopation)	"Did trip it on the toe" is an old-fashioned way of saying "danced elegantly," and a steady beat returns here, without syncopation	

Q Student FAQs

I can't hear the shift in meters in the music. What should I do?

Try beating time, as if you were playing a drum to back up the singers. The opening section is fairly regular (1-2, 1-2, 1-2, etc.). When you get to the shift at 0:19, shift to three beats, with the heavy beat on "1" (1-2-3, 1-2-3, 1-2-3, etc.). At 0:29, shift back to 1-2, 1-2, etc. This physical pattern may help you hear the shifting meters.

Are those men or women singing the higher voices?

This recording features a woman singing soprano and a man singing alto, using **falsetto**, a technique by which a singer bypasses the voice box (larynx), thereby creating a sound in the very high range. In the 1960s, the Beach Boys (shown here) became famous for this kind of singing.

73

PROFILE   Thomas Weelkes (ca. 1575–1623)

A Shakespearean Composer

Weelkes belonged to that generation of English composers who lived during the age of Shakespeare, a period of great cultural achievements under the reigns of Elizabeth I and James I. Like Shakespeare, Weelkes and his contemporaries were fascinated by Italian poetry and music: Many of Shakespeare's plays, it should be remembered, take place in Italy. The Italian madrigal came to England toward the end of the sixteenth century, and Weelkes lost no time imitating these Italian models. In an era of great poets and playwrights—Shakespeare, Ben Jonson, Christopher Marlowe, and Philip Sydney, among others—English composers had no difficulty finding new texts to set to music.

Like most composers of his day, Weelkes was a professional musician. He received a bachelor of music degree from New College, Oxford; served as organist at Chichester Cathedral; and wrote a great deal of sacred music in addition to madrigals. His career ended badly, however, when he was dismissed from his position for drunkenness and blasphemy. No likeness of him survives.

Chichester Cathedral, where Thomas Weelkes served as organist.

 EXPAND YOUR PLAYLIST: THE ENGLISH MADRIGAL

- **William Byrd,** "This Sweet and Merry Month of May"
- **John Farmer,** "Fair Phyllis I Saw Sitting All Alone"
- **Orlando Gibbons,** "The Silver Swan"
- **Thomas Morley,** "Now Is the Month of Maying"

- **Thomas Weelkes,** "As Vesta Was from Latmos Hill Descending"; "Hark, All Ye Lovely Saints"
- **John Wilbye,** "Weep, Weep, Mine Eyes"

HISTORICAL CONTEXT   Musicians as Spies

Being a musician and a spy might seem an odd combination, but in Elizabethan England at the end of the sixteenth century, playing an instrument provided the perfect cover for gathering intelligence. Over the course of the sixteenth century, England had gone back and forth between Protestant monarchs (Henry VIII) and Catholic monarchs (Mary I). Throughout the long reign of Elizabeth I (1558–1603), a Protestant, England was awash in rumors and actual plots to overthrow the monarchy and invade the country. As in today's global struggles, good intelligence about the intentions and resources of one's enemies carried a very high value. A coded message, intercepted by a spy, led to the arrest and eventual execution of Mary, Queen of Scots, in 1587.

Musicians were in an ideal position to carry secret messages between households, to eavesdrop on conversations, and to observe the comings and goings of the great households in which they were engaged. And good musicians were always in demand: No large-scale upper-class entertainment was complete without dancing, and dancing required musicians; musicians were able to pass easily among the servants, and those servants always knew about what was going on in their households. Musicians at the royal court were routinely loaned out to loyal supporters of the queen, with the understanding that these employees would also report on any events or rumors they had witnessed; they presumably received an extra tip for particularly useful information. For an underpaid musician, spying provided a good source of supplementary income.

A group of musicians—perhaps musician-spies—playing at a 16th-century ball.

 EXPAND YOUR PLAYLIST

The Italian Madrigal

The English madrigal, which blossomed at the end of the sixteenth century, was directly indebted to the Italian madrigal, which had been flourishing for more than half a century earlier. Indeed, the earliest English-language madrigals were direct translations from the Italian. Here are some of the composers that were admired (and imitated) by the English:

Jacob Arcadelt (ca. 1505–1568)
- "The White and Gentle Swan" ("Il bianco e dolce cigno"). Judging from the number of published editions, this was one of the most popular of all Italian madrigals in the sixteenth century. The text is about the swan, a bird who is mute throughout its life, yet according to legend sings just before dying.

Cipriano de Rore (1516–1565)
- "Once Again in Parting" ("Ancor che col partire"). A four-voice madrigal about the pain of parting lovers, a favorite subject of Renaissance madrigalists.

Luzzascho Luzzaschi (1545–1607)
- "I Love You, My Life" ("T'amo mia vita"). This madrigal for three women's voices was written for the celebrated Consort of Ladies ("Concerto delle donne"), a group of extraordinarily talented women musicians at the court of Ferrara, in northern Italy.

Lucca Marenzio (1553 or 1554–1599)
- "Alone and Pensive" ("Solo e pensoso"). For five voices, with lyrics by fourteenth-century poet Petrarch, this madrigal expresses loneliness and despair.

Claudio Monteverdi (1567–1643)
- "I Love You, My Life" ("T'amo mia vita"). A setting of the same text as Luzzaschi's earlier madrigal, but in the new style of the Baroque (see Part 3 of this book), with instrumental accompaniment an essential element of this five-voice work.

9

William Byrd
"Sing Joyfully"
Composed: 1590

Byrd's "Sing Joyfully," a sacred work to be sung in church, exemplifies the rich sound of six-voice polyphony from the late Renaissance. The text comes from the Book of Psalms.

Listen to This First

Texture

Try to hear the six distinct voices, all of equal weight. Listen also for passages in which one voice presents a musical idea that the other voices then imitate in quick succession. ■

Form

Notice how each new section of the text receives its own new musical idea. ■

Word–Music Relationships

Listen to how Byrd captures in music the feeling of the text's key words, such as "joyfully" and "sing loud." Note the word painting on certain phrases, such as "blow the trumpet," which imitates the sound of the trumpet. ■

LEARNING OBJECTIVES

9.1 Discuss the challenges of setting sacred music polyphonically.

9.2 Define the genres of anthem and motet.

9.3 Listen for the imitative counterpoint in six voices in William Byrd's "Sing Joyfully."

9.4 Listen for and describe the relationship between the structure of the text and sectional form of the music in "Sing Joyfully."

9.5 Describe the options for performance of Renaissance choral music.

9.6 Discuss Byrd's work as a Catholic composer and publisher in Protestant England.

Words and music seem made for each other, but their marriage is not always a happy one. What creates verbal clarity—monophonic texture and syllabic text setting—does not always create musical beauty. And what often creates musical beauty, such as long lyrical melodies, melismatic text setting, and rich polyphonic textures, can often obscure the text being sung.

This challenge of blending words and music had grown particularly acute by the end of the Renaissance, when compositions for six voices, like William Byrd's "Sing Joyfully," had become the norm. The musical effect of this full-bodied sound can be irresistible. Reverberating off the high ceilings and stone walls of the large churches and cathedrals for which this work was written, Byrd's music is rich and luxuriant. Even if we did not understand the words at all, the music alone is capable of moving us, of giving us a heightened sense of spirituality. Yet Byrd and other composers of his time also wanted to project the words being sung in a way that could be grasped by listeners. The challenge was to do this in a way that also exploited the potentials of six-part polyphony.

Byrd's "Sing Joyfully" takes as its text the first four verses of Psalm 81. He called his setting an **anthem**, the English equivalent of what composers in other countries called a **motet**, a sacred choral work (see Chapter 10). It is an example of *a cappella* choral music: **Choral music** because there is more than one singer to a part, and *a cappella* (Italian for "in the church style") because it is meant to be sung without instrumental accompaniment of any kind.

Texture: Polyphony in Six Voices

One of the ways in which Byrd projected the text to be sung even while writing for six independent parts was to use a technique known as **imitative counterpoint**. Counterpoint is basic to all polyphony: It is the technique used to meld contrasting voices into a satisfying whole. Imitative counterpoint is a particular type of counterpoint in which one voice, entirely by itself for a short time, introduces each new theme and is answered (imitated) by other voices that enter in succession shortly afterward, even as the first voice continues to sing. Imitative counterpoint, or simply **imitation**, as it is often called, has been of great importance for composers of all eras from the Renaissance onward.

At the very beginning of this work, only four voices enter in imitation, and two of them (Soprano 1 and Alto 2, see notation below) enter together (at 0:03). But by the time only four voices have entered (0:07), we would be hard put to say exactly what words they are singing, for at no given point are they all singing the same word, at least not here in the opening. At the point marked with an asterisk in the example below, one of the voices is singing the word "God," while another sings the "un-" syllable of the word "unto," and the third the "-to" syllable in "unto." If this were three or four different people all talking at the same time, it would be a complete jumble. Fortunately, each voice is differentiated by its range, so they do stand out from one another, even when they are singing together. And because the first voice began by itself, we are able to hear this first full statement of the opening text as a unit; when we hear the other voices enter with the same words, we know that they are singing the same text even if we cannot make out every word in every voice at all times. Finally, like other composers of his era, Byrd liberally repeats the text in all the parts several times before moving on, to help impress upon us the words being sung.

Sectional Form

The form of the music follows the form of the text. Each new line of the text receives its own melodic idea, which is shared to at least some extent by all the voices. Each line of text, in turn, ends with a **cadence**, marking the end of a section. These cadences vary in strength; the strongest one comes (naturally enough) at the very end, to signal the conclusion of the entire work. Somewhat less strong is the full but brief stop at the end of line 6. The weakest cadences of all are those in which some of the voices come to a stop but others enter before we hear a pause in all the voices. This last kind of cadence is called an **elided cadence**. (To elide something is to skip over it, as in the unvoiced "a" sound of "I'm" or the "o" sound of "can't.") Between lines 1 and 2 of the text, for example, the music introduces line 2 before line 1 has completely finished. Elided cadences help break up the text into smaller units even while allowing the music to continue its forward flow.

Word–Music Relationships: The Music Paints the Words

Byrd sets the opening phrase—"Sing joyfully"—to a lively, upward-moving musical motive. And at "Blow the trumpet" (1:03), we hear a clear instance of word painting, with the voices imitating the kind of fanfare-like figure associated with that instrument, complete with echoes. A more subtle instance of **word painting** can be found toward the end (1:50) on the words "For this is a statute for Israel." After a brief pause, all the voices sing the words "For this" in exactly the same rhythm, which creates the kind of declamatory sound fitting the public proclamation of a law or statute.

Now listen to this piece again, using the Listening Guide.

Listening Guide

William Byrd Composed: 1590
"Sing Joyfully" (2:46)

Time	Text	Form: Musical Ideas	Texture	Word–Music Relationships
0:00	1. Sing joyfully unto God our strength,	A	Polyphonic, with imitation among all the voices	Lively, upward-moving motif for "joyfully"
0:20	2. Sing loud unto the God of Jacob.	B: B A	Elided cadence: **B** begins before **A** has ended.	Long notes on "Sing loud"
0:35	3. Take the song and bring forth the timbrel,*	C	Imitation	
0:49	4. The pleasant harp and the viol.*	D	Imitation	Lyrical, flowing melody matches the sound of these two soft instruments
1:04	5. Blow the trumpet in the new moon,	E	Imitation	Fanfare-like theme on the word "trumpet"
1:23	6. Ev'n in the time appointed, and at our feast day,	F	Imitation; section ends with a strong cadence.	
1:50	7. For this is a statute for Israel,	G	Imitation	All voices sing in the same rhythm on the words "For this," as suits a public proclamation
2:00	8. And a law of the God of Jacob.	H	Strongest cadence at the very end of the work.	

*A timbrel could mean either a small drum or a tambourine. A viol is a bowed string instrument.

 ## Student FAQs

I still can't understand the words. Is that a problem?

Many listeners in Byrd's time complained about the same thing—not just for his music, but for a great many works of polyphony. Even with imitative counterpoint and the exposed declamation of certain passages, the words do tend to get lost at points. This is one of the issues that composers of the early Baroque era were keen to address (see Chapters 13 and 14).

Are those boys' voices in the upper range?

No, those are women singing in a style meant to imitate boys' voices, which is what choirs in Byrd's time would have used. The sopranos and altos in this particular recording are singing with very little vibrato (vibration) in their voices, which creates a sound quality similar to that produced by boys. For an illustration of what an all-male choir sounds like, see "Performance: The Sound of the All-Male Choir."

PROFILE   William Byrd (1542–1623)

A Catholic Composer at a Protestant Court

As a Roman Catholic in England, William Byrd had to negotiate his way carefully through the intrigues in and around the court of the Protestant queen, Elizabeth I. This was the same queen, after all, who had ordered the execution of her Catholic cousin, Mary, Queen of Scots, in 1587. Byrd was harassed at various times because of his faith: Authorities searched his house on at least one occasion and kept him under varying degrees of surveillance for years on the suspicion that he was harboring "papists"—the catch-all term of the day for Catholics disloyal to the Crown because of their allegiance to the Pope. Byrd's talent as a composer seems to have provided him sufficient protection from serious persecution, however. The fact that he also wrote large quantities of music to be performed in Anglican (Protestant) services—including the anthem "Sing Joyfully"—certainly helped Byrd avoid the fate of many other Catholics in Protestant England.

Widely regarded as the greatest English composer of the Renaissance, Byrd was also the most important English music publisher of his time.

Queen Elizabeth I being carried through the streets of London by her courtiers. She was herself an accomplished lute player and supporter of all the arts, including music.

EXPAND YOUR PLAYLIST: BYRD

- **Mass for Four Voices.** A setting of the Mass Ordinary, in Latin.

- **O Lord, Make Thy Servant Elizabeth.** A motet for the Anglican service of worship, which included a prayer for the monarch.

- **Sadness and Anxiety (Tristitia et anxietas).** A motet with powerful settings of its key words.

- **"This Sweet and Merry Month of May."** One of Byrd's many madrigals, a secular song (see Chapter 8).

PERFORMANCE The Sound of the All-Male Choir

With few exceptions, women were not permitted to sing in church choirs until well into the eighteenth century, and in some locales even into the nineteenth. It was feared that women might create a distraction; many choruses, moreover, used students from a church or cathedral school, and the pupils at such schools were almost invariably boys. In any event, the sound of an all-male chorus, with boys singing the soprano and alto lines and men singing the tenor and bass lines, became a sound ideal that has persisted in some churches down to the present day. Listen in particular for the different quality of the upper voices.

There are some excellent albums offering examples of the all-male chorus. One that features Byrd's "Sing Joyfully" is *An English Chorister's Songbook*, by the Salisbury Cathedral Choir (Metronome MET 1016). Other all-male choirs that have recorded extensively include the Choir of King's College (Cambridge), Christ Church Cathedral Choir (Oxford), and New College Choir (Oxford).

The Choir of King's College, Cambridge University, consisting of men and boys, has provided music for daily services more or less continuously for more than 500 years.

    EXPAND YOUR PLAYLIST

Music of the Reformation

In an age of spiritual strife, Catholics and Protestants alike recognized the power of music to sway the hearts and minds of the faithful. The intense spirituality of the age gave rise to some of the most moving sacred music ever written. While the Roman Catholic Church retained a liturgy entirely in Latin, the leaders of the Protestant Reformation encouraged followers to conduct services primarily in the everyday language of the local people. This included the texts of music to be sung.

English
- Thomas Tallis (ca. 1505–1585). "I Have Never Put My Hope in Any Other but You" ("Spem in alium"). This sacred Latin motet, for 40 different voices (eight choirs, each with five voices), is one of the monumental works of Renaissance vocal music.

- Tallis. "Verily I Say Unto You." A much more modest anthem, for four voices, written for a typical Anglican church choir.

German
- Martin Luther (1483–1546). "A Mighty Fortress Is Our God" ("Ein' feste Burg ist unser Gott"). Luther wrote both the words and music of what would come to be known as the anthem of the Protestant Reformation.

- Johann Walter (1496–1570). "A Mighty Fortress Is Our God" ("Ein' feste Burg ist unser Gott"). One of many elaborate settings of Luther's hymn. Walter, like many other Protestant composers, used this well-known melody as a basis for a more extended work.

French
- Louis Bourgeois (ca. 1510-15–1559). Monophonic Pslams for the Calvinist Psalter, a French rendition of the Psalms set to monophonic melodies. Calvinists embraced simplicity in their worship and rejected polyphonic music and the use of instruments in the church.

Giovanni Pierluigi da Palestrina
Pope Marcellus Mass, "Gloria"
Composed: 1555

The "Gloria" from Palestrina's *Pope Marcellus Mass* conveys its sung text with exceptional clarity and richness in a six-voice texture for voices alone, without instruments.

Listen to This First

Timbre
Listen for the sound of unaccompanied voices, without instruments of any kind. ■

Texture
Try to hear the six distinct voices, high to low. Listen for the contrast between moments when only some voices are singing and those when all six voices are singing. ■

Rhythm
Listen for the steady, even flow of the music and the occasional cadences that punctuate this flow at various points. ■

Harmony
Listen for the contrast between consonance—a "sweet" sound—and the occasional dissonance—a "harsh" sound. ■

LEARNING OBJECTIVES

10.1 Discuss the sixteenth-century debate over sacred music within the Catholic Church and how Palestrina provided a model for polyphonic music of the Counter-Reformation.

10.2 Explain the ritual of the Catholic Mass and how music is used within it.

10.3 Recognize how Palestrina creates different textures in *Pope Marcellus Mass* by varying the number of voices from phrase to phrase.

10.4 Listen for the steady, even flow of the rhythm and how Palestrina uses elided cadences to keep the music moving forward.

10.5 Recognize passages where Palestrina has strategically introduced dissonance.

10.6 Discuss highlights of Palestrina's life.

For every force there is an equal and opposite reaction, and the Protestant Reformation of the sixteenth century, led by Martin Luther, evoked a vigorous response from the established church. This movement is now known as the Counter-Reformation. In 1545, Pope Paul III convened an extraordinary council of church officials—cardinals, archbishops, and bishops—who met in the city of Trent, in northern Italy, to debate at length what measures the Catholic Church could take to stem the "protest" at the heart of Protestantism.

Most of the debate concerned church doctrine, but music was also on the agenda of what came to be known as the Council of Trent, an assembly that met on-and-off over a period of almost two decades, from 1545 until 1563. Church officials acknowledged that a great deal of sacred music had become so intricate that the words being sung could not be understood by members of the congregation. And the words, after all, were at the heart of any service of worship. The purpose of music, according to the final decree of the Council of Trent, should not be "to give empty pleasure to the ear," but rather to enhance the meaning of the words. The Council called for a style of music whose words could "be clearly understood by all," set in such a way that the hearts and minds of listeners would be drawn toward "a desire for the harmonies of heaven."

Another resolution of the Council of Trent was to eliminate settings of the Mass that used tunes from popular—secular, worldly—songs. It was not at all uncommon before the middle of the sixteenth century for composers to set the text of the Mass to melodies that listeners would have known from outside the church, including some that had nothing to do with faith or religion. This resulted in Mass setting with titles like "My Mistress" or "The Peacock's Tail." As far as music was concerned, then, the Council of Trent was about purification: Music should be beautiful without being too elaborate or too secular, and the words being sung had to be easily understood.

Palestrina's *Pope Marcellus Mass* falls squarely into the middle of the debates that raged during the Council of Trent. It takes its name from its dedication to Pope Marcellus II, who reigned for only 22 days before his death in 1555. (A more literal translation of its Latin title, *Missae Papae Marcelli*, would be "Mass in Honor of Pope Marcellus.) In this Mass, Palestrina sought to fulfill the mandates of the Council of Trent's emerging consensus on the nature of which kind of music would be appropriate for the church.

The *Pope Marcellus Mass* is the most famous of the 104 Masses Palestrina wrote, largely because of the legend (since disproven) that grew up around it. The Council of Trent, it was rumored, was considering abolishing polyphonic music altogether and returning exclusively

HISTORICAL CONTEXT   The Mass

The Mass is the ritual re-enactment of Christ's Last Supper with the Disciples, in which Jesus blessed and distributed bread and wine to his followers. (The Last Supper was itself a gathering for the Jewish feast of Passover, and hence Easter and Passover often fall very close together in the calendar.) In the Mass, a priest blesses and distributes bread and wine—the Holy Sacrament—to those who have come forward to take communion.

The ritual of the Mass consists of a combination of texts that never change and texts connected to specific seasons, weeks, or days in the church calendar. The texts that never change are called the *Ordinary* ("ordinary" in the sense of everyday). The texts that change throughout the year are called the *Propers* because they are "proper" only for specific times of the year or occasions, such as Advent, Christmas, Easter, or a particular Saint's day. Until the mid-1960s, all the elements of the Mass, both Ordinary and Propers, were always said or sung in Latin; most Catholic churches now use the vernacular, that is, the everyday language of the country in which the

Mass is being celebrated. (Protestant sects, some of which have retained the Mass in whole or in part, switched to the vernacular early on, during the Reformation in the sixteenth century.)

A Mass can be performed with no singing at all, but the five parts of the Ordinary have often been set to music to generations of composers, including Machaut, Josquin des Prez, Haydn, Mozart, and Beethoven. The Ordinary consists of five parts:

1. Kyrie eleison   Seeks God's mercy
2. Gloria   Praises God's glory
3. Credo   Professes faith in God and the church
4. Sanctus   Proclaims God's holiness
5. Agnus Dei   Asks for God's mercy and for peace

The selection heard in this chapter—the "Gloria" from Palestrina's *Pope Marcellus Mass*—is roughly the first half of the Gloria.

A priest celebrates Mass. Here, he elevates the host (the bread or wafer).

to **plainchant** (see Chapter 3), which with its single melodic line was extremely effective at projecting the text being sung. When Palestrina presented his *Pope Marcellus Mass* to the Council, though, the assembled church officials recognized that polyphony, too, could be effective in projecting a text, and with harmonies that could indeed cause listeners to desire "the harmonies of heaven." Like many good stories, this one is more dramatic than what actually happened. What we know with certainty is that Palestrina provided a model for polyphonic music of the Counter-Reformation, and that subsequent generations of church composers imitated what came to be known as the "Palestrina Style."

 ## A capella Timbre

Like most polyphonic choral works of the sixteenth century, the *Pope Marcellus Mass* is for unaccompanied voices. Like William Byrd's "Sing Joyfully" (Chapter 9), this is an example of **choral music** sung *a capella*: choral music because there is more than one singer to a part, and *a capella* (Italian for "in the manner of the chapel") because it is meant to be sung without instrumental accompaniment of any kind.

 ## Varied Polyphonic Textures

Palestrina calls for the standard four vocal lines—soprano, alto, tenor, bass—with an extra tenor and bass line to make six voices altogether. But he rarely uses all six at any given moment. Instead, he creates different textures by using three, four, five, or occasionally all six voices at the same time. The effect is very subtle, but if you listen closely, you can hear how the texture of the music changes with almost every phrase of the text. Let's look at one specific passage in detail:

1. At the words "Deus Pater omnipotens ("God the Father Almighty") we hear three voices: one high (soprano), one medium (tenor 2), one low (bass 1). These three voices cadence but the music does not stop because other voices come in before the cadence has finished. This is called an **elided cadence**, and it was a favorite technique of sixteenth-century composers because it allowed the music to pause in certain voices without coming to a halt altogether. ("Elided" comes from "elision," the omission of something; what is omitted here is the silence one would hear at the end of a full cadence.)
2. The text continues with "Domine Fili, unigenite . . . " ("O Lord, the only begotten Son . . . ") and here Palestrina uses four voices: two high (soprano, alto), one medium (tenor 1), one low (bass 2). Thus in the span of a few short seconds, all six voice parts have sung, but in two different combinations.
3. At the repetition of the words "Domine Fili" we hear all six voices for the first time in the entire Gloria. This is a special moment in the Gloria, as it pronounces an important article of faith, and Palestrina highlights by repeating this one phrase of text with all the forces at his command. The voices move in exactly the same rhythm, emphasizing the word "Domine" ("Lord") still further.
4. At "unigenite" ("only begotten") the texture drops to five voices and then four.

Changing textures

 Flowing Rhythm

The music moves in a consistently steady, even flow, but it never becomes monotonous because Palestrina inserts brief passages of faster rhythmic motion to provide variety. The rhythm of the movement as a whole accelerates slightly as it progresses, moving from a stately opening to a more active middle. Each phrase of the text receives its own particular melodic idea, which in turn features a rhythmic pattern slightly different from what had come before and what comes after. And each phrase concludes with a cadence of some kind, usually elided, which keeps the music moving forward. The cadence at the end of this selection is a full cadence, followed by a definite pause, for it marks the end of a distinctive passage of text in the Gloria.

CONNECT YOUR PLAYLIST

Dissonance and Consonance

Example: Imogen Heap, "Hide and Seek" (2005)
Here the close (electronic) harmonies of the vocals alternate dissonance with consonance.

 Consonant and Dissonant Harmonies

One of the reasons Palestrina's music became a model for sacred music in its time was his careful and strategic use of **dissonance**, the harsh sound created when two or more notes clash and do not seem to belong together. **Consonance** is the opposite of dissonance, and we hear consonance whenever contrasting notes create a harmony that sounds "sweet" and pleasing. Palestrina's music is largely consonant, but he knew that a piece with no dissonance at all would become dull and lifeless—too bland. Dissonance is often likened to a "spice" in a dish: It's something that enhances the dominant flavor but does not overwhelm it.

A specific example will help illustrate the contrast between consonance and dissonance. Listen at 0:35 for the word "Adoramus" ("We praise"). It begins with a consonance, moves to a dissonance, but then quickly resolves back to a consonance. The same happens on the word "Glorificamus" ("We glorify").

Dissonance and consonance

Giovanni Pierluigi da Palestrina Composed: 1555

Pope Marcellus Mass, "Gloria" (2:39)

Time	Latin Text	English translation	Texture
0:00	Gloria in excelsis Deo	Glory be to God on high	monophonic (solo)
0:09	et in terra pax hominibus bonæ voluntatis.	And on earth peace to men of goodwill	4 voices
0:26	Laudamus te,	We praise thee,	4 voices
0:30	benedicimus te,	We bless thee,	4 voices
0:35	adoramus te,	We worship thee,	4 voices
0:39	glorificamus te,	We glorify thee,	4 voices
0:44	Gratias agimus tibi	We give thanks to thee	5 voices
0:54	propter magnam gloriam tuam,	for thy great glory,	3 voices
1:03	Domine Deus, Rex cælestis,	Lord God, heavenly King,	4 voices
1:12	Deus Pater omnipotens.	God the Father Almighty.	3 voices
1:20	Domine Fili unigenite, Iesu Christe,	O Lord, the only begotten Son, Jesus Christ	6 voices, then 5
1:54	Domine Deus, Agnus Dei, Filius Patris.	Lord God, Lamb of God, Son of the Father.	4 voices, then 6

Q Student FAQs ✱

Why is there a solo singer at the beginning?

A soloist typically "intones" the Gloria with a brief phrase of plainchant (see Chapter 3) on the words "Glory be to God on high." This helps all the singers find the right pitch on which to enter, and it serves as a clear announcement to the congregation that the Gloria has begun. A single voice singing solo, after all, allows the words to be projected across a large space with maximum clarity.

How big is an a cappella choir?

The size can vary quite a lot. Much depends on the size of the church or concert hall in which the group performs. The Tallis Scholars, heard on the recording here, is an ensemble of 10 voices, but Palestrina's *Pope Marcellus Mass* could just as easily be performed by a much larger ensemble.

The Tallis Scholars

PROFILE   Giovanni Pierluigi da Palestrina (1525 or 1526–1594)

"The Prince of Music"

Giovanni Pierluigi da Palestrina took his name from the town Palestrina, near Rome, where he was probably born in 1525 or 1526. He spent his entire career as a musician in churches and around Rome, sometimes at Saint Peter's Basilica in the Vatican, sometimes at other major churches in the city. He was incredibly prolific, composing 104 settings of the Mass, more than 270 **motets** (sacred choral works, some for as many as 12 voices), and both sacred and secular madrigals. Unlike most composers of the sixteenth century, Palestrina's music continued to be performed long after his death. His tomb in Saint Peter's, Rome, bears the words *Princeps musicae*—"Prince of Music."

At a time when the music of most composers was forgotten soon after their death, Palestrina's reputation actually increased over time. Later composers looked back to his music as a model of the way in which the complexities of four- to six-part counterpoint could be projected with clarity, beauty, and grace. This style of writing is still known today as the "Palestrina Style."

The composer Palestrina (right) presents his First Book of Masses to Pope Julius III (1554) and receives a blessing in return.

 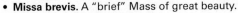

EXPAND YOUR PLAYLIST: PALESTRINA

- **Missa brevis.** A "brief" Mass of great beauty.
- **Tu es Petrus.** A motet on Jesus' words, "Thou art Peter, and upon this rock I will build my church." This statement in effect made Saint Peter the first pope.

- **Stabat mater.** A motet for eight voices on a hymn text of Mary's sorrows at the crucifixion of Christ.
- **Vestiva i colli.** A secular madrigal for five voices on a pastoral text.

The Council of Trent, a gathering of high church officials, addressed changes in the liturgy, doctrine, and practices of the Roman Catholic church, including music.

EXPAND YOUR PLAYLIST

Music of the Counter-Reformation

The Counter-Reformation is generally considered to have begun with the Council of Trent (1545–1563) and ended with the close of the Thirty Years' War (1618–1648). Composers who maintained allegiance to Rome continued to set texts in Latin and in the process produced a remarkable repertory of new music.

- **Tomás Luis de Victoria (ca. 1549–1611). "O Great Mystery" ("O magnum mysterium").** A sacred motet for four voices by the greatest Spanish composer of the Renaissance.

- **Cristobál de Morales (ca. 1500–1553). "Magnificat on the First Tone" ("Magnificat primi toni").** Morales was another important composer of the Iberian Peninsula. His Magnificats were written specifically for the Papal Chapel in Saint Peter's Basilica.

- **Orlande de Lassus (1530 or 1532–1594). "The Sibylline Prophecies" ("Prophetiae sibyllarum").** A mystically inspired text of ancient Greek oracles, the Sibyls, who prophesied the coming of Christ.

- **Gregorio Allegri (1582–1652). "Have Mercy on Me, Lord" ("Miserere mei Deus").** A setting of Psalm 51. This work was performed in the Papal Chapel with increasing quantities of melodic embellishment until well into the eighteenth century.

Rhyming Singers of the Bahamas

"My Lord Help Me to Pray"

Recorded: 1965

Polyphony, the singing of multiple independent parts simultaneously, is a worldwide phenomenon. In the Bahamas sometime during the nineteenth century, sponge fishermen passing time on their boats developed a genre known as *rhyme song*. It features three vocalists who sing distinct melodic lines.

Listen to This First

🌐 Texture	🎵 Melody	💬 Word–Music Relationships	🏛 Form
Listen for the contrasting register and timbre of the three voices: high, middle, and low. ■	Listen for the distinctive melodic contour of each voice. ■	Notice how the singers change and add words while maintaining the basic textual framework. ■	Listen for the alternation between the call (lead vocalist) and response (chorus). ■

Rhyme songs, based on gospel texts, are sung in three parts, each with its own words and own independent melody. In this way, rhyme songs resemble Byrd's "Sing Joyfully"(Chapter 9), in which the words of the individual voices often contrast with one another. This recording of the rhyme song "My Lord Help Me to Pray" is performed by three singers from Mores Island in the Bahamas: Bruce Green (lead singer), his cousin Clifton Green (bass), and their friend Tweedie Gibson (treble).

The singers of this piece are from Mores Island in the Bahamas. Often sponge fishermen would sing when they brought their catch to Nassau.

LEARNING OBJECTIVES

11.1 Recognize polyphonic singing as a global phenomenon.

11.2 Listen for call-and-response in the Rhyming Singers of the Bahamas's performance of "My Lord Help Me to Pray."

11.3 Listen for and describe the three parts of rhyme, treble, and bass in "My Lord Help Me to Pray."

11.4 Listen for the contrasts among the different sections of "My Lord Help Me to Pray."

11.5 Discuss Bob Marley and the beginning of reggae.

CONNECT YOUR PLAYLIST

Call-and-Response

Find a piece that contains a lead vocalist who states the melody ("call") and a vocal group that responds to him or her ("response").

Example: Whiskey Shivers, "Graves" (2014)
The soloist sings each verse, while the chorus responds with a refrain on the same tune.

 Texture: Monophony versus Polyphony

At the beginning of "My Lord Help Me to Pray," it is easy to hear the alternation between the **monophonic texture** of the lead singer (known as the **rhyme singer**) and the **polyphonic texture** of the other two voices (one higher, one lower) when they respond together. This alternation is known as **call-and-response**: The lead singer calls and the other parts respond. As the rhyme song progresses, the calls and responses overlap to an increasing degree, creating a thick polyphonic texture.

Call-and-response and the overlap of parts are important structural elements of African music and African-derived music in the Americas. Rhyme singing is an African American **syncretism**, which means that it combines different forms of belief and practice. The songs are mostly Christian spirituals, but they are mixed with local Bahamian religious beliefs: The rhyme part is associated with the wind, the treble part with the sky, and the bass part with the earth. In the same way, rhyme singing combines Christian gospel texts with African call-and-response.

 Intoning the Melody

What we may hear as singing in "My Lord Help Me to Pray," Bahamian culture actually considers "intoning," referring more specifically to the act of "saying words in tones." While those outside Bahamian culture have come to call these pieces "songs," Bahamians call them "rhymes." Thus, the melodic lines sung by each of the three singers are called **intonations**.

Each line has its own intonation model:

- **Rhyme line.** Varied and often improvised, but always descending in motion. Each phrase ends on its lowest tone.

- **Treble line.** Consists of two halves, *a* and *b*. The *a* ascends and pauses on the highest tone of the phrase, sounding like an unresolved question. The *b* descends and resolves on the lowest tone of the phrase, giving finality.

- **Bass line.** Varied slightly, but primarily two essential tones that provide the basic harmonic support. At times, the bass line occurs under the rhyme line as additional support.

Here is a graphic representation of each:

HISTORICAL CONTEXT   Bob Marley and the Birth of Reggae

Caribbean music is as rich and varied as the many islands that dot the ocean from Cuba and Haiti to Barbados and Aruba. Over the past few decades, American popular styles—particularly rock 'n' roll—have been heard throughout the Caribbean thanks to radio stations and recordings reaching the islands. Local styles have evolved that take elements of American pop and wed them wlth local rhythms. One of the most popular of the styles to emerge in this cultural melting pot has been reggae, and its greatest star was Bob Marley (1945–1981).

Reggae is closely associated with the Rastafarian religion. The Rastafarians combine elements of Western and African religious beliefs and venerate as their leader Haile Selassie I, who led Ethiopia from the 1930s through the mid-1970s. Its emphasis on black liberation, culture, and artistic expression had strong appeal in Jamaica, the impoverished nation where Marley lived and worked.

Marley was a performer, composer, and political activist who embodied for many the best of reggae music. Marley and his group, the Wailers, set the basic style of reggae, with its loping rhythm and topical lyrics. Among Marley's best-known songs are "I Shot the Sheriff" (popularized in a cover by Eric Clapton), "One Love" (used as a theme song on Jamaican tourism commercials), "No Woman, No Cry" and "Jammin'. "

Marley died of skin cancer in 1981, but his recordings and message have only grown since then.

Bob Marley, songwriter, performer, and political activist, who popularized reggae music around the world in the mid-1970s.

 # Word–Music Relationships

The "rhyming" consists mostly of repetitions that occur within the couplets (pairs of metered lines) intoned by the rhyme part. After a spoken introduction of the title, the rhyme singer begins the first couplet by praising a soul of faith. The others repond with the song's title, "My Lord help me to pray." This pattern then repeats.

Subsequent couplets use different text for each line, but the response is always "My Lord help me to pray."

Later, at 0:43, the rhyme part breaks the couplet pattern and sings an embellished version of "The Lord's Prayer" ("Our Father, who art in heaven, hallowed be Thy name . . . "). The other voices likewise embellish their parts with added words. Listen particularly at 0:31 and at 0:56, where the bass begins to improvise words around his part. The treble continues to sing the response, less altered. By the song's end, the parts have become polyphonically and textually quite intricate and complex.

Now listen to this piece again, following the Listening Guide.

Listening Guide

Rhyming Singers of the Bahamas Recorded: 1965
"My Lord Help Me to Pray" (2:03)

Time	📀 Form	🌐 Texture	🎵 Melody	♀ Word–Music Relationships
0:00	Introduction	Spoken	Introduction	The rhyme singer states the title.
0:05	Call-and-response	The treble and bass are in harmony.	Interlocking melody among the three singers.	The first singer calls a rhyme, praising a soul of faith, and is followed by the response, the words of the song's title: "My Lord help me to pray." Followed by different rhymes in call-and-response with the treble and bass.
0:31	Metered song set by the rhythm of the treble and bass.	Polyphonic—the call-and-response overlap to create a thick texture.	Interlocking melodies continue.	Rhyming becomes improvised in all three parts.
0:43		Polyphonic overlapping maintains the sense of thick texture.	"The Lord's Prayer" melodically embellished.	The rhyme singer improvises words and rhythms around the text of "The Lord's Prayer."
0:56		Polyphonic overlapping creates an increasingly intricate texture.	The bass improvises as the treble stabilizes.	The rhyme singer improvises rhymes until the end. The bass improvises more words.

 Student FAQs ⚙

Why are many work songs set in call-and-response style?

Call-and-response is one way of helping a large group of people work together. The rhythm of the song and the repeated structure facilitate finishing a tough job, such as lifting heavy nets or laying railroad track. The "call" by the leader coincides with the first part of a movement (such as the lifting of hammers to lay railroad track) and the "response" with its culmination (the banging of the hammer down onto the spike).

Is rap related to Bahamian rhyme songs?

Rhyming or intoning is found in many African and African-influenced cultures around the world. Rap has many roots, including the African American

practice of the "dozens" in which rhymed insults are traded between two or more people and the practice of mobile Jamaican deejays who traveled in sound trucks, setting up impromptu dances and using rhymed introductions to attract a crowd.

Is call-and-response heard in other religious song traditions?

Call-and-response is quite common in religious singing throughout the world. "Lining out" a hymn in American shape note singing is one form of call-and-response: A leader sings a line, and then the congregation repeats it. This is a way of learning the song. Eventually the leader may just sing a guiding word or two—between the actual lines of the hymn—to remind the congregation of what is coming next.

Cover of an early record by Lord Invader recorded in New York City in 1946. He was one of several Caribbean artists who made calypso music popular throughout the world, beginning in the middle of the 20th century.

 EXPAND YOUR PLAYLIST

Music of the Caribbean

Music of the Caribbean
- Caribbean Party. *Putamayo* 132.
  A good, short collection of representative dance recordings from throughout the Caribbean.

Jamaica
- Bongo, Backra & Coolie. *Jamaican Roots, Vol. 1*, Folkways 4231.

- Bongo, Backra & Coolie. *Jamaican Roots, Vol. 2*, Folkways 4232.
  Roots music from various different Jamaican cultural groups recorded by Kenneth Bilby in the early 1970s.

Reggae
- *Bob Marley: Natty Dread*, Tuff Gong 422-846204-2.
  Considered by many to be Marley's finest studio album.

- *Babylon by Bus*, Tuff Gong 422-846197-2.
  Influential live album recorded during Marley's European tour in 1978.

Bahamas
- *The Real Bahamas, Vols. 1 and 2*, Nonesuch Explorer 72013 and 72078.
  Recordings of various performers, including legendary guitarist Joseph Spence, made in 1965.

Calypso
- Lord Invader. *Calypsos in New York*, Smithsonian Folkways 40454.
  Calypso was very popular in the 1950s in New York, and many island musicians made their home there working at local clubs. This gathers recordings of Lord Invader, one of Calypso's major stars, made from the 1940s through the 1950s.

Tielman Susato
Moorish Dance
Composed: ca. 1550

Dance music is rhythmically clear and consistent to match the repeated steps of the dancers. This *Moorish Dance* consists of many small units of the same size that are joined to create a larger whole. Many of the Renaissance instruments in this recording are different from instruments in common use today.

Listen to This First

🎵 Timbre

Listen for instruments from different families of instruments: percussion, woodwinds, and brass. ■

🥁 Rhythm

Listen for the underlying metrical regularity of the music, in duple meter (**1**-2 | **1**-2 | **1**-2 | etc.). ■

🏛 Form

Listen for the repetition and alternation of the dance's two sections: The first features the higher, brighter sound of the woodwind instruments, while the second features the fuller sounds of the brass instruments. ■

LEARNING OBJECTIVES

12.1 Explain the function of dance in Renaissance society.

12.2 Describe the different timbres in Tielman Susato's *Moorish Dance*.

12.3 Explain the relationship between meter and dancing.

12.4 Identify the binary form of Susato's *Moorish Dance*.

12.5 Discuss Susato's role as a publisher.

12.6 Describe why music publishing was difficult.

12.7 Identify other examples of instrumental music from the Renaissance.

In an era when public physical contact between the sexes was largely prohibited and closely monitored, dance was a vital element of social life. "Dancing," as the leading manual on the subject put it in 1589, "is practiced to reveal whether lovers are in good health and sound of limb, after which they are permitted to kiss their mistresses in order that they may touch and savor one another thus to ascertain if they are shapely or emit an unpleasant odor as of bad meat. Therefore, from this standpoint, quite apart from the many other advantages to be derived from dancing, it becomes an essential to a well-ordered society."*

Without music, of course, there could be no dance, and Renaissance composers like William Byrd (Chapter 9) and Tielman Susato supplied the public with copious quantities of music for dancing. Pavanes, galliards, allemandes, sarabandes, and gigues are just a few of the many kinds of dances that flourished in the Renaissance and beyond. Each had its distinctive tempo, meter, and rhythm, depending on the dance step for which it was written.

Susato's *Moorish Dance* (*La Moresca*) was one of the most popular dance tunes of its day. Although we have no clear account of exactly how the *moresca* was danced, it seems to have depicted a ritualized combat between Moors (Muslims) and Christians. Most evidence suggests that it was performed by professional troupes as entertainment at large social gatherings,

* Thoinot Arbeau, *Orchesography* (1589), trans. Mary Stewart Evans (New York: Dover, 1967), p. 12.

in parades at Carnival time, or between the acts of a dramatic entertainment. Certain elements of the *moresca*—some of the dancers are in blackface, others wear bells on their legs—are also found in the English tradition of Morris dancing, whose name probably derives from the same root word (*Moorish/Morris*).

 ## A Rich and Varied Timbre

The ensemble in this performance is very large by Renaissance standards. It consists of the following:

Percussion:

Tabor (drum)

Tambourine

Woodwinds:

shawms (a straight double-reed instrument)

crumhorns (a curved double-reed instrument)

dulcian (a lower double-reed instrument, forerunner of the bassoon)

Brass:

sackbuts (a forerunner of the trombone)

cornetto (a forerunner of the trumpet)

Piffaro: The Renaissance Band is one of today's leading ensembles of Renaissance wind music. The instruments shown here are (from left to right): bagpipes, dulcian (also known as the curtal, a forerunner of the bassoon), soprano recorder, sackbut (a forerunner of the trombone), shawm (a forerunner of the oboe), and great bass recorder.

Dancing to Rhythmic Units

By its very nature, dance music must be rhythmically clear and consistent. The meter, whether duple or triple, has to come through strongly enough for the dancers to perform their steps in a set pattern, and the melody has to fall into a series of smaller rhythmic units that correspond to the steps of the dance. A "step" is a series of body movements—at least two, more typically four to six—that together bring the dancer back to the position in which he or she began. A typical dance repeats the basic step many times. In *Moorish Dance*, each basic rhythmic unit—the step—consists of eight beats, and the entire dance consists of twelve units. The percussion instruments provide the steady beat underneath for the dancers from beginning to end.

All social dance music today is constructed on this principle of repeated musical units played to a steady beat. Line dancing, square dancing, ballroom dancing, swing dancing, and club dancing all follow this basic kind of design. Even less formal styles of dancing—such as street dancing, hip-hop, or funk dancing—are typically performed against a steady beat, though the dancers have a greater degree of freedom in coordinating their moves to the music.

Binary Form

Like a great many dances of earlier times, this one divides into two large units (**A** and **B**), each of which is repeated in performance. This structure of two repeated halves is known as **binary form**. Binary form can be represented graphically with the symbols |: :|, which are used in musical notation to indicate that everything between these two signs is to be repeated immediately after it has been played the first time:

BINARY FORM

||:   **A**   :||:   **B**   :||

In performance, the above would be played as **A A B B**.

This is the basic structure of *Moorish Dance* as written down by Susato. In performance, however, this would make for an extremely short dance: The dancers would probably just be getting warmed up by the end of **AABB**. For this reason, ensembles often repeat an entire dance (often with varied instrumentation), as in the performance here, where the musicians play the complete binary form twice, creating this pattern:

A A B B A A A A B B A A

Other recordings (see the Susato playlist later in this chapter) may or may not feature the additional repeats heard here, but all of them will include at a very minimum the pattern of **AABB**.

Now listen to this piece again, using the Listening Guide.

CONNECT YOUR PLAYLIST

Brass Instruments

Find a piece that makes prominent use of brass instruments.

Example: Shakira, "Hips Don't Lie" (2006)
Throughout this song the Colombian singer-songwriter Shakira samples a prominent brass section from the song "Amores Como El Nuestro" (1992) by the salsa singer Jerry Rivera.

Listening Guide

Tielman Susato Composed: ca. 1550
Moorish Dance (1:59)

Time	Form	Timbre	Rhythm
0:00	Introduction	Drum, tambourine	Duple meter (**1**-2 | **1**-2)
0:09	A theme	Woodwinds	
0:17	A repeated	Brass	
0:25	B theme	Woodwinds	
0:33	B repeated	Brass	
0:42	A	Full ensemble	
0:51	A repeated		
0:59	A	Woodwinds	
1:07	A repeated	Brass	
1:16	B embellished	Woodwinds	
1:24	B embellished and repeated	Brass	
1:33	A embellished	Woodwinds	
1:42	A embellished and repeated	Full ensemble	

Q Student FAQs ⚙

Why didn't Susato indicate what instruments this music is for?

Very few composers of the Renaissance wrote music for specific instruments, and performers were expected to use whatever instruments they had on hand. The only limitations were ones of range: A bass viol, for example, could play only relatively low notes, while a soprano recorder could play in only a high register. Remember, too, that by leaving the instrumentation open, Susato could sell more copies of his music than if he specified a precise group of instruments.

I can't hear the difference between a sackbut and a trombone. Is the sound really all that different?

It's similar but definitely different. If you listen to a recording that uses trombones (see the Susato playlist later in this chapter for suggestions), you can better compare the two instruments, and you might find that the sound of the sackbut is lighter, more delicate, and more like that of the human voice.

PROFILE   Tielman Susato (ca. 1510–ca. 1570)

The Composer as Publisher

Tielman Susato is remembered today both as a composer and as a publisher. He lived in Antwerp, a major commercial center on the coast of what is now Belgium, and began his career as a calligrapher in the cathedral *scriptorium*, a copy shop in which all copying was done by hand. He also played the sackbut and other wind instruments in the town band. By 1543, he had established his own music printing business, the first successful enterprise of its kind in the Low Countries (present-day Belgium and the Netherlands). No image of Susato has survived.

Susato published dozens of music books during his lifetime, many of which include compositions of his own. He was particularly interested in promoting local composers: Many of his publications are songs with Flemish (Dutch) texts. The *moresca* here first appeared in Susato's *The Third Book of Music* (*Het derde musyck boexken*), published in Antwerp in 1551, which he marketed as "a set of all kinds of dances . . . which can be played pleasantly and comfortably on all musical instruments."

No image of Tielman Susato has come down to us from the sixteenth century. We do, however, have many accounts and images of the *Moresca* dance, including this figure, carved by the German craftsman Erasmus Grasser in 1480. Grasser's dancer conveys the physicality of the *Moresca*, with its large leaps and high steps. Notice, too, the bells on the dancer's legs. This figure is only one in a much larger collection. If you search online you can find others in this colorful and intriguing set.

HISTORICAL CONTEXT   The Business of Music Publishing

The invention of printing by movable type in the mid-fifteenth century created the world's first information explosion. What had once been copied out painstakingly by hand could now be produced on a massive scale in far less time. By the early sixteenth century, printing and publishing had become a major business.

Music publishing was slower to follow than book publishing because a page of printed music involved far more than just a series of letters on a series of lines. By the early sixteenth century, however, Ottaviano Petrucci, a printer working in Venice, had developed an efficient method of printing staff lines, notes, and texts on a single page.

As with any commercial enterprise, quality and consumer demand combined to drive the nature of the product. Just as recording labels promote certain musicians based on artistry and popular tastes, Petrucci marketed his early publications toward a public that wanted printed music by the leading composers of the day, including Josquin des Prez (see Chapter 7). Tielman Susato, working far to the north half a century later, followed these same business principles and sold mostly dance music and popular songs.

A page from one of Petrucci's early publications. Like all early book printers, Petrucci tried to create printed materials that resembled manuscripts as closely as possible.

Moorish Dance

Moorish Dance in various versions. Susato left no indications about the instrumentation of the music for this dance, and a number of groups have recorded it in a variety of different arrangements.

- **Piffaro.** *A Flemish Feast*, Archive 457609. A performance on period instruments by one of the leading ensembles specializing in early instrumental music.
- **Ensemble Terpsichore.** *Musique vocale et instrumentale de la Renaissance*, Gall 567. Another performance on an ensemble of period instruments.
- **Rupert Gough.** *Popular Organ Music, Vol. 3*, Priory Records 595. An arrangement on the organ, recorded at Wells Cathedral, England.
- **Philip Jones Brass Ensemble.** *Greatest Hits*, Decca 467746. This version (*Mohrentanz* or *Moorish Dance*) is on modern-day brass instruments (trumpet, horn, trombone, tuba).
- **Canadian Brass.** *Renaissance Men*, RCA 68018. Another performance on modern-day brass instruments.

Instrumental Music of the Renaissance

Many Renaissance musical instruments disappeared over time or evolved into different forms. Only in the last 40 years or so have performers begun to recover these instruments and thereby recreate the Renaissance in sound. These albums will allow you to hear some of these instruments in greater depth.

Flautando Köln
- *Ancor che col partire*, Harmonia Mundi HMC 90 5234. A wide selection of Renaissance vocal music arranged for recorder quartet, with works by Cipriano de Rore, Andrea Gabrieli, and the Spanish composer Antonio de Cabezón.

His Majestys Sagbutts and Cornetts
- *The Canzonas and Sonatas from Sacrae Symphoniae (1597)*, Hyperion 66908. A collection of brass music written by the great late-sixteenth-century Venetian composer Giovanni Gabrieli. Includes the celebrated *Sonata pian' e forte*, which features contrasting loud (*forte*) and soft (*piano*) passages.

Phantasm
- *The Four Temperaments*, Avie 2054. A wide sampling of viol music by composers active in England in the sixteenth and early seventeenth centuries, including Thomas Tallis, William Byrd, and Alfonso Ferrabosco.

PART 2 Summary

	Middle Ages	Renaissance
Texture	Monophonic and polyphonic	Polyphonic, including imitative counterpoint
Melody	Flowing, largely conjunct, divided into sections by cadences; melodies based on scales of the medieval modes	Flowing, but with greater use of disjunct motion; divided into sections by cadences; melodies based on scales of the medieval modes
Rhythm	Free (plainchant) and metrically structured	Relatively smooth and flowing rhythms within a metrically structured framework
Timbre	No sharp distinction between instrumental and vocal music	No sharp distinction between instrumental and vocal music; a growing number and variety of instruments
Harmony	A by-product of counterpoint	A by-product of counterpoint
Form	Based on repetition, variation, and contrast	Based on repetition, variation, and contrast; primarily sectional; binary form for dance music
Word–Music Relationships	Syllabic settings to project texts clearly; melismatic settings to emphasize key words	Limited use of word painting

IN REVIEW: Renaissance Style

Polyphonic texture Although monophonic plainchant continued to be used in sacred services, new music is almost entirely polyphonic. Imitative counterpoint becomes increasingly important (Byrd). Four-voice texture is the norm at the beginning of the Renaissance (Josquin); six-voice texture is the norm by the end (Byrd).

- Josquin, "The Cricket" (Chapter 7)
- Weelkes, "Since Robin Hood" (Chapter 8)
- Byrd, "Sing Joyfully" (Chapter 9)
- Palestrina, *Pope Marcellus Mass* (Chapter 10)
- Susato, *Moorish Dance* (Chapter 12)

Melody Greater use of disjunct motion; melodies still based on medieval modes.

- Josquin, "The Cricket" (Chapter 7)
- Weelkes, "Since Robin Hood" (Chapter 8)
- Byrd, "Sing Joyfully" (Chapter 9)
- Palestrina, *Pope Marcellus Mass* (Chapter 10)
- Susato, *Moorish Dance* (Chapter 12)

Rhythm Metrical structure provides a framework for rhythms that are usually fluid (Josquin, Weelkes, Byrd), though in the case of dance music these rhythms are more repetitive (Susato).

- Josquin, "The Cricket" (Chapter 7)
- Weelkes, "Since Robin Hood" (Chapter 8)
- Byrd, "Sing Joyfully" (Chapter 9)
- Palestrina, *Pope Marcellus Mass* (Chapter 10)
- Susato, *Moorish Dance* (Chapter 12)

Word painting Setting specific words to music that imitates the meaning of those words.

- Josquin, "The Cricket" (Chapter 7)
- Weelkes, "Since Robin Hood" (Chapter 8)
- Byrd, "Sing Joyfully" (Chapter 9)

Binary form The most common form for dance movements, consisting of two sections, each repeated in performance.

- Susato, *Moorish Dance* (Chapter 12)

PART 3

1600–1750

The Baroque Era

The period between roughly 1600 and 1750 was first called the **Baroque Era** by historians who wanted to characterize the period between the Renaissance and the Classical Era. By using the term *baroque*, historians were calling attention to the extravagant and even bizarre qualities of the music and art. Indeed, music's textures, harmonies, and forms tend to be more free and unpredictable in Baroque music than in the music of the Renaissance. The standard texture of polyphony now made room for homophony in which one voice was clearly more important than any of the others. Putting one voice in the musical foreground meant that a solo singer could portray on stage the thoughts and actions of a single dramatic character. The new use of homophony beginning around 1600 made possible the emergence of opera, a sung drama. Composers extended the expressive possibilities of solo singing into sacred music as well, creating the genre of the oratorio, which was essentially an unstaged opera on a sacred topic. The new texture of homophony also made possible the instrumental genre of the concerto, in which a soloist or small group of soloists could stand out against the backdrop of a larger ensemble. Singers and instrumentalists alike began to display their virtuosity with pride, improvising and embellishing their parts as never before, and playing music that made increasingly greater technical demands on their abilities as musicians.

The Baroque Era was a period of energy and motion, of ornamentation and extremes. New contrasts between light and dark appeared in painting; similarly, musical compositions exhibited bold contrasts in sounds, between high and low, soft and loud. Painting and sculpture gained a new sense of motion; music, likewise, propelled itself forward by the continuous unfolding of small groupings of notes. Architecture became increasingly ornate; musical lines, too, came to be decorated by ornamental flourishes and trills (notes next to each other that are played in alternation very rapidly). In all the arts, the expression of one particular emotion, known as an *affect*, became all-important. Baroque composers and performers were committed to representing the passions through music. These passions are not to be understood as personal self-expression, however. Like good actors, Baroque musicians could move their audiences by the artful portrayal of emotion.

A Musical Interlude, by Dutch painter Jan Verkolje (ca. 1674). Like a work of Baroque music, this painting uses a strong sense of movement to depict a single "affect," or emotion. The gentleman has turned away from the keyboard in a sudden moment of passion and grasped the hand of his musical partner, a woman holding a viol.

Louis XIV's palace at Versailles, west of Paris, depicted in 1722 by Jean-Baptiste Martin. The grounds included a magnificent opera house.

Projecting Cultural Power through Music

During the Baroque Era, a nation's splendor was measured in cultural terms as well as political and economic terms. The arts were an important means of projecting power and authority. Rulers vied with one another to find and retain the best artists, poets, composers, and musicians. When the ruler of Hanover (Germany) became King George I of England, he took with him his court composer, Georg Friedrich Händel, who Anglicized his name to George Frideric Handel. Handel's fame as a composer throughout Europe reflected well on the new king. Across the English Channel from England, Louis XIV, who ruled France from 1643 until his death in 1715, spared no expense on the arts and was particularly passionate about music and dance, sponsoring such composers as Jean-Baptiste Lully, Antonia Bembo, and Elisabeth Jacquet de la Guerre (see "Historical Context: Female Composers in the Baroque Era" in Chapter 16). On a much smaller scale but still very much in the same tradition, the Christian Ludwig, Margrave of Brandenburg (1677–1734) assembled an orchestra of virtuosos; Johann Sebastian Bach wrote his Brandenburg Concerto no. 2 (1720) for this ensemble. Visitors to the court were no doubt impressed by the Margrave's ability to assemble such talent.

Chapter 19
Bach: Brandenburg Concerto No. 2

The Baroque Era

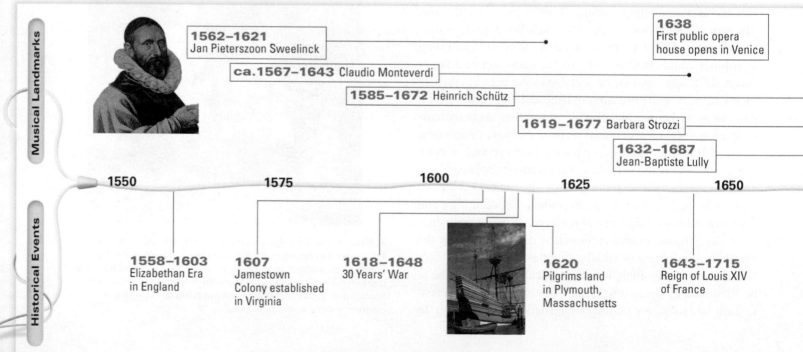

Musical Landmarks

1562–1621 Jan Pieterszoon Sweelinck

1638 First public opera house opens in Venice

ca.1567–1643 Claudio Monteverdi

1585–1672 Heinrich Schütz

1619–1677 Barbara Strozzi

1632–1687 Jean-Baptiste Lully

1550   1575   1600   1625   1650

Historical Events

1558–1603 Elizabethan Era in England

1607 Jamestown Colony established in Virginia

1618–1648 30 Years' War

1620 Pilgrims land in Plymouth, Massachusetts

1643–1715 Reign of Louis XIV of France

The Splendor of the Church

The arts served also to project the power of the church. The same theatricality and intense artistic expression designed to arouse earthly passions could awaken religious passion as well. Churches spent large sums of money on lavish decoration that would both convey the church's authority and inspire religious fervor. Filling these brilliant interiors was the sound of the Baroque organ, an instrument whose powerful resonance and striking variety of timbre was unsurpassed in creating awe. Churches invested small fortunes in their organs, and organ-building enjoyed its golden age in the Baroque Era. Johann Sebastian Bach, who composed many works for organ including the Fugue in G Minor (1705), made frequent trips to towns and cities around central Germany to test the craftsmanship of newly installed instruments.

Chapter 18
Bach: Fugue in G minor, BWV 578

Music also served as an important means of conveying the teachings of the church, and sacred music could be every bit as elaborate as sacred architecture. The first movement of Bach's Cantata no. 140, *Awake, a Voice Calls to Us* (1731), is based on a relatively simple and well-known hymn tune. Bach constructed an intricate and extended structure around it, while leaving the melody itself more or less intact. Listeners of all levels could thus easily follow the course of this intricate movement and be uplifted by its glorious sound.

Chapter 20
Bach: Cantata No. 140, *Awake, a Voice Calls to Us*

1653–1713 Arcangelo Corelli

1678–1741 Antonio Vivaldi

1653–1706 Johann Pachelbel

1685–1759 G. F. Handel

ca.1659–1685 Henry Purcell

1685–1750 J. S. Bach

1660–1725 Alessandro Scarlatti

1668–1733 François Couperin

1650   1675   1700   1725   1750

1653–58 Oliver Cromwell takes power in England following the beheading of Charles I in 1649

1660 "The Restoration" era begins in England with the return of Charles II to the throne

1686 Isaac Newton explains planetary motion by the principles of gravity in his *Principia mathematica*

1688 "Glorious Revolution" brings William and Mary to power in England

1703 Peter the Great establishes St. Petersburg as Russia's capital city

The organ loft of the 18th-century Augustinian Monastery church in Herzogenburg, Austria. Scarcely a square inch of surface is left unadorned. In a similar manner, Baroque musicians embellished composers' works.

Not all productions of opera and oratorio were successful. In fact, arson became a serious problem in the opera world for a time during the Baroque Era; in an attempt to recoup losses, unscrupulous investors were known to set fire to opera houses to collect insurance money.

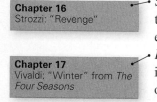

Chapter 16
Strozzi: "Revenge"

Chapter 17
Vivaldi: "Winter" from *The Four Seasons*

Opera, Oratorio, and the Entrepreneurial Spirit

The earliest operas, including Claudio Monteverdi's *Orpheus* (1607), were performed in private theaters at the courts of the nobility and royalty. But a growing spirit of entrepreneurship made the arts increasingly accessible to the public, most notably in Italy and England. The first public opera houses opened in Venice in 1637, and by the early eighteenth century even some theaters under the control of ruling monarchs began opening their doors to paying customers (see "Closer Look: The Baroque Opera House"). Opera was slow to develop in England: Henry Purcell's *Dido and Aeneas* (1689) remains an outstanding exception. But by 1710, opera had become big business, not only in London but across all of Europe. Impresarios (producers) invested heavily in new productions and paid enormous sums to the singers who could ensure the success of a new work. When the church prohibited performances of operas during Lent (a somber period of fasting and penance preceding Easter), these same impresarios filled their opera houses by hiring the same singers and instrumentalists to perform oratorios. The oratorio was essentially identical to opera in its musical form, but it was unstaged, and the libretto was usually based on a sacred subject. The oratorio we will hear, Handel's *Messiah* (1747), moves audiences today as it did in 1742 when it was first performed.

Chapter 14
Purcell: *Dido and Aeneas*

Chapter 21
Handel: *Messiah*

The Virtuoso

The Baroque Era was an age of opulence, and that opulence extended to the world of sound. Virtuoso singers and instrumentalists were coveted by rulers and the public alike. As soloists, these musicians were expected to embellish the parts written for them. What is preserved in the notated score today is by many accounts only an outline of what these skilled soloists actually performed. In Barbara Strozzi's song "Revenge" (1651), we will hear a soprano soloist of today recreate the highly ornamented, improvisatory style of the early eighteenth century. Antonio Vivaldi's violin concerto "Winter," from his *Four Seasons* (1720), places extraordinary demands on the soloist. And in his Brandenburg Concerto no. 2, Bach created a vehicle by which not one but four different soloists—on trumpet, oboe, violin, and recorder—can display their talents (Chapter 19).

Castrati—singers who had been castrated as young boys so as to preserve the high range of their voices—were in especially high demand. Through their art, the most successful castrati became the equivalent of millionaires. They possessed both the high range of a woman's voice and the physical power of a man's voice, and the effect could be stunning. The castrato was an entirely unnatural phenomenon, of course, and barbaric by today's standards, but for Baroque audiences, the pursuit of vocal beauty justified even the most drastic measures.

Stefano Dionisi in the title role of the 1994 film *Farinelli*. Carlo Broschi (1705–1782), who used "Farinelli" as his stage name, was the most celebrated castrato of the 18th century. The producers of *Farinelli* recreated his singing voice by blending two separate recordings—one by a woman, one by a man—onto a single soundtrack.

CLOSER LK   The Baroque Opera House

The earliest operas were performed only in private theaters of the nobility. Eventually, however, opera moved into public theaters open to paying customers. This 1740 painting shows an opera being performed at the Teatro Regio in Turin, in what is now northern Italy. The "Royal Theater" was funded by the Grand Duke of Tuscany, who could enter the hall directly from his palace without going outside. The magnificence of the staging, costumes, singing, and orchestral playing helped the duke impress visiting dignitaries and thereby enhance his standing within the cultural politics of Europe.

The more elite members of the audience sit in stalls or **"boxes"** on the theater's upper levels. Each box was rented privately for an entire season.

Audience behavior at operas was rather relaxed. In this first row, one member of the audience gestures toward the stage, while his neighbor studies the words being sung by following the **libretto** (literally "little book"), which contains the complete text of the opera. And one of *his* neighbors is not even facing the stage!

Stage design was a major element of the theatrical spectacle. Here, an elaborate backdrop gives the illusion of depth to a fairly small stage.

Soloists sing their parts wearing dazzling costumes, a standard feature in most Baroque operas.

The orchestra occupies the **"pit,"** a lowered area between the audience and the stage. Two sets of basso continuo are visible here on each side of the orchestra: one accompanies the recitatives, while the other accompanies arias and other numbers that call for a full orchestra.

A **bailiff** maintains order in the theater. Although his function is largely ceremonial, his physical presence is a reminder to all that this is a royal theater.

A **merchant** sells refreshments to members of the audience. In the Baroque Era, vendors moved up and down the aisles throughout the performance.

13 Claudio Monteverdi
Orpheus, selection from Act II
Composed: 1607

Opera was the most important new genre of the Baroque Era, and Monteverdi's *Orpheus* is one of the earliest operas. This scene presents the moment in which the legendary poet and singer Orpheus learns of the death of his wife, Euridice; the chorus, following the conventions of Greek drama, responds with an outburst of communal grief.

Listen to This First

Texture

Listen for homophony at the beginning: The solo singer carries the melody, while a small group of instruments provides support. Toward the end, when the chorus enters, listen for the change to polyphonic texture: All voices have equal importance. ■

Word–Music Relationships

Listen to the way in which the music heightens the expressive emotion of what the characters are saying. Notice how the soloist's singing style differs from that of the chorus. ■

LEARNING OBJECTIVES

13.1 Outline the origins of opera, using Claudio Monteverdi's *Orpheus* as an example.

13.2 Define basso continuo and its significance in homophonic texture.

13.3 Define recitative.

13.4 Listen for the difference between homophonic and polyphonic settings of the text in this selection from *Orpheus*.

13.5 Outline Monteverdi's career as a composer.

13.6 Identify the difference between the older style of the *prima prattica* and the newer style of the *seconda prattica*.

While the idea of a sung drama with one performer singing the part of each character may seem perfectly obvious to us today, it was the object of heated debate in the early years of the Baroque Era. The monophonic dramas of the Middle Ages, like Hildegard von Bingen's *Play of Virtues* (Chapter 1), had long since been forgotten. It was not until the decades around 1600 that a small group of philosophers, musicians, and poets began meeting in Florence (present-day Italy) to consider how they might revive the synthesis of music and drama they knew had been practiced by the ancient Greeks. The result was **opera**, a drama sung from beginning to end. For all its changes over the ensuing centuries, the genre of opera has remained devoted to its original purpose: to convey a story onstage through characters who express their thoughts and emotions by singing.

Monteverdi's *Orpheus* (*L'Orfeo*) is the most frequently performed of all early operas. The music is richly varied, with elaborate songs and choruses for the singers and lively instrumental music for the dancers. And while the story itself is based on myth, the music makes the characters seem very human, their emotions very real.

Orpheus, the legendary singer of Greek mythology, learns from a messenger that his beloved Euridice has died from the bite of a serpent. The selection here, from Act II, begins just after the messenger has delivered this terrible news. Orpheus is stunned; the on-stage **chorus** (consisting of nymphs and shepherds) echoes his grief. Later in the opera, Orpheus uses the power of music to persuade the guardians and gods of the underworld (Hades) to allow him to cross the River Styx and bring Euridice back from the dead to "see the stars once more." He is allowed to do so on the condition that he not look behind him on his ascent out of the underworld. But he cannot resist the temptation to look back, and Euridice is lost to him once again. Monteverdi's setting of the myth has a bittersweet ending in which Euridice herself takes her place among the stars as a constellation.

Homophonic Texture: One Character, One Voice

The texture of **homophony**—a single principal voice with subordinate accompaniment—is essential in opera, for it allows one singer to represent a single character onstage. The group of instruments accompanying the singer here is known collectively as the **basso continuo** ("continuous bass"). This small ensemble, as its name suggests, plays more or less continuously, and it provides a bass line and harmonies that support the melody above. The basso continuo typically consists of two instruments: one that can sustain long notes (such as a bass viol, a cello, or a bassoon), and one that can play chords (such as a lute or a harpsichord). The organ was one of the few instruments that alone could both sustain a sound *and* play chords. In the recording here, the basso continuo part is performed by a combination of organ and lute. In practice, musicians of the Baroque Era used whatever number and combination of instruments were available.

Homophonic texture also made it much easier for audiences to understand the text being sung. A single singer carrying the melodic line, with a subordinate accompaniment (the basso continuo), could articulate the words clearly without competition from other voices. The rich sound of polyphonic texture came at the expense of textual clarity. Listen again to William Byrd's "Sing Joyfully" (Chapter 9), without following the text in the book, and see how well you can understand the words. Even the best choirs cannot project every word with equal clarity: This kind of writing for four, five, or six voices is simply too thick.

The new homophonic texture restored a greater sense of balance between text and music. Composers who used this new manner of writing argued that the text should determine the nature of the music and not vice versa—even if the expressive portrayal of certain words sometimes involved breaking long-standing conventions of harmony and counterpoint. Composers who believed in the text as a driving force called this new way of writing the *seconda prattica* (the "second" or "later" practice). This newer compositional style came to be seen in opposition to the *prima prattica* (the "first" or "older" practice), the older style in which musical richness took priority over textual expression (see Expand Your Playlist).

Word–Music Relationships: Between Speech and Song

The selection opens with an extended **recitative** by Orpheus. The word "recitative" derives from the same root word as "recite," and this style of singing lies somewhere between singing and speaking. It is still singing—we hear sustained pitches and definite rhythms—but the **syllabic** setting of the text, with one note per syllable, makes it closer to speech than the more **melismatic**, lyrical kind of singing we hear more frequently, with many notes per syllable. The great advantage of recitative over more conventional styles of singing is that it allows the words to be projected with special clarity: The beauty of the melody is less important than the clarity of the words. In this sense, recitative is rather like plainchant (discussed in Chapter 1), but with the addition of supporting instruments underneath the vocal line.

The chorus that follows is written in the older **polyphonic** style. As in the sung dramas of Greek antiquity, the chorus—here, the gathering of nymphs and shepherds—comments from time to time on what has just occurred. The texture is necessarily polyphonic because the chorus represents the reactions of the many characters onstage who are witnessing the drama. The textures in Monteverdi's *Orpheus* thus include both homophony and polyphony; this coexistence of old and new textures is typical of music throughout the Baroque Era.

Now listen to the excerpt again, using the Listening Guide.

CONNECT YOUR PLAYLIST

Soloist and Chorus

Find a song where a soloist and chorus interact.

Example: The Rolling Stones, "You Can't Always Get What You Want" (1969)
In this song a boys' choir contrasts effectively with the timbres of the rock band.

Listening Guide

Claudio Monteverdi Composed: 1607

Orpheus, selection from Act II (6:10)

Time	Form	Italian Text	English Translation	Texture	Word–Music Relationships
0:00 0:39 1:02 1:13 1:24 1:38 1:50 1:59 2:18	Recitative: Orpheus	Tu se' morta, mia vita, ed io respiro? Tu se' da me partita Per mai più non tornare, ed io rimango? No, che se i versi alcuna cosa ponno, N'andrò sicuro a' più profondi abissi; E intenerito il cor del Re dell'ombre, Meco trarrotti a riveder le stelle. O, se ciò negherammi empio destino, Rimarrò teco in compagnia di morte. Addio terra, addio cielo e sole, addio.	Thou art dead, my life, and I still breathe? Thou art departed from me, Never to return, and I remain? No, if my verses still hold any power, I shall descend to the deepest depths; And I shall soften the heart of the king of shadows And bring thee back with me to see the stars again. Or if impious fate denies me this, I shall remain there in the company of the dead. Farewell, earth, farewell, sky and sun, farewell.	Homophonic (voice and accompanying basso continuo)	Recitative (syllabic). Word painting on *abissi* ("depths"): melody descends. Melody rises up to the word *stelle* ("stars") and sinks down again on *morte* ("the dead").
2:54 3:52 4:04	Chorus: Nymphs and shepherds	Ahi caso acerbo, ahi fat'empio e crudele. Ahi stelle ingiuriose, ahi cielo avaro. No si fidi uom mortale Di ben caduco e frale, Che tosto fugge, e spesso A gran salita il precipizio è presso. (Alessandro Striggio)	Ah, bitter event! Ah, impious and cruel fate! Ah, misaligned stars! Ah, voracious heaven! Let no mortal trust in transient and frail happiness, for it soon flies away, and often the great height is close to the precipice. (Transl. MEB)	Polyphonic (chorus of five parts, all equal)	Lyrical singing. Word painting on *acerbo* ("bitter"), with sharp dissonance (conflicting notes). Word painting on *fugge* ("flies"), with rapid rhythms, and on *salita* ("height"), with rising melodic line.

🔍 Student FAQs ⚙

If recitative makes it so much easier to understand the words, why isn't the whole opera written in recitative?

So far as text intelligibility is concerned, recitative has definite advantages over lyrical singing. If an opera consisted entirely of recitative, however, we would likely miss the more musical elements that lyrical singing has to offer. Composers of opera typically use a combination of different singing styles and instrumental and vocal combinations to create a wide variety of timbres and textures.

Does the basso continuo play when the chorus sings?

Yes it does, though it is not as noticeable because the alto, tenor, and bass voices provide the necessary harmonic support to the upper line. Once the basso continuo took hold in the early seventeenth century, it was used for homophonic and polyphonic textures alike.

PROFILE   Claudio Monteverdi (1567–1643)

Master of Old and New Styles

Claudio Monteverdi's career straddled the Renaissance and the Baroque Era, and he mastered both the old and new textures of composition. The madrigal "Luci serene e chiare," featured in the playlist, is a good example of the earlier polyphonic style. The "Lamento della ninfa," on the other hand, reflects his shift to the new homophonic way of writing. Monteverdi served for many years at the court of Mantua, where he produced *Orpheus* (1607), the first opera to win widespread acclaim. In 1613, he became director of music at St. Mark's Basilica in Venice, where he lived the rest of his life. He was constantly trying new styles and new genres. In addition to operas for an elite audience at court, he also wrote works for the new public opera houses that began to open in Venice at the end of the 1630s. His music remained a touchstone for all subsequent seventeenth-century composers.

This portrait of Monteverdi dates from around 1613, when he was appointed music director at St. Mark's in Venice, one of the most prestigious musical positions in all Italy.

EXPAND YOUR PLAYLIST: MONTEVERDI

- **The Coronation of Poppea** (*L'incoronazione di Poppea*). This opera is based on the historical figures of the Emperor Nero (who fiddled while Rome burned) and his lover, Poppea, who schemes and plots to eliminate everyone who stands in her way of becoming empress of Rome.

- **The Return of Ulysses to His Homeland** (*Il ritorno d'Ulisse in patria*). The libretto of this opera draws on the end of Homer's *Odyssey*.

- **Psalm 100** (*Confitebor tibi*). Written for soloist, chorus, and orchestra, this piece is one of many sacred works Monteverdi wrote at San Marco in Venice.

- **"Serene and clear eyes"** ("Luci serene e chiare"). This madrigal is composed in the earlier polyphonic style.

- **"The Western Wind Returns"** ("Zefiro torna"). This is an Italian-language madrigal for two tenors and basso continuo, to a text by the fourteenth-century Italian poet Petrarch.

- **"Lament of the Nymph"** ("Lamento della Ninfa"). Here is an extended madrigal for vocal soloists, chorus, and basso continuo.

- **Vespers in Honor of the Blessed Virgin Mary** (*Vespro della Beata Vergine*). Monteverdi wrote this work when he was music director at the Basilica of San Marco in Venice. Its various movements present both old and new styles, the *prima prattica* and the *seconda prattica*.

Orpheus, with his lyre, greets one of the nymphs celebrating the joys of love. He has not yet learned that Euridice, his bride, has been bitten by a snake and died. To bring her back to life, he will use his music to gain entry to Hades.

 EXPAND YOUR PLAYLIST

Old and New Practices in the Seventeenth Century

The music of the early Baroque Era encompasses both old (*prima prattica*) and new (*seconda prattica*) styles, sometimes in the same work. These composers bridged the gap between Renaissance polyphony and Baroque homophony.

Giovanni Gabrieli (ca. 1554/57–1612)
- Gabrieli was the most celebrated composer working in Venice in the decades before Monteverdi's arrival. His *Oh Great Mystery (O magnum mysterium)* is a sacred piece for chorus, brass ensemble, and solo vocalist, combining elements of the old and new practice in a single work.

Heinrich Schütz (1585–1672)
- Schütz was the leading German composer of the seventeenth century. He studied composition in Venice, possibly with Monteverdi.
- "Sing Unto the Lord a New Song" ("Cantate domino canticum novicum"), a setting of Psalm 96, in Latin, is written in the *prima prattica* for four-part chorus.

- "Sing Unto the Lord a New Song" ("Singet dem Herren ein neues Lied") is a version of the same psalm in German. It is written in the newer *seconda prattica*, for solo voice, two violins, and basso continuo. The vocal and instrumental parts are quite florid and virtuosic.

Francesco Cavalli (1602–1676)
- Cavalli was Monteverdi's successor as music director at St. Mark's in Venice. Like Monteverdi, he composed in many genres, including operas and sacred music. *Dido (La Didone)* is an opera based on the same plot as Purcell's *Dido and Aeneas* (see Chapter 14), a story taken from Virgil's *Aeneid*.

14 Henry Purcell
Dido and Aeneas, selections
Composed: 1689

Purcell's *Dido and Aeneas* is one of the first operas written in English. The arias and recitatives help delineate the characters who are singing them. The story comes from Virgil's *Aenead*, which is about the aftermath of the Trojan War and the eventual founding of Rome.

Listen to This First))

⚡ Timbre

Listen for the variety of timbres. Following the instrumental overture, we hear a vocal recitative answered by a chorus, then an aria ("song") for solo voice, then another recitative, and finally another chorus. The final selection is Dido's celebrated lament toward the end of the opera. ■

🌐 Texture

Listen for the contrast between homophonic and polyphonic textures in the individual numbers. ■

🎧 Word–Music Relationships

Listen for the way in which certain words are emphasized through repetition and set to music in ways that enhance their meaning. ■

LEARNING OBJECTIVES

14.1 Outline the story of Dido and Aeneas.

14.2 Describe Henry Purcell's use of "numbers" as structural units by listening to *Dido and Aeneas*.

14.3 Explain the features and function of the operatic overture in general and the French overture in particular.

14.4 Discuss issues surrounding the singing of opera in English.

14.5 Listen for the differences between recitative and aria.

14.6 Listen for and define ostinato (ground bass).

14.7 Outline Purcell's career as a composer.

The early performance history of *Dido and Aeneas* is shrouded in mystery. The first documented production was sometime in 1689 at a school for young ladies in Chelsea (west of London at the time, now a part of the city), but it may have been performed as early as 1685. The work seems to have disappeared from the stage shortly afterward. It was not revived until 1700, almost five years after the composer's death, in a drastically altered version. *Dido and Aeneas* may have been suppressed for political reasons, either by Purcell himself or by the Crown, on the grounds that it could have been perceived as an unflattering commentary on the dual reign of King William, a foreigner, and Queen Mary, daughter of James II. The opera's plot, after all, deals with a foreign prince (Aeneas) who promises to marry the Queen of Carthage (Dido) but then abandons her, driving her to suicide.

The chief characters of the opera are the following:

• Dido, the queen of Carthage (soprano; the highest vocal range)

• Aeneas, a Trojan prince (baritone; the middle-low male voice)

• Belinda, Dido's maidservant (soprano)

Aeneas is a refugee from Troy, which has just fallen to the Greeks and their Trojan Horse. Fulfilling a promise from the gods, Aeneas and his companions are now on their way from Troy to the Italian peninsula, where he is destined to establish the city of Rome. On the coast of northern Africa (what is now Tunisia), they land at Carthage, ruled by the widowed Queen Dido. True to operatic convention, Dido and Aeneas immediately fall in love. He pledges to abandon his mission to found Rome, but when a witch disguised as Mercury, the messenger of the gods, orders him to leave, he obeys and departs. A grief-stricken Dido kills herself, but not before singing a long lament at the very end of the opera.

Form by the Numbers

Purcell moves the plot forward through a series of brief, self-contained units known as "numbers":

1. **Overture.**   There had to be some way to get the audience to settle down and be quiet. Far from the well-trained classical audiences of today, who file in respectfully to hear an esteemed musical work, audiences in Purcell's time (and, indeed, for the century and a half that followed) could be quite boisterous and noisy. For one thing, the music they were about to hear was new and had not yet entered the ranks of cherished masterworks. For another, people regarded the opera as a supreme social event, as many people still do today. A purely instrumental opening, or **overture**, signaled to the audience that it was time to leave the socializing and direct their attention to the stage, where the singers would soon appear.

   The form of this particular overture—a slow introduction followed by an imitative fast section—was very common in French operas of the time and for that reason is known as a **French overture**. We hear two typical characteristics of the French overture here:

   a. The slow introduction features a consistent alternation between long and short notes (a "LONG-short-LONG-short" pattern).

   b. The fast section begins with **imitation** among the voices: the same theme introduced by different instruments of the orchestra in succession.

2. **Scene and Chorus.**   An **aria**, sung by Queen Dido's maidservant and confidante, Belinda ("Shake the cloud from off your brow"). "Aria" is Italian for "air" or "melody," and is used to describe any lyrical movement or piece for solo voice, usually with some kind of instrumental accompaniment. The **chorus** then joins in, reinforcing this same sentiment with different words ("Banish sorrow, banish care").

3. **Song.**   Another aria, this one more elaborate. Dido laments her state ("Ah! Belinda"). She sings her melody over an **ostinato** pattern in the bass, a short array of nine notes repeated over and over. ("Ostinato" comes from the same root word as "obstinate.") This kind of pattern is also known as a **ground bass** or simply a **ground**.

4. **Recitative.**   Belinda and Dido in dialogue ("Grief increases by concealing"). The **recitative**, as we saw in Chapter 13, provided a way of delivering text quickly and clearly in a singing style similar to speech. The accompaniment is a simple **basso continuo**, played by harpsichord and cello in this case, providing harmonic support to the singers' lines.

5. **Chorus.**   In the manner of the chorus in an ancient Greek tragedy, the chorus comments on what has just happened on the stage, reinforcing Belinda's advice that Troy and Carthage join forces in the union of Dido and Aeneas ("When monarchs unite").

6. **Song.**   Toward the very end of the opera, Dido resolves to take her own life and sings this one last song of farewell (popularly known as "Dido's Lament") to Belinda. Once again we hear an ostinato pattern in the bass, similar to but different from the one that had figured in her briefer lament from Act I (number 3 above).

Belinda (Lucy Crowe, right) consoles Dido (Sarah Connolly) in the closing scene of Purcell's *Dido and Aeneas*, in a recent production from the Royal Opera House, Covent Garden, London.

Word–Music Relationships: Speaking, Expressing, Commenting

Purcell was influenced by composers of both French opera (especially Lully; see Expand Your Playlist) and Italian opera (including Alessandro Scarlatti, among others), who had begun moving more and more toward a clear division between recitative and aria.

When Purcell's characters need to talk to each other, he gives them something between speech and song: the recitative. When his characters need to convey some deeper feeling, he gives them lyrical arias in which they can linger expressively over individual words. The chorus, observing and feeling for us at closer range, punctuates these longer melodic expressions with comments communicated clearly and intelligibly, with one syllable per note. Each unit of the opera is dominated by a single *affect*, or emotion. Belinda is agitated in her opening number: She sings in uneven rhythms (short-LONG, short-LONG), particularly on the word "shake." Dido, in turn, sings her first lament (no. 3 in Listening Guide) to a repeated bass pattern that mirrors her state of constant sorrow. The chorus "When monarchs unite," with its lively, dance-like rhythms and major mode, injects a note of optimism into the musical narrative.

The concluding number of the opera, "Dido's Lament," uses a different ostinato bass that consists of a falling line, a pattern that listeners of Purcell's time would have immediately recognized as an emblem of lament. The ostinato is repeated no fewer than eleven times, but never overstays its welcome because Purcell skillfully layers the voice above it in ways that at times coincide with the bass line and at times do not. This helps give a very slow piece a strong sense of dramatic forward motion.

Now listen to the piece again, using the Listening Guide.

CONNECT YOUR PLAYLIST

Ostinato

Find a piece that uses an ostinato.

Example: One Direction, "Never Enough" (2015)
The same "doo-wop"–influenced bass line continues through almost the entire song.

PERFORMANCE   **Opera in English**

Why aren't there more operas in English? Most of the works in the operatic repertory were written in other languages, particularly Italian (opera began on the Italian peninsula, after all), but also French and German. Some claim that English by its nature is not as singable as Italian with all its sustainable vowels. But the enormous repertory of English-language songs offers compelling evidence that English words lend themselves to singing just as well. In our day, many operas are being written in English, partly because it has become a language of worldwide significance—much as Italian was in the seventeenth and eighteenth centuries. Benjamin Britten's operas from the 1940s and 1950s (*Peter Grimes, The Turn of the Screw*) are staples of the repertory. More recent contributors include Thea Musgrave (*Mary, Queen of Scots*), John Adams (*Nixon in China*), and Philip Glass (*Einstein on the Beach*; see Chapter 61).

Should foreign-language operas be sung in English? The advantage is obvious: Audiences could easily understand what's being sung onstage. But there are drawbacks, too. It's difficult to create translations that retain the sense of the original and still mesh well with the composer's music. A composer might write a melodic phrase in such a way as to reach the highest note on one particular word, and a good translation must take that into account. Finally, English is a challenging language when it comes to rhyme: French, German, and especially Italian offer many more possibilities for rhymed words, and rhyme often plays an important role in opera texts.

Recently, opera houses have begun to address these challenges. Many use super-titles during performances. Listeners who want to follow the text can see the translations projected above the stage. A few opera houses have begun trying out personalized screens on individual seats that gives the listener the freedom to pick any language as a translation.

PROFILE   Henry Purcell (ca. 1659–1695)

Inspired by the Stage

Purcell was born into a family of musicians and served in his early years as a composer and organist at the English court and later at Westminster Abbey, where he is buried. He contributed songs and instrumental music to dozens of plays but wrote only one true opera, *Dido and Aeneas.* The English public was largely hostile to opera during the seventeenth century, in part because of England's strong tradition of spoken theater. Shakespeare had called for songs or instrumental music at many points in a number of his plays, but the idea of singing an entire drama from beginning to end was something most English theatergoers considered absurd. Not until the early eighteenth century would opera take hold in England, and when it did, the rage was for opera sung in Italian, not English. It would be another 50 years before audiences would begin to accept the idea of English-language opera. Purcell, in short, was far ahead of his time. When *Dido and Aeneas* was rediscovered in the late eighteenth century, it helped establish his eventual reputation as the greatest of all seventeenth-century English composers.

Purcell in the 1690s, toward the end of his brief life.

EXPAND YOUR PLAYLIST: PURCELL

- **Chaconne in G minor, Z. 730.** A purely instrumental ground bass (ostinato) for four stringed instruments and basso continuo.

- **"Sound the Trumpet"** from *Ode for Queen Mary's Birthday.* A duet for tenors and basso continuo, with the voices imitating trumpets.

- **"One Charming Night"** from *The Faerie Queen.* An aria from a semi-opera, set to a text by Sir Edmund Spenser.

- **"Lord, What Is Man?"** A song for solo voice and basso continuo.

- *My Heart Is Inditing.* A full anthem (Chapter 9) in the tradition of English sacred music, for chorus and string orchestra.

Listening Guide

Henry Purcell Composed: 1689
Dido and Aeneas, Selections (8:11, 4:05)

The Overture

Time	🏛 Form	🌐 Texture	🥁 Rhythm
0:00	1. Overture: Slow introduction (**A**)	Melody in the uppermost voice; prominent basso continuo part below.	Uneven rhythms (LONG-short) figure prominently.
0:45	Literal repeat of slow introduction (**A**)		
1:26	Fast section (**B**)	Begins with imitative entries.	Theme consists of notes of equal value.
1:57	Literal repeat of fast section (**B**)		

Act I

When the curtain goes up on Act I, we see the Palace of Carthage, with Queen Dido accompanied by Belinda, her maidservant and confidante, and other members of the court. Dido laments her current state: Her husband has died, she has not remarried, and her kingdom, as a result, is vulnerable and unstable.

Time	Form	Character(s) Singing	Text	💬 Word–Music Relationships
2:31	2. Scene and Chorus	Belinda	Shake the cloud from off your brow, Fate your wishes does allow; Empire growing, pleasures flowing, Fortune smiles and so should you.	Rapid uneven rhythms on "shake" (short-LONG) as if to mimic the act of shaking.
3:04		Chorus	Banish sorrow, banish care, Grief should ne'er approach the fair.	
3:30	3. Song (Aria)	Dido	Ah! Belinda, I am pressed With torment not to be confessed, Peace and I are strangers grown. I languish till my grief is known, Yet would not have it guess'd.	Ground bass (ostinato), a brief pattern repeated in the bass line throughout the entire number, reflecting the unceasing nature of Dido's torment.
7:21	4. Recitative	Belinda and Dido	**Belinda:** Grief increases by concealing. **Dido:** Mine admits of no revealing. **Belinda:** Then let me speak; the Trojan guest Into your tender thoughts has pressed; The greatest blessing Fate can give Our Carthage to secure and Troy revive.	The first part of the dialogue stands between speech and song. Belinda's last two lines stand out because they are more lyrical and because she repeats these words.
7:57	5. Chorus	Chorus	When monarchs unite, how happy their state, They triumph at once o'er their foes and their fate.	The syllabic setting helps make the words more intelligible.

Act III

Aeneas has abandoned Dido, who, in her grief, takes her own life and sings one last song before she dies.

Time	Form: Instrumental	Form: Text	Word–Music Relationship
0:00	Statement 1		Slow, descending chromatic bass line announces that this will be a song of lament, full of pain.
0:17	Statement 2	When I am laid, am laid in earth, May my wrongs create	The voice enters, slow and steady, moving in a narrow range.
0:43	Statement 3	No trouble, no trouble in thy breast;	
1:05	Statement 4	When I am laid, am laid in earth, May my wrongs create	
1:25	Statement 5	No trouble, no trouble in thy breast;	
1:47	Statement 6	Remember me, but ah! forget my fate	The voice moves into a higher range.
2:08	Statement 7	Remember me, but ah! forget my fate	The same words, but now even higher and more intense.
2:31	Statement 8	Remember me, but ah! forget my fate	
2:52	Statement 9	Remember me, but ah! forget my fate.	
3:16	Statement 10		The ostinato line, present throughout, seems more prominent now that the voice has ceased singing. On the stage, this part of the song is sometimes staged as Dido's actual death.
3:41	Statement 11		

Q Student FAQs

Why is there so much repetition of the words?

Text repetition is common in many operas from different times and places. Repeating the words gives listeners a better chance of understanding them, and altering the music with each statement of the words allows the composer to bring out ever-deeper levels of meaning in them.

How long is this opera?

For an opera, it's very short: most performances run somewhere between 50 minutes and an hour. Most operas, by contrast, run at least two hours and often three or more, not including intermissions.

Baroque Opera

The most important repertories of later Baroque opera were in Italian and French. Italian opera enjoyed international acclaim; French opera was limited to France. Today, both repertories are performed.

Italian Opera

- **George Frideric Handel** (1685–1759), although German by birth, wrote many Italian operas during his years in London. These operas were often based on subjects from Classical history (Roman emperors, for example) or myth.

- The aria "Or la tromba" ("Now the trumpet") from *Rinaldo* is a **da capo aria**, which is very typical of **opera seria** (or "serious opera"), as Italian opera of this kind was called. A da capo aria opens with two contrasting sections, **A** and **B**; at the end of the **B** section, the singer returns to the beginning of the **A** section, following the direction in the score of *da capo*—literally, "from the head," or as we would say, "from the top." When the singer performs this **A** section a second time, he or she embellishes it heavily. The typical opera seria consists of an alternation of recitatives, which move the action forward, and da capo arias, in which the singers reflect on what has just happened on the stage.

- "Piangerò," a lament by Cleopatra from *Giulio Cesare*, is also a da capo aria. The **A** section is slow, and the **B** section is fast.

French Opera

- **Jean-Baptiste Lully** (1632–1687) was the favorite composer of King Louis XIV of France. The aria "Enfin, il est en ma puissance" from the opera *Armide*, is a stirring monologue by the sorceress Armida, who contemplates murdering the sleeping Renaud (Rinaldo) but cannot bring herself to do it because of his beauty.

- **Marc-Antoine Charpentier** (1643–1704) was another French composer who lived during the reign of Louis XIV. Charpentier's *Andromède* provides instrumental music for a play based on the Greek myth of Andromeda. In the aria "Quelle est lente, cette journée," you hear the very fluid rhythms typical of Baroque French homophony.

- **Jean-Philippe Rameau** (1683–1764) was the greatest composer of French opera in the eighteenth century. In "Rossignols amoureux" ("Amorous nightingales"), an aria from the opera *Hippolyte et Aricie*, both voice and instruments imitate the song of the nightingale.

Mbuti Pygmies

"Marriage Celebration Song"

Recorded: 1958

GLOBAL CONNECTION

OSTINATO

15

Ostinato, such as we heard in Dido's two arias from *Dido and Aeneas* (Chapter 14), is a formal device that has been used in the music of many different times and places. In the "Marriage Celebration Song" of the Mbuti Pygmies of central Africa, the repetition of a single pattern of notes and rhythms throughout the entire song provides a unifying structure above which a variety of melodies are presented.

Listen to This First

🎛 Form	🌐 Texture	🥁 Rhythm
Listen for the repetition of one basic unit. How would you describe the construction of this unit? ■	How many different vocal lines can you identify? Compare how they function independently and work together. How do the inner voices support each other on the same part? ■	Listen to how the parts are arranged rhythmically. Do the voices seem to function rhythmically as individuals, or do they work together? ■

The Mbuti Pygmies from the northeastern region of the Democratic Republic of the Congo (DRC, formerly known as Zaire) use **ostinatos** as the basis for complex musical structures involving **polyphony**, interlocking rhythms, and the alternation of voices to create a melody. In recent years, the music of the Pygmies has found growing interest among Western audiences, and its influence has extended to various pop, jazz, and world beat genres.

The Mbuti Pygmies inhabit the Ituri Forest. Although they are officially citizens of the DRC, the majority of Pygmy groups maintain a semiautonomous hunting-and-gathering existence. The Mbuti Pygmies are nomads, camping for a few weeks at a time in different locations of the forest in search of game. The hunt is a communal affair in which men string nets in semicircles, and women and children beat the brush to scare game into the nets. Food is shared. A political

LEARNING OBJECTIVES

15.1 Identify where the Mbuti Pygmies live and describe their social structure.

15.2 Discuss music in the communal culture of Mbuti Pygmies.

15.3 Recognize the use of ostinato in "Marriage Celebration Song."

15.4 Listen for heterophony in "Marriage Celebration Song."

15.5 Listen for interlocking parts of heterophonic lines in "Marriage Celebration Song."

The Mbuti Pygmies live in the Ituri Forest.

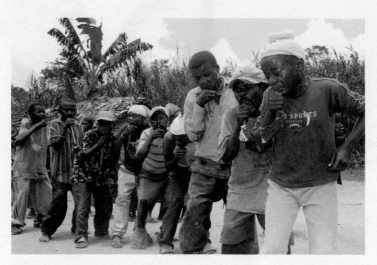

Mbuti Pygmies making music. The pipes they are blowing into are made of leaves; each member of the group plays a single note.

hierarchy is absent because survival depends on cooperation and not competition. In the same way, musical parts in Pygmy songs are distributed equally and coordinated carefully. The contribution of each separate part reflects every member's contribution to food gathering in the rainforest.

Form: A Call-and-Response Ostinato

The ostinato in this song consists of a brief **call-and-response** that may be represented as four phrases, **ABBB**, covering a total of eight beats. A lead singer sings the call (A) and the other singers in this group respond with a series of three short phrases (B). This basic melodic unit repeats over and over to create the ostinato.

Texture: Layers upon Layers

The ostinato is the unchanging "foundation" of this song. Around it, the other voices weave a complex texture made of multiple layers that overlap and interlock in intriguing ways. Beneath the call-and-response structure, two heterophonic lines are stacked. **Heterophony** is the simultaneous playing or singing of two or more versions of a melody. Thus, the line marked "Heterophonic voice 1" in the diagram on page 123 actually consists of multiple voice lines all singing similar melodies but not identical pitches. (The same is true of the line marked "Heterophonic voice 2.") Heterophony is a basic way of creating harmonic support without using harmony built from chords. It gives a thicker texture to the polyphony.

The two heterophonic lines are further layered by a **hocket** construction. Hocket is a form of polyphony consisting of two or more rhythmically **interlocking voices**. When voices interlock, one voice fills the spaces left by another's rests to complete a melodic unit. In other words, the melody is distributed throughout the parts, and each part contains only its constituent notes, sounded at the precise time. Hockets were also particularly popular in medieval France.

Think of a game where each player can speak only one word. Each person would then have to say this word at precisely the right moment to fit into a sentence:

Voice I:	I
Voice II:	am
Voice III:	a
Voice IV:	girl.

Now imagine that each person sings just one note in a melody. The same effect would be created by having each person chime in when his or her note is needed:

Voice I:	Hap-py		day
Voice II:		Birth-	
Voice III:			to
Voice IV:			you.

In Pygmy hocketing, this is made more complicated by the fact that each singer may sing two or three different notes, but the basic challenge of fitting these notes together into a melody remains.

Interlocking Rhythms

The rhythmic complexity of African hocket comes partly from the number of different parts that interlock and partly from the complexity of each individual part. No single line stands on its own. Each larger unit is built from interlocking subunits. The hocket thus occurs on many levels, as shown in the diagram.

	A *Call*	**B** *Response Voices 1*	**B** *Response Voices 2*	**B** *Response Voices 3*
Call/Response				
Heterophonic Voice 1				
Interlocking Voice with Heterophonic Voice 1				
Heterophonic Voice 2				
Interlocking Voice with Heterophonic Voice 2				

CONNECT YOUR PLAYLIST

Interlocking Rhythms

Find a piece that contains interlocking rhythms.

Example: Santana's recording of "Oye Como Va" (1970)—originally recorded by the great percussionist Tito Puente—has a complex accompaniment that uses interlocking rhythms.

Now listen to this excerpt again, using the Listening Guide.

Listening Guide))

Mbuti Pygmies Recorded: 1958
"Marriage Celebration Song" (1:02)

Time	🏛 Form	🌐 Texture
0:00	The song is already in progress.	Polyphonic throughout, with heterophony in each phrase subunit. The hocket is already established.
0:01	Ostinato cycle 1. **A:** the call.	Thick throughout.
0:02	**B, B, B:** the responses. One singer sets the intonation for the first response voices.	Thinner than the call. Voices overlap.
0:07	Ostinato cycle 2, beginning once again with the call.	Texture remains the same: polyphonic.
0:13	Ostinato cycle 3.	Polyphonic throughout.
0:20	Ostinato cycle 4. The lead singer of the call is heard over the group for the first time on this recording.	
0:26	Cycle 5	
0:32	Cycle 6	
0:38	Cycle 7	
0:44	Cycle 8	
0:51	Cycle 9	
0:57	Cycle 10	

Note: The selection begins midway through the song, and the lead singer is absent in the first three cycles but rejoins the song on the fourth cycle. Thus, in the early seconds of the excerpt, a different singer leads the response and sets the intonation.

Rhythm

Eight beats per cycle, built of four interlocking phrases. Each phrase is built from interlocking voices.

A long sung tone followed by two shorter sung tones, descending.

The first of the three interlocking responses is sung.

A varied response this time.

The responses continue to be varied each time.

 ### Student FAQs

How do Pygmies learn and remember these songs if there is no written notation?

Traditional singers and musicians around the world have developed a way of learning music without using any system of notation. Often, master musicians of one generation will teach students, either formally or informally, passing on their knowledge. Of course, with no recordings or written documentation, songs may change as they are sung over time. This is called "oral transmission" by ethnomusicologists because nothing is put in writing.

Why do Pygmies sing?

They sing for the same reason that most people do. However, many Pygmy songs have associations with specific rituals. For instance, the song featured in this chapter is linked to the wedding ceremony. Singing is a group activity in which everyone takes part, rather than one where a professional performs and others merely listen (as in many Western cultures).

How hard is it to sing in a hocketing style?

Try it with a group of friends! It's not that hard to learn your individual part, but synchronizing your singing with everyone else is very difficult if you've never tried it before. Add the idea that different melodies are occurring simultaneously (perhaps in different rhythms), and you'll get some sense of the skill of these Pygmy singers.

HISTORICAL CONTEXT Do I Repeat Myself?

The use of an ostinato bass—a repeating bass part—onto which a melody line is overlaid is common in many different forms of music. A great example in American popular music is the doo-wop vocal music of the 1950s.

How does doo wop work? In the vocal quartet, each voice has its own role. The bass singer handles the repeated foundation part, often in the form of a short phrase of nonsense syllables.

Think of the classic "Sh'Boom" by the Chords. The bass part is a simple repeated part. Above this bass line floats the melody. Between melody and bass, the other two voices fill in by also singing short melodic fragments. These four parts—fairly simple and seemingly independent—actually fit together to form one musical experience. We don't hear the individual parts as separate (although we can listen for them if we want) but instead experience the piece as a coherent whole.

How is this similar to the Pygmy music that we're hearing in this chapter?

The Chords, a 1950s doo-wop group famous for their recording of "Sh'Boom."

 EXPAND YOUR PLAYLIST

Singing in the Rain (Forest)

Mbuti Pygmies of the Ituri Rainforest
- Smithsonian Folkways Recordings SFW40401.
  Colin Turnbull was among the first Western anthropologists to spend considerable time studying and recording the Mbuti Pygmies in Africa. His landmark book, *The Forest People*, published in 1960, is considered a classic study of these people and helped introduce their culture to Western audiences. These recordings were made in the late 1950s and include many examples of the hocketing vocal style that we've studied in this chapter.

Heart of the Forest: The Music of the Baka Forest People of Southeast Cameroon
- Hannibal HNCD 1378.
  The Baka Forest people have their own unique form of vocal and instrumental hocketing. This recording includes a wide range of music, including performances on the single-string musical bow, and the distinctive vocal "yodeling" practiced by this tribe.

Centrafique: Anthologle de la Musique des Pygmees Aka
- Ocora C559012 13.
  Recorded by Pierre Toureille for UNESCO, this two-CD set documents the music of the Aka Forest peoples. Along with Turnbull's earlier recordings, this is considered a classic collection for those who love this musical style.

The Spirit Cries: Music from the Rainforests of South America & the Caribbean
- Rykodisc RCD 10250.
  Edited by percussionist Mickey Hart of the Grateful Dead, this collection of field recordings goes beyond Africa to trace related musical styles found across the ocean in South America and the Caribbean. The mixture of European and African influences is striking in these recordings.

Barbara Strozzi

"Revenge"

Composed: 1651

Barbara Strozzi's "Revenge" ("La Vendetta") allows the singer to display great vocal agility and makes effective use of contrasting timbres. The music requires only a small group of musicians: one singer, two violinists, and a basso continuo consisting in this chapter's performance of two instrumentalists, one playing the cello, the other playing the lute.

Listen to This First

🎵 Melody

Listen for the contour of the melodic lines and the way in which the singer embellishes these lines. Many of the longer notes are ornamented with shorter ones before or after. ∎

🎼 Form

Notice the alternation of the two contrasting melodies, one in a lively duple meter, the other in a slower triple meter. ∎

〰️ Timbre

Listen for the relationship of the two violins to the voice. The instruments echo the last phrase of each line of the text. Listen, too, for the way in which the instruments in the basso continuo (harpsichord, cello, and lute) support the vocal line. ∎

A poetic text that expresses a jilted lover's thirst for revenge demands energetic, extroverted music, and that is exactly what Barbara Strozzi gave "Revenge." Music like this was meant to be performed for private gatherings in relatively small rooms or "chambers," hence the term *chamber music*. In chamber music, we hear only one performer on each part, in contrast to orchestral music, which features multiple players on most parts.

🎵 Decoration of the Melody

In this performance of "Revenge," the singer adds extra notes to the notated melody line, decorating it more elaborately as the piece progresses. Listeners of the Baroque Era expected soloists to add this kind of ornamentation; the melodic lines written by the composer were only a starting point for performance. Music of the Baroque Era is in many respects like jazz today: Musicians embellish a basic tune in a highly individual and often quite spontaneous manner. The opening melody returns twice (at 0:52 and at 1:45) and becomes more florid with each appearance. It is as if the jilted lover is becoming ever more agitated as she describes the revenge she will exact. **Homophony** made this kind of improvisation possible. With two or more independent melody lines, players would have to agree in advance just how their embellishments would work together.

LEARNING OBJECTIVES

16.1 Listen for the use of vocal embellishments in successive repetitions of the same melodic line in Barbara Strozzi's "Revenge."

16.2 Recognize the relationship between the structure of the poem and the structure of the music.

16.3 Describe the relationship between the voice and the instruments in this work.

16.4 Identify trio-sonata texture in "Revenge."

16.5 Outline Barbara Strozzi's career as a composer.

16.6 Discuss the challenges for women composers during the seventeenth century.

Form: Contrast and Repetition

Strozzi alternates the two contrasting melodies—the first in duple meter, the second in triple meter—to create a large-scale structure that can be diagrammed in this way:

A   **B**   **A**   **B**   **A**

Duple   Triple   Duple   Triple   Duple

The contours and rhythms of the two melodies differ markedly: The first moves mostly downward, with short, quick notes, while the second moves mostly upward, using longer notes. The return of each melody creates a sense of coherence for the piece. This combination of contrast and return is basic to a great deal of Baroque music. The opening melody (**A**) gives the work an anchor, while the contrasting melody (**B**) provides variety.

The **A** melody

The **B** melody

The words to the **A** melody do not change. This device—bringing back the same words with the same basic melody at regular intervals over the course of a work—is called a **refrain**. Refrains had been used in song since the Middle Ages, and they continue to be used today. Many popular songs rely on the use of refrains. Here are a few examples:

- "With a knick-knack paddy-whack . . . " ("This Old Man")
- "Oh Susanna, oh don't you cry for me . . . " ("Oh Susanna")
- "Glory, glory hallelujah . . . " ("Battle Hymn of the Republic")

Timbre: Contrast and Punctuation

In addition to the **basso continuo** (harpsichord, cello, and lute), Strozzi uses two violins to great effect. They punctuate the end of every line in the refrain (the **A** section), each time providing an echo to what the soprano has just sung. This kind of back-and-forth between instruments and voices is another new element in Baroque music and has remained a basic compositional technique to the present day. The violins drop out entirely during the **B** sections of the work, further emphasizing the contrast between the **A** and **B** sections. The basso continuo part also participates in this interplay between instruments and voices. In the middle of the **B** section (at 0:36), you can hear the roles of voice and instruments reversed: The cello introduces the basic thematic idea before the soprano picks it up.

The combination of instruments heard in this song—two violins and basso continuo—was a favorite in the Baroque Era. Many works of chamber music from this time feature two high instruments (violins, flutes, oboes, recorders, or any mixture of these various instruments) and basso continuo. Such a combination produced what is known as **trio-sonata texture**, with three main voices: two in the soprano and one in the bass (the basso continuo). Arcangelo Corelli, J. S. Bach, and Handel all wrote trio sonatas (see Expand Your Playlist).

Now listen to this arietta, or "little aria" as Strozzi called it, using the Listening Guide.

An ensemble plays a sonata for two violins and basso continuo. The basso continuo group here consists of a harpsichord and a chitarrone, a lute-like instrument. A clear delineation between a leading voice or voices (here, the two violins) and supporting instruments (the basso continuo) marks a decisive break with the predominantly polyphonic style of the Renaissance.

Barbara Strozzi Composed: 1651

"Revenge" (2:14)

Time	Original Italian Text	English Translation	Timbre	Meter	Form (melodic idea)	Melody
0:00	La vendetta è un dolce affetto, il dispetto vuol dispetto, Il rifarsi è un gran diletto.	Vengeance is a sweet emotion; spite desires spite, and getting even is a great pleasure.	Soprano, basso continuo, two violins	Duple	**A**	Moves primarily downward in short, rapid notes
0:24	Vane son scuse e ragioni per placar donna oltraggiata, non pensar che ti perdoni! Donna mai non vendicata pace ha in bocca e guerra in petto.	Excuses and reasons are useless in placating an outraged woman; do not think that she will pardon you! A woman who has never avenged herself has peace on her lips and war in her heart.	Soprano, basso continuo	Triple	**B**	Moves primarily upward in longer, sustained notes
0:52	La vendetta è un dolce affetto il dispetto vuol dispetto, il rifarsi è un gran diletto.	Vengeance is a sweet emotion; spite desires spite, and getting even is a great pleasure.	Soprano, basso continuo, two violins	Duple	**A'**	Embellished further
1:17	Non perdona in vendicarsi all'amante più gradito che l'adora e vuol rifarsi quand'il fiero insuperbito verso lei perd'il rispetto.	She does not pardon, when taking vengeance, even the most agreeable lover who adores her and wants to make up with her when the proud and arrogant man loses respect for her.	Soprano, basso continuo	Triple	**B' (embellished)**	Embellished further
1:45	La vendetta è un dolce affetto il dispetto vuol dispetto Il rifarsi è un gran diletto.	Vengeance is a sweet emotion; spite desires spite, and getting even is a great pleasure.	Soprano, basso continuo, two violins	Duple	**A"**	Embellished still further

---

🔍 Student FAQs

How do performers know how to embellish this music?

At least some performance practices of the Baroque Era are documented in the books that taught musicians how to sing or play instruments. But these are really only starting points. Now, as then, musicians must use artistic judgment and embellish the music as they see fit. Opinions about what constitutes too much or too little embellishment vary widely.

If chamber music is performed by one musician to a part, is there a limit on the number of parts for it to still be considered chamber music?

A nonet—nine different parts—is generally considered to be the largest group of performers in a work of chamber music. With more than nine musicians, the "chamber" becomes rather crowded.

PROFILE   Barbara Strozzi (1619–1677)

"Secure from the Lightning Bolts of Slander"

Being a female composer—and a supremely talented one, no less—was not easy in the seventeenth century. In 1644, Barbara Strozzi dedicated her first published work, a collection of madrigals, with this note of awareness about criticism of her gender:

> To the august name of Your Highness I do reverently consecrate this first work, which I, as a woman, send forth into the light all too anxiously, so that under an oak tree of gold it may rest secure from the lightning bolts of slander prepared for it.

Her anticipation of "slander" was not without foundation. Rumors surrounded Strozzi's life. She had been adopted by the poet Giulio Strozzi and may in fact have been his natural daughter, born out of wedlock. She grew up in a family at the center of Venice's intellectual and cultural life and attended meetings of poets and philosophers that did not normally include women. Her chastity seems to have been a source of repeated satire and jest in the late 1630s as well.

Strozzi's achievements as a composer are all the more impressive in this light. By the end of her life, she had published eight volumes of music, including about 125 individual works of music, more than all but a few of her male contemporaries. What's more, she accomplished all this without benefit of a secure professional position in music and without extended support from any one patron.

The Gamba Player, by Bernardo Strozzi, ca. 1640. The woman depicted here may be Barbara Strozzi.

EXPAND YOUR PLAYLIST: STROZZI

- **"With New Bad News, I Cannot Sing"** ("Con male nuove, non si puo' cantare") is a lament for soprano and basso continuo.

- **"Proud Eyes"** ("Gl' occhi superbi") is a love song for soprano and basso continuo.

- **"Betrayal!"** ("Tradimento!") is a song from the perspective of a jilted lover for soprano and basso continuo.

- **"Between Hope and Fear"** ("Tra le spiranze e 'l timore") is a dialogue—for a single voice and basso continuo—between hope and fear.

HISTORICAL CONTEXT   Women Composers in the Baroque Era

Barbara Strozzi was one of a relatively small number of women in the Baroque Era who were able to publish their own compositions. The success of countless women composers in more recent times may make us wonder why there were so few in the past.

While many women received musical training as performers—particularly as singers or as keyboard players—very few enjoyed the benefit of instruction in composition. Francesca Caccini (1587–ca. 1641) and Elisabeth Jacquet de la Guerre (1665–1729), two accomplished composers of the Baroque period, were both daughters of musicians and learned harmony and counterpoint at home. Others, like Barbara Strozzi, grew up in highly cultured households in which musicians and composers circulated freely. But for the most part, women simply did not have access to the kind of rigorous instruction needed to learn the art of composition.

Part of the reason for this is that there were virtually no professional prospects for women composers. Unless they worked in convents, women could not hold positions associated with composing. Of the women who published music on the Italian peninsula between 1566 and 1700, more than half were nuns. Isabella Leonarda (1620–1704) was easily the most prominent and prolific of this group, publishing some 20 volumes of her own compositions, mostly sacred vocal music but also some instrumental works as well. Even Barbara Strozzi, with all her talents, struggled to make ends meet in the later years of her life. In spite of her prowess as a composer, she would never have been considered as a potential successor to Monteverdi as music director of St. Mark's Basilica in Venice. That honor went instead to Monteverdi's pupil (and Strozzi's teacher) Francesco Cavalli. From a strictly economic point of view, there was no reason for parents to encourage their daughters in this direction.

Without an appointment at a church or court or some other institution, it was just not possible for a composer to earn a decent living.

These conditions would change little over the next two centuries. So while there are many examples of women performers from the Renaissance onward, including many noted virtuosos, the number of women composers in relation to men remained disproportionately small until well into the twentieth century. Only with the advent of compulsory public education and the broadening of career options to women did the phenomenon of the female composer cease to be unusual.

The first woman to write an opera in French, Elisabeth Jacquet de la Guerre was also widely admired for her abilities on the harpsichord.

EXPAND YOUR PLAYLIST

Baroque Chamber Music

Baroque composers wrote unprecedented quantities of chamber music, both for voices and instruments and for instruments alone. One genre they cultivated with special intensity was the *sonata*, a word whose literal meaning is "that which is played" (as opposed to the *cantata*, "that which is sung"; see Chapter 20). Composers wrote sonatas for many combinations of instruments; the most popular variety involved two high-ranged instruments (such as two violins, two oboes, or two flutes) and basso continuo. This combination was known as the *trio sonata*. Sonatas could be performed in the home (the *sonata da camera*, or "chamber sonata") to provide entertainment, or in the church (the *sonata da chiesa*, or "church sonata") during sacred services to provide devotional music.

Arcangelo Corelli (1653–1713)

• Corelli wrote many trio sonatas of both kinds. His Trio Sonata in A Major, op. 3, no. 12, a chamber sonata, features much interplay between the two solo violins over a basso continuo. His Trio Sonata in F Major, op. 1, no. 1, is a church sonata. His Sonata in D Major, op. 5, no. 1, is for a single violin and basso continuo and allows the violinist ample opportunity to display virtuosity on the instrument.

Johann Pachelbel (1653–1706)

• Pachelbel wrote the Canon and Gigue in D Major, for three violins and basso continuo, which is one of the best-known works of the entire Baroque Era. This piece features three violins that play a canon over an ostinato bass. A canon is another word for round, in which each voice sings or plays exactly the same melody with staggered entries (as in "Row, row, row your boat").

Marin Marais (1656–1728)

• Marais composed much virtuosic music for the viola da gamba, a forerunner of today's cello. The second book of his *Pièces de violes* (*Works for Viol*) contains several suites for viol and basso continuo; a suite is a series of loosely connected movements. Marais and his music were featured in the 1991 film *All the Mornings of the World* (*Tous les matins du monde*).

17 Antonio Vivaldi
The Four Seasons, "Winter," first movement
Composed: 1720

This work for solo violin and string orchestra portrays, through sound alone, the season of winter. It follows the outline of a brief text (probably by Vivaldi himself) that describes ice, snow, wind, stamping feet, and chattering teeth.

Listen to This First

〰 Timbre

Listen for the contrast in sound between the solo instrument (the violin) and the ensemble (a small orchestra of stringed instruments, plus basso continuo). Notice how the soloist stands out from the orchestra at some points and not at others. ■

▦ Form

Listen for the alternation of long sections with and without the soloist. ■

◉ Word–Music Relationships

Vivaldi called this work "Winter." Do you hear any sounds that might suggest this season of the year? ■

LEARNING OBJECTIVES

17.1 Define concerto.

17.2 Listen for the application of the ritornello principle through the use of contrasting tutti and solo sections in the first movement of Antonio Vivaldi's *The Four Seasons*, "Winter."

17.3 Define program music and discuss its relationship to *The Four Seasons*, "Winter," first movement.

17.4 Discuss the elements that contribute to both the unity and variety of this movement.

17.5 Discuss the social and cultural context of Vivaldi's work in Venice in the 1720s.

17.6 Describe the basic mechanism by which the violin produces its distinctive sound.

A concerto is an instrumental work for a soloist (or sometimes more than one soloist) and a larger ensemble. This particular **concerto** is for a solo violin and an orchestra of stringed instruments, plus **basso continuo**. It is the last of four concertos for this same combination of instruments that Vivaldi designated collectively as *The Four Seasons*. Although each of these concertos—"Spring," "Summer," "Fall," and "Winter"—stands on its own, the four together represent the cycle of the seasons, a favorite theme of painters and poets alike. "Winter," like most other concertos of its time, consists of three movements in the sequence fast-slow-fast. The movement here is the first of the three.

〰 Contrasting Timbres

The concerto emerged as a particularly popular genre for Baroque audiences because it featured a dramatic contrast between the sound of a solo instrument and the combined sound of all the other instruments. The two forces sometimes work together and sometimes clash in opposition. Baroque audiences also thrilled to the virtuosic displays characteristic of most concertos. The solo parts in a concerto are almost always demanding and often downright flamboyant. Both as a composer and as a player, Vivaldi took the art of **virtuoso** violin playing to new levels. He worked in a time and a place—early eighteenth-century northern Italy—in which violin making and violin playing were at their very peak: To this day, the best violins such as those made by Antonio Stradivari or "Stradivarius" (the Latinized form of his name) are from that time. How the great violin makers produced their instruments is not entirely known to us today, but the features of the violin basically remain the same (see "Closer Look: The Violin").

The appeal of the concerto's contrasting timbres and its inherent virtuosity lasted beyond the Baroque period and into the present day. The concerto has undergone changes over the centuries but remains a popular genre among composers and audiences alike. Many modern symphony orchestra concert programs feature a concerto—from the Baroque or from a later period—and Vivaldi's masterful opposition of a soloist against a larger ensemble of strings has given *The Four Seasons* lasting fame.

 # Form: The Ritornello Principle

This movement consists of a series of alternating sections between the orchestra (also known as the **tutti**, Italian for "all") and the soloist. Each statement and return of the full ensemble is known as the **ritornello** (Italian for "little [i.e., brief] return"). This formal design of alternating ritornello and solo sections is known as the **ritornello principle** and is basic to almost all concerto movements of the Baroque Era. The form of this movement, based on the ritornello principle, can be represented graphically in this way:

Ritornello 1	Solo 1	Ritornello 2	Solo 2	Ritornello 3	Solo 3	Ritornello 4

The form of the movement is also structured around large-scale changes of key area. A *key area* is a set of harmonies that all have a distinctive relationship to one particular note, known as the **tonic**. At the beginning and end of this movement, the tonic note is F, and because the mode is minor, this central key area is called "F minor." F minor acts as the "home" key, and it is by definition the key in which the movement begins and ends. If it closed in a different key, the ending would not sound as conclusive. But if the entire movement were in a single key, it would sound monotonous, and so Vivaldi moves the music to key areas other than the tonic—including some in the major mode. These other key areas provide a sense of harmonic variety.

Section:	Ritornello 1	Solo 1	Ritornello 2	Solo 2	Ritornello 3	Solo 3	Ritornello 4
Key Area:	F minor	C minor	F minor	F minor	E♭ Major	E♭ Major → C minor	F minor

Variety: Modulates to different (nontonic) keys

Unity: Begins and ends in F minor (the tonic key) and reestablishes F minor in the middle

The ritornello principle is found not only in concertos, but in almost every Baroque work that contrasts a soloist or group of soloists against a larger ensemble. Operatic arias, for example, routinely open with an instrumental ritornello (Ritornello 1), followed by the entrance of the voice (Solo 1), a brief return of the orchestra without the voice (Ritornello 2), a reentry of the voice (Solo 2), and so on. Composers and audiences of the Baroque relished the sound of contrasting forces, and the ritornello principle provided the perfect means by which to present such contrasts.

Word–Music Relationships: Program Music

The form of this particular concerto is also shaped by its relationship to a poem ("Winter") that Vivaldi appended to the first publication of the score in 1725. He indicated quite precisely which lines of the following poem corresponded to specific points of the concerto, and those lines of poetry are typically published in the program notes of today's concerts. This concerto is thus an example of **program music**, an instrumental work that is in some way associated with a story, event, or idea. A composer can indicate such connections by a suggestive title, a prose or poetic narrative, or both. A listener may choose to listen to the piece with the program in mind—in the case of Vivaldi's "Winter," hearing the strings shaking as if cold in Ritornello 1, a stamping of feet in Ritornello 2, and a chattering sound in the Solo 3—or simply listen to the piece as music that does not represent anything at all outside of itself. Indeed, some composers (for example, Berlioz—see Chapter 33) have gone back and forth about whether their audiences should be aware of a program or simply be allowed to hear the music as it unfolds.

CONNECT YOUR PLAYLIST

The Concerto

Find a piece that features a contrast between a solo instrument and a larger ensemble.

Example: Stevie Ray Vaughan, "Say What" (1985)
This song, featuring almost no words, is essentially a concerto for solo electric guitar (it also features an organ solo, though less prominently).

"Winter"

First movement:	To tremble from cold in the icy snow
	In the harsh breath of a horrid wind
	To run, stamping our feet every moment
	Our teeth chattering in the extreme cold.
Second movement:	Before the fire to pass peaceful, contented days,
	While the rain outside pours down.
Third movement:	To walk on the ice and, at a slow pace
	For fear of falling, move carefully.
	To make a bold turn, slip, fall down.
	To go on the ice once more and run hard
	Until the ice cracks and breaks up.
	To hear the Sirocco [the north wind], Boreas [the south wind], and all
	The winds at war leave their iron gates:
	This is winter, but even so, what joy it brings![1]

[1]Lyrics here and on page 138: Vivaldi, "Winter," Copyright © 1999 Dover Publications, Inc.

PROFILE   Antonio Vivaldi (1678–1741)

Composing for Orphans

Known as the "Red Priest" because he was red-haired and ordained, Antonio Vivaldi served for many years as director of music at Venice's Ospedale della Pietà ("Hospice of Compassion"), a large orphanage for girls. Being the music director of an orphanage might strike us today as a strange job for one of the most famous composers of his time, but judging from the music Vivaldi wrote for the young women at this particular institution, they must have been quite talented indeed. He actually wrote most of his concertos while in service to the orphanage.

Vivaldi was extremely prolific. He wrote almost 350 solo concertos (about two-thirds of which are for solo violin) and 45 double concertos (more than half of which are for two violins). His music was widely published and admired throughout Europe during his lifetime.

 J. S. Bach arranged several of Vivaldi's concertos for the organ and in the process taught himself how to write concertos "in the Italian style." Bach and Handel may have had greater facility at counterpoint, but Vivaldi was a master of melodic invention and formal novelty. Almost every one of Vivaldi's concertos contains some unusual twist that makes it different from all the rest.

Antonio Vivaldi was famous both as a composer and as a violinist during his lifetime. His red hair is covered by his wig.

EXPAND YOUR PLAYLIST: VIVALDI

- **The Four Seasons:** "Spring." The opening theme (Ritornello 1) is now a popular ringtone for cell phones.

- **The Four Seasons:** "Summer." The finale depicts a violent thunderstorm.

- **The Four Seasons:** "Fall." The finale depicts a hunting scene.

- **Concerto for Mandolin,** RV 532. More typically associated with bluegrass music, the mandolin was already a popular instrument in the Baroque.

- **Gloria,** RV 589, for chorus and orchestra. A thrilling setting of the Gloria portion of the Mass Ordinary.

- **Concerto for Flute, Strings, and Basso Continuo,** op. 10, no. 1. Nicknamed "The Tempest at Sea" because of its stormy sound.

Now listen again to the movement, using the Listening Guide.

Listening Guide

Antonio Vivaldi Composed: 1720

The Four Seasons, "Winter," first movement (3:33)

Time	Timbre	Form	Harmony: Key Area	Word–Music Relationships (1): The Poetry
0:00	Orchestra	Ritornello 1	F minor	To tremble from cold in the icy snow
0:37	Solo violin and orchestra	Solo 1	C minor	In the harsh breath of a horrid wind
0:59	Orchestra	Ritornello 2	F minor	To run, stamping our feet every moment
1:26	Solo violin and orchestra	Solo 2	F minor → unstable	
2:05	Orchestra	Ritornello 3	E♭ major	
2:25	Solo violin and orchestra	Solo 3	E♭ major → C minor	Our teeth chattering in the extreme cold
3:04	Orchestra	Ritornello 4	F minor	

Q Student FAQs ⚙

I can't hear the difference in key areas between the sections. How can I learn to hear these changes?

With digital technology, it's easy to make side-by-side comparisons. Using the Listening Guide, start the music at 0:37. (In the interactive Listening Guide, click on "Solo 1" from the Form line.) The long note to which the solo violinist keeps returning is C, the tonic of C minor. Let the music run through 1:00, the end of Solo 1. Vivaldi again

and again emphasizes this new key area of C minor. Now go back to the beginning, which is in F minor. Hear the difference? The main note at the beginning is F, the root of the tonic key of F minor. Now let the music run through and listen for the change of key between the opening and 0:37. This may take some time at first, but once you start listening for changes of key, it gets easier to recognize them. And even if you don't always hear the key changes consciously, you will appreciate that they affect the way the music sounds by providing both harmonic unity (the tonic) and variety (all other keys).

What does the violin soloist do during the tutti sections?

The soloist actually plays along with the first violin section of the orchestra. But because the sound of the solo instrument blends into the sound of the orchestra, the soloist cannot be heard as a separate, distinct voice in these sections.

Word–Music Relationships (2): The Music

Repetitive figure in the strings suggests trembling.

The solo violin also "trembles" and moves from high to low, like the wind.

Faster rhythms ("running"); the music begins to "stamp" at 1:12.

The soloist bounces the bow very rapidly against the string, creating a "chattering" sound (2:35–3:03).

Which is more important, the musical or the programmatic form?

The two work in tandem and reinforce each other. We do not know if Vivaldi began with the poem and wrote a concerto around it, or if he began with a concerto and wrote a poem around it. It's also possible that the two processes took shape simultaneously.

 EXPAND YOUR PLAYLIST

Program Music

Program music—instrumental music explicitly connected in some way with a story, person, or idea outside the music itself—has long fired the imaginations of composers and listeners.

Johann Kuhnau, *Six Biblical Sonatas* (1700)
- Each of these six sonatas for harpsichord depicts a famous story from the Bible. When David defeats Goliath, we "hear" the stone hurled toward the giant and the enormous thud when he falls to the ground.

Marin Marais, *An Image of Abdominal Surgery* (1725)
- A lengthy work for solo viola da gamba, it depicts in great detail the removal of a gallstone. The score includes such comments as "The Incision," "Blood Flows," and "The Stone Is Removed."

Ludwig van Beethoven, *Wellington's Victory*, op. 91 (1813)
- Depicts the victory of the English general over Napoleon's forces at the Battle of Vittoria (Spain). The opening mimics the trumpet calls of the armies, and the percussion simulates the sounds of cannon and musket fire.

Hector Berlioz, *Symphonie fantastique* (1830)
- The story of an ill-fated love affair in which She dumps Him (see Chapter 33).

George Gershwin, *An American in Paris* (1928)
- This work recreates, in sound, impressions of Paris, including honking horns of the traffic, French speech, and an American's homesickness for his native country.

John Adams, *A Short Ride in a Fast Machine* (1986)
- The title suggests the acceleration and tremendous speed of this work for large orchestra.

CLOSER LOOK   The Violin

There are more violins in an orchestra than any other instrument. The violin is also the prototype for two larger versions: the mid-range viola and the low-range cello. The basic principles of the instrument are simple: A player draws a bow perpendicularly across the strings and sets them in motion, controlling the pitch by depressing the fingers onto the individual strings. The violinist controls the volume of the instrument by pressing the bow into the strings with greater or lesser pressure, and by moving the bow at a faster or slower speed. No two instruments are identical: The slightest variations in wood quality, the size and placement of the bridge, the exact shape of the f-holes, and even the nature of the varnish can affect the quality of an instrument's sound.

The **horsehair**—from a horse's tail—is the part of the bow that sets the violin's strings in motion, creating sound.

The **tuning pegs** are turned clockwise or counterclockwise to increase or decrease tension on the strings, thereby raising or lowering the pitch of the strings as they are being tuned.

Four **strings** on the pitches G, D, A, and E. The lowest-sounding string, on the left, is the thickest; the highest string, on the right, is the thinnest.

The **fingerboard**. The violinist presses the strings onto the fingerboard, thereby shortening the length of the vibrating portion of the string. The shorter the vibrating length, the higher the pitch.

The **stick** is the wooden part of the bow that supports the horsehair.

The **bridge**, made of wood, elevates the strings and provides a fixed point at the opposite end from the top of the fingerboard. The bridge also transmits the vibration of the strings to the body of the instrument, and it is the vibration of the body's wood that amplifies the sound naturally, without any electronics.

The **f-holes** (so called because they resemble the letter "F" in italics) direct some of the vibration of the body directly out into the air.

The small metal **screw** at the end of the bow can be turned clockwise or counterclockwise to increase or decrease the tension on the horsehair.

The **tailpiece** supports the strings. Optional small metal knobs allow for fine-tuning the strings.

The **chin rest** helps the player to hold the instrument securely under the chin.

The **body** of the instrument is made of specially treated and carefully carved wood covered with a varnish that both protects the wood and enhances the instrument's sound. The interior of the instrument is hollow to allow the vibrating body to resonate more fully; a **sounding post**—a small dowel of wood inside this space and not visible here—helps transmit energy from the front (top) of the instrument to its back.

Johann Sebastian Bach

Fugue in G Minor, BWV 578 ("Little" Fugue)

Composed: 1705

This chapter presents two versions of Bach's Fugue in G minor: (1) in its original version for organ, and (2) in an arrangement for orchestra made by Leopold Stokowski in 1940. The notes are exactly the same in both versions, but the timbres are very different.

Listen to This First �»))

⟿ Timbre

Listen for the range of sounds in each version. The organ and orchestra are both capable of enormous timbral variety. Every "voice" (melodic line) in the work has its own distinctive sound. ■

🎵 Melody

There is only one real theme in this work, and we hear it many times. It appears all by itself at the very beginning. Listen to how it begins slowly and then picks up speed as it progresses. ■

🌐 Texture

Listen for the way in which the theme is first presented by a single voice, then imitated in a second voice, then imitated yet again with the entrances of the third and fourth voices. See how many of these iterations of the main theme your ear can pick out: in the high voice, the low voice, and (perhaps most difficult of all) the middle voices. ■

A fugue is a polyphonic work based on a central theme. Fugues are easy to recognize: They typically begin with the theme in one voice, which is imitated by all the other voices in succession, each presenting its own statement of the theme. "Fugue" comes from the same root word as "fugitive" and refers to the tendency of voices to "chase" one another: A theme presented in one voice is "pursued," as it were, by a second (and often third or fourth) voice that brings in the same theme but slightly later. The fugue represents the continuing fascination of composers and listeners alike with the intricacies of polyphonic texture. Many composers of the Baroque regarded the fugue as the touchstone of a composer's art, for it demanded more than just the invention of a good tune. That tune also had to be capable of being played against other, independent voices derived from the tune itself.

This particular fugue for organ is an early work by Bach, written when he was only about 20 years old. He probably composed it during his years in Arnstadt, where he was the organist of the town's church (see "Closer Look: Bach's World").

Timbres of the Organ, Timbres of the Orchestra

The organ is sometimes called the "King of Instruments" because of its size, power, and variety of tone. No other acoustic (that is, nonelectric) instrument possesses the range of volume and timbre found in the organ (see "Closer Look: The Baroque Organ"). The organ has a tremendous range from the lowest notes (played by the feet on wooden pedals) to the highest notes (played on the keyboard or **manual**). Air passing through the largest pipes produces the lowest notes, while air

LEARNING OBJECTIVES

18.1 Listen for and identify the subject, fugal exposition, and episodes by listening to J. S. Bach's "Little" Fugue in G minor.

18.2 Explain the organ's nickname "The King of Instruments" and describe the basic mechanisms of the Baroque organ.

18.3 Explain why it is important for a fugue to have a distinctive opening theme.

18.4 Identify differences in timbre between Bach's original version of the "Little" Fugue in G minor for organ and Stokowski's later arrangement for orchestra.

18.5 Outline Bach's professional career.

passing through the smallest pipes—some of them not bigger than a pencil—produces the highest notes. By engaging a series of *stops*—small knobs that control the flow of air through the pipes—the organist can choose the particular set or even sets of pipes and give different melodic lines their own distinctive sound. Organists can even change the stops "on the fly," in the middle of a performance, giving even greater variety of sound within a single work. The number of possible sound combinations on a large organ can range well into the hundreds.

In Leopold Stokowski's much later orchestral arrangement of Bach's Fugue in G minor, his reworking of the piece for orchestra, the timbral contrast among the various voices is even more readily audible. Taking advantage of the full range of the modern orchestra, Stokowski kept Bach's notes, but distributed the work's voices among various instruments or combinations of instruments. The opening theme, for example, is played first by the solo oboe, then by the English horn, then the bassoon, then the bass trombone. Other instruments pick up the various voices throughout the work as a whole.

Arrangements, also known as transcriptions, have been common throughout the history of music. Bach himself arranged (transcribed) a number of works by other composers. In one instance, he arranged a concerto for string orchestra and two violins by Antonio Vivaldi for solo organ—the opposite, in effect, of what Stokowski would do with this fugue by Bach, originally written for the organ.

♫ A Distinctive Melody

The theme of this work appears many times, and its slow and stately entrance (section **A**) stands out even among a welter of fast-moving voices. After its slow beginning, the theme begins to accelerate, moving in shorter note values (section **B**). Finally, it kicks into high gear and moves very rapidly (section **C**). This rhythmic progression—slow to faster to fastest—gives the theme a strong sense of forward progression. And because this is the only real theme in the work, this sense of constant rhythmic motion extends to the work as a whole.

CLOSER LOOK   The Baroque Organ

In many large churches, the organist is hidden behind pipes and casings that obscure the console, the organ's "control panel" seen here. From the console the organist determines the timbre and volume of the sound. An elaborate mechanism of knobs and pedals allows the player to control which pipes will sound at any given moment. There is no standard size or configuration for the organ: The number of keys and pipes can vary consider-ably. The largest pipes, which can be up to 16 feet high, produce the lowest notes, while the smallest pipes, some as small as a pencil, produce the highest notes. While every organ is distinctive, the principal elements of the Baroque organ can be seen in this photograph of the console at Sint Jans, a large church in Gouda, The Netherlands. This organ dates from 1732 (during Bach's lifetime).

The **stops** (circular pull knobs) control which set of pipes sounds when a specific keyboard (or **manual**) is played. The organ's pipes offer a wide variety of timbres, ranging from pipes that imitate the sound of a trumpet, oboe, or even the human voice (called the "Vox Humana" from the Latin). The player controls which pipes sound by opening the related stop, which allows air to flow through its related pipes. Organists can use either one stop at a time or a combination of stops, and each keyboard can be linked to a specific stop or group of stops. The number of possible sound combinations is enormous.

The organist can play low notes by depressing the **pedals** with his or her feet, even while playing the manuals by hand. Very rapid pedalwork can place great technical demands on the performer.

The **music stand** displays the organist's printed or manuscript music.

Manuals are the multiple keyboards found on larger organs. Each manual is connected to particular sets of pipes, which in turn create specific kinds of sound. With multiple manuals, a player can move back and forth quickly between the different sound qualities that have been pre-set for each manual with the knob-like stops on either side of the console.

PERFORMANCE **Changing the Sound, but Not the Notes**

Leopold Stokowski (1882–1977) ranks among the most influential conductors of the twentieth century. After immigrating to the United States from his native England in 1905, he helped develop the Philadelphia Orchestra into one of the world's leading ensembles. He also played a key role in bringing classical music to Hollywood. When he appeared with Mickey Mouse in Walt Disney's *Fantasia* in 1940, Stokowski was already a celebrity himself. Musical purists looked down on Stokowski's many orchestral arrangements of works originally written for other instruments, but countless listeners have admired the way in which his arrangements illuminate the workings of the inner voices, particularly in a densely contrapuntal work like Bach's Fugue in G Minor.

Leopold Stokowski (1882–1977) was one of the first conductors to abandon the baton (the conductor's "stick") and use only his hands while leading an orchestra. He felt that hands communicate emotions more effectively to the musicians. Stokowski had a magnetic personality: He had an affair with the movie star Greta Garbo in the 1930s and was married to the actress and socialite Gloria Vanderbilt from 1945 until 1955.

 ## Fugal Texture

A fugue typically begins with its central theme, also known as a **subject**, in one voice all by itself. This subject is often quite distinctive—instantly recognizable—in its first few notes so that we can immediately recognize it upon its entrance in subsequent voices and its return later throughout the fugue. Some characteristic feature—a melodic leap, a distinctive rhythm—typically makes the subject stand out as it enters in the second voice, then the third, and so on, even as the other voices continue their independent lines. The type of polyphony used in a fugue is known as **imitative counterpoint**. The voices "imitate" one another, each sounding against ("countering") the others at the same time.

Fugue has more to do with texture—the way the voices relate to each other—than with form. Still, most fugues tend to unfold according to a conventional pattern. The opening entry of all the voices on the main subject is known as a **fugal exposition** because it "exposes" the main idea of the work. Beyond this exposition, the only formal convention is that the main theme must reappear at some point within the later course of the movement; in actual practice, it usually reappears at many points. These later entries of the subject are known as **middle entries**. Passages in which the main subject (the main theme) is absent are called **episodes**, though not every fugue has them. But the typical fugue, including this one, consists of a fugal exposition and a series of middle entries, interspersed with episodes.

Fugues—for all kinds and combinations of instruments and voices—were extremely common throughout the Baroque Era in many different genres. The finale of Bach's Brandenburg Concerto no. 2 (see Chapter 19) is a fugue for solo instruments and orchestra; portions of the "Hallelujah Chorus" (see Chapter 21) are, in effect, brief fugues for chorus and orchestra. In the centuries following the Baroque Era, composers continued to take up the challenge of writing fugues, both as practice exercises in composition and as works for performance. Fugal writing still turns up today in music of varying styles and genres.

Now listen to Bach's fugue again in both versions—the original for organ and the later arrangement for orchestra—using the Listening Guides.

Listening Guide

Johann Sebastian Bach Composed: 1705
Fugue in G Minor, BWV 578, Bach's Original
Version for Organ (4:06)

Time	Form: Section	Melody: Fugue Subject
0:05	Exposition	0:05 in highest voice (soprano)
		0:21 in next-highest voice (alto)
		0:40 in next-lowest voice (tenor)
		0:56 in lowest voice (bass)
1:09	Episode 1	(Subject is absent.)
1:18	Middle Entry 1	In tenor voice and then soprano voice (1:24)
1:37	Episode 2	(Subject is absent.)
1:44	Middle Entry 2	In alto voice
1:58	Episode 3	(Subject is absent.)
2:09	Middle Entry 3	In bass voice
2:23	Episode 4	(Subject is absent.)
2:38	Middle Entry 4	In soprano voice
2:52	Episode 5	(Subject is absent.)
3:18	Final Entry	In bass voice

 Student FAQs

What forces air through the organ pipes?

Nowadays, the airflow in an organ is generated by an electric pump. In Bach's day, someone—usually a small boy—had to tread on a large set of bellows that operated somewhat like a stair-climber machine in a modern-day gym. This produced a steady flow of air through the pipes. Even older organs that have been restored now use an electronically generated airflow.

So the modern organ is electronic?

Only the airflow is generated electronically. What we call the electronic organ is really a different instrument altogether. It looks and sounds like a manual organ, but it produces sound through a system of electromagnetic currents, an amplifier, and speakers. Laurens Hammond (1895–1973), an American inventor, created the first mass-market, portable electronic organ in the 1930s.

Listening Guide ♪)

Johann Sebastian Bach Arranged: 1940
Fugue in G Minor, BWV 578, Leopold
Stokowski's Orchestral Arrangement (3:29)

Time	🏛 Form: Section	🎵 Melody: Fugue Subject	〰 Orchestral Timbre
0:00	Exposition	0:00 in highest voice (soprano) 0:14 in next-highest voice (alto) 0:31 in next-lowest voice (tenor) 0:44 in lowest voice (bass)	0:00 solo oboe 0:14 English horn 0:31 bassoon 0:44 bass clarinet and contrabassoon
0:57	Episode 1	(Subject is absent.)	Flutes enter
1:06	Middle Entry 1	In tenor voice	Subject = clarinets, then flutes
1:22	Episode 2	(Subject is absent.)	Winds
1:29	Middle Entry 2	In alto voice	Subject = violas
1:41	Episode 3	(Subject is absent.)	Violas, then various winds
1:51	Middle Entry 3	In bass voice	Subject = double basses
2:03	Episode 4	(Subject is absent.)	Strings
2:17	Middle Entry 4	In soprano voice	Subject = violins
2:29	Episode 5	(Subject is absent.)	Various winds, then full orchestra
2:55	Final Entry	In bass voice	Subject = trombones

PROFILE   Johann Sebastian Bach (1685–1750)

New Jobs, New Genres

Born into a family of musicians, Johann Sebastian Bach earned his living through music. He changed jobs often between the ages of 18 and 38, and with every new position, he wrote whatever music was required of him (see "Closer Look: Bach's World"). When he was a church organist early in his career, he wrote the majority of his organ works, including the Fugue in G Minor discussed in this chapter. Later, as violinist and concertmaster at a court orchestra (Weimar) and as music director (Cöthen), he wrote the bulk of his orchestral music, including the Brandenburg Concerto no. 2 (see Chapter 19). When he became cantor of St. Thomas's Church in Leipzig in 1723, he began writing new cantatas for use in the services there (see Chapter 20). By the time he died, Bach had written at least one work in virtually every genre of music except for opera. Why no opera? The reason is simple: Bach never held a job that required him to write one.

Bach's two marriages—his first wife died in 1720—produced 20 children, 10 of whom survived into adulthood. Several of the sons became renowned composers in their own right. Carl Philipp Emanuel Bach (1714–1788) would become more famous than his father during the elder Bach's lifetime. Johann Christian Bach (1735–1782), sometimes called the "London Bach" because of his eventual home, was one of Mozart's favorite composers. Wilhelm Friedemann Bach (1710–1784), said to be perhaps the most musically gifted of all Bach's sons, met repeated misfortunes in his career and died in poverty.

Bach in the 1740s. Proud of his abilities as a composer, Bach chose to have himself portrayed holding a particularly complex work of imitative counterpoint of his own invention.

 EXPAND YOUR PLAYLIST: BACH

- **St. Matthew Passion,** BWV 244.
  An extended work for vocalists and orchestra, with choral movements, recitatives, and arias. This three-hour work narrates the betrayal and crucifixion of Christ and is built around texts from the Gospel of St. Matthew.

- **Partita no. 2 for Violin,** BWV 1004: Chaconne.
  Bach's self-imposed challenge was to write a contrapuntal work for an instrument—the violin—that is essentially melodic and normally plays only one musical line at a time.

- **The Well-Tempered Clavier,** Book 1, BWV 846–69.
  Two sets of keyboard preludes and fugues in all 24 major and minor keys. Bach wrote these works for teaching purposes.

- **A Musical Offering,** BWV 1079.
  In 1747 Bach visited his son Carl Philipp Emanuel Bach, who was a musician at the court of King Frederick II of Prussia. Frederick—himself a composer and flute player—gave Bach a particularly difficult theme on which to improvise. Later, Bach composed and sent Frederick an enormous set of different works, all based on this same theme, a "musical offering" to the king.

CLOSER LOOK **Bach's World**

Johann Sebastian Bach lived and worked within a relatively small area of what is now north-central Germany. Unlike Handel, his contemporary, Bach never traveled widely. The distance between Arnstadt and Cöthen, his two places of employment farthest apart from each other, is only a little over 100 miles. Within this small space, however, he held a number of different kinds of positions that required him to write music in every major genre except opera.

1. Eisenach. Bach is born here on March 21, 1685, the son of a town musician. Both of his parents die when he is 10, and he is raised afterward by an older brother who is also a musician.

2. Arnstadt, 1703–1707. Bach's first full-time job is as a church organist. The congregation complains that his harmonizations of the chorales (hymns) are confusing and too elaborate. He probably writes his Fugue in G minor here (see Chapter 15).

3. Mühlhausen, 1707–1708. Again, Bach serves as organist for a church and continues to write a great deal of music for that instrument.

4. Weimar, 1708–1717. Bach is the organist and later chamber musician at the court of the Duke of Weimar. He gains a reputation as a performer and as a judge of newly built organs. Because he breaks his contract to move to Cöthen, he spends time in the duke's prison as punishment.

5. Cöthen, 1717–1723. Bach serves as music director ("kapellmeister") to the Prince of Anhalt. This position requires him to write a good deal of chamber music and orchestral music, including the concertos that would eventually be dedicated to the Margrave of Brandenburg (the "Brandenburg" Concertos).

6. Leipzig, 1723–1750. Bach is cantor of St. Thomas's Church and director of music for the city of Leipzig. Here he composes and supervises the performance of music for Leipzig's major churches, provides music for civic events, and teaches in St. Thomas's boys' school. He writes the large majority of his sacred cantatas, including Cantata 140 (see Chapter 17), in Leipzig.

 EXPAND YOUR PLAYLIST

Baroque Organ Music

Jan Pieterszoon Sweelinck
- *"Echo" Fantasia* (*Ionian*) (early seventeenth century). A native of what is now the Netherlands, Sweelinck wrote a great deal of organ music. A fantasia is a freely constructed work, meant to sound improvised as if it were being thought up on the spot. This is one of several fantasias in which Sweelinck uses special echo effects.

Dietrich Buxtehude
- Praeludium in G Minor, BuxWV 149 (ca. 1675–1689). Buxtehude was the greatest organist in the generation before Bach. This prelude ("praeludium" is the Latin term) is a multisectional work: Parts of it are free, and parts of it are fugal.

Johann Sebastian Bach
- Toccata and Fugue in D Minor, BWV 565 (ca. 1705). Perhaps the most famous work of organ music ever written, this has been used in countless horror movies to provide "scary" music. A toccata is a "touch piece," one that calls for a light and rapid touch on the keys.
- "Jig" Fugue, BWV 577. This work may not actually be by Bach, but whoever wrote it certainly knew how to write fugues. The rhythm is so compelling that audiences have been known to clap along with it.
- *Chorale Prelude* (*Wachet auf, ruft uns die Stimme*), BWV 645. An organ version of one of the movements from the Cantata 140, arranged by Bach himself (see Chapter 20).

Johann Sebastian Bach

Brandenburg Concerto no. 2 in F Major,
BWV 1047, finale

Composed: 1720

Bach's Brandenburg Concerto features multiple soloists: a trumpet, oboe, violin, and recorder. The soloists function with and against a larger ensemble of stringed instruments. The movement presented here is the last one in a three-movement concerto Bach wrote for the Margrave of Brandenburg.

Listen to This First

〰 Timbre

Listen for the contrasting sounds of the four solo instruments, which enter in this order:

- The trumpet, a brass instrument, has a loud, bright sound.

- The oboe, a woodwind instrument, has a piercing, slightly nasal sound.

- The violin, a stringed instrument, has a resonant, lyrical sound.

- The recorder, a woodwind instrument, has a high, gentle sound similar to that of a flute.

Also listen for the way in which the sound of the four solo instruments as a group contrasts with the sound of the larger ensemble, which is a small orchestra of stringed instruments (violins, violas, cellos, basses) and basso continuo. ■

🏛 Form

Listen for the alternation between the soloists as a group and the orchestra as a whole. Like all concertos of the Baroque Era, this one is built around the ritornello principle, in which sections played by the soloists alone (accompanied only by the basso continuo) alternate with sections played by the full orchestra. ■

🌐 Texture

Listen for the way in which the melody is presented successively by each of the soloists at the beginning and then taken up by each voice in turn repeatedly over the course of the movement. This entire movement is a fugue. ■

Not all concertos are for only one soloist. Baroque composers also cultivated the genre of the **concerto grosso**—in Italian, this means literally "big concerto"—with multiple soloists. Bach's Brandenburg Concerto no. 2 is one of six such works dedicated to the Margrave of Brandenburg (a region in what is now eastern Germany) in 1721. Bach's six Brandenburg concertos feature unique instrumental combinations and contain three or four movements each. The movement here is the last of three.

LEARNING OBJECTIVES

19.1 Define concerto grosso.

19.2 Describe the ritornello principle as it applies to the finale by listening to Bach's Brandenburg Concerto no. 2 in F Major.

19.3 Listen for and describe the contrasting timbres in this movement.

19.4 Discuss how areas of large-scale harmonic stability and instability contribute to the overall form of this movement.

19.5 Identify how the principles of the fugue apply to this movement.

19.6 Discuss the nature of the Baroque trumpet and its differences from the modern trumpet.

149

An outdoor evening instrumental concert in the town square of Jena in the 1740s. The large orchestra includes trumpets and timpani. J. S. Bach led a similar ensemble in nearby Leipzig for a time.

Extreme Timbres

Central to the solo concerto and concerto grosso is timbral contrast: soloist(s) versus orchestra. In this particular work, the solo instruments provide unusual contrast among themselves. The trumpet is one of the loudest and most penetrating of all instruments, while the recorder is one of the softest and gentlest. The oboe and violin lie between these two extremes. Bach clearly relished the challenge of combining such a wide spectrum of solo instruments in the same concerto. It was a new and bold measure to group such different instrumental timbres together.

Form: The Ritornello Principle Returns

As in Vivaldi's concerto for solo violin and orchestra (see Chapter 17), this movement is based on the **ritornello principle**: Sections for the soloists (Solo 1, Solo 2, etc.) alternate with sections for the **tutti**, the full orchestra (Ritornello 1, Ritornello 2, etc.). The soloists—or at least some of them—also play along with the full orchestra during the ritornello sections. The **basso continuo** instruments—harpsichord and cello—live up to their name, playing continuously throughout the movement.

Section:	Solo 1	Ritornello 1	Solo 2	Ritornello 2	Solo 3	Ritornello 3	Solo 4	Ritornello 4
Key Area:	F Major	C Major	C Major → D minor	D minor	D minor	B♭ Major	B♭ Major → F Major	F Major

Variety: Modulates to different (nontonic) keys

Unity: Begins and ends in F Major (the tonic key)

Like Vivaldi in his solo concerto "Winter," Bach uses different key areas to establish a sense of a beginning, a contrasting middle, and an ending that brings harmonic closure to the whole. The movement opens and closes in the key of F major; in between, it moves through a variety of different key areas. If the movement did not **modulate**—that is, move to a different key area—the theme would not sound as fresh as it does each time it comes back (and it comes back often). If it ended in a key other than the **tonic**—its primary key area, the one in which it began—it would sound open-ended and inconclusive.

Fugal Texture

Although Bach did not label it as such, this entire movement is a **fugue**: A central theme is introduced and then imitated by subsequent voices. As we have seen (Chapter 18), fugue is more a function of texture—imitative polyphony—than of form, but as in Bach's Fugue in G Minor, BWV 578, the fugal finale of Bach's Brandenburg Concerto no. 2 employs some of the structural features most commonly found in fugues:

- **Fugal exposition**. This section gets its name from the fact that it "exposes" the theme in each of the solo instruments in turn.
- **Middle entries**. These are passages (throughout the movement) that reintroduce the subject, often in imitation with other instruments.
- **Episodes**. Here the subject does not appear at all. In this movement, the episodes happen to coincide with the tutti sections, in which all the instruments of the orchestra play.

Now listen to this movement again, using the Listening Guide.

CONNECT YOUR PLAYLIST

Imitation

Find a piece that contains imitation between two or more voices.

Example: John Kander and Fred Ebb, "The Cell-Block Tango," from *Chicago* (1975)
Toward the end of this song, the main melody is sung in imitation: The lead singer sings a line, and the remaining singers echo it slightly later, creating an overlapping effect.

Listening Guide

Johann Sebastian Bach Composed: 1720
Brandenburg Concerto no. 2 in F Major, BWV 1047, finale (3:00)

Time	Form: Ritornello/Solo	Timbre	Texture: The Fugue	Harmony: Key Areas
0:00	Solo 1	0:00 Trumpet alone 0:08 Oboe enters 0:26 Violin enters 0:33 Recorder enters 0:51 Trumpet reenters	Fugal exposition	F major
0:59	Ritornello 1	Tutti and soloists	Episode 1	C major
1:11	Solo 2	Recorder and violin; subject in oboe at 1:23	Middle Entry 1	C major → D minor
1:31	Ritornello 2	Tutti and soloists	Episode 2	D minor
1:47	Solo 3	Oboe and violin together, then recorder, then trumpet	Middle Entry 2	D minor
2:03	Ritornello 3	Tutti and soloists	Episode 3	B♭ major
2:15	Solo 4	Trumpet and oboe together, subject in oboe; recorder at 2:23	Final Entry	B♭ major → F major
2:30	Ritornello 4	Tutti and soloists	Final Entry (cont'd.)	F major

---

Q Student FAQs

Did Bach ever write programs for his concertos the way Vivaldi did?

No. In fact, very few of Bach's instrumental works give any hint at a story or idea outside the music. He did write a work for harpsichord he called *Capriccio on the Departure of a Beloved Brother*, BWV 992, and he labeled individual sections with such titles as "Friends gather and try to dissuade him from departing," "They imagine the dangers which might befall him," and "The Friends' Lament," but on the whole, these verbal cues are the exception rather than the rule in Bach's music.

Is the basso continuo part of the ritornello or the solo group?

Both. Its function is to support whatever other instruments are playing at the moment, so it plays in both the solo and ritornello sections.

PERFORMANCE The Art of Trumpet Playing, Lost and Found

When Bach died in 1750, most of his music soon disappeared from the active repertory. Keyboard performers still knew and played some of the works that he had written for harpsichord and for organ, but the choral and orchestral music were largely forgotten. When performers began rediscovering Bach's music in the nineteenth century, they were baffled by how to perform some of it, including the very difficult trumpet part of Brandenburg Concerto no. 2.

Both trumpets and the art of trumpet playing had changed drastically over the centuries. In the nineteenth century, the instrument began to be produced with valves and keys that allowed players to produce a wider range of notes with a more uniform quality of sound. But the art of playing the "natural"—valveless—trumpet gradually disappeared. In Bach's time, and for centuries before that, trumpet playing had been strictly regulated; the trumpet was an aural symbol of military and political power, and not just anyone could pick up the instrument. Trumpeters had to join guilds to practice their art, and the secrets of the art, as in all guilds, were transmitted largely by word of mouth. When restrictions on trumpet playing began to be lifted in the late eighteenth century, the guilds soon disappeared, and with them the knowledge of how to perform the kinds of high, rapid passagework so prevalent in Bach's Brandenburg Concerto no. 2.

In the late nineteenth century, a few trumpet players began experimenting with specially designed instruments (so-called Bach trumpets) that would allow them to play this earlier music. Over time, more and more musicians became interested in using original instruments or accurate reproductions of them. Today, the lost art of playing the high range of the Baroque trumpet has been recovered, and we can hear Bach's Brandenburg Concerto no. 2 in a manner that more closely resembles the sound of what Bach himself heard when he conducted it.

Binding
The bell and tubing sections are kept separate by a wooden block. Heavy woolen cord holds them together.

Bell
Often has an embossed rim, bearing the maker's name, the name of the town, and the date.

Back bow

Knop
Strengthens the joint between bell and tube.

The Baroque ("natural") trumpet. There are no keys or valves, only one long piece of coiled tubing. Bach wrote his Brandenburg Concerto no. 2 for a smaller trumpet that could reach a higher range but that similarly lacked keys or valves.

Mouthpiece **Valves** **Bell**

First valve tube **Second valve tube** **Third valve tube** **Water key** **Tuning slide**

The modern trumpet. Notice the valves and multiple coils of tubing, both of which allow the trumpeter to lengthen or shorten the column of air, thereby making it easier to produce a wider range of notes.

The Baroque Concerto

Baroque listeners responded enthusiastically to the emergence of a genre highlighting contrasts among instruments and performing forces. Here are some of the best-loved concerto composers and their works, all of which are still performed regularly today.

Arcangelo Corelli (1653–1713)

Corelli was one of the first composers to write large-scale concertos, all with two violins and basso continuo as soloists, accompanied by a string orchestra.

- Concerto Grosso in G Minor, op. 6, no. 8, known as the "Christmas Concerto" because it ends with a pastoral-like movement thought to depict the shepherds and their flocks who came to see the infant Jesus in the manger.

Antonio Vivaldi (1678–1741)

In addition to his Four Seasons (see Chapter 17), Vivaldi wrote literally hundreds of concertos, both for solo instruments and for groups of solo instruments. Like Bach, Vivaldi seems to have been attracted to the idea of writing for unusual instruments and unusual combinations of instruments.

- Concerto in C Major for Mandolin and Strings, RV 425. The first movement of this work has been used in several movie soundtracks, including *Casanova* (2005) and *The Royal Tenenbaums* (2001), as well as for a 2005 episode of *The Sopranos*. The slow movement is a favorite for wedding ceremonies.
- Concerto in C Major for 2 Trumpets and Strings, RV 537. The two trumpets play together, often creating echo effects.

George Frideric Handel (1685–1759)

Handel wrote many concertos, mostly during his time in England, and many imitating the style of Corelli.

- Concerto Grosso in B-flat Major for 2 Recorders, 2 Oboes, 2 Bassoons, Violin, and Strings, op. 3, no. 1. Handel gives the wind instruments unusually prominent roles in this work.

Johann Sebastian Bach

All six of his Brandenburg Concertos are well worth knowing.

- Concerto no. 1 in F Major, BWV 1046. There are no true soloists in this concerto; every instrument is treated virtuosically. Written for two horns, three oboes, bassoon, violino piccolo (a type of small violin tuned slightly higher than the standard violin), strings, and basso continuo.
- Concerto no. 3 in G Major, BWV 1048. For strings alone, with no soloists. Each of the stringed instruments (violins, violas, cellos) is subdivided into three separate parts, creating a nine-voice texture, all above the basso continuo.
- Concerto no. 4 in G Major, BWV 1049. The soloists are two recorders and violin; the orchestra consists of strings and basso continuo. The finale is a rousing fugue.
- Concerto no. 5 in D Major, BWV 1050. The soloists are a flute, violin, and—an innovation in this work—a harpsichord, which at times plays as a member of the basso continuo, at times as a true soloist.
- Concerto no. 6 in B-flat Major, BWV 1051. The scoring is limited entirely to low strings. The soloists are two violas, accompanied by viola da gambas, cellos, and basso continuo.

Johann Sebastian Bach

Cantata 140: *Awake, a Voice Calls to Us*, selections

Composed: 1731

In the Protestant church, the chorale (hymn) was the basic musical element of the church service. The entire congregation would know the words and melodies by heart and sing as a group. In this work, Bach used one of the most popular of all chorale melodies as the basis for an elaborate opening movement performed by a chorus and orchestra.

Listen to This First

🎵 Melody

- *First Movement:* Listen to how the individual phrases of the chorale are separated by long passages of contrasting music.
- *Last Movement:* Listen to how the original chorale is presented in a straightforward fashion, with only brief pauses between its individual phrases. ■

〰 Timbre

- *First Movement:* Listen for the contrast between the chorus and the orchestra.
- *Last Movement:* Listen for the *lack of* contrast between the chorus and orchestra. ■

🌐 Texture

- *First Movement:* Listen for the polyphonic texture. The chorale appears in the uppermost voice, but the lower voices present contrasting, important melodic material of their own.
- *Last Movement:* Listen for the homophonic texture, with the melody in the uppermost voice and accompanying voices beneath. ■

🎹 Form

- *First Movement:* Listen for the orchestral ritornello that introduces the chorale and then returns between the chorale's individual phrases.
- *Last Movement:* Listen for the absence of any ritornellos in this movement. ■

When J. S. Bach became music director at St. Thomas's Church in Leipzig in 1723, he agreed to provide music for the Lutheran worship services each Sunday, and it was in this position that he wrote the vast majority of his more than 200 **cantatas**. The word *cantata* means simply "that which is sung," and cantatas can range from a single movement for one vocal soloist to an extended cycle of movements for soloists, chorus, and orchestra, such as Cantata 140. Had Bach written these works over the span of his 27 years in Leipzig, the accomplishment would be remarkable enough. But through detailed studies of paper, handwriting, and other evidence, scholars have discovered that Bach actually wrote about 150 cantatas within his first three years in Leipzig, at the rate of roughly one a week.

When one considers the time needed to compose a new work, write down the score, supervise the copying of the parts, rehearse the new work, and then perform it on Sunday—all in addition to his duties as a teacher at St. Thomas's School—Bach's achievement seems almost superhuman. What motivated him to write such elaborate music week after week, year after year? We cannot know for sure, but he clearly embraced the opportunity to express his faith through music. Just as the resident preacher would write a sermon each Sunday expounding on the biblical readings for that day, Bach would compose a cantata expressing through music the ideas or lessons gleaned from those readings.

LEARNING OBJECTIVES

20.1 Define cantata and chorale and explain their use in Protestant services during the Baroque Era.

20.2 Describe the similarities and differences between the final-movement chorale and the first-movement chorus in J. S. Bach's Cantata 140.

20.3 Listen for the use of the ritornello principle in the first movement of this cantata.

20.4 Describe the contrasting timbres used by Bach to create the first-movement chorus.

20.5 Outline the ways in which J. S. Bach's responsibilities at St. Thomas's church shaped his output as a composer.

Awake, a Voice Calls to Us (*Wachet auf, ruft uns die Stimme*) was written for the 27th Sunday after Trinity in 1731. The Gospel reading for that Sunday is Matthew 25:1–13, which is the parable of the wise and foolish virgins who attend a wedding. The wise ones are prepared for the bridegroom's arrival: They have brought extra oil for their lamps in case he is late. The foolish ones are unprepared: They must leave to buy oil, and the bridegroom arrives in their absence, at midnight. The message implicit here has to do with Christ's return at the end of the world: Who will be ready?

(1) The Chorale: Movement Seven

Awake, a Voice Calls to Us derives some of its text and a good bit of its musical material—as well as its name—from a hymn tune or **chorale** that was in circulation long before Bach wrote this cantata. In fact, the easiest way to approach this particular cantata is by starting with the last of its seven movements, in which Bach presents the chorale melody in its simplest form. The melody is in the uppermost voice, in a syllabic setting (one note per syllable) with three voices singing in harmonization below it. The words here are the last stanza of the hymn, but the melody is identical to the one used in the opening movement.

Unified Timbre

The instruments of the orchestra **double** the voices—that is, the instruments play the same notes sung by the chorus: High instruments like the violin, flute, and oboe double the soprano line, while lower instruments (violas, cellos, basses) double the lower voice lines. When instruments double the voices, the contrast between chorus and orchestra is minimized, and the combined forces create a powerful sense of unity, symbolizing the unified belief of the congregation.

A Familiar Melody

The chorale melody is in the uppermost voice, and the lower voices provide a fairly simple harmonization of the tune, one that would have been familiar to every member of Bach's congregation in 1731. It is even possible that worshippers sang along with the chorus in this particular movement. Lutherans, like other Protestants, placed a high importance on the personal connection of each believer to God. Chorale melodies played a role in making this connection, as they were easy to sing and the melodies were memorable, which enabled everyone to participate. Using the vernacular—that is, the everyday language of the people, in this case, German—was another way Protestants aimed to facilitate direct communication between ordinary people and God.

The melody opens with a fanfare-like figure that suits the words of the first stanza ("Sleepers, Awake!"). Notice the contour: The opening phrase (**A**) keeps moving upward before finally settling back down. The individual phrases are brief enough to be sung by untrained singers, and the space between phrases allows the congregation plenty of time to take a good breath. Phrase **A** is sung twice. The contrasting phrase (**B**) that follows has a different contour: It begins high and moves downward before making a long climb to reach the highest point of the melody and then descending once again, ending on the same note on which the melody began.

The chorale melody

 Bar Form

The movement consists of one verse of the chorale melody, and so the form of the movement reflects the form of the melody: **AAB**. The opening phrase (**A**) is sung twice, and the melody concludes with a contrasting section (**B**). This **AAB** pattern is so common that it has its own name: **bar form**. It is sometimes also called song form because many popular songs from later eras—including "The Star-Spangled Banner"—follow this pattern.

Homophonic Texture: To Hear the Words

The texture is **homophonic**, with the melody in the uppermost voice and all four parts moving in equal or nearly equal rhythm. The bass voice, which moves at a slightly faster speed, keeps the chorale moving forward and provides rhythmic variety. But the three upper voices begin their articulation of nearly every syllable at the same time, which makes the words particularly clear to listeners.

The opening of the chorale, showing the synchronized motion of the three upper voices.

St. Thomas's Church in Leipzig, where Cantata 140 (*Awake, a Voice Calls to Us*) received its premiere in 1731. Bach is buried inside this church.

(2) The Chorus: Movement One

Bach uses this same chorale melody in a spectacular manner in the opening movement of the cantata. **Dotted rhythms** (LONG-short LONG-short LONG, etc.) and a steady pace suggest a march, the kind of procession described in the cantata's text. Bach's listeners would have heard these dotted rhythms as a reference to the pomp of royalty, as in the French overture (see Chapter 14). As in the chorale itself (movement 7), the melody is sung from beginning to end by the soprano voices. But instead of a straightforward harmonization, Bach weaves elaborate lines of **counterpoint** underneath the melody with the other voices and with the instruments of the orchestra.

Melody Interrupted

The melody is sung in the soprano voices, as in the finale, but in this opening chorus, Bach creates substantial pauses after each line and even longer pauses between the main sections (**A | A | B**). These interruptions in the uppermost voices are filled in by the orchestra (which plays constantly throughout) and by the other voices in the chorus. The music between the sections of the chorale melody thus provides both contrast and commentary.

Like other Protestant composers of his time, Bach often worked chorale melodies into larger, more complex movements. In his Cantata 80, for example, Bach wove the well-known chorale "A Mighty Fortress Is Our God," or some variation of it, into three of the work's eight movements (see Expand Your Playlist). His Cantata 78 (also in the playlist) follows a similar pattern.

Form: The Ritornello Principle

The first movement presents the chorale melody in its entirety in very long, drawn-out note values (in the soprano line), with an instrumental **ritornello** (the full orchestra) on each end as well as between major text sections. In this way, the ritornello provides a "frame" for the chorale melody on multiple levels: It introduces and concludes the movement, and it also introduces and concludes the individual melodic subunits. The ritornello principle here is very similar to the one Vivaldi used in the first movement of "Winter" from *The Four Seasons* (see Chapter 17).

Section:	Ritornello 1	Chorale A	Ritornello 2	Chorale A	Ritornello 3	Chorale B	Ritornello 4
Timbre:	Orchestra	Orchestra & Chorus	Orchestra	Orchestra & Chorus	Orchestra	Orchestra & Chorus	Orchestra

Now listen to the movements again, using the Listening Guide. As suggested earlier, you may find it easier to listen to the last movement first in order to hear the chorale in its simplest, most straightforward form.

The Composer Speaks **Bach's Working Conditions**

We have observed how churches and noble patrons competed for the best and brightest musicians, in part because of the influence and prestige the arts could confer. But Bach had a very high estimation of his self-worth, and he was not the easiest of employees. He quarreled almost constantly with his employers about his pay and working conditions no matter where he was. He even spent a month in prison for signing a contract for a new job in Cöthen against the wishes of his then-employer, the duke of Weimar (see "Closer Look: Bach's World," Chapter 18). In 1730, about six years after moving to Leipzig, Bach wrote to a lifelong friend, venting some of his frustration about his position there:

 I am still here [in Leipzig], by God's will. But as I now find that (1) this position is not nearly as agreeable as I had been led to believe; (2) many supplemental sources of income have been taken away from this position; (3) this is a very expensive place to live; and (4) the powers-that-be here are remarkably uninterested in music, I find myself in a state of such constant annoyance, envy, and persecution that I am now compelled to seek my fortune elsewhere.

My current salary is approximately 700 thalers, and when there are more funerals than usual, the supplemental income rises accordingly. But when the air is wholesome, this income declines accordingly, as it did last year, when I had to forego more than 100 thalers from funerals. In Thuringia I can do more with 400 thalers than in this place with double that amount, due to the extremely high cost of living here in Leipzig.

Source: Letter to Georg Erdmann, 28 October 1730, trans. MEB.

EXPAND YOUR PLAYLIST

Sacred Music of the Late Baroque

Baroque composers wrote vast quantities of music for services of different faiths, including Catholicism and the various Protestant sects. The cantata was used in both Catholic and Protestant services, but it was more important in the latter and more closely connected to the traditions of the chorale. J. S. Bach wrote more than 300 cantatas, of which about 200 survive, including the following:

- **A Mighty Fortress Is Our God** (*Ein' feste Burg ist unser Gott*), BWV 80, is based on the words and melody of the well-known hymn by Martin Luther. One of Bach's sons later added trumpets and timpani to the score; this version is most often performed today.

- **Praise God in All Lands** (*Jauchzet Gott in allen Landen*), BWV 51, for soprano solo, trumpet solo, strings, and basso continuo. The two solo parts (one vocal, one instrumental) are spectacular—and spectacularly difficult.

The **motet**, similar to the cantata, was used widely in both Protestant and Catholic services. Here are some examples:

- **Sing Unto God** (*Cantate Domino*) **by Michel-Richard Delalande** (1657–1726) is a good example of the French motet, for tenor soloist, chorus, and orchestra. The text is in Latin, and the tenor part is highly virtuosic.

- **Sing Unto the Lord a New Song** (*Singet dem Herrn ein neues Lied*), BWV 225, is a motet for chorus alone, without soloists or instruments.

The Mass is the central liturgical service of the Catholic Church, recreating, in symbolic fashion, Christ's Last Supper with his disciples. Although retained in the Protestant service to some extent (usually in the language of the people), the Mass in Latin was associated primarily with the Catholic Church.

- The **Saint Cecilia Mass** (*Missa Santa Cecilia*) by **Alessandro Scarlatti** (1660–1725) is an elaborate setting of the Mass text, with spectacularly florid parts for the vocalists.

- Though a Lutheran himself, Bach also wrote an important Mass for the Catholic court at Dresden, near Leipzig. The B-Minor Mass, BWV 232, is for chorus, soloists, and orchestra, and it is widely considered the greatest of all Baroque Masses.

****

The oratorio (see Chapter 21) is musically very similar to an opera—usually for soloists, chorus, and orchestra—but it is unstaged and often based on a sacred topic:

- Giacomo Carissimi's *Jephthe* depicts the story of an Israelite caught between his duty to God and love of his family.

- George Frideric Handel (1685–1759) was the most celebrated composer of oratorios in the Baroque Era. Audiences responded enthusiastically to his *Messiah* (see Chapter 21), *Samson*, and other oratorios.

Johann Sebastian Bach Composed: 1731

Cantata 140: *Awake, a Voice Calls to Us*, Movement I: Chorus (6:06)

Time	🏛 Form	Original German Text	English Translation
0:00	Ritornello 1		
0:28	Chorale A	Wachet auf, ruft uns die Stimme, der Wächter sehr hoch auf der Zinne, wach auf, du Stadt Jerusalem.	"Awake," a voice calls to us, the watchman high in the tower: "Awake, thou city of Jerusalem."
1:32	Ritornello 2		
2:00	Chorale A	Mitternacht heißt diese Stunde, sie rufen uns mit hellem Munde, wo seid ihr klugen Jungfrauen?	Midnight the hour is called; they call to us with bright voices: "Where are you, wise virgins?"
3:04	Ritornello 3		
3:24	Chorale B	Wohlauf, der Bräut'gam kömmt, steht auf, die Lampen nehmt, Alleluia! Alleluia! Macht euch bereit zu der Hochzeit, ihr müsset ihm entgegengehn.	Behold, the bridegroom comes; rise up and take your lamps, Alleluia! Alleluia! Prepare yourselves for the wedding, you must go to meet Him.
5:32	Ritornello 4		

Movement VII: Chorale (1:25)

Time	Form	Original German Text	English Translation
0:00	A	Gloria sei dir gesungen, mit Menschen- und englischen Zungen, mit Harfen und mit Zimbeln schon.	Let Gloria be sung to You with mortal and angelic tongues, with harps and even cymbals.
0:24	A	Von zwölf Perlen sind die Pforten, an deiner Stadt sind wir Konsorten der Engel hoch um deinen Thron.	Of twelve pearls the portals are made, in your city we are consorts to the angels high around your throne.
0:47	B	Kein Aug' hat je gespürt, kein Ohr hat je gehört solche Freude, des sind wir froh, io, io, ewig in dulci jubilo.	No eye has ever glimpsed, no ear has ever heard such joy which makes us glad, io, io eternally, with sweet rejoicing!

Melody

	Texture
Dotted rhythms, march-like feeling.	Polyphonic
Chorale melody in the highest (soprano) voice, which enters first. "Wachet auf" ("Awake") set to fanfare-like figure (using skips), rather like a trumpet that would awaken a sleeper.	
Dotted rhythms; same melody as in Ritornello 1.	
Same melodic phrase as Chorale A.	
Same melody as in previous ritornellos.	
Chorale melody enters after the other voices, at 3:26.	
Same melody as in previous ritornellos.	

Melody

	Texture
Fanfare-like opening (disjunct, upward). Leaps upward again on "mit Menschen" and again on "mit Harfen." Otherwise conjunct motion or repeated notes.	Homophonic
Same music as above, with upward motion at the beginning and leaps upward again on "an deiner Stadt" and "der Engel hoch."	
First two lines: Descending conjunct motion. Next line ("sol-che Freude"): ascends and descends by conjunct motion. "Des sind wir froh" ("which makes us glad"): ascends by conjunct motion to highest pitch of the chorale.	

🔍 Student FAQs ⚙

What are the other movements of this cantata like?

The second movement is a recitative for tenor and basso continuo; the third movement is a duet for soprano and bass, with a solo violin and basso continuo accompaniment; the fourth movement presents the chorale melody as sung by the tenors of the chorus, with a contrapuntal line weaving around it played by the violins and violas; the fifth movement is a recitative for bass; and the sixth movement is another duet for soprano and bass, with an oboe solo.

How large was Bach's chorus?

This has been a matter of heated debate among scholars in recent years. Documentary evidence has come to light that indicates that for at least some performances there was only one singer to a part. But there is no consensus on whether this represented standard practice or an exception. Conductors today must take into account the quality of the singers in their ensemble and the size of the space in which they are performing. There is no one "right" size for a chorus when performing this work.

This satirical depiction of a chorus, by the English artist William Hogarth (1697–1764), shows a conductor who has gotten so caught up in the moment that he has literally flipped his wig. Only one of the singers seems to notice.

21

George Frideric Handel
Messiah, selections
Composed: 1747

The "Hallelujah Chorus" is one of the most famous works of music ever written. What many people do not realize is that it is only one movement out of a much larger work called *Messiah*. In addition to the "Hallelujah Chorus," this chapter includes the recitative and aria that immediately precede it.

Listen to This First

〰️ Timbre	🎵 Melody	🔄 Word–Music Relationships	🌐 Texture
Listen to the expanding variety of timbres, from (1) solo voice and basso continuo in the recitative to (2) solo voice, basso continuo, and violins in the aria to (3) a large group of singers and a large orchestra in the chorus. ■	Notice that the aria has just one distinctive melody from beginning to end, in keeping with the single-mindedness of the text. By contrast, listen to the multiple melodies in the chorus, which reflect its more varied text. ■	Try to identify specific ways the music supports and describes the words being sung. ■	Listen to the variety of textures, from homophony in the recitative and aria, to a full array in the chorus: homophony, monophony, and polyphony. ■

LEARNING OBJECTIVES

21.1 Identify the similarities and differences between oratorio and opera.

21.2 Identify the distinguishing features of recitative, aria, and chorus in George Frideric Handel's *Messiah*.

21.3 Listen for Handel's use of word painting in the recitative and aria pairing of "He that dwelleth in . . . heaven" and "Thou . . . shalt break them."

21.4 Listen for the structural use of varied textures and timbres in "Hallelujah!"

21.5 Discuss Handel's use of contrasting musical textures in each of these three movements from *Messiah*.

21.6 Explain why people traditionally stand for "Hallelujah!"

21.7 Outline Handel's career as a composer.

Throughout the Baroque Era, the church remained deeply ambivalent toward opera. On the one hand, authorities recognized the power of music to move the spirits of the faithful, and a number of composers in the seventeenth century even wrote operas on sacred subjects, such as the lives of particular saints. On the other hand, opera had become such a spectacle—both visual and aural—by the end of the seventeenth century that the church could no longer sanction such elaborate productions during the penitential seasons of Lent (40 days in early spring before Easter) and Advent (30 days in the fall before Christmas). These were periods of time when the faithful were supposed to give up worldly pleasures and devote themselves to inward contemplation. Fortunately, the new genre of the **oratorio** offered a way out of this dilemma that satisfied both the church and music lovers alike.

Musically, an oratorio is virtually identical to an opera: It includes **recitatives**, **arias**, and **choruses**, and the singing can be quite elaborate. But unlike opera, an oratorio is not staged—there are no costumes, no sets—and is usually based on a sacred topic. The word *oratorio* is the Italian word for "prayer hall," which is where these works were performed in the seventeenth century. The genre soon spread across Europe and became a standard substitute for opera during the penitential seasons of Lent and Advent.

Most oratorios have characters and a plot, just as in an opera. Handel's *Messiah*, the most popular of all oratorios, is actually somewhat unusual in this regard. There are no characters and no plot, although it does progress from prophecy and the birth of Christ (Part 1) to the crucifixion and resurrection (Part 2) to meditations on the eternal life of the soul (Part 3). The text is drawn from various biblical passages, including both Old and New Testaments. Musically, however, *Messiah* is typical in that it uses the basic conventions of opera. The movements presented here include a recitative, an aria, and a chorus.

(1) Recitative ("He That Dwelleth in Heaven") and Aria ("Thou Shalt Break Them")

This pair of movements, both for tenor soloist, forms a sequence of recitative and aria that would have been familiar to Handel's original audiences from opera. The brief recitative ("He that dwelleth in heaven"), for tenor and **basso continuo** alone, introduces the more extended aria, for tenor and a reduced orchestra of violins and basso continuo.

 ## Form: Paired Movements

The declamatory recitative sets up the more musically elaborate aria that follows. The aria is built on the **ritornello principle**, in which the ensemble (the orchestra) and the soloist (the tenor) alternate. The text of the aria is also quite brief, but Handel, like a great many composers of his time, spins a few short phrases into an extended aria by repeating the words several times and by writing long **melismas** (many notes for a single syllable) in setting certain key words.

> Thou shalt break them with a rod of iron,
> Thou shalt dash them to pieces like a potter's vessel.
> *(Psalm 2:9, King James Version)*

 ## Word–Music Relationships: Virtuosic Word Painting

Those being "broken" and "dashed" in the text are the heathen, the unbelievers who scorn God. Handel captures the violence of this text from the very start with a back-and-forth shaking figure in the violins, two rapidly alternating notes repeated several times.

Shaking figure   Large leap downward

Word painting

He also sets the words "dash them" at several points to a large downward leap, a moment of **word painting** that suggests an object being thrown from a great height. The words "potter's vessel"—that is, a clay pot—receive elaborate melismatic settings at several points: The many notes sung to these words can be heard to represent the many pieces into which these objects will be broken. The elaborate melodic line of the aria interprets the text and allows the singer to display his virtuosity as a musician. It also gave audiences the kind of florid singing they would not otherwise have been able to hear during the periods of the year when operatic performances were banned.

A Single Melody

The brief text of the aria speaks of one thing and one thing only: destruction. The first half of Psalm 2:9 is about the tool of destruction ("a rod of iron"), and the second half is about the nature of that destruction ("dash them to pieces like a potter's vessel"). Handel responds to this text with a single melodic idea. He does not use any kind of melodic contrast in his music because there is no real contrast within the text itself.

Homophonic Texture

The **homophonic texture** in both the recitative and aria allows the solo singer to project his words with great clarity. In the aria, the instruments present the "shaking" melody repeatedly so that it is not merely subordinate to the voice. But the voice stands out, particularly in those passages of the aria in which it is accompanied only by the basso continuo.

A Stark Timbre

The recitative is accompanied only by the basso continuo, following standard practice. But when the tenor's aria begins, only the violins join in. This not only falls well short of the full orchestra—Handel is saving that larger sound for the chorus to follow—but it does not even include all the stringed instruments. Moreover, both sections of violins (Violin 1 and Violin 2) play exactly the same notes, which creates a strong single line that contrasts markedly with both the basso continuo and the solo tenor voice. The result is a stark timbre of only three lines: the voice, the violins, and the basso continuo.

(2) Chorus ("Hallelujah")

Just as the recitative introduces the aria, the aria introduces the chorus, the celebrated "Hallelujah." The text now jumps from the Old Testament to the New Testament. The words of this chorus are a compilation of different verses from the Book of Revelations:

Hallelujah, for the Lord God Omnipotent reigneth, Hallelujah! (*Revelation 19:6*)

The Kingdom of this world is become the Kingdom of our Lord, and of His Christ; and He shall
    reign for ever and ever, Hallelujah! (*Revelation 11:15*)
King of Kings, and Lord of Lords, and He shall reign for ever and ever, Hallelujah!
    (*Revelation 19:16*)

 ## Sectional Form

Handel allows the form of the text to shape the form of the music. Each verse or half-verse
receives its own melodic material so that there are four large sections within the chorus as a whole
(labeled **A**, **B**, **C**, and **D** in the Listening Guide). After the introductory, narrative singing style of
the recitative and the highly ornamented, reflective style of the aria, the clear and mostly syllabic
singing style of the culminating "Hallelujah" chorus makes it easy to understand the jubilant and
victorious text. It also enhances these joyous words, which provide the conclusion to (Part 2) of
Messiah.

 ## The Same Melody for the Same Words

Even though the text draws on three different biblical verses, they contain a good bit of repetition.
All three end with the opening word of the entire chorus ("Hallelujah") and the phrase "And He
shall reign for ever and ever" appears in two of the three verses. Handel, accordingly, uses the
same melodic ideas when these words return later in the text.

    Melody 1 consists of short notes that repeat or move in mainly conjunct (stepwise) motion.

Melody 2 is a unison line (a single melodic line, without any harmony) that rises and falls.

Melody 3 is a long, descending line with a dramatic leap up at "the Kingdom of our Lord."

Melody 4 is a disjunct line, with several leaps up and down but a generally downward contour.

and He shall   reign for   ev - er and   ev - er,

Melody 5 consists of very long notes in a unison line that rises quite slowly.

King   of   Kings, _____   and Lord of   Lords, _____

Sometimes, different melodies appear at the same time. At 0:45, melodies 1 and 2 appear together; at 1:48, we hear both 1 and 5; and at 2:29, melodies 1, 4, and 5 join for a grand polyphonic climax.

Varied Textures

This movement features all three basic textures of music: monophony (a single melodic line), homophony (melody with accompaniment), and polyphony (multiple lines of equal importance). The textures are driven in large part by the text. We hear homophony at the beginning ("Hallelujah"), monophony on the line that emphasizes God's power ("For the Lord God Omnipotent reigneth"), and polyphony whenever these texts are combined with other texts. All this contributes to a sense of variety reinforced by the new words, new melodies, and new timbres in each section of the chorus.

Varied Timbres

In the aria immediately preceding this chorus ("Thou shalt break them"), Handel had used a reduced orchestra of only violins and basso continuo. As a result, the full orchestra in this chorus of exaltation ("Hallelujah") sounds even fuller. The timbre also varies within the movement itself. It begins with strings and basso continuo (0:00), which are soon joined by the full chorus and oboes (0:06), and later still by trumpets and timpani (0:29). As the movement progresses, instruments drop out and reenter, building to a climax at the end on the final word, "Hallelujah."

Now listen to these movements again, using the Listening Guide.

Listening Guide))

George Frideric Handel Composed: 1747

Messiah, selections

(1) Recitative: "He that dwelleth in heaven" (2:20)

Time	Text	⊕ Texture	〰 Timbre	◔ Word–Music Relationships	♪ Melody
0:00	He that dwelleth in heaven shall laugh them to scorn; the Lord shall have them in derision.	Homophonic	Tenor (voice) and basso continuo (in this performance, harpsichord and cello)	Line goes up to word "heaven," descends on "laugh"	Recitative

Aria: "Thou shalt break them"

Time	Form: Ritornello/Solo	Text	Timbre	Word–Music Relationships	Melody
0:17	Ritornello 1		Sharp contrast between the violins above and the basso continuo below.	Minor mode and melody establish the violent mood of the text	Theme 1 here and throughout; there is no contrasting melody
0:33	Solo 1	Thou shalt break them with a rod of iron;	The tenor soloist enters.	Downward leap on "break them"	
0:43		Thou shalt dash them in pieces like a potter's vessel.		Downward leaps on "dash them" and "in pieces." Long melisma on "potter's," evoking the many pieces of a smashed clay pot	
1:06	Ritornello 2		Violins and basso continuo alone.		
1:13	Solo 2	Thou shalt break them with a rod of iron;	The tenor solo returns. Violins recede or drop out entirely on melismas in this section, exposing the emphasized words still further.	Long melisma on "rod"	
1:28		Thou shalt dash them in pieces like a potter's vessel.		Long melisma on "potter's"	
2:04	Ritornello 3				

Listening Guide 🔊

George Frideric Handel Composed: 1747
Messiah, selections
(2) Chorus: "Hallelujah" (3:33)

Time	🏛 Form: Section	🎵 Melody	Text	🌐 Texture
0:00	Introduction			Homophonic
0:06	**A**	Melody 1	Hallelujah,	Homophonic
0:23		Melody 2	for the Lord God Omnipotent reigneth,	Monophonic
0:45		Melodies 1 & 2 together	Hallelujah, for the Lord God Omnipotent reigneth, Hallelujah!	Polyphonic
1:09	**B**	Melody 3	The Kingdom of this world is become the Kingdom of our Lord, and of His Christ;	Homophonic
1:26	**C**	Melody 4	and He shall reign for ever and ever,	Polyphonic (imitative)
1:48	**D**	Melodies 5 & 1 together	King of Kings, and Lord of Lords, and He shall reign for ever and ever, Hallelujah!	Polyphonic
2:29		Melodies 1, 4, & 5 together	And He shall reign for ever and ever, King of Kings and Lord of Lords, Hallelujah!	Polyphonic

Word–Music Relationships	Timbre
	Strings and basso continuo.
Melody 1: Rhythm of music matches two different ways of saying "Hallelujah," either with a long first syllable (HA-le-lu-jah), or with a long third syllable (Ha-le-LU-jah).	The full chorus and oboes join in.
Melody 2: Large leap down and up on "omnipotent," as if to show the range of God's power.	
Melodies 1 and 2 together when their texts are combined.	Trumpets and timpani join in at 0:51.
Melody 3: Notes moving from high to low suggest the "Kingdom of our Lord" descending to "the Kingdom of this world," that is, Earth. The leap upward suggests that Earth and heaven are now connected.	Chorus, strings, oboes, bassoons, and basso continuo only. Then trumpets and timpani join in.
Imitative entries give the impression that this section might continue indefinitely ("for ever and ever").	
"King of Kings" in uppermost (soprano) line, literally above all the other notes, perhaps to parallel God's position in relation to Earth. The melodic line reaches its highest point at 2:21.	Trumpets and timpani join in at 1:50.
Melodies 4, 5, and 1 together. Movement ends with the same melodic idea with which it began (1), suggesting the idea of God's eternal power.	Chorus, strings, oboes, bassoon, and basso continuo only. Trumpets and timpani join in at 2:39.

Q Student FAQs

Is the title of this work The Messiah or Messiah?

Handel called it simply *Messiah*, though the definite article started creeping into accounts of the work almost at once. Everyone would know what you mean if you called the work *The Messiah*, but *Messiah* is the correct title.

Why is this work performed so often around Christmas?

Part 1 has a definite Christmas theme to it: the prophecy and birth of Christ. But Parts 2 and 3 belong more appropriately to Easter, as they deal with the Crucifixion and Resurrection. But like the tradition of standing for the "Hallelujah" chorus (see "Historical Context: Why Stand?"), any tradition, once started, can take on a life of its own. And as shown here, choruses attract people of all ages.

So the "Hallelujah" is not the end of the work?

No. It's the end of Part 2, and if the work is performed in its entirety, all of Part 3 follows. *Messiah* concludes with an enormous chorus on the word "Amen" that in its own way is as impressive as the "Hallelujah" chorus.

HISTORICAL CONTEXT   Why Stand?

If you have ever attended a live performance of Handel's *Messiah*, chances are good that the entire audience stood up for the singing of the "Hallelujah" chorus. It is widely believed that this replicates the actions of King George II, who, during the London premiere of the work in 1743, was moved to rise because of the sheer beauty and majesty of the music. And when the king stands, everyone else stands, too—so the audience rose.

It is a good story, and it may even be true, but the fact is that we have no record of the king having attended any performance of any of Handel's oratorios after 1739. Newspapers and diarists of the time routinely took note of the king's comings and goings, especially to public events, so it seems likely that someone would have recorded this event had George II in fact attended *Messiah* at some point. The first report of the king's response comes to us from 1780, long after the death of not only Handel but of George II (1683–1760) as well.

Yet who is to say whether this actually happened or not? Proving a negative ("King George II never attended a performance of *Messiah*") is virtually impossible. Whatever its origin, the tradition of rising for the "Hallelujah" chorus has grown over time and today symbolizes the emotional connection listeners feel with this music.

A performance of Handel's *Messiah* in Westminster Abbey in 1784, with a massive chorus and orchestra.

 EXPAND YOUR PLAYLIST

Covering the "Hallelujah Chorus"

When an artist interprets a song made famous by another artist, we call the new version a "cover." Musicians have been covering the celebrated "Hallelujah" from Handel's *Messiah* since the late eighteenth century, altering the orchestration, the tempo, and even the notes themselves. Here are some examples:

Wolfgang Amadeus Mozart
• *Der Messias* (1789). Mozart arranged several of Handel's oratorios for performance in Vienna, using a German translation of the text, lengthening and shortening some numbers, and adding new instruments—flutes, clarinets, bassoons, horns, and trombones.

Johnny Mathis
• "Hallelujah Chorus" (1972). A relatively standard version with orchestra and chorus, but with Mathis alone singing the tenor part.

The Roches
• "Hallelujah Chorus" (1982). An *a cappella* version—three voices, no instruments—by an ensemble of three women.

Quincy Jones (producer)
• *Handel's Messiah: A Soulful Celebration* (1992). A gospel-style rendition of *Messiah* performed by a variety of different artists, this album won the Grammy Award for Best Contemporary Soul Gospel Album in 1992.

Marin Alsop
• *Too Hot to Handel* (1993). A gospel-jazz-rock-funk version by a noted conductor who now directs the Baltimore Symphony Orchestra.

Mannheim Steamroller
• "Hallelujah" (2004). A purely instrumental version of the chorus, on rock instruments and synthesizers.

Relient K
• "Handel's Messiah: The Hallelujah Chorus" (2006). A rock interpretation that adds some counterpoint to the original in places and subtracts it in others.

PROFILE   George Frideric Handel (1685–1759)

The Well-Traveled Composer

Geoge Frideric Handel and J. S. Bach were born within a month of each other and less than 100 miles apart, but they never met, and their careers as composers could scarcely have been more different. Bach spent his entire life in central Germany (see "Closer Look: Bach's World," Chapter 18), whereas Handel traveled widely throughout Europe. He moved to Italy in 1706 and soon established a name for himself as a composer of operas and oratorios. He returned to Germany as music director for the elector of Hanover in 1710, but he soon journeyed to England, where his operas won great acclaim.

When the ruler of Hanover ascended the English throne as George I in 1714, Handel was still in his service and thus perfectly positioned to enjoy the new king's patronage and support. Over the course of his long career in England, Handel wrote many operas and oratorios that met with great public success. He abandoned opera altogether in 1741 and turned his attention toward the oratorio.

Music historian Charles Burney, who knew Handel personally, wrote this reminiscence:

> The figure of Handel was large, and he was somewhat corpulent, and unwieldy in his motions; but his countenance, which I remember as perfectly as that of any man I saw but yesterday, was full of fire and dignity; and such as impressed ideas of superiority and genius. He was impetuous, rough and peremptory in his manners and conversation, but totally devoid of ill-nature or malevolence; indeed there was an original humor and pleasantry in his most lively sallies of anger or impatience . . . *

*Charles Burney, *An Account of the Musical Performances in Westminster-Abbey . . . in Commemoration of Handel* (London: T. Payne, 1785), 31–32.

Handel as a young man, composing at the keyboard. Like many men of the day, he kept his head shaved to better accommodate a wig, which he always wore in public.

 EXPAND YOUR PLAYLIST: HANDEL

- **Saul** (oratorio). One of Handel's many oratorios on a story from the Old Testament. The text deals with the relationship between Saul, King of Israel, and the young David.

- **Rinaldo** (opera). Handel's first operatic hit premiered in London in 1711.

- **Giulio Cesare** (opera). One of Handel's most enduring operas, the tale of Caesar and Cleopatra in ancient Egypt.

- **Alexander's Feast** (ode). Set to a text by poet and playwright John Dryden, this work for soloists, chorus, and orchestra extols the power of music even over Alexander the Great, ruler of the world's greatest empire in his day.

PART 3 Summary

	Renaissance	Baroque
Texture	Polyphonic	Polyphonic and homophonic coexist
Melody	Lyrical, rarely virtuosic	Lyrical and declamatory (recitative) coexist; often virtuosic
Rhythm	Relatively smooth and flowing	Wider range of extremes, from smooth and flowing to choppy and irregular
Timbre	No sharp distinction between instrumental and vocal music	Sharp distinction between vocal and instrumental parts
Harmony	Harmony as a by-product of the relationship among polyphonic voices	Harmony as an underlying basis for melody
Form	Primarily sectional	Greater variety of formal principles: sectional form, theme and variations, ostinato
Word–Music Relationships	Limited use of word painting	Even greater use of word painting; texture and musical affect strongly support text

IN REVIEW: Medieval Style

Homophonic Texture A texture in which one voice predominates and the others support it.
- Monteverdi, *Orpheus* (Chapter 13)
- Purcell, *Dido and Aeneas* (Chapter 14)
- Strozzi, "Revenge" (Chapter 16)

Basso Continuo The group of instruments accompanying the lead voice in homophonic texture, playing the bass line ("basso") continuously, thereby allowing the solo voice to pursue its own melody, drop out, and return.
- Almost all the works in this part fall into this category except Bach's Fugue in G Minor, a purely polyphonic work for organ.

Recitative A style of singing midway between lyrical song and speech, usually syllabic (one note per syllable).
- Monteverdi, *Orpheus* (Chapter 13)
- Purcell, *Dido and Aeneas* (Chapter 14)
- Handel, *Messiah* (Chapter 21)

Word painting While not an entirely new development, word painting—the depiction of specific words through music that imitates the meaning of those words—becomes particularly important in the Baroque Era.

- Monteverdi, *Orpheus* (Chapter 13)
- Purcell, *Dido and Aeneas* (Chapter 14)
- Strozzi, "Revenge" (Chapter 16)
- Bach, Cantata 140 (Chapter 20)
- Handel, *Messiah* (Chapter 21)

Ritornello Structure The regular alternation between sections for contrasting ensembles (soloist versus orchestra; voices versus instruments).
- Vivaldi, *The Four Seasons*, "Winter" (Chapter 17)
- Bach, Brandenburg Concerto no. 2 (Chapter 19)
- Bach, Cantata 140 (Chapter 20)

Program Music Instrumental music that is in some way associated with a story, event, or idea.
- Vivaldi, *The Four Seasons*, "Winter" (Chapter 17)

Ostinato A short repeated pattern of notes.
- Purcell, *Dido and Aeneas* (Chapter 14)

Counterpoint Two independent melodies, played simultaneously.
- Bach, Fugue in G Minor (Chapter 18)

PART 4

1750–1800

The Classical Era

A classic is something that endures. The music of what we now call the **Classical Era** was the first to thrive without interruption long after its time. Joseph Haydn (1732–1809) (Chapters 22 and 24) and Wolfgang Amadeus Mozart (1756–1791) (Chapters 25–27), the two leading composers of this era, wrote music that has never really gone out of fashion. The term *classical* also refers to Greek and Roman antiquity, which strongly influenced the arts and architecture of this period. As a new kind of thinking took hold, the Baroque love of ornamentation, virtuosity, and expressive extremes gave way to more classical ideals of balance, clarity, and naturalness.

The eighteenth century as a whole, but particularly the period between about 1720 and 1790, is known as the Age of Enlightenment. **Enlightenment** thought held that reason could bring humankind to a new age of splendor, freed from the dark superstitions of the past (hence "en*light*enment"). Science became more important during the Enlightenment. For Enlightenment artists and thinkers, the power to convince lay not in overwhelming displays of opulence or in larger-than-life drama aimed to influence the emotions, but rather in critical thinking and reasoned discussion, which persuaded the mind.

The music of the Classical Era reflects these principles of clarity, proportion, and what critics of the day called "naturalness." Classical Era melodies are on the whole more tuneful, less complicated, and more balanced than those of the Baroque Era. More symmetrical melodic phrasing, based on the rhythms

The Classical Era

Musical Landmarks

1714–1788 C. P. E. Bach

1714–1787 Christoph Willibald Gluck

1732–1809 Joseph Haydn

1735–1782 Johann Christian Bach

1746–1800 William Billings

1700 **1725**

Historical Events

1714 Peace of Utrecht ends War of the Spanish Succession, leading to England becoming a major global power

1732 *Poor Richard's Almanac* by Benjamin Franklin

1740 Alaska discovered by Capt. Vitus Bering

of dance music, extended itself across all genres, both vocal and instrumental. Critics of the day praised homophonic texture for its clarity and grace, and the dense textures of counterpoint became the exception rather than the rule. But this does not mean that music of the Classical Era is somehow simpler, for a typical movement of music from this period features more internal contrasts than its Baroque counterpart. A movement in sonata form, the most important new structural innovation of the Classical era—one used in Mozart's Symphony no. 40 in G Minor (1788)—juxtaposes multiple themes that differ markedly in their melody, rhythm, harmony, dynamics, and timbre.

> **Chapter 25**
> Mozart: Symphony no. 40 in G Minor, K. 550

Music as the Language of the Heart

The string quartet—a work for two violins, viola, and cello—was another innovation of the Classical Era, and it is no coincidence that critics of the time spoke of works like Joseph Haydn's String Quartet in C Major, op. 76, no. 3 (1797), as a rational conversation among four intelligent individuals. In the second movement, each of the instruments presents the theme in succession while the other three weave an ever-changing commentary around that theme.

> **Chapter 22**
> Haydn: String Quartet in C Major, op. 76, no. 3

This intriguing image captures the Enlightenment's ideal of the mind—the seat of reason—as the focal point of all perception.

1756–1791 Wolfgang Amadeus Mozart

1750   1775   1800

1756–1763 7 Years' War

1775–1781 American Revolution

1793 Eli Whitney's cotton gin introduced

1760 George III crowned king of England

IN CONGRESS, JULY 4, 1776. A DECLARATION BY THE REPRESENTATIVES OF THE UNITED STATES OF AMERICA, IN GENERAL CONGRESS ASSEMBLED.

1776 Declaration of Independence

1789 U.S. Constitution

1789 French Revolution

1751–1777 Diderot's Encyclopedie published

Thomas Jefferson's University of Virginia, shown in an early engraving. Jefferson designed the Rotunda after the Pantheon of ancient Rome. Symmetry is important in Classical architecture as well as in the music of the Classical Era, though on closer inspection very few structures—or melodies—prove entirely symmetrical. Each of the large houses for faculty in this "academical village" is slightly different from the others.

The melody itself, like many Classical melodies, consists of an opening (antecedent) and closing (consequent) phrase. Writers of the Enlightenment recognized the structural parallels with language and began to call instrumental music the "language of the heart." Instrumental music lacked the specificity of words (the "language of the mind") but the perception of it as a language of any kind helped raise the prestige of such genres as the string quartet, the symphony, and the concerto.

Music and Revolution

The plot of Wolfgang Amadeus Mozart's comic opera *The Marriage of Figaro* (1786) (Chapter 27) would have been unthinkable only a generation before. Count Almaviva, a nobleman, is outwitted by his servants. This opera

Chapter 27
Mozart: *The Marriage of Figaro*

captures the growing mood of discontent with the established order of society in the decades leading up to the French Revolution. Basic ideas about human rights ("life, liberty, and the pursuit of happiness," to quote the U.S. Declaration of Independence) won growing acceptance during this time. Enlightenment social critics such as Voltaire (1694–1778) and Jean-Jacques Rousseau (1712–1778) argued for the innate goodness of human beings and for the rational pursuit of personal and societal betterment. The Declaration of Independence is a quintessential document of the Enlightenment, for it recognizes the inherent dignity of the individual. Its principal author, Thomas Jefferson, established the University of Virginia (see image) on the premise that the institution would be "based on the illimitable freedom of the human mind. For here we are not afraid to follow truth wherever it may lead, nor to tolerate any error so long as reason is left free to combat it."

The American Revolution (1775–1781) established the independence of the United States from Great Britain, and the French Revolution (1789) overthrew the power of what until that point had been the world's most powerful monarchy. The results affected not just the countries immediately involved, but ultimately every nation in the Western world. National independence and democracy, if not always realized in practice, became new ideals of social order. Music could help foster these ideals, through such songs as the stirring "La Marseillaise" in France and "Chester" in the United States, which became the unofficial anthem of the American Revolution.

Chapter 29
Billings: "Chester"

Music and the New Economy

The second half of the eighteenth century witnessed the beginnings of an even more powerful revolution, one that would change everyday life throughout the Western world. Rapid advances in technology—the steam engine, the cotton gin, and the principle of manufacturing based on interchangeable parts, to cite just a few examples—made it possible

George Washington (on the brown horse at right) accepts the surrender of British troops at Yorktown in 1781, marking the end of the Revolutionary War. The military band present at the occasion played "Chester," "Yankee Doodle," and a tune called "The World Turned Upside Down."

A family making music together in late 18th-century England.

to produce goods on a far greater scale than ever before. Many national and local economies based on agriculture began to shift toward industry. Cities grew rapidly and this growth in urban populations in turn created new demands for cultural institutions of all kinds, including music.

While the churches and royal courts remained important centers of culture, theaters and concert halls open to the paying public began to flourish for the first time on a widespread scale. We see these changes in the careers of both Haydn and Mozart. Haydn worked almost all his adult life in the service of one aristocratic family, composing symphonies, sonatas, and operas according to the desires of his employers. By the 1790s, however, Haydn was lured away to England to write symphonies, including the Symphony no. 102 in B♭ Major (1795), for a series of public concerts organized by a musical entrepreneur. Mozart left his native Salzburg at the age of 25 to seek his fortune in Vienna. He tried unsuccessfully to land a secure job at the imperial court there, but he managed to support himself reasonably well (for a time, at least) by giving public concerts, by writing operas, and by composing works that could be published and sold to music-loving amateurs. Composers had to write in ways that would appeal to this expanded audience even while maintaining the high standards of their craft. Works like the Piano Concerto in A Major, K. 488 (1786) were the perfect lure for audiences intrigued by Mozart's virtuosity both as a composer and as a performer.

> **Chapter 24**
> Haydn: Symphony no. 102 in B♭ Major

> **Chapter 26**
> Mozart: Piano Concerto in A Major, K. 488

The Art of the Natural

Throughout the Classical Era, artists in every field looked to nature as a model. The ideal work of art, according to this view, was one that hid its artifice, that concealed its mechanical elements, and that appeared to be the product of effortless—natural—genius. Composers still had to learn technique and to study such topics as harmony and counterpoint with great diligence. The goal of all this study was not to show off one's art, but rather to touch the hearts of listeners in a manner that was direct and (seemingly) spontaneous.

This new aesthetic manifested itself in music in many ways. Melodies and ornamentation became less ornate. Textures on the whole tended more toward homophony than polyphony, homophony being the more "natural" of the two textures because it allowed the ear to focus on a single melody. In opera, plots and characters became more realistic. Mozart and others devoted great energies to the new genre of opera buffa or "comic opera," which portrayed real-life characters and situations, as opposed to the mythological and historical figures that populate so much of Baroque opera. In Mozart's *The Marriage of Figaro* (Chapter 27), we can immediately identify with the emotions and actions of the characters because they are presented in a manner that is true to life, in a manner that is, in a word, natural.

Joseph Wright, *An Experiment on a Bird in the Air-Pump,* 1768. A scientist demonstrates the effect of a vacuum jar on a small bird. The young boy at the right lowers the cage for the bird, which will be revived when air is reintroduced to the bowl. Empirical science and the application of reason dominated Enlightenment thought.

22

Joseph Haydn
String Quartet in C Major, op. 76, no. 3, second movement
Composed: 1797

The string quartet is often compared to a conversation among four friends. In the second movement of Joseph Haydn's String Quartet in C Major, op. 76, no. 3, each of the instruments—two violins, a viola, and a cello—presents the melody in succession while the other three weave their own "commentary" around it.

Listen to This First

 Timbre

Listen to how the sounds of the four instruments blend together and stand apart. The registers of these instruments range from high (the two violins) to medium (the viola) to low (the cello), but their sound quality is similar. ∎

 Texture

Notice how the melody always appears in one of the instruments while the other three move around it. Is the texture homophonic or polyphonic? Also listen for the passages in which not all of the instruments are playing. ∎

🎵 **Melody**

Listen for the pauses that break the melody into sections known as phrases. Which phrases sound like endings? Which demand a continuation of the music? Which phrases are repeated? ∎

 Form

Listen to the way the melody is first presented by one of the violins and then repeated with very little change by each of the other instruments across the course of the movement. ∎

LEARNING OBJECTIVES

22.1 Describe the typical sequence of movements of a string quartet in the Classical period.

22.2 Listen for the differences among the timbres of the violins, viola, and cello within the ensemble of the string quartet.

22.3 Describe how Haydn treats texture in his String Quartet op. 76, no. 3, second movement.

22.4 Recognize and describe the periodic phrase structure underlying the melody.

22.5 Listen for and define the form of theme and variations.

22.6 Discuss the ways in which Haydn's professional career shaped the genres in which he wrote.

22.7 Discuss the practice of musical appropriation and give examples of it.

A good melody is worth hearing again and again. But at some point, we also want to hear something different, either a different version of the melody or a different melody altogether. Composers use a combination of repetition, variation, and contrast to satisfy and sustain our interest as listeners. The second movement of Haydn's String Quartet in C Major, op. 76, no. 3, offers a good example of how music can deliver repetition, variation, and contrast all at the same time. The melody is from a song Haydn himself had written a few months earlier for the birthday of Holy Roman Emperor Franz II, who resided in Vienna. The song, set to the words "God save Franz, the Emperor," was an immediate hit with the public and soon became Austria's unofficial national anthem.

The melody was so closely associated with the emperor that Haydn faced a dilemma in writing variations on it. He decided he could not alter the melody itself, for the ideal emperor is steadfast and not subject to change. So he created an ingenious solution to this problem by repeating the emperor's theme more or less unchanged four times in succession, varying only the instrument that played it and writing contrasting musical lines to surround the theme each time. Thus, though the theme remains essentially the same throughout, it stays fresh because the voices surrounding it are constantly changing.

In setting this theme with variations for four instruments of similar timbre, Haydn imposed an additional challenge on himself. Without the full orchestra at his disposal, he could not rely on winds, brass, or timpani to create varieties of sound. This makes his accomplishment—a movement that sustains interest while repeating a melody four times—all the more remarkable.

Haydn was not the first to write string quartets, but he did more than any other composer to establish this new genre's significance from the middle of the eighteenth century onward. Not in spite of its timbral constraints but *because* of them, Haydn, Mozart, and later Beethoven all took up the challenge of writing for the string quartet repeatedly throughout their careers. By the end of the eighteenth century, the string quartet had acquired the reputation of being the most demanding of all musical genres, one that allowed composers to demonstrate their talents more fully.

The quartet is a decidedly intimate genre. In Haydn's time, it was usually performed in the home and only rarely in public concerts. Unlike the concerto, no soloist or small group of soloists stands out; instead, all four instrumentalists operate on an equal footing. Commentators since Haydn's day have repeatedly likened the string quartet to a conversation among four equal participants. The conversational aspect of the genre reinforced the sense that these works were written primarily for the pleasure of the performers. Listeners in private settings sometimes even compared themselves to eavesdroppers.

The typical string quartet of the Classical Era consisted of four contrasting movements:

1. The first movement, usually in a fast tempo, is most often written in what came to be known as "sonata form," the most significant new form to come out of the Classical Era. We take up the sonata form in Chapter 25 of this book, with Mozart's Symphony no. 40.
2. The second movement is usually in a slow tempo and a contrasting key. Slow movements could assume many different forms: Sonata form, theme and variations, and **ABA** are the most common. (The movement that we are listening to here is a set of variations on a theme.)
3. The third movement is usually a minuet, a lively, stylized dance in triple meter, in the tonic key. We take up the minuet in Chapter 24 of this book, with Haydn's Symphony no. 102.
4. The fourth movement, also known as the **finale** because it is the final movement, is somewhat lighter and usually very fast. The most common forms used in finales are sonata form and rondo. We take up the rondo in Chapter 24 of this book, with Haydn's Symphony no. 102.

 ## The Timbre of the String Quartet

The string quartet creates an unusually homogeneous timbre, for its instruments are all variants of the same basic instrument. The viola and cello are essentially larger and therefore deeper versions of the violin. Together, these four instruments correspond to the four standard ranges of the singing voice:

HIGHEST	Soprano:	Violin 1
	Alto:	Violin 2
	Tenor:	Viola
LOWEST	Bass:	Cello

Like any good vocal ensemble, the instruments of a string quartet can blend together to sound almost like a single instrument, or they can be played in ways that emphasize their differences. The violin has a sweet, piercing sound, whereas the cello has a more resonant, richer tone.

The Kronos String Quartet in performance. From left to right: violin 1, violin 2, viola, and cello.

The viola creates a sound somewhere between these two extremes of high and low. It is particularly easy to compare the differences between the sounds of the individual instruments in this movement because Haydn gives the main theme to each at some point.

Changing Textures

Haydn expands the variety of this movement by changing textures throughout. The theme is first presented in a hymn-like fashion, with the melody in the top voice (Violin 1) and the other instruments supporting it, moving at the same pace, rather like the chorale in the last movement of Bach's Cantata no. 140 (see Chapter 20). The texture is **homophonic**. In Variation 1, Violin 2 carries the theme, while Violin 1 weaves an intricate accompanimental figure around it: This is two-part homophony. In Variation 2, the cello carries the theme, with the three other voices weaving around it. Variation 3 begins with only three voices, with the melody in the viola and the cello silent; when the cello enters, Violin 1 drops out. Only later in this variation do we hear all four voices together. Variation 4 features four-part polyphony from beginning to end.

Melody: Periodic Phrase Structure

The melody of this movement is made of five phrases, each marked at the end by a cadence, a brief resting point:

1. The first two phrases (labeled **A**) are the same.
2. They are followed by a phrase that is not repeated (**B**).
3. This is followed by two final phrases (**C**) that are the same.

Neither the **A** phrase nor the **B** phrase sounds complete at the end: With each, we expect the music to continue. Not until the end of the **C** phrase do we feel a sense of conclusion.

The structure of these units (**A**, **B**, and **C**) can be compared to the elements that make up a sentence. The opening **A** and **B** sections act as **antecedent phrases** (*ante* = before), while **C** functions as a **consequent phrase** (*sequent* = following). As in a sentence, an antecedent phrase sets up a consequent phrase and the two together make a complete sentence.

Antecedent phrase 1	Antecedent phrase 2	Consequent phrase
If I'm still here tomorrow,	and if you're back,	I'll stop by your place.
Comma	*comma*	*Period*

Neither of the antecedent phrases here is complete: We expect each to continue. In Haydn's melody, neither the **A** nor the **B** phrase of the melody sounds complete because neither finishes on the tonic (home) note of the key. Phrases **A** and **B** both end on the note D, which creates a certain sense of arrival but not closure. These points of arrival are called **half cadences**: They create a moment of punctuation more like a comma than a period. But the melody of the **C** phrase ends on the main note of the tonic key (G) and, for that reason, we call it a **full cadence**, and we hear its arrival as a moment of closure.

PROFILE   Joseph Haydn (1732–1809)

Writing to Order

It's hard to imagine any individual having his or her own orchestra at home nowadays, but that's exactly what Prince Nicholas Esterházy had in his three different palaces throughout the Austrian Empire during the second half of the eighteenth century.

For almost three decades, Joseph Haydn was the prince's music director, responsible for writing new music, conducting the orchestra, and keeping order among the musicians, who could be a rowdy bunch at times. Fortunately for Haydn, Prince Nicholas (known far and wide as "The Magnificent") was willing to spend huge amounts of money on music, and Haydn was thus in charge of one of the best orchestras in all of Europe.

"My Prince was satisfied with all of my works," Haydn told one of his biographers late in life, "and I received applause. As the director of an orchestra, I could make experiments, observe what elicited or weakened an impression, and thus correct, add, delete, take risks. I was cut off from the world, no one in my vicinity could cause me to doubt myself or pester me, and so I had to become original." Haydn wrote whatever works the prince requested: string quartets, operas, sonatas. In fact, his original contract required him to appear in uniform every morning before the prince and receive instructions as to what kinds of works he was to compose.

The death of Prince Nicholas in 1790 opened a new chapter in Haydn's life. He made two extended tours to England, where he composed symphonies, songs, and a number of works for piano. After returning to Vienna for good in 1795,

Joseph Haydn, in a portrait done during his years in London in the 1790s.

he produced two highly successful oratorios (*The Creation* and *The Seasons*), a handful of Masses, and several of his finest string quartets. The young Ludwig van Beethoven was one of his last composition pupils.

EXPAND YOUR PLAYLIST: HAYDN

- String Quartet in E♭, op. 33, no. 2 (nicknamed "The Joke" because of its comical ending)
- String Quartet in D Major, op. 76, no. 5
- Piano Sonata in E♭ Major, Hob. XVI: 52
- *The Creation*. An oratorio based on the book of Genesis; the opening is a purely instrumental representation of Chaos.

Music is often used in ways its composers could never imagine. **Musical appropriation** is the use or adaptation of a work to serve something other than its original purpose. The melody Haydn wrote in honor of Emperor Franz II became so popular that many different poets set new words to it:

- One text praised the people of Hamburg.
- Several praised rulers other than Franz II.
- Another text (in Latin) came from the Book of Psalms.
- Several other texts praised God.

The most famous of all the new texts, though, was "Germany Above All Else" ("Deutschland über alles"), written in 1841 by German poet August Heinrich Hoffmann von Fallersleben. This song would eventually become the German national anthem, though only the third strophe is used today.

A work setting new words to an established melody is known as a **contrafactum**. Nothing prevents any person or institution—a political party, a nation, a church—from appropriating an existing melody, often in ways that are quite different from the purpose of the original. (Whether that reuse is legal or not is a different matter altogether.) Often new lyrics turn the original song on its head. The British national anthem, "God Save the King," provided the melody for "My Country, 'tis of Thee," one of the most popular of all patriotic songs in the breakaway colonies of North America. The tune now known as "The Star-Spangled Banner" first accompanied a text that was originally a drinking song.

This kind of phrase structure, with antecedent and consequent units that together make a larger whole, is called **periodic phrase structure**. The term "periodic" comes from the Latin word for sentence (*periodus*), named after the mark of punctuation that indicates the end of a sentence. This terminology reflects the parallels between verbal and musical "sentences." Periodic phrase structure provides the basis for many melodies from different eras of music, but it is particularly associated with music of the Classical Era.

Theme and Variations Form

Theme and variations form was an extremely popular musical form throughout the Classical Era and indeed is found in musical cultures throughout the world (see Chapter 23). It is basically a simple structure: A theme is presented and then altered in some way—through harmony, melody, texture, dynamics, or some combination of these—in a succession of individual variations.

Composers often used well-known themes as the basis of new variations. Mozart, for example, wrote a set of variations on the French song "Ah, vous dirai-je, maman" (better known as "Twinkle, Twinkle, Little Star"; see Expand Your Playlist), and Beethoven later wrote a set on the melody to "God Save the King" (better known in the United States as "My Country, 'tis of Thee").

Haydn's unusual move—to keep the theme almost completely intact in each variation, altering only its register (the instrument) and changing the other three voices around the theme—takes on symbolic significance when one considers that the theme began as a birthday melody celebrating his emperor. The constancy of the melody can be heard as a portrait of the constancy of Emperor Franz. Circumstances around him may change, the music seems to say, but the emperor himself remains unchanged.

Now listen to this movement again, using the Listening Guide.

CONNECT YOUR PLAYLIST

Musical Appropriation

Find a work that has been appropriated for a purpose quite different from that for which it was originally created.

Example: Aretha Franklin, "Respect" (1967)
Franklin transformed this Otis Redding song into a feminist anthem by flipping traditional gender roles.

Listening Guide

Joseph Haydn Composed 1797
String Quartet in C Major, op. 76, no. 3, second movement (6:46)

Time	🏛 Formal Section	🎵 Melodic Phrases	〰 Timbre
0:00	Theme	A (0:00) A (0:15) B (0:30) C (0:47) C (1:02)	Theme in the first violin
1:18	Variation 1	A (1:18) A (1:32) B (1:45) C (1:59) C (2:12)	Theme in the second violin
2:27	Variation 2	A (2:27) A (2:42) B (2:57) C (3:13) C (3:29)	Theme in the cello
3:45	Variation 3	A (3:45) A (3:59) B (4:14) C (4:28) C (4:42)	Theme in the viola
4:58	Variation 4	A (4:58) A (5:14) Theme now in a higher range from here to the end of this variation B (5:30) C (5:46) C (6:01)	Theme in the first violin
6:15	Coda	Concluding passage	Material from the theme in first violin

Texture

Homophonic. Hymnlike, with all four voices moving at the same speed.

Homophonic. The first violin plays a rapid accompanimental figure, while the lower voices (viola and cello) are silent.

Polyphonic. The other three voices are playing lines that have distinctive profiles of their own and are not merely accompanimental.

Polyphonic. As in Variation 2, the other three instruments play lines that have distinctive profiles of their own and are not merely accompanimental.

Polyphonic. Same as in Variations 2 and 3.

Q Student FAQs

I can't always tell the difference among the four instruments. The cello in Variation 2 and the viola in Variation 3 sound almost the same. Is this a problem?

The three kinds of instruments used in a string quartet all overlap to some degree. So a cello, like the one pictured here, playing in a high range is in fact playing some of the same pitches as a viola, and a viola in its high range covers many of the notes available on the lower end of the violin's range. There is a difference in the quality of sound of the instruments, however, and it is worth listening closely for this difference. If you are able to experience a live performance of this work, or at least watch the video of the live performance included in this chapter, you will see that the visual cues help reinforce the individual qualities of the instruments.

Without a conductor, who leads the quartet in performance?

As any string player will tell you, playing in a quartet is very different from playing in an orchestra. A quartet is a collaborative enterprise: The players discuss and agree among themselves in rehearsal about such matters as tempo, phrasing, and dynamics. In performance, the first violinist, such as the one pictured on page 180, gives subtle indications to lead the other players, often through a glance, a raised eyebrow, or a slight gesture of the head. But at times other players might give such signals, depending on which instrument leads at any given moment. The longer a group has performed together, the better the individual members know one another's manner of playing, and the more subtle the gestures.

EXPAND YOUR PLAYLIST

Chamber Music and Solo Keyboard Music of the Classical Era

The second half of the eighteenth century witnessed a tremendous growth in amateur music making at home. New printing technologies had reduced the cost of sheet music, and the fortepiano (a new instrument, the forerunner of the modern-day piano) was less expensive than the harpsichord (the principal domestic keyboard instrument of the Baroque Era). The string quartet was one of several genres intended primarily for use in the home.

Joseph Haydn

- String Quartet in E♭ Major, op. 76, no. 6. The first movement is a set of variations on a theme.
- Piano Trio in G Major, Hob. XV: 25. The piano trio is an ensemble consisting of a piano, a violin, and a cello.

Wolfgang Amadeus Mozart

- String Quartet in C Major, K. 456. The slow introduction to the first movement has so many clashing sounds that the entire quartet is known as the "Dissonance" Quartet.
- String Quartet in D Major, K. 575. One of three quartets Mozart wrote for the king of Prussia, who was a cellist, this work includes an unusually prominent cello part.
- Variations on "Ah vous dirai-je, maman," K. 265. A set of variations for piano on the tune known as "Twinkle, Twinkle, Little Star."

- Piano Sonata in A Major, K. 331. The finale is "alla Turca" ("in the Turkish style"), imitating what Mozart and others of his time thought music from the Ottoman Empire sounded like.

Carl Philipp Emanuel Bach

- Fantasia in C Minor, H. 75. A fantasia is a work that follows no formal conventions, guided only by the composer's fantasy. A writer set the words of Hamlet's celebrated monologue "To be or not to be . . . " to this fantasia. C. P. E. Bach (1714–1788) was one of several of Johann Sebastian Bach's sons who had distinguished musical careers.

Johann Christian Bach

- Keyboard Sonata in D Major, op. 5, no. 2. The young Mozart liked this solo sonata (which could be played on harpsichord or piano) so well that he rearranged it as a piano concerto. J. C. Bach (1735–1782), another son of J. S. Bach, was known as the "London Bach" because he lived there for so long.

Master Musicians of the Ikuta-ryu

Cherry Blossom

Recorded: ca. 1965

23

GLOBAL CONNECTION: THEME AND VARIATIONS FORM

A theme followed by a series of variations is a basic musical form used in cultures throughout the world. In *Cherry Blossom* the koto, a plucked stringed instrument from Japan, plays a Japanese folk melody that provides the basis for a series of six variations.

Listen to This First

◍ Timbre

Listen for the variety of sounds produced by different plucking and strumming techniques. ∎

♬ Melody

Listen to the three different sections of the melody and to the direction in which each moves. ∎

▥ Form

Identify the melody when it enters, then listen for the ways it is varied throughout the piece. ∎

◍ Texture

Listen to the way the texture changes from homophonic to polyphonic in the middle of the piece, and then back again to homophonic. ∎

The koto is a plucked zither with 13 silk strings stretched over its wooden board. The strings of the **koto** are tightly stretched across the board and are supported by 13 movable bridges that are adjusted during tuning. The player wears three ivory *plectra* (picks) on the right thumb and first two fingers for plucking the strings. Traditionally, players used the left hand to the left of the bridge to press a string to raise its pitch and, conversely, to pull a string to lower its pitch. In the modern technique used in this chapter's performance of *Cherry Blossom*, the player's left hand plucks in alternation with the right hand to execute rapid passages.

Koto music originated in the Japanese court as early as the eighth century, when a variety of instruments were brought there from the Korean peninsula. Early koto music does not survive because it was an **oral tradition**; that is, it was learned and transmitted without the aid of written notation. The koto was used for the private entertainment of the nobles, and it was also integrated with other court instruments for ceremonies.

During Japan's Edo Period and the reign of the Tokugawa Shoguns (Japanese rulers), from 1603 to 1867, the theme and variations form became well developed in this part of the world. This period happens to coincide in part with the era in which Joseph Haydn wrote his String Quartet in C Major, op. 76, no. 3 (which we discussed in Chapter 22), though there is no evidence of influence in either direction. Cultural and commercial contacts between Japan and the Western world were extremely limited at this time. What this similarity of musical forms demonstrates, instead, is the ways in which different cultures have applied similar means to achieve very different musical ends.

LEARNING OBJECTIVES

23.1 Listen for the structural principle of varying a theme as basic to the music of many cultures throughout the world.

23.2 Discuss the koto as an instrument.

23.3 Describe the extramusical connotations in *Cherry Blossom*.

23.4 Listen for the pentatonic melody in *Cherry Blossom* and its variations.

23.5 Describe the life of a geisha.

23.6 Locate other examples of zither-like instruments from around the world.

The koto originated in the region that includes what is now Japan and Korea.

Through the centuries, koto masters have often been women, many of them geisha—"geisha" translates literally as "arts person" (see "Historical Context: Geisha in Japanese Life"). The koto is now used in ensembles and for vocal accompaniment as well as for solo works such as *Cherry Blossom*. Modern Japanese composers still compose for it.

The Timbre of the Koto

The focused, penetrating sound of the koto comes from the tension of its strings, which produce few overtone partials and thus a very "pure" sound. As we saw in the Elements section under "Timbre," partials are frequencies that resonate with the fundamental sound wave to create a richer quality of sound. Western violins and acoustic guitars, for example, produce more partials than the koto and have a correspondingly fuller tone. The characteristically tense timbre of the koto is highly valued within traditional Japanese musical culture, and a similar tone may also be heard in Japanese vocal music. The use of **tremolo** in *Cherry Blossom* adds to this sense of tension. The term means "trembling" in Italian and refers to the rapid back-and-forth plucking of a single note that gives it a shimmering or even shivering quality.

This close-up of a koto shows the strings stretched across its soundboard. They are held by 13 footed bridges that can be moved to change the tuning of the instrument.

Melody: The Wilt of Sorrow

The main melody of *Cherry Blossom* divides into three subunits (labeled "A," "B," and "C" in the Listening Guide). The melody, known as *sakura* ("cherry blossom") is a popular Japanese folk tune with a sad sentiment; cherry blossoms are beautiful but short lived, and the Japanese perceive this as sorrowful. The variations on *Cherry Blossom* portray the successive stages of blossoming and wilting. In a broader sense, they symbolize the human life cycle. Like the *Cherry Blossom* variations, many Japanese melodies have **extramusical** connotations, which means that the music refers to ideas (such as a dying flower) beyond the realm of sound. This is in some ways similar to the concept of program music in Western music (see Chapter 17). The piece is shaped by its relationship to the title, and a title may be associated with an idea, story, or event. A listener may choose to listen to the piece with or without the extramusical idea in mind.

On this recorded example of *Cherry Blossom*, the master musician first plucks through a short section devoted to testing and tuning the instrument's strings. This tuning is considered part of the performance, and it serves as a prelude. After this short prelude, the musician introduces the *Cherry Blossom* melody. It is in the *in* mode, a particularly sorrowful-sounding Japanese tonal sequence similar to the European minor mode. The *in* mode consists of five tones. Five-tone modes, also known as **pentatonic scales**, have long appeared in Asian music and in the folk music of Europe and the Americas, but were not taken up by Western classical composers until the nineteenth century. To hear what one kind of pentatonic scale sounds like, play only the black keys on a piano up or down.

Theme and Variations Form

Cherry Blossom is an example of **theme and variations form**. After the theme is played, the master koto musician then performs six variations on it, all with different plucking and strumming techniques that create rhythmic and timbral variety. Before the final variation, the koto master performs an improvisation around the theme's phrases, A, B, and C. The variations are learned by rote, but the improvised section is freely played from the musician's inner creativity, which is part of what goes into being a master.

Textural Variety on the Koto

Although this work is performed by only one musician, the technique of right- and left-hand alternation results in the performance sounding as though it were played by two musicians, sometimes homophonic and other times polyphonic. The right hand steadily plays the theme's phrases each time they occur, while the left hand creates variations around them.

Now listen to this piece again, using the Listening Guide.

CONNECT YOUR PLAYLIST

Theme and Variations

Find a piece that contains a melodic theme followed by a series of variations.

Example: Jerry Lee Lewis, "Good Golly, Miss Molly" (1964) Each successive statement of the theme is varied.

Listening Guide

Master Musicians of the Ikuta-ryu Recorded: ca. 1965
Cherry Blossom (3:08)

Time	🏛 Form: Section	🎵 Melody	〰 Timbre
0:00	Tuning Prelude	Introduction	Penetrating and focused tones plucked melodically throughout the instrument's range.
0:19	Theme	A (0:18) B (0:23) C (0:28) B (0:32) C (0:37) A (0:40) Ending (0:46)	Theme plucked by the right hand; the accompaniment is plucked by the left hand.
0:52	Variation 1	A (0:51) B (0:56) C (1:01)	The right hand plucks the theme in three-note rhythmic groupings.
1:06	Variation 2	A (1:05) B (1:10) C (1:14)	Rapid left-hand variation.
1:20	Variation 3	B (1:19) C (1:24) Slight pause before next variation (1:28)	
1:30	Variation 4	A (1:29) B (1:36) C (1:43)	Theme played slowly, with right-hand tremolo, which creates a "shivering" effect.
1:50	Variation 5	A (1:49) B (1:56)	Theme with more rapid tremolo, further intensifying the "shivering" effect. There is then an adjusted tuning, giving a different timbre to those changed tones.
2:08	Improvisation	Through-composed variations on fragments of the theme.	The musician plucks with extreme speed.
2:33	Variation 6	A (2:31) B (2:34) C (2:37) A (2:40) B (2:43) C (2:46) A (2:49) B (2:52)	Theme played with extreme speed. Each repetition of the theme is faster.

Texture

Monophonic. Strings are individually tested and tuned by both hands in alternation.

Homophonic.

Homophonic.

Polyphonic. The left-hand variation is independent.

Polyphonic. The left-hand variation is in triplets, rhythmic groupings of three.

Homophonic.

Homophonic. The left hand continues to strum in accompaniment to the theme.

Homophonic.

Homophonic.

Q Student FAQs

Why does Japanese music sound foreign to me?

Like other forms of world music, Japanese music uses a "gapped" scale; instead of having seven notes, typically Japanese scales have only five notes. (These are also called pentatonic scales.) Western ears are used to hearing melodies based on seven tones, and so these missing notes—or gaps—can make the music sound odd or foreign to us.

Why is the koto so soft compared to Western string instruments?

The koto's strings are made of silk, while the strings on many modern violins are made of a synthetic material such as nylon or steel. The silk strings are also at a lower tension than violin strings, so they don't vibrate as efficiently. The koto soundboard is a simple, slightly arched board that does little to amplify the vibrations of the strings, whereas the violin's sound chamber—the inside of the instrument's body—is very efficient at amplifying the sound of its strings (see "Closer Look: The Violin," Chapter 17). All these factors combine to make the sound produced by the koto very soft. Because the koto was designed to be played in small rooms or with only a few other instruments, there was no need for it to be louder. In modern concert halls, the koto's sound is usually amplified by a microphone.

The stereotyped image of the geisha as a paid companion who caters to the whims of her male patrons is—like many stereotypes—only partially true. In fact, geisha are more like paid performers than they are servants or—as commonly believed—prostitutes. Geisha are paid for their accomplishments as musicians, dancers, and experts in the tea ceremonies and other ceremonial practices enjoyed by their clients.

To become geisha, young girls were often sold into a kind of indentured service by their parents. They went through rigorous training that took years to complete. The final part of this training focused on the traditional arts, and many geisha became renowned for their talents at playing traditional instruments, including the koto or *shamisen* (a kind of plucked lute), and singing and dancing.

Geisha must be single. They often have a sole patron who supports them by underwriting their education, clothing, and other expenses. However, the relationship is not necessarily sexual. A geisha must retire if she marries, and many retired geisha become music and dance teachers. Arthur Golden's *Memoirs of a Geisha*, published in 2005, provides a sensitive portrait of a geisha.

Two women playing the koto. The long-bodied zither is placed either on a table or directly on the floor. The movable bridges regulate the tuning of the strings.

 EXPAND YOUR PLAYLIST

Zither-Dee-Dee

The koto is one type of zither; various other types are found around the world.

Japan

- Nanae Yoshimura. *The Art of the Koto, Vol. 1.* Celestial Harmonies B00004X0T4.
  This is the first of five CDs showing the development of koto music from the seventeenth century to today.

- Satomi Saeki, koto, and Alcvin Takegawa Ramos, shakuhaci. *Japanese Traditional Koto and Shakuhachi Music.* Oliver Sudden Productions B000CQNIHY.
  Traditional pieces played on the low-voiced Japanese flute (shakuhachi) and koto.

China

- Zhiming Han on yangqin and Hsinmei (Cynthia) Hsiang on zheng (Chinese zither). *Celestial Echo: Live Performance on Yangqin—Chinese Butterfly Harp and Zheng.* Plectrum Recordings B000W1MJV0.
  Duets on the Chinese hammer dulcimer (or yangqin) and the zheng (a long zither, similar to the Japanese koto).

Austria

- *Anton Karas: First Man of the Zither.* Jasmine Music B00006J9M2. Played on the Austrian zither, Karas's famous theme for the 1949 thriller *The Third Man*, starring Joseph Cotton and Orson Welles, was a top pop hit in its day..

United States

- *Dulcimer World: Kevin Roth.* Star Gazer Productions B000CAKC3I. A selection of popular and traditional melodies played on a range of Appalachian dulcimers.

Joseph Haydn

Symphony no. 102 in B♭ Major, third and fourth movements

Composed: 1795

The third and fourth movements of Haydn's Symphony no. 102 are part of a four-movement symphony written for a concert series in London in 1795. The thlrd movement is a minuet, a stylized dance movement, while the fourth movement is a rondo, a rollicking finale to the symphony as a whole.

Listen to This First

Timbre

Listen for the breadth of sound from the full orchestra: many strings (first and second violins, violas, cellos, double basses), winds (flutes, oboes, bassoons), brass (horns and trumpets), and percussion (timpani, also known as "kettledrums"). ■

Dynamics

Listen for the frequent changes in dynamics between very loud and very soft. ■

Form

Listen for the return of the opening idea in each movement. ■

Listeners hear music against the backdrop of their times. In the middle of World War II, audiences in the United States rejected Igor Stravinsky's unusual harmonization of "The Star-Spangled Banner" for orchestra. Twenty-five years later, during the Vietnam War, listeners at Woodstock embraced Jimi Hendrix's jarring, distorted rendition of the melody on the electric guitar.

The backdrop in London 1795 was revolution and its aftermath. Among the audience at the premiere of Haydn's Symphony no. 102 in B♭ Major were French aristocrats who had only recently fled the bloody Reign of Terror that followed the French Revolution. The English press and public were now debating at length how to reconcile the three goals of the French Revolution: "liberty and equality"—personal freedom and democracy—with "fraternity," the need for social order.

Some in Haydn's audience heard this social ideal realized in the sound of this **symphony**. A large number of varied instruments—strings, winds, percussion—contributed uniquely and in equal measure to an all-encompassing harmony. It was a mirror of the ideal society. And unlike chamber music works such as the string quartet, played in small spaces and private homes, the symphony brought large numbers of the public together to hear music give voice to their personal and collective aspirations.

Haydn's London audiences could not get enough of his symphonies. By the time he had finished his two extended visits to the English capital (1791–1792, 1794–1795), he had written 12 altogether. Each of these "London" symphonies follows a standard pattern of four movements, along the lines of the typical string quartet (see Chapter 22).

LEARNING OBJECTIVES

24.1 Discuss the social setting in which Joseph Haydn's "London" symphonies were first performed in the 1790s.

24.2 Listen for the use of dynamics in the third movement of Haydn's Symphony no. 102.

24.3 Define the terms *symphony*, *minuet*, and *rondo*.

24.4 Recognize the use of rounded binary form in the minuet.

24.5 Listen for the contrasting formal section used in both the third and fourth movements of Haydn's Symphony.

24.6 Describe the makeup for a chamber orchestra.

24.7 Describe Haydn's reactions to being in London.

24.8 Discuss concert manners in the Classical Era.

1. *First movement:* A substantial movement in a fast tempo, usually in what is known as *sonata form* (we discuss this form in Chapter 25).
2. *Second movement:* Another substantial movement, but in a slow tempo and in a contrasting key. Slow movements assume many different forms: sonata form, theme and variations, and **ABA** are the most common.
3. *Third movement:* A minuet, a lively, stylized dance in triple meter, in the tonic key and in the pattern ABA. The third movement we are listening to follows this form.
4. *Fourth movement:* A somewhat lighter and often very fast movement. The most common forms used in the finale are sonata form and rondo. The finale of Haydn's Symphony no. 102 is a rondo.

The Timbre of the Full Orchestra

The size of an orchestra performing a symphony can vary widely, depending on the composer's instructions, the availability of players, and the size of the concert hall. In Haydn's time, a large orchestra would have consisted of strings (about 8–10 first violins, 6–8 second violins, 4–6 violas, 3–4 cellos, and 2 double basses), winds (2 flutes, 2 oboes, 2 bassoons, 2 trumpets, and 2 horns), and percussion (timpani, also known as "kettledrums"). (See "Closer Look: The Chamber Orchestra.") Listen to the ways in which these various instruments and groups of instruments combine and contrast with one another. Haydn uses the full orchestra judiciously. We hear all the instruments playing together at times, but more often we hear smaller groups of instruments: just the strings, or just the winds, or just the winds and percussion. The variety of sound available from the possible combinations is enormous.

The Dynamics of Surprise

Changes in dynamics can help guide our listening. The entire middle section ("trio") of the third movement of Symphony no. 102, for example, is played softly, which helps set it off against the two mostly loud outer sections. Whether we realize it or not, we also have certain expectations about dynamics. When we hear a very soft passage for a long stretch, we begin to anticipate the music getting loud again. Haydn always obliges, but not always in the ways we expect. Sometimes the music stays unusually soft for much longer than we think it will, such as at the very beginning of the finale (the fourth movement). When the full orchestra comes in, after almost a whole minute, we feel a sense that what we have long anticipated has at last arrived.

While the full orchestra often plays at a very loud volume, as might be expected, dynamics operate independently of the number or combination of the instruments that happen to be playing. Even a large number of instruments playing together can create a soft sound.

(1) Third Movement: Minuet

The minuet is a courtly, elegant dance, although it often assumes a playful character in Haydn's hands. Like all minuets, this one is in triple meter, with an accent on the first beat of each measure (**1**-2-3, **1**-2-3, etc.).

CONNECT YOUR PLAYLIST

Dynamics

Find a piece that makes use of sharply contrasting dynamics.

Example: Radiohead, "Paranoid Android" (1997)
This song makes dramatic shifts between loud and soft at several points.

Minuet Form

In **minuet form**, the opening section, known as the minuet proper (**A**), is followed by a contrasting trio (**B**), which is followed by a repeat of the minuet proper, thus creating the pattern **ABA**. This structure is called **ternary form**.

A: The minuet proper

- This section of the minuet is in **binary form**. It is called "binary" because it consists of two sections, each of which is repeated in performance.
- About halfway through the second section, the opening idea returns in the tonic key, "rounding out" the form. This creates what is known as **rounded binary form**.

B: The trio

- This is also in rounded binary form (two sections, with a return of the opening idea about halfway through the second section).
- The trio provides a contrasting theme and mood to the minuet proper.
- At the end of the trio stands the Italian phrase *da capo*, meaning literally "from the head," or as we would say more colloquially in English, "from the top" or "from the beginning." This indicates that the orchestra is to play the minuet proper again.

A: The return of the minuet proper

- The performers return to the beginning, and the movement as a whole ends with the end of the minuet proper (the **A** section).
- Many modern-day ensembles omit the repetition of these sections the second time around.

    To summarize, minuet form is a ternary form (**ABA**) whose individual units (**A** and **B**) are each in binary form. This structural pattern was used frequently in the Classical Era, throughout the nineteenth century, and even into the twentieth.

(2) Fourth Movement: Finale

The last movement of Haydn's Symphony no. 102—its **finale**—is lighter in tone than the other movements, a "happy ending" to the cycle of the work's four movements. In this respect, it is very typical of the symphonic finale in the Classical Era. Haydn, Mozart, and other composers of the time liked to use the rondo form in the finale of symphonies and other multimovement works (sonatas, string quartets, etc.) because rondos are jaunty and bright, and their principal melodies are often quite catchy.

The Composer Speaks　Haydn in London

Written a week after Haydn arrived in England, this fascinating letter was addressed to Maria Anna von Genzinger, a talented pianist who lived in Vienna. It reminds us of the physical and emotional distance the composer had traveled from his native Austria. When Haydn arrived in London, he was already a celebrity. He granted interviews to three newspapers and received invitations to dine at the highest levels of English society. Only a few months before, he had been going about his daily routine in remote Esterháza, his patrons' palace in the Hungarian countryside.

Haydn's journey to London took more than two weeks.

66My arrival caused a great sensation throughout the entire city. I was carted around to all the newspapers for three straight days. Everyone wants to meet me. I have had to dine out six times already, and if I wanted to, I could accept invitations for every day. But I have to think first of all about my health and also about my work. . . . I have charming, comfortable, but very expensive lodgings. My landlord is Italian, and also a cook, and he prepares four good meals for me every day. Not including wine and beer, it costs 1 florin and 30 kroner daily, but everything is shockingly expensive here.

Yesterday I was invited to a concert [of the Academy of Ancient Music], but I got there a bit late. . . . I was not allowed in but was taken instead to a small room, where I had to wait. . . . Finally the door opened, and I was led by the impresario through the middle of the concert hall to general applause, up to the front of the orchestra pit, where I was showered with a string of English compliments, everyone staring at me all the while. I was assured that this honor had not been bestowed on anyone in the past fifty years.

After the concert I was led into another adjacent hall, where a table had been laid for more than 200 persons. . . . I was told I must sit at the head of it. But I had already eaten out that day, and had eaten more than usual. So I declined this honor and said that I was not feeling entirely well. I nevertheless had to drink to the harmonious health of all those present with Burgundy [wine], and they had to reciprocate. At that point, I was allowed to be taken home.99

Source: Joseph Haydn, Letter to Maria Anna von Genzinger, January 1791; translated by Mark Evan Bonds.

Rondo Form

In **rondo form**, an opening theme (**A**) returns repeatedly over the course of the movement, interspersed with contrasting ideas (**B**, **C**, etc.). In this instance, the pattern is **ABACADACA**. In Italian, a *rondo* is a "round dance," in which any one dancer in a circle of dancers repeatedly moves away from his or her starting point and then returns to it. In a similar fashion, the musical form of the rondo keeps moving away from and returning to its opening idea (**A**).

The main theme (**A**) of a rondo is typically brief and simple, which makes it that much easier to recognize when it returns. The main theme of this particular rondo is almost instantly recognizable because of the distinctive rhythm of its opening (da-da-DUM).

From the listener's perspective, rondos are easy to follow—no matter how intricate the music might be at any given point, even the most casual listener can anticipate and recognize the return of the opening theme. But rondos are not always so simple underneath the surface. Haydn (and later, Beethoven) liked to play with listeners' expectations of the form. In the finale of Symphony no. 102, Haydn repeatedly teases the listener into thinking that the opening theme is about to return, only to deflect (or delay, at least temporarily) this return. The net result is a movement that is at once simple and sophisticated.

Now listen to the third and fourth movements of this symphony again, using the Listening Guide.

HISTORICAL CONTEXT   Concerts and Concert Manners in the Classical Era

Concerts in Haydn's time were far longer than today, with many of them lasting four hours or more. On the other hand, audience members were not expected to sit as still and silent as statues through the entire performance. As in the Baroque Era, sizeable portions of the audience socialized during concerts and felt free to converse even while the music was being played.

Audiences were also much more open about expressing their reactions to performances, both favorable and unfavorable. Composers could always tell which portion of a particular symphony or concerto an audience liked best, because listeners clapped immediately. Sometimes a movement would even be encored in its entirety.

Contemporary accounts tell us that eighteenth-century audiences could burst into applause even *while* the music was playing—much as what occurs today after a jazz solo, for example. Mozart once described in a letter to his father how he had counted on this custom while composing the finale of one of his symphonies:

> Having observed that all finales as well as opening Allegros begin here [in Paris] with all the instruments playing together and generally in unison, I began mine with two violins only, *piano* [softly] for the first eight measures, followed instantly by a *forte* [loud outburst]. The audience, as I expected, said "hush" at the soft beginning, and when they heard the *forte*, began at once to clap their hands. [Letter of 3 July 1778]

In short, concert manners in the late eighteenth century were rather more like concert manners at a rock or jazz concert today. The gap between "serious" art and "popular" entertainment was not nearly as wide in Haydn's time as it is today.

CLOSER LOOK   The Chamber Orchestra

What counted for a large orchestra in Joseph Haydn's time is relatively small by modern standards. Today we call an ensemble that would have been used to perform a work like Haydn's Symphony No. 102 a **chamber orchestra.**There are no standard numbers of instruments or players for a chamber orchestra: Four of the twelve symphonies Haydn wrote call for clarinets, for example, while eight of them (including Symphony No. 102) do not. The Chamber Orchestra of Europe, pictured here, reflects the approximate size and makeup of the orchestra that first performed Haydn's Symphony No. 102 in 1795.

Conductor

Double basses (3) The largest of the string instruments, the **double basses** sound exactly one octave lower than the cellos. In Haydn's time, they usually doubled the line being played by the cellos, giving additional richness and color to the bottom end of the orchestral register.

Cellos (5) The **cellos** typically provide the harmonic underpinning for other melodic instruments (such as the violins or woodwinds), but they can carry the principal melody on their own as well.

Timpani (1) The **timpani** ("kettledrum") was often the only percussion instrument in the orchestras of Haydn's time. The pitch of each drum is controlled by tightening or loosening the pressure on the surface of the drumhead. In earlier times, the drumhead surface was made of dried animal skin. It is now made of a synthetic material.

Violas (6) In orchestral music of the Classic Era, the **violas** rarely came to the fore with an independent melodic line of their own. Instead, they supplied the important inner lines between the higher violins and the lower cellos and double basses.

Trumpets (2) The brightest and most penetrating of the brass instruments, the **trumpet** began as a valveless instrument but later acquired a mechanism so performers could play a wider range of notes more readily.

Bassoons (2) The **bassoon** is the lowest of the woodwinds. This double-reed instrument often doubles or plays the same notes as the cellos or double basses, though it can also carry the principal melody on its own.

First violins (12) Violins are divided into two sections, first and second. The **first violins** are usually larger in number because they carry the principal melodic line most often. The leader of this section, called the concertmaster or concertmistress, is the "lead player" not only within this group, but for the orchestra as a whole. In some ensembles the concertmaster doubles as the conductor, leading the performance from his or her seat while playing.

Second violins (8) The **second violins** sometimes double the first violins—playing exactly the same line—but more often complement them, enriching the harmony or adding a different contrapuntal line.

Flutes (2) The highest of the woodwinds, **flutes** were made of wood in Haydn's time but have more recently been constructed from metal, as shown here. The timbre of the metal is slightly different, but the range is the same.

Oboes (4) A double-reed instrument, the **oboe** is often regarded as the woodwind instrument that most closely resembles the human voice. It is particularly adept at projecting a lyrical, "singing" line that can stand out through the orchestra as a whole.

Horns (3) Sometimes called "French" horns, these instruments evolved out of the early hunting horn. In Haydn's time, the natural (valveless) horn was the norm. The musicians here hold valved instruments, which emerged during the first half of the nineteenth century and made it easier for players to negotiate a wider range of notes.

Listening Guide 🔊

Joseph Haydn Composed: 1795

Symphony no. 102 in B♭ Major,
(1) third movement: Minuet (4:46)

Time	🏛 Form	Subsection	〰 Timbre	▦ Dynamics
0:00	A (minuet proper)	First section: Melody is very disjunct.	Full orchestra: The melody is primarily in the first violins.	Frequent alternations between loud and soft.
0:20		Repeat of first section.		
0:39		Second section: begins with three low notes, tossed from cellos and basses to violas, up to the violins; opening idea of minuet returns at 0:56.		
1:27		Repeat of second section; opening idea of minuet returns at 1:44.		
2:16	B ("trio")	First section: melody more lyrical, mostly conjunct.	Reduced orchestra: Trumpets and timpani are silent throughout. The melody is carried primarily by the winds (oboes and bassoons).	Entirely soft.
2:32		Repeat of first section.		
2:48		Second section, with return of the B section's opening idea at 2:56.		
3:12		Repeat of second section, with return of the B section's opening idea at 3:20. Section ends with the instruction "da capo," indicating that the orchestra returns to the beginning of the minuet.		
3:36	A (return of the minuet proper)	Return of first section of minuet proper (this recording does not repeat the first section here).	Full orchestra: The melody is primarily in first violins.	Frequent alternations between loud and soft.
3:55		Return of the second section of the minuet proper; opening idea returns at 4:12 (this recording does not repeat the second section here).		

Listening Guide

Joseph Haydn Composed: 1795

Symphony no. 102 in B♭ Major,
(2) fourth movement: Rondo (4:53)

Time	🏛 Form	🎵 Melody	〰 Timbre	🔊 Dynamics	👤 Harmony: Key Area
0:00	A (main theme)	Rapid stepwise motion.	Reduced orchestra (strings and woodwinds alone).	Soft	Tonic (B♭ major)
1:00	B	Wide leaps, dotted rhythms.	Full orchestra: Horns, trumpets, and timpani join in.	Loud	
1:26	A	Rapid stepwise motion.	Strings alone.	Soft	Not tonic (F major)
1:33	C	Meandering melody over a drone bass—a single note repeated over and over.	Full orchestra.	Loud/soft/loud; much contrast of dynamics within this section	
2:16	A	Rapid stepwise motion.	Strings and flute, then full orchestra (but softly, starting at 2:25), with back-and-forth between winds and timpani (high) and strings (low).	Soft	Tonic (B♭ major)
2:46	D	Leaping melody striding upward.	Full orchestra.	Loud	Tonic (but in minor mode—B♭ minor), then unstable (moves through various key areas)
3:25	A	Rapid stepwise motion; note how the theme is interrupted at 3:32.	Strings, alone, then winds join in.	Soft	Tonic (B♭ major)
3:40	C	Meandering melody over a drone bass.	Full orchestra.	Loud/soft/loud	
4:04	A	Rapid stepwise motion; note how Haydn plays with our expectations of how a piece should end.	Winds, then strings, then full orchestra.	Soft/loud	

 🔍 Student FAQs ⚙

Why is there no basso continuo in the orchestra?

Most performances of Haydn's later symphonies dispense with the basso continuo for the simple reason that it's not necessary: the voices are sufficiently full without it. Some ensembles do use a basso continuo, however, for there is evidence that Haydn himself conducted from the keyboard in London. Whether he actually played while sitting at the harpsichord or piano is not clear, but he did write a surprise solo passage for himself into the finale of his Symphony no. 98.

Why does the recording omit the repeats when playing the da capo portion of the minuet proper?

Listeners today tend to be less tolerant of literal repetition than their eighteenth-century counterparts. When all the repeats are observed, the minuet proper (that is, the opening two sections of the minuet movement, excluding the trio) is heard altogether four times. But repetition was basic to dance music, and Haydn's audiences would not have considered so many repeats unusual in any way.

EXPAND YOUR PLAYLIST

Haydn's Symphonies

Haydn wrote 106 symphonies, and each is distinctive. Here are some of the more famous:

Symphony no. 8 in G Major
- ("Evening/Le soir")
  The third of three programmatic symphonies depicting the times of day (no. 6 is Morning/Le matin; no. 7 is Noon/Le midi). Haydn wrote these works shortly after arriving at the Esterházy court, and he ingratiated himself with the leading members of the orchestra by giving them important solo passages. The evening concludes with a tempest, complete with lightning.

Symphony no. 45 in F# Minor
- ("Farewell")
  While the Esterházy castle was still under construction, the musicians had to live some distance away from their families for the whole of the summer. When the prince kept delaying his return to Eisenstadt, Haydn wrote a finale to remind him that the musicians longed to go home. In the finale of this symphony the players stop playing, one by one, and exit the stage so that at the end only two violinists are left. They, too, extinguish their candles and leave the stage.

Symphony no. 94 in G Major
- ("Surprise")
  "I wanted to create a sensation" was Haydn's explanation for the wholly unprepared and—yes—surprisingly loud chord near the beginning of the slow movement. Everyone remembered this effect, and the symphony received the nickname of "Surprise," which has stuck ever since.

Symphony no. 101 in D Major
- ("Clock")
  This work takes its nickname from the persistent tick-tock rhythm of the slow movement. It is one of the 12 (nos. 93–104) Haydn wrote for London audiences.

Wolfgang Amadeus Mozart

Symphony no. 40 in G Minor, K. 550, first movement

Composed: 1788

Mozart's Symphony no. 40 in G Minor is one of three symphonies that he wrote in Vienna in 1788, probably for a concert he organized himself, although no record of the event survives. The first movement, presented here, is full of dramatic contrasts. It is in sonata form, the most important structural convention to emerge from the Classical Era.

Listen to This First

Form

Listen for the repeated return of various themes over the course of this movement. Notice, too, the sharp contrast between the character of the themes. The opening is quietly agitated, but within less than a minute, we hear themes that are louder and brighter and still others that are softer and calmer. ■

👤 Harmony

Listen for the contrast between key areas early in this movement. The change in keys coincides with a change in mode: the opening theme is in the minor mode, the next main theme is in major. Which sounds darker? Which sounds brighter? Which mode predominates in this movement? ■

🎵 Melody

How would you characterize the themes of this movement? What makes them different from each other? ■

If we think of themes as different characters, we hear all the essential elements of a good drama in this movement: memorable personalities (melodies), conflict (the juxtaposition and transformation of those melodies), and resolution (the restoration of these melodies in their more-or-less original form). The events of this musical drama without words unfold in the same kind of logical sequence that we see in a three-act play presented on the stage:

- We meet the main character and the supporting characters (Act 1).
- We witness their interaction and transformation: They fall in or out of love, they fight, they search or struggle for something (Act 2).
- We experience some kind of resolution in the end: It may be a happy or an unhappy ending, or something in between, but we recognize it as an ending because all the strands of the plot are resolved (Act 3).

How does Mozart present this drama in purely musical terms? He organizes the first movement of this symphony around a musical structure known as **sonata form**, a form that was new in the Classical Era and that allowed for the presentation, development, and resolution of multiple themes within a single movement. From roughly 1750 to the present day, composers have written literally thousands of movements in sonata form, for it provides a versatile framework for creating a drama without words.

LEARNING OBJECTIVES

25.1 Discuss how the themes of a sonata-form movement function like characters.

25.2 Listen for and describe the basic features of sonata form, including exposition, development, recapitulation, and coda.

25.3 Listen for and identify the role of modulation to a new key and the return to the original key in a sonata-form movement.

25.4 Describe the ways in which sonata form creates a dramatic musical structure.

25.5 Listen for and recognize the parts of sonata form in Mozart's Symphony no. 40, first movement.

25.6 Outline Mozart's professional career.

25.7 Discuss Mozart's sister as a musician in eighteenth-century society.

Sonata Form

The three acts of a drama outlined previously correspond to the three parts of sonata form:

> Act 1: The **exposition** introduces us to—*exposes* us to—all the movement's thematic ideas. By the end of the exposition, we have met all the musical "characters."
>
> Act 2: The **development** is the middle part of a sonata-form movement, in which the thematic ideas are most intensively *developed*, both thematically and harmonically. Themes are taken apart, combined in different ways, and tried in different keys.
>
> Act 3: The **recapitulation** comes in the last third of the movement. The themes we heard in the exposition are *recapitulated* or *recapped*. This provides a resolution to all we have heard before.

Sonata form emerged around the middle of the eighteenth century as an expansion of a form already well established, **rounded binary form**. Rounded binary form consists of two sections in which the opening idea and the tonic key return simultaneously about a third of the way through the movement. (We saw this structure in the minuet of Haydn's Symphony no. 102, discussed in Chapter 24.) In sonata form, two important new elements are added:

1. The first section—the exposition—always modulates, presenting themes in a new, contrasting key area.
2. The theme(s) presented in the new key area in the exposition are repeated in the recapitulation *in the tonic*—that is, in the original key of the movement. This is what helps give a sense of resolution to any sonata-form movement.

Sonata form thus consists of three sections—exposition, development, and recapitulation—that are superimposed on a binary form. The exposition takes up the whole of the first binary section. The development and recapitulation both fall within the second binary section. Almost by definition, the second binary section is longer than the first, because it develops the themes *and* recapitulates them. Graphically, this form can be represented as follows:

Sonata Form

In practice, no two sonata-form movements are entirely alike. Sonata form is a broad and flexible scheme, and composers were extremely adept at manipulating it. There are, however, several predictable features that a listener can recognize:

- There is always a modulation from a primary to a secondary key area in the exposition.
- The first binary section (the exposition) is always repeated; the second binary section (the development and recapitulation) may or may not be repeated.

- The development moves through various keys other than the tonic and rarely settles on any one of them for very long. This section features bits and pieces of one or more earlier themes, transformed and combined in different ways.

- There is always a return to the primary key area (tonic) in the recapitulation, and it almost always coincides with the return to the opening idea in its original form. This is the onset of the recapitulation, and it is often a dramatic moment in a sonata-form movement. After the unpredictability and instability of the development, we are now finally back on familiar ground, both thematically (the opening idea) and harmonically (the tonic key).

- The sequence of themes in the recapitulation usually follows the sequence of themes as presented in the exposition.

- The recapitulation always stays in the tonic throughout.

The first movement of Mozart's Symphony no. 40 in G Minor follows the conventions of sonata form fairly closely:

- It opens with an exposition that modulates from the tonic of G minor to the contrasting key area of B♭ major. The contrast of mode between the **minor mode** (the tonic) and the **major mode** (the new key area) helps make the contrast between the two key areas more audible.

- The development is quite unstable harmonically, and it features an intense manipulation of the movement's opening theme.

- The onset of the recapitulation provides a strong and dramatic sense of return: The music comes back to the tonic, and the opening theme reappears more or less in its original guise.

- Later in the recapitulation, what had been heard outside the tonic in the exposition is now presented in the tonic: Again, the contrast of mode (B♭ major in the exposition, G minor in the recapitulation) makes the resolution easier to hear. What we heard in B♭ major in the exposition now returns in G minor, and the difference is striking.

The movement concludes with a brief **coda**. *Coda* is the Italian word for "tail," and it brings the movement to a close after the recapitulation. Codas stand outside of the sonata-form structure itself and may or may not be present in a sonata-form movement.

Harmony: Minor to Major

Harmony plays an important role in the sonata-form structure, as we have seen, and to sustain a musical argument across such a long span of time, Mozart uses different key areas to create variety. The **modulation** in this movement from the tonic to the new key area is particularly clear because it coincides with a change in mode. The first key area is G minor; the mood is dark and brooding. The new key area is B♭ major; here, the music sounds brighter and more optimistic. But when the themes presented in this new key area return in the recapitulation, they are played in G minor (the tonic), and now they, too, sound dark and brooding. It is as if all the melodies— all the "characters"—have finally come under the spell of the tonic, thereby creating a sense of resolution and closure.

CONNECT YOUR PLAYLIST

Modulation

Find a song that modulates.

Example: Johnny Cash, "I Walk the Line" (1956)
This song modulates with each new verse.

🎵 Contrasting Principal Melodies

The dramatic interest of this movement depends not just on forms and harmonies but also on the compelling and contrasting nature of the principal melodies. The music begins with an accompanimental figure in the low strings that sets both a mood (quietly agitated) and a mode (minor). When the first theme enters in the violin soon after, we hear many repetitions of a brief downward step. The melodic line sounds almost like a series of short sighs.

Theme 1

After an energetic transitional theme (labeled Theme 2 in the Listening Guide), we hear a strongly contrasting theme (labeled Theme 3) in the new key area of B♭ major. It consists of much longer notes, and the agitated accompanimental figure is no longer present. This, together with the major mode, creates a mood that is much calmer and relaxed.

Theme 3

Both themes are constructed around a series of antecedent (opening) and consequent (closing) phrases. But the opening theme stretches out over a much longer span of time. Even though it establishes the tonic key, the restlessness of this theme gives it a sense of constant forward motion. Theme 3 in the new key area, by contrast, moves in a slower rhythm and is much more regular and compact.

Throughout the development, Mozart dismantles and puts back together the opening theme and a portion of the transitional theme (Theme 2 in the Listening Guide). He varies them in multiple ways by presenting them in different keys and by giving them to different instruments

The Drama of Sonata Form

If sonata form can be thought of as a drama in three acts, perhaps there are dramas that can be thought of in terms of sonata form. The original movie version of *The Wizard of Oz*, for example, bears striking parallels. The chart below shows how scenes in the movie correspond to sections of sonata form. Think of the characters as themes and the places where the action occurs as the key areas. The black-and-white scenes at the beginning and end of the movie function as the exposition and recapitulation, respectively. We meet all the main characters of the story in two different places: first at home (the tonic key area)—Dorothy, Miss Gulch, and the three farmhands—and then, after Dorothy runs away from home (the transition) at Professor Marvel's caravan, which is near home (the secondary key area) but not too far away. In the "development"—the bulk of the movie, in color, which takes us through many different places (from Munchkinland, along the Yellow Brick Road, to Oz itself)—those same characters are transformed. At the end, even Professor Marvel, whom Dorothy had met away from home, drops by her house. He is the same person, but now he is in a different place, in Dorothy's home—in musical terms, her tonic key. It is a satisfying conclusion to the whole, in which the characters have all covered a great deal of ground but all return home.

Dorothy wakes up in her room toward the end of *The Wizard of Oz*. The characters from the black-and-white "exposition" (Professor Marvel and the three farmhands) who were transformed in the color "development" (into the Wizard of Oz, the Scarecrow, the Tin Woodsman, and the Cowardly Lion) are now reunited in the black-and-white "recapitulation" in their original form on Dorothy's home ground (the tonic or "home key" of the film).

Sonata Form	Musical "Drama"	*The Wizard of Oz*
EXPOSITION	The themes of the movement are "exposed" to us.	In the opening black-and-white section, we meet all the major characters of the story.
Tonic	Theme(s) are presented in the tonic, the "home" key.	Dorothy at home on her farm; we meet the farmhands and the dreaded Miss Gulch.
→ modulates to	→ modulates to	→ runs away from home
Secondary key area	A new theme or themes are presented in a key area that is not the tonic, away from the "home" key.	Away from home, Dorothy meets a new character, Professor Marvel.
DEVELOPMENT	Harmonically unstable. Themes are transformed so that they are different from how we first heard them, yet are recognizably the same.	The film turns to color, and all the characters are transformed: Miss Gulch has become the Wicked Witch of the West; the farmhands are now the Scarecrow, the Tin Woodsman, and the Lion; and Professor Marvel has turned into the Wizard of Oz.
RECAPITULATION	Return to the "home" key of the tonic. All themes heard in the exposition are now presented in the tonic.	Dorothy returns to her home in Kansas and the film returns to black and white. The characters of the opening scenes (even Professor Marvel, whom Dorothy had met away from home) all reappear in their original form and visit at her bedside.

or combinations of instruments. In this way, even though Mozart adheres to the conventions of sonata form, he manipulates its content in surprising and unusual ways.

Now listen to this movement again, using the Listening Guide.

Listening Guide

Wolfgang Amadeus Mozart Composed: 1788

Symphony no. 40 in G Minor, K. 550, first movement (8:10)

Time	🎹 Sonata Form	🎵 Melody
0:00	Exposition	1 = "Sighing" theme, repeated and then interrupted by the transitional theme.
0:33		2 = Transitional theme, sudden shift in dynamics (loud) and mode (major); ends with a rapid upward-moving, scale-like figure.
0:51		3 = Calm theme, divided between strings and winds.
1:28		4 = Very similar to opening theme, but now in the new key area and thus conveying a different mood.
2:02	Exposition Repeat	1 = "Sighing" theme.
2:35		2 = Transitional theme.
2:53		3 = Calm theme.
3:30		4 = Similar to opening theme, but in the new key area.
4:07	Development	1 = Opening theme, fragmented and harmonically unstable.
4:21		1 = Fragment of opening theme; highly contrapuntal passage, combining theme 1 with the rapid upward-moving scale-like figure from theme 2. Winds, high strings, and low strings present different ideas simultaneously.
4:49		1 = Opening theme fragmented and transformed still further. Beginning of a long passage leading back to the recapitulation.
5:23	Recapitulation	1 = Return of the opening theme in the tonic key, with slight alterations in the orchestration (notice the added bassoon part here).
5:54		2 = Transitional theme, but altered here in the recapitulation so as not to modulate.
6:36		3 = Same as theme 3 in exposition, but now in the tonic (G minor).
7:19		4 = Same as theme 4 in exposition, but now in the tonic (G minor).
7:43	Coda	1 = Sudden intensification, return of opening theme in tonic, with a full cadence to end the movement.

Harmony: Key Area

Tonic (G minor)

Modulating to

New key area (B♭ major)

Tonic (G minor)

Modulating to

New key area (B♭ major)

Unstable: moves through many different key areas, avoids tonic

Tonic (G minor)

Q Student FAQs

I don't hear the modulations within the sonata form. Is that a problem?

Everyone hears differently, but digital technology makes it easier to improve your ability to perceive changes in key. For this particular movement, try listening up to the point just before the recapitulation begins (at 5:25), then hit the button that takes you back to the very beginning of the entire movement and listen through the end of the exposition. What you will have heard, in effect, is a recapitulation that modulates and does not end in the tonic; the effect is quite different from the actual recapitulation, which stays in the tonic throughout.

What are some other examples of modulation?

Modulation—moving from one key to another—is a very common device in music. Here are some other examples that may already be familiar to you, even if you've never thought about them in these terms:

- *Hymns with many stanzas.* Organists will often modulate up a step for the last stanza to give the music renewed freshness.
- *The "Final Jeopardy" theme song of the well-known game show.* Listen carefully next time you watch this show. The theme is stated once in the tonic; the second time around, it is presented in a new key.
- *Most popular songs.* Almost every popular song that lasts more than a couple of minutes will modulate for the sake of variety, usually in the middle or toward the end of the song.

PROFILE   Wolfgang Amadeus Mozart (1756–1791)

The Composer as Chameleon

"I can write in any style I choose," Mozart once commented. This wasn't bragging: it was simply the truth. This extraordinary flexibility was due to Mozart's innate genius and his education. His father, Leopold Mozart, a composer of some renown, quickly recognized the musical talent of his young son early on and took him on a number of extended journeys throughout Europe to perform and learn from others (see "Closer Look: Mozart's World"). By the time he was twenty, Mozart had experienced more different kinds of music than any living composer of his day.

Like many child stars today, Mozart had difficulty in making the transition to adulthood. He found his native Salzburg increasingly provincial, but a series of job searches across Europe proved fruitless. Against his father's wishes, Mozart left Salzburg in 1781 for Vienna hoping to land a position at the imperial court there. Unfortunately, the vicious world of Viennese musical politics did not embrace Mozart. He was rather eccentric and rarely said anything nice about contemporary composers (Haydn was the exception). It must have been painful for Mozart to see court appointments go to lesser composers like Antonio Salieri. Although fictionalized to some degree, Peter Shaffer's play *Amadeus* (1980) brilliantly captures the sense of mutual frustration between the competent Salieri and the genius Mozart.

While waiting for an appointment, Mozart supported himself and his new wife, Constanze, by giving public performances on the piano, selling his published compositions, and giving lessons in piano and composition. He did fairly well for a time but for reasons that remain

The Mozart family, ca. 1780. Leopold Mozart (right) was an accomplished violinist and a composer; Nannerl, the composer's sister, excelled as a keyboard player. Mozart's mother, whose portrait hangs on the wall, had died a few years earlier.

obscure—the fickleness of Viennese tastes, hard economic times, or perhaps compulsive gambling—he was in serious debt by the early 1790s and had to borrow money from friends. He died at the age of 35, just when his popularity (and income) seemed to be on the rise again.

 EXPAND YOUR PLAYLIST: MOZART

- **Mass in C Minor**, K. 427. Unfinished, but a magnificent setting for soloists, chorus, and orchestra, with unusually demanding parts for the vocal soloists.

- **A Musical Joke** (*Ein musikalischer Spaß*), K. 522. A chamber work for string quartet and two horns, this piece is full of intentional mistakes and pokes fun at bad composers.

- **A Little Serenade** (*Eine kleine Nachtmusik*), K. 525. A suite for strings, among Mozart's most popular works.

- **String Quintet in G Minor**, K. 516. Similar in mood to the Symphony in G Minor (the same key), this work is scored for string quartet plus an additional viola.

- **Requiem**, K. 626. Mozart's last work, a funeral Mass commissioned by a mysterious stranger, a count (not Salieri!) who later tried to pass it off as his own composition.

CLOSER LK   Mozart's World

Before he turned 18, Mozart had met more famous musicians and heard more kinds of music in more cities than probably any other composer in all of Europe. His father, Leopold, a talented composer and violinist in his own right, took his son from Salzburg on tours across the continent from the time Wolfgang was seven. Some of these trips lasted more than a year. At each stop, the Mozarts would meet the local composers, perform in public, and absorb different styles of composition and performance. Mozart continued traveling on his own from Vienna after 1781, often in search of a full-time position.

Berlin: Mozart visits the Prussian capital in hopes of securing a position at the court of the new king, who is an avid cellist. He writes some string quartets with prominent parts for the cello, but otherwise comes away empty-handed.

London: The young boy astonishes the English public with his keyboard skills, at one point dazzling his audience by playing on a keyboard covered with a cloth.

Paris: Mozart makes three extended visits to Paris. On the last of these, he seeks a position at the court, but without success.

Italy: With its long tradition of music-making, Italy attracts performers and composers from all over Europe. The Mozarts make the arduous trek across the Alps three times in five years, visiting all the major cities, including Milan, Bologna, Mantua, Florence, Rome, Naples, and Venice. In Rome, Pope Clement XIV makes the 16-year-old Wolfgang a knight of the Golden Spur.

Prague: Mozart is a huge favorite in Prague, more so than in Vienna. The theater there commissions his *Don Giovanni,* which premieres in 1787.

Vienna: At 25, Wolfgang moves to Vienna and continues his travels from there. He establishes himself as a composer and keyboard virtuoso, but dies 10 years later before securing a major position at the imperial court.

Salzburg: Mozart is born here on January 26, 1756. His father has just published his *Method of Playing the Violin,* soon to become a standard in the field. From Salzburg, Leopold and Wolfgang set out on many trips to London, Paris, and Italy.

MOZART'S TRAVELS

London 1764–65

Berlin: 1 trip 1789

Berlin 1789

England: 1 trip 1764–65

The Hague 1765–66

Frankfurt 1763, 1790

Prague 1787

Prague: 4 trips 1787 (2x) 1789 1791

Paris

Paris: 3 trips 1763–64 1766 1778

Dijon 1766

Lyons 1766

Milan 1770, 1772–73

Verona 1769

Venice 1770

Bologna

★ Vienna (resides 1781–91)

★ Salzburg (resides 1756–81)

N

Italy: 3 trips 1769–71 1771 1772–73

Florence

Rome 1770

Naples

HISTORICAL CONTEXT · Mozart's Sister

Maria Anna ("Nannerl") Mozart (1751–1829) was as much a child prodigy on the keyboard as her younger brother. A notice in a German newspaper of the time described her as "a young girl of eleven" who "played with the greatest clarity and an effortlessness scarcely to be believed" the "most difficult sonatas and concertos of the great masters on the harpsichord or on the piano, all with the greatest taste." Their father, Leopold, took both children on concert tours across Europe, and gave her, not Wolfgang, top billing when the family visited London in 1765.

But for reasons that remain unclear, Nannerl eventually stopped traveling with her father and brother. She did not accompany them on two extended tours of Italy in the late 1760s and early 1770s. This may have been by her own choice, her father's choice, or some combination of the two. In any case, Leopold seems to have made a conscious decision to invest his primary energies in the promotion of Wolfgang's career, affording him extensive training in composition as well as performance. All that survives of Nannerl's compositions are a few brief exercises. Professional outlets for women composers were virtually nonexistent in that place and time.

On the other hand, women could and did enjoy successful careers as performers, especially in Vienna. Wolfgang tried to persuade his sister to join him there in 1781: "Believe me, you could earn a great deal of money in Vienna . . . playing at private concerts and by giving piano lessons. You would be very much in demand—and you would be well paid." Nannerl chose not to pursue a career as a performer, however. Her father arranged for her to marry a baron in 1784, and she bore three children by him—one of whom she named Wolfgang—but she apparently did not perform in public again. After her husband died in 1821, Nannerl returned to Salzburg and gave piano lessons for the rest of her life.

A portrait of Maria Anna ("Nannerl") Mozart. Notice her unusually long fingers, which undoubtedly served her well as a pianist.

 EXPAND YOUR PLAYLIST

Mozart's Symphonies

Mozart, like Haydn, seems to have relished the challenge of writing for a large ensemble. Here are some of his better-known symphonies:

Symphony no. 1 in E♭ Major, K. 16.
- A small-scale work, but nevertheless an impressive accomplishment for an eight-year-old composer.

Symphony no. 25 in G Minor, K. 185.
- Known as the "Little" G Minor symphony, this work is featured prominently in Milos Forman's film version of Peter Shaffer's play *Amadeus*.

Symphony no. 38 in D Major, K. 504.
- Known as the "Prague" symphony because of its popularity there during Mozart's lifetime. The first movement opens with an extended slow introduction, and the symphony lacks a minuet movement, unlike Mozart's other late symphonies.

Symphony no. 41 in C Major, K. 551.
- Nicknamed the "Jupiter" symphony sometime after Mozart's death because of its size and exuberant nature. The finale is a remarkable synthesis of fugue and sonata form.

Wolfgang Amadeus Mozart

Piano Concerto in A Major, K. 488, first movement

Composed: 1786

In his Piano Concerto in A Major, K. 488, Mozart explores a variety of moods across three movements, from the serene but passionate first movement to the dark, contemplative second movement to the rousing, exuberant finale. Here, we are listening to the first movement alone.

Listen to This First

～ Timbre

Listen to the fluid relationship between the solo instrument—the piano—and the ensemble, an orchestra of strings and winds. Like characters in a drama, they cooperate at times, oppose each other at times, and appear by themselves, without the other at times. ■

♪ Melody

Listen to the number and variety of the melodies, each with its own distinct character. Notice, too, how these melodies rarely appear in exactly the same guise twice. ■

▥ Form

Listen for the entrance of the soloist and then later on for the return of the opening idea about two-thirds of the way through the movement, which marks the onset of the recapitulation. ■

When Mozart moved to Vienna in 1781, he was determined to make an impression on the Imperial Court and the public, both as a pianist and as a composer. His piano concertos provided him with the ideal vehicle for achieving this dual goal: Audiences marveled at the young man's virtuosity at the keyboard and his ingenuity as a composer. Over the span of less than 10 years, Mozart composed 17 piano concertos, including this one from 1786. Like so many of Mozart's works, the Piano Concerto in A Major, K. 488, seems effortless and natural, clear and unforced. On closer listening, however, we can hear that what sounds effortless is in no way simple. The concertos of the Classical Era combine the ritornello principle of the Baroque Era with the newer sonata form.

～ Timbre: The Drama of Contrast

The driving force behind any concerto lies in the inherently dramatic tension between the soloist and the orchestra. The two forces collaborate at times and compete at others; on still other occasions, each appears alone. There are five basic scenarios:

1. Orchestra alone
2. Soloist alone
3. Orchestra supporting the soloist
4. Soloist supporting the orchestra
5. Soloist and orchestra on an equal footing

LEARNING OBJECTIVES

26.1 Discuss why Mozart wrote piano concertos.

26.2 Listen for the various possible timbral relationships between the soloist and the orchestra in a concerto.

26.3 Describe Mozart's use of melody in his Piano Concerto K. 488, first movement.

26.4 Listen for the integration of sonata form and the ritornello principle in this first movement.

26.5 Listen for the cadenza and describe its nature.

26.6 Describe the relationship between sonata form and double-exposition concerto form in Mozart's Piano Concerto K. 488, first movement.

26.7 Describe how the type of piano is a consideration in a performance of Mozart's piano music.

Listen once through this movement to identify these five different combinations. Here are some examples:

Possible Combinations	Timing	Relationship of Orchestra and Solo
1. Orchestra alone	0:00	The orchestra plays by itself at the beginning.
2. Soloist alone	2:04	When the piano enters for the first time, it plays alone briefly.
3. Orchestra supporting the soloist	2:12	When the orchestra reenters, it supports the piano.
4. Soloist supporting the orchestra	3:18	The orchestra carries the melody, while the piano supports it.
5. Soloist and orchestra on an equal	3:33	The orchestra and piano engage in dialogue, tossing the theme back and forth between each other.

By varying the timbre so frequently and by using so many different combinations, Mozart is able to sustain our interest across a relatively long movement.

🎵 Melodic Generosity

One feature that sets Mozart's music apart from that of almost all his contemporaries is the sheer number and variety of musical ideas within a given movement. Indeed, some critics of the time complained that Mozart's music presented them with too many ideas, and that his melodies moved from one to the next faster than audiences could follow. Where another composer might be satisfied with two different melodies, for example, Mozart provides his listeners with three or four or five. This first movement of this concerto offers a good example of Mozart's melodic generosity, as well as the way in which he alters the combination of dynamics, texture, and rhythm to create a sense of variety.

Theme 1
The opening idea is serene and balanced, a statement that sets the mood for the movement as a whole. The texture is homophonic (melody above, harmony below), the dynamics soft. The melodic contour is a mixture of conjunct (stepwise) and disjunct (leaping) motion, moving down at first and then up, ending where it began.

Theme 2

The second idea is more agitated, more propulsive: It moves in a faster rhythm (with shorter note values). The texture is homophonic, the dynamics loud. The melodic motion is marked by prominent upward leaps, and the contour moves largely upward.

Theme 3

This theme also uses shorter note values, but it restores a sense of calm because its many repeated notes help create an impression of not hurrying anywhere. The texture is homophonic, the dynamics soft. The melodic motion is primarily conjunct, and the contour moves largely downward.

Theme 4

This theme is also calm, but the effect comes from the longer note values that make it move more slowly. The texture this time is polyphonic, with some imitation between the voices. The dynamics are soft, and the melodic motion is marked by an initial down contour followed by upward leaps.

PERFORMANCE   Mozart on Modern Instruments

The recording here presents Mozart's music played on the kinds of instruments he would have known in his lifetime. These differ in subtle but noticeable ways from modern instruments. The violins, violas, cellos, and basses of the eighteenth century, for example, all used strings made from catgut, not wire as they are today; this made their sound warmer, softer, and less penetrating than the sound of modern instruments.

The piano, in particular, has changed considerably since Mozart's day. It is a much longer, heavier, and louder instrument. In Mozart's time, the hammers that struck the strings were covered with leather, not felt, producing a lighter, more percussive sound. The fortepiano, as it was known back then, is a more delicate and intimate instrument than today's grand piano. It produces far less volume, but this was not a drawback, as concert halls in Mozart's time were much smaller. Many musicians and listeners today prefer the sound of Mozart's music on the fortepiano than on the modern piano.

Which is better? That is entirely a matter of taste. Advocates of the fortepiano argue that we should try to re-create the sound that Mozart had in mind when he wrote his music. Advocates of the modern piano make the case that in proportion to the size of today's concert halls, the modern piano alone creates a sound that fills the space; they also point out that the fortepiano had already begun to grow in size and volume during Mozart's lifetime, and that Mozart himself embraced these developments.

Fortunately, as listeners in today's music world, we have plenty of choices. The following are some good recordings of Mozart's Piano Concerto in A Major, K. 488 on modern instruments:

- Alfred Brendel, piano. Academy of St. Martin in the Fields, Neville Marriner, conductor. Philips 000552102.
- Murray Perahia, piano. English Chamber Orchestra, Murray Perahia, conductor. Sony 87230.
- Ingrid Haebler, piano. London Symphony Orchestra, Witold Rowicki, conductor. Eloquence 468171.

The soloist Emmanuel Ax performs a piano concerto by Mozart on a modern grand piano with the Swedish Chamber Orchestra, conducted by Thomas Dausgaard.

Kristian Bezuidenhout on fortepiano with members of Freiburg Baroque Orchestra performing Mozart's Piano Concerto No. 20 in D Minor. Notice the considerably smaller size of the instrument compared to a modern piano.

Form: Double-Exposition Concerto Form

Like other composers of his time, Mozart adapted **sonata form** (see Chapter 25)—which was new in the middle of the eighteenth century—to the concerto. But he also retained elements of the contrast between ritornello and solo that was so basic to the Baroque concerto (see Chapters 17 and 19). Mozart organized the melodic and harmonic structure of the first movement of the Piano Concerto in A Major, K. 488, around a form known as the **double-exposition concerto form**. Although based on the same principles as sonata form, double-exposition concerto form differs in several important respects:

Standard Sonata Form	Double-Exposition Concerto Form
• One exposition, repeated literally	• Two different expositions: one for the orchestra, and one for the soloist and orchestra together.
• Exposition modulates from tonic	• The first exposition (for the orchestra alone) stays in the tonic. Only the second exposition (for soloist and orchestra together) modulates to new key area.
• Development avoids the tonic	• Same
• Recapitulation restates themes from the exposition, but now with all of them in the tonic.	• Same
• No cadenza	• At the end of the recapitulation, the soloist plays a *cadenza*—an elaborate improvisation on themes heard earlier in the movement, with no accompaniment at all from the orchestra.

The only entirely new element in double-exposition concerto form is the **cadenza**, a moment when the soloist can display his or her virtuosity to the fullest. Mozart actually wrote down cadenzas for many of his own concertos, but in performance, improvisation was the order of the day. A long trill from the soloist was the standard signal to the orchestra that the cadenza was about to end, and with a gesture from the soloist, the orchestra resumed playing its written parts. Mozart conducted his music from the keyboard; conductors did not arrive on the scene until the early nineteenth century.

Graphically, the double-exposition concerto structure can be represented in this manner:

Double-Exposition Concerto Form

Formal Section	Tutti Exposition (orchestra alone)	Solo Exposition (soloist & orchestra)	Development (soloist & orchestra)	Recapitulation (soloist & orchestra)	Cadenza (soloist alone, improvised)	Coda (orchestra alone)
Key Area	Tonic	Tonic → New key area	Not Tonic (unstable)	Tonic	Unstable	Tonic

Now listen to the first movement of this piano concerto again, using the Listening Guide.

Listening Guide

Wolfgang Amadeus Mozart Composed: 1786
Piano Concerto in A Major, K. 488, first movement (10:54)

Time	🏛 Form: Section	🎵 Melody	〰 Timbre
0:00	Tutti exposition (orchestra alone)	1 = lyrical, begins with long notes, downward contour	Strings alone present the theme, which is then repeated by the winds alone.
0:32		2 = more energetic theme, begins with repeated notes but then has several upward leaps and a generally upward contour	Full orchestra
0:56		3 = another lyrical theme, largely conjunct, downward contour	Strings alone at first, winds join in later
2:04	Solo exposition (soloist and orchestra together)	1 = a more elaborate presentation of the theme	Soloist alone, joined gradually by orchestra
2:32		2 = begins as above, but continues differently so that it modulates, taking the music to a new key area	Orchestra alone, joined by soloist
3:03		3 = as above, but now in the new key area	Soloist alone, joined by the orchestra (at 3:18)
4:27		4 = a new theme, not heard in the tutti exposition; long notes, disjunct motion, generally downward contour	Orchestra (strings alone), joined by soloist (at 4:37)
4:52	Development (soloist and orchestra together)	4 = dialogue between soloist and orchestra on fragments of this theme	Winds alone at first, joined by soloist and strings
6:12	Recapitulation (soloist and orchestra together)	1	Orchestra (with winds now), soloist joins in (at 6:27)
6:40		2	Orchestra, then soloist
7:10		3	Soloist, then orchestra
8:12		4	Soloist, then orchestra
8:55		2 (brief return)	Orchestra alone
9:07		4 (brief return)	Orchestra alone
9:20	Cadenza	Improvisation on themes heard earlier in the movement	Soloist alone
10:20	Coda (orchestra alone)	3 (fragment)	Orchestra alone

Harmony: Key Areas

Tonic (A major)

Tonic

→ (modulating to). . .

New key area (E major)

Unstable: the music moves quickly through many key areas

Tonic: a strong sense of arrival at the beginning of the recapitulation, both to the opening theme and to the opening key

Does not modulate; stays in the tonic

Tonic

Unstable, returns to tonic only at the end

Tonic

 Q **Student FAQs**

Isn't the piano soloist playing very softly with the orchestra in the tutti exposition?

Yes, and you have an extremely good ear if you can hear this.

The piano's very discreet (almost inaudible) part here represents a holdover from the days when the keyboard soloist would perform double duty as both a soloist and as a member of the basso continuo. In modern performances that strive to replicate eighteenth-century performance practice (as in the recording here), the soloist helps support the basso continuo in the tutti exposition and at the end, in the coda, fills out harmonies here and there without really calling attention to him- or herself.

How could Mozart have conducted from the keyboard while playing? Didn't he need his arms to conduct?

Yes, but playing the lead on the piano created a basic beat for the musicians to follow. Also, Mozart could use his head and eyes to gesture to the musicians while playing. In those passages in which the orchestra took the lead (as in the tutti exposition), Mozart probably did conduct with one or both arms.

Did Mozart really improvise his cadenzas on the spot?

It's hard to say for sure—even if we could ask him, would we believe his answer? It seems likely, though, that Mozart would have given at least some advance thought to how he might improvise on the themes of a concerto movement, combining those premeditated strategies with genuine improvisation at the moment of performance. Jazz musicians today often do the same thing: To varying degrees, their solo riffs represent a combination of both the planned and the spontaneous.

HISTORICAL CONTEXT   Mozart's Concerts: The Bottom Line

When Mozart moved to Vienna from Salzburg in 1781, he was taking a calculated risk, believing that he could secure a steady position at the Imperial Court or, failing that, earn enough money from concerts, opera commissions, publications, and teaching to support himself (and, after he married, his family).

For a time, at least, Mozart's gamble paid off. His concert series in the years 1783–1786 were a great success and attracted many subscribers, including wealthy aristocrats whose opinions could make or break the career of any new musician who had just arrived in Vienna. Mozart kept his expenses down in part by doing almost everything himself.

The actor Tom Hulce in the role of Mozart in *Amadeus* (1984). Mozart was in fact fascinated with the game of billiards, and the image of him composing on a billiard table is entirely plausible.

He wrote the music for his concerts (symphonies and, above all, piano concertos), performed the music himself as soloist and conductor (sometimes filling both functions simultaneously), hired the musicians, and even sold the tickets from his own apartment. (Mozart was affluent enough to afford a servant, and it was presumably the servant, rather than Mozart himself, who actually sold the tickets.)

One recent estimate of Mozart's balance sheet for his 1784 subscription concert series suggests that he in fact made a healthy profit on his venture:

Income:

150 subscribers @ 13.5 Gulden ea. for 6 concerts =	2,025 Gulden

Expenses:

Orchestra musicians (estimated):	420 Gulden
Concert hall rental	80
Lighting, printing, and other miscellaneous expenses:	100
Total Expenses:	600 Gulden
Net Profit:	1,425 Gulden

To give some sense of what this meant in terms of purchasing power, the rent for Mozart's apartment at this time was 460 Gulden per year. His subscription series of six concerts thus generated more than three times his annual housing costs. Beyond the subscription concerts, of course, Mozart was also free to give special additional concerts as well.

   EXPAND YOUR PLAYLIST

The Classical Concerto

Carl Philipp Emanuel Bach (1714–1788), one of J. S. Bach's sons, wrote more than 50 keyboard concertos. The Concerto in G Minor, H. 442, is from the mid-1750s.

Johann Christian Bach (1735–1782), like his much older half-brother, Carl Philipp Emanuel Bach, wrote dozens of keyboard concertos. J. C. Bach's Concerto in B♭ Major, op. 7, no. 4 (1770) is written in a more modern style, closer to that of W. A. Mozart.

W. A. Mozart wrote concertos for a variety of different instruments, including not only piano (27 of them) but also violin (5), horn (4), bassoon (1), and flute and harp (1), among others. Here are some recommendations for further exploration:

- Piano Concerto in D Minor, K. 466. This is one of the darker and more turbulent of the 27 piano concertos Mozart wrote for himself.

- Concerto for Two Pianos in E♭, K. 365. Mozart wrote this to be performed jointly with his sister Nannerl, an accomplished pianist in her own right.

- Sinfonia Concertante in E, K. 364. A "concerto-like symphony," grand in scale and sound, for solo violin and viola, with orchestra.

- Clarinet Concerto in A Major, K. 622. Mozart's last concerto for any instrument, written for a friend of his, the clarinetist Anton Stadler.

Joseph Haydn's most celebrated concertos are the Cello Concerto in D Major, Hob. XIIb: 2 and the Trumpet Concerto in E♭, Hob. VIIe:1.

Marianne Martinez (1744–1812), who in her youth studied composition with Haydn, wrote three concertos for piano.

Wolfgang Amadeus Mozart

The Marriage of Figaro, Act I, "Cosa sento"

Composed: 1786

The dramatic contrasts, modulations, and sudden changes so characteristic of instrumental music in the Classical Era provided composers with the means by which to enhance dramatic action on the stage. In this chapter's excerpt from Mozart's opera *The Marriage of Figaro*, the music gives added depth to the words and actions of the characters on stage.

Listen to This First

🗣 Word–Music Relationships	🎹 Form	🎵 Melody
Listen to the contrasting singing styles of Susanna (soprano), Basilio (tenor), and the Count (bass). The three personalities are shaped not only by the words, but by the way each character sings them. ■	Much of the drama is in the music itself. Listen to the increasing and decreasing tension of the music over the course of this one selection. These three characters are singing to one another, not just to the audience. ■	Listen for the return of the opening melody at various points. In the middle of the scene, notice the sudden change in the Count's singing style from lyrical to declamatory. ■

In this trio from Mozart's opera *The Marriage of Figaro* (*Le nozze di Figaro*), words and music combine to create a moment of intense confrontation full of both suspense and humor. The text enriches the music, and the music enriches the text. The scene occurs toward the end of the opera's first act. The three characters singing in this selection are the following:

- Count Almaviva (bass), who is married to the Countess but has his eyes on Susanna.
- Susanna, the Countess's maidservant. Susanna is engaged to be married to Figaro, the Count's manservant.
- Basilio, the music teacher at the court. He is meddlesome and loves to gossip.

There is actually a fourth character on stage as well, but Cherubino (a page boy) is silent in this scene because he is hiding. When he is discovered, about midway through the selection, he is too mortified to sing.

How did we get into this situation? Cherubino is infatuated with women in general and the Countess in particular. In the scene just prior to this one, Cherubino has been asking Susanna's help in calming the anger of the Count, who the day before has caught him making advances on Barbarina, the young daughter of the gardener. But while Cherubino and Susanna are discussing the matter in the Countess's chamber, the Count arrives unexpectedly, and Cherubino must hide behind a large chair. (The audience, of course, can see everyone on the stage.) In the process of

LEARNING OBJECTIVES

27.1 Summarize the plot of Mozart's *The Marriage of Figaro*.

27.2 Listen for the contrasting dramatic qualities of the voices and melodic styles of the three characters.

27.3 Identify contrasting melodies associated with specific characters.

27.4 Listen for recurring themes as related to the text being sung.

27.5 Listen for the passage of accompanied recitative within this excerpt.

trying to seduce Susanna, the Count is in turn interrupted by the impending arrival of the music teacher, Basilio. So now the *Count* must hide, and he goes to conceal himself behind the very same chair where Cherubino is crouching. Using her quick wits, Susanna steps between the Count and the chair and directs Cherubino to slip onto the seat itself and conceal himself underneath one of the Countess's dresses that happens to be lying there. Just as the Count assumes his position behind the chair, Basilio enters the room. He is a meddlesome creature, and he teases Susanna about the Count's interest in her. He then goes on to tell her about Cherubino's interest in the Countess, which by now has become common knowledge at the court. At this moment an indignant Count bursts out from his hiding place. "I heard that!" he roars ("Cosa sento!"). And with that, our scene begins.

Mozart's *The Marriage of Figaro* is a **comic opera** or *opera buffa*, to use its Italian name. *Buffa* comes from the same root word as "buffoon." The genre uses many of the same conventions as serious opera—arias, recitatives, ensembles, choruses—but the plots do not revolve around mythical or historical figures. Instead, comic operas tend to deal with very believable characters who behave as individuals, not as symbols, and we can relate to all of them to varying degrees. Mozart's music makes them even more believable.

Word–Music Relationships: The Character of Each Voice

Even without music, this is a highly dramatic scene. The witty **libretto**—the text of an opera—by Italian poet Lorenzo da Ponte (1749–1838), is based on a stage play of the same name by French dramatist Pierre Augustin Caron de Beaumarchais (1732–1799). A great deal happens here within a short span of time. As soon as the Count emerges from his hiding place ("Cosa sento!"—"I heard that!"—he exclaims), Basilio backtracks and apologizes, claiming that what he had just been saying about Cherubino and the Countess was merely a suspicion rather than a fact. But the Count is all the more determined now to banish Cherubino from his court. He tells Susanna and Basilio about his encounter with the page the day before and describes exactly how he had discovered Cherubino under the table by lifting the tablecloth. He illustrates his discovery of the previous day by lifting the dress off the chair—only to find Cherubino cringing before him, hiding yet again.

The duplicity and irony of it all is hilarious, for the Count himself had been hiding behind this very same chair only moments before. The Count had come to seduce Susanna (on the day of her wedding!) and yet when he overhears Basilio talking about Cherubino's infatuation with the Countess, he becomes outraged. And just what was the Count doing at Barbarina's house the day before, when he discovered Cherubino there? She was "more flustered than usual," the Count observes; this clearly was not the first time the Count had visited Barbarina.

This scene illustrates Mozart's uncanny ability to capture the essence of individual characters and at the same time move a plot forward through the music. What Mozart's music portrays so convincingly in this brief trio is the fluidity of each character's emotions. We witness the following changes:

1. The Count moves from outrage (on hearing of Basilio's suspicions about Cherubino and the Countess) to astonishment at discovering Cherubino in hiding once again, for the second time in two days.

2. Basilio moves from embarrassment (on realizing that the Count has overheard his gossip about the Countess) to triumph when Cherubino's presence in the Countess's chamber bears out what Basilio had at first called "mere suspicions."

3. Susanna moves through states of increasing humiliation that her reputation has been compromised by the presence of all three male visitors, none of whom should really be where they are and certainly should not be alone with her on the day of her own wedding.

These contrasting and evolving emotional states are reflected in the contrasting melodies Mozart gives to each character.

Contrasting Melodies

Mozart associates distinctly different melodies with each of the emotional states of the three characters. The Count's opening theme (Theme 1 in the Listening Guide, later in this chapter)—a slow, rising line—reflects his determination to banish Cherubino from the court. Basilio's whiny and slightly hesitant descending line (Theme 2) matches his embarrassment at having been overheard repeating malicious gossip about the Countess. Susanna's agitated melody (Theme 3) sounds like it is shaking: It moves up and down, back and forth with a very narrow register, reflecting her personal agitation; at this point, she alone knows that Cherubino, who is the object of all this gossip, is still hiding in the room.

Later on (at 2:12), when the Count tells about his encounter with Cherubino the day before, he suddenly shifts to a more syllabic, declamatory style of singing. This is **accompanied recitative**—recitative accompanied by the orchestra, as opposed to the more standard recitative accompaniment of basso continuo alone. This passage stands in marked contrast to the rest of the scene, for it is a narration of something that has already happened.

CONNECT YOUR PLAYLIST

Simultaneous Contrasting Melodies

Find a song that features two different voices singing different musical lines and different words at the same time.

Example: Stephen Schwartz, "What Is This Feeling?" from *Wicked* (2003) In this duet from the Broadway musical *Wicked*, the two main melodies combine near the end, creating polyphonic texture.

Dramatic Form, Musical Form

As in any opera, the form of this selection is built around its text. Mozart structures the music around a recurring musical theme that reflects the scene's recurring dramatic theme: the Count's resolve to send Cherubino away from the court. We hear some variation of this theme ("1" in the Listening Guide) three times:

- At the very beginning, when the Count reacts to Basilio telling Susanna about Cherubino's interest in the Countess

- After Susanna's "fainting" spell, when Basilio apologizes for what he has said about Cherubino and the Countess

- After the Count discovers Cherubino hiding under a dress on the chair

These moments are separated by two dramatic interruptions. Susanna pretends to faint to draw attention away from Cherubino.

The Count makes advances toward an unwilling Susanna while Cherubino hides behind a chair. When Basilio arrives soon afterward, the Count will be forced to hide as well. This scene is from a 2012 production at the Glyndebourne Festival Opera in England.

Listening Guide

Wolfgang Amadeus Mozart Composed: 1786

The Marriage of Figaro, Act I, "Cosa sento" (4:07)

Time	Character(s) Singing	Original Italian	English Translation	
0:00	Count	Cosa sento! Tosto andate, e scacciate il seduttor!	I heard it all! Go at once and throw the seducer out!	
0:16	Basilio	In mal punto son qui giunto; perdonate, o mio signor.	I have arrived at an unfortunate moment; forgive me, my lord.	
0:25	Susanna (*as if fainting*)	Che ruina! me meschina! Son' oppressa dal dolor!	What a catastrophe! I am ruined! I am oppressed with sadness!	
0:47	Basilio and Count (*supporting Susanna*)	Ah, già svien la poverina, Come, oh Dio, le batte il cor!	The poor child has fainted! My Lord, how her heart is beating!	
	(*Basilio and the Count draw Susanna toward the chair to set her down in it—the chair on which Cherubino is hiding under a dress.*)			
1:05	Basilio	Pian pianin: su questo seggio.	Gently, gently, to this chair.	
1:09	Susanna (*reviving*)	Dove sono? cosa veggio? Che insolenza, andate fuor.	Where am I? What do I see? What insolence, get away.	
	(*She frees herself from both of them.*)			
1:17	Count and Basilio	Siamo qui per aiutarti, [Count]: Non turbarti, o mio tesor. [Basilio]: è sicuro il vostro onor.	We're here to help you, [Count]: Don't be alarmed, my dear. [Basilio]: Your honor is safe.	
1:34	Basilio (*to the Count*)	Ah del paggio quel ch'ho detto Era solo un mio sospetto!	What I was saying about the page Was merely a suspicion I had!	
1:43	Susanna	È un'insidia, una perfidia, Non credete all'impostor.	It's a snare, a lie; Don't believe this impostor.	
1:53	Count	Parta, parta il damerino!	The young girly-boy must go!	

Form: Parallels to Rondo Form	Melody	Word–Music Relationships
A	(1) Rising contour	This theme recurs whenever the Count reacts to news about Cherubino's amorous advances.
	(2) Falling contour	This theme recurs whenever a character refers to his suspicions about Cherubino's attempted seductions.
	(3) Narrow range, static motion: the melody winds around on itself	The rapid, fluttering notes of this theme reflect Susanna's agitation.
B	(4) New melody, rising contour	This theme recurs whenever the Count and Basilio try to assist Susanna.
		Susanna "faints" in a low register but suddenly starts singing in a high one when she realizes she is about to be put on the same seat where Cherubino is hiding.
	(4) Same as 0:47	Again, the two men assist Susanna.
	(2) Same as 0:16	Basilio apologizes for having suggested that the Countess and Cherubino have been meeting in secret.
	(3) Variant of earlier melody (at 0:24)	Susanna is agitated again; she has barely managed to conceal Cherubino's presence.
A	(1) Return to opening theme	Varied return of the opening theme emphasizes the Count's resolve to banish Cherubino from the court.

Student FAQs

Why are they singing in Italian? Wasn't German the language that was spoken in Vienna?

Yes, but Italian was the international language of opera throughout Europe at this time, even in England. Most of the leading singers of Mozart's day were Italian by birth, as was Mozart's librettist, Lorenzo da Ponte. *Don Giovanni* and *Così fan tutte*, two other librettos he wrote for Mozart, are also in Italian. And although German was the standard language in Mozart's Vienna, many audience members also spoke and understood Italian; those who did not could buy a copy of the libretto—a word whose literal meaning in Italian is "little book"—with parallel texts in Italian and German.

Why is there so much repetition of the text in the singing?

This is standard practice in operas. Music gives added emotional depth to the words, but it can also make those words more difficult to understand. Repetition helps audiences grasp the actual words being sung. This is especially important when two or more characters are singing at the same time. When the Count narrates his discovery of Cherubino from the day before, on the other hand, he does so in recitative, which allows him to present quite a large quantity of text in a short time; because recitative stands halfway between speech and song, it is easier to comprehend its words.

(Continues)

Time	Character(s) Singing	Original Italian	English Translation
1:56	Susanna and Basilio	Poverino!	Poor boy!
2:02	Count	Poverino! Ma da me sorpreso ancor.	Poor boy! But I have found him out yet again.
2:07	Susanna	Come?	How's that?
2:08	Basilio	Che?	What?
2:12	Count	Da tua cugina L'uscio ier trovai rinchiuso, Picchio, m'apre Barbarina, Paurosa fuor dell'uso. Io dal muso insospettito, Guardo, cerco in ogni sito,	At your cousin's yesterday I found the door locked; I knocked, and Barbarina opened it, more flustered than usual. My suspicions aroused, I looked in every corner,
2:31		Ed alzando piano pianino Il tappeto al tavolino, Vedo il paggio!	And lifted, ever so quietly, The tablecloth on the table, And there I saw the page!
2:40	(*He illustrates his action of the day before by raising the dress draped over the chair, only to discover Cherubino once again.*)		
2:47	Count	Ah, cosa veggio!	Ah! What do I see?
2:50	Susanna	Ah, crude stelle!	Ah, cruel fate!
2:52	Basilio (*laughing*)	Ah, meglio ancora!	Ah, it's getting even better!
2:56	Count	Onestissima signora! Or capsico come va.	O madame of highest virtue, Now I see how things are.
2:58	Susanna	Accader non può di peggio; Giusti Dei! che mai sarà?	Nothing worse could happen now; Ye gods of justice! What will happen?
3:03	Basilio	Così fan tutte le belle Non c'è alcuna novità.	All beautiful women act the same! There's nothing new about this.
3:21	Basilio (*to the Count*)	Ah del paggio quel ch'ho detto Era solo un mio sospetto!	What I was saying about the page Was merely a suspicion I had!
3:29	Count, Susana, Basilio	(All three repeat their texts from 2:56–3:20)	(All three repeat their texts from 2:56–3:20)

Form: Parallels to Rondo Form	Melody	Word–Music Relationships
		Susanna and Basilio sing a continuation of the Count's theme (1). For the first time, the two agree on something.
C	(5) Declamatory	Accompanied recitative, not very melodic, as the Count narrates yesterday's events.
	(2)	The "suspicion" theme returns.
A	(1) Opening theme again	The Count reacts again to news of Cherubino.
		Susanna is mortified, the Count feels vindicated, and Basilio gloats over the misfortunes of others.
B	(2)	Basilio repeats his earlier apology, but this time it sounds triumphant: the "suspicion" has turned out to be true.
A	(1)	The Count and Basilio feel vindicated, Susanna feels humiliated. (But she will get her revenge in Act 4!)

Q Student FAQs

Why do characters sing different texts at the same time? They seem to cancel each other out.

In a play, when two or more characters are talking at the same time, it's almost impossible to understand either one. In opera, however, each character sings in a distinctive vocal range (soprano, tenor, and baritone in this case), which allows listeners to distinguish among the lines more easily. The repetition of texts also helps us understand what is being sung.

Why is Cherubino played by a woman?

Cherubino is a young teenager whose voice has not yet broken, and for this reason the role is always sung by a woman dressed as a man. This kind of role—a woman playing the part of a young man—is known as a "trousers role."

227

But she has to "revive" quickly so as not to be placed on top of him, for the two men are trying to help her sit down on the very chair where he is hiding. The second interruption comes from the Count himself when he narrates the events of the day before, describing how, while visiting Barbarina (another young girl he is pursuing), he had discovered Cherubino hiding under the table. He demonstrates to Susanna and Basilio how he had lifted the tablecloth, using the dress on the chair as a prop to demonstrate his actions of the previous day—only to find Cherubino once again.

This sequence of dramatic events suggests a musical form rather like the rondo. In a rondo, an opening melodic idea returns repeatedly over the course of a movement, and these points of return are separated by a series of contrasting melodic ideas. Mozart seems to have recognized a parallel between rondo form and the dramatic situation in this particular scene, and he set the action to music following the conventions of rondo form, with the moments of musical and dramatic return and interruption closely coordinated.

Now listen to **The Marriage of Figaro** *excerpt again, using the Listening Guide.*

EXPAND YOUR PLAYLIST

Opera in the Classical Era

Opera remained the most prestigious (and lucrative) genre in the Classical Era and inspired some of its greatest music. Mozart and Christoph Willibald Gluck are generally considered the two principal composers of opera in this period. A sampling of their works follows:

Wolfgang Amadeus Mozart

- *Don Giovanni*, K. 527. The story of Don Juan ("Don Giovanni" in Italian) and his many amorous conquests. The libretto is by Lorenzo da Ponte, who also wrote the text for *The Marriage of Figaro*.

- *Così fan tutte*, K. 588. "All women act that way" is a loose translation of the title. The libretto, again by da Ponte, traces the fate of two couples and a bet by the men that their fiancées will not be unfaithful. The men lose their bets.

- *The Magic Flute* (*Die Zauberflöte*), K. 620. A fairy-tale *Singspiel*—a play combining spoken text with music—about a prince and his birdlike companion and their search for knowledge (and a princess).

Christoph Willibald Gluck (1714–1787)

Gluck was born in what is now Germany but spent much of his life in Italy, England, France, and Austria. He worked to bring a sense of naturalness to opera, avoiding excessive displays of virtuosity.

- *Orfeo ed Euridice*. Another setting of the legend of Orpheus and his use of music to bring his beloved Eurydice back from Hades to the land of the living. Gluck also produced a French-language version of this same opera (*Orphée et Eurydice*).

- *Alceste*. Based on the Greek legend of Queen Alceste, who offers to sacrifice her own life to save that of her husband, King Admetus. The music includes extensive choral numbers and accompanied recitatives as well as arias.

Jingju
"The Reunion"
Recorded: ca. 1995

GLOBAL CONNECTION: OPERA

28

The term *opera* has been applied to many forms of sung theater throughout the world. Jingju is the principal form of Chinese opera today. Because it developed in China's capital city of Beijing, it came to be known as *jingju* (which means "capital theater") in China. In the West, it is known as Peking or Beijing Opera.

Listen to This First ◊))

♫ Melody	☺ Word–Music Relationships	〰 Timbre	⊕ Texture	▥ Rhythm
How are the melodies constructed? ■	How do the words shape the tones? ■	Do certain instruments have a more penetrating sound than others? Do the sounds of the instruments have different purposes? ■	Listen to how instruments accompany the singing. Are they working together or independently? ■	Describe how the rhythm changes. How are percussion rhythms used for musical meaning? ■

In the late 1700s, many genres of Chinese theater were performed in the capital city of Beijing. **Jingju** developed out of these styles into a new, lavish art form. Its first imperial patron was the Empress Dowager (1835–1908), who brought its performance into the Forbidden City (the Imperial Palace, located in the heart of Beijing) and developed a court troupe. The period of jingju's development coincided with the era of European operatic composers such as Giuseppe Verdi and Richard Wagner, about seventy years after Mozart (see Chapters 41 and 43).

Jingju dominated Beijing entertainment for over 100 years, until the Cultural Revolution (1966–1976) of Mao Zedong banned the performance of traditional-style jingju and replaced it with revolutionary jingju. The Communists considered all traditional Chinese opera to be a by-product of elitist culture. After Mao Zedong's death in 1976 and the end of the Cultural Revolution, however, traditional forms of opera, including jingju, slowly reemerged.

There are about two hundred plays in the jingju repertoire, drawing mainly from popular legends, historical events, narratives, and novels. The characters in all the operas are categorized into a limited number of role types, each with its own style of acting, speaking, singing, costume, and makeup. On stage, there is no scenery, and the action usually takes place in front of a curtain.

Jingju singing includes short phrases and songs that may be compared to recitative and aria in European opera. Recitative-like phrases and heightened speech narrate dramatic action, and

LEARNING OBJECTIVES

28.1 Define and describe the origins of *jingju*.

28.2 Identify the two parts of "The Reunion" by their melodic distinctions.

28.3 Explain the use of heterophony in "The Reunion."

28.4 Identify the sections of metered and unmetered music in "The Reunion."

28.5 Distinguish between recitative and aria in "The Reunion."

28.6 Describe the effect of the Cultural Revolution on jingju.

28.7 Identify other examples of traditional Chinese music.

arias express the lyrical sentiments of the characters. The arias are created by setting the text using different preexisting "tune families." The most commonly used tune families, or modes, are *xipi* and *erhuang*. *Erhuang* is typically used for lyrical or tragic scenes of moderate tempo; the livelier *xipi* is employed in more positive situations.

The jingju instrumental ensemble is divided into two groups: the *wenchang*—the civic, or melodic, group—and the *wuchang*—the military, or percussive, group. The melodic ensemble includes strings and wind instruments. It accompanies singing and it provides introductions and interludes. The *jinghu*, the lead instrument, is a two-string fiddle. *Jinghu* literally means "capital fiddle," and since it is the major supporting sound to the singing, it must have a strident timbre. The percussion group provides rhythmic punctuation for singing, movements, entrances, sound effects, and moods. In the early days of *jingju*, women were banned from the stage to protect them from moral corruption. Men therefore trained to sing women's roles using a **falsetto** voice. Mei Langfang (1894–1961) was a famous male singer of female roles, and he brought the first Peking Opera troupe to the United States. In this listening example, his god-daughter Lisa Lu (b. 1931) plays the Princess Lady Precious Stream and sings of her devotion to her gardener husband.

An ensemble of characters from a recent production of Beijing opera.

HISTORICAL CONTEXT **Jingju and the Cultural Revolution**

When Mao Zedong and the Chinese Communist Party took over the rule of China in 1949, they immediately developed and employed new cultural policies. Under communism in Russia, traditional arts had been transformed to convey the new message of collective life and communist ideology to the common people. China would follow in these footsteps particularly during the Cultural Revolution (1966–1976), led by Mao's wife Jiang Qing. She targeted jingju, along with other traditional arts, for reform, eliminating the older plots and replacing them with messages more appropriate to the revolution. The new propagandistic plots centered on workers battling the evils of capitalism or imperialist forces.

With the close of the Cultural Revolution, traditional jingju repertoire eventually returned to the stage. New operas have also been written, some of which incorporate some of the musical and singing innovations developed during the Cultural Revolution. State-supported training schools were once again opened, too.

 ## A Mandarin Word-Melody

The melody is in two parts: the recitative-like phrases in *erhuang* and the metered aria in *xipi*. The melody of this recitative emphasizes the highly elaborate treatment of the Mandarin word-melody. When the aria begins at the start of the *xipi* meter (0:54), the melody follows a pentatonic (five-toned) scale (see also Chapters 45 and 50). At points in the aria (at 1:23 and 1:55), the singer improvises above the accompaniment to create contrast but each time returns to the original melody (at 1:36 and 2:10).

 ## Timbre and Texture

Because it is the lead melodic instrument, the timbre of the *jinghu* is strident. The *jinghu*'s part mirrors—but is not identical to—the singer during the recitative; this style is known as **heterophony** (two or more parts that are nearly the same sounding simultaneously). Heterophony is also heard during the aria, between the voice and the various accompanying melody instruments. The percussion ensemble provides a textural contrast as it punctuates musical segments.

 ## Rhythm and Punctuation

The aria is set in a four-beat rhythm and follows the unmetered recitative. The melody enters on the third beat. In our listening example, once the melody has started, a high-pitched drum strikes beats three and one to clarify the rhythm.

Now listen to this piece again, using the Listening Guide.

CONNECT YOUR PLAYLIST

Opera

Find a recording that tells a story through music.

Example: The Who, *Tommy* (1969) The rock group The Who created a new genre of music when they issued *Tommy*. Widely hailed as the first "rock opera," the series of songs told the story of a disabled young man who found hope and faith through playing pinball.

Listening Guide 🔊

Jingju Recorded: ca. 1995
"The Reunion" (2:41)

Time	Form	Timbre and Texture	Rhythm
0:00	Introduction	A wooden clapper punctuates the start of the recitative, followed by one strike on the drum, and then two strikes on a small gong.	Free
0:04	Recitative	Heterophony. The voice sings with the *jinghu* (two-stringed fiddle) a short motive based on word tones of spoken Mandarin.	
0:14		A brief instrumental interlude.	
0:21		Heterophony. Voice returns. The timbre of the *jinghu* is prominent.	
0:46		Brief interlude in which we hear the *wuchang* (percussion group).	
0:54	Aria	Throughout, the *wuchang* plays a melody—*xipi*—in four beats.	The four-beat *xipi* rhythm begins loosely and then becomes steady to the end of the aria.

🔍 Student FAQs ⚙️

Why does so much Chinese music sound so different to Western ears?

All musical cultures employ their own ideals of what sounds beautiful and what does not. One of the most striking areas of difference is that of vocal timbre and production. In addition, some forms of Chinese music use a five-tone (or pentatonic) scale. You can approximate one type of pentatonic scale by playing these notes on the piano keyboard: C-D-E-G-A-C. The gaps in the scale give it a distinctive tonality often associated with Eastern music. Western composers—particularly for films—often use a pentatonic scale when they are imitating Chinese music. However, jingju often uses all seven tones of its scale.

Why do some characters paint their faces in elaborate, colorful patterns in jingju?

Elaborate face painting is used for characters that belong to the "painted face" category of roles. The patterns and colors give key insights into the character's psychology and intrinsic personality. A symmetrical pattern indicates that the character is well balanced; complicated, asymmetrical patterns indicate instability. Colors all have meaning, too. For example, red face paint signals bravery and loyalty; yellow reveals a fierce, ambitious, but cool-headed personality. A touch of gold indicates the presence of another worldly spirit or god. Stylized face painting allows the knowledgeable audience to immediately read a character's essential characteristics.

Why do the musicians sit on stage, in full view of the audience?

The musicians play a key role in jingju productions, and are in many ways equal to the actors in setting the mood, expressing feelings, and signaling changes in the action. It's important to remember that jingju productions are not meant to be realistic in the sense of Western theater; the lack of sets, the use of face painting, and placing the musicians on stage all remind the audience that they are watching an artistic event. The "illusion of reality" that we expect in Western theater productions is simply not found in many other cultures.

EXPAND YOUR PLAYLIST

Traditional Chinese Music

Here are some recordings of other types of traditional Chinese music.

Chine: L'Art du Qin, Li Xiangting, Ocora 560001
Music on the traditional Chinese *qin* or zither, similar in style to the Japanese koto.

Chinese Music for the Pipa, Wu Man, Nimbus NI-5368
Wu Man is a modern virtuoso of the Chinese *p'ip'a*, or four-string lute. She plays both traditional and modern compositions on this recording.

The Art of the Chinese Erhu, Zhou Yu, Arc 1555
The *erhu* is a bowed lute, something like a violin, found in traditional Chinese music (see Chapter 62). This recording again combines traditional and more modern styles.

Vocal Music of Contemporary China, Vol. 1: The Han People, Folkways Records FW04091

Vol. 2: The National Minorities, Folkways Records FW04092
Two-volume set of vocal music in various styles.

Music of Chinese Minorities, King World Music Library 5142
Musical styles of six minority groups from China. These represent various different traditions (Korean, Mongolian, etc.) found within China that are not part of mainstream (i.e., government-sponsored) traditional Chinese music.

29 William Billings
"Chester"
Composed: 1770

"Chester" was the unofficial anthem of the American Revolution. Composed by William Billings of Boston, a tanner by trade, its melody and words stirred the hearts of colonists fighting for their freedom from Great Britain. It follows the musical conventions of hymnody, with four voices moving in rhythm together.

Listen to This First

♪ Melody

The melody in each of the five verses is sung by the tenor voice. Listen for the antecedent-consequent structure of the melody's four phrases. ■

🌐 Texture

In this recording, the tenors and basses sing the first verse, with the melody in the tenor, the higher of the two voices. Listen for the growing texture as the sopranos enter in the third verse, and the altos enter in the fourth. ■

👤 Harmony

Listen for the growing richness of the harmony with each verse as new voices come in. ■

LEARNING OBJECTIVES

29.1 Describe the role music played in the American Revolution.

29.2 Listen for the periodic phrase structure within the melody of William Billings's "Chester."

29.3 Listen for the contrasting melodic contours among the individual phrases of "Chester."

29.4 Recognize the nature of counterpoint among the four voices in "Chester."

29.5 Distinguish between two- and three-part harmony in "Chester."

29.6 Describe Billings's use of texture and harmony to delineate the text in "Chester."

29.7 Outline William Billings's career as a composer.

Virtually every war and every revolution has fostered its own songs, and among the colonists fighting for their independence in the American Revolution, the two most popular songs by far were "Yankee Doodle" and "Chester." Unlike many songs of the time, neither of these had been imported from Great Britain; both the words and music of "Chester" were written by a native of Boston. William Billings embodied the ideals of Yankee independence and self-reliance: A tanner by trade, he had taught himself how to write music, and his first publication, *The New-England Psalm-Singer* (1770), enjoyed great commercial success.

"Chester" is a song that follows the musical conventions of a **hymn**: Its four voices move in rhythm for the most part together. The musical style is very similar to that found in the chorale that ends Bach's Cantata 140 (see Chapter 20). The text setting is largely syllabic (one note per syllable), with a few melismas (multiple notes per syllable) that give added emphasis to key words. Groups singing this work could have sung the melody alone (in the tenor voice), or they could have sung all four independent parts. Unlike most hymns, however, "Chester" has a text that is largely secular. It begins and ends with praises of God but devotes itself largely to a description of the struggle for American independence. Only the first verse of text ("Let tyrants shake . . . ") appeared initially in 1770; over time Billings added new verses that reflected events and personages of the war. The second verse even singles out a series of British generals—Howe, Burgoyne, Clinton, Prescott, and Cornwallis—by name.

A recreation of a Revolutionary-era marching band celebrates Patriots Day in Concord, Massachusetts. During the Revolutionary War, an instrumental arrangement of Billings's "Chester" would have been a staple of the group's repertory.

A Structured Melody

The melody of "Chester" is built on the same principles of **periodic phrase structure** common in other works of the Classical Era. The structure of the tune reflects the structure of the text, which consists of two antecedent and two consequent phrases. Recall from Chapter 22 that an **antecedent phrase** introduces a sentence (*ante* = "before") and a **consequent phrase** completes it (the "consequence" of what was stated at the beginning of the sentence). Musical phrase structure works in the same way: An antecedent phrase cannot stand on its own because it ends off the tonic, but a consequent phrase completes the statement by ending on the tonic. In "Chester," the root note of the melody and the key as a whole is F.

Phrase	Text	Grammatical Structure	Melodic Structure	Melodic Contour
1	Let tyrants shake their iron rod,	Antecedent phrase: The thought is incomplete and ends with a comma.	Begins and ends off the tonic (C); an antecedent phrase	Arching: The melody begins and ends on the same note and moves up and down in between.
2	And Slav'ry clank her galling chains,	Completes the antecedent phrase as a whole, but the two lines together do not constitute a satisfying whole; again, this line ends with a comma.	Begins and ends off the tonic (G); a second antecedent phrase	Downward

(Continues)

CONNECT YOUR PLAYLIST

Periodic Phrase Structure

Find a song with a melody based on the principle of periodic phrase structure.

Example: Aloe Blacc, "Wake Me Up" (2014)
Both the verses and the chorus of this song demonstrate regular period phrase structure.

Phrase	Text	Grammatical Structure	Melodic Structure	Melodic Contour
3	We fear them not, we trust in God,	Completes the thought, although the comma indicates that this is not in fact the end of the text.	Begins off the tonic but ends on tonic note (F), but in a high register; a weak consequent phrase	Upward
4	New England's God forever reigns.	Completes the thought conclusively by providing reasons why "we fear them not" and why "we trust in God."	Begins and ends on tonic note (F) in lower register, the lowest note in the entire melody; a strong consequent phrase	Downward

Billings uses the melodic contour of each phrase to reinforce its antecedent or consequent function:

- The first phrase ("Let tyrants shake . . . ") begins and ends on the same note: It arches upward in the middle but in the end does not "go" anywhere. In terms of contour, it provides a neutral opening.

- The second phrase ("And Slav'ry . . . ") begins on this same note but moves decidedly lower in a downward contour. We have the sense now of having "gone" somewhere. We also have a sense that we need to return to the tonic.

- The third phrase ("We fear them not . . . ") begins on the same opening note as phrases 1 and 2 but moves upward now, and ends on the tonic. To some extent, this sounds like an ending—we have, after all, returned to the tonic—but our voices are high, and when we make an assertion in speech, we usually lower the pitch. (We raise the pitch, by contrast, to ask a question.)

- The fourth phrase ("New England's God . . . ") moves from the pitch we landed on at the end of the third phrase—the high tonic note, "F"—and descends rapidly, with shorter, faster notes, to the lower "F." This is in fact the lowest note of the melody, and it reinforces the sense of an ending.

Schematically, then, the phrase structure of the music can be represented in this way:

Antecedent		Consequent	
Antecedent 1	Antecedent 2	Consequent 1	Consequent 2
Let tyrants . . .	And Slav'ry . . .	We fear them not . . .	New England's God . . .

 ## Changing Textures

When Billings published this work, he wrote out the full parts for all four voices (soprano, alto, tenor, bass), with the melody always in the tenor. In this recording, however, the group sings the first verse with only two voices (tenor and bass), then adds the soprano in the second verse, and the alto in the third verse. In the fourth verse, all four voices continue, but now the sopranos switch to the independent line notated in Billings's original score. The fifth stanza retains the texture of the fourth.

 ## Changing Harmonies

The changing textures allow us to hear with special clarity the changing harmonies of the various verses. The first verse is in two-part harmony (tenor and bass). This two-part harmony continues in the second verse even though a third voice (soprano) has joined in. Because the soprano is doubling the tenor line (the melody), we hear a richer texture but not a richer harmony. In harmonic terms, the sopranos and tenors are singing the same line, even though they are an octave apart, with one of them higher than the other.

True three-part harmony begins with the third verse, when the altos join in with their own independent line. And four-part harmony begins with the fourth verse when the sopranos stop singing the melody and switch instead to their own distinctive line, different from all the others. Only now do we hear true four-part harmony, with each voice singing its own distinctive line. The fifth verse is also in true four-part harmony, with the same music but different words as the fourth verse.

With these points in mind, listen again to "Chester," using the Listening Guide.

William Billings Composed: 1770
"Chester" (2:15)

Time	Verse	Text	🌐 Texture	⬛ Harmony	🎵 Melody
0:00	1	Let tyrants shake their iron rod, And Slav'ry clank her galling chains, We fear them not, we trust in God, New England's God forever reigns.	Tenor and Bass	Two parts	In the Tenor here and in all five verses
0:25	2	Howe and Burgoyne and Clinton too, With Prescott and Cornwallis join'd, Together plot our Overthrow, In one Infernal league combin'd.	Tenor and Bass, with Soprano entering an octave above the Tenor: still basically two-part harmony	Two parts	
0:51	3	When God inspir'd us for the fight, Their ranks were broke, their lines were forc'd, Their ships were Shatter'd in our sight, Or swiftly driven from our Coast.	New Alto part joins in with its own independent line	Three parts	
1:17	4	The Foe comes on with haughty Stride; Our troops advance with martial noise, Their Vet'rans flee before our Youth, And Gen'rals yield to beardless Boys.	As in Verse 3, but now the Soprano part sings its own independent line	Four parts	
1:42	5	What grateful Off'ring shall we bring? What shall we render to the Lord? Loud Halleluiahs let us Sing, And praise his name on ev'ry Chord.	As in Verse 4	Four parts	

 🔍 Student FAQs ⚙️

Why is it called "Chester"?

It was customary in Billings's time to give song and hymn tunes a distinctive name because these tunes could be (and often were) sung to different texts. Many of Billings's tune names appear to have been arbitrary: One of his finest hymns is called "Africa," but it has no connection with that continent any more than do the tunes he called "Asia" and "Europe." "Chester" is a town in western Massachusetts; Billings named a series of other tunes after cities and towns in the Bay State, such as "Lexington," "Medford," and "Waltham."

The last chord sounds strange. Why is that?

Even when there are four independent lines (as in verses 4–5 in this recording), the last chord contains only two different notes, an F and a C, which together make up the interval of a fifth. A fifth all by itself, without a third (which in this case would be the note "A"), sounds "empty" or "hollow" to our ears.

PROFILE **William Billings** (1746–1800)

Independent Composer

Born in Boston, Billings trained as a tanner and was largely self-taught as a composer. He was an enthusiastic supporter of the Revolution and counted Paul Revere among his friends. Billings's *The New-England Psalm Singer* (1770) remains a landmark in the history of American music: It was the first published collection of musical works by an individual native-born composer.

Billings would go on to publish another five major collections of his works—more than 300 compositions in all, almost all for four-part chorus—and would establish or help set up several different schools in Massachusetts and Rhode Island. But without copyright laws, he could not support himself financially as a composer. He died in poverty and was buried in an unmarked grave, presumably in the old Central Burying Ground on the edge of the Boston Common. In a fitting if posthumous tribute, Billings was inducted into the Songwriters Hall of Fame in 1970. He was in many respects the first great American songwriter.

The frontispiece to Billings's *New-England Psalm Singer* shows a group of men seated at a round table singing a round ("Wake ev'ry breath"), in which all voices sing the same tune, but each enters at a different point (in the manner of "Row, row, row your boat"). The melody itself encircles the musicians. This engraving was done by one of Billings's Boston friends and fellow patriots, the silversmith Paul Revere, better known for his ride from Boston to Lexington to warn the people of advancing British troops.

EXPAND YOUR PLAYLIST: BILLINGS

- **Wake Ev'ry Breath.** This canon (round) for six voices over a contrasting bass line is depicted in the illustration above.
- **Lamentation Over Boston.** An anthem written after American troops had evacuated Boston following the battle of Bunker Hill in 1775. The text ("By the Rivers of Watertown we sat down and wept, / we wept when we remember'd, O Boston . . . ") is a variant on Psalm 137, sung by the exiled Israelites ("By the rivers of Babylon there we sat down / yea, we wept, when we remembered Zion").
- **I am the Rose of Sharon.** An anthem on a text from the Song of Solomon, 2:1–11.
- **Africa.** A stirring hymn to words by the great English hymnodist Isaac Watts.

THE COMPOSER SPEAKS   Billings on the Rules of Nature

Billings seems to have been quite proud to have taught himself composition. In the introduction to his *New-England Psalm Singer*, he argued that nature was the true source of all art. The excerpt here preserves Billings's idiosyncratic spelling and syntax.

❝Perhaps it may be expected that I should say something concerning Rules for Composition; to those I answer that Nature is the best dictator, for all the hard, dry, studied Rules that ever was prescribed, will not enable any Person to form an Air [i.e., melody] any more than the bare Knowledge of the four and twenty Letters, and strict Grammatical Rules will qualify a Scholar for composing a Piece of Poetry, or properly adjusting a Tragedy, without a Genius. It must be Nature, Nature who must lay the foundation. Nature must inspire the Thought. . . . For my own part, as I don't think myself confin'd to any Rules for Composition, laid down by any that went before me, neither should I think (were I to pretend to lay down Rules) that any one who came after me were in any ways obligated to adhere to them, any further than they should think proper: So in fact I think it best for every Composer to be his own Carver. Therefore, upon this Consideration, for me to dictate, or pretend to prescribe Rules of the Nature for others, would not only be very unnecessary, but also a great Piece of Vanity.❞

Source: William Billings, Introduction to *The New-England Psalm Singer* (Boston, 1770).

EXPAND YOUR PLAYLIST

Music of the American Revolution

"The Liberty Song"
- Set to an old English tune, the lyrics, by John Dickinson, of Pennsylvania, begin, "Come, join hand in hand, brave Americans all, / And rouse your bold hearts at fair Liberty's call."

"Yankee Doodle"
- This popular tune served literally hundreds of different texts, including "Yankee Doodle's Expedition to Rhode Island."

"The World Turned Upside Down"
- An old English ballad supposed to have been played when Cornwallis surrendered to Washington at Yorktown, Virginia. (Coldplay would record an entirely different song of the same name more than 225 years later.)

"The British Grenadiers"
- A popular song among the British forces at the time.

Making Connections: Music of the Baroque and Classical Eras

		Baroque	Classical
	Texture	Polyphonic and homophonic coexist	Both polyphonic and homophonic, but on the whole more homophonic
	Melody	Lyrical and declamatory (recitative) coexist; often virtuosic	Growing importance of periodic phrase structure in all genres of music, not just in dance
	Rhythm	Wider range of extremes, from smooth and flowing to choppy and irregular	More smoothly flowing melodies
	Timbre	Sharp distinction between vocal and instrumental parts	Establishment of the modern orchestra (strings, winds, percussion)
	Harmony	Harmony as an underlying basis for melody	Harmony becomes increasingly important as a large-scale structural element (tonic/nontonic/tonic)
	Form	Greater variety of formal principles: sectional form, binary form, theme and variations, ostinato	Theme and variations, minuet, rondo, sonata form, double-exposition concerto form
	Word–Music Relationships	Even greater use of word painting Texture and musical strongly support text	Word painting still present, but not as prevalent and often more subtle

IN REVIEW: Classical Style

Periodic phrase structure Melodies are constructed of antecedent (opening) and consequent (closing) phrases.

- Haydn, String Quartet in C Major, op. 76, no. 3, second movement (Chapter 22)
- Haydn, Symphony no. 102 in B♭ Major, third and fourth movements (Chapter 24)
- Mozart, Symphony no. 40 in G Minor, K. 550, first movement (Chapter 25)
- Billings, "Chester" (Chapter 29)

Theme and variations A modular form, with a theme followed by a series of discrete units, each of which presents a varied restatement of the theme.

- Haydn, String Quartet in C Major, op. 76, no. 3, second movement (Chapter 22)

Binary form A structure consisting of two sections, each of which is repeated in performance.

- Haydn, Symphony no. 102 in B♭ Major, third movement (Chapter 24)

Minuet form A **ternary form** (**ABA**) with a strong sense of contrast between the **A** and **B** sections, each of which is itself a binary form.

- Haydn, Symphony no. 102 in B♭ Major, third movement (Chapter 24)

Rondo form A structure in which the opening idea (**A**) returns repeatedly after the presentation of contrasting ideas (**B**, **C**, **D**, etc.), creating the pattern **ABACADA**.

- Haydn, Symphony no. 102 in B♭ Major, fourth movement (Chapter 24)

Sonata form An expanded type of binary form in which the music modulates to a secondary key area in the first section and then returns to the tonic about midway through the second section. A sonata form movement consists of an exposition, a development, and a recapitulation.

- Mozart, Symphony no. 40 in G Minor, K. 550, first movement (Chapter 25)

Double-exposition concerto form A type of sonata form often used in concertos of the Classical Era, with two separate expositions, the first for the orchestra (which does not modulate) and the second for the soloist and orchestra together (in which the music does modulate). The development and recapitulation follow the standard pattern of sonata form.

- Mozart, Piano Concerto in A Major, K. 488, first movement (Chapter 26)

The orchestra An ensemble of strings, winds, and percussion. The orchestra would expand in size and range later in the nineteenth and twentieth centuries, but its nucleus established itself in the second half of the eighteenth century.

- Haydn, Symphony no. 102 in B♭ Major, third and fourth movements (Chapter 24)
- Mozart, Symphony no. 40 in G Minor, K. 550, first movement (Chapter 25)
- Mozart, Piano Concerto in A Major, K. 488, first movement (Chapter 26)

Accompanied recitative A type of recitative in which the orchestra (and not merely the basso continuo) accompanies the singer.

- Mozart, *The Marriage of Figaro*, Act I, "Cosa sento" (Chapter 27)

PART 5 The Nineteenth Century

In the nineteenth century, the rationality of the Enlightenment gave way to a new fascination with imagination, individual emotion, and longing. **Romanticism**, as this movement was called, does not refer to a kind of love; it derives its name from a literary genre—the "romance," forerunner of today's novel—that was largely free of structural or narrative conventions. For the Romantic, dreams were as important as the intellect, and art—particularly music, which did not rely on words or the representation of objects—offered access to a realm beyond logic and the physical world. It was less a new style of art than a new way of thinking about art.

The music of the nineteenth century reflects this increased sense of freedom from convention. Composers felt obligated to develop their own distinctive voices. To make their music original, they explored musical extremes of all kinds. They wrote for orchestras that were bigger and louder than ever before. They emphasized extreme contrasts of texture between the simple and the complex. They wrote music that ranged from the disarmingly simple to the fiendishly difficult, often within the course of the same work. They gave growing importance to program music, writing instrumental music that illustrated a story, sometimes in very specific detail: The "March to the Scaffold" of Hector Berlioz's *Symphonie fantastique* (1830)

> **Chapter 33**
> Berlioz: *Symphonie fantastique*

depicts an artist being led to his execution, with music so graphic that we hear the sound his head makes when it falls into the bucket at the base of the guillotine. Felix Mendelssohn's *Overture to A Midsummer Night's Dream* (1826) explores the world of Shakespeare's comedy with a passage that imitates the sound

> **Chapter 32**
> Mendelssohn: *Overture to A Midsummer Night's Dream*

of a braying donkey. In short, the range of each musical element available to composers— melody, rhythm, harmony, dynamics, timbre, texture, form— grew exponentially in the nineteenth century.

"Most Romantic of All the Arts"

The way audiences listened to music—especially instrumental music—also changed in the nineteenth century. Because it lacked words, instrumental music had long been perceived as somewhat vague, not "about" anything in particular. Romanticism changed all that. Precisely *because* it lacked words, instrumental music could engage the imagination of listeners more directly and evoke ideas and emotions that could not be captured by nouns, verbs, and adjectives. This new way of listening is captured in a review of Beethoven's Fifth Symphony (1808) by

> **Chapter 30**
> Beethoven: Symphony no. 5 in C Minor, op. 67

Caspar David Friedrich's *The Wanderer* (1818) captures the Romantic fascination with dream, contemplation, and the infinite.

E. T. A. Hoffmann (best known as the author of *The Nutcracker* and other fantastical tales) in 1810. "Beethoven's music sets in motion the machinery of awe, of fear, of terror, of pain," Hoffmann declared, "and awakens that infinite yearning which is the essence of Romanticism." For Hoffmann music was "the most Romantic of all the arts," for it "opens to mankind an unknown realm, a world that has nothing in common with the outer world of the senses that surrounds him." This was particularly true of instrumental music, he felt, because it was unencumbered by words. Hoffmann's review won widespread praise because it articulated a fundamental shift from eighteenth-century thinking, which had held that the verbal arts gave form to the highest expressions of thought (see "Closer Look: The Power of Music").

Originality

Composers, once seen as artisans providing musical goods made to order, were now perceived to have a window on the infinite and the spiritual. Audiences thus expected that every new work would be a revelation. Originality became imperative: Each new symphony, each new opera, had to be somehow different from any before it. Composers of the nineteenth century were more conscious of their place in history than those of any previous time: To produce something original, they had to study all the more carefully what had come before. Johannes Brahms's Symphony no. 4 (1885)

Chapter 43
Brahms: Symphony no. 4 in E Minor, op. 98

builds on traditions of the past even while pushing forward the boundaries of the present. In the realm of opera, Giuseppe Verdi's *La Traviata* (1853)

Chapter 40
Verdi: *La Traviata*

and Richard Wagner's *The Valkyrie* (1856) both incorporate and

Chapter 41
Wagner, *The Valkyrie*

extend the norms of music for the stage. And Peter Ilyich Tchaikovsky's *Swan Lake* (1876),

Chapter 42
Tchaikovsky: *Swan Lake*

one of the first full-length ballets, showed that it was possible to tell an extended story through dance alone, entirely without words.

Nineteenth Century

Musical Landmarks

1770–1827 Ludwig van Beethoven

1809–1849 Frédéric Chopin

1810–1856 Robert Schumann

1797–1828 Franz Schubert

1803–1869 Hector Berlioz

1804–1847 Fanny Mendelssohn Hensel

1813–1883 Richard Wagner

1813–1901 Giuseppe Verdi

1775   1800   1810   **1819–1896** Clara Schumann

Historical Events

1804 Napoleon crowns himself Emperor of France

1815 Napoleon defeated at Waterloo

1825 Erie Canal completed

A Piano in Every Home

Chapter 31
Schubert: "Erlkönig"

Today, one is most likely to hear songs like Schubert's "Erlkönig" (1815) or Robert Schumann's "Dedication" (1840) in the concert hall,

Chapter 36
Robert Schumann:
"Dedication"

with a highly trained singer and a skilled pianist performing from the stage for a quiet audience. These songs were composed, however, to meet the growing nineteenth-century demand for music that could be played at home because in the nineteenth century pianos became a common fixture of middle-class households. The Industrial Revolution, which had begun toward the end of the eighteenth century, made it possible to manufacture goods on a scale never before imagined, which in turn made them cheaper to produce and sell. Demand grew steadily through the century for piano compositions, songs, and chamber music, and composers wrote works to meet this demand, including chamber music like Fanny Mendelssohn Hensel's Piano Trio in D Minor, op. 11, for piano, violin, and cello.

Chapter 34
Hensel: Piano Trio in
D Minor, op. 11

A British piano factory in the early 20th century. The scale of production reduced costs and made it possible for most middle-class households to own an instrument.

Music as Political Force

"Leave the dreaming and hesitation behind/Without fatigue, go forward!" With these words set to music in 1848 by Clara Schumann in her song "Forward!" the Dresden Choral Society exhorted listeners to work—and fight, if necessary—for a united and democratic

Chapter 36
Clara Wieck Schumann:
"Forward!"

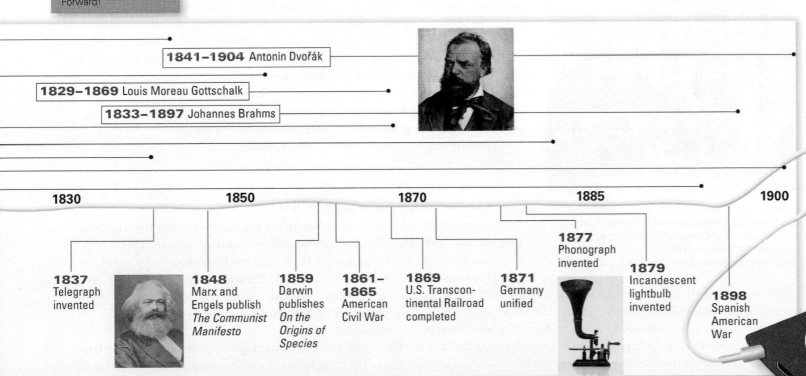

1841–1904 Antonin Dvořák

1829–1869 Louis Moreau Gottschalk

1833–1897 Johannes Brahms

1830	1850	1870	1885	1900

1837
Telegraph
invented

1848
Marx and
Engels publish
*The Communist
Manifesto*

1859
Darwin
publishes
*On the
Origins of
Species*

**1861–
1865**
American
Civil War

1869
U.S. Transcontinental Railroad
completed

1871
Germany
unified

1877
Phonograph
invented

1879
Incandescent
lightbulb
invented

1898
Spanish
American
War

Street fighting in Berlin, 1848. Barricades were constructed by ordinary citizens to block the movement of the royal armies.

Germany. This push was part of a broader impulse throughout Europe to achieve the goals set out by the French Revolution of 1789: freedom through representative government, equality through the abolition of hereditary class privilege, and fraternity through rights of assembly and association. A series of uprisings in 1848–1849 throughout continental Europe was largely unsuccessful at the time but helped pave the way for later political reforms.

Music proved an important vehicle for expressing political sentiment throughout the nineteenth century. In the United States, Louis Moreau Gottschalk's *Union* (1862) for piano sought to rally support for the northern cause during the Civil War by incorporating such patriotic tunes as "The Star-Spangled Banner" and "Yankee Doodle."

> **Chapter 38**
> Gottschalk: *Union*

Nationalism

Another political impulse that developed over the course of the nineteenth century was **nationalism**. More and more peoples began to perceive their social identities on the basis of a shared language and cultural practices in a community that extended far beyond any one locale or region.

But not all groups united by language and culture had their own nation-states. Many ethnic Czechs and Hungarians, for example, were subjects of the Austrian Empire, whose capital (Vienna) and official language (German) were foreign to them. Poles, in turn, fell under the rule of the Prussian or Russian Empires at various times and places. Music proved a powerful outlet for the expression of nationalistic feelings. Often more powerfully than language, composers could express in sound their sense of national pride by using the characteristic melodic and rhythmic elements of their peoples. Frédéric Chopin, living in Paris, felt deep sympathy for the plight of his native Poland. His Mazurka in B♭ Major, op. 7, no. 1 (1830s), was one of numerous pieces he wrote using elements of Polish folk music. Chopin's Polonaises, in particular—piano works based on the proud national dance of Poland—were described by one contemporary as "cannons wrapped in flowers."

> **Chapter 37**
> Chopin: Mazurka in B♭,
> op. 7, no. 2

The End of Poland (*Finis Poloniae*) shows a Polish officer comforting two disconsolate comrades after the Battle of Ostrolenka (1830), in which the Russian army defeated Polish forces. Polish nationalism was a driving force behind the uprising.

The Revolution in Transportation

Increased mobility on both land and sea in the nineteenth century fostered commercial and cultural connections that would have been unthinkable only a few generations before. In the summer of 1893, Antonín Dvořák was able to travel from New York City to the Czech-American community of Spillville in northeastern Iowa in less than three days, where he would compose a string quartet he called "American." Music publishers could distribute their music on a global basis for the first time. European musicians could tour the United States and American musicians could tour Europe with ease.

> **Chapter 44**
> Dvořák: String Quartet in F
> Major, op. 96 ("American")

Even though the world's population increased dramatically in the nineteenth century, technological innovations like the telegraph, telephone, railroads, and steamships made the world a smaller place. The completion of the transcontinental railroad in 1869 reduced the six-month travel time from New York to San Francisco to one week. On the water, steam-powered engines replaced sails, cutting the ocean voyage from Europe to the United States to as little as six days.

This photograph shows the ceremony marking the completion of the Transcontinental Railroad in 1869, linking the eastern and western United States by rail for the first time.

CLOSER LOOK   The Power of Music

Josef Danhauser's *Franz Liszt at the Piano* (1840) shows the composer and pianist Franz Liszt surrounded by a gathering of famous writers and musicians. The literary figures, including Alexandre Dumas, Victor Hugo, and George Sand, have all interrupted their reading to listen to Liszt play. This group portrait idealizes the power of music—it could be more important than drama, poetry, and fiction. Even the great writers of the era stop reading to listen to the music!

The Italian composer and violin virtuoso **Niccolò Paganini** (1782–1840). He is to the violin what Liszt is to the piano. Paganini is widely rumored to have made a pact with the devil in exchange for his talent; he does nothing to dispel the story.

Gioacchino Rossini (1792–1868), the enormously successful and beloved composer of Italian opera. He stands arm-in-arm with Paganini listening to Liszt.

Victor Hugo (1802–1885), the greatest literary figure in nineteenth-century France. He is famous for his poetry, dramas, criticism, and above all his novels, which include *Les Misérables* and *The Hunchback of Notre Dame.*

A portrait of the English poet **George Gordon, Lord Byron** (1788–1824). Byron had died fighting for Greece's independence from the Ottoman Empire and was beloved in death both as a poet and as a fighter for freedom.

Alexandre Dumas *père* (1802–1870), author of *The Count of Monte Cristo* and *The Three Musketeers.*

A bust of the composer **Ludwig van Beethoven** (1770–1827). Beethoven cast a long shadow over musicians in the nineteenth century and is accorded pride of place here. While others contemplate Liszt, Liszt contemplates Beethoven.

The novelist **George Sand** (1804–1876), whose real name is Amandine-Aurore-Lucile Dudevant. She wrote under a man's name, dressed in men's clothes, and smoked in public. In the 1830s she was Chopin's lover.

Franz Liszt (1811–1886), virtuoso pianist and composer.

Marie d'Agoult (1805–1876), French author who writes under the pen name "Daniel Stern." She lived with Liszt in the late 1830s and bore him three children. One of their children, Cosima, eventually marries the composer Richard Wagner (see Chapter 36).

▲ Josef Danhauser, *Franz Liszt at the Piano*, 1840.

30 Ludwig van Beethoven

Symphony no. 5 in C Minor, op. 67

Composed: 1808

Beethoven's Fifth Symphony is one of the most famous works of music ever written, and with good reason: its energy and drive have proven irresistible to generations of listeners. It helped redefine the symphony as a genre that carried meanings beyond the notes themselves.

Listen to This First

🎵 Rhythm

You may already know the opening motif: "short-short-short-LONG." Listen for how this basic rhythmic idea is varied not only in the first movement, but in all four movements. ■

📊 Dynamics

Notice the repeated and sudden contrasts between loud and soft, not only in the first movement, but in all four movements. ■

〰️ Timbre

Listen to how Beethoven varies the sound of the full orchestra by using all of it at times and only a small portion of it at others (just strings, or just winds). Be ready for the addition of new instruments (especially trombones) at the beginning of the finale. ■

🏛️ Form

Listen for the variety of forms among the four movements:
- **1:** Sonata form.
- **2:** Variations on two different themes, one soft and one loud.
- **3:** Ternary form (**ABA′**), with the return of **A** varied.
- **4:** Sonata form. ■

LEARNING OBJECTIVES

30.1 Describe the opening motif of Ludwig van Beethoven's Symphony no. 5 in terms of rhythm.

30.2 Listen for the transformations of the opening theme.

30.3 Describe how Beethoven uses dynamics in the first movement of Symphony no. 5.

30.4 Discuss how Beethoven uses instruments in the first movement of Symphony no. 5.

30.5 Explain how Symphony no. 5 is cyclic.

30.6 Outline Beethoven's career as a performer and composer.

The opening of Beethoven's Fifth Symphony is quite possibly both the briefest and best-known theme in all of music: It is instantly recognizable. Generations of listeners around the world have heard this theme as an aural symbol of strength and resolve precisely because it is so simple and straightforward. Like an acorn that grows into a giant oak tree, this theme provides the basic rhythmic motif for almost every theme in the work. Even though Beethoven gave no indication in the score of an extramusical meaning of this work, critics from his time onward have interpreted it as a progression from struggle (in the first movement) to triumph (in the finale), from the darkness of C minor to the brightness of C major.

Beethoven never wrote a program for the work, but when asked the meaning of this opening idea, he is said to have grumbled in response: "Thus Fate pounds at the portal." Whether the report is true or not—it was first published long after the composer's death by a notoriously unreliable witness—it has been repeated many times over. This symphony does indeed seem to "describe" a process that moves from struggle (in the first movement) to triumph (in the finale).

Beethoven's symphonies—he wrote nine altogether—helped establish his reputation as the greatest instrumental composer of his time. Works like the Fifth Symphony helped redefine the symphony as a genre that carried meaning beyond the notes themselves, without the aid of a sung text or program. Beethoven's last symphony, the Ninth, includes voices and a text in its finale, and his Sixth Symphony ("Pastoral") is programmatic. But in the Fifth Symphony, Beethoven created a work that challenged listeners to create their own sense of meaning.

Rhythm: The Power of Four Notes

CONNECT YOUR PLAYLIST

Unison Opening

Find a work that opens with a statement in unison.

Example: Pink, "So What" (2008) One critic described the opening of this song as ideal for "massive car singalongs."

The Fifth Symphony opens with a distinctive but deceptively simple theme. It consists of only four notes and two different pitches. The instruments play in **unison**, and we hear no harmony of any kind. The rhythm is what gives this idea its real identity: short-short-short-LONG—that is, three notes of equal length followed by one longer note. One of the things that make this symphony so remarkable is the fact that Beethoven transforms this simple musical idea in so many different ways.

In the first movement, the process of transformation begins almost instantly:

1. 0:00   Opening statement of the *s-s-s-L* figure, with last note held out long by the strings in unison (monophonic texture).
2. 0:03   Restatement of the *s-s-s-L* figure, moved down a step. The texture is still monophonic—the strings are still playing in unison—and the rhythm is still the same, but the notes are different.
3. 0:06   Restatement of the *s-s-s-L* figure in different voices in quick succession (polyphonic texture) and on different pitches. Now the texture *and* the notes are different; only the rhythm remains the same.

This transformation continues throughout all the movements that follow. The pitches, harmonies, and textures are constantly shifting, but the same basic rhythmic idea—short-short-short-LONG—remains recognizable from the beginning of the symphony to the very end. Only occasionally does it leave the stage, and when it does, it always comes back.

Dynamics: Loud versus Soft

One of the more striking features of the Fifth Symphony is its treatment of dynamics. The music repeatedly moves without warning from extremely loud to extremely soft and vice versa. The very opening establishes this contrast: The loud unison is immediately followed by a soft passage. These dynamic contrasts are especially prominent at the end of the third movement, where the music remains extremely quiet for a very long time before moving without a break into the finale, which erupts in an explosion of sound. Composers had exploited dynamic contrasts long before the early nineteenth century, but the number of sudden changes, their rapidity, and, above all, the wide extremes of volume in this work were unprecedented.

0:00 **(1)** Opening statement of the *s-s-s-L* motif, with last note held out long (unison). All instruments play G-G-G-E flat.

0:03 **(2)** Restatement of the *s-s-s-L* motif, moved down a step (unison) and held out longer. All instruments play F-F-F-D.

0:07 **(3)** Restatement of the *s-s-s-L* motif in different voices in rapid succession and on different pitches (polyphonic texture). Only the rhythm remains the same.

Timbre: The Orchestra Grows

The contrast in dynamics between the end of the third movement and the beginning of the finale is reinforced by the addition of new instruments at that point. The piccolo and contrabassoon enrich the upper and lower ranges of the orchestra, respectively, and the trombones help create an even fuller sound in the middle ranges.

Already, in the first movement, Beethoven repeatedly contrasts wind instruments (flute, clarinet, oboe, bassoon, horns, and trumpets) against the stringed instruments (violins, violas, cellos, and double basses). The oboe has an unusual and wholly unexpected solo in the recapitulation of the first movement. The double basses have an unusually prominent and difficult passage in the middle (**B**) section of the ternary-form third movement. By using these instruments in such distinctive ways, Beethoven creates an enormous sense of breadth within a small space: The Fifth is among the shortest symphonies he wrote. Later composers of the nineteenth century would extend the range of orchestral timbre still further.

Four Movements, Cyclic Form

Each of the four movements has its own individual form:

- First movement: **sonata form**: Exposition (repeated), development, recapitulation, coda.
- Second movement: **double variations**. This is a set of variations that alternate between two different themes, one soft and one loud.
- Third movement: ternary form (**ABA′**), with the return of **A** varied. This is similar to the minuet form of the eighteenth-century symphony (see Chapter 24), but the return of **A** is varied. And while the meter is still triple (as in the eighteenth-century's minuet), nineteenth-century composers like Beethoven tended to call this kind of ternary movement a **scherzo**, from the Italian word for "joke," because it often assumes a playful and sometimes biting character.

  This third movement leads without a break into the next one.

- Fourth movement: sonata form, but with a surprising twist. The music from the close of the third movement returns at the end of the development, just before the beginning of the **recapitulation** when the fourth movement's opening theme comes back in the tonic.

  The third and fourth movements, as noted, are connected both in time (the third leads without a break into the fourth) and in their musical material (the closing portion of the third movement returns unexpectedly in the middle of the fourth). All four movements are further linked through various permutations of the *short-short-short-LONG* figure. When the individual movements of a work are linked in such tangible and distinctive ways (usually through the use of a common musical idea) we say that the work as a whole is in **cyclic form**. Other composers of symphonies in the nineteenth century would follow Beethoven's lead by integrating individual movements into a more tightly integrated—cyclic—whole.

Listening Guide

Ludwig van Beethoven Composed: ca. 1808
Symphony no. 5 in C Minor, op. 67, first movement (7:53)

Time	Form: Sonata–Form Section	Melody	Rhythm: The Short-Short-Short-LONG Motif	Timbre
0:00 (1:32)*	**Exposition** Tonic (C minor)	1: the *s-s-s-L* motif in its original form	First in the powerful unison, then in polyphony	Strings alone at first, then alternating with full orchestra
0:30 (2:02)	Transition	2: constant motion	In the bass	Full orchestra
0:47 (2:20)	Secondary key area (E♭ major)	3: more lyrical, a sense of relative rest after the turmoil of the opening	In the beginning by the horn, then in the bass	Strings with horns; strings and other winds enter gradually.
1:12 (2:44)		4: triumphant	Same as 1, but in a different key and in the major mode	Full orchestra
3:05	**Development** (harmonically unstable)	1	In unison horns, then in many different voices (polyphony)	Full orchestra
3:44		3	In unison strings, then polyphonic. The music seems to lose its drive momentarily.	Strings alternate against winds
4:33	**Recapitulation** Tonic (C minor)	1	In the theme	Full orchestra in union; even louder and more powerful than the opening
4:53		Oboe "cadenza": mournful, slow, rhythmically free	Motif disappears momentarily	Solo oboe, a complete surprise
5:05		2	In many voices	Full orchestra
5:28		3	First unison, then polyphonic	Starts with bassoons, then full orchestra
5:58		4	In many voices	Full orchestra
6:16	**Coda**	1	In many voices	Full orchestra
6:33	Tonic	3	In many voices	
6:49		New theme: march-like	*s-s-s-L* motif absent here	
7:05		1	Returns in strings, then full orchestra (unison, 7:05), then polyphonic (7:15) before final cadence	

* Second timing in parentheses = exposition repeat

Second movement: Andante con moto (11:55)

Time	Form	🎵 Melody	Rhythm: The Short-Short-Short-LONG Motif	〰️ Timbre
0:00	**A** Tonic (A♭ Major)	Theme 1	At the close of the theme (0:42, 0:55, etc.)	Low strings at beginning, then dialogue between strings and winds
1:07	B (C Major)	Theme 2	At the beginning of the theme (1:09) and repeated throughout	Strings and winds; then full orchestra, including trumpets and drums, at 1:26
2:28	A′ (A♭ Major)	Theme 1 varied		Low strings at beginning, then dialogue between strings and winds
3:30	B′ (C Major)	Theme 2 varied		Strings and winds; then full orchestra, including trumpets and drums
4:47	A″ (A♭ Major)	Theme 1 varied		Running figure in lower string, with accompanying winds above; then full orchestra
7:01	B″ (C Major)	Theme 2 varied		Begins with full orchestra, including trumpets and drums, then grows softer
7:55	A‴ (A♭ Minor)	Theme 1 varied		Starts with mostly winds, then erupts with bright trumpets and timpani (8:43)
9:44	Coda	Theme 1 varied, with a slightly faster pace at the beginning		Melody in winds, then full orchestra (10:02)

Third movement: Allegro (5:12)

Time	Form	Form	Rhythm: The Short-Short-Short-LONG Motif	Timbre
0:00	**A (C minor)**	Theme 1: rising figure, soft	In the melody at the very beginning	Mostly low strings
0:21		Theme 2: repeated notes, loud	In the melody at the very beginning	Horns, then full orchestra
0:40		Theme 1, varied slightly		Mostly low strings
1:02		Theme 2		Full orchestra
1:21		Theme 1 returns, varied yet again		Mostly low strings
1:47		Theme 2		Full orchestra
1:52	**B (C Major)**	Theme 3: rapid, upward moving	At the end of the theme, several times in quick succession (2:05, 2:06, 2:07)	Starts in low strings and moves upward; polyphonic texture as voices enter one by one
3:24	**A′ (C minor)**	Theme 1 varied		Strings and winds, very quietly
3:43		Theme 2 varied		Strings play pizzicato (plucked); all very soft this time
4:02		Theme 1 varied yet again		Strings continue to play pizzicato
4:34	**Coda**	Theme 1 varied		Low rumbling in the bass; strings play with the bow once again; leads without a break into the fourth movement

Q Student FAQs ⚙

Why isn't the short-short-short-LONG motif present in every theme?

It is rarely absent for very long, but Beethoven no doubt wanted to avoid having the theme overstay its welcome. He created sufficient variety by transforming the motif both within and across movements, and also by providing some contrast in the form of themes that don't use the motif at all.

What do the extra musicians who come in at the beginning of the finale do during the first three movements?

Nothing. They must sit quietly and wait their turn. They are nevertheless paid at the same rate as the musicians who have been playing throughout.

Fourth movement: Allegro (8:57)

Time	Form: Sonata form section	🎵 Melody	🥁 Rhythm (*s-s-s-L* motif)	〰️ Timbre
0:00	**Exposition** Tonic (C Major)	Theme 1: upward moving, triumphant	In the melody at many points (0:08, 0:11, etc.)	Full orchestra, now joined for the first time by trombones, contrabassoons, piccolo
0:24	Transition	Theme 2: rushing	Not present	Mostly strings
0:35	Secondary key area (G Major)	Theme 3: broad, lyrical	In the bass many times (0:46, 0:48, etc.)	Horns carry the main melody at first
1:02		Theme 4: sweeping, energetic	At the beginning of the theme and repeated often	Full orchestra
1:29		Theme 5: descending, more stately	In the repeated notes of the theme (1:31, 1:33, etc.)	Full orchestra
2:00	**Development** (harmonically unstable)	Theme 4	In the theme and later (2:50) in the bass as well	Full orchestras; trombones are particularly prominent beginning at 2:37
3:34		Unexpected return of the opening theme from the third movement	At the beginning of the theme, as In the third movement	Low strings and winds, all very quiet
4:13	**Recapitulation** Tonic (C Major)	Theme 1	In the melody at many points	Full orchestra
4:37		Theme 2	Not present	
4:48		Theme 3	In the bass many times	Full orchestra
5:19		Theme 4	In the theme and later in the bass as well	
5:45		Theme 5	In the repeated notes of the theme	
6:48	**Coda** Tonic (C Major)	**Theme 3**	Not present	Begins in winds, then full orchestra
7:43		Theme 5, pace of the music accelerates; Theme 1 returns toward the very end (8:00)	In the repeated notes of the theme	Full orchestra

PROFILE   Ludwig van Beethoven (1770–1827)

Composing through Deafness

Deafness was only one of many obstacles Beethoven faced as a composer. He was exploited as a child by his father, a court musician in Bonn (in present-day northern Germany), who lied about his son's age to make the boy's talents as a pianist seem even more remarkable. More seriously, his father's alcoholism forced the young Beethoven to become the principal breadwinner for his family while still in his mid-teens. But a grant from the ruler of Bonn allowed him to travel to Vienna to study composition with Joseph Haydn (among others), and Beethoven quickly established a reputation there both as a piano virtuoso and as a composer. He would spend the rest of his life in Vienna.

When Beethoven began to go deaf in his late 20s, he became increasingly withdrawn from society. It is unclear exactly what caused this deafness, but we know from his letters that it caused him great psychological pain. He eventually had to stop performing in public altogether, and his despair at one point drove him to contemplate suicide. "It was only *my art* that held me back," he confessed to a friend in 1802. "Ah, it seemed to me impossible to leave the world until I had brought forth all that I felt was within me."

Beethoven's contemporaries found his music demanding. Still, he was widely recognized at the time as the greatest living composer of instrumental music, and he enjoyed the financial support of an important group of aristocratic patrons in Vienna. The last 15 years of his life were nevertheless filled with difficulties. He suffered from chronic poor health, his deafness grew even worse, and he became embroiled in a bitter custody battle with his sister-in-law over her son, Karl. Beethoven held his sister-in-law in low regard—as did the courts, who awarded him custody of the boy in 1816. But Beethoven was ill-prepared to become the single parent of a teenager, and constant struggles over the next decade, both in and out of court, took their toll emotionally and financially.

When he died in 1827, Beethoven was hailed as a national hero. His funeral was attended by throngs of spectators who wanted to catch a last glimpse of the great composer who called himself a "tone poet," a poet who created with musical sounds rather than words.

Beethoven came of age after the French Revolution (1789), and like most others of his generation did not wear a wig. While this may seem merely a matter of changing fashion, the practice of showing one's own hair reflected a broader change in attitudes toward each self as a distinct individual. It also reflected a gradual leveling of social hierarchies that Beethoven himself endorsed: no more "big wigs."

EXPAND YOUR PLAYLIST: BEETHOVEN

- **Piano Sonata in C# Minor, op. 27, no. 2** ("Moonlight")
- **Piano Sonata in D Minor, op. 31, no. 2** ("Tempest")
- **Piano Sonata in F Minor, op. 57** ("Appassionata")
- **String Quartet in F Major, op. 59, no. 1** ("Razumofsky")
- **Violin Concerto in D Major, op. 61**
- **Piano Concerto in E ♭ Major, op. 73** ("Emperor")

Beethoven's Symphonies

- **Symphony no. 1 in C Major, op. 21**

- **Symphony no. 2 in D Major, op. 36**
  Beethoven's first two symphonies are similar in format and scope to Haydn's late symphonies.

- **Symphony no. 3 in E♭ Major, op. 55**
  Called the "Eroica" ("Heroic") Symphony by Beethoven himself, this is widely viewed as Beethoven's breakthrough symphony, a work almost twice as long as any previous symphony by any other composer. Beethoven originally intended to dedicate the work to Napoleon but became disillusioned when Napoleon crowned himself Emperor of France. He finally issued it instead "In memory of a great man."

- **Symphony no. 4 in B♭ Major, op. 60**
  An energetic work in four movements.

- **Symphony no. 6 in F Major, op. 68**
  Called the "Pastoral" by Beethoven, this is the most programmatic of his symphonies.

- **Symphony no. 7 in A Major, op. 92**
  A large work in four movements, one of the most popular of all the symphonies. Sarah Brightman's 2000 hit "Figlio Perduto" ("Lost Son") is based on the music of this symphony's second movement.

- **Symphony no. 8 in F Major, op. 93**
  A relatively small-scale work and more playful than Beethoven's other symphonies.

- **Symphony no. 9 in D Minor, op. 125**
  The finale incorporates vocal soloists and a chorus singing Schiller's "Ode to Joy." This is the symphony that was performed in celebration of the fall of the Berlin Wall in 1989.

31 Franz Schubert

"Erlkönig," D. 328
Composed: 1815

Schubert's song "Erlkönig" presents a drama in miniature, the story of a father riding on horseback through the night, holding his ill child. The song uses only one singer and a pianist to portray a narrator, three different characters, and one highly emotional series of events.

Listen to This First

🏛 Form	🎧 Word–Music Relationships
Listen for the way in which the same basic musical idea is presented in each strophe of the text, but in a new guise each time. ■	Listen to how the song captures the rhythms of the horse's hooves beating along the road. Notice the way in which this conveys the perspectives of four different characters—the narrator, the father, the child, and the Erlking—by changes in register (high versus low), dynamics (loud versus soft), and harmony (minor versus major). ■

LEARNING OBJECTIVES

31.1 Define ballad and *Lied*.

31.2 Define modified strophic form.

31.3 Listen for the ways in which the voice and piano together differentiate the roles of the narrator, the father, the child, and the Erlking in Franz Schubert's "Erlkönig."

31.4 Listen for the ways in which melody, harmony, and rhythm differ from strophe to strophe in Schubert's "Erlkönig."

31.5 Outline Schubert's career as a composer.

Schubert's song opens with a loud, fast, repetitive figure that evokes the sound of a galloping horse. The narrator tells us about the father and child on horseback. We hear a dialogue between father and son: The feverish boy imagines that he hears and sees the malicious Erlking, a shadowy figure from the land of the spirits, who has come to take him away from the land of the living; the father tries to comfort the child, telling him that his visions come from the wind and from wisps of cloud. And then we hear the voice of the Erlking himself, who at first tries to attract the child with promises of a wonderful realm of games, dance, and beautiful clothing, but who eventually tires of this and resorts to force to carry the child away. At the end, the narrator returns to tell us the grim conclusion.

The text of Schubert's song is a poem written in the 1780s by celebrated German poet Johann Wolfgang Goethe (1749–1832). Goethe's "Erlkönig" is a **ballad**, a poem that tells a story, and Schubert's setting of it, also known as a ballad, makes the poetry even more intense. Just as a speaker giving a dramatic reading can shape a poem's sound and meaning by emphasizing certain words, varying the speed of delivery, or altering the register and volume of the voice, so can a composer shape the sound and meaning of the text by manipulating these same elements—rhythm, tempo, register, dynamics—and by incorporating other elements unique to music, such as melody and harmony. Schubert's setting is longer and more musically varied than any of the many earlier settings of the poem: The piano part is more important and technically demanding, and the voice part covers a wider range than ever before.

Songs for voice and piano were so widespread and popular in Germany from the late eighteenth century onward that we often use the German term today to identify this genre: *Lied* (pronounced "leet") is the German word for "song" (the plural, *Lieder*, is pronounced "leader"). Schubert wrote hundreds of *Lieder* for voice and piano during his short life. "Erlkönig" is one of his earliest: He wrote it when he was only 18.

Modified Strophic Form

Almost every composer who writes a song begins with the text. In this case, Schubert began with Goethe's poem of eight strophes (also known as stanzas). He could have set each strophe to the same music, creating a song in simple strophic form. Or he could have written entirely new music for each strophe. In the end, he chose a middle path: He set each strophe to the same basic melody and rhythms presented in the first strophe, but he varied the music with every subsequent strophe. If there were no words to this song, we would hear, in effect, a set of variations (strophes 2–8) on a theme (strophe 1). But because there are words, we call the form of this song **modified strophic form**. Each strophe, as we shall see, is varied (modified) to fit the text in a particular way.

 Word–Music Relationships: Creating Characters

Like any good song composer, Schubert studied the content, meter, and rhyme scheme of the poem very carefully before deciding on an appropriate musical setting, and he used these musical elements to connect the music with the words:

- **Rhythm:**   Schubert uses a repetitive rhythmic figure at the very beginning of his setting to capture the constant forward movement of the pair on horseback and the thundering of the horse's hooves.

- **Register:**   There are three characters and a narrator in this dramatic poem, all of them sung by a single voice. Schubert differentiates among them by placing each in a particular range or register of the voice. The narrator occupies a neutral space in the middle, the father's words are always sung in the lowest register, and the words of the child and the Erlking both sound in the highest range.

- **Dynamics:**   Schubert indicates gradations of volume with great care in this song. The father is unchanging: He always sings **forte** (the Italian word for "loud"). The child starts softly but grows louder and louder. The Erlking starts softly and grows even softer before erupting at the end, when he loses patience and finally seizes the child.

- **Harmony:**   Schubert begins and ends in the key of G minor but moves through several different keys in between to provide harmonic variety. He even shifts to the major mode when the voice of the Erlking enters.

Now listen to the piece again, using the Listening Guide.

CONNECT YOUR PLAYLIST

The Ballad

Find an example of a musical ballad.

Example: The Dixie Chicks, "Goodbye Earl" (2000)
This darkly comic "murder ballad" tells the story of two women killing an abusive husband.

Moritz von Schwind, *A Schubert Evening with Joseph von Spaun*. In this scene from a Viennese salon, Schubert plays the piano while the singer sits beside him. The salon was a gathering in a home, where guests conversed, ate, drank, and entertained one another with song, poetry readings, or reenactments of scenes from dramas. During Schubert's lifetime, the *Lied* was a distinctly domestic genre. Only later did it move into the concert hall.

Listening Guide �))

Franz Schubert Composed: 1815
"Erlkönig," D. 328 (4:00)

Form:⟨⟩ Strophe	Character	Melody:♪ Register	German Original	English Translation
Introduction	Piano solo			
1	Narrator	Middle	Wer reitet so spät durch Nacht und Wind? Es ist der Vater mit seinem Kind; er hat den Knaben wohl in dem Arm, er fasst ihn sicher, er hält ihn warm.	Who rides so late through night and wind? It is the father with his child; He holds the boy fast in his arms. He holds him tightly, he keeps him warm.
2	Father	Low	Mein Sohn, was birgst du so bang dein Gesicht?	My son, why do you hide your face so anxiously?
	Son	High	Siehst, Vater, du den Erlkönig nicht? den Erlkönig mit Kron und Schweif?	Do you not see, father, the Erlking? The Erlking with crown and train?
	Father	Low	Mein Sohn, es ist ein Nebelstreif.	My son, it is a streak of clouds.
3	The Erlking	High	"Du liebes Kind, komm, geh mit mir! gar schöne Spiele spiel' ich mit dir; manch bunte Blumen sind an dem Strand, meine Mutter hat manch gülden Gewand."	"You dear child, come with me! Such wonderful games I will play with you; So many beautiful flowers are on the shore, My mother has many a golden robe."
4	Son	High	Mein Vater, mein Vater, und hörest du nicht, was Erlenkönig mir leise verspricht?	My father, my father, do you not yet hear, What the Erlking softly promises me?
	Father	Low	Sei ruhig, bleibe ruhig, mein Kind: in dürren Blättern säuselt der Wind.	Be calm, stay calm, my child: Through the dry leaves rustles the wind.
5	The Erlking	High	"Willst, feiner Knabe, du mit mir gehen? meine Töchter sollen dich warten schön; meine Töchter führen den nächtlichen Reihn und wiegen und tanzen und singen dich ein."	"Will you, dear child, come with me? My daughters shall wait on you well; my daughters dance at night and will cradle and dance and sing to you."

Time	Dynamics	Rhythm	Harmony: Key Area
0:00	Forte (loud)	Driving, repetitive triplets	G minor
0:00	Forte	Driving, repetitive triplets	-
0:50	Forte		
1:03	Piano (soft)		
1:20	Forte		
1:29	Pianissimo (very soft)	Lilting triplets	B♭ major
1:50	Forte	Driving, repetitive triplets	Unstable
2:04			
2:13	Pianississimo (extremely soft)	Flowing triplets	C major

(Continues)

Q Student FAQs

Could this song be performed by a female singer?

Yes. This song has been performed and recorded many times by men and women alike. Songs are often transposed—reset in a different key—to fit the range of the singer.

What do singers do with their bodies while singing? Do they act out the drama of these songs?

This is always a challenge. Singers can't (and don't) remain completely motionless; such woodenness would distract from the emotional content of the song. At the same time, overly emphatic gesturing with the hands and arms might be even more distracting to an audience. So singers generally try for something in between: subtle gestures, changes of pose, slight movement of the body and expressions of the face, but nothing excessive.

What does "Erlkönig" mean?

In German, *König* means "king" and *Erl* means "alder," a type of birch tree. But the legend of the Erlking, a figure visible only to those who are about to die, originated in Denmark as *ellerkonge*, which means "elf king." At some point in the eighteenth century *ellerkonge* became "Erlkönig" in German.

Form: Strophe	Character	Melody: Register	German Original	English Translation
6	Son	High	Mein Vater, mein Vater, und siehst du nicht dortErlkönigs Töchter am düstren Ort?	My father, my father, do you not see there Erlking's daughters in the desolate place?
	Father	Low	Mein Sohn, mein Sohn, ich seh es genau, es scheinen die alten Weiden so grau.	My son, my son, I see it clearly, The old fields appear so gray.
7	The Erlking	High	"Ich liebe dich, mir reizt deine schöne Gestalt, und bist du nicht willig, so brauch ich Gewalt."	"I love you, your lovely form charms me, and if you're unwilling, then I'll use force."
	Son	High	"Mein Vater, mein Vater, jetzt fasst er mich an!Erlkönig hat mir ein Leids getan!"	"My father, my father, now he seizes me! Erlking has done me harm!"
8	Narrator	Middle	Dem Vater grauset's, er reitet geschwind, er hält in Armen das ächzende Kind, erreicht den Hof mit Müh und Not; in seinen Armen das Kind war tot.	The father, filled with horror, rides fast, He holds in his arms the groaning child, Reaches the courtyard with toil and trouble, In his arms the child was dead.

The first edition of Schubert's "Erlkönig," billed as a "Ballad by Goethe, set to music for a solo voice with piano accompaniment . . . by Franz Schubert." The name of the dedicatee, Count Moriz von Dietrichstein (one of Schubert's patrons), is considerably larger than the composer's name. The vignette illustration shows the Erlking hovering over the father and the son on horseback.

Time	Dynamics	Rhythm	Harmony: Key Area
2:30	Forte	Driving, repetitive triplets	Unstable
2:44			
2:55	Pianissimo		D minor
3:11	Fortississimo (extremely loud)		
3:25	Forte	Recitative (free rhythm)	G minor
3:47			

PROFILE   Franz Schubert (1797–1828)

Turning Poetry into Music

Franz Schubert was an astonishingly prolific composer of songs for voice and piano. The most recent recording of all his songs fills no fewer than 37 compact discs—quite an accomplishment for a composer who died so young, at the age of 31. In the year 1815 alone, when he was 18, he composed 144 songs, including "Erlkönig." Even more remarkably, each song is distinct.

Schubert was constantly looking for poetry to set to music. Some of his *Lieder* are settings of verse by the greatest writers of the day; others draw on works by poets who are largely forgotten today. He approached each new text on its own terms, trying to interpret, through music, the words he had chosen to set. As if his song output alone were not impressive enough, Schubert composed many other works: nine symphonies, dozens of piano sonatas, and dozens of works for various chamber ensembles. He never achieved widespread fame during his life, however. He enjoyed a devoted following in Vienna and probably would have attracted a wider audience had he not died so young (five years younger than Mozart at the time of his death).

Franz Schubert, ca. 1825, by W. A. Rieder. As in many portraits of composers from this time, he sits near a piano, quill pen in hand.

EXPAND YOUR PLAYLIST: SCHUBERT

- **"The Trout"** ("Die Forelle"), D. 550. A strophic song about the brevity of all forms of life, not just that of fishes.
- **Piano Quintet in A Major** ("The Trout"), D. 667. For violin, viola, cello, double bass, and piano; the nickname comes from Schubert's song "The Trout," whose melody is the basis for the theme-and-variations fourth movement.
- **"Death and the Maiden"** ("Der Tod und das Mädchen"), D. 531. A brief song about Death's visit to a young woman.
- **String Quartet in D Minor, D. 810** ("Death and the Maiden")
- **Symphony no. 8 in B Minor, D. 759** ("Unfinished")
- **Symphony no. 9 in C Major, D. 944**

EXPAND YOUR PLAYLIST

Schubert's Songs

"Erlkönig" is only one of many hundreds of songs written by Schubert. Some others worth exploring include the following:

- **"Gretchen am Spinnrade"** ("Gretchen at the Spinning Wheel"). The song is taken from Goethe's drama *Faust*. Gretchen muses over her agitated state (she is in love), and the music of the piano imitates the motion of her spinning wheel.

- **"Prometheus."** A stirring song set to another text by Goethe, narrated by Prometheus, the god who gave fire to mortals and was punished for his deed.

- **"Ständchen"** ("Serenade"). One of Schubert's best-known melodies, a song from a lover to his beloved.

Felix Mendelssohn
Overture to A Midsummer Night's Dream
Composed: 1826

Mendelssohn's *Overture to A Midsummer Night's Dream* captures the spirit of Shakespeare's play through music alone. Without any words at all, it evokes many of the leading characters in that comedy.

Listen to This First

⊙ Word–Music Relationships

As you listen for the first time, try to identify which passages might be associated with fairies, kings and queens, lovers, and a donkey. (The last one is particularly obvious!) ■

Form

This one-movement work is in sonata form, but without a repeat of the exposition. Listen for those elements of the form that you have learned to expect: a modulation to a new key early on, a development section, and a return to the tonic key and opening idea in the recapitulation, about two-thirds of the way through. ■

Mendelssohn's overture to Shakespeare's play *A Midsummer Night's Dream*, written when he was just 17, captures the chaotic, magical spirit of an enchanted forest. An **overture** is a purely instrumental work performed before the curtain goes up on the play or opera that follows, and Mendelssohn's work certainly captures the essentials of Shakespeare's comedy, which is full of collisions between the world of fantasy and the world of reality. Mendelssohn translates these two worlds into music by using melodies that can be readily associated with the play's principal characters, which range from the real (two pairs of human lovers) to the unreal (fairies) to the real transformed into the unreal (a weaver whose head is changed into that of a donkey). The title alone supplies the verbal cue to these links, for in this composition Mendelssohn creates a purely instrumental work that embodies the spirit of the play, its main characters, and its overall dramatic shape.

This kind of music—a purely instrumental work openly linked in some way to an object, story, or idea outside of the music—is a good example of **program music**. Program music was not new in the nineteenth century (see Chapter 17), but it became increasingly important during that time as artists sought to integrate purely instrumental music with ideas.

LEARNING OBJECTIVES

32.1 Define program music.

32.2 Listen for themes that can be associated with principal characters in Shakespeare's play *A Midsummer Night's Dream*.

32.3 Discuss Mendelssohn's use of the orchestra to create moods associated with the various characters of the drama.

32.4 Listen for Mendelssohn's application of the conventions of sonata form in his *Overture to A Midsummer Night's Dream*.

32.5 Outline Mendelssohn's life and work as a composer.

Word–Music Relationships: Creating Characters through Sound

All the principal thematic ideas in this piece can be linked to characters in Shakespeare's play. The number identifying each of the following themes is the same as that used in the Listening Guide.

1. **Theme 1.** The opening five measures, given entirely to the winds, draw us into the enchanted forest that is the setting for much of the play.

2. **Theme 2.** The scurrying, high-pitched figure in the strings that begins at 0:21 conjures up the kingdom of the fairies, led by Oberon and Titania.

3. **Theme 3.** This loud, pompous theme (beginning at 1:05) reflects the heavier world of the humans and its ruler, Theseus.

4. **Theme 4.**   The first theme in the secondary key area (beginning at 2:01) corresponds to the two pairs of human lovers who over the course of the play, through magic, fall in and out of love with one another and in various combinations.

Crescendo (gradually louder)   Decrescendo (gradually softer)

5. **Theme 5.**   The loud, braying theme at 2:54 is clearly associated with Bottom, the weaver, who figures prominently in Shakespeare's play-within-the-play, when he appears on stage with the head of a donkey.

Accent marks

Hee-haw   Hee-haw

 ## The Drama of Sonata Form

This one-movement work follows the basic conventions of sonata form. Mendelssohn introduces all the principal characters to us in the exposition. In the development section (beginning at 3:42; the exposition does not repeat), the scurrying theme associated with fairies predominates. Mendelssohn captures the sometimes chaotic magical spirit of the midsummer night's forest by having different sections of the orchestra play in simultaneously contrasting dynamics. At 4:17, for example, he brings in the horns fortissimo—"with all force"—even as the strings and high winds maintain their elfin pianissimo—extremely quiet—figure. The recapitulation brings all the main themes back in the tonic, and the coda ends the work as it began, with the sound of long-held notes high in the winds.

With this framework in mind, listen to this piece again, using the Listening Guide.

CONNECT YOUR PLAYLIST

Dynamic Contrast

Find a work that makes effective use of contrasting dynamics (loud versus soft).

Example: Katy Perry, "Roar" (2013) The dynamics alternate between the relatively quiet verses and the "roar" of the chorus.

Listening Guide

Felix Mendelssohn Composed: 1826

Overture to A Midsummer Night's Dream (11:29)

Time	Form: Sonata (Section)	Melody	Word–Music Relationships: Character or Setting
0:00	**Exposition** (tonic)	Theme 1 (long-held notes in winds only)	World of fantasy
0:21		Theme 2 (scurrying figure in strings)	Fairies
1:05	Tonic, with modulation beginning around 1:33	Theme 3 (full orchestra, loud)	Theseus, the ruler of the humans: a loud, pompous theme
2:00	Secondary key area	Theme 4 (lyrical, first in clarinet, then in strings)	The two pairs of human lovers
2:54		Theme 5 (loud, braying sound: full orchestra)	Bottom, the weaver dressed as a donkey
3:25		Theme 3 again, but now in new key area (full orchestra)	Theseus's theme, varied
3:42	**Development** (unstable harmony)	2 (scurrying figure)	Confusion in the dark woods
5:24		4 (lyrical)	Lovers' theme, now in minor; the pairs of lovers become separated
5:53	**Recapitulation** (tonic)	1 (long-held notes in winds)	Return of the opening theme and key
6:18		2 (scurrying theme)	Fairies again, but now with added winds and timpani
6:53		4 (lyrical)	Lovers' theme, now in the tonic
7:47		5 (braying)	Bottom's theme (the donkey)
8:48		3 (pompous)	Theseus's theme
9:17	**Coda** (tonic)	2 (scurrying)	Fairies
10:06		4 (lyrical)	Lovers' theme, now in major mode and much slower
11:00		1 (long-held notes)	Opening phrase closes the work

Student FAQs

I don't know Shakespeare's play. Can the music still make sense?

Yes. Composers can never really be certain that their listeners will have a program in hand, or in their heads, and so they generally try to write music that can function on its own, in purely musical terms. Mendelssohn's overture is no exception to this pattern. While our understanding of it can be enriched through knowledge of Shakespeare's play, we can enjoy the work even without being aware of its connections to the drama.

Why is there no repeat of the exposition?

By the end of the eighteenth century, it had become common to omit the exposition repeat in opera overtures, and Mendelssohn continues that tradition with this overture to a spoken play.

PROFILE   Felix Mendelssohn (1809–1847)

The Cosmopolitan Composer

Perhaps the most cosmopolitan composer who ever lived, Mendelssohn spoke fluent English, French, and Italian—in addition to his native German—and he could read ancient Greek and Latin with ease. He was as much at home in England as he was in Germany. He even excelled at painting and created a number of watercolors of very high quality.

Mendelssohn was born into a prominent family whose fame was based not on music, but on philosophy and finance. His grandfather, Moses Mendelssohn, was one of the leading philosophers of his day, and his father, Abraham Mendelssohn, was one of Berlin's most successful bankers.

Felix was the greatest child prodigy of his age, both as a composer and as a pianist. As a young child, he traveled across Europe in much the same manner Mozart had half a century before. By the time he was 17, he had already written the Octet for Strings, op. 20, and the *Overture to A Midsummer Night's Dream*, op. 21. He also excelled as a conductor. In 1828, on the hundredth anniversary of its premiere, he led a hugely successful performance of J. S. Bach's *Saint Matthew Passion*, a then-forgotten work he had helped rediscover.

Mendelssohn on one of his many trips to England, painted by James Warren Childe. Mendelssohn was a particular favorite of Queen Victoria.

A 19th-century depiction of Felix Mendelssohn's workroom in Leipzig. In the foreground, a square piano is covered with a cloth; by the window, a writing desk is visible where the composer could work on scores.

EXPAND YOUR PLAYLIST: MENDELSSOHN

- **Complete Incidental Music to *A Midsummer Night's Dream*.** Sixteen years after writing this stand-alone overture to Shakespeare's play, Mendelssohn composed music for all the songs in Shakespeare's play (Shakespeare had provided only the poetry, not the music), along with other incidental music—marches, dances, intermezzos, and the like—including the celebrated "Wedding March."

- **Symphony no. 3 in A Minor** ("Scottish")
- **Symphony no. 4 in A Major** ("Italian")
- **Violin Concerto in E Minor**
- ***Elijah*.** An oratorio for soloists, chorus, and orchestra, written for the Birmingham Festival of 1846 during one of the composer's many visits to England.

THE COMPOSER SPEAKS Mendelssohn Reflects on His *Overture to A Midsummer Night's Dream*

Mendelssohn never issued a program to accompany this work, but in a letter to his publisher, he explained the relationship between the musical elements of the overture and the drama on the stage. He acknowledged broad parallels between his overture and Shakespeare's play, but he stopped short of drawing direct equivalencies between the two. This reflects the feelings of many composers about attaching specific meanings to their music. Clearly, Mendelssohn wanted his listeners to associate his overture with Shakespeare's play—otherwise, he would not have given it the title that he did—but he also wanted listeners to accept the work on its own terms, as music.

In the 1999 film version of *A Midsummer Night's Dream* directed by Michael Hoffman, Nick Bottom (Kevin Kline) and Titania (Michelle Pfeiffer) spin out love's sweet dream. The soundtrack uses Mendelssohn's overture and some of the additional incidental music he wrote for the play much later, in 1842. The music Mendelssohn added later includes the celebrated "Wedding March."

66 The piece is . . . closely associated with the play, and thus it might perhaps be quite appropriate to indicate to the public the main events of the drama. . . . I believe it would suffice to recall how the elf-royalty, Oberon and Titania, appear with all their train throughout the play, at one moment here, at another there; then comes Duke Theseus of Athens, who goes hunting in the forest with his bride-to-be; then the two pairs of tender lovers, who lose and find one another; and finally the troop of clumsy, coarse tradesmen, who pursue their heavy-handed amusements; then the elves once again, who tease all of them—it is precisely out of all this that the work is constructed. When at the end everything is resolved and the main characters depart fortunate and happy, the elves follow them, bless the house, and disappear as the morning dawns. So ends the play, and my overture too. I would prefer it if on the printed program you would summarize only this content and say nothing further about my music, so that it can simply speak for itself, if it is good; and if it is not good, then no explanation will help at all. 99

Source: Felix Mendelssohn, *Briefe an deutsche Verleger* (Berlin: de Gruyter, 1968), pp. 25–26. Translation, MEB.

 EXPAND YOUR PLAYLIST

Shakespeare in Music

Many of Shakespeare's plays call for moments of instrumental music, song, or both. A good anthology of settings by Shakespeare's contemporaries is available in *Shakespeare's Songbook*, ed. Ross Duffin (New York: Norton, 2004).

- **Hector Berlioz**, *Roméo et Juliette*. A symphony consisting of both instrumental and vocal movements for soloists, chorus, and orchestra.

- **Franz Liszt**, *Hamlet*. An orchestral work loosely based on Shakespeare's play.

- **Giuseppe Verdi**, *Macbeth* (1847), *Otello* (1887), and *Falstaff* (1893). All three are operas. The last of these draws on *The Merry Wives of Windsor* and the *Henry IV* plays for its libretto.

- **Pyotr Ilich Tchaikovsky**, *Romeo and Juliet, Fantasy-Overture*. A work for orchestra.

- **Sergei Prokofiev**, *Romeo and Juliet*. A ballet.

- **Cole Porter**, *Kiss Me, Kate*. A Broadway adaptation of *The Taming of the Shrew*.

- **Leonard Bernstein**, *West Side Story*. A Broadway adaptation of *Romeo and Juliet* (see Chapter 58).

Hector Berlioz

Symphonie fantastique, fourth movement
("March to the Scaffold")
Composed: 1830

The fourth movement of this symphony depicts a nightmare through music alone. A sensitive young artist dreams that he has killed his unfaithful lover and that he is now being led away to the scaffold, where he will be executed by guillotine.

Listen to This First

〰 Timbre

Listen for the massive sound of the orchestra, especially in the brass (trumpets, horns, trombones, and tubas) and percussion (timpani, snare drum, cymbals, and bass drum). ■

☺ Word–Music Relationships

Berlioz's *Symphonie fantastique* is a work of program music. How does the music reflect the scenario outlined here? ■

🏛 Form

Listen for the alternation between large sections of music in the minor mode and large sections in major mode. What happens at the very end of the movement? ■

This "Fantasy-Symphony" recreates, in music, the thoughts, dreams, and nightmares of an artist. Originally titled *Episode in the Life of the Artist: Symphonie fantastique*, this work is one of the most celebrated instances of **program music** in the entire concert repertory. The French composer Berlioz himself wrote a detailed prose narrative to be distributed at performances. It is the story of a dream (the "fantasy" in the title) that moves from blissful reverie (in the opening movement) to nightmare (in the fourth and fifth movements). The artist dreams about his beloved and her eventual rejection of him. In the fourth movement, the "March to the Scaffold" (presented here), the

"Before" and "After" views of the guillotine at work. The basket used to catch the severed head is clearly visible in front of both machines. At the time of the French Revolution, the guillotine was hailed as a humane form of execution because of its swiftness. The guillotine remained the only legal means of execution in France until the abolition of the death penalty there in 1981. Public executions ended in 1939.

LEARNING OBJECTIVES

33.1 Outline how the fourth movement of Hector Berlioz's *Symphonie fantastique* is representative of Romanticism.

33.2 Discuss Berlioz's use of the instruments of the orchestra.

33.3 Define *idée fixe* and its application in Berlioz's *Symphonie fantastique*.

33.4 Listen for the *idée fixe* in "March to the Scaffold."

33.5 Describe the way in which the character and form of the fourth movement of the *Symphonie fantastique* relates to Berlioz's prose program.

33.6 Outline aspects of Berlioz's life that relate to this work.

33.7 Describe the relative range of dynamics in the orchestra as compared to daily life.

271

artist dreams that, having killed his beloved, he is being led up to a large platform (the scaffold), where he is beheaded by a guillotine. The music is so detailed that we even hear his head plop into the basket placed below and slightly in front of the blade.

The *Symphonie fantastique* captures Romanticism's fascination with the world of the gothic and the grotesque. The artist who "dreams" this symphony dreams not of glory, but of his own downfall and death. In this work, Berlioz paints a musical picture of darkness and despair, and he uses the full resources of the orchestra to portray this nightmare in sound.

The Modern Orchestra

Berlioz is widely acknowledged as the first great master of **orchestration**, the art of arranging music for the instruments of the orchestra. He came of age at a time when concert halls—and thus orchestras—were becoming larger and larger, and he incorporated a wider variety of instruments into his compositions than anyone before. Berlioz achieved novel and spectacular orchestral effects, and even his detractors praised his ability to draw new sounds out of the orchestra by combining individual instruments or groups of instruments to create timbres that had never been heard before. The brass section in this particular movement is unusually prominent, and the percussion section (timpani, bass drum, and snare drum) comes to the fore in ways that no one had ever imagined. Berlioz would go on to write an important treatise on orchestration. Then, as now, any composer who wanted to write a work of music for orchestra must know the particular characteristics of every instrument, starting with its range (what notes are within its reach) and extending to what kinds of melodies or figures work best for it (see Elements: Timbre).

Word–Music Relationships: The Program

Berlioz wrote a detailed program for his *Symphonie fantastique* and gave each of its five movements a distinctive title. "A young musician of morbidly sensitive temperament and fiery imagination poisons himself with opium in a fit of lovesick despair," he explains in the introduction to his program. "The dose of the narcotic, too weak to kill him, plunges him into a deep slumber accompanied by the strangest visions, during which his sensations, his emotions, his memories are transformed in his sick mind into musical thoughts and images. The loved one herself has become a melody to him, an *idée fixe* as it were, that he encounters and hears everywhere."

This *idée fixe* is a melody whose form changes from movement to movement but that appears at some point in all five, transformed to fit the emotion of the moment. In the fourth movement, presented here, the *idée fixe* is heard only once, just before the end (at 4:14). Its appearance marks the last living thought of the artist, a split second before the blade of the guillotine chops off his head.

Here are the titles of all five movements and a summary of the program of each:

1. "Dreams—Passions." The artist fixates on his beloved and imagines her in the form of a melody, the *idée fixe* or "obsessive idea" heard in every movement in one guise or another.
2. "A Ball." The artist imagines he sees his beloved at a ball, during a waltz.

CONNECT YOUR PLAYLIST

Autobiographical Music

Find an example of a work of music that is autobiographical.

Example: Dolly Parton, "Coat of Many Colors" (1968)
This song relates an incident in Parton's youth in rural East Tennessee.

3. "Scene in the Countryside." A slow movement in which the artist dreams he is in the countryside. The scene begins peacefully, but he is soon seized by panic, thinking that his beloved has been unfaithful to him.
4. "March to the Scaffold." Having murdered his beloved for her unfaithfulness, the artist is led to the scaffold, a large elevated platform supporting a guillotine. There, he dreams of her one last time, but her musical image—the *idée fixe*—is interrupted by the fall of the guillotine's blade. The artist dies, at least in his dream.
5. "Dream of a Witches' Sabbath." In this dream within a dream, the artist finds himself "in the midst of a frightful troop of ghosts, sorcerers, and monsters of every kind, gathered for his funeral." The beloved, in the form of her melody, the *idée fixe*, now appears in grotesque form, for in the artist's nightmare, she has become a witch. In the end, evil triumphs over good.

Musical Form, Programmatic Form

The form of this movement is fairly straightforward. It consists of two contrasting sections based on two contrasting themes—the opening **A** section is in the minor mode, the contrasting **B** section is in the major mode. The movement as a whole is framed by an introduction and coda. Graphically, the form of this movement can be represented as

Introduction A / B / A / B / A Coda

But this tells only half the story of the music's form, which would seem to be dictated every bit as much by the prose of Berlioz's program:

> He [the artist] dreams he has killed his beloved, and that he is condemned to death and led to the scaffold. The procession moves forward to the sounds of a march that is at times gloomy and ferocious, at times solemn and brilliant. Noisy outbursts are followed without pause by the heavy sound of measured footsteps. At the end, the *idée fixe* appears for a moment, like a last thought of love broken off by the fatal blow [of the guillotine's blade].

"At times gloomy and ferocious, at times solemn and brilliant": This description is reflected directly in the form of the music in the alternation between the minor-mode **A** section ("gloomy and ferocious") and the major-mode **B** section ("solemn and brilliant"). The ending is particularly graphic, because the *idée fixe*, the musical image of the beloved, is interrupted—almost literally "cut off"—with the sudden fall of the guillotine's blade represented by a thundering chord played by the entire orchestra.

With these points in mind, listen once again to this movement, using the Listening Guide.

Listening Guide

Hector Berlioz Composed: 1830

Symphonie fantastique, fourth movement
("March to the Scaffold") (4:47)

Time	Form: Section	Harmony: Mode	Word–Music Relationships: Berlioz's Program	Timbre
0:00	Introduction	Minor	He [the artist] dreams he has killed his beloved, and that he is condemned to death and led to his execution. The procession moves forward to the sound of . . .	Rumblings in the low strings, low winds, and low brass
0:27	**A**	Minor	. . . a march, at times gloomy and ferocious . . .	March-like theme in low strings, descending by step
1:39	**B**	Major	. . . at times solemn and brilliant. Noisy outbursts . . .	Brass and winds predominate
2:11	**A**	Minor	. . . are followed without pause by the heavy sound of measured footsteps.	March-like theme, descending by step
2:22	**B**	Major		Brass and winds predominate
2:53	**A**	Minor		March-like theme, descending by step
4:14	Coda	Major	At the end, the *idée fixe* appears for a moment [4:14, on the clarinet], like a last thought of love broken off by the fatal blow [of the guillotine's blade, at 4:24].	The severed head falls into the bucket (pizzicato figure at 4:25) and the crowd (the full orchestra) roars its approval (4:27).

Q Student FAQs ⚙

Did audiences in Berlioz's time know about the program?

Sometimes yes, sometimes no. Berlioz once wrote that "at concerts where this symphony is to be performed, it is essential that this program be distributed in advance in order to provide an overview of the dramatic structure of this work." Later in life, however, he felt that the program was actually drawing attention *away* from the music, and he declared that the names of the individual movements would suffice.

Does the program account for everything in the music?

No. As is almost always the case with program music, many details are left to the listener's imagination. As Berlioz himself noted, the purpose of the program was to give listeners "an overview of the dramatic structure of the work," not an explanation of its every detail.

PROFILE   Hector Berlioz (1803–1869)

Music as Autobiography

Berlioz wrote his personal life into his music. The *Symphonie fantastique* mirrors his obsession with Harriet Smithson. He wrote his second symphony, *Harold en Italie* (*Harold in Italy*), which was loosely based on Byron's epic poem *Childe Harold*, after a two-year stay in Italy. His sequel to the *Symphonie fantastique*, titled *Lelio; or, The Return to Life*, has often been seen as a thinly veiled marriage proposal to Harriet Smithson.

Berlioz had to struggle to establish himself in music. His father wanted his son to follow in his footsteps and become a doctor, so he sent the young Hector off to Paris to study medicine. But the younger Berlioz was more interested in music; he stopped attending medical classes and began spending more and more time at the national conservatory of music, where he eventually enrolled as a student. His teachers thought him talented but undisciplined. He had to supplement his income for some time by writing music criticism, and only late in life did he enjoy the accolades of a public that for decades had not quite known what to make of his music.

Hector Berlioz in a portrait from 1832, two years after the premiere of the *Symphonie fantastique*. Caricatures invariably exaggerated the composer's dramatic hairstyle (see the image in the Performance box). One contemporary compared Berlioz's hair to a "forest growing on the edge of a steep cliff."

EXPAND YOUR PLAYLIST: BERLIOZ

- *Symphonie fantastique (complete).*
- *Harold in Italy (Harold en Italie).* A symphony loosely based on Byron's epic poem *Harold in Italy*, with a prominent part for solo viola.
- *Roméo et Juliette.* A symphony based on Shakespeare's play, for soloists, chorus, and orchestra.

- *Requiem.* A mammoth setting of the Catholic service for the dead, requiring multiple choruses and instrumental ensembles.
- *The Infancy of Christ (L'enfance du Christ).* An oratorio for soloists, chorus, and orchestra.

PERFORMANCE How Loud Is Too Loud?

Volume is relative: what is unbearably loud to some seems perfectly acceptable to others. And perceptions of volume have changed over time. In an era before amplified sound, few things were louder than a large orchestra playing with full force. Berlioz's contemporaries were quick to point out the physical pain associated with the volume of sound he could elicit from a large ensemble of instruments.

The decibel is the standard measurement of sound volume: the higher the decibel level, the louder the sound. Most experts consider prolonged exposure to anything over 80 decibels (dB) as potentially dangerous. Decibels increase logarithmically: an increase of 10 dB, for example, means that a sound becomes 10 times louder. A large orchestra playing at peak volume can reach potentially painful levels, as high as 110 dB. Earbuds for portable listening equipment often produce decibel levels of over 120 dB. Hearing damage is a function not only of the decibel level but also of the duration of exposure to that level. As little as 15 minutes of exposure to 100 dB can cause permanent hearing damage.

Berlioz conducts. This caricature reflects the reactions of contemporaries to the sheer level of sound called for in certain passages in Berlioz's music, including the "March to the Scaffold" from the *Symphonie fantastique*. While clearly exaggerated—a cannon spews notes and giant hammers strike the timpani—the reactions of Berlioz's contemporaries are not without foundation.

Decibels	Sound Source	Relative Musical Dynamic
130	Jet engine (100 feet away)	
120	Jackhammer	
120	Rock concert	
90	Large orchestra (25 feet away, full volume)	fff (*fortississimo*—extremely loud)
90	Noisy kitchen	ff (*fortissimo*—very loud)
80	Busy street noise	f (*forte*—loud)
60	Ordinary conversation, 3 feet away	mp (*mezzo piano*—fairly soft)
40	Average voice, 5 feet away	p (*piano*—soft)
10	Whisper	ppp (*pianississimo*—extremely soft)

 EXPAND YOUR PLAYLIST

The Music of Dreams

Berlioz's *Symphonie fantastique* is only one of many musical compositions that deal with dreams.

- **Vincenzo Bellini**, *La Sonnambula* (*The Sleepwalker*; 1831). An opera whose plot turns on the heroine's walking in her sleep (she sings, too).

- **Felix Mendelssohn**, *Overture to A Midsummer Night's Dream* (see Chapter 32).

- **Robert Schumann**, "Träumerei" ("Dreaming," 1838) is one of a group of short pieces for solo piano in a collection called "Scenes from Childhood."

- **Edward Elgar**, *The Dream of Gerontius* (1900). An oratorio for soloists, chorus, and orchestra that traces the fate of a soul from death through purgatory.

- **Thelonious Monk**, *Monk's Dream* (1963). A work created and performed by the jazz pianist.

- **Elvis Costello**, *Il Sogno* ("The Dream," 2004). Costello's ballet, based on Shakespeare's *Midsummer Night's Dream*, combines classical and jazz idioms in a work for large orchestra.

Fanny Mendelssohn Hensel
Piano Trio in D Minor, op. 11, third movement ("Song")
Composed: 1846

The third movement of Hensel's Piano Trio in D Minor, op. 11, is a song that has no words. The composer specifically labeled this movement a "Song," suggesting that it might have a hidden text behind it, even though it is for instruments alone.

Listen to This First

Timbre

Listen to the interplay of the three instruments: piano, violin, and cello. How would you describe their relationship? Is any one instrument more important than the others? ■

Word–Music Relationships

Why might the composer have called this movement a "song"? What kind of poetic text would fit the mood of this movement? ■

Melody

There is only one melody in this entire movement, but it returns repeatedly in a varied form. Listen for these differences across the course of the movement. ■

In an era before recorded sound, people who wanted to hear music at home had to play it themselves. Pieces for solo piano and songs formed a major part of the domestic repertory. No medium proved as versatile and wide-ranging as the **piano trio**, an ensemble consisting of piano, violin, and cello. The third movement of Fanny Mendelssohn Hensel's Piano Trio in D Minor, op. 11, offers an excellent example of the genre and invites us to imagine what it must have been like to make music in a nineteenth-century parlor. Because so many homes had pianos, the piano trio lent itself particularly well to music making in the home. We can hear the intimacy of the setting in the intimacy of the music, which presents a single melody in ever-changing guises.

The Timbre of the Piano Trio

The piano trio had been a popular medium ever since the middle of the eighteenth century: Haydn, Mozart, Beethoven, Schubert, and Felix Mendelssohn (Fanny's brother) had all written piano trios. Part of the appeal of this ensemble was the breadth of sound available from only three instruments: The violin and cello are melodic instruments in the high and low ranges, respectively, while the piano can play chords as well as melodies in all registers. Because so many amateur musicians owned and played at least one of these instruments, piano trios enjoyed special popularity in the nineteenth century. Indeed, many musicians and listeners of the time heard the symphonies of Haydn, Mozart, and Beethoven performed more often in the home in arrangements for piano trio than in their original orchestral setting in the concert hall.

LEARNING OBJECTIVES

34.1 Define and describe a piano trio.

34.2 Explain why Fanny Mendelssohn Hensel called the second movement of her Piano Trio, op. 11 a "song," even though it has no words.

34.3 Listen for the trochaic tetrameter rhythm used throughout the movement.

34.4 Listen for the modified strophic form of the second movement of the Piano Trio, op. 11.

34.5 Outline Fanny Mendelssohn's career as a composer and discuss the challenges faced by female composers in the nineteenth century.

34.6 Name other women composers of the nineteenth century.

CONNECT YOUR PLAYLIST

Trochaic Meter

Find a work, either vocal or instrumental, whose underlying rhythm is based on trochaic meter (LONG-short).

Example: Britney Spears, "Womanizer" (2008)
This song highlights a rhythm that reflects the LONG-short-LONG-short pattern of the title's lone word.

In this particular movement, the piano takes the lead from the very beginning, introducing the melody in an extended solo passage and then playing continuously throughout. The violin and cello each has its turn of presenting the melody as well. In the end, the three instruments blend to create a full, rich sound.

A Song Without Words

Fanny Mendelssohn Hensel placed the word *Lied*—"Song"—at the head of this movement. It is a provocative title, for the music has no words. How can a song not have words? Fanny and her brother Felix had in fact already written a number of piano pieces with precisely this title: *Songs Without Words*. These are short, lyrical works that imitate songs, both in their form and in their texture, with a clear melodic line throughout. In this movement, Fanny Mendelssohn Hensel creates a song without words for piano, violin, and cello.

What are we, as listeners, to make of this wordless song? The title serves as an invitation to us to create our own lyrics. What kind of text would best fit the music? Is this song lyrical (describing an emotional state) or is it a ballad (narrating a story)? Are there points at which the "voice" drops out?

This meter is called *trochaic tetrameter*. Trochaic indicates that the basic unit is a trochee, in the pattern LONG-short (or TUM-ta); tetrameter means that each line consists of four basic units (*tetra* = "four"). Henry Wadsworth Longfellow's *Song of Hiawatha* is written in this meter, and the words in fact fit the opening theme of this piano trio's movement quite well:

> **By** the **shores** of **Git**che **Gu**mee,
> **By** the **shi**ning **Big**-Sea-**Wa**ter,
> **Stood** the **wig**wam **of** No**kom**is,
> **Daugh**ter **of** the **Moon**, No**kom**is.

Can you think of other texts in this meter that might fit this music, or create your own?

Melodic Metamorphosis

This is a song in modified strophic form (see Chapter 31). We hear only a single melody, but the composer skillfully alters it each time it returns, changing the notes slightly, changing the instrument in which it appears, or changing the nature of the accompaniment. This creates a sense of both variety and unity. Each instrument has a chance to come to the fore, making the movement satisfying for performers as well as listeners.

Now listen to this movement again, using the Listening Guide.

Fanny Mendelssohn Hensel Composed: 1846
Piano Trio, op. 11, third movement (2:14)

Time	Melody	Timbre	Word–Music Relationships
0:00	**A**	Piano alone; violin joins in at 0:18, cello at 0:20.	The imagined text is presented in its original form.
0:29	**A1**, more somber, with minor mode inflections	Piano alone at first; cello and violin join in shortly afterward.	The "text" begins similarly but takes a darker and more circuitous turn.
1:02	**A2**	Violin has the melody.	The "text" reappears closer to its original form in the violin and reaches its most intense point toward the end of this section.
1:36	**A3**	Cello has the melody at first, then all three instruments (1:33).	The "text" reappears in its original form, now in the cello, with a confident and affirmative ending.

Q Student FAQs ⚙

Does the piano always have the leading role in piano trios?

The piano is the biggest, loudest, and widest-ranging of the three instruments, and so in fact it usually does play more often than either of the other two. The violin and cello might occasionally have a passage to themselves as soloists or as a duet, but the piano is rarely out of the spotlight for long in a piano trio.

Not all songs have words. What makes the lack of a text here significant?

In English, many people tend to use the word *song* rather loosely to mean any work of music. Technically, however, a song is a piece of music that has a text to be sung. Particularly in German, the word placed at the head of this movement by Fanny Mendelssohn Hensel—*Lied*—strongly suggests the presence of a text, which makes the absence of one here all the more surprising.

PROFILE   Fanny Mendelssohn Hensel (1805–1847)

Overcoming Obstacles

As a composer, Fanny Mendelssohn faced two major obstacles. The first was the immense fame of her younger brother Felix, who was an international celebrity as both a performer and composer while still in his teens. In spite of her own accomplishments as a pianist and composer, Fanny was inevitably known as "Felix's sister." Only recently have critics and historians begun to discover the full range of her talents as a composer of more than 200 songs, more than 100 works for piano, and more than 24 works for chorus, as well as various works for chamber ensembles.

The second obstacle was her gender. Fanny grew up in an era when musical composition was not considered an appropriate profession for women, and she grew up in a family in which women were not expected to pursue a vocation of any kind. Her father, Abraham Mendelssohn, wrote to her in 1820—she was 15 at the time—that while Felix might pursue a musical career, music "for you will always remain but an ornament; never can or should it become the foundation of your existence." This helps explain why for most of her life, Fanny published her music under her brother's name. Only later—just a year before her death, as it turned out—did she begin issuing compositions under her own name.

Felix and Fanny were extremely close not only in childhood but in their adult years as well, even after Fanny married painter Wilhelm Hensel in 1829. She shared her brother's interest in the music of J. S. Bach and remained his closest musical confidante until her sudden death at the age of 41. Felix himself died only six months later.

Fanny Mendelssohn Hensel.

EXPAND YOUR PLAYLIST: FANNY MENDELSSOHN HENSEL

- *Gartenlieder*, Six Songs for Soprano, Alto, Tenor, and Bass, op. 3

- Six Songs, op. 9

- Four Songs (Without Words) for Piano, op. 2 op. 6. Two sets of Songs Without Words—that is, short, lyrical works for solo piano.

- Prelude in F Major, for Organ

- *Das Jahr* (*The Year*). A cycle of 12 pieces for piano, each a portrait of a month of the year.

HISTORICAL CONTEXT   Women Composers of the Nineteenth Century

Fanny Mendelssohn Hensel was one of a growing number of women in the nineteenth century who won fame through their compositions. Like women in many other professions of the time, most of these composers struggled to win recognition in a sphere dominated and controlled by men. Women were widely encouraged to sing or play the piano, but rarely encouraged to pursue a career in composition.

Maria Szymanowska (1789–1831), born in Warsaw (Poland), toured extensively as a piano virtuoso throughout Europe before settling in St. Petersburg (Russia) in 1827. She wrote primarily for her own instrument, the piano, and was an important precursor of Chopin (also a native Pole), writing mazurkas (Polish folk dances) and nocturnes (serenades from lover to beloved).

Louise Farrenc (1804–1875) wrote three symphonies, a piano concerto, four piano trios, and many other chamber works, in addition to a large number of works for piano. She was the only woman in the nineteenth century to hold a permanent chair at the Paris Conservatory, where she taught piano.

Clara Wieck Schumann (1819–1896) pursued a highly successful career as a soloist and teacher. Critics hailed her as one of the great piano virtuosos of her generation. Her compositions include a piano concerto, a piano trio, and many short piano works and songs for voice and piano.

Augusta Holmès (1847–1903) was born in France of Irish parents and added the accent to her last name when she became a French citizen in 1871. Her *Triumphant Ode* was commissioned as the musical centerpiece of the 1889 World's Fair, which gave us the Eiffel Tower. It is an enormous work for soloists, chorus, and orchestra, requiring more than 1,000 musicians to perform.

Cecile Chaminade (1857–1944), a native of Paris, achieved both critical and commercial success through her compositions for solo piano, as well as larger-scale compositions like her *Concertstück* for piano and orchestra and her Concertino for flute and orchestra. The French government awarded her the prestigious Order of the Legion of Honor in 1913 for her achievements in music.

Teresa Carreño (1853–1917), born in Venezuela, studied piano with Louis Moreau Gottschalk. Her piano technique was so powerful that she was known as the "Valkyrie of the Piano." She played in the White House for both Abraham Lincoln (in 1863) and Woodrow Wilson (in 1916); she also sang in and conducted operas. Carreño composed almost exclusively for solo piano.

Amy Marcy Cheney Beach.

Amy Marcy Cheney Beach (1867–1944) was born in New Hampshire but spent most of her life in Boston. She performed as a piano soloist several times with the Boston Symphony Orchestra, beginning in 1885. After marrying that year, she turned her attention away from performance and toward composition. She wrote in many genres, from chamber music to orchestral music to choral music, and her output includes such works as a piano concerto and a Mass. Her "Gaelic" Symphony (1897) shows the influence of Dvořák and was the first symphony written by an American woman.

    EXPAND YOUR PLAYLIST

Chamber Music of the Nineteenth Century

Chamber music enjoyed great prestige throughout the nineteenth century. Composers, performers, and listeners all approached it as a serious and demanding category of music. It also became increasingly public over time, moving more and more into the concert hall, even as it continued to be cultivated in the home.

- **Ludwig van Beethoven: Piano Trio in B♭ Major, op. 97 ("Archduke").**
  The most famous of Beethoven's six piano trios, so named because he dedicated it to one of his composition pupils, Archduke Rudolph of Austria.

- **Ludwig van Beethoven: String Quartet in A Minor, op. 132.**
  One of Beethoven's "late" quartets, written in the last years of his life. The slow movement is labeled "Song of Holy Thanksgiving from a Convalescent to the Almighty."

- **Franz Schubert: Piano Trio in B♭ Major, D. 898.**
  One of two lengthy piano trios by Schubert, as long as many symphonies of the time.

- **Felix Mendelssohn: Piano Trio in C Minor, op. 66.**
  One of two piano trios by Fanny's brother Felix. The finale incorporates a sacred chorale (hymn tune).

- **Johannes Brahms: Piano Quintet in F Minor, op. 35.**
  Densely textured but richly melodic, this quintet resembles a symphony in its scope and tone.

- **Johannes Brahms: Clarinet Quintet in B Minor, op. 115.**
  Brahms became attracted to the clarinet as a solo instrument relatively late in life; this work is one of the few of its kind in the repertory.

35

Robert Schumann
"Dedication"
Composed: 1840

Schuman's "Dedication" is an example of a nineteenth-century song for voice and piano by one of the greatest composers who worked in the genre. Unlike Schubert's "Erlkönig," a ballad, this is a lyrical love song.

Listen to This First

🎹 Form

Listen for the ternary form (**ABA**) of this *Lied*. Try to identify the beginning of the contrasting middle section (**B**) and the subsequent return of the opening section (**A**). How does the middle section differ from the two outer sections? ■

👤 Harmony

Listen for the unusual modulation in the middle section of this song. ■

🎵 Melody

Listen for the contour of the melody, its rise and fall, and its highest and lowest points. How does the melody of the middle (**B**) section differ from that of the opening (**A**) section? ■

🕐 Rhythm

Notice the difference in the rhythmic patterns underlying the vocal line at various points in the song. ■

LEARNING OBJECTIVES

35.1 Define *Lied*.

35.2 Explain the connection between Robert Schumann's "Dedication" and his marriage to Clara Wieck.

35.3 Describe the unconventional harmony in "Dedication."

35.4 Describe how Schumann uses melody and rhythm to create a ternary form in "Dedication."

35.5 Describe Schumann's work as a critic.

Few love songs are as intense as Robert Schumann's "Dedication" ("Widmung"). The fast tempo and the uneven, impatient rhythms of the piano convey a sense of urgency and intensity even before the voice enters. The soaring vocal melody evokes in sound the kinds of passionate emotion that romantic love can produce. The distant harmony of the middle section transports us to a world far removed from that of the opening. The poetry is direct and heartfelt, and Schumann's music matches it perfectly.

In 1840, the year he wrote this song—or *Lied*, to use the German term—Schumann was finally able to marry Clara Wieck (see Chapter 36), the daughter of his piano teacher. After a long and difficult courtship—Clara's father was adamantly opposed to the marriage, and the couple eventually had to elope—Robert seemed to have found inspiration in setting love poems to music. He surely had Clara in mind while writing "Dedication." In fact, it is very easy to imagine the two of them performing it together, even taking turns singing it to each other, with the other playing the piano. And Clara's inspiration did not stop with "Dedication." In that same year, Robert wrote almost 150 *Lieder*, an astonishing number that translates to roughly one new song every two days, with Sundays off for rest.

Ternary Form

The form of this song is simple enough: it falls into three main sections, with a variation of the first returning at the end (**ABA'**). This structure is clearly suggested by the poem itself, in which the opening four lines return at the end but conclude with a new line of text. What makes the music of this **ternary form** extraordinary is the way in which Schumann sets the middle section apart: He uses a melody and a harmony that are strikingly different.

 # Unconventional Harmony

At the end of the first section, the music seems to find a whole new center, to relocate and take the careful listener right along with it. We feel we are in a completely different place. The reason is that there has been an unusual **modulation**, an unconventional shift from one key area to another.

As we have seen in many earlier works, composers modulate to provide a sense of variety and freshness; staying in the same key too long would make the music seem monotonous. Indeed, modulation is a central element in the exposition of sonata form movements. But the modulations we have seen thus far, in sonata-form expositions and elsewhere, have always been to a key that is closely related to the original.

What does it mean for keys to be "closely related"? Music theory includes the study of the relationships of certain keys to other keys, in part to understand the effects of these relationships on the listener. For any given key area, there is a set of key areas that relate closely and easily to it, and another set of key areas that do not. It's rather like a color wheel, in which one can identify complementary colors and colors that do not normally match. What Schumann has done at the beginning of the second section, with the words *Du bist die Ruh'* ("You are rest"), is to choose a key that does not normally match because in harmonic terms it is related only very distantly to the key of the first section. In this way, it is a very different choice from the kinds of modulation we have heard in works by Haydn, Mozart, or Beethoven. This kind of modulation to increasingly distant keys was becoming more and more common over the course of the nineteenth century, however. Beethoven used it increasingly in his later works (those written after the Fifth Symphony).

Technically, a music theoretician would say that Schumann has moved from "tonic to the flat submediant." Emotionally, the effect is melting.

 # Melody and Rhythm: Creating Contrast Together

Schumann reinforces the contrast between the **A** and **B** sections of his ternary form by basing them on two strongly contrasting melodies. In the accompaniment, as well as in the melody, rhythm also creates contrast.

- **Melody 1**, the basis of the **A** section, unfolds in the voice over a repetitive rhythmic pattern in the piano characterized by a steady flow but with a sudden "catch" just before it reaches the

CONNECT YOUR PLAYLIST

Ternary Form

Find an example of a popular song in ternary form.

Example: The Beatles, "We Can Work It Out" (1966)
This song alternates between a major-keyed melody (A) and a contrasting melody that is more ominous (B); the first melody is sung by Paul McCartney, while the contrasting one is sung by John Lennon.

top, almost like a heart skipping a beat. The voice line makes several dramatic leaps upward. The rhythmic values in the melody line are short, so this melody moves not only through a wider range of pitches than the second melody, but also simply through more pitches, and it sounds energetic.

- **Melody 2**, the basis of the **B** section, unfolds over an entirely different repetitive rhythmic figure in the piano. Here we have triplets (rhythmic groupings of three: (**1**-2-3 **1**-2-3 **1**-2-3, etc.), in the piano, without the agitation of the opening. The voice occupies a lower register and sings in longer, more measured notes. This section of the text, after all, is about "rest" and "peace."

Now listen to this song again, using the Listening Guide.

Robert Schumann Composed: 1840

"Dedication" (2:22)

Time	Original German Text	English Translation	🏛 Form: Section
0:00	Du meine Seele, du mein Herz, Du meine Wonn', o du mein Schmerz, Du meine Welt, in der ich lebe, Mein Himmel du, darein ich schwebe, O du mein Grab, in das hinab Ich ewig meinen Kummer gab.	You my soul, you my heart, You my bliss, o you my pain, You my world, in which I live; My heaven, you, in which I float, O you my grave, into which I cast my grief forever.	A
0:38	Du bist die Ruh, du bist der Frieden, Du bist vom Himmel mir beschieden. Daßdu mich liebst, macht mich mir wert, Dein Blick hat mich vor mir verklärt, Du hebst mich liebend über mich, Mein guter Geist, mein beßres Ich!	You are rest, you are peace, You have been granted me from heaven. That you love me makes me worthy of myself, Your gaze transfigures me before myself; You elevate me lovingly above myself, My good spirit, my better self!	B
1:23	Du meine Seele, du mein Herz, Du meine Wonn', o du mein Schmerz, Du meine Welt, in der ich lebe, Mein Himmel du, darein ich schwebe, Mein guter Geist, mein beßres Ich!	You my soul, you my heart, You my bliss, o you my pain, You my world, in which I live; My heaven, you, in which I float, My good spirit, my better self!	A'
1:52			[Piano coda]

Melody and Rhythm   Harmony: Key Areas

Melody and Rhythm	Harmony: Key Areas
Theme 1 = repeated rhythmic pattern in the piano; several dramatic leaps upward in the voice line, as on the words *Seele* ("soul"), *Wonn'* ("bliss"), and *Himmel* ("heaven")	Tonic (A♭ major)
Theme 2 = triplet rhythms in piano (1-2-3 1-2-3, etc.); lower register for both the voice and the piano, and longer notes in the vocal melody	Not tonic (E major). This is a very remote key area from the tonic, and the sudden shift is striking.
Theme 1 = varied return of opening theme, with highest note of all on the next-to-last word, *beßres* ("better").	Tonic (A♭ major)

Q   Student FAQs   ✦

I don't hear the contrast between the keys of the A and B sections. What am I supposed to be listening for here?

Play (or ask a friend to play) an A♭ major chord on the piano. This is the tonic of the song. Now play (or ask your friend to play) an E♭ major chord. This is one of the predictable keys to which the song might have modulated. But this song goes to E major, not E♭ major. Listen to the difference now between the move from A♭ to E, as opposed to A♭ to E♭.

Why does the piano have such a long "outro" at the end?

Schumann put the voice and piano on almost equal footing in his songs, and here the piano not only introduces the song (standard practice among many song composers, even today) but also closes it out, providing a kind of wordless commentary on what has gone before.

PROFILE   Robert Schumann (1810–1856)

The Composer as Critic

I t is no coincidence that Schumann was such a prolific composer of songs. He was an avid reader of poetry and fiction of all kinds, constantly in search of new poems to set to music. He was also one of the first great composer-critics, and his critical writings on music are themselves of a very high literary quality. Schumann took on the more conservative elements of the musical establishment with an "us versus them" attitude, dubbing his own group the Davidsbund (Band of David), in honor of the young David of the Bible, who against all odds slew the giant Goliath, a member of the Philistine tribe. Schumann and his "Band of David" saw themselves fighting the many "Philistines" of the 1830s. (To this day, the term *Philistine* is still used to indicate a person of limited artistic sensibilities.)

Schumann enjoyed the advantage of editing his own journal, the *Neue Zeitschrift für Musik* (*New Journal of Music*), which he and a few partners set up in 1834. He was thus in a position to see and pass judgment on a great many new works being published and performed. As a critic, Schumann was one of the first to praise Berlioz's *Symphonie fantastique* (see Chapter 33), and he was the first major figure to recognize publicly the compositional genius of both Chopin and Brahms.

The last years of Schumann's life were not happy ones. Having established himself as a successful conductor in both Dresden and Düsseldorf, he began to show signs of mental instability in 1853 and attempted suicide in 1854. He was eventually committed to a mental institution, where he died.

Robert Schumann and Clara Wieck Schumann in 1850.

EXPAND YOUR PLAYLIST: ROBERT SCHUMANN

- *Dichterliebe* (*Poet's Love*), op. 48. A cycle of 16 songs for voice and piano to poetry by Heinrich Heine.
- *Kreisleriana*, op. 16. A set of piano pieces inspired by the spirit of Johannes Kreisler, an eccentric fictional musician created by the author E. T. A. Hoffmann.
- Piano Concerto in A Minor, op. 54
- Symphony No. 3 in E-flat Major, op. 97 ("Rhenish"). A five-movement work that moves from a dark, highly contrapuntal fourth movement to a bright, lyrical finale.

EXPAND YOUR PLAYLIST

The Song in the Nineteenth Century

Franz Schubert and Robert Schumann were only two of many composers in the nineteenth century to write songs for voice and piano. This rich repertory extends across many languages. Here is a sampling:

German
- Johannes Brahms, "Wiegenlied" ("Cradle Song"). The famous lullaby.
- Brahms, "Feldeinsamkeit" ("Loneliness of the Field"). A dark, somber song about solitude.
- Hugo Wolf, *Möricke-Lieder*. A collection of songs on texts by German poet Eduard Möricke.
- Gustav Mahler, *Des Knaben Wunderhorn* (*From the Youth's Magic Horn*). A collection of songs on folk poetry for voice and orchestra.

French
- Gabriel Fauré, *La bonne chanson* (*The Good Song*). A collection of songs to texts by French symbolist poet Paul Verlaine.

- Claude Debussy, *Chansons de Bilitis*. Three songs that evoke the world of nymphs and fauns, with texts by French poet Pierre Louÿs.

Russian
- Modest Moussorgsky, *The Nursery*. A collection of songs on life as seen by a child.

English
- Stephen Foster, "Beautiful Dreamer." One of many famous songs by the American composer (1826–1864); others include "My Old Kentucky Home," "Oh! Susanna," and "Old Folks at Home" (probably best known for the lyric "Way down upon the Swanee River . . . ").

36

Clara Wieck Schumann
"Forward!"
Composed: 1848

The public uprisings that began with the French Revolution of 1789 opened up new ways of connecting music and politics. Every mass political movement since then has had its songs. This song for *a cappella* chorus captures the progressive spirit of its time and place.

Listen to This First 🔊

〰️ Timbre

Listen for the range of voices from highest (soprano) to lowest (bass). Notice that there are no instruments at all in this work. ■

🎵 Melody

Listen for the return of the opening melody at later points in the work, and listen for the way it is varied each time. Also listen for the contrasting melody between these returns of the opening theme. ■

💬 Word–Music Relationships

Listen for the ways in which the melodic contour or texture of the music emphasizes certain words in the text. Which words—even if on first hearing you do not understand their meaning—*sound* the most important? ■

LEARNING OBJECTIVES

36.1 Outline the political context of Clara Schumann's "Forward!"

36.2 Define *a cappella* and describe the social and musical nature of *a cappella* choruses in the nineteenth century.

36.3 Describe the ways in which the music amplifies the meaning of the text.

36.4 Listen for changes in the texture of the music throughout from monophonic to polyphonic.

36.5 Outline Clara Schumann's career as a performer and composer.

36.6 Discuss the ways in which music can be used for political purposes.

This work began as a birthday present. Clara Schumann wrote it as a gift to her husband, Robert Schumann, on his 38th birthday, on June 8, 1848. She even arranged a performance of it on that day in their home, engaging members of the Dresden Choral Society, a group her husband had founded earlier that same year.

But the text of "Forward!" ("Vorwärts!") is political, not personal. The poem was written in 1840 by the poet Emanuel Geibel, and its title was a slogan for those who believed in a united and democratic Germany. What we now think of as Germany was at the time divided into a myriad of large and small states including Prussia, Swabia, Baden, Saxony, and others. Each state had its own monarch, laws, and currency. The idea of unifying these various states into a single nation (Germany) with provisions for representative government was the chief goal of the revolutionaries who fought in the streets during the uprisings of 1848 and 1849. These outbreaks of violence were scattered and sporadic and ultimately failed. Not until 1871 did Germany emerge as a united country under the leadership of the former king of Prussia, with a limited form of representative government.

When Clara Schumann wrote this work, in the early summer of 1848, revolution was in the air, and she was well aware of the political implications of Geibel's text. Her husband did not participate actively when revolution broke out in Dresden a year later, but he did follow the events closely in the newspapers and even wrote to a colleague in 1849 that he felt a responsibility "to tell, in music, of the sorrows and joys that motivate the times." In "Forward!," Clara Schumann had beaten him to the punch.

A Cappella Timbre

An ensemble of unaccompanied voices is called an ***a cappella*** chorus. The voices in this particular work are "mixed," consisting of both women (sopranos, altos) and men (tenors, basses). The practice of *a cappella* singing goes back to the Middle Ages and Renaissance, so the timbre itself was not new in the nineteenth century, even if the harmonies now moved in a wider range, the rhythms were more jagged and irregular, and the dynamic contrasts were more pronounced. But performances of choral music took on special social significance in German-speaking lands in the nineteenth century, where laws of association strictly regulated and limited large social gatherings of any kind. Choruses of all varieties were permitted on the grounds that they were artistic and not political. In reality, everyone knew that these groups were to some extent political organizations giving voice to what they could otherwise not say in public.

 ## Contrasting Melodies

Clara Schumann's setting of the text follows the form of the poem's five strophes (stanzas), three of which (1, 3, and 5) begin with or culminate in the word *Vorwärts* ("Forward"). She sets these three strophes to a loud, rhythmically energetic melody, varying it with each strophe. The other two strophes (2 and 4), which speak to the temptations of complacency and fatigue, are set to a very different melody that is softer and more rhythmically smooth. Here, too, the melody is varied when it returns. The contrasting melodies become the basis of contrasting sections, creating a form that approximates that of a rondo (**A B A′ B′ A″**).

 ## Painting Revolutionary Words

The key word of the text, *Vorwärts* ("Forward"), is a charged one. The composer goes to great lengths to emphasize it at its first appearance, at the end of the first strophe, where she sets it in unison to a phrase that sounds like a trumpet call. Passages that speak of calm and peace—the contrasting strophes 2 and 4—are set to a low dynamic (piano), and the music hits its registral high point on the word *Himmel* ("heaven") just before the very end. All of these are good examples of **word painting**, in which individual words are "painted" with music that matches their meanings.

Now listen to this work again, using the Listening Guide.

Clara Wieck Schumann Composed: 1848

"Forward!" (1:25)

Time	Original German Text	English Translation	🎵 Melody	🏛 Form: Section
0:00	1. Lass das Träumen, lass das Zagen, Unermüdet wandre fort! Will die Kraft dir schier versagen, "Vorwärts!" ist das rechte Wort.	Leave the dreaming and hesitation behind, Without fatigue, go forward! If you simply run out of energy, "Forward!" is the right word.	1 = rising figure, using agitated, dotted rhythms (Long-short)	A
0:15	2. Darfst nicht weilen, wenn die Stunde Rosen dir entgegenbringt, Wenn dir aus des Meeres Grunde Die Sirene lockend singt.	You may not dally, if the day Brings you roses, Or if from the depths of the ocean the siren sings seductively to you.	2 = higher register, leaps up, then moves down	B
0:27	3. Vorwärts, vorwärts! Im Gesange Ringe mit dem Schmerz der Welt, Bis auf deine heisse Wange goldner Strahl von oben fällt,	Forward, forward! In song wrestle with the suffering of the world, Until on your hot cheek, a golden ray from above should fall,	1 (varied)	A′
0:39	4. Bis der Kranz, der dichtbelaubte, Schattig deine Stirn umwebt, Bis verklärend überm Haupte Dir des Geistes Flamme schwebt.	Until the crown, thickly woven, wraps itself with shadows around your head, Until above your head transfigured the flame of the spirit hovers before you.	2 (varied)	B′
0:50	5. Vorwärts drum durch Feindes Zinnen, Vorwärts durch des Todes Pein, Wer den Himmel will gewinnen, Muss ein rechter Kämpfer sein!	Forward, then, through the enemy's lines, Forward through the pain of death, Whoever would gain entry to heaven Must be a true fighter! Transl. MEB	1 (varied)	A′

⦿ Word–Music Relationships

Unison trumpet-like figure on the word
Vorwärts! ("Forward!") (0:10)

Soft dynamics for passage of text
describing a lack of conflict in life.

Goldner Strahl von oben ("Golden ray from
above") moves from high to low.

Soft dynamics describing the transport of
the soul to heaven.

Highest note of the entire work on the word
Himmel ("heaven") at 0:57.

🔍 Student FAQs

How many singers are in an a cappella *chorus?*

The number can vary. Some
a cappella groups, like the
one pictured here, have
only one or two singers
on each part (thus, four to
eight singers in total), while
others might have as many
as eight or ten to a part. In
the recording here, we hear
a group of about two dozen
singers.

Whatever happened to the tradition of a cappella *singing?*

It continues to this day. Many colleges in the United States feature
a cappella groups (men, women, or mixed). The Fisk Jubilee
Singers, of Fisk University in Nashville, Tennessee, is one of the
oldest groups of this kind. The original members consisted of
emancipated slaves, and they broke racial barriers when they
began touring with their repertory of spirituals and "slave music"
in 1871. Today, it is estimated that there are more than 1,500
a cappella ensembles on U.S. college campuses. Many of these
groups specialize in a particular
repertory of music, such as classical,
popular, gospel, or jazz.

The Fisk Jubilee Singers of
Fisk University, ca. 1880. This *a
cappella* ensemble was one of
the first of many such groups
established at American colleges
in the 19th century. Its repertory
included many songs with political implications.

PROFILE Clara Wieck Schumann (1819–1896)

Independent Spirit

Clara Wieck's father, Friedrich Wieck, was adamantly opposed to the idea of his daughter marrying a musician, particularly a composer of such limited means as Robert Schumann. The situation was complicated by the fact that Wieck was Robert Schumann's piano teacher. The young couple eventually eloped without her father's approval. Clara and her father were estranged for many years, and at one point she had to go to court to recover her piano from him.

Schumann's independence of spirit grew even stronger after her husband's death. Finding herself a young widow in her mid-30s, she went on to pursue a highly successful career as a soloist and teacher. Her performances of Beethoven's sonatas and concertos, Chopin's piano pieces, and her husband's compositions were legendary in their time. Critics hailed her as one of the great piano virtuosos of her generation. Her compositional output includes a piano concerto, a piano trio, and many short piano works and songs for voice and piano. Later in life, she edited the first complete edition of her husband's musical works.

Clara Wieck, ca. 1840, around the time of her marriage to Robert Schumann.

 EXPAND YOUR PLAYLIST: CLARA WIECK SCHUMANN

- *Three Songs on Texts by Rückert*
- *Variations on a Theme by Robert Schumann.* A set of variations on a theme by her husband.
- **Piano Trio in G Minor, Op. 17**
- **Piano Concerto in A Minor, Op. 7.** An early work written to showcase her talents both as a performer and composer.

HISTORICAL CONTEXT   Music and Politics

Rulers from all periods and all corners of the world have used music as a way to demonstrate their material and cultural power. In the early nineteenth century, when Beethoven was at one point considering leaving Vienna for good, the city's nobility and aristocracy considered it a point of civic and national pride to keep him there, so they raised sufficient funds to persuade him to stay. Beethoven responded by writing a number of works on overtly political texts that glorified Austria. For many composers before the nineteenth century, having a patron, an influential person who supported them, was the only way they could earn a living in music.

The public uprisings that began with the French Revolution of 1789 opened up new ways of connecting music and politics. Communal singing became an important means of fostering solidarity among a large and diverse population, and the idea that every nation should have its own national song or anthem took root around this time. Every mass political movement since then has had its songs. In the twentieth century, protesters for and against many different causes used music to galvanize support. Labor unions, supporters of the civil rights movement, and opponents of the Vietnam War all developed extensive repertories of songs.

Politicians have also perceived certain kinds of music as threats at various times. Some types of jazz were prohibited in Nazi Germany and the Soviet Union. Even in the United States there have been movements to ban types of rock, rap, and hip-hop music, or at least give them ratings so people are aware of the "dangerous" content (see "Profile: Public Enemy" in Chapter 68). More often than not, however, such controversies have centered on lyrics, not on musical styles. Still, it seems unlikely that any American presidential candidate in the near future will be using a punk soundtrack in his or her television ads.

August 28, 1963: Marian Anderson (1897-1993) sings to the crowd assembled at the Lincoln Memorial in Washington, D.C. Music played an important role in the March on Washington, a key event in the civil rights movement. The climax of the day's events was Dr. Martin Luther King's "I Have a Dream" speech.

 EXPAND YOUR PLAYLIST

Political Music

Music has a long history of being used to promote political causes. Some examples follow:

The French Revolution
- "La Marseillaise"
- "Ça ira"

The Civil War
- "The Battle Hymn of the Republic"

The Civil Rights Movement
- "The Battle Hymn of the Republic"
- "If I Had a Hammer"
- "We Shall Overcome"

The Vietnam War
- Country Joe and the Fish, "I-Feel-Like-I'm-Fixin'-to-Die Rag" (1965)
- Creedence Clearwater Revival, "Fortunate Son" (1969)

37

Frédéric Chopin
Mazurka in B♭ Major, op. 7, no. 1
Composed: 1830s

Certain kinds of music carry strong national associations, even without words. This mazurka by Chopin uses the characteristic rhythms of a Polish folk dance. In the context of its time and place—Paris in the 1830s—listeners would have recognized at once its national implications, for Chopin's native Poland had recently ceased to exist.

Listen to This First

🌐 Texture
Notice the clear homophonic texture throughout, with the melody in the uppermost voice and the lower voices playing a strictly supporting role. ■

🎵 Melody
Listen for contrasting contours of the melodies: up, down, and undulating. ■

📖 Rhythm
Listen carefully to the opening rhythm, which repeats itself many times, and then see if you can tap it out yourself afterward. ■

🎼 Form
Listen for the return of the opening idea and the way in which themes introduced later contrast with the opening. ■

LEARNING OBJECTIVES

37.1 Describe Chopin's association with nationalism.

37.2 Describe Chopin's approach to composing for the piano.

37.3 Listen to how Chopin uses scales in different directions in the Mazurka in B♭, op. 7, no. 1.

37.4 Listen for the contrast between the alternating sections of the Mazurka in B♭, op. 7, no. 1.

37.5 Listen for the drone bass in the Mazurka in B♭, op. 7, no. 1.

37.6 Recognize and describe tempo rubato.

37.7 Outline Chopin's career as a performer and composer.

For many, Frédéric Chopin epitomizes Romanticism. His piano music is passionate and direct. A renowned piano virtuoso, he was able to evoke a wide range of emotions in the works he composed for his instrument. Without recourse to words, he created poetry for the keyboard that still speaks in a profound way to pianists and audiences today. His repertory consists mainly of what are called **character pieces**, relatively short works that capture a particular character—not in the sense of a character in a story, but in the sense of a mood. The titles of these works always provide a clue to the character they seek to establish.

A **mazurka** is a Polish **folk dance** in triple meter, often with a heavy accent on the second or third beat of each measure (1-**2**-3 | 1-**2**-3 or 1-2-**3** | 1-2-**3**) instead of the usual accent on the first beat (**1**-2-3 | **1**-2-3). Folk dances, like folk music in general, are passed down from generation to generation by a living tradition. They are typically associated with particular rhythms and dance steps. No one knows who wrote them, and they are transmitted by **oral tradition**, without the aid of notation. Chopin, who was born in Poland but later moved to France, was inspired by Polish folk dances and composed a number of mazurkas and other dances that reflect his intense national pride for the spirit of his native land. The Mazurka in B♭ is thus an example of musical **nationalism**. Chopin was neither the first nor the last composer to draw on folk music for inspiration, but the particular context of a work like the mazurka—Poland was under Russian occupation at the time—gave this music a sense of political meaning that was quite obvious to his contemporaries, regardless of their nationality.

PERFORMANCE Speeding Up and Slowing Down: Robbed Time

Listen carefully to almost any recording of Chopin's solo piano music and you will notice that the performer does not always maintain a strict tempo but instead speeds up and slows down. The changes are not dramatic, but they are noticeable and effective. These subtle changes of tempo applied by the performer are known as tempo rubato—literally "robbed time"—or simply rubato.

Many accounts of Chopin's piano playing mention his use of rubato. One particularly intriguing account has come down to us from one of his students:

> In keeping time, Chopin was unrelenting, and it will surprise many to learn that the metronome never left his piano. Even in his oft-derided *tempo rubato*, he always played in strict time with the hand providing the accompaniment, while the other hand, playing the lyrical melody, would either hesitate, undecided, or rush ahead, faster, with impatient force, as if in passionate speech.

The key phrase here is "as if in passionate speech." Music that imitates singing must capture the flexible delivery so characteristic of singers. Just as we speak with varying speeds—speeding up here, slowing down there for emphasis—so, too, do operatic performers vary the pace of their delivery, altering the rhythm of their words to match the emotion. Pianists imitating singers have a corresponding obligation to play this kind of music with a sense of expression, as "passionate speech."

Source: Carl Mikuli, Preface to his edition of *Chopin's Pianoforte-Werke*, vol. 4: *Balladen* (Leizpig: Kistner, 1879), iii. Transl. MEB.

The metronome is a mechanical device developed in the early 19th century for measuring musical time more precisely. By raising or lowering the weight on the stick, the user can decrease or increase the pace of the clicking sound produced by the back-and-forth motion of the pendulum.

Texture: The Singing Piano

Chopin advised young pianists to listen carefully and often to great singers and to imitate at the keyboard their manner of projecting the voice. In composing, he put this advice into practice. He endowed one part with a beautiful melody—as though giving a line to a singer—and created other parts to support and enhance the melody—as though giving the singer a truly inspired and creative accompanist or backup. This homophonic texture worked particularly well on the piano because it is an instrument that can play both lyrical melodies and accompaniment at the same time. In this piece, the right hand carries the melody, in a higher register, while the left hand provides the accompaniment.

About two-thirds of the way through (at "C" in the Listening Guide), the accompaniment changes markedly. It moves from a series of varied chords to a **drone bass**, a single pair of notes repeated over and over, rather like the sound of a bagpipe. This static harmony creates a strong sense of contrast between this section and those before and after. It also reinforces the folk-like origins of the mazurka as a genre, for the bagpipe is an instrument associated almost exclusively with the music of the countryside.

Melody: Scales Going Up, Scales Going Down

If you ever learned to play an instrument or sang in a choir, you probably learned to play or sing scales (or "Do-Re-Mi's"). Maybe you even wondered why you were asked to spend time practicing something other than actual songs. If you have not played or sung much music yourself, you have probably still heard of scales as a building block of music, and wondered what they actually have to do with the music itself. This mazurka is an example of how scales can form important parts of melodies, and also how different scales can create completely different-sounding music.

This mazurka, a very popular one with pianists, opens with a theme that consists quite simply of an ascending scale—a series of steps up. Pianists who have practiced their scales conscientiously will have an easier time playing this scalar melody. Because it is a major scale, it sounds bright and optimistic. (You may come up with slightly different terms, because the quality of a sound remains subjective.) The top note of this scale is marked by a trill (two notes a step apart played in alternation so rapidly it can be difficult for the listener to separate them).

Later, at 1:05, the mood changes to one of perhaps mystery or contemplation, and we hear a scale going downward. But it is not the downward motion that creates this unusual sound with a completely different feel. It is the kind of scale that it is: a variation on a minor scale—which, as we have already heard, imparts a sadder or more somber quality to music. You hear that the dynamics are suddenly very quiet, which enhances the minor mood or mystery.

Between these two melodies, at 0:34, we hear a gentler melody that has neither a long trajectory upward or downward nor wide leaps. It moves within a limited range of notes.

 ## Form: Repetition, Variation, Contrast

Chopin uses just a few brief melodic ideas to create a larger whole. Here, the various sections (**A**, **B**, **C**) are restated without significant variation to create a rondo-like pattern, in which **A** returns repeatedly after the interjection of contrasting ideas (**B** and **C**):

A A B A B A C A C A

 ## Rhythm: The Pride of Poland

The rhythm that you hear at the beginning is found in some guise in every mazurka Chopin wrote—and he wrote at least 57, all in triple meter. They encompass many different moods, from melancholy to exuberant, but all contain this rhythm typical of Polish folk dance, with an accent on the second beat of a three-beat measure ("2") rather than on the downbeat ("1"):

Now listen to the Mazurka again, using the Listening Guide.

Listening Guide

Frédéric Chopin Composed: 1830s
Mazurka in B♭ Major, op. 7, no. 1 (2:10)

Time	Form/ Melody	Harmony	Texture
0:00	**A** (= a long ascending scale with sudden downward leaps; major mode)	Major	Homophonic
0:17	**A**		
0:34	**B** (= a much narrower range; major mode)		
0:46	**A**		
1:05	**C** (= a downward trajectory)	Minor	Homophonic, with drone bass
1:18	**A**	Major	Homophonic
1:37	**C**	Minor	Homophonic, with drone bass
1:50	**A**	Major	Homophonic

Student FAQs

How is the mazurka actually danced?

As a folk dance, the mazurka emphasizes the off-beat accents (on "2" of each measure) by calling on the dancers to click their heels or stamp their feet. More stylized forms of the dance emerged later, allowing the dancers relatively great freedom to improvise steps and gestures of the hands.

Would anyone have actually danced to Chopin's mazurkas?

Probably not, at least not in public. Even though this is dance music, with a steady beat, it was meant to be heard rather than serve as the accompaniment to an actual dance.

This 1844 Polish drawing shows two enthusiasts dancing the mazurka.

PROFILE   Frédéric Chopin (1809–1848)

A Polish Composer in France

The son of a French father and a Polish mother, Chopin never felt quite at home in either land. After early training in his native Poland, he set out on an extended tour of Western Europe and never returned. But Poland was never far from his mind. When Russia annexed all but a tiny portion of the country in 1831, the cause of Polish nationalism burned even brighter in the nation's exile community. Chopin's cultivation of such national dances as the polonaise and mazurka manifests his deep feelings toward his native land.

Thanks in part to the large number of Polish expatriates in Paris, Chopin was able to circulate in the highest levels of society. He made a good living from his teaching and sales of his own music, along with the occasional public concert, though he avoided these as much as he could, especially in his later years. In 1837, he began a decade-long liaison with novelist Amandine Lucile Aurore Dudevant (1804–1876), better known by her pen name, George Sand. In 1838–1839, the two wintered on the island of Majorca, off the Spanish coast in the Mediterranean. There, local doctors diagnosed Chopin's growing illness as tuberculosis. In spite of his poor health, Chopin continued to compose steadily until the last few months of his life.

Most of Chopin's music is for solo piano, and even the small number of works that are not—such as songs, concertos, and a piano trio—include the piano.

Chopin was one of the first composers to have been photographed. This image was made only a few months before his death.

EXPAND YOUR PLAYLIST: CHOPIN

- **Preludes, op. 24.** A collection of 24 short pieces for solo piano in each of the major- and minor-mode keys.

- **Etudes, op. 10 and op. 25.** Two sets of "studies" for solo piano, each of which emphasizes a particular technical skill, such as playing in octaves or in contrasting rhythms in the two hands.

- **Ballade no. 1 in G Minor, op. 25.** A wordless "story" for solo piano.

- **Berceuse in D♭ Major, op. 57.** A "cradle song" for solo piano that features a constant rocking rhythm.

- **Polonaise in A Major, op. 40, no. 1 ("Military").** One of Chopin's most famous polonaises, another stylized Polish dance for solo piano.

- **Piano Concerto no. 1 in F Minor, op. 21.** The more popular of Chopin's two concertos for piano and orchestra, a highly dramatic work.

CLOSER LK The Piano

The piano is an extremely versatile instrument: it has an enormous register of more than seven octaves and can play melodies and harmonies simultaneously in a variety of timbres.

Technically, the piano is a percussion instrument because the hammers inside the instrument strike the taut strings to produce sound.

Strings: Piano strings vary from quite thick (the lowest strings) to thin (the highest). To balance out the sound, there are three strings for each pitch in the high registers and two per pitch in the middle registers. Altogether, a piano can have as many as 236 strings.

Keyboard: The standard modern keyboard consists of 88 keys, with the lowest on the left and the highest on the right. Each key is one half-step removed from the one above and below it. The configuration of white and black keys allows for easier movement of the hands across the keys.

Pedals: The three pedals modify the sound of the instrument. The soft pedal, on the far left, reduces the volume of sound. The sostenuto pedal, in the middle, sustains notes for keys that have already been depresssed (but not subsequently played notes). The damper pedal, the one most often used by pianists, sustains the sound of all the notes being played; its effect continues until the pedal is lifted.

Lid: The lid is used to direct the sound of the instrument outward in a specific direction. In solo performances, the lid is usually opened all the way; when accompanying other instruments, it is often opened only a small bit so as not to overpower the sound of the ensemble as a whole.

Frame: The frame, made of cast-iron metal, holds the strings and other hardware in place. The metal construction allows for the strings to be stretched to an extremely high tension, which in turn provides for a fuller sound.

Hammers: The wooden hammers, covered in felt, are connected to each key by a complex mechanism that allows the pianist to strike each string or set of strings with varied force, producing loud or soft dynamics.

 EXPAND YOUR PLAYLIST

Piano Music of the Nineteenth Century

Many of the nineteenth century's leading composers were themselves pianists, and they wrote extensively for the instrument.

Ludwig van Beethoven's 32 compositions include the "Moonlight" (op. 27, no 2) and "Appasionata" (op. 57) Sonatas.

Robert Schumann's *Carnaval*, op. 9, has a festive theme.

In Franz Liszt's Sonata in B Minor, a central idea is transformed across an entire work.

Johannes Brahms's deceptively simple Intermezzo, op. 118, no. 2, is one of his most beloved piano miniatures.

Louis Moreau Gottschalk
Union: Concert Paraphrase on National Airs
Composed: 1862

Gottschalk wrote *Union* in response to the outbreak of the American Civil War. Although born and raised in New Orleans, he was an ardent Unionist who opposed slavery and secession. To express his political convictions and national pride, he composed a work that incorporated three well-known patriotic tunes: "Yankee Doodle," "Hail, Columbia," and "The Star-Spangled Banner."

Listen to This First

♫ Melody

Listen for the three well-known patriotic tunes. Listen, too, for the way in which Gottschalk has the piano imitate the sound of distant and approaching drums at one point. ■

🌐 Texture

Listen for differences in texture in the way these melodies are presented. "The Star-Spangled Banner" and "Hail, Columbia" are homophonic (melody with accompaniment). But when "Yankee Doodle" is introduced toward the end, it is combined with "Hail, Columbia" to produce a polyphonic texture, two independent melodies played at the same time. ■

Union **did more than help galvanize Northern sentiment in support of the war**: it gave Gottschalk a vehicle by which to display his talents both as a composer and (in performance of the work) as a piano **virtuoso**. Gottschalk was the first American-born piano virtuoso to achieve international fame. His solo recitals were legendary, and his repertory consisted almost entirely of music he had written himself, because it allowed him to display his technical abilities to greatest effect. He performed *Union* to great acclaim throughout the United States—at least in the North—and in Latin America. Gottschalk noted in his diary that a performance of *Union* in Philadelphia during the Civil War elicited "unheard-of enthusiasm. . . . Recalls, encores, hurrahs, etc.!"[1]

Many of Gottschalk's works incorporate national or ethnic elements. His piano piece *The Banjo*, for example, imitates the sound of that quintessentially American instrument and includes a reference to Stephen Foster's beloved song "Camptown Races." Another of Gottschalk's piano works, *Bamboula*, incorporates the rhythms of African American dances of the mid-nineteenth century.

LEARNING OBJECTIVES

38.1 Explain why Gottschalk composed *Union: Concert Paraphrase on National Airs.*

38.2 Describe the role of music in the American Civil War.

38.3 Listen for familiar patriotic themes in *Union.*

38.4 Describe how Gottschalk manipulates textures in *Union: Concert Paraphrase on National Airs.*

38.5 Describe the virtuosic nature of this work.

38.6 Outline Gottschalk's career as a performer and composer.

[1] Louis Moreau Gottschalk, *Notes of a Pianist*, ed. Clara Gottschalk, trans. Robert E. Peterson (Philadelphia: Lippincott, 1881), p. 81.

HISTORICAL CONTEXT Music in the Civil War

Works like Gottschalk's *Union* remind us of the power of music to arouse intense feelings of community spirit, whether for a school, a faith, or a nation. When giving a concert in Maryland—a slave state that had not seceded and whose citizens' loyalties were deeply divided between North and South—Gottschalk realized that he could not play both *Union* and "Dixie" on the same program without risking a riot, so fierce were the sentiments that could be aroused by certain works of music.

Some songs had more universal appeal. "All Quiet Along the Potomac Tonight," for example, was sung on both sides of the conflict. The words had been written as a poem in 1861 by Ethel Lynn Beers, a New Yorker. Two years later, South Carolinian John Hill Hewitt set them to music while living in Georgia. The song speaks to the quiet fate of an enlisted soldier killed by a sniper; the newspapers the following day report no action along the Potomac River—the river separating Virginia from Maryland, South from North—but the soldier's family knows better.

With the advent of war, old tunes received new texts: A newly minted Confederate version of "Yankee Doodle," issued early in the Civil War, begins,

Yankee Doodle had a mind
To whip the Southern "traitors,"
Because they didn't choose to live
On codfish and potaters.

Several Northern poets, in turn, penned new words to the melody of "Dixie," including these:

Away down South in the land of traitors,
Rattlesnakes and alligators,
Right away, come away, right away, come away.
Where cotton's king and men are chattels,
Union boys will win the battles,
Right away, come away, right away, come away.

Music provided a source of comfort and inspiration to both soldiers in the field and their families back home. And for the soldiers, music was more than entertainment: Every unit had its allotted number of musicians, who conveyed orders across wide distances (through musical signals), mustering the troops, and moving them into position for both drill and battle.

Band of the 107th U.S. Colored Infantry at Fort Corcoran, Arlington, Virginia, in 1865. The most common band instruments of the Civil War were trumpets, fifes (a small, high flute, similar to the piccolo), and many different kinds of drums. The large instruments in the front row are saxhorns, a brass instrument named after Adolphe Sax, who also invented the saxophone. Players carried the instrument over their shoulders, with the bell pointing backward, which allowed troops in the rear to hear their music.

Patriotic Melodies Made Virtuosic

The "national airs" that Gottschalk incorporates in this piece—"The Star-Spangled Banner," "Hail, Columbia," and "Yankee Doodle"—were all closely identified with the Union cause. The work presents no original melodies of its own but offers instead, as its title promises, a "paraphrase" on these "national airs." The patriotic melodies themselves are fairly simple, but Gottschalk embellished them in ways that allowed him to demonstrate his abilities as a piano virtuoso. This work is fiendishly difficult to play, and contemporary audiences were probably responding not only to the nationalism inherent in the music, but also to the sheer skill it took to perform it. With its rapid runs, large leaps, and complicated rhythms, all played for the most part at a very rapid speed, *Union* is the kind of work that only the most technically skilled pianists can perform convincingly. The virtuosity demanded in this work is in many respects physical, similar in kind to that required by a figure skater to execute a difficult maneuver.

 ## Same Melodies, Different Textures

The texture of this work builds from homophonic at the beginning to polyphonic at the end. The harmonization of "The Star-Spangled Banner" is unusual, but the texture is clearly homophonic: melody above, accompaniment below. When "Yankee Doodle" enters clearly for the first time, however, it is combined not with a simple accompaniment underneath, but with another well-known melody, "Hail, Columbia." Both melodies are clearly audible at the same time. Even more remarkably, Gottschalk proceeds to reverse the relative position of these two "national airs," moving "Hail, Columbia" to the uppermost voice and placing "Yankee Doodle" underneath it. Writing two different melodies that work together is difficult enough; writing two melodies whose positions can be reversed is even harder. (The technical term for this kind of polyphony is "invertible counterpoint.") Even though Gottschalk wrote neither of these melodies, he recognized their compatibility and was thus able to demonstrate his skills as a composer and performer at the same time.

Now listen to this piece again, using the Listening Guide.

CONNECT YOUR PLAYLIST

Virtuosity

Find a work that places extreme demands of virtuosity on its instrumentalists.

Example: DragonForce, "Through the Fire and Flames" (2006) This song is known for its extremely difficult instrumental solos. That's why it's featured in the final challenge of the popular video game *Guitar Hero III: Legends of Rock* (2007).

Listening Guide

Louis Moreau Gottschalk Composed: 1862
Union (7:24)

Time	Form	Melody	Texture	Rhythm: Meter
0:00	A	Fragments of "Yankee Doodle" (in minor mode), beginning at 0:24	Homophonic	Duple
1:36	B	"The Star-Spangled Banner" ("with melancholy")		Triple
3:22	A	Fragments of "Yankee Doodle" in minor mode		Duple
3:39	C	Imitation of trumpets (3:39), followed by "Hail, Columbia" (4:00). This section begins softly, grows in volume (4:59), and recedes (5:44)—as if played by a band approaching, marching by, and departing.		
6:06	D	"Yankee Doodle" (upper voice) and "Hail, Columbia" (lower voice); voices switch positions at 6:20. "Yankee Doodle" returns to its usual major mode in this section.	Polyphonic	
6:29	A	Fanfare-like figure from the beginning	Homophonic	
6:43	D	"Yankee Doodle" (upper voice) and "Hail, Columbia" (lower voice); voices switch positions at 6:58.	Polyphonic	

 Student FAQs

Why is "The Star-Spangled Banner" section marked "with melancholy"?

We can't know for certain what Gottschalk had in mind here, but it seems likely that this reflects the dissolution of the Union at the beginning of the Civil War (April 1861). The melody does eventually regain its original form, though, which would reflect the Union's resolve to preserve it.

I've never heard of "Hail, Columbia" before. Was it well known in Gottschalk's time?

"Hail, Columbia" was widely known in the nineteenth century and served as a kind of unofficial national anthem, along with "The Star-Spangled Banner." For reasons that remain unclear, the tune fell out of use in the early twentieth century.

CLOSER L👓K   Gottschalk's 1862 Concerts

In 1862 during the Civil War and after almost six years in Latin America, Louis Moreau Gottschalk returned to the United States. He concertized extensively throughout the North, including one tour of some 15,000 miles by train in which he gave 85 concerts over the course of 18 weeks. Some of his concert stops are presented here with excerpts from his diary.

1. February 22. Gottschalk premieres *Union* in New York City to great acclaim on Washington's birthday.

2. Spring. In St. Louis, Gottschalk writes, "The Germans (they are numerous here, as throughout the West) have organized a Philharmonic Society, which performs the works of Beethoven, Mendelssohn, Schumann, and Wagner."

3. April 18. On his way east from Chicago, Gottschalk witnesses a convoy of wounded soliders recently arrived from the Battle of Shiloh in Tennessee. "I have never in my life seen a more heart-rending sight than the spectacle of these heroic victims of our monstrous war," he writes.

4. June 6. In Portland, Maine, Gottschalk observes, "The hall contains twenty-five hundred persons, and is one of the finest in the world for its acoustic properties. The public are desirous that I should return and give another concert. Extraordinary enthusiasm."

5. June 28. In Springfield, Massachusetts, Gottschalk "visited a large manufactory of guns belonging to the government, where as many as twelve hundred rifles are made daily by a machine. Three thousand workmen are employed here."

6. November 26. Gottschalk is not impressed by Toledo: "Nothing interesting. Audience stupid. In the Artist's Room there was a bill attached to the wall: 'If, before commencing the concert, the performers do not pay the rent of the hall, the porter has orders from the proprietors to turn off the gas.'"

7. Early December. In Madison, Wisconsin, Gottschalk writes, "This town is hardly more than twelve years old, and nevertheless is already remarkable. The cathedral (Catholic) and the marble capitol are superb."

8. December 15. Indianapolis according to Gottschalk: "Whistling is here applause carried to its highest point... Another annoyance is the people who arrive late at the concert, and who traverse the hall in the middle of a piece, marching as if they were marking time for a battalion of raw recruits."

CANADA

U.S.A.

Portland, ME 4

Madison, WI 7

Springfield, MA 5

Chicago, IL 3   6   New York, NY 1

Toledo, OH

Indianapolis, IN 8

2   Washington, DC

St. Louis, MI

N

Confederate States of America

PROFILE   Louis Moreau Gottschalk (1829–1869)

The Musician as Showman

Wherever he performed, Gottschalk won over audiences with a combination of superb piano technique, good looks, and showmanship. He always made a ceremony of taking off his white gloves before performing at the piano, and critics raved about his ability to play even the most difficult passages with ease.

Orchestras around the country featured Gottschalk as a soloist in showpieces he wrote to display his own talents, like the *Grand fantasie triomphale*, a series of brilliant variations on the Brazilian national anthem, or the *Grande tarentelle* for piano and orchestra, based on the traditional Italian dance said to cure the bite of a tarantula. Other nineteenth-century musicians took full advantage of the concerto as a vehicle for showing off their talents as both composers and performers. Franz Liszt wrote two fiendishly difficult piano concertos—he was one of the few musicians of his time who could do justice to them—and Felix Mendelssohn, Frédéric Chopin, and Johannes Brahms also wrote piano concertos in addition to solo piano pieces (see Expand Your Playlist).

A native of New Orleans, Gottschalk studied piano in Paris, where his playing was praised by Chopin, Berlioz, and other leading European musicians. He returned to the United States in 1853 and soon became one of the nation's most popular soloists, touring the country extensively and playing almost entirely works he had composed himself (see "Closer Look: Gottschalk's 1862 Concerts"). He died of yellow fever in Rio de Janeiro, Brazil, during an extended tour of Latin America.

Louis Moreau Gottschalk, ca. 1860. He had a long-standing business relationship with Chickering, a major piano manufacturer, endorsing their instruments and performing on them whenever possible. Notice the bust of Beethoven in the background, much like the bust of Beethoven in the group portrait with Liszt at the piano (see "Closer Look: The Power of Music" in the Part 5 introduction).

EXPAND YOUR PLAYLIST: GOTTSCHALK

- *The Banjo.* This work for solo piano imitates the strumming and plucking sound of the title instrument.

- *Bamboula.* For solo piano; the bass line imitates the bamboo drum of African American musical traditions.

- *Souvenir de Puerto Rico.* A work for solo piano that captures the characteristic rhythms of the Caribbean island.

- **Symphony no. 1** ("A Night in the Tropics"). The finale incorporates a Latin-inspired dance melody.

- *Grande Tarantelle.* A concerto-like work for piano and orchestra. Its central theme uses the rhythm of the tarantella, a traditional Italian dance.

EXPAND YOUR PLAYLIST

The Nineteenth-Century Virtuoso

Audiences throughout Europe and the United States paid big money to hear the great virtuosos of their time perform, either in one-person recitals or as soloists with an orchestra, in concertos. Virtuosos were part musician, part showman. Many of these individuals, like Gottschalk, wrote and performed their own music.

Niccolò Paganini (1782–1840) was the greatest violin virtuoso of the nineteenth century. He did nothing to dispel rumors that he had made a pact with the devil to achieve his mastery of the instrument.

• *Caprices*, op. 1, no. 24. This is a fiendishly difficult set of variations on a short theme.

• Violin Concerto no. 2 in B Minor, op. 7, finale. The main theme of this rondo sounds like the ringing of bells.

Franz Liszt (1811–1886) was the greatest piano virtuoso of the nineteenth century. As a child, he met Beethoven; one of his daughters married the composer Richard Wagner; and he almost single-handedly created the public solo piano recital.

• Hungarian Rhapsody no. 2. This is the most famous of the 19 solo piano works Liszt wrote in a quasi-Hungarian style. Although Liszt was born in present-day Hungary, his native language was German, and he started to learn Hungarian only later in his life.

• Piano Concerto no. 2 in A Major. This is one of two concertos Liszt wrote to perform himself.

• *Grandes etudes de Paganini*, no. 3 in G-sharp Minor ("La Campanella"). Liszt's reworking of the finale of Paganini's Violin Concerto no. 2 (see earlier), for piano, adds extra lines to make the music even more difficult.

Ignacy Jan Paderewski (1860–1941) was famous as a piano performer, composer, and statesman. In later life, he served briefly as prime minister of his native Poland and was active in the Polish government-in-exile during World War II.

• *Humoresques de concert*: Minuet in G Major. The most famous of Paderewski's many works for solo piano.

39

Ravi Shankar
Raga Sindhi-Bhairavi
Recorded: 1968

Instrumental virtuosity plays a role in the music of many cultures around the world. In this work for solo sitar—an Indian plucked string instrument—famed Indian sitarist Ravi Shankar (1920–2012) demonstrates his musicianship through music that is extremely difficult to play.

Listen to This First

Timbre	Melody	Texture	Form	Rhythm
The sitar includes strings that are plucked and produce pitches and also strings that simply resonate when other pitches sound. Listen for the difference between these two kinds of sounds. Also listen for other instruments as well. ■	Listen to the melodies produced on the sitar. Do some notes sound more important than others? ■	Is the texture homophonic or polyphonic? How many instruments do you hear? How does the texture change throughout the piece? ■	Listen for four different sections and the way each section changes in texture and rhythm. ■	Listen to how the rhythm begins freely but becomes more established throughout. ■

LEARNING OBJECTIVES

39.1 Discuss virtuosity as a quality common to many musical cultures around the world.

39.2 Describe the sitar, an Indian stringed instrument.

39.3 Discuss Ravi Shankar's virtuosity and his role in introducing the sitar to Western popular music audiences.

39.4 Describe the nature of *raga*.

39.5 Identify the tambura and the tabla.

39.6 Listen for the four sections in Ravi Shankar's *Raga Sindhi-Bhairavi*.

39.7 Define *tala*.

During India's Mughal Period—which lasted from the early sixteenth to the mid-nineteenth centuries—the *raga* flourished as a genre of North Indian music. *Raga*, which means "mood," "color," or "musical scale," is a term that refers to an instrumental performance featuring a soloist who played to color the emperor's mood or day. The dissolution of the Mughal court after 1720 led to the dispersal of Hindustani musicians and raga performance throughout northern India. Today, schools for *raga* performance exist throughout the world.

Timbre: The Sound of the Sitar

The **sitar** is a plucked string instrument that usually has 18 strings (*tar* is the Indian word for "string"). The strings are arranged in three sets: the playing strings, the drone strings, and the sympathetic strings. The playing strings are fretted and produce the melody. (Frets are made of a thick twine that is wrapped around the neck of the instrument. They determine the pitch of a note when the nonplucking hand presses down against the top of the fret.) The main melody string is played by bending it far across the frets to produce a wide range of pitches. One of the drone strings is struck periodically to resonate with an important note in the melody. The sympathetic strings are located under the frets and vibrate when a corresponding pitch on a main melody string is sounded. At the very beginning and very end of a *raga*, including the one heard here, players can also strum the sympathetic strings directly.

All the strings of a sitar are fastened to a wooden neck with pegs. The base of the neck of the sitar is attached to a large gourd resonator, and at the top of the neck is often attached a smaller gourd resonator. For plucking, the player wears a wire plectrum ("pick") around the index finger of the right hand. Players perform seated.

Ravi Shankar was widely considered the finest sitarist of his generation. He was certainly the most famous sitarist in the Western world. Here he performs with his daughter Anoushka (b. 1981).

Melody of the Sunrise

Raga (also the plural form of the word) are scalar patterns of five to nine notes, each with its own distinct manner of performance. Each *raga* has a certain character, or mood, that is believed to affect the universe. North Indian classical music uses far more tones than European classical music does. Theoretically, thousands of *raga* exist; however, 72 *raga* are known and performed today. Based on the larger vocabulary of available tones, new *raga* may still be invented.

Raga Sindhi-Bhairavi is a morning *raga*. It was created by Shankar, who was a composer, improviser, and **virtuoso**. From the sixteenth through mid-nineteenth centuries, a morning raga could be performed at the court only at sunrise to regulate the sun's movement over the horizon. A different type of *raga* performed at that time of day, or a morning *raga* played with mistakes, was believed to throw off the entire day because the musical vibrations would be "out of synch" with the vibrations of the universe at that moment. Today, as concert pieces, any *raga* can be performed at any time of day.

CONNECT YOUR PLAYLIST

Instrumental Virtuosity

Find a recording that showcases a performer's virtuosity on an instrument.

Example: Charlie Daniels, "The Devil Went Down to Georgia" (1979) The song, about a fiddling contest between the devil and a boy named Johnny, features two extended instrumental sections in which each character displays his talents.

HISTORICAL CONTEXT   The Sitar in Popular Music

Ravi Shankar (1920–2012), who was born in Benares, India, was already well known in Western classical and jazz circles when George Harrison first heard his playing in the mid-1960s. The lead guitarist for the Beatles, Harrison first played sitar on their recording of the song "Norwegian Wood." Soon after, Brian Jones of the Rolling Stones played a sitar part on that group's hit single "Paint It Black." Harrison remained deeply devoted to Indian music and philosophy, studying with Shankar and also incorporating Indian tonalities and instruments into several of his songs, most notably "Within You, Without You" on *Sgt. Pepper's Lonely Heart's Club Band.*

Shankar's fame in rock circles grew after he appeared at several major festivals in the late 1960s, including the Monterey International Pop Music Festival in 1967 and the famous Woodstock festival in 1969. His best-known appearance was at the Concert for Bangladesh at New York's Madison Square Garden in 1971. Shankar had approached Harrison after hearing of the devastating floods in the Bangladesh region, situated between India and Pakistan. Harrison enlisted other rock artists—including Bob Dylan, Eric Clapton, and Ringo Starr—to perform at the benefit concert. The concert opened—as did the

Benares, on the Ganges River, is one of the world's oldest cities still inhabited today.

later three-album record set—with a half-hour performance by Shankar on sitar.

Shankar continued to perform a mix of traditional *ragas* with his own compositions and to cross genres to work with classical orchestras and jazz and pop ensembles. His daughter Anoushka is also a noted sitar artist; another daughter, Norah Jones, is well known as a pop singer, songwriter, and pianist.

British pop musician George Harrison, right, of the Beatles, with seven top Indian instrumentalists, singers, and dancers. Ravi Shankar is third from the right, holding a sitar.

At the opening of this performance, Ravi Shankar demonstrates the ascending and descending scales that form the basis of this *raga*. Note that these scales are not identical; the descending scale has more notes than the ascending one and also more up-and-down motion. Note also the ornaments and small "bends" he applies to certain notes by easing into or out of them. This style of playing is part of what gives this particular raga its distinctive sound.

A *raga* solo always begins with the sounding of the tones of the *raga* scale in descending motion. Then, throughout the first three unmetered sections, the soloist freely improvises themes using the tones of this particular *raga*. Each *raga* has scale tones that are more important than others; you can hear during the improvisations that Shankar lingers on certain notes longer (for example, from 0:36 to 0:54), or decorates them with brief upward or downward motions while basically remaining on the same note (for example, from approximately 1:29 to 1:35). These key notes are the ones that will be used to build the principal melody of the *raga*, known as a *gat* (see the following discussion).

Virtuosity and improvisation are basic features of *raga* performances. The *raga* improvisations gain in intensity throughout and culminate in the statement of the principal theme of the melody (at 5:48).

A Triple Texture

In addition to the texture created by the sitar's numerous strings, Indian music requires three players to produce the layers of musical activity: a melodic soloist (sitar or other instrument), a separate drone instrument, and an accompanying drummer. *Raga* performance by a sitarist is always accompanied by two instruments: the tambura and the tabla. The **tambura** is a plucked string instrument like the sitar, but it has four to six strings and is used only to provide a drone.

The **tabla** is a set of two drums struck with the fingertips. The tabla enters in the fourth and final section of the *raga*, when the meter becomes established. The tabla player is able to vary the pitch of each drum by pressing his or her hand against the drum head, creating a sliding sound something like the bending of the melody string on the sitar. So the tabla part can combine rhythm and melody, and can "answer" the melodies stated by the sitar.

 ## Form by Four Sections

The improvisation of the raga takes place over four sections of music:

1. The *alap* is the introductory section. The sitar soloist is accompanied only by the tambura. The alap section allows a free-ranging exploration of the raga without a regular meter or pulse. It starts out in free rhythm and increases through a series of plateaus until the listener has a sense of a regular rhythmic pulse.
2. The *jor* is the section of the pulsed improvisation that develops from the *alap*. The *jor* tempo is faster than the *alap*, and the density of the rhythm increases.
3. The *jhala* section, the second type of pulsed improvisation, involves repeatedly striking a jhala (drone) string on the sitar.
4. The *gat tora* section introduces the meter set by the tabla drums. The *gat*, mentioned previously, is a short composed melody, and the primary theme of the song. *Tora* are the alternated, improvised passages between the *gat* statements.

 ## Rhythm: From Free to Established

Tala are fixed, repeated cycles of pulses. Certain pulses receive accents and are thus more important than the others. *Tala* is absent from *alap*, *jor*, and *jhala* sections because these sections build from free rhythm to a constant unmetered pulse. The *tala* is always established at the *gat tora* section of a *raga*. As Shankar says in his introduction, the basic rhythm can be played at various speeds, in this case at a medium and fast tempo.

There are many *tala* patterns. In *Raga Sindhi-Bhairavi*, the *tala* is *tintál*, a 16-beat cycle. The 16 beats are further broken down into groups of 4, with the first beat of each grouping receiving extra emphasis: **1**-2-3-4 **5**-6-7-8 **9**-10-11-12 **13**-14-15-16. In the *gat tora*, the soloist and tabla player can exchange roles, one improvising for a rhythmic cycle or two, while the other plays the fixed melody or rhythmic pattern.

Now listen to this piece again, using the Listening Guide.

Listening Guide ◀))

Ravi Shankar Recorded: 1968

Raga Sindhi-Bhairavi (14:59)

Time	🏛 Form	🎵 Melody	🌐 Texture
0:00	Shankar demonstrates the *raga*'s tones and describes the rhythmic pattern of the piece. In his narration, Shankar refers to "two pieces" of the *raga*: The first piece consists of the first three sections (*alap, jor,* and *jhala*), which are played in a free rhythm, without a fixed meter; and the second piece is the longer *gat*, played in a metrical pattern called a *tintál*, a cycle of 16 beats.		
0:28	*Alap:* the introductory section	The piece begins with freely improvised short melodic phrases. Listen to how some phrases lead up to the highest tone of the *raga,* while other phrases feature lower tones of the *raga*. Bending of the strings is used in an expressive and decorative style.	Homophonic: drone harmony. The tambura provides a soft drone to the freely improvised introduction of the *raga* scale.
4:26	*Jor:* improvisatory section	The soloist strikes a string to create a pulse and continues improvising now with a rhythmic pulsation.	
4:54	*Jhala:* a second improvisatory section	The soloist features a repeatedly struck *jhala* or open string to build the first part of the piece to a climax.	
5:48	*Gat tora*	The *gat* theme begins with a brief flourish by the sitar, which is answered by the entrance of the *tabla*.	Homophonic. The drone continues and the tabla drums enter.
11:26		Second, faster, and final section of the raga, highly improvisatory. The faster tempo helps build the performance to a climactic finish.	

Rhythm

Free rhythm

Rhythm established but in unmetered pulsations.

Rhythm continues in unmetered pulsations.

Tintál begins on the first tone of the *gat*. It is a 16-beat cycle.

Tintál rhythm cycle continues.

Q   Student FAQs

What are sympathetic strings? How do they work?

A sound wave creates physical movement in the air around it. When a string is plucked, its vibrations move through the air; if another string is nearby, even if it is not touched by a pick or finger, it is set into vibration by the original sound. This is described as a "sympathetic vibration," although of course the second string doesn't feel any sympathy for the first!

How are drone strings different from sympathetic strings?

Both sympathetic and drone strings play only one note and are not "fretted" by the sitar player. However, the drone strings are regularly played with the pick to sound throughout the piece. Sympathetic strings are never struck; rather, they simply vibrate on their own when the sound of another string sets them into motion.

How does a sitar player play different ragas if each raga has a different set of scale notes?

The sitar player can adapt his or her instrument to different scales by moving the frets on the fingerboard. Unlike a guitar, which has frets permanently placed into the neck, the sitar's frets are arched metal pieces attached to the back of the neck by thick twine to stay in place. To play a different scale, it is easy to slide the frets into different positions.

EXPAND YOUR PLAYLIST

Raga

Ravi Shankar

- *Three Ragas*, Angel 67310.
- First issued in 1956, this recording captures Shankar at his youthful prime playing three traditional ragas.
- *At Woodstock*, BGO 117.
- Three ragas recorded live at the famous 1969 rock festival.
- *Improvisations*, Angel 67049.
- Originally released in 1961, this album features Shankar playing with two American jazz musicians, Bud Shank on saxophone and Gary Peacock on bass. It represents an early attempt at "fusion" of North Indian *raga* and American jazz music.

Anoushka Shankar

- *Anoushka*, Angel 53729.
- The 2000 debut album by Ravi's talented daughter is a program of original compositions in the style and spirit of classical *raga*.

Ali Akbar Khan

- Khan is a master of the sarod, a 25-string fretless lute that features a skin head stretched over the gourd-shaped body. The use of metal strings and neck and the skin head produce a much sharper and louder sound than is heard on the sitar.
- *Signature Series No. 1: Three Ragas*, Aamp 7500.

  The "Signature Series" brings onto CD classic recordings by Khan and represents some of his best works. This CD includes the night *raga* "Chandranandan."

George Harrison, Ravi Shankar, and Others

- *The Concert for Bangladesh*, Sony 4688352.
- The famous live concert from 1971, featuring a wonderful traditional performance by Ravi Shankar.

Giuseppe Verdi

La Traviata, Act I, selection ("Follie!")
Composed: 1853

40

In Verdi's opera *La Traviata*, Violetta, a high-class prostitute, thinks she may be falling in love with Alfredo, a young gentleman she has just met at a party. Alone back in her apartment, she moves from recitative at the beginning—simple, declamatory, syllabic—to a virtuosic aria at the end. Her singing is interrupted by Alfredo, whom she hears but does not see, singing his own aria to her from the street. At the end of this excerpt, we hear two separate melodies—two separate arias—being performed simultaneously.

Listen to This First

♫ Melody

Listen to the contrast between the melodic styles of Violetta's recitative, the aria, and the purely lyrical nature of Alfredo's singing. ▪

🗨 Word–Music Relationships

Listen to the contrast between the introspective nature of the opening recitative and the growing exuberance of the music that leads into the aria. Note in particular Verdi's setting of the key word "*gioir*" ("enjoy"), set melismatically and in an extremely high register. Listen for the changes in tempo and melody later in the aria that reflect Violetta's attraction to Alfredo. ▪

This scene takes us on an emotional roller coaster. Violetta and Alfredo, a young gentleman, have fallen in love. But Violetta is already suffering from the consumption (tuberculosis) that will eventually kill her. She senses that her days are numbered, and she must decide whether to keep her freedom or commit to one man alone (Alfredo). The music she sings here ranges from uncertainty and fear of abandonment to the ecstasy of freedom to the crippling pain of love.

Verdi projects these profoundly contrasting emotions through a variety of singing styles. In this scene, we hear passages of recitative-like outbursts flowing in and out of more lyrical, aria-like sections. We hear spectacularly virtuosic singing and extremely high notes—the kind that can sometimes break glass—and a moment later, simple song. By writing long units of music that encompass both lyrical and declamatory moments, Verdi is able to move the plot forward (through recitative) and at the same time provide plenty of space for both the lyrical and virtuosic singing that opera audiences love so dearly. In this scene, in fact, Violetta's aria becomes a duet, for about halfway through this scene, Alfredo joins in. We do not see him onstage—he is singing his serenade of love to her from the street up to her balcony. This is a melody Alfredo had sung to her earlier in Act 1, and the combined sound of Alfredo's voice and this hauntingly lyrical melody causes Violetta to doubt her own resolve to live freely, alone and independent of anyone else's demands.

LEARNING OBJECTIVES

40.1 Outline the basic story and describe the two central characters of Verdi's *La Traviata*.

40.2 Describe the ways in which the virtuosic singing in this selection from *La Traviata* is motivated by the dramatic situation.

40.3 Listen for the declamatory, virtuosic, and lyrical styles of singing in this selection from *La Traviata*.

40.4 Listen for the contrasting timbres and melodies of the music sung by Violetta and Alfredo in the selection.

40.5 Discuss Verdi's career as a composer and social reformer.

40.6 Discuss the nature of the diva in culture today.

Julia Roberts and Richard Gere at the opera house in the 1990 film *Pretty Woman*. They are watching Verdi's *La Traviata*, which provides the basis for much of the plotline of *Pretty Woman*.

Verdi's *La Traviata* exemplifies the best elements of nineteenth-century Italian opera. It showcases the voice and uses the orchestra sparingly but effectively. Above all, it is dramatically realistic—who has not been torn between the desire for freedom and the pull of love?—and musically satisfying. Even if we do not understand the words, we can hear the sound of the emotions expressed by the singers.

Melody: Declamatory, Lyrical, Virtuosic

Verdi uses three distinct types of melody in this brief scene:

- **Declamatory.** Violetta begins her monologue by singing in **accompanied recitative**. The style is declamatory—that is, delivered as if in a speech, with great feeling—and syllabic (one note per syllable), making the text easy to understand. The melody is quite simple: At one point, Violetta sings the same note repeatedly, as if talking to herself—which, in fact, she is. The focus here is on the text.

- **Virtuosic.** At the exclamation *"Gioir!"* ("Enjoy!"), the music suddenly becomes melismatic (more than one note per syllable). The text is not so easy to understand at this point, for intelligibility has taken a back seat to the expression of emotions, which we hear more in the *way* she sings than in *what* she sings. And what she sings is extremely **virtuosic**: She hits some extremely high notes (at 0:36 and 0:56) and navigates through difficult runs at a rapid pace. When the **aria** begins (at 1:07), the orchestra introduces the principal melody but then gives way to Violetta, who continues to sing in a highly virtuosic style throughout the aria portion of the scene. When a soprano sings this role well, few things can be more thrilling in the world of opera.

- **Lyrical.** When Alfredo (or to be more precise, Alfredo's voice) enters the scene, we hear a very different kind of singing. The tempo is slower, the notes are longer and smoother, and the declamation is for the most part syllabic. There are no enormous leaps to the extreme end of the tenor's vocal range, no breathtaking runs. The music is sustained and lyrical.

Word–Music Relationships: Signs of Contemplation, Ecstasy, Love

Like every good opera composer, Verdi captures the drama of the text through music. The contrasting styles of singing noted earlier—declamatory, virtuosic, and lyrical—correspond to the emotional states of the characters singing them. When Violetta is unsure of what to do, she sings in recitative. But at the moment when she decides to devote herself to a life of pleasure, her whole manner shifts quite suddenly. When she sings *"gioir"* ("enjoy"), we can almost feel with her the bodily pleasure she takes in singing the word, lingering over it, repeating it, hitting the highest range of her register. Even if we do not understand the word itself, we know that her emotion is one of ecstasy. She reinforces this sense with the way she goes on to sing the word *"vortici"* ("vortices," in the phrase "Perish in the vortices of pleasure!"), spiraling downward from a high note to a low one.

Love—emotional love, as opposed to merely physical love—appears in the guise of Alfredo's lyrical melody. Dramatically, the sound of Alfredo's voice derails Violetta's ecstatic singing. She suddenly shifts to her original mood of contemplation and sings in the manner of recitative once again, punctuating the phrases of Alfredo's melody. When she once again rejects the path of emotional commitment and returns to her ecstatic, virtuosic style of singing (2:43), she sings a variation of the aria's opening text and music that is even more spectacular than before. This highly virtuosic moment of intensification is motivated by the drama itself, for Violetta has contemplated her choices (as heard in the sections of accompanied recitative) and opted for pleasure (as heard in her virtuosic singing).

With these points in mind, listen to this scene once again, using the Listening Guide.

CONNECT YOUR PLAYLIST

Vocal Virtuosity

Find an example of vocal virtuosity.

Example: Whitney Houston, "I Will Always Love You" (2000) This song emphasizes Houston's impressive vocal abilities throughout.

The Russian-born soprano Anna Netrebko as Violetta in a production of *La Traviata* at the Salzburg Festival in 2005. New opera productions often update the scenery and staging of the original.

Giuseppe Verdi Composed: 1853

La Traviata, Act I, selection (4:49)

Time	Character	Original Italian Text	English Translation
0:00	Violetta	Follie! Delirio vano è questo! Povera donna, sola, abbandonata In questo popoloso deserto Che appellano Parigi, Che spero or più? Che far degg'io?	It's madness! Empty delirium! A poor woman, alone, abandoned In this populated wasteland They call Paris; What can I now hope? What should I do?
0:26		Gioir! Di voluttà ne' vortici perir!	Take delight! Perish in the vortices of pleasure!
0:49		Gioir!	Take delight!
1:07		Sempre libera degg'io Folleggiare di gioia in gioia, Vo' che scorra il viver mio Dei sentieri del piacer.	Always free I must Frolic from pleasure to pleasure, I want to glide through my life Along the paths of pleasure.
1:31		Nasca il giorno, oil giorno muoia, Sempre lieta ne' ritrovi,	As each day dawns, or as each day dies,
1:44		A diletti sempre nuovi Dee volare il mio pensier.	I shall always be joyful in discovering Constantly new pleasures that make my spirit soar.
2:06	Alfredo [underneath the balcony]	Amor è palpito . . .	Love is the pulse . . .
2:14	Violetta	Oh!	Oh!
2:15	Alfredo	. . . dell'universo intero . . .	. . . of the entire universe . . .
2:22	Violetta	L'amore!	Love!
2:24	Alfredo	Misterioso, altero, Croce e delizia al cor.	Mysterious, proud, The torment and delight of the heart.
2:43	Violetta	Follie!	It's madness!
2:58		Gioir!	Take delight!
3:14		Sempre libera degg'io Folleggiare di gioia in gioia, Vo' che scorra il viver mio Dei Sentieri del piacer.	Always free I must Frolic from pleasure to pleasure, I want to glide through my life Along the paths of pleasure . . .
3:26		Nasca il giorno, oil giorno muoia, Sempre lieta ne' ritrovi,	As each day dawns, as each day dies, I shall always be joyful in discovering
3:40		A diletti sempre nuovi Dee volare il mio pensier	Constantly new pleasures That make my spirit soar.
4:02	Alfredo and Violetta	Amor è palpito . . . dell'universo intero . . .	Love is the pulse . . . of the entire universe . . . [transl. MEB]

Melody	Word–Music Relationships
Accompanied recitative (syllabic, many repeated notes)]	Violetta contemplates and sings in declamatory manner.
Virtuosic	Resolved to dedicate herself to pleasure, she begins to sing virtuosically.
Aria	She continues to sing in a virtuosic fashion.
Aria (to words and a melody Alfredo had sung to Violetta earlier in the opera)	Lyrical melody: long, sustained notes, no high leaps or rapid runs.
Accompanied recitative	
Aria	
Accompanied recitative	
Aria	
Accompanied recitative (resumes)	Once again, Violetta rejects emotional love and returns to a virtuosic style of singing.
Virtuosic	
Aria	
	We again hear both voices at the same time, each singing in its own way.
Aria	

Q Student FAQs

Can high notes like the one in this aria really break glass?

Yes, although crystal is easier to break than glass. If you tap a fine crystal wineglass, you will hear a tone: This is the pitch that corresponds to the structures of the crystals that make up the glass. If a singer hits precisely this pitch and sings loudly enough, the glass can break. The crystals in a normal pane of glass, or in a beer bottle, are irregular enough to resist this kind of breakage.

Are operas amplified with microphones and speakers when they are performed?

Sometimes they are, especially if they're being performed outside or in an extremely large arena. But for the most part, opera companies tend to avoid amplified sound. Opera singers are trained to fill large spaces with their voices, and most opera lovers want to hear voices in their purest form. Even the very best amplification systems distort sound in subtle ways.

PROFILE   Giuseppe Verdi (1813–1901)

The Composer as Social Reformer

The story of *La Traviata* mirrors Giuseppe Verdi's own life in certain respects. Audiences were scandalized by the portrayal of an unwed couple living together, but this is exactly the situation in which Verdi found himself while composing *La Traviata*. He and Giuseppina Strepponi, a soprano, had been living together openly since 1848; they eventually married (in 1859), but Verdi experienced firsthand the same kind of scorn cast at those who, like his operatic characters Violetta and Alfredo, defy social conventions.

Through his art, Verdi sought to reform political conventions as well. Several of his operas incorporate thinly veiled appeals for the unification of Italy, which at the time was still a loose confederation of small states, many of them under the domination of the Austrian Empire. The chorus of captive Israelites in ancient Babylon in Verdi's *Nabucco* (1842) became the unofficial anthem of the simmering Italian uprising that would eventually liberate and unify Italy. Verdi himself was elected to the newly constituted Italian parliament in 1860, though by his own admission he spent little time there. He was too busy fulfilling commissions for new operas from around Europe, including France, Russia, and even Egypt. His *Aïda* (1871), set in ancient Egypt, was written to celebrate the opening of the Suez Canal.

For all his accomplishments, Verdi remained a private and modest individual, spending most of his life in Italy (see "Closer Look: Verdi's World"). A few years before his death, he established a home for retired musicians unable to support themselves, and he consigned all royalties for the 30 years after his death to this institution.

Giuseppe Verdi.

EXPAND YOUR PLAYLIST: VERDI

- ***Il Trovatore*** ("The Troubadour"). An opera about a series of loves and rivalries among a group of gypsies.

- ***Rigoletto.*** An opera about a hunchback court jester (Rigoletto) and a lascivious duke.

- ***Aïda.*** An opera commissioned to celebrate the opening of the Suez Canal; the story takes place in ancient Egypt.

- ***Requiem.*** A Mass for the dead, composed in honor of Italian writer Alessandro Manzoni, this work is for chorus, soloists, and orchestra. It is quite operatic in its style, despite its being written for the church.

CLOSER LOOK Verdi's World

Except for a few years in Paris and occasional extended visits to London and Vienna, Giuseppe Verdi spent most of his life on the Italian peninsula. His professional career was closely linked to the major opera houses of the region, and most of his stage works received their premieres in Italy.

Many of Verdi's operas premiere in **Milan** at the Teatro alla Scala, one of the world's leading opera houses. These include *Otello* (1887) and *Falstaff* (1893), the last operas Verdi composes. He dies in Milan January 27, 1901.

Verdi is born in Roncole, a small village near **Busseto**, in 1813, the son of an innkeeper and small landowner. In the 1840s Verdi acquires a house (known today as the "Villa Verdi") in nearby Sant' Agata and lives here off and on throughout his life.

Macbeth, based on Shakespeare's drama, premieres in **Florence** in 1847.

In 1850 *Stiffelio* premieres in **Trieste**. The plot, centering on adultery, creates a furor with the censors.

In **Venice**, several of Verdi's operas premiere, including *Rigoletto* (1851) and *La Traviata* (1853) at the Teatro La Fenice. True to its name, the "Phoenix Theater" has twice been rebuilt after serious fires, the most recent of which occurred in 1996.

Several of Verdi's operas, including *Il Trovatore* (1853), one of his most popular, premiere in **Rome** at the Teatro dell' Opera di Roma.

In 1849 *Luisa Miller,* an early work based on a drama by Friedrich Schiller, opens in **Naples** at the Teatro San Carlo.

 EXPAND YOUR PLAYLIST

The Art of the Diva

A comparison of different artists performing the same work—here, the excerpt from Verdi's *La Traviata*—quickly reveals the enormous difference singers can make in bringing a work to life. Listen for differences in interpretation—tempo, rhythm, articulation, dynamics—and above all, the quality of the voice itself. The recording here is by famed Spanish soprano Monserrat Caballé (b. 1933), renowned not only for the quality of her singing but also the remarkable range of dramatic roles at her command.

- **Renata Tebaldi** (1922–2004) was widely perceived as the greatest rival of Maria Callas. Like Callas and Sutherland, she excelled in Italian opera. Opera d'Oro 1276.

- **Joan Sutherland** (b. 1926) was one of the great sopranos of her generation until her retirement from the stage in 1990. Born in Australia, she established her reputation singing Italian opera of the nineteenth century. The Italians dubbed her *"La stupenda"* ("The stupendous one"). Decca 430491.

- **Kiri Te Kanawa** (b. 1944) began her career in her native New Zealand singing in clubs. She is of both Maori and European descent and was made Dame Commander of The Order of the British Empire in 1982. Philips 464982.

- **Anna Netrebko** (b. 1971) was born in Krasnodar, Russia, and became an Austrian citizen in 2006. She has entranced audiences around the world with both her voice and striking physical appearance. DG 000692209.

HISTORICAL CONTEXT **The Diva**

Diva is an Italian word that means "goddess" and in the world of opera, it is used to describe that small handful of singers in each generation whose voices and personalities together capture the imagination of opera lovers. Some of the great divas of the last 50 years include Maria Callas, Joan Sutherland, Marilyn Horne, and Leontyne Price.

The diva is more than just a singer: She is a phenomenon, a force whose life story fascinates as much as her artistic accomplishments. Soprano Maria Callas (1923–1977) attracted an enormous following during her lifetime, and through her recordings, her reputation has grown still greater. She remains one of the top-selling operatic vocalists to this day, more than 30 years after her death.

Callas's voice was spectacular, with an enormous range, a huge variety of colors, and an unmistakable sound that belonged to her and to no other soprano. Her personal life was equally distinctive. She was notoriously temperamental and demanding, and she was romantically linked for many years to Aristotle Onassis, a Greek shipping magnate. But when Onassis abandoned Callas in 1968 to marry Jacqueline Kennedy, widow of the late U.S. president, the diva was once again in the news, even though she had retired from the stage three years before.

There is a male counterpart to the diva—the divo—but the image has not sparked nearly the same response in audiences. The idea of the diva, however, has extended itself beyond the opera house to include any female entertainer whose off-stage persona is as eagerly followed as her on-stage presence and who can be difficult or demanding. One might call these entertainers modern divas: Liza Minnelli, Barbra Streisand, Diana Ross, Whitney Houston, Mariah Carey, and Lady GaGa.

Maria Callas (left) and Lady GaGa (right). Every true diva knows how to strike a meaningful pose.

Richard Wagner

The Valkyrie, Act III, selection ("Wotan's Farewell")
Composed: 1856

The excerpt here is the closing scene of *The Valkyrie* (*Die Walküre*), the second opera in a cycle of four operas known as *The Ring of the Nibelung* (*Der Ring des Nibelungen*). Wotan, the chief of all gods, is bidding farewell to his daughter, Brünnhilde, who has disobeyed him. As punishment, Wotan deprives her of her supernatural powers and puts her into a deep sleep, surrounded by a circle of fire.

Listen to This First

Texture

Listen to the relationship between the voices and the orchestra. In traditional opera, the orchestra supports the voice; in Wagner's operas, the two blend into a single unit. ■

Word–Music Relationships

Listen for the return of certain musical themes or fragments of themes and their relationship to what is being sung or acted on the stage. ■

Richard Wagner's *Ring of the Nibelung* **traces the fate of a magic golden ring** that has supreme powers of both good and evil. The **libretto**, by Wagner himself, is a text that draws heavily on northern European mythology, including many of the same sources used by J. R. R. Tolkien in his *Lord of the Rings* (see "Historical Context: Wagner and Tolkien: A Tale of Two Rings"). There are many strands running through the plot. In *The Valkyrie*, the principal characters are Wotan, the supreme god of Norse mythology, and his daughter Brünnhilde, a warrior-like Valkyrie. Against Wotan's explicit command, Brünnhilde has interceded on behalf of a human couple (Siegmund and Sieglinde). Enraged, Wotan condemns his daughter to death. But she pleads for a lesser sentence, and because she is his favorite offspring, her father relents. He strips Brünnhilde of her godlike powers, encloses her in a deep sleep, and surrounds her with a circle of fire that can be crossed only by a person who has no fear of Wotan's spear, an object that represents his authority over the universe. As it turns out, in the next opera of the *Ring* cycle, Brünnhilde will be awakened by Siegfried (the offspring of Siegmund and Sieglinde), who has in fact in the meantime shattered Wotan's spear. For the moment, though, all this still lies in the future. In the scene here, a Wotan full of mixed emotions bids farewell to his beloved Brünnhilde, puts her into a deep sleep, and then summons Loge, a shifty, firelike figure, to create the circle of magic fire that will protect her from those ordinary mortals who would fear the fire.

LEARNING OBJECTIVES

41.1 Outline the story of *The Valkyrie*.

41.2 Describe the ways in which Wagner sought to change the nature of opera and specifically the relationship between voice and orchestra.

41.3 Define *Leitmotif*.

41.4 Listen for the *Leitmotifs* associated with Wotan's spear, Loge, and Fate.

41.5 Outline Wagner's career as a composer.

41.6 Identify the ways in which the idea behind each of the *Leitmotifs* in Richard Wagner's *The Valkyrie*, Act III, selection ("Wotan's Farewell") is conveyed through purely musical means.

HISTORICAL CONTEXT　Wagner and Tolkien: A Tale of Two Rings

J. R. R. Tolkien vehemently denied any connection between his *Lord of the Rings* and Wagner's *Ring of the Nibelung*. "Both rings were round, and there the resemblance ceases," he once declared. But the parallels are too strong for us to accept this assertion at face value. We know, in fact, that Tolkien collaborated on a translation of *The Valkyrie* with his friend C. S. Lewis (author of *The Chronicles of Narnia*); unfortunately, the translation was never finished.

Tolkien may or may not have borrowed directly from Wagner, but both artists drew on the same Nordic myths for their subject matter. Thus the characters, events, and themes of the two works exhibit striking similarities. See the following examples:

1. Each cycle consists of four works, the first of which (Wagner's *Das Rheingold*, Tolkien's *The Hobbit*) serves as a prelude to the central sequence of three.

2. In both cycles, a golden ring holds great power but also brings grief to any owner who covets that power.

3. The plots center on efforts to own and control the ring.

4. Both cycles begin in a state of innocence (the Rhine; the Shire) that is corrupted and then ultimately restored.

5. Both cycles feature giants, dragons, dwarves who are great metalworkers, a riddling match, and a shattered sword recast into one even more powerful.

Nikolai Putilin performs as Alberich with the Kirov Opera. Alberich, the dwarf in Wagner's *Ring of the Nibelung*, owns the magic ring for a brief time; he wins it by renouncing love, but it is later stolen from him.

Gollum (Andy Serkis) holds the Ring in Peter Jackson's film adaptation of Tolkien's *Lord of the Rings*.

Texture: The Relationship of Voice and Orchestra

Wagner and Verdi were contemporaries, but the styles of singing in their operas are very different. In Verdi's *La Traviata*, the voices predominate over the orchestra and dazzle with their virtuosic runs, elaborate melismas, and spectacular high notes. Wagner felt that this kind of singing sacrificed the intelligibility of the text (the libretto) for the sake of musical effect. In fact, he considered conventional opera—by Mozart, Verdi, and others—to be based on a fundamentally false premise: that the words being sung constituted little more than an excuse for virtuosic singing. The "error of opera," Wagner declared, was that "a means of expression"—the music—had become an end in its own right while the goal of that expression—the drama—"had been made a means." Wagner wanted to restore dramatic integrity to opera by creating a style of singing that was at once musically satisfying and readily intelligible. Thus in Wagnerian opera, the vocal writing tends to be more syllabic—one note per syllable of text—and not nearly so virtuosic. There is also very little repetition of text: Just as actors in a spoken drama rarely repeat their lines, singers typically sing their words only once. The melodies also tend to be more open-ended and generally avoid strong cadences.

In a particularly memorable turn of phrase Wagner called the drama—the events transpiring on the stage—"deeds of music made visible." What happens on the stage, in other words, is a tangible reflection of what is going on in the orchestra pit. Ideally, then, one should be able to follow the course of a Wagnerian "music drama" through the music alone, without the aid of words, by tracing the fate of its various musical ideas. These musical ideas would eventually come to be known as *Leitmotifs* (see the following discussion).

Word–Music Relationships: The Themes and the Drama

Minimizing virtuosity and projecting the text more clearly were only two of Wagner's strategies for integrating text, voices, and instruments. Another important element of Wagnerian opera is the technique of **Leitmotif**, a brief musical phrase or idea connected dramatically to some person, event, or idea in the drama. These "leading motifs" are meant to lead—direct—our minds in such a way as to help us understand what we see happening onstage. A modern example of this technique is found in the *Star Wars* movies: Every time Darth Vader appears on screen we hear the theme associated specifically with him. In the excerpt here, the bright but constantly shifting music heard at 0:09, 0:31, 1:00, and so on, is consistently associated with the character of Loge, who in the world of northern European mythology is half-creature, half-flame, a cunning figure who resists taking on solid shape. The musical *Leitmotif* for Loge reflects this unstable nature: The theme, like the character himself, darts around and avoids any clearly defined shape. Thus, whenever we hear Loge's *Leitmotif*—his "signature tune," as it were—we know that Loge or fire (or both) are about to figure in the plot.

The Valkyrie, Act III: Wotan puts Brünnhilde into a deep sleep and surrounds her with a ring of magic fire; only a hero with no fear of Wotan's spear will brave the flames to awaken her. This image is from the original 1876 production of the *Ring* in Bayreuth, Germany.

High register, bright timbre (piccolo, harp)

p

"Flickering" rhythms
(short notes are *very* short)

The other *Leitmotifs* heard in this excerpt are the following:

1. **Wotan's spear**   (0:00–0:07, 0:27–0:31). This is a steady, confident, downward-striding figure in the brass. The character of this theme captures the solidity and confidence of Wotan's authority, in contrast to the flitting, ever-changing form of Loge's fire-music. All the laws of the world are carved on Wotan's spear; in the excerpt here, it represents Wotan's duty to punish Brünnhilde, who has broken one of these laws.

2. **Sleep**   (1:37–1:51). Also a descending line, but this time it is played softly by winds and high strings (as opposed to the loud brass of Wotan's spear). The sleep *Leitmotif* is also highly **chromatic**. This means that it contains many notes that do not naturally occur in the scale or key area on which it is based. These extra notes undermine the sense of a harmonic center or goal. This motif thus gives the impression of gentle falling, as in falling asleep. Even if you don't play the piano, you can produce a chromatic line by simply playing any series of adjacent notes—both black keys and white keys—in succession. You'll notice that no matter where you stop, there is no sense of closure, no center of melodic or harmonic gravity. This is the essence of chromaticism.

3. **The Sword**   (2:01–2:29, 2:32–2:58). The sword is the magic talisman that Siegfried will eventually use to shatter Wotan's spear. The theme is loud, bright, and confident, rather like a fanfare. Wotan sings it to the words "Whoever fears the point of my spear shall never pass

through the fire!" Siegfried, brandishing the magic sword, is the one mortal who has no fear of Wotan's spear; thus when Wotan sings this *Leitmotif*, he is (consciously? unconsciously?) anticipating the future. The words do not tell us this, but the music does.

Wotan.

Wer   mei - nes   Spee   -   res   Spit   -   ze   fürch -
Whoever   fears   the   tip of   my

tet   durch - schrei   -   te   das   Feu   -   er   nie!
spear   shall   never   pass through   the   fire!

4. **Fate** (3:49–3:55, 3:56–4:02). A brief, open-ended, rather questioning phrase associated throughout the *Ring* with the idea of destiny, of what must be.

"Magic fire" leitmotif
(piccolo, strings, harp)

mp   *pp*

"Fate"
leitmotif
(brass)

Of particular importance is the way in which these *Leitmotifs* transform themselves and combine with one another. These are not inert themes, but flexible ideas that are developed in much the same way that themes in the development section of a sonata-form movement are developed.

Now listen to this selection again, using the Listening Guide.

CONNECT YOUR PLAYLIST

The *Leitmotif*

Find an example of a dramatic work (musical, opera, or film) that uses musical *Leitmotifs*.

Example: John Williams's music to the *Star Wars* films features many *Leitmotifs*: We hear variations of the same basic theme whenever Darth Vader appears on screen, for example, and a very different theme when Princess Leia appears.

Listening Guide

Richard Wagner Composed: 1856
The Valkyrie, Act III, selection ("Wotan's Farewell") (4:34)

Time	Original German Text	English Translation
0:00	*Wotan, having put Brünnhilde into a deep sleep, kisses her on her closed eyes and turns away from her slowly. Then he strides with solemn resolution to the middle of the stage and points his spear toward a massive, rocky cliff.*	
0:09	Loge, hör'! Lausche hieher! Wie zuerst ich dich fand, als feurige Glut, wie dann einst du mir schwandest, als schweifende Lohe; wie ich dich band, bann ich dich heut'!	Loge, hear! Listen here! As I found you first, a fiery ember, as you once fled from me, a flitting flame; as I tamed you, so I call on you today!
0:33	Herauf, wabernde Loge, umlodre mir feurig den Fels!	Come, flickering glow, Surround the rock for me with flames!
0:48	*(He strikes his spear three times on the rock.)* Loge! Loge! Hieher!	*(He strikes his spear three times on the rock.)* Loge! Loge! Appear!
1:00	*A flash of flame comes out of the rock and gradually swells into a glowing fire. Bright flickering erupts. Wotan directs the flame to form a circle around the sleeping figure of Brünnhilde. He then recedes into the background, even as the flames continue to glow.*	
2:01	Wer meines Speeres Spitze fürchtet, durchschreite das Feuer nie!	Whoever fears the tip of my spear shall never pass through the fire!
2:01	*He stretches out his spear as if to cast a spell, then looks with pain back upon the figure of Brünnhilde (2:57) and turns slowly to depart (3:25). He looks back once again (3:46), before disappearing through the fire (4:00). The curtain drops.*	

⊙ Word–Music Relationships: Musical *Leitmotifs*

- Spear (= Wotan's authority) at 0:00
- Loge (= fire) at 0:07

- Loge (= fire) at 0:09
- Spear (= Wotan's authority) at 0:27 on Wotan's command that Loge appear.

- Loge (= fire) at 0:31

- Loge (= fire) at 0:49

- Magic fire music at 1:00, a variant of Loge's *Leitmotif*, but much brighter and in a higher register, representing the flames that rise up to surround Brünnhilde.
- Sleep at 1:37, representing Brünnhilde's sleep within the circle of fire.

- The sword at 2:01, again at 2:32. The music tells us that a sword will in fact eventually destroy Wotan's spear, and that Siegfried will awaken Brünnhilde from her sleep.
- Magic fire music throughout. This *Leitmotif*, in the high register, plays simultaneously with the one above and throughout this entire section.

- Magic fire music throughout.
- Fate at 3:49, 3:56. Wotan knows what must happen (fate), but it pains him nevertheless.

Q   Student FAQs

How did Wagner's original audience know the meaning of the Leitmotifs when this work was first performed?

Wagner believed that anyone following the plot would associate the music they heard with the action on the stage. Whether they made these associations consciously or unconsciously did not matter to him. He was in fact quite reluctant to attach names to specific musical motifs, and only later did critics begin to compile guides to the *Leitmotifs* in *The Ring*.

Is it true that Brünnhilde is the Fat Lady in the saying "It ain't over 'til the Fat Lady sings"?

Yes. After Siegfried slays the dragon guarding the ring, he awakens Brünnhilde and gives her the ring as a token of his love, not understanding its full power. When Siegfried is killed in the last opera of *The Ring of the Nibelung*, Brünnhilde sings an enormously long passage, at the end of which she throws the ring back into the Rhine, where it came from in the first place. When she finishes singing, *The Ring*—all four nights of it—is over.

PROFILE   Richard Wagner (1813–1883)

The Composer as Radical

Worshipped by some, reviled by others, Wagner and his music have provoked extreme reactions from the middle of the nineteenth century to the present day. Those who admired him during his lifetime considered him the most progressive composer of his day, advancing the harmonic idiom of music into new and exciting realms. His detractors assailed his music as ear-splitting noise. One caricature from the 1860s captures this sense of pain quite graphically (see the accompanying image).

Wagner's influence, moreover, went well beyond the realm of music. His operas are full of social and political ideas. George Bernard Shaw, for one, interpreted the massive *Ring of the Nibelung* as an allegory on capitalism and communism. *Tristan and Isolde* was seen by many as an impassioned plea for free love, an assault on the institution of marriage. And *Die Meistersinger von Nürnberg* has long been viewed as a monument to German political and cultural nationalism. Drawing on Wagner's well-documented anti-Semitism, the Nazis would later use his music to promote their own racial and social agendas.

Born in Leipzig, Wagner immersed himself in the music of Beethoven and secured a series of increasingly prestigious appointments as a conductor. His participation in the uprisings of 1848, however (see Chapter 31) forced him to flee to Switzerland to avoid arrest. After a decade of exile, he won the support of King Ludwig II of Bavaria, who spared no expense to support the composer and his art. The final phase of Wagner's life centered around Bayreuth, a small city about halfway between Munich and Berlin, the respective capitals of Bavaria and Prussia, where he built an opera house that is still in operation (see "Closer Look: Wagner's World").

For many of Wagner's contemporaries, the composer's chromatic harmonies were literally painful. In this French caricature from 1869, Wagner hammers away at the modern ear, using a quarter-note as a chisel.

 EXPAND YOUR PLAYLIST: WAGNER

- ***The Ring of the Nibelung*** (*Der Ring des Nibelungen*)
  - ***The Rhine Gold*** (*Das Rheingold*)
  - ***The Valkyrie*** (*Die Walküre*)
  - ***Siegfried***
  - ***Twilight of the Gods*** (*Götterdämmerung*)
- ***The Flying Dutchman*** (*Der fliegende Holländer*)

- ***Tannhäuser***
- ***Lohengrin***
- ***Tristan und Isolde***
- ***The Mastersingers of Nuremberg*** (*Die Meistersinger von Nürnberg*)
- ***Parsifal***

CLOSER LK   Wagner's World

In 1872, when Wagner moved to Bayreuth, a city between Munich and Berlin, Germany had just become a unified nation. It was Wagner's aim to build a *Festspielhaus*—a "festival drama house"—that would unify Germany culturally as well. He oversaw every detail of the building and the performances to be held within it. Thus, when the *Ring* received its premiere there in 1876, Wagner could legitimately claim not only to have written the libretto and the music, but also to have built the opera house. Wagner's descendants still control the *Festspielhaus* in Bayreuth. Here is a look into Wagner's world.

1. Leipzig. Wagner is born here in 1813, the son of a police clerk.

2. Riga, 1837–1839. Wagner works as musical director of the theater in Riga (now the capital of Latvia). He eventually must flee to escape his creditors.

3. Paris, 1839–1842. By making arrangements of works by others and writing music criticism, Wagner ekes out a living. He fails to get any of his own works performed in Paris at this time.

4. Dresden, 1842–1849. Wagner is court conductor at one of Europe's leading theaters. His fame spreads but his career in Dresden is cut short by his revolutionary activities in 1848–1849. He flees to Switzerland after a warrant is issued for his arrest.

5. Zürich, 1849–1863. Wagner continues to compose and also writes many of his most important treatises on music, society, and the nature of opera.

6. Munich, 1864–1872. Wagner comes under the protection and patronage of Ludwig II of Bavaria, who pays off the composer's debts and finances the production of his stage works.

7. Bayreuth, 1872–1883. Wagner designs and builds a "festival drama house" for the production of his works. The first Bayreuth Festival takes place in 1876. It eventually becomes a yearly event that continues to the present.

8. Venice. Wagner dies on February 13, 1883.

Opera in the Nineteenth Century

Operas written in the nineteenth century form the core repertory of most opera houses. Italian opera (by Rossini, Bellini, Verdi, and Puccini, among others) dominated the stage across all of Europe, but operas in French (by Bizet) and German (by Weber, Wagner, and others) had strong followings as well.

Italian Opera

- Gioacchino Rossini: *The Barber of Seville* (*Il Barbiere di Siviglia*). Like Mozart's *Marriage of Figaro*, this opera is based on a play by Beaumarchais and even includes many of the same characters (Figaro, the Count, the Countess).

- Vincenzo Bellini: *Norma*. A Romeo-and-Juliet-style story set in ancient Gaul. Norma is a Druid, her lover a Roman.

- Giuseppe Verdi: *La Traviata*. See Chapter 40. The story of Violetta and Alfredo, who have fallen in love. Violetta is suffering from the consumption (tuberculosis) that will eventually kill her. She senses that her days are numbered, and she must decide whether to keep her freedom or commit to one man alone (Alfredo).

- Giacomo Puccini: *La Bohème*. The story of struggling young artists, set in late nineteenth-century Paris. The Broadway musical *Rent* draws on the plotline of this opera.

- Giaccomo Puccini: *Madama Butterfly*. The story of the relationship between a young American naval officer and the Japanese woman he marries and then abandons.

French Opera

- Georges Bizet: *Carmen*. The story of an enchantress (Carmen) and her ill-fated lover (Don José), who is torn between love and duty.

German Opera

- Carl Maria von Weber: *The Free Shooter* (*Der Freischütz*). A hunter makes a pact with the devil to win a shooting competition, and with it, the hand of the woman he loves.

English Opera

- Arthur Sullivan: *The Pirates of Penzance*. The most successful operas in English in the nineteenth century were the operettas (literally, "little operas") by Arthur Sullivan and his librettist, W. S. Gilbert. Together, Gilbert and Sullivan created a long series of what we today call musicals: spoken dialogue interspersed with musical numbers (arias, duets, choruses, etc.).

Peter Ilyich Tchaikovsky

Swan Lake, Act IV, finale
Composed: 1876

42

A ballet is a story told through music and dance. It is essentially an opera without words. The gestures and movements of the human body, combined with music, produce a powerful and eloquent form of art that operates beyond the reach of language. Tchaikovsky's *Swan Lake* is among the most popular of all ballets.

Listen to This First

🎵 Melody

Listen for the return of the opening melody throughout this excerpt. It is always varied in some way each time it appears. ■

〰️ Timbre

Listen for the contrasts in orchestration, from the sparse opening (oboe and strings) to the full orchestra (including many percussion instruments) in the middle, to the extended section with harp at the end. ■

💬 Word–Music Relationships

Although there are no words to this ballet, the music accompanies a drama onstage. Try to listen for moments that suggest agitation, conflict, and resolution. ■

The union of music and dance to tell a story is probably as old as music itself. The spectacle of **ballet** was especially popular in royal courts in the seventeenth and eighteenth centuries, and ballets often provided entertainment between the acts of operas. But it was not until the last quarter of the nineteenth century that composers began to write full-length ballets with an extended plot. Tchaikovsky's *Swan Lake* is one of the first such ballets, and it has retained its hold on audiences down to the present. In 2010, the director Darren Aronofsky made it the centerpiece of his film *Black Swan*.

The plot of *Swan Lake* revolves around the lovers Siegfried, a young prince, and Odette, a young princess who has been kidnapped by the evil sorcerer Rothbart. To keep her for himself, Rothbart has cast a spell on Odette; by day, she is a swan, though by night she returns to her human form. Siegfried discovers Odette in the forest one night and falls in love with her, but she forbids him from killing Rothbart before the spell over her is broken. In the end, however, Odette realizes that the spell will continue as long as she lives, and so in the finale—the excerpt heard here—she leaps to her death; Siegfried follows her, and Rothbart collapses, powerless.

Tchaikovsky's music provides clear points of reference for the most dramatic moments of the tale, but **choreographers**, who design the dance, have always exercised their freedom to interpret the wordless depiction of this drama in a variety of ways. A comparison of various productions of this finale reveals a wide of range of possibilities: Some productions end in tragedy, with the lovers united only in death, while others feature a miraculous reunion of the two

LEARNING OBJECTIVES

42.1 Describe the evolution of ballet as an art form.

42.2 Outline the story of *Swan Lake*.

42.3 Listen for the ways Tchaikovsky has varied the "Swan Theme" in the finale.

42.4 Identify the contrasts in orchestration.

42.5 Describe how the music supports and heightens the onstage drama.

42.6 Outline Tchaikovsky's career as a composer.

In the film *The Black Swan* (2010), Natalie Portman plays a dancer struggling with the role of Odile—Rothbart's daughter and Odette's darker mirror image. In the film as in ballet companies, the roles of Odile and Odette are danced by the same ballerina yet demand very different emotional acting.

alive. In any case, the extended sequence for harp toward the very end of the finale (beginning at 4:04) suggests an ultimate triumph of good over evil.

The "Swan Theme"

The melody we hear at the very beginning of this excerpt has come to be known as the "Swan Theme" because it is so consistently associated throughout the entire ballet with the character of Odette (the swan-princess) and her "court" of accompanying swan-maidens. The solo oboe orchestration here at the beginning gives the melody a sense of plaintive longing, while the **syncopated** (off-beat) accompaniment of the strings creates a strong sense of agitation. Listen to the **contour** of the Swan Theme, how it moves up and falls back repeatedly but stays in a high register at the end. Some have compared this motion to that of a bird taking flight.

Orchestrating Events

Tchaikovsky was an acknowledged master of **orchestration**—the manner in which different instruments of the orchestra are employed—and he uses timbre to great effect throughout *Swan Lake*, including the very ending, heard here. The effective use of the oboe at the opening has already been noted. Listen as well to how this theme is then transferred to the violins as it becomes fragmented (starting at 0:40)—that is, in the on-stage struggle between Siegfried (the prince) and Rothbart (the sorcerer). The timbre changes yet again when the "Swan Theme" is presented by the full orchestra at the moment when Odette leaps to her death (1:52). At the true climax of the finale, the moment of triumph (3:08), we hear the same melody in the full orchestra with all the percussion instruments fully engaged—timpani, bass drum, side drum, cymbals, and triangle. It is a stirring moment.

CONNECT YOUR PLAYLIST

Changing Tempo

Find a piece that changes tempo.

Example: Dexy's Midnight Runners, "Come on Eileen" (1982)
At about 3:00 into this song, the tempo suddenly slows and begins to gradually accelerate back to the original tempo.

Telling a Story through Music and Movement

The **scenario** of a ballet establishes the basic outline of the story to be told through dance. It also guides the composer in writing the music. With the music in hand, the choreographer—the "director" of the dance—then draws up a series of specific movements coordinated with the music. Thus, while there are no word–music relationships in the conventional sense—there is no text to be sung—there is a close relationship between the words of the scenario and the music the composer writes for it.

How a choreographer interprets a ballet's scenario can differ considerably: No two productions are alike. In the case of *Swan Lake*, the differences can be particularly striking. Records of the original production at the Bolshoi Theater of Moscow in 1877 have only recently come to light, and many productions over the years have followed in the tradition of French-Russian choreographer Marius Petipas (1818–1910), who prepared a substantially revised version of the ballet in 1895 in Saint Petersburg, Russia. As a result, some productions of the ballet today end with both lovers united in death, while others end with the death and transfiguration of Odette, while still others end with both lovers alive and reunited. The uplifting music of the very end of the finale supports all three interpretations.

Now listen to this selection again, using the Listening Guide.

Prince Siegfried, Odette, and the Swan Maidens in a production of *Swan Lake* at Moscow's Bolshoi Theatre in 2005.

Peter Ilyich Tchaikovsky   Composed: 1876
Swan Lake, Act IV, finale (5:10)

Time	Form	Melody	Timbre	Word-Music Relationships
0:00	Swans	The "Swan Theme"	Oboe, with accompanying strings.	This theme is always associated with Odette (the princess) and her flock of fellow swan-maidens.
0:40	Conflict	The "Swan Theme" is interrupted by agitated music. When it returns, it is fragmented—we hear only the first phrase—suggesting the sense of a struggle.	Full orchestra	Often staged as confrontation between Siegfried (the prince) and Rothbart (the sorcerer), with Odette in the middle of it all.
1:02		The "Swan Theme" disappears for the moment, overwhelmed by a different theme.	Full orchestra, including timpani, bass drum, and cymbals	Often staged in a way that conveys the immense powers of the evil Rothbart.
1:52		The "Swan Theme" returns, but now in a more menacing tone.	Full orchestra, including now the tam-tam.	Often staged as the moment when Odette leaps to her death.
3:08	Turning Point	The "Swan Theme" returns, but now in the bright major mode.	Full orchestra, with even greater use of the percussion instruments. The "Swan Theme," played by the trumpets, is now triumphant.	The breakthrough from minor to major mode suggests a dramatic moment of triumph. This is sometimes staged as the moment of Rothbart's defeat, sometimes as the moment when Siegfried leaps to his own death.
4:04	Transfiguration	A new theme, a series of simple arpeggios (broken chords) rising upward. The string accompaniment is no longer syncopated but now on the beat, suggesting a sense of calmness, not agitation.	Harp, followed by triumphant sound of the brass (beginning at 4:34).	The new theme and the timbre of the harp suggest a resolution of the conflict. This is sometimes staged as an apotheosis (in which Odette appears as if floating in the sky), sometimes as a reunion of the two lovers.

 Q   Student FAQs

If there are no words in a ballet, how does the ace actually know what is going on?

It's remarkable how much can be conveyed through gesture alone. Beyond this, however, a "scenario"—a printed plot synopsis—is usually distributed to ballet audiences in advance.

How is dance notated?

There are several different systems by which choreographers record how they want a particular ballet to be danced. With the advent of film in the early twentieth century, it became possible to record choreography in far greater detail. Dancers also rely heavily on oral tradition: "Petipa did it this way. . . ." and similar such statements get handed down from generation to generation of dancers and choreographers.

PROFILE   Peter Ilyich Tchaikovsky (1840–1893)

Russian Romantic

Tchaikovsky was a late bloomer. He had already secured a position as a government clerk before entering a musical conservatory at the age of 21. Within five years, however, he was teaching harmony at the prestigious Moscow Conservatory. A wealthy widow, Nadezhda von Meck, provided him with a long series of generous commissions that allowed him to resign his teaching position in 1878 and devote himself entirely to composition. He was an intensely private individual who acknowledged his homosexuality within his immediate circle but otherwise kept it concealed for fear of public condemnation. The strain of this concealment, some have speculated, contributed to his repeated bouts of depression.

The circumstances surrounding Tchaikovsky's death have long been controversial. He died apparently of cholera during an epidemic of the disease in St. Petersburg. Some maintain that he knowingly drank contaminated water, effectively committing suicide, but nothing in his correspondence suggests that he was unusually depressed at the time.

Tchaikovsky's ballets, symphonies, concertos, and operas have been perennial favorites among concert-goers for more than a hundred years.

 EXPAND YOUR PLAYLIST: Tchaikovsky

- **Ballets**: *Sleeping Beauty* (1889) and *The Nutcracker* (1892), the latter a staple of Christmas productions, based on the short story by E. T. A. Hoffmann.

- **Operas**: *Eugene Onegin* (1879) and *Queen of Spades* (1890). Tchaikovsky was a major figure in the development of Russian-language opera.

- **Symphonies**: Symphonies nos. 4 (1880), 5 (1888), and 6 ("Pathétique," 1894) are all staples of the concert-hall repertory today.

- **Concertos**: The Piano Concerto no. 1 (1879) and the Violin Concerto (1888) are two of the most popular concertos of any kind today.

- **Overture**: The *1812 Overture* (1882) written to commemorate the Russian victory over Napoleon's invading army. It incorporates the French and Russian national anthems and concludes with a blast of cannons.

EXPAND YOUR PLAYLIST

Russian Music of the Nineteenth Century

Tchaikovsky was only one of many Russian composers who rose to prominence over the course of the nineteenth century. The cities of Saint Petersburg and Moscow developed highly sophisticated musical cultures at this time and attracted many of the world's leading composers and performers, both in opera and in orchestral music. Some of the Russian composers whose works are most frequently performed today include:

- **Mikhail Glinka** (1804–1857). The operas *A Life for the Tsar* and *Ruslan and Ludmila*. The overture of the latter is often performed in orchestral concerts.

- **Alexander Borodin** (1833–1887). *In the Steppes of Central Asia*, an orchestral work; String Quartet no. 2; the opera *Prince Igor*, which includes the popular *Polovtsian Dances*.

- **Modest Mussorgsky** (1839–1881). *Boris Godunov*, a staple of the operatic repertory today. *Pictures at an Exhibition* for piano, later orchestrated by Maurice Ravel, is also extremely popular.

- **Nikolai Rimsky-Korsakov** (1844–1908). *Scheherazade*, for orchestra, is based on *One Thousand and One Nights*; the *Capriccio Espagnol*, also for orchestra, evokes the spirit of Spain.

Johannes Brahms
Symphony no. 4 in E Minor, op. 98, finale
Composed: 1885

43

The finale of Brahms's Fourth Symphony is a kaleidoscope of emotions: The 30 brief variations on a very short theme present a series of constantly shifting moods. Each group of instruments—strings, winds, brass, and percussion—comes to the fore at various points.

Listen to This First

Form	Timbre
Listen for the succession of varied restatements of the central melodic idea. This movement is in the form of theme and variations. Also listen for the change in tempo (to slow) and mode (to major) in the middle of the movement. ■	Each variation has its own distinctive sound, depending on which instrument or group of instruments predominates. The textures created by these groupings are sometimes quite thick, and sometimes quite transparent. ■

The changes in Brahms's Fourth Symphony from one variation to the next are at times subtle, at times sudden. The theme makes its first appearance in a majestic, grandiose fashion in the winds and brass. The first variation is subdued and reticent, played by the timpani and low brass. The winds create a new, more wistful mood when they join in for the second variation. The third variation is more rhythmically lively, and the violins take over with a lyrical counter-melody in the fourth variation. The shifting moods continue as each variation establishes its own sound world.

Brahms wrote only four symphonies, but all four are mainstays of today's concert repertory. His Fourth Symphony calls for a large orchestra to match the growing size of concert halls in the last decades of the nineteenth century. It also synthesizes the old and new in ingenious ways. Brahms takes both the form and theme of the finale of his Fourth Symphony from the Baroque Era. **Theme and variations form** had been popular in Bach's time, and the theme itself is in fact derived from a work by Bach (see the following discussion). But Brahms creates harmonies, textures, and timbres that were novel in their day. The harmonies often extend well beyond what was then conventional, and the textures tend to be richly layered and dense. The timbres range from the bright to the dark, but in this movement, more often than not, they veer toward a somber, serious kind of sound that many listeners find lush and—to use a metaphor drawn from the world of food—ripe. Brahms demands our attention when we listen, and his music repays the effort.

LEARNING OBJECTIVES

43.1 Describe the form of the finale of Brahms's Fourth Symphony, op. 98.

43.2 Describe the nature of the theme on which the 30 variations of this movement are based.

43.3 Listen for the transformations of the theme in each variation.

43.4 Listen to the ways in which Brahms's orchestration provides variety across the movement as a whole.

43.5 Describe the role of the orchestral conductor.

43.6 Outline Brahms's career as a composer.

Form: Theme and Variations Plus

The theme consists of only eight notes. This type of form—many variations on a very short theme—was tremendously popular during the Baroque Era. Purcell had used it in the ostinato bass of Dido's aria in Act I of *Dido and Aeneas* in the late seventeenth century (see Chapter 14), and Johann Sebastian Bach had used this kind of structure in a number of works.

Brahms borrowed the theme from Bach's Cantata no. 150, and it is extremely simple. Notes 1–6 move up, step by step, then drop down (note 7), only to end up (note 8) exactly where the theme had begun. This simplicity works to the listener's advantage because Brahms subjects the theme to an increasingly complex series of variations. But because the theme itself is so simple, listeners can hear it more easily. This movement represents what might be called compositional virtuosity, for Brahms demonstrates his ability to construct a great deal out of very little.

There is no end of melodic richness in this movement. Each variation uses the eight notes of the theme as a framework for its own counter-themes. The texture throughout is strongly polyphonic, for in many variations we hear the original theme played against a new and different counter-melody. At other times, Brahms adds many additional notes around the theme, so that it is in effect embedded within a new and different theme (as in Variation 12). In still other variations, Brahms distributes the notes of the theme across different instruments.

On a larger scale, Brahms creates a **ternary form** (**ABA**) by making the middle variations (10–15) markedly different from the others. They are all slower, and the first three of them (13–15) are in E major rather than E minor. This creates a strong sense of contrast in the middle of the movement (the **B** section of the **ABA** form). The sense of a ternary form superimposed on a set of theme and variations is reinforced by the clear return of the opening theme of the movement in variation no. 16 (the second **A** in the **ABA** form).

 ## Timbre: The Drama of Orchestration

Brahms's **orchestration**—the way in which he distributes the music to be played among all the different instruments of the orchestra—also helps create a sense of forward movement and contrast among the 30 different variations. The winds and brass announce the theme together at

CONNECT YOUR PLAYLIST
Same Theme, Different Timbres

Find a work that presents the same theme in two different timbres.

Example: Louis Armstrong, "Ain't Misbehavin'" (1929)
In this classic recording of a jazz standard, Armstrong first plays the melody on the trumpet and then immediately afterward sings it.

the very beginning with great force. The focus then moves to the timpani and the plucked low strings (Variation 1), after which the winds join in (Variation 2), followed by the full orchestra (Variation 3). At times, a pair of variations share the same basic orchestration (Variations 5 and 6, Variations 8 and 9), but more often than not each new variation differentiates itself from the one before through its timbre. The theme itself appears in all the different instruments (except timpani) at one point or another.

This movement is remarkable in its emotional sweep. It embraces an ever-changing series of moods that might be described as extending from angry at first, to brooding, energetic, melancholic, docile, pleading, devotional, anxious, and in the end triumphant; each listener will find slightly different adjectives. The last movement of Brahms's last symphony sums up an entire century of symphonic composition: Its orchestration is rich, its textures varied, its harmonies advanced.

Now listen to this symphony finale again, using the Listening Guide.

PERFORMANCE The Conductor

Exactly what does a **conductor** do? It's a good question, and the answer is not so obvious, particularly because most concertgoers tend to see only the conductor's back during performances.

Even from the back, however, conductors' styles can vary enormously. Some are like gymnasts on the podium: They jump, twist, crouch. Others are more reserved and seem to move scarcely at all. Some use a baton, others use only their hands.

For all these outward differences, all conductors have a basic responsibility of keeping performers playing together, in time. They do this by beating the basic meter of the music during performance; every player can see the conductor, so all the performers can follow the same beat together. The more rhythmically complicated the work at hand, the greater the need for a conductor. In the finale of Brahms's Fourth Symphony, for example, Brahms calls on the orchestra to change to a slow tempo at Variation 12. But how slow? That is up to the conductor to decide, and the players follow the conductor's lead.

At a deeper level, conductors also shape the interpretation of the work at hand through such elements as dynamics, rhythm, texture, and timbre. Are the trumpets playing too loud? Are the flutes too soft? Are the violins entering sharply enough? These are just a few of the many questions conductors have to answer when rehearsing with an orchestra. Even in performance, there is room for spur-of-the-moment changes: holding a long note just a fraction of a second longer, slowing down just a little more, or making a loud passage even louder.

Like all conductors, Marin Alsop uses her hands, her eyes, and her entire body to communicate with the musicians in her orchestra. Like most but not all conductors, she also uses a baton; many orchestral musicians say that this small stick helps them see the conductor's beat out of the corner of their eyes, which are largely focused on the notated music on their stands.

No two performers play the same music exactly the same way: Each has an individual style. This is true for conductors as well, whose instrument is in effect the orchestra. Listen to multiple recordings of the finale of Brahms's Fourth Symphony—or of any other work in this book, for that matter—and you will immediately realize the enormous freedom performers have in bringing a work of music to life.

Listening Guide))

Johannes Brahms Composed: 1885
Symphony no. 4 in E Minor, op. 98, finale (10:36)

Time	Form: Theme and Variations	Ternary Form	Timbre
0:00	Theme	**A** (E minor)	Winds and brass
0:15	Variation 1		Pizzicato (plucked) strings, with percussion and low brass
0:30	Variation 2		Winds join in
0:46	Variation 3		Full orchestra
1:01	Variation 4		Strings
1:18	Variation 5		Strings and winds
1:32	Variation 6		
1:48	Variation 7		High strings and winds
2:04	Variation 8		Strings and winds
2:20	Variation 9		
2:36	Variation 10		Strings and winds
2:53	Variation 11		Strings, winds, horns
3:14	Variation 12		Flutes, horn, and strings
3:57	Variation 13	**B** (E major)	Winds and strings in dialogue
4:37	Variation 14		Brass enter with hymn-like sound, all parts moving together in a slow, stately rhythm
5:17	Variation 15		Winds join in
6:03	Variation 16	**A'** (E minor)	Return to opening theme: winds and brass, then strings join in
6:16	Variation 17		Strings (tremolo) and high winds in dialogue

🎵 Melody

Theme in high winds; long note values

Theme in pizzicato (plucked) strings

Theme stays in pizzicato (plucked) strings

Theme in violins

Theme in low strings; counter-melody in violins

Theme in low strings; counter-melody in high strings and winds

Theme in low strings; counter-melody of dotted rhythms (short-LONG-short-LONG, etc.) in high strings and winds

Theme in low strings; rapid figure in violins

Theme in strings; longer note values give the impression of slowing down

Theme in low strings; syncopated figure in high strings (off the beat)

Theme embedded within flute's counter-melody

Theme distributed among various instruments

Theme distributed among trombones

Theme in high winds; new counter-melody in violins

Theme in syncopated high winds

(Continues)

Time	🏛 Form: Theme and Variations	🏛 Ternary Form	〰 Timbre
6:28	Variation 18		Full orchestra
6:40	Variation 19		
6:53	Variation 20		
7:05	Variation 21		
7:19	Variation 22		High winds and low strings
7:31	Variation 23		Full orchestra
7:44	Variation 24		
7:57	Variation 25		Full orchestra, strings tremolo
8:11	Variation 26		Full orchestra
8:26	Variation 27		Winds and strings in dialogue
8:40	Variation 28		
8:54	Variation 29		
9:08	Variation 30		Full orchestra
9:29	**Coda**	Coda (E minor)	Full orchestra

Melody

Theme distributed among high winds

Theme distributed among various instruments; strings with fast triplet figure
(*1-2-3- 1-2-3- 1-2-3*)

Theme distributed among various instruments

Theme distributed among various instruments

Theme clearly presented in horns

Theme in high strings

Theme distributed among various instruments

Theme distributed among horns and winds; somewhat calmer

Theme embedded in counter-melody in strings

Theme embedded in counter-melody in winds

Theme embedded in pizzicato strings in syncopation

Theme distributed among various instruments; counter-melodies in both strings
and winds

Theme clearly stated in brass and winds at the beginning of this section, but the
music continues beyond this in a free fashion for the first and only time in the
movement.

 Student FAQs

I can't always hear the theme. Is that a problem?

No. Brahms's self-imposed challenge was to say the same thing in a different way 30 times in a row. For this reason, he wanted to mask the theme often enough so that it would not become tiresome. Some of the variations in the **B** section (Variations 13–15) hide the theme so well it becomes very difficult to hear. As you become more familiar with the movement, you will probably hear the theme more clearly in most variations with each new listening.

Is there any consistent meter in this movement?

The theme and every variation are always in triple meter, though Brahms creates a good deal of variety by skillfully varying the underlying rhythms and (in the middle of the movement) the tempo.

PROFILE   Johannes Brahms (1833–1897)

The Composer as Hedgehog

In an age of flamboyant composer-celebrities who wrote and talked endlessly about themselves and their own music, Johannes Brahms was by comparison a recluse. He preferred to let his works speak for themselves and remained an intensely private individual to the end of his life. One particularly revealing caricature of him done during his lifetime shows him walking next to a hedgehog: The prickly composer and prickly animal bear a striking resemblance.

Perhaps Brahms became a bit prickly because of the criticism he received during his lifetime. Part of this can be traced to the unrealistic expectations projected on him by no less a figure than Robert Schumann, editor of one of the leading music journals of the day (the nineteenth-century equivalent of *Rolling Stone* or *Spin*). Brahms was a virtually unknown 20-year-old when Schumann introduced him as the savior of music, a messiah who had arrived on the scene "fully developed," ready to assume the mantel of the deceased Beethoven. This publicity cut both ways for Brahms: He was an instant celebrity, but the public expected more than he was prepared to offer, at least at that point in his career. As in the musical world of today, the best artists can withstand criticism, and Brahms eventually proved that Schumann was right in the end. By the time he died in 1897, Brahms had become the last of the "three Bs" of German music—Bach, Beethoven, Brahms—and he would be buried next to Beethoven in Vienna's Central Cemetery.

Brahms's links to Bach and Beethoven rest on more than mere alliteration. He was deeply interested in the music of the past, and in the music of the two other "Bs" in particular. He helped edit works by Bach and zealously collected sketches by Beethoven. The finale of the Fourth Symphony, in a sense, represents Brahms's synthesis of the two: He presents Bach's technique of varying a brief theme within Beethoven's most challenging genre, the symphony. Brahms uses this traditional form and genre to create what is nevertheless a thoroughly modern work.

Brahms (right) and Johann Strauss, Jr. (1894). Brahms deeply admired Johann Strauss, Jr., the "Waltz King" of Vienna known for such favorites as *The Beautiful Blue Danube* and *Tales from the Vienna Woods*. The difference in appearance of the two composers is striking, especially when we realize the grandfatherly Brahms was almost eight years younger than the dapper Strauss. Brahms was 61 and Strauss was 69 at the time this photograph was taken.

    EXPAND YOUR PLAYLIST: BRAHMS

- Symphony no. 1 in C Minor, op. 68.
- Symphony no. 2 in D Major, op. 73
- Symphony no. 3 in F Major, op. 90. A dramatic and emotionally wide-ranging work.
- Piano Concerto no. 2 in B♭ Major, op. 83

- Violin Concerto in D Major, op. 77
- *A German Requiem,* op. 45 (for chorus, orchestra, and soloists). A setting of German-language biblical texts relating to death and resurrection, written after the death of the composer's mother.

Brahms and the hedgehog.
A contemporary caricature
by Otto Bohler.

EXPAND YOUR PLAYLIST

The Art of the Conductor

You can learn more about what goes into leading an orchestra by listening to recordings of the same work by different conductors. Here are some alternative performances of the finale of Brahms's Fourth Symphony. Listen carefully for different approaches to tempo, dynamics, phrasing, and balance among the instruments.

- **Felix Weingartner** (1863–1942) was one of the leading conductors of his day. His style, in a recording made with the London Symphony Orchestra in 1938, reflects a more flexible approach to rhythm and phrasing than would be fashionable later in the century. Centaur 2128.

- **Arturo Toscanini** (1867–1957) was born in Italy but immigrated to the United States in the late 1930s to escape the Fascist government. In New York, NBC created an orchestra expressly for Toscanini, and he made many recordings and radio broadcasts with it. His style of conducting attracted an almost cult-like following. RCA Red Seal 55838.

- **Leonard Bernstein** (1918–1990) was the first American-born conductor to lead the New York Philharmonic, one of the premier orchestras in the nation. A composer as well as a conductor, he was known for promoting modern music and the music of other American composers. Sony 61846.

- **Marin Alsop** (b. 1956) is one of a growing number of female conductors who have enjoyed both artistic and commercial success. She is currently director of the Baltimore Symphony Orchestra. Her performance, recorded with the London Philharmonic Orchestra in 2007, combines both flexibility and drive. Naxos 8570233.

44

Antonín Dvořák

String Quartet in F Major, op. 96 ("American"), third movement

Composed: 1893

In the nineteenth century, composers began to write works for the concert hall that incorporated musical devices associated with folk music. When he lived in the United States, Czech composer Antonín Dvořák wrote a string quartet he called "American." The third-movement scherzo of this quartet uses a number of folk-like elements.

Listen to This First

〰 Timbre

Listen to the call-and-response of various combinations of the four instruments—two violins (high register), a viola (medium), and cello (low)—at the very beginning of the movement and at later points as well. Listen, too, for extended passages in which only the two highest or the two lowest of the four instruments are playing. ■

🎵 Melody

Listen for the folk-like sound of the various melodies of this movement. What makes this music sound like folk music? ■

🏛 Form

Consider the basic principles of form—repetition, variation, and contrast—as you listen for the musical elements listed earlier. Can you identify the distinct sections of this movement? ■

LEARNING OBJECTIVES

44.1 Listen for call-and-response sections in Antonín Dvořák's String Quartet in F Major, op. 96 ("American"), third movement.

44.2 Describe the folk-like melodies of this movement.

44.3 Listen for the **ABA** form of Dvořák: String Quartet in F Major, op. 96 ("American"), third movement.

44.4 Discuss Dvořák's efforts to encourage composers to develop a truly American style of composition.

44.5 Discuss the nature of the string quartet as an ensemble of four instrumentalists.

44.6 Outline Dvořák's career as a composer, including the circumstances by which he came to write a string quartet in Iowa in 1893.

Antonín Dvořák wrote his String Quartet in F Major, op. 96, in Iowa, more than 5,000 miles from his native Prague. In the United States on a two-year contract as director of the National Conservatory of Music in New York City, Dvořák welcomed the opportunity for a change of scenery. He spent the summer of 1893 in Spillville, a small town recommended by his personal assistant who had grown up there. Most of Spillville's approximately 350 inhabitants were immigrants or the children of immigrants from Dvořák's native Bohemia (a region corresponding roughly to today's Czech Republic).

Shortly after arriving in Iowa, Dvořák set out, by his own account, "to write something really melodious and simple." Of course, writing good melodies is not easy, and what seems simple is often difficult to craft. But he must have been inspired by his new surroundings, for in just a little over two weeks, he completed a four-movement string quartet he called "American." The selection here is the third movement of this quartet.

Originally from Prague, Dvořák crossed the Atlantic to spend two years in the United States.

Timbre: Call-and-Response between Strings

Dvořák had been a professional violist earlier in his career, and he knew the instruments of the string quartet from the inside out. In the very opening of this movement, he creates a kind of **call-and-response** pattern that begins with two instruments (second violin and cello, 0:00) answered by the full ensemble (0:04). The music continues with the upper three instruments (0:07) punctuated by the lowest, the cello (0:08). This kind of back-and-forth between individual instruments or groups of instruments continues throughout the movement and creates timbral variety. Call-and-response is a basic element of many kinds of **folk music**, particularly in African music (see Chapter 15) and music cultivated by the descendants of Africans in the Americas, such as the blues (see Chapter 52). In emphasizing this kind of pattern, Dvořák was at the same time emphasizing the folk-like nature of his quartet.

 ## Folk-Like Melodies

The movement features two principal melodies, each of which is based on a limited number of notes. The antecedent phrases of the two melodies use only four and three notes, respectively; the consequent phrases add only two and one. Although not based on a strictly **pentatonic scale** of only five notes—something that makes a good deal of folk music sound "folkish"—these melodies convey a feeling of simplicity because they use fewer than the standard seven notes in the diatonic scale that is so common in Western music. In this way, Dvořák creates a folk-like sound. The clarity of the antecedent–consequent phrase structure (see Chapter 22) also contributes to the apparent simplicity of the melodies.

The first part of the second principal theme consists of only *four* notes:

But what is the "folk" in question here? Like other composers of his time, Dvořák felt that composers should draw on the folk or indigenous music of their countries, and he wrote the "New World" Symphony and "American" String Quartet to provide examples for composers of the United States (see "The Composer Speaks: The Sources of an American Musical Style"), using pentatonic melodies in both. Dvořák himself once observed that pentatonic melodies were common to the music of African Americans, Native Americans, and (remarkably enough) "the music of Scotland." Pentatonic or quasi-pentatonic melodies also figure in the folk music of Dvořák's native Bohemia, so it is hard to say clearly which tradition this quartet represents. In any case, its unmistakably folk-like feel contrasts with the more formal sound of Haydn's string quartet from more than 100 years before (Chapter 24).

Scherzo Form: Repetition, Variation, Contrast

This third movement is a **scherzo**. *Scherzo* is the Italian word for "joke," and a musical scherzo is often a light-hearted movement in a fast tempo and in triple meter. Over the course of the nineteenth century, the scherzo gradually replaced the minuet (see Chapter 24) as one of the internal movements of a four-movement cycle in a symphony, sonata, string quartet, or other similar instrumental work. The scherzo retained the basic **ABA** form of the minuet, but sometimes with the addition of an extra trio section and conclusion (**ABABA**), as in this particular movement. The overall form can be represented graphically in this way:

A	B	A′	B′	A
Scherzo Proper	Trio I	Scherzo Proper (varied)	Trio II (varied)	Scherzo Proper (literal repetition of A)

Dvořák uses all three principles of form in this movement:

- **Repetition.**   The scherzo proper is repeated literally ("da capo") at the end of the movement. The movement thus ends with exactly the same section of music with which it began.

- **Variation.**   Both the scherzo proper and the trio are subject to variation: **A** becomes **A′**, and **B** becomes **B′**.

- **Contrast.**   **A** and **B** differ markedly in their melodies, harmonies (modes), and timbres. The differences in the melodies of **A** and **B** have already been noted earlier. The two sections are also in contrasting modes: **A** is consistently in F major, while **B** is consistently in F minor. The timbres of the two sections also contrast markedly: The **A** section is quite expansive, covering a wide register, while **B** tends to move in a more narrow range, with the instruments closer together.

Now listen to this movement once again, using the Listening Guide.

Forming a string quartet is really no different from putting together a rock band. Two or more players know one another well and look for others to fill out the group, musicians who can bring their own creative ideas to the table. And like rock bands, string quartets often transform themselves over time. The Juilliard String Quartet, based at the Juilliard Conservatory of Music in New York City, has over the course of more than 60 years featured two different first violinists, five second violinists, two violists, and three cellists.

Artistic collaborations invariably involve artistic differences: Quartet members can (and often do) disagree about how to perform a particular work or a passage in a work, but the best groups work through these differences to create performances that are fresh and exciting. There is no conductor in a string quartet; the four players have to agree on just about everything, including where and what to perform. By the same token, a single player who has fundamentally different ideas about how to make music likely will not last very long in a quartet.

The group bond performing at the Classical Brit Awards, 2005. The instruments of this string quartet are electric, its repertory eclectic.

Not all quartets play the standard stringed instruments. The Kronos Quartet, formed in 1973 and based in San Francisco, was one of the first to use electronic as well as acoustical instruments and incorporated many special lighting and stage effects into their concerts. In 1991, the group started taking "roadies" on its tours to handle this end of its performances. More recently, bond (the group uses a lowercase "b" to avoid copyright infringements with 007) has moved to exclusively electronic instruments (violins, viola, cello), performing a repertory that ranges from classical to pop to New Age. The group's first album sold more than two million copies. In 2001, bond performed with the tenor Luciano Pavarotti at his annual all-star charity concert and collaborated with the Royal Philharmonic Orchestra on their 2003 album *Classified*.

Listening Guide

Antonín Dvořák Composed: 1893
String Quartet in F Major, op. 96 ("American"), third movement (3:46)

Time	🎵 Melody	🏛 Form: Section	〰 Timbre
0:00	Theme 1 = disjunct, clear antecedent–consequent phrase structure	**A** = Scherzo proper (F major)	Call-and-response interplay between individual instruments and groups of instruments
0:46	Theme 2 = narrow range, begins with only four notes; clear antecedent–consequent phrase structure	**B** = Trio I (F minor)	Passages for two instruments (0:46–0:52; 1:06–1:12) contrast with passages for all four instruments
1:26	Theme 1, but this time it begins quietly, with the themes in different instruments from the first time around	**A'** = Variation of Scherzo proper: (F major)	
2:15	Theme 2, again it begins quietly, now in a much higher register than before	**B'** = Trio II (in fact a variation of Trio I) (F minor)	Higher register than before; all four instruments together throughout
2:57	Theme 1	**A** = Literal repeat of Scherzo proper (F major)	

🔍 Student FAQs ⚙

Did Dvořák ever actually hear any music performed by Native Americans?

He did when he was in Iowa, although it's not entirely clear just what kind of Native Americans were performing, and we should remember that musical styles vary widely from tribe to tribe. We also know that Dvořák read at least one account of Native American music.

Why does the movement end so softly? It doesn't sound like a real ending.

Quiet endings are not all that uncommon, actually. Keep in mind that this is the third movement of a four-movement string quartet, and that a very lively finale begins shortly after this movement ends. By not ending this movement with a bang Dvořák is able to start the next movement with one.

PROFILE   Antonín Dvořák (1841–1904)

In Search of National Sounds

Even before he arrived in the United States in 1892, Antonín Dvořák was known as a composer who drew widely on the folk music of his native Bohemia. As director of the (now defunct) National Conservatory of Music in New York City, he felt a responsibility to show American composers how to incorporate the characteristic sounds and inflections of the folk music of their own country. He studied with interest the melodies of African Americans—freed slaves and their first-generation descendants—and of Native Americans and discovered that pentatonic scales figured prominently in both repertoires. He wrote pentatonic melodies into his next symphony, which quickly became known as the "New World" Symphony. Composers, critics, and audiences took note, for all were eager to find a way by which the United States could establish its own musical sound, distinct from the traditions of European music.

Dvořák was less interested in borrowing from specific African American or Native American songs than he was in seeking an idiom based in the spirit of all those who made music outside the concert hall, outside the traditions of "learned" music. He seems to have been seeking a kind of nationalism that would speak to the varied ethnic backgrounds of the American people, no matter what the color of their skin (see "The Composer Speaks: The Sources of an American Musical Style"). In the end, though, in spite of being so closely associated with American music, Dvořák remained true to his roots. His personal assistant, Josef Kovařík, the man of Czech descent who took him to Iowa, reports Dvořák saying,

Dvořák (right) and his family shortly after their arrival in the United States in 1892.

So I am an American composer, am I? I was, I am, and I remain a Czech composer. I have only showed them the path they might take—how they should work. But I'm through with that! From this day forward I will write the way I wrote before.

Source: Michael Beckerman, *New Worlds of Dvořák* (New York: Norton, 2003), 16.

 EXPAND YOUR PLAYLIST: DVOŘÁK

- **Piano Quintet in A Major, op. 81.** A chamber work of large dimension, particularly notable for its lengthy, slow movement.
- **Cello Concerto in B Minor, op. 104.** The most frequently performed of all cello concertos in the concert repertory today.
- **Slavonic Dance for Orchestra, op. 46, no. 8.** One of many orchestral dances inspired by ethnic rhythms and melodies.
- **Symphony in E Minor, op. 96** ("New World"). Written during Dvořák's years in the United States, at least some of the themes have been attributed variously to Native American or African American melodies.

DVOŘÁK: THE SUMMER OF 1893

Sept. 7: Returns to Spillville

August 12: Arrives in Chicago, conducts concert at World Columbian Exposition

Sept. 10: Arrives in Niagara Falls

Sept. 4: Visits St. Paul

Minnesota

Ontario

New York

St. Paul

Niagara Falls

Nebraska

Spillville

Chicago

New York City

August 2: Visits Omaha

Omaha

Iowa

Sept. 12: Returns to NYC

June 5: Arrives in Spillville, completes "American" String Quartet June 23

N

Illinois

U.S.A.

June 2: Leaves with family for Iowa

Dvořák's travels in America in the summer of 1893.

The Composer Speaks The Sources of an American Musical Style

O n his arrival in America, Dvořák was impressed by the "native" music that he heard, particularly the music of Native Americans and African Americans. Two years after writing his "American" Quartet, Dvořák wrote an essay entitled "Music in America," published in *Harper's New Monthly Magazine*.

❝A while ago I suggested that inspiration for truly national music might be derived from the Negro melodies or Indian chants. I was led to take this view partly by the fact that the so-called plantation songs are indeed the most striking and appealing melodies that have yet been found on this side of the water, but largely by the observation that this seems to be recognized, though often unconsciously, by most Americans. All races have their distinctively national songs, which they at once recognize as their own, even if they have never heard them before. When a Tcech [Czech], a Pole, or a Magyar [Hungarian] in this country suddenly hears one of his folk-songs or dances, no matter if it is for the first time in his life, his eyes light up at once, and his heart within him responds, and claims that music as his own. So it is with those of Teutonic or Celtic blood, or any other men, indeed, whose first lullaby mayhap [perhaps] was a song wrung from the heart of the people. . . .

It matters little whether the inspiration for the coming folk songs of America is derived from the Negro melodies, the songs of the creoles, the red man's chant, or the plaintive ditties of the homesick German or Norwegian. Undoubtedly the germs for the best in music lie hidden among all the races that are commingled in this great country. The music of the people is like a rare and lovely flower growing amidst encroaching weeds. Thousands pass it, while others trample it under foot, and thus the chances are that it will perish before it is seen by the one discriminating spirit who will prize it above all else. The fact that no one has as yet arisen to make the most of it does not prove that nothing is there.❞

Source: Antonin Dvořák, "Music in America," *Harper's New Monthly Magazine*, February 1895, pp. 433–434.

EXPAND YOUR PLAYLIST

Nationalism in Nineteenth-Century Music

Dvořák was one of many composers working in the late nineteenth century who sought to infuse at least some of his works with nationalistic elements, though not necessarily from his own country. Just as Dvořák (a Czech) wrote at times in an "American" style, Brahms (a German) sometimes wrote in a "Hungarian" style, and Chabrier (a Frenchman) wrote in a "Spanish" style.

- **Bedřich Smetana** (1824–1884), *The Moldau*. This symphonic poem paints a picture of the most important river in Smetana's native Bohemia (present-day Czech Republic).

- **Louis Moreau Gottschalk**: *Union*. See Chapter 38. Although born and raised in New Orleans, Gottschalk was an ardent Unionist who opposed slavery and secession. This piece was written in response to the outbreak of the American Civil War.

- **Johannes Brahms**: *Hungarian Dances*. These piano pieces (later orchestrated by the composer) incorporate characteristic Hungarian rhythms and melodic turns of phrase. Brahms lived most of his life in Vienna, not far from present-day Hungary.

- **Alexander Borodin** (1833–1887): *Polovtzian Dances* from the opera *Prince Igor*. Borodin's native Russia extended eastward into Asia, and these dances capture its flavor.

- **Emmanuel Chabrier** (1841–1894): *España*. This single-movement work for large orchestra reflects the Frenchman Chabrier's fascination with Spain.

- **Nikolai Rimsky-Korsakov** (1844–1908): *Scheherazade*. This suite for orchestra narrates, without words, episodes from a series of stories originating in ancient Persia, *The Book of One Thousand and One Nights*. Rimsky-Korsakov's music evokes many effects associated with music of the Near East.

PART 5 Summary

Making Connections: Music of the Classical Era and the Nineteenth Century

		Classical Era	Nineteenth Century
🌐	**Texture**	Both polyphonic and homophonic, but on the whole more homophonic	Both homophonic and polyphonic
🎵	**Melody**	Growing importance of periodic phrase structure in all genres of music, not just in dance	Periodic phrase structure continues, but also more fragmented thematic ideas; some use of pentatonic scales. Growing tendency toward virtuosic writing for both voices and instruments
🥁	**Rhythm**	More smoothly flowing melodies	Highly varied, from simple to complex
〰️	**Timbre**	Establishment of the modern orchestra (strings, winds, percussion)	Orchestra continues to grow, with addition of trombones, tubas, piccolos, contrabassoon, and more percussion instruments
👤	**Harmony**	Harmony becomes increasingly important as a large-scale structural element (tonic/not-tonic/tonic)	Harmony becomes increasingly chromatic
🏛️	**Form**	Theme and variations, minuet, rondo, sonata form, double-exposition concerto form	Sonata form, ternary forms, theme and variations, modified strophic form
💬	**Word–Music Relationships**	Word painting still present, but not as prevalent and often more subtle	Greater importance of program music

IN REVIEW: Nineteenth-Century Style

Program music Although not new in the nineteenth century, program music took on increasing importance as composers attempted to connect purely instrumental music with the wider world of events and ideas.

- Mendelssohn, *Overture to A Midsummer Night's Dream* (Chapter 32)
- Berlioz, *Symphonie fantastique* (Chapter 33)
- Gottschalk, *Union* (Chapter 38)

Virtuosity While most composers continued to write for amateur performers in many instances, at least some devoted their energies to writing for performers of exceptional talent, creating music that was notoriously difficult to perform.

- Gottschalk, *Union* (Chapter 38)
- Verdi, *La Traviata* (Chapter 40)

Nationalism At least some nineteenth-century music expresses the aspirations of national groups united either politically or ethnically.

- C. Schumann, "Forward!" (Chapter 36)
- Chopin, Mazurka in B♭, op. 7, no. 1 (Chapter 37)
- Gottschalk, *Union* (Chapter 38)
- Dvořák, String Quartet in F Major, op. 96 (Chapter 44)

Song The song (German: *Lied*) became an important domestic genre, noted for its lyricism and intimacy of tone. These works were mostly for voice and piano, but the style could be applied in almost any medium, including solo piano music or the piano trio.

- Schubert, "Erlkönig" (Chapter 31)
- Hensel, Piano Trio, op. 11 (Chapter 34)
- R. Schumann, "Dedication" (Chapter 35)

The growth of the orchestra The orchestra continued to expand throughout the nineteenth century, growing in both the number and variety of instruments.

- Beethoven, Symphony no. 5 (Chapter 30)
- Mendelssohn, *Overture to A Midsummer Night's Dream* (Chapter 32)
- Berlioz, *Symphonie fantastique* (Chapter 33)
- Brahms, Symphony no. 4 (Chapter 43)

Opera and ballet as a fusion of music and drama Leading composers used different means to integrate music and drama. Verdi created large-scale units that move fluidly between declamatory and lyrical singing; Wagner created even larger units in which the voice and orchestra present ideas on an equal footing.

- Verdi, *La Traviata* (Chapter 40)
- Wagner, *The Valkyrie* (Chapter 41)
- Tchaikovsky, *Swan Lake* (Chapter 42)

6 Since 1900

The pace of musical change—like the pace of life itself—increased dramatically in the twentieth century. Thanks to advances in technology—sound recordings, radio, film, television, and the computer, to name only a few—listeners gained greater access to more diverse kinds of music than ever before. Musical styles were changing just as rapidly. By the 1930s, listeners could choose to listen to music that went beyond long-standing principles of harmony, melody, rhythm, and timbre. Many composers created entirely novel approaches to music by writing works without a tonal center and without a clear sense of meter or regular rhythm. Others incorporated sounds from the music of non-Western cultures. Still others opened up the realm of timbre by using old instruments in new ways or by exploiting the wealth of electronically generated sounds that were becoming available for the first time. And some composers wrote works that called into question the nature of music itself.

But novelty did not always mean a rejection of the past. Twentieth-century listeners could also choose from a wide variety of fresh and innovative music that remained tonally based and rhythmically regular, from the concert hall to the jazz club. Ragtime, jazz, and the blues developed novel ways of applying tonal harmonies and metered rhythms. Indeed, music became such a lucrative business in the twentieth century that many talented composers and musicians earned fortunes writing for a mass-market audience. These new genres of popular music both appealed to and reflected the tastes of a musical public that was now broader and more diverse than

Since 1900

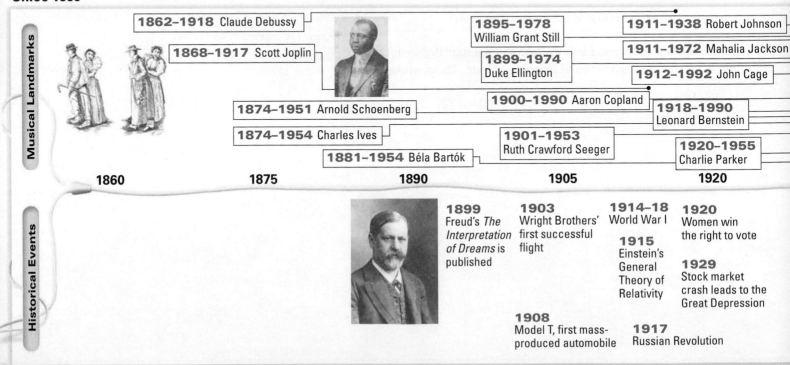

Musical Landmarks

1862–1918 Claude Debussy

1868–1917 Scott Joplin

1874–1951 Arnold Schoenberg

1874–1954 Charles Ives

1881–1954 Béla Bartók

1895–1978 William Grant Still

1899–1974 Duke Ellington

1900–1990 Aaron Copland

1901–1953 Ruth Crawford Seeger

1911–1938 Robert Johnson

1911–1972 Mahalia Jackson

1912–1992 John Cage

1918–1990 Leonard Bernstein

1920–1955 Charlie Parker

1860　　1875　　1890　　1905　　1920

Historical Events

1899 Freud's *The Interpretation of Dreams* is published

1903 Wright Brothers' first successful flight

1908 Model T, first mass-produced automobile

1914–18 World War I

1915 Einstein's General Theory of Relativity

1917 Russian Revolution

1920 Women win the right to vote

1929 Stock market crash leads to the Great Depression

Modernism

Paris, May 1913: Composer Igor Stravinsky sits expectantly in the auditorium at the premiere of his ballet *The Rite of Spring*. After the first few bars, some audience members begin to laugh derisively. Stravinsky slips out into the backstage wings and listens with astonishment. Before long, the dancers can hardly hear the irregular beats of the music, and they begin to dance out of step with each other. General chaos in the audience ensues, and the press reports a "riot" at the performance.

This scene exemplifies the relationship between many artists and the public in the early decades of the twentieth century. Stravinsky was writing in a new—and to many listeners, shocking—manner. Other composers working in the early twentieth century began to call into question the age-old basis of tonality, choosing instead to write works without any tonal center at all, or with a jarring juxtaposition of tonal and nontonal idioms.

ever. The influence of African American and Latin composers and musicians became particularly pronounced in all realms of music—recorded and live, popular and classical.

For some audiences, the pace of musical change in the 20th century was a bit too fast. This cartoon is based on an actual scuffle that occurred at one of Arnold Schoenberg's concerts in 1913 (see Chapter 47). Schoenberg continues to conduct, apparently perceiving the noise of the riot as music. The musicians use their instruments as weapons with which to assault listeners. A figure resembling Franz Schubert (see Chapter 31) lies sprawled in the foreground.

Chapter 46
Ives: *The Unanswered Question*

Chapter 47
Schoenberg: *Pierrot lunaire*

Chapter 53
Crawford: *Piano Study in Mixed Accents*

b. 1932
John Williams

b. 1937
Philip Glass

b. 1943
Tania León

b. 1977
Corey Dargel

b. 1984
Austin Wintory

1935   **1950**   **1965**   **1980**   **2000**

1933
Franklin D. Roosevelt launches "New Deal" to fight the Great Depression

1939–45
World War II

1945
Atom bomb

1950–53
Korean War

1954
Desegregation of U.S. schools begins

1964–73
Vietnam War

1964–65
Civil Rights and Voting Rights Acts

1969
First man on the moon; Woodstock; First message sent over Arpanet (later known as the Internet)

1982
CD introduced

1989
Berlin Wall falls; Cold War ends

1991
WorldWideWeb introduced by Tim Berners-Lee

1999
Napster revolutionizes file sharing of music

2001
iPod introduced by Apple

2001
9/11 attacks on the U.S.

2015
Spotify reaches 75 million subscribers worldwide

Wassily Kandinsky, *Improvisation No. 7* (*Storm*), 1910. Russian modernist Kandinsky was among the first painters to abandon the idea of representation, preferring instead to create images based on forms and colors.

A new spirit, known as **modernism**, had taken hold in all the arts, and it represented a disregard for tradition and a quest for novelty that far exceeded any such drive in the past. Ironically, the work that unleashed a riot at its premiere is now one of the most popular works in today's concert halls, a staple of the orchestral repertory. A similar pattern of shock followed by acceptance can be seen in the other arts as well. Many modernist painters rejected the time-honored idea that a painting had to represent a particular object exactly; abstract art, based on color and form, became a touchstone of modernism. Even artists who created representational images began to do away with the illusion of perspective (depth) in their paintings. Viewers were scandalized at first, but eventually they came to accept and even embrace such new approaches. In architecture, modernists advocated a style of design based on the spirit of contemporary times. Modernist architects eliminated elements of ornamentation and focused on smooth, clean lines. Novelists experimented with such techniques as writing in an unbroken "stream of consciousness," in which readers were often at a loss to decipher any clear story line. While these approaches no longer seem unusual to us today, they were unsettling in their time.

Not all composers embraced this ultra-modern aesthetic. In a counter-reaction to modernism known as **neoclassicism**, some composers in the 1920s and 1930s sought to synthesize old and new styles in a more accessible idiom. **Postmodernism**, at the end of the century, attempted to achieve the same ends by different means. Others drew on folk tunes as a source of melodic inspiration. Still other composers cultivated traditional genres like the art song, the concerto, and the musical, a more popular form of opera.

Chapter 54
Tailleferre: Concertino for Harp and Orchestra

Chapter 55
Still: "A Black Pierrot" from *Songs of Separation*

Chapter 63
León: "Guaguanco" from *A la par*

Chapter 57
Bartok: *Concerto for Orchestra*

Chapter 58
Bernstein: "Tonight" from *West Side Story*

Audio Technology

Perhaps the single most remarkable aspect of music in the twentieth century is that for the first time listeners could hear music when and where they wanted to. We take the portability of music—on radio, CDs, and through the Internet—for granted nowadays, but being able to hear music without the physical presence of performing musicians marked a radical change in the history of music. In theory at least, anyone could hear anything at any time, anywhere.

Thomas Edison invented the cylinder disk in 1877, but the earliest recordings were poor and served only to emphasize the gulf between live and recorded sound. With the advent of 78 rpm (revolutions per minute) disks in 1897, the availability and quality of recorded music began to expand exponentially. For the first time, listeners could hear the same performance more than once, and they could listen to music without any performers present. Radio stations, which first appeared in the early 1920s, radically changed the music industry by broadcasting everything from grand opera to hillbilly music to audiences who had never had the chance to hear those performances live. Eventually, film, television, and the Internet gave listeners even more choices and easier access to music. Film and video music became new genres in their own right, designed to enhance the cinematic and gaming experience in ways that are both obvious and subtle.

Chapter 69
Williams: *Star Wars*

Chapter 65
Wintory: *Journey*

This revolution in listening changed the way music was produced. Traditional written notation became irrelevant to many musical styles. With the ready availability of audiotape beginning in the 1940s, composers could for the first time manipulate sound by splicing and rerecording taped sounds. It was now possible to use the recording studio not merely to refine the sound of a recording, but actually to forge integral elements of the work. In 1990, rap group Public Enemy relied on studio manipulation of sounds from other albums to create the musical accompaniment for their lyrics in "Fight the Power." Some composers took the classical tradition into a whole new realm of experimental electronic sounds and recording techniques, and some performers gave up live performance completely in favor of the recording studio, where they had complete control over quality.

Chapter 68
Public Enemy:
"Fight the Power"

Chapter 64
Dargel: "On This Date"

Social Diversity

When Duke Ellington and his orchestra recorded the swing hit *Cotton Tail* in 1940, American society was sharply divided along racial lines. Most institutions, including the military and schools as well as housing, restaurants, hotels, and professional sports, were segregated either by law or by practice. And yet in dance halls like New York City's Savoy Ballroom, where Ellington frequently played, whites and African Americans alike thronged to hear the hottest bands and dance the newest steps. By 2000, Americans as a whole were far more accepting of the idea of social diversity than they had been 100 years before. Over the course of the twentieth century, the image of a social melting pot had given way to the idea of society as a mosaic of different cultures and traditions, each contributing in its own distinctive way toward the larger whole.

Music played an important role in this change. Styles with roots in the traditions of African American culture in particular helped bridge the divide between the races. As early as the 1930s, whites and blacks were playing together in instrumental ensembles. Ragtime, the blues, jazz, rock, and hip-hop all became a part of mainstream American culture. But the move across racial and social divides was never easy. At different times, every one of these very same kinds of music erupted as a flashpoint of social conflict. In the 1920s, many white parents expressed open opposition to the sexual overtones in ragtime and jazz. Many of their children, in turn, were shocked in the

Chapter 49
Joplin: *Maple Leaf Rag*

Chapter 50
Johnson "Terraplane Blues"

Chapter 52
Parker: *Ornithology*

Chapter 66
Berry: "School Day"

"HIS MASTER'S VOICE"

"Little Nipper" listens to "His Master's Voice." This 1899 painting by English artist Francis Barraud served as the logo for the HMV record label (and later RCA and JVC) for most of the 20th century. The gramophone is playing a 78 rpm shellac disk that contains only about three minutes' worth of music. The machine operated on a windup hand crank; speakers and electrical wiring came only later.

More than any other kind of music, jazz promoted racial integration for audiences and performers alike. Here, the celebrated pianist Count Basie leads an ensemble in 1945 that includes Illinois Jacquet (saxophone), Tommy Dorsey (trombone), Artie Shaw (clarinet), and Lionel Hampton (vibraphone).

1950s when white teenagers began listening (and worse, dancing) to rock 'n' roll, music heavily influenced by a style traditionally associated with the music of African Americans. Throughout the twentieth century, pop music has been an integral part of social change and protest—gospel in the civil rights movement of the 1950s and 1960s, psychedelia in the antiwar movement of the 1960s and 1970s, punk as an outcry against economic repression in the 1970s and 1980s, and hip-hop as a statement on racism and discrimination at the end of the century and beyond.

Globalization

It was a revelation for French composer Claude Debussy when, in 1889, he heard the Java-nese musical ensemble known as the gamelan play at Paris's International Exposition (the same event that gave us the Eiffel Tower). A gamelan includes many percussion instru-ments—drums, gongs, and xylophones, among others—and its music has what Western ears often perceive as a floating, nondirectional quality that operates outside the conventions of Western harmony. Debussy was so impressed by this kind of sound that he incorporated elements of it into his *Voiles*, for piano, in 1910. In an age before recordings, such cross-cultural musical encounters were rare. Few gamelan ensembles had ever performed outside of what is now Indonesia, and if Debussy had wanted to travel there it would have taken him several weeks by steamship. Thanks to air travel, gamelan ensembles perform all over the world today, and recordings make their music even more widely available. By the late 1940s, the American composer John Cage knew the sound of the gamelan from recordings, and the influence of this timbre is amply evident in some of his music for "prepared piano," a stan-dard instrument altered in such a way to produce both pitched and unpitched sounds. Still later in the century, Philip Glass used the repeating small rhythmic and melodic patterns of the gamelan repertory in many of his works.

> **Chapter 45**
> Debussy: *Voiles*

> **Chapter 59**
> Cage: *Sonatas and Interludes*

> **Chapter 61**
> Glass: *Einstein on the Beach*

The growing ease of telecommunications and transportation made the world of 2000 a far smaller place than it had been in 1900. Telephones, fax machines, video transmissions, and the Internet made it possible to communi-cate from almost any point on the globe to almost any other. National economies grew increas-ingly dependent on one another. Disparate cultures mingled even within individual composers and performers, who often rebelled against the notion that they or their music belonged strictly to one tradition or another. Whether in the concert hall, the jazz club, or on the dance floor, music had become a global phenomenon.

Claude Debussy
Voiles
Composed: 1910

45

Debussy's *Voiles*, a short piece for solo piano, represents a major shift in musical styles. Many of the nineteenth century's standard elements of music are used in new ways to create a distinctively modern sound for the twentieth century.

Listen to This First 🔊

〰️ Timbre	🎵 Melody	📊 Dynamics	🥁 Rhythm	👤 Harmony	🏛️ Form
How would you describe the sound of the piano in this work? How is it different from the sound of other works for piano (for example, the Mazurka by Chopin discussed in Chapter 37)? ◼	How many distinct themes can you identify? ◼	What is the predominant volume of this work? Does it change at any point? ◼	Is the basic meter of this work duple or triple? ◼	Listen for a sense of a harmonic center. Can you hum a note that sounds like home base, or *do* (as in do-re-mi)? ◼	Listen for the return of the opening idea toward the end of the work. ◼

Debussy's title is deliberately ambiguous: The French word *voiles* (pronounced like "wall" with a "v" immediately before the "w") can mean either "sails" (as in the sails on a boat) or "veils." Thus, we cannot be sure which (or both?) of these meanings the composer might have had in mind. Debussy placed this title at the end of the written score rather than at the beginning. The music, too, suggests rather than states: The timbre is muted, melodies appear and disappear without development or conclusion, harmonies remain unresolved, and the rhythm never establishes any strong sense of meter. In this sense, it fits both meanings of the word *voiles*, for both sails and veils are light and fluttering and constantly in motion.

This quality of suggesting rather than stating is basic to an artistic movement known as **Impressionism**. Impressionism was particularly important in the realm of painting (see "Historical Context: Impressionism"), where artists focused more on sensations, perceptions, and light than on the direct representation of objects. Although paintings by Monet and Renoir are among the most familiar and treasured images in art museums today, at the time of their creation, they met with considerable skepticism and at times outright derision. Were the paintings even finished? Critics and viewers of the time wondered. Similarly, the music of Debussy confronted listeners with an entirely new sound that ignored conventions and defied expectations. In this way, Debussy's music was an early manifestation of **modernism**, for it challenged critics and audiences to understand it. At the time, many of them did not.

LEARNING OBJECTIVES

45.1 Define Impressionism and how it relates to the music of Claude Debussy.

45.2 Describe the ways in which Debussy elicited new timbres from the piano.

45.3 Identify possible sources of Debussy's inspiration of these new sounds.

45.4 Listen for Debussy's use of dynamics in *Voiles*.

45.5 Describe how Debussy manipulated rhythm in an innovative way in "Voiles" from *Preludes*, book 1.

45.6 Listen for Debussy's use of whole-tone scales in "Voiles" from *Preludes*, book 1.

45.7 Outline Debussy's career as a composer.

In literature, a group of French poets known as Symbolists (including Stéphane Mallarmé, Arthur Rimbaud, and Paul Verlaine) used comparable techniques with words, avoiding clear syntax and using symbols to suggest rather than articulate ideas. Debussy was drawn to their texts, setting some of them as songs, and he regularly attended readings by his friend Mallarmé.

Timbre: A Nonpercussive Sound

It may surprise some people to learn that the piano is a percussion instrument, but consider its action: The performer strikes a key, which in turn activates a hammer that strikes metal strings, which vibrate and produce sound. When pianists play a melodic line, they must work to make this sound as lyrical and nonpercussive as they can. But Debussy asks performers to go even further here, to play the piano as if it were (in his own words) an "instrument without hammers." The ultra-smooth lines and the persistently soft volume create a timbre that is more intimate and more inward than the often bold, crisp sound of the piano.

Where did Debussy come up with such an unusual idea? Debussy heard a Javanese ensemble known as the **gamelan**, a large collection of drums, gongs, xylophones, and plucked string instruments (see Chapter 60) at the International Exposition in Paris in 1889. He was fascinated by the gentle, floating timbres of what is essentially a percussion ensemble. The gongs in a gamelan, in particular, can be set in motion by the softest of touches, and it would seem that Debussy was trying to recreate this kind of sound on the piano. A French composer absorbs and reinterprets the sound of Javanese music: *Voiles* thus reflects the growing globalization of music in the twentieth century.

We also know that Debussy was intent on exploring musical timbre in much the same way that the French Symbolist poets—all of them his contemporaries, some of them his friends—explored sound for sound's sake, unconstrained by logic or syntax. Debussy's rich sonic palette particularly inspires performers to listen and make careful choices regarding touch and pedaling, so that the exploration continues with each new performance.

Melody: Fragments

Instead of clear themes, Debussy presents what sounds more like fragments of themes than actual self-sufficient melodies:

①= a downward contour, ending with a leap upward (first presented at 0:00)

②= a single repeated note in the bass (first presented at 0:10)

③= a slow, rising three-note figure (first presented at 0:15)

④= a turning figure (first presented at 1:01): the music moves in a wave-like motion

⑤= a glissando (harp-like) figure (first presented at 2:08)

None of these themes has a particularly sharp profile: Each is as fluid as a sail or veil, altered slightly every time it returns. The music as a whole avoids any sense of strong direction; we do not feel any point as if it is moving toward a goal or climax. Instead of a kind of musical narrative, Debussy is presenting something more like a succession of slowly changing images.

Glissando (harp-like) figure ⑤

pp
"Like a very smooth glissando"

② Repeated note in bass

Dynamics: Whispering, Hinting

Except for one very brief passage in the middle (2:08–2:20), the entire work is written at the level of *piano* (soft) or *pianissimo* (very soft). This extremely low dynamic reinforces the nonpercussive timbre of the instrument, as the pianist touches the keys lightly, even wiping or caressing them rather than striking them. It also allows the one *forte* (loud) moment to stand out all the more markedly. In this manner, dynamics assume a kind of structural importance, providing a point of contrast against an otherwise unchanging plane of softness.

Rhythm: Where's the Downbeat?

Although notated in duple meter, *Voiles* provides the listener with almost no sense of a fixed metrical pattern. Most music in duple meter would follow a pattern of **1**-2 **1**-2 **1**-2, but Debussy's music resists any such pattern. Instead, the music seems to float or drift, again evoking the images suggested by the work's title.

The repeated B-flats in the lower register help obscure the meter of the work even more. At times they fall on the beat, at times off it. This repeated note seems to operate in its own little world and never quite synchronizes with the upper voices. It disappears, returns, and then disappears again. It is as unpredictable as a flowing veil or as a sail flapping in a light breeze.

Harmony: A Centerless Center

The piece opens in a relatively high register, but at 0:10, a single, low note—the note B♭—enters in the bass. This B♭ is repeated in various rhythms throughout the entire work until just before the very end (it drops out at 3:29). Yet the constant presence of this one note actually *reduces* the sense of any harmonic center. Because it is always there, it recedes into the background and contributes still further to the sense of floating or drifting created by the timbre, dynamics, and rhythm. It is a little like the sound of wind flapping against a sail: We hear these sounds if we listen for them, but after a while, we stop hearing them precisely because they never stop.

Another element that undermines any sense of a harmonic center is the use of the **whole-tone scale**. A scale, as we have seen (see "The Elements of Music," as well as Chapter 37), is an ordered arrangement of notes that together make up a kind of palette for melodies. The standard Western-music scale, known as the **diatonic scale**, consists of a combination of whole steps and half steps.

- A **half step** is the smallest distance between two adjacent notes on a piano (white or black), such as C-C♯ (see illustration below); it is also the smallest distance you can comfortably sing.
- A **whole step** is a little bigger. An example on the keyboard is C-D, which skips C♯. In other words, one whole step equals two half steps.
- The standard diatonic scale uses a combination of whole and half steps to emphasize the tonal center of any given key. The placement of those half steps tells your ear which note is home base, or the **tonic**.

But a whole-tone scale has no half steps, and this eliminates a sense of a tonal center.

A Diatonic Scale

W = Whole step   H = Half step

A Whole-Tone Scale

W = Whole step

Debussy's use of the whole-tone scale in *Voiles* helps give the music the sense that it has no tonic, that all notes are equally important. In this way, too, the music may offer an impression of a drifting cloud or a billowing sail. Western listeners tend to associate the whole-tone scale with the music of East Asia. And as noted earlier, Debussy was in fact influenced by certain repertories from this part of the world, particularly the gamelan from Indonesia (see Chapter 60).

Debussy was one of several composers working in the early twentieth century who was questioning **tonality**, which for many centuries had been the primary system of organizing pitch. Other composers would take the challenge still further, until it became possible to compose using an entirely nontonal or "atonal" style altogether (see Chapters 47 and 53).

 ## Form: Nondirectional

All the elements discussed to this point—timbre, dynamics, rhythm, harmony—combine to create a sense of nondirectional form. The music never seems to be moving toward a particular goal. There is a climax of sorts in the middle, when the music becomes rhythmically more animated and loud for a brief moment before returning to its original tempo and dynamic. This creates a vague sense of an overall **ABA'** form. But even this change in the middle comes as something of a surprise: It simply arrives, one more event in a series of seemingly random events. And thanks to the whole-tone scale, we do not have a sense that the music is moving away from or back toward a tonic key at any point. Even the ending seems inconclusive. The music stops, but it does not convey any strong sense of closure.

With these points in mind, listen to the work again, using the Listening Guide.

Listening Guide 🔊

Claude Debussy Composed: 1910
Voiles (3:55)

Time	🎵 Melody	🎁 Rhythm	👤 Harmony	💿 Dynamics	🎹 Form
0:00	1 (descending line, ending with leap up). Debussy's instructions to the pianist: "Moderately, in a rhythm without rigor and caressingly"	Begins with dotted rhythms	Whole-tone scale is established by the first five notes.	p (*piano*, soft)	A
0:10	2 (single low note repeated in bass)	Slow, irregular	Low note is disconnected from harmonies above.	pp (*pianissimo*, very soft)	
0:15	3 (rising three-note figure)	Slow, regular	Octaves imply no harmony at all.		
0:26	1 and 2 and 3 simultaneously, in various combinations.		The three voices are seemingly unconnected.		
1:01	4 (turning figure), to be played "very supply." Combined with 2 (repeated bass note), which continues throughout	Moderately fast, regular	Based on whole-tone scale		
1:38	3 (rising three-note figure) added to 4 and 2				
2:08	5 (harp-like glissando figure). "Becoming more animated." Combined with 2 underneath.	Fast, regular	Based on pentatonic scale	p growing to f (*forte*, loud)	B
2:44	5 and 2 and 3. "As at the beginning of the work."	Slow, regular		**pp**	A'
3:15	1 returns. "Very calmly and growing increasingly faint from here to the end." Combined with 5; 3 (repeated bass note) drops out for first time.				

🔍 Student FAQs ⚙

Is this music difficult to play?

Yes and no. It's not difficult to hit the right notes, but it is very difficult to sustain such a quiet sound for this length of time. It's a little like holding one's hand still in midair: It's easy to do it for a short time, but after a while it becomes a challenge. The performer has to pay attention to every subtle nuance in this work, and that requires a high degree of musicianship.

I can't really hear the difference between "piano (soft)" and "pianissimo (very soft)." Is that a problem?

Not all pianists bring out the difference clearly, but most do, and given the limited range of dynamics in this work, it's a difference worth listening for. You should be able to hear the one "*forte* (loud)" moment as quite clearly different, though.

PROFILE   Claude Debussy (1862–1918)

The Path Less Taken

Debussy's life straddled two centuries—he was born during the U.S. Civil War and died a few months before the end of World War I—yet he is widely regarded as the first great composer of the twentieth century. The inevitable association of his style with the label of Impressionism tends to obscure the wide-ranging novelties of his music: No other single figure of his era did more to expand the possibilities of form, harmony, and timbre.

Debussy was born on the outskirts of Paris and studied piano and composition at the renowned Conservatory of Paris, where he won a prestigious prize in composition. But from that point on, Debussy pursued a highly unconventional career as a composer. He never held a public post, accepted no students on any regular basis, and rarely appeared in public as a pianist or conductor. Instead, he pushed the boundaries of composition with increasing intensity, exploring new ways of applying the basic elements of music to his works. He rejected many of the conventions of composition and sought to create sounds that had never before been heard. He was a master of orchestration and drew sounds from the orchestra that had never been heard before. Like the Impressionist artists and symbolist poets who were his contemporaries, Debussy often worked in obscurity. Works that are now recognized as masterpieces, like *The Afternoon of a Faun*, were initially greeted with indifference and occasionally scorn.

Ultimately, Debussy was vindicated in his drive to extend the boundaries of music. He had many imitators (*Debussyistes*, as they were known), and his death was widely mourned throughout the musical world. In 1920, a group of prominent composers—Igor Stravinsky, Béla Bartók, Paul Dukas, Manuel de Falla, Maurice Ravel,

and Erik Satie—honored his memory with a series of short piano pieces issued in a commemorative volume called *Le tombeau de Claude Debussy* ("The Tomb of Claude Debussy").

Debussy on the beach at Houlgate, on the Normandy coast of France, 1911.

EXPAND YOUR PLAYLIST: DEBUSSY

- *Suite bergamasque.* A series of movements for piano, including the famous *Clair de lune*.

- *Préludes, Books 1 and 2.* Two collections of works for solo piano, including *Voiles*.

- *Children's Corner.* A suite of dances about childhood, for piano, including the famous *Golliwogg's Cake-Walk*, a quasi-ragtime piece.

- *Prélude à l'après-midi d'un faune* ("Prelude to the Afternoon of a Faun"). A ballet later made famous by Nijinsky and the Ballets Russes (see Chapter 48).

- *Pelléas et Melisande.* Debussy's only completed opera, based on a drama by Maurice Maeterlink about a doomed love affair in legendary times.

HISTORICAL CONTEXT   Impressionism

Debussy's music is often associated with Impressionism, an artistic movement spearheaded by French painters like Claude Monet, Pierre Auguste Renoir, and Edgar Degas in the late 1860s. These artists used an accumulation of short, visible brushstrokes instead of a continuous line to produce not so much a representation of an object as the sensation—the impression—produced by it. They were particularly interested in the effects of light on our perception of an object. Color took precedence over line. Because the idea was to capture a moment in time, Impressionists worked quickly to reproduce on canvas the fleeting appearance of a scene, and then moved on to the next painting, leading some critics to call their works unfinished.

In music, the Impressionist style is similarly based on a blurring of harmonies, rhythms, and forms. It tends to avoid clear cadences and rhythmic patterns, and the music often seems to ebb and flow with a fluid sense of motion. Above all, Impressionist composers placed great emphasis on the color (timbre) of sound. Debussy, the leading composer in this style, brought new sounds out of the orchestra and piano alike. Early critics were not so enthralled. One took the composer to task for writing "unprecise harmonies and fleeting phrases." Another said of his opera *Pelléas et Melisande* that "Debussy has definitely discounted all melody. . . . He lets us hear only chords. . . . The score resembles a curiosity shop of tangled harmonies . . . which makes a less disagreeable impression only because it falls on our ears in soft and discreet half fading tones."

Debussy himself intensely disliked the term *impressionism*, especially if it was applied to music. He insisted he was more concerned with making "something new—realities—as it were." An impression, he maintained, was reality reconstructed in the mind from our sensory perceptions of the world. These mental reconstructions offered, in effect, an alternative reality of ideas to the reality of the physical world.

Claude Monet's painting *Impression: Sunrise* (1872) supplied the name of the movement that would later be known as "impressionism." Though a few objects in this painting—two boats and the sun, for instance—are recognizable, Monet's emphasis is on capturing the mood of early morning on the water.

 EXPAND YOUR PLAYLIST

Impressionism

Debussy is regarded as the great master of Impressionism, but other composers wrote in this style as well.

Maurice Ravel
- "Mirrors" (*Miroirs*). A suite of movements for piano, including "Sad Birds" and "Valley of the Bells."

Frederick Delius
- *Appalachia*. This "American Rhapsody," for orchestra, records the impressions of an English composer who spent considerable amounts of time in the southern United States.

Charles Griffes
- *The White Peacock*. This "tone poem" for orchestra is by the leading American composer associated with the Impressionist movement.

Manuel de Falla
- "Nights in the Gardens of Spain" (*Noches en los jardines de España*). Though often categorized as a composer who expressed nationalist sentiments through his music for his native Spain, de Falla was also influenced in at least some of his compositions by the Impressionist idiom, including this work for piano and orchestra.

46 Charles Ives
The Unanswered Question
Composed: 1908

Ives, like other modernists working in the early twentieth century, was trying to find new means of musical expression that went beyond standard conventions of harmony and melody. Nowhere is this struggle between old and new styles more evident than in *The Unanswered Question*.

Listen to This First

⌁ Timbre

Listen for the distinctive sound of three different groups of instruments: strings, solo trumpet, and a quartet of wind instruments (two flutes and two clarinets). ▪

♫ Melody

Listen for the contrast in the melodies played by each of the three groups of instruments. ▪

⊕ Texture

Listen for the layered texture of these instruments. Notice that the strings play continuously, while the trumpet and the quartet of winds come and go. ▪

☺ Harmony

Which group plays the most conventional-sounding musical harmonies? Which plays the most unconventional musical harmonies? ▪

LEARNING OBJECTIVES

46.1 Explain how Charles Ives tried to change conventional notions of musical correctness.

46.2 Listen for the three contrasting ensembles within Ives's *The Unanswered Question*.

46.3 Listen for the harmonic contrasts among the various ensembles in Ives's *The Unanswered Question*.

46.4 Listen for the rhythmic contrasts among the three ensembles as you listen to *The Unanswered Question*.

46.5 Discuss the nature of the "question" identified by the work's title.

46.6 Discuss Ives's dual career as a composer and insurance executive.

Ives both absorbed and rebelled against almost every musical tradition of his time. "Please don't try to make things nice. All the wrong notes are right," he once implored a scribe he had hired to copy some of his music. But what makes notes "wrong" or "right"? Ives, along with many other modernists working in the early twentieth century, was trying to change conventional notions of musical correctness.

Contrasting Timbres

The music is performed by three contrasting groups of instruments:

- **Strings:** A small string orchestra of violins, violas, cellos, and double basses plays throughout the entire work from beginning to end, without pause.

- **Solo trumpet:** A single trumpet interjects what Ives called "The Unanswered Question" at five different points over the course of the piece.

- **Wind quartet:** An ensemble of four wind instruments (two flutes and two clarinets) responds to the trumpet's "question," each time with a different "answer."

Layered Texture

Many composers had used contrasting groups of instruments before—think of Vivaldi's "Winter" from *The Four Seasons* (violin versus string orchestra; see Chapter 17) or Mozart's Piano Concerto in A Major, K. 488 (piano versus full orchestra; see Chapter 26)—so the idea of having two groups of instruments in dialogue with one another was certainly not new. What is unusual here is the manner in which the strings seem utterly oblivious to the dialogue taking place between the two groups of wind instruments (the solo trumpet and the flute quartet). The result is a kind of layered texture in which three blocks of sound—the strings, the solo trumpet, and the winds—are moving completely independently of one another.

 Atonal versus Tonal Harmony

Ives uses these contrasting timbres and textures to highlight, in microcosm, the conflict between two very different harmonic languages: **tonal** and **atonal**.

- Tonal music establishes a harmonic center of gravity, a central note (the tonic) that provides a strong sense of resolution and closure. We have talked about the role of the tonic in Chapters 19 and 41, for example. There is an experiment that you can use to help clarify the significance of the tonic. When we sing the end of "The Star-Spangled Banner" ("... home of the *brave*"), the note for "brave" is the tonic, also known as the "tonal center," of the melody. Try singing the last phrase but not the last note ("O'er the land of the free, and the home of the ...": if you end on the word "the," you will immediately sense the strength and pull of the tonic note in tonal music. You want to go there!

- Atonal music, by contrast, has no harmonic center of gravity. No single note exerts the kind of force, the attraction, that we find in the tonic note in tonal music. Or, to put it more positively, all notes in atonal music are of equal weight: No particular note is more important than any other. Without a tonal center, everything our ears have come to expect notes to do, in the music we have listened to so far in this book and in the music we hear most often in the world around us, simply does not happen. Not only do notes not follow other notes the way we expect, but notes do not line up together the way we expect to hear them, and often they sound like they clash—like they are wrong. This sound is called a **dissonance**. (The opposite sound, the one our ear finds naturally right, is called a **consonance**.) A dissonance gives us the sense that something has not quite been finished or resolved.

In *The Unanswered Question*, the strings play in a decidedly tonal fashion, moving in a slow, steady pace, almost as if playing a very slow hymn. What little dissonance we hear is carefully resolved: Nothing is left open-ended or unresolved.

The solo trumpet, by contrast, repeatedly poses a five-note figure—the "Question"—that implies no tonal center at all and is completely open-ended. Its contour is jagged, moving first down before leaping upward dramatically. The instruments of the wind quartet respond with music that is even more tonally uncentered and that becomes increasingly agitated as the work progresses.

CONNECT YOUR PLAYLIST

Dissonance

Find a work (or an extended portion of a work) that is dissonant.

Example: Sonic Youth, "I Don't Want to Push It" (1981)
This song employs dissonance for dramatic effect throughout, particularly in the guitar.

Dissonance: Play these two notes at the same time

The Contour of the Trumpet's "Question"

The "3s" indicate rhythmic groupings

Dissonance in the Wind Quartet

The "3s" indicate rhythmic groupings

Ives himself hinted at the symbolism behind these contrasting elements of tonal (strings) and atonal (trumpet, wind quartet). He compared the strings to "Druids" who "know, see, and hear nothing." The trumpet, by contrast, poses what Ives called "The Perennial Question of Existence," in exactly the same manner each time and without variation. The quartet of flutes, in turn, attempt to answer the trumpet but becomes increasingly turbulent each time and eventually begins to "mock" the trumpet's question. By the end, only the sound of the strings remains, and the question remains unanswered.

It is revealing that Ives chose to represent this metaphysical debate through a contrast of the musical old (conventional harmony and regular rhythms within a single tempo) and the musical new (unconventional harmony and irregular rhythms across shifting tempos). Like other modernist composers of the early twentieth century, he was trying to shock listeners out of what he perceived to be their all-too-comfortable habit of listening to "beautiful" music—listeners who, like the "Druids" of *The Unanswered Question*, are content within themselves and oblivious to all that is around them. Ives elsewhere noted that music is all too often treated as a "narcotic," something that dulls the senses rather than arouses them. And a narcotic, he maintained, was no basis for progress. For Ives, progress in music was an imperative, and that meant challenging listeners to hear with fresh ears.

Now listen to this work once again, using the Listening Guide.

 EXPAND YOUR PLAYLIST

Tonal versus Atonal

Ives was not the only composer of his generation to write music that openly contrasts tonal and atonal blocks of sound.

Arnold Schoenberg

• *Pierrot lunaire*, op. 21, no. 1, "O alter Duft." The music of the finale of this song cycle (see Chapter 47), which has been entirely atonal to this point, becomes surprisingly tonal.

• String Quartet no. 2, op. 10. The third movement includes a distorted version of the children's folksong "O du lieber Augustin" (known in English as "The More We Get Together" or "Did You Ever See a Lassie?").

Alban Berg

• Violin Concerto, finale. Berg quotes a well-known chorale melody "Es ist genug" ("It is enough") in the finale, along with J. S. Bach's harmonization of it, in an otherwise atonal work.

Béla Bartók

• String Quartet no. 5, third movement. This scherzo "Alla bulgarese" ("In the Bulgarian Style") juxtaposes an intentionally cheap-sounding tonal melody against music that, while not atonal, is not clearly tonal either.

Listening Guide

Charles Ives Composed: 1908
The Unanswered Question (4:34)

Time	Timbre	🎵 Melody	🌐 Texture	👤 Harmony
0:00	Strings	Strings play a hymn-like tune, slow and stately	Homophonic throughout by themselves, like a harmonized hymn-tune	Strings tonal throughout
1:08	Trumpet	Trumpet plays the "Question"	Monophonic by itself; polyphonic when heard against strings throughout	Trumpet atonal throughout
1:27	Wind quartet	The winds respond	Polyphonic by itself; more densely polyphonic still when heard against strings	Wind quartet atonal throughout
1:42	Trumpet	Trumpet repeats the "Question"		
1:54	Wind quartet	The winds respond, more dissonantly this time		
2:14	Trumpet	Trumpet repeats the "Question"		
2:26	Wind quartet	The winds answer with an even greater degree of dissonance		
2:46	Trumpet	Trumpet repeats the "Question"		
2:56	Wind quartet	The winds respond quite dissonantly now, and loudly		
3:15	Trumpet	Trumpet repeats the "Question"		
3:27	Wind quartet	The winds now answer in a wholly uncoordinated manner, each instrument going its own way		
3:39	Trumpet	Trumpet repeats the "Question"		
3:47	Wind quartet	The winds mock the "Question" and end on a shrill high note		Strings land on final (tonic) chord at 4:10 and sustain to the end.
4:14	Trumpet	Trumpet repeats the "Question"		

🔍 Student FAQs ⚙

What does Ives mean by the strings representing "The Silence of the Druids"?

Druids were Celtic priests in pre-Christian Britain and Ireland. It's not entirely clear what Ives meant by this remark, but the Druids are (or were) mystical figures of the distant past who practiced ancient rituals—which seems consistent with the role Ives assigns to the strings in this work: tonal, brooding, slow-moving, unchanging.

How did early critics respond to this work?

Remarkably, *The Unanswered Question* did not receive its first performance until 1946, almost 40 years after it was written. By that point, critics had begun to realize just how far ahead of his time Ives really was, and they responded positively. Had it been performed at the time of its composition, the work would probably not have been received nearly as well.

PROFILE   Charles Ives (1874–1954)

Against the Grain

I ves both absorbed and rebelled against almost every musical tradition of his time. The son of a Civil War bandmaster, he grew up in Danbury, Connecticut, where he learned many different kinds of music: the orchestral repertory of the concert hall, church hymns, band music, and popular songs in the parlors of the town's homes. Ives worked all of these idioms into his own music, often in the same work.

As a composer, Ives's career path also went against the grain. If a composer "has a nice wife and some nice children," he once asked, "how can he let them starve on his dissonances?" His "day job" was in insurance, and as it turned out, Ives did quite well for himself. He composed in his spare time, but his music was rarely performed or published during his lifetime. Declining health forced him to more or less give up composition after 1918. Only toward the end of his life did critics and performers begin to take note of his music. By the time he died, he was recognized as a pioneer who had challenged convention and gone against the grain well before other American composers would take up the cause of modernism.

Charles Ives in his study, ca. 1947. He would not achieve widespread fame as a composer until after his death, when he began to be recognized as one of the pioneers of musical modernism.

EXPAND YOUR PLAYLIST: IVES

- ***Piano Sonata no. 2: Concord, Mass., 1840–60.*** A solo sonata with movements devoted individually to Emerson, Hawthorne, the Alcotts, and Thoreau.

- **String Quartet no. 2.** In Ives's own words, this work depicts "four men who converse, discuss, argue . . . fight, shake hands, shut up—then walk up the mountainside to view the firmament."

- ***Three Places in New England.*** A series of orchestral movements based on specific locales. The second is "Putnam's Camp," about the dream of a small boy who falls asleep during a Fourth of July celebration at the site of a Revolutionary War camp.

- **Symphony no. 2.** This piece uses thematic material derived from patriotic tunes, Stephen Foster melodies, gospel hymns, and a college song.

47

Arnold Schoenberg

"Columbine" from *Pierrot lunaire*

Composed: 1912

Can anguished thoughts be expressed through beautiful music? "Columbine," one of a set of 21 songs for soprano and a small ensemble of instruments from Arnold Schoenberg's *Pierrot lunaire*, offers one answer.

Listen to This First

🔊 Timbre

How would you describe the vocalist 's sound? Is it singing? Speech? ■

👤 Harmony

Does the music feel at rest anywhere, or as though it finds resolution in a certain place? In other words, do you hear a tonal center? ■

💬 Word–Music Relationships

The text being sung here expresses the despair of a spurned lover. How does the music capture this feeling? ■

LEARNING OBJECTIVES

47.1 Define Expressionism and identify the motivations that led to this artistic movement.

47.2 Define and listen for *Sprechstimme* as a technique of vocal performance.

47.3 Define atonality and give examples of how composers might use it.

47.4 Listen for and describe what musical devices Schoenberg uses to illustrate Pierrot's anguish in "Columbine" from *Pierrot lunaire*.

47.5 Characterize Expressionism in arts outside of music, especially film.

47.6 Outline Schoenberg's career as a composer.

"Columbine" is not beautiful in any conventional sense. Schoenberg purposely set this anguished text to music that is equally tormented. He saw no point in trying to project pain through beauty. Instead, his music captures pain itself.

Schoenberg's *Pierrot lunaire* represents **Expressionism**, a broad artistic movement that flourished in music, painting, and literature in the early decades of the twentieth century. Expressionist painters used exaggerated imagery and sometimes garish colors to create art that was not so much beautiful as probing. Their concern was not with the representation of external objects, but rather with the expression of inner moods and thoughts. Expressionism sought to give voice (expression) to the unconscious, to make apparent humanity's deepest and often darkest emotions. In Freudian terms, Expressionist art bypasses the ego—the conscious self—and aims straight for the id, the unconscious bank of basic instincts and drives. Expressionist art rejects conventional techniques of representation, favoring instead devices that exaggerate and distort. Psychological truth comes before beauty, and inner emotion comes before any sense of external reality. Widely dismissed by more conservative critics in its time, Expressionist art has since come to be recognized as one of the most important outcomes of modernism in the twentieth century.

Pierrot is the pale, moonstruck clown of the *commedia dell'arte*, a type of improvisational theater that originated during the Renaissance in Italy but eventually spread across Europe. Its stock characters include such figures as Harlequin and Punch and Judy. These figures always behave according to type: The cunning Harlequin is constantly playing tricks; the anarchic Punch is constantly swinging at other characters with his stick; and the lovesick Pierrot is forever pining away, unduly influenced by beams of moonlight (*lunaire* = "lunar"). Pierrot's view of life is

HISTORICAL CONTEXT **Expressionist Film**

Expressionism came of age in the years just after World War I, when filmmaking was becoming a serious art form. A number of prominent directors around this time, especially in Germany, made movies that reflect the Expressionist outlook. These films tend to be dark, severe, and highly stylized. They are often gruesome and surreal. The plots of these movies rarely involve action and revolve instead around issues of insanity and the psychologically abnormal.

Fritz Lang (1890–1976) is widely regarded as the greatest of all expressionistic directors. Like Schoenberg, he immigrated to the United States because his Jewish ancestry put him at risk in Nazi Germany. Lang's most famous German films, *Metropolis* (1927) and *M* (1931), won international acclaim and still hold their own in movie houses today. The tradition of Expressionist film lives on in the work of such modern-day directors as Tim Burton (*Batman Returns*, *Edward Scissorhands*) and David Lynch (*Eraserhead*, *Lost Highway*).

A still from *The Cabinet of Dr. Caligari*, an early (1920) German Expressionist film about the head of an insane asylum who is himself a serial murderer. Notice the distorted use of perspective, the grotesque costumes and makeup, and the stylized decor of the room.

darkly tragic yet at the same time laughable; he can scarcely control his own emotions and takes himself so seriously that we alternately sympathize with and scorn him.

Pierrot was in this sense the perfect vehicle for Expressionist art, which sought to remove all inhibitions on personal expression. Schoenberg was drawn to the surreal, violent, and eerie imagery in Albert Giraud's *Pierrot lunaire*, a cycle of poems that had recently been translated from their original French into German. The text of the selection here, the second of the 21 songs in Schoenberg's cycle, concerns Columbine or Columbina, another character from the commedia dell'arte. She is a sharp-witted maidservant and is usually linked romantically to Harlequin. Here, Pierrot laments that Columbine has rebuffed him; he sings the lament of a rejected lover.

 Timbre: The *Sprechstimme*

Throughout *Pierrot lunaire*, Schoenberg calls on the soprano to sing in a manner that is halfway between speech and song. He called this device **Sprechstimme**, which means literally "Speech-Voice," with "voice" understood here in the sense of "singing voice." Everyday speech has its own notes, but we do not sustain those notes. In *Sprechstimme*, Schoenberg calls for the singer to hit—but not sustain—precise pitches. Thus when the singer hits the note, she drops her voice. This creates an eerie, disassociated sort of sound that fits well with the eerie, disassociated texts of *Pierrot lunaire*.

CONNECT YOUR PLAYLIST

Sprechstimme

Find a work that incorporates the technique of *Sprechstimme*.

Example: Bob Dylan, "Like a Rolling Stone" (1965)
Dylan's distinctive vocal timbre is often more akin to *Sprechstimme* than traditional singing.

A recent Pierrot. The facial expression captures the character's sense of longing and anxiety. Pierrot's mood is subject to sudden and unpredictable changes—exuberant one moment, anguished the next. Like a true Expressionist, he wears his heart on his sleeve.

Sprechstimme is similar to the recitative of earlier eras (see Chapters 13, 14, 26, and 40) in some respects but different in important ways. Like conventional recitative, it is syllabic (one note per syllable), which makes it more like speech and less like lyrical song. But in *Sprechstimme*, the notes are delivered slowly enough so that the sound of the voice actually tails off at the end of each word, creating something that sounds like someone talking in an exaggeratedly slow fashion. The vocalist has to sustain the tone to connect the words, but the tone is not sustained as it would be in conventional singing: The vocalist hits the specified pitch but then releases it almost at once. The effect is eerie and somehow surreal.

 ## Harmony: Atonality

Debussy had used the whole-tone scale in *Voiles* (see Chapter 45) to create a harmonic idiom in which all notes are of equal weight and no single note forms a center of attraction (a "tonic"). Ives, similarly, had explored the possibility of writing melodies or melodic fragments also lacking a tonal center (see Chapter 46). Yet both composers had kept one foot squarely in the tonal universe: Debussy by using a single tone underneath the entire work to ground it all, and Ives by playing off the atonal trumpet and wind instruments against the thoroughly tonal strings. In *Pierrot lunaire*, Schoenberg breaks all ties with the tonal tradition to create a work that is thoroughly **atonal**, without any sense of a tonal center or resolution or harmonic closure. From its first performance until today, many listeners have found this kind of composition jarring and unpleasant, while others have found in it a powerful means of expression. What better way to convey the agony of rejection and Pierrot's overwhelming sense of alienation from the world than by ignoring the tonal tradition?

 ## Word–Music Relationships: Expressing Anguish

Pierrot is suffering from an inability to express his emotions through action. He wants to scatter white rose petals on Columbine's hair but lacks the courage to pluck even a single rose. He sings in mostly very short notes, often broken by short pauses, creating a sense of breathlessness. One repeated phrase comes in for special treatment: Whenever he sings of the "miraculous white roses," the music makes large leaps or descends to the very lowest range of the singer's register, or both.

When Pierrot begins to describe the way in which he would pluck the petals off the roses and strew them in Columbine's hair, the music makes a sudden shift: The flute and clarinet, silent up until this point, enter with a repeated three-note figure that seems to mimic the sound of petals dropping. The music is as quietly desperate as Pierrot himself.

With these points in mind, listen again to this selection, using the Listening Guide.

Listening Guide

Arnold Schoenberg Composed: 1912
"Columbine" from *Pierrot lunaire* (1:44)

Time	Original German Text	English Translation	Timbre	Word–Music Relationships
0:00	Des Mondlichts bleiche Blüten, Die weißen Wunderrosen, Blühn in den Julinächten— O bräch ich eine nur!	Moonlight's pale blossoms, The miraculous white roses, Blossom in the nights of July—Oh, if I could pluck just one!	Vocal soloist (*Sprechstime*), piano, and violin, which alternates between bowed and plucked (pizzicato) passages.	Conjunct (stepwise) motion for most words except those describing the "miraculous white roses," which are set to large leaps. Notes are short, broken, breathless.
0:27	Mein banges Leid zu lindern, Such ich am dunklen Strome Des Mondlichts bleiche Blüten, Die weißen Wunderrosen.	To still my anxious suffering, I seek alongside the dark stream Moonlight's pale blossoms, The miraculous white roses.		The notes of "the miraculous white roses" go extremely deep in the singer's range.
0:52	Gestillt wär all mein Sehnen, Dürft ich so märchenheimlich, So selig leis —entblättern Auf deine braunen Haare Des Mondlichts bleiche Blüten!	All my longing would be stilled If I could, in fairy-tale fashion, Secretly and softly—pluck onto your brown tresses Moonlight's pale blossoms!	Vocal soloist (*Sprechstime*), flute and clarinet enter for the first time at 1:13, on the word *entblättern* ("pluck").	Repetitive three-note pattern in the wind instruments, beginning at 1:13, reflects the image of Pierrot dropping the white rose petals onto Columbine's brown hair.

🔍 Student FAQs

Why would anyone want to listen to such ugly music?

"Ugly" is in the ear of the listener. Besides, works of art don't always have to be beautiful to be moving. For many listeners, a work like Schoenberg's is appealing not because it is beautiful, but because it is true, because it confronts the reality of the mind and doesn't try to sugar-coat things.

After leaving Europe to flee Nazi persecution, Arnold Schoenberg taught composition in the United States, first (briefly) at the University of Southern California and then for many years at the University of California, Los Angeles.

Why Sprechstimme*?*

Schoenberg probably felt that normal singing would sound too, well, normal. So he settled on a technique that would make the voice seem stylized and distorted, the sonic counterpart of Expressionist painting and (later) Expressionist film (see Historical Context, "Expressionist Film").

PROFILE Arnold Schoenberg (1874–1951)

The Composer as Outsider

Schoenberg was a tortured soul, an outsider who longed to be accepted yet never felt comfortable regardless of his place in the world. Widely perceived as a musical radical, he considered himself a traditionalist who was extending the heritage of Bach, Beethoven, and Brahms. Born Jewish, he converted to Christianity but later went back to Judaism. An Austrian by birth, he moved back and forth between Vienna and Berlin, finally immigrating to the United States when the Nazis assumed power in Germany. (It was in the United States that he changed the spelling of his name from Schönberg to Schoenberg.) He eventually moved to Los Angeles and bought a home in Brentwood, across the street from Shirley Temple and only a few doors down from what would become O. J. Simpson's house.

As composers challenged tonality and then finally pushed beyond it entirely, Schoenberg began a relentless search for a new system for organizing music. What he came up with, in the 1920s, completely altered the way composers thought about their craft. **Twelve-tone composition**, as his system was called, organized pitches into rows of 12 different notes. Each of the 12 tones had equal weight, and none was repeated before all the others had been played. We take a closer look at the principles of 12-tone composition when we look at the work of Ruth Crawford (Chapter 53).

Arnold Schoenberg (center), ca. 1920, with critic Erich Steinhard (left) and noted pianist Eduard Steuermann (1892–1964).

In 1935 Schoenberg was appointed to the faculty of the University of Southern California; he later taught at UCLA, and he became an American citizen in 1941. He had many pupils in the United States and exerted a powerful influence. Every subsequent generation of composers has studied Schoenberg's music carefully, and in this sense he stands as one of the most influential composers of the entire century—maybe *the* most influential.

EXPAND YOUR PLAYLIST: SCHOENBERG

- **Chamber Symphony no. 1 in E Major, op. 9.** One of Schoenberg's last works to bear a key designation ("E Major").
- **Variations for Orchestra.** A 12-tone work that is a series of variations on a 12-tone theme.
- **Erwartung.** A "monodrama" for soprano and orchestra, a stream-of-consciousness monologue from a woman who discovers the corpse of her lover in the woods.
- **A Survivor from Warsaw.** A cantata for narrator, male chorus, and orchestra, based on a report of Jews being shipped to the gas chambers in World War II bursting into the *Shema Yisrael*, a sung prayer.
- **Moses und Aron.** An opera based on Moses and the Israelites in the wilderness.

EXPAND YOUR PLAYLIST

Expressionism

Schoenberg was the leading composer of the Expressionist movement, but others followed his lead and developed their own personal varieties of Expressionism.

Anton Webern

- Six Bagatelles, op. 9. These aphoristic works for string quartet, by an Austrian protégé of Schoenberg, are highly atonal and intense. The title ("Little Trifles") is ironic. These works are anything but trifles, in spite of their size.

- *Five Pieces for Orchestra*, op. 10. Like all Webern's works, these are brief but concentrated. Webern's music does not "scream" in the same way that some of Schoenberg's does, but it can be quietly desperate.

Alban Berg

- *Wozzeck*. This expressionist opera, by another Austrian disciple of Schoenberg, is a mainstay of the operatic repertory today; its story, about the fate of a poor soldier, still exerts a powerful effect on audiences around the world.

- *Lulu*. Another highly successful expressionist opera, this one about the rise and fall of a *femme fatale*.

Ernst Křenek

- *Jonny spielt auf!* (*Johnny Strikes Up the Band*). This opera, by an Austrian composer of Czech ancestry, mixes jazz idioms with atonal Expressionism.

48

Igor Stravinsky
The Rite of Spring, Part One
Composed: 1913

Stravinsky's ballet *The Rite of Spring* (*Le Sacre du printemps*) was so new and different that the audience at its premiere in Paris in 1913 rioted. Many found the harmonies, melodies, and rhythms to be beyond the limits of the acceptable, and they let their feelings be known. Yet within a few years it became an audience favorite around the world and remains so today.

Listen to This First

🎧 Harmony

Are the harmonies here tonal or atonal? Do you hear a harmonic center of gravity? ■

🎵 Melody

Listen for the fragmentary nature of the melodies, which seem to start and stop suddenly, without warning. ■

🥁 Rhythm

What is the meter of this work? Can you tap a regular pattern of beats? Are some sections more regular than others? ■

〰 Timbre

The enormous size of the orchestra for this ballet was virtually without precedent. Listen for the variety of sounds in all families of instruments: woodwinds, brass, strings, and percussion. ■

🌐 Word–Music Relationships

The dancers present through movement and gesture the storyline of the ballet. What images, events, or moods come to mind as you listen to this music? ■

LEARNING OBJECTIVES

48.1 Explain Igor Stravinsky's *The Rite of Spring* as a ballet.

48.2 Define polytonal.

48.3 Define pentatonic.

48.4 Describe the size and makeup of the orchestra and listen for the timbre of key instruments.

48.5 Explain what is meant by "scenario" in ballet.

48.6 Outline Stravinsky's career as a composer.

48.7 Characterize the business of dance.

In ballet, music tells a story through movement. The idea of interpreting sound through gesture on stage has a long history, dating back to ancient times. Many operas, from the Baroque Era onward, have incorporated dance scenes. But the ballet as an independent genre—the focus of an evening's entertainment—did not come into its own until the nineteenth century. It has flourished since that time, however, thanks to works like Stravinsky's *The Rite of Spring*.

Stravinsky's *Rite* was commissioned by Sergei Diaghilev for his Ballets Russes (The Russian Ballet), a company of largely Russian dancers whose home base was in Paris (see "Historical Context: The Business of Dance"). The score follows a plot outline Stravinsky himself recalls as having first conceived in "a fleeting vision which came to me as a complete surprise. . . . I saw in my imagination a solemn pagan rite. Sage elders, seated in a circle, watched a young girl dance herself to death. They were sacrificing her to propitiate the God of Spring. I heard and I wrote what I heard. I am the vessel through which *Le Sacre* passed." In the end, the scenario for the ballet was drawn up by Stravinsky and Nikolai Roerich, a leading expert in Russian folklore and ancient ritual. Originally called *The Great Sacrifice*, the ballet was eventually divided into two parts: (1) The Adoration of the Earth, and (2) The Sacrifice.

PERFORMANCE The Audience Riots

The audience at the premiere of *The Rite of Spring* in Paris in May 1913 was scandalized by the music and the dancing, which by the composer's own account was seriously out of step with the music. Stravinsky later recalled standing in the wings beside Nijinsky, the choreographer, and watching the debacle unfold. Nijinsky was screaming out the rhythms to the dancers in a vain attempt to hold them together. Diaghilev repeatedly ordered the lighting crew to flash the house lights off and on in an attempt to quiet the crowd. Stravinsky claims to have been surprised at the audience's response because everything had gone so smoothly at the public dress rehearsal the day before.

Noted Parisian critic Pierre Lalo spoke for many of his contemporaries when he characterized the work in these terms:

> *Le Sacre du Printemps* is . . . the most dissonant and the most discordant composition that has ever been written. . . . Never before has the system and cult of the wrong note been applied with such industry, zeal, and obstinacy. From the first measure of the work to the last, whatever note one expects is never the note that follows. . . . Whatever the previous chord, the chord one actually hears, and this chord and this note are used expressly to produce the impression of falseness that is acute and almost excruciating. When two themes are superimposed, the composer scarcely uses themes that might work together; quite to the contrary, he chooses themes whose superimposition produces the most irritating friction and grating that can be imagined.[1]

But the riot soon turned to Stravinsky's advantage. Within a few short months, audiences across Europe were greeting *The Rite of Spring* with great enthusiasm, and the initial rejection of the work served to rally all artists of modernist tendencies.

[1] *Le Temps*, Paris, June 3, 1913.

Polytonal Harmonies

Does Stravinsky's *The Rite of Spring* lack a tonal center, as Schoenberg's *Pierrot lunaire* and parts of Ives's *Unanswered Question* do? Is this atonal music? No, it is not. The reason the harmonies of *The Rite of Spring* sound different, and the reason the tonal center is hard to find, is not because there isn't one, but because at any given moment there is often *more* than one. The repetitive chords at 3:36, for example, juxtapose two conventional harmonies in a way that creates a new **dissonance** of its own. Each of the two chords is tonal in its own right, but when combined, they clash. This kind of harmony is called *polytonal*.

To hear this clash of tonalities, ask someone who knows how to play the piano to play an E-major chord with the left hand (the notes marked in red in the illustration on the next page). Then ask that person to play an E-flat-seventh chord with the right hand (the notes marked in green). Separately, the two chords sound perfectly consonant. Finally, ask the person to play the two chords together. Simultaneously, they sound dissonant. This is an example of **polytonality**.

Pentatonic Melodies

Many of the melodies in *The Rite of Spring* are built on the **pentatonic scale**. As its name implies (*pent* = "five," as in the word *pentagon*), this scale consists of five notes instead of the conventional seven. An example of a melody based on a pentatonic scale may be found at the beginning of the "Spring Round Dance" (8:22).

Like Dvořák before him (see Chapter 44), Stravinsky was trying to capture a folk-like sound. The setting of this ballet, after all, is "Pagan Russia," before the arrival of Christianity there in the tenth century. In the context of this ballet, the pentatonic melodies—some of which Stravinsky found in transcriptions of Russian folksong—give the work an exotic sound, very different from that of the musical traditions of Western Europe. The melodies tend to be brief and full of repetitions—small fragments repeated and varied many times in succession—and they always seem to arrive and depart without warning.

Irregular and Regular Rhythms

One of the most novel elements of this music is its frequent use of irregular rhythms. Notice, for example, how the melody at the beginning of the "Spring Round Dance" (see the previous musical example) changes meter three times within three measures: The first measure has five beats, the second has seven, and the third has six.

This kind of rhythmic irregularity is offset by the frequent use of **ostinato** figures, in which a single rhythmic or rhythmic-melodic gesture is repeated over and over again, many times. Listen, for example, to the ostinato in the low strings beginning at 8:48. This figure repeats itself no fewer than 32 times over the next two-and-half minutes. Similar extended ostinato patterns can be found throughout the work.

A recent production of *The Rite of Spring*, performed by the Kirov Ballet, using recreations of the original 1913 costuming and choreography.

Timbre and the Mega-Orchestra

The orchestra for Brahms's Fourth Symphony (1885) seems like a chamber ensemble by comparison to the orchestra of Stravinsky's *The Rite of Spring*. Stravinsky's work calls for an ensemble consisting of the following:

Woodwinds:

1 piccolo

3 flutes, 1 doubling on second piccolo

1 alto flute

1 English horn

4 oboes, 1 doubling on second English horn

1 E♭ clarinet

3 clarinets, 1 doubling on second bass clarinet

1 bass clarinet

4 bassoons, 1 doubling on second contrabassoon

1 contrabassoon

Brass:

8 French horns, 2 doubling on tenor tubas

1 high trumpet (D trumpet)

4 trumpets

1 bass trumpet

3 trombones

2 tubas

Percussion: Timpani, bass drum, cymbals, gong, guero ("scraper"), tambourine, triangle

Strings: Violins 1 and 2, violas, cellos, double basses

Unsung Words: The Scenario

In ballet, the dancers present, through their movement, a story line known as the **scenario**. The words of the scenario are not sung, but they shape the form of the music directly. In the spring of 1913, Stravinsky made the following comments about the scenario of the ballet's Part One:

> In the Prelude, before the curtain rises, I have confided to my orchestra that great sense of dread that weighs on every sensitive spirit before an event of great import. . . . The fragile sound of a flute can embody this import with great power, and it expands to the full orchestra. . . .
>
> In the first scene, some adolescent boys appear with an old—very old—woman. Her age and era are unknown but she herself knows the secrets of nature and teaches her children the art of predicting the future. She runs, bent over the earth, half-woman, half-beast. The adolescent boys beside her are the Augurs of Spring, who mark in their movements the rhythm of Spring, the pulsing beat of Spring.
>
> Meanwhile, the adolescent girls arrive from the river. They form a circle that meshes with the boys' circle. These are not fully formed entities: their sex is both single and double, like that of a tree. The two groups mix; but in their rhythms one senses the cataclysm of groups that are forming. In reality, they divide, right and left. This is the form in which they realize themselves, a synthesis of rhythms, and the thing that is now formed produces a new rhythm.
>
> The two groups separate and compete against each other. . . . But they await the arrival of a procession. It is the saint who arrives: the sage, the pontifex, the elder of the clan. A sense of great terror seizes all. The sage gives his blessing to the earth, lying flat on his stomach, arms and legs extended, himself becoming one with the soil. His benediction is like a signal for a rhythmic gushing forth. All cover their heads and run in spirals, gushing continuously, as if with the new energies of nature. This is the Dance of the Earth.
>
> Source: "Ce qui j'ai voulu exprimer dans *Le Sacre du Printemps*," *Montjoie!* 29 June 1913, p. 13. Transl. MEB.

In Part Two, the "Chosen One," a young woman, is sacrificed to the gods to ensure the repeated return of Spring the following year.

In writing *The Rite of Spring*, Stravinsky gave each of these scenes its own distinctive music. The form of the work is **through-composed**. There is very little repetition of music between individual sections.

With these points in mind, listen once again to Part One of Stravinsky's **The Rite of Spring,** *using the Listening Guide.*

CONNECT YOUR PLAYLIST

Ostinato

a piece that uses an ostinato at some point.

Example: Jonathan Larson, "Seasons of Love" from *Rent* (1993) This song from the musical *Rent* begins with an ostinato figure in the piano, which continues unchanged through much of the song.

HISTORICAL CONTEXT   The Business of Dance

Sergei Diaghilev (1872–1929) had a great eye for talent. As director of the Ballets Russes in Paris, he encouraged the still relatively unknown Igor Stravinsky to write music for his company. In addition to Stravinsky, he engaged groundbreaking composers such as Claude Debussy, Maurice Ravel, Erik Satie, Richard Strauss, Sergei Prokofiev, and Francis Poulenc. And he worked with an equally impressive array of artists on set designs, including Pablo Picasso, Leon Bakst, and Juan Gris. Many of the dancers and choreographers in his company became legends in their own right, including Vaslav Nijinsky (chief choreographer for *The Rite of Spring*), Anna Pavlova, and Georges Balanchine, the last of whom became a leading force in the world of American ballet.

Diaghilev combined his sense of taste with the skills of a businessman. The early years of the Ballets Russes, from its founding in 1909 until the outbreak of World War I in 1914, were the most financially successful. The musical repertory consistently included new works by promising young composers, which were always a topic of conversation among the Parisian elite. Even the riot at the premiere of *The Rite of Spring* produced excellent press for the company (see "Performance: The Audience Riots").

The years after the war were less rewarding. Cultural life did not return to its earlier level for several years, and Diaghilev had to use great ingenuity to keep his company afloat. The revival of *The Rite of Spring* in 1920 offers a case in point. The work was in great demand—audiences *wanted* to hear the

Sergei Diaghilev, the Russian impresario who found great success in Paris through his collaborations with Stravinsky, Picasso, and others.

work now, not shout it down—but the orchestra demanded by the score was enormous, almost twice the size of the company's normal ensemble, and all 97 musicians had to be paid. Diaghilev turned to fashion designer Gabrielle ("Coco") Chanel for help, and she contributed a large sum of money that made the production possible. After Diaghilev's death, the Ballets Russes struggled, changing its name and locale at various times but never recreating its earlier success.

"The Elect" from Stravinsky's *Rite of Spring* in the original 1913 production. The innovative costumes and masks were by Russian designer N. K. Roerich and were part of what made the original production so shocking to audiences.

CLOSER LOOK The Mega-Orchestra

By the early twentieth century, the size of orchestras had grown considerably compared to those in use during Haydn's lifetime (see pages 198–199). The image here shows a large orchestra similar (but not identical) to that called for in Stravinsky's *Rite of Spring*.

Horns. Sometimes called "French horns," this versatile member of the brass family covers a wide range of both pitches and timbres, from bold to mellow.

Percussion. Works that call for percussion typically require only a fraction of the large number of instruments in this family. Seen here, from left to right, are chimes, a snare drum, cymbals, a bass drum, and timpani ("kettle drums").

Woodwinds. These instruments include (from highest range to lowest) piccolo, flute, oboe, English horn, clarinet, bassoon, contrabassoon, and bass clarinet.

Trumpets. Trumpets come in different sizes and ranges but typically produce a bright, piercing sound.

Harp. This is another stringed instrument but one that is plucked rather than played with a bow.

Second violins. In an orchestra, playing "second fiddle" is by no means a secondary task. This group, about equal in number to the first violin section, often plays its own independent line.

First violins. Although the seating of the other stringed instruments can vary, the first violins are always found on the left side of the stage. The violinist closest to the conductor is the concertmaster, the orchestra's equivalent of a team captain.

Conductor. The conductor holds everything together. All eyes are on him—or at least should be!—as he controls tempo, phrasing, and the overall balance of sound among the many instruments and instrument groups.

Trombones. These often operate in groups of three, corresponding to the alto, tenor, and bass ranges of the voice. The sliding mechanism allows trombones to "slide" into and out of pitches quite easily.

Tuba. The lowest-sounding of the family of brass instruments.

Double basses. This instrument is even larger (and louder) than the cello. In this ensemble, only five double basses are required to balance the sound of the other stringed instruments.

Violas. Slightly lower in range than the violins but much higher than the cellos, the violas often provide the harmonies of the inner voices between high and low. They can carry the principal melodic line at times as well.

Cellos. These instruments are, in effect, very large violins—so large, in fact, that they must be played upright, held between the legs. Because a cello produces a much larger volume of sound than a violin, an orchestra requires far fewer cellos. In this ensemble, there are only 8, as opposed to the 14 first and 14 second violins.

Listening Guide 🔊

Igor Stravinsky Composed: 1913
Rite of Spring, Part One (16:40)

Time	🎵 Word–Music Relationships: The Scenario	〰️ Timbre	🥁 Rhythm
0:00	**Introduction** (the curtain remains down). Stravinsky later said that this introduction "should represent the awakening of nature" after a long Russian winter, "the scratching, gnawing, and wiggling of birds and beasts."	Wind instruments predominate. Each instrument seems to function independently of the others, from the solo on the bassoon at the opening through the gradual addition of horns, clarinets, English horn, oboes, and flutes.	Free
3:14	*The Spring celebration. The pipers pipe and young men tell fortunes. The old woman enters. She knows the mystery of nature and how to predict the future.*	The entrance of the fortuneteller (3:14) is signaled by the appearance of an ostinato motif in the violins (pizzicato).	
3:36	**The Harbingers of Spring; Dances of the Adolescents.** *Young girls with painted faces come in from the river in single file. They dance the Spring dances.*	Full orchestra. Strings enter in force for the first time.	Same chord repeated many times, but with no predictable pattern of accent.
6:56	**Game of Abduction.** *The games start.*	Full orchestra, including heavy beating of timpani and bass drum.	Frenzied pace, fast rhythm.
8:22	**Spring Round Dance.** *The Spring Khorovod* (a traditional Russian circle dance).	High winds introduce the main melody, played on clarinets.	A slow, stately dance, which transforms the preceding mood of frenzy into one of calm. Ostinato bass begins at 8:48.
12:16	**Games of Rival Tribes.** *The people divide into two opposed groups.*	Percussion and low brass open this section.	Another energetic section based on a succession of ostinato patterns.
14:16	**Procession of the Sage.** *The holy procession of the wise old men. The oldest and wisest interrupts the Spring games, which come to a stop.*	Steady drum beat, with prominent brass parts.	Another section based on a slow, steady, ostinato pattern. Comes to a sudden and extremely abrupt stop.
14:58	**Adoration of the Earth.** *The people pause trembling before the Great Action. The old men bless the earth. The Kiss of the Earth.*	Sustained low winds, with high notes on double bass, punctuated by timpani.	For the first time, the forward momentum of the music stops.
15:20	**The Dance of the Earth.** *The people dance passionately on the earth, sanctifying it and becoming one with it.*	Full orchestra.	Ostinato pattern in bass.

Melody

Fragments are mostly based on a pentatonic scale. Several of the melodies are based on Russian folk tunes that Stravinsky knew from a published source.

The ostinato figure that occurs here will come back later.

Ostinato figure throughout (3:46, 4:01, 5:02, etc.); melodic fragments above and below.

Short fragment running up and down, repeated many times.

Pentatonic melody at 8:22. The theme sounds extremely simple at first but becomes more complicated as it progresses.

Many thematic fragments simultaneously, in layers of the orchestra.

Again, many fragments in layers of the orchestra.

The "kiss" is an eerily quiet chord played on a group of 14 solo string instruments (violins, violas, cellos, double basses).

The "kiss" unleashes a frenzy of motion. Once again, the music builds over a sustained ostinato pattern. And once again, the music comes to an abrupt halt.

 ## Q Student FAQs

Is this work always performed as a ballet?

No. In fact, ballet performances of it are fairly rare. Stravinsky's *The Rite of Spring* has become a staple of the concert hall, where it is enjoyed without the added dimension of dance.

Why did the first audience riot?

Some were offended by the music's unconventional nature. Others found the choreography preposterous: Ballet dancers had always emphasized grace, but Nijinsky's choreography called for the dancers to do many ungraceful moves, like a rapid series of standing vertical leaps. And there is speculation that Diaghilev, dance company director, may have encouraged a scandal at the opening. A scandal meant publicity, and publicity meant ticket sales, not only for this ballet, but for others produced by the Ballets Russes.

PROFILE Igor Stravinsky (1882–1971)

"Modernsky"

Like many pop artists—Bob Dylan, David Bowie, Madonna—Stravinsky was constantly reinventing himself. The son of a famous Russian operatic bass singer, many of Stravinsky's early works, including *The Rite of Spring*, reflect his Russian ancestry. By 1917 he was at the forefront of a new movement, **Neoclassicism**, which turned its back on the huge orchestras and complex textures of his own earlier music. In this period, Stravinsky wrote music that was more clearly tonal, using forms and rhythmic patterns that owed much to the music of the eighteenth century. Many other composers followed his lead.

With the advent of World War II, Stravinsky continued his travels, settling in Los Angeles and becoming a U.S. citizen in 1945. Late in life, to everyone's astonishment, he began writing 12-tone music, the most intellectually rigorous and severe form of atonal music. Even at an advanced age, the old composer could learn new tricks.

From the 1920s onward, Stravinsky was widely regarded as one of the century's two greatest composers, together with Arnold Schoenberg (see Chapter 47). Unlike Schoenberg, however, Stravinsky was able to connect with audiences so that he had quite a following despite his modernism (one clever critic dubbed him "Modernsky"). He had no direct students, but his influence on subsequent generations of composers has been profound.

Stravinsky (seated) visiting Claude Debussy, a composer whose works he admired enormously, ca. 1912. Like Debussy, Stravinsky sought to expand the vocabulary of music.

STATIONS IN STRAVINSKY'S LIFE

1. Oranienburg (Lomonosov). Born June 17, 1982.

2. St. Petersburg, 1901–11. Studies law and music. First successes as a composer.

3. Paris, 1911–14. Collaboration with Sergei Diaghilev and the Ballets Russes.

4. Switzerland, 1914–20. Escapes World War I.

5. Paris, 1920–39. Becomes French citizen in 1934. Flees to escape World War II.

6. Cambridge, Massachusetts, 1939–40. Delivers Norton Lectures at Harvard University.

7. West Hollywood, California, 1941–69. Becomes American citizen in 1945.

8. New York City, 1969–71. Dies April 6, 1971.

9. Venice. Buried near Serge Diaghilev.

Stravinsky was at various stages in his life a citizen of Russia, France, and in the end the United States.

EXPAND YOUR PLAYLIST: STRAVINSKY

- *Petrouchka.* A ballet written for Diaghilev shortly before *The Rite of Spring*, also based on Russian themes.

- *Pulcinella.* A ballet in the Neoclassical style, again for Diaghilev, based in part on actual melodies from the eighteenth century.

- *Symphony in Three Movements.* Another Neoclassical work that includes a fugue.

- *The Rake's Progress.* An English-language opera set to a libretto by English poet W. H. Auden, tracing the decline and fall of a libertine.

- *Canticum sacrum.* A late, 12-tone work for tenor, baritone, chorus, and orchestra.

EXPAND YOUR PLAYLIST

Ballet Music

Ballet can be danced to almost any kind of music, but from the middle of the nineteenth century onward, a number of prominent composers have written works expressly to be danced onstage.

Adolph Adam
- *Giselle.* One of the earliest (1841) full-length ballets to establish itself in the repertory. A love story, full of intrigues and disguises.

Leo Delibes
- *Coppélia.* An intricate plot centered around a pair of lovers. It premiered in 1870 at the Paris Opera.

Pyotr Ilich Tchaikovsky
- *The Nutcracker, Swan Lake* (Chapter 42), *Sleeping Beauty.* Tchaikovsky's three ballets are standards of the repertory today.

Francis Poulenc
- *Les biches.* Commissioned by Diaghilev and the Ballets Russes in 1922, the scenario of this ballet (whose title translates awkwardly as "The Female Deer") takes place at a fashionable party in contemporary Paris. Poulenc was a member of the French group of composers who called themselves "Les Six" (see Chapter 54).

Sergei Prokofiev
- *Romeo and Juliet.* This 1935 score, commissioned by the Kirov Theater of Leningrad (St. Petersburg), follows the basic outline of Shakespeare's tragedy.

49

Scott Joplin
Maple Leaf Rag
Composed: 1899

When Scott Joplin published *Maple Leaf Rag* in 1899, the piece became an immediate hit, selling half a million copies over the next 10 years and inspiring countless musicians to perform it, create new arrangements of it, and imitate it. Joplin and other composers were discovering that there was an enormous public appetite for works inspired by the traditions of African American music making, including the musical style known as ragtime.

Listen to This First

🎵 Rhythm

Find the basic beat of the piece, and then listen for rhythmic accents. Do they occur on the beat or off the beat? ■

🎵 Melody

Can you identify any melodies that contain wide leaps? If you were asked to sing back the melody of the piece, what would you sing? Are there ever multiple melodies audible at the same time? ■

🎹 Form

Do you hear discrete musical sections? Do any of them repeat or return later in the recording? How long are the sections? ■

LEARNING OBJECTIVES

49.1 Define ragtime and discuss its origins.

49.2 Listen for the use of syncopation in Scott Joplin's *Maple Leaf Rag*.

49.3 Listen for "stride" bass in the pianist's left-hand accompaniment.

49.4 Recognize the form of *Maple Leaf Rag*.

49.5 Explain what the "piano roll" rendition of *Maple Leaf Rag* tells us about ragtime performance.

49.6 Outline Scott Joplin's career as a composer.

Ragtime is a style of music that emphasized rhythmic syncopation (musical accents that occur off the beat) while continuing many of the characteristics of marches, cakewalks, two steps, and popular songs from the late nineteenth century. **Ragtime** music during the first decade of the twentieth century included solo piano pieces, songs (with lyrics), and pieces for small dance ensembles, but most listeners today know the piano solos best.

The style originated in the Midwest when musicians improvised catchy rhythmic variations of popular songs, a technique known as "ragging" a tune. In 1893, Chicago hosted the World's Columbian Exposition, which drew musicians and performers from around the country. African American musicians excluded from the official entertainment performed outside the exposition in countless venues, exchanging musical ideas and learning one another's styles. Musical developments at these and similar gatherings brought ragtime into existence. The first pieces titled "Ragtime" or "Rag" appeared in 1897 in Chicago, and the style spread rapidly across the country.

In the first years of the twentieth century, ragtime was perceived as a threat to the "moral, spiritual, mental, and even physical well being" of the nation (as historian Edward Berlin explained).[1] One reason was that the music was associated with saloons, brothels, and illicit establishments, all of which frequently hired ragtime pianists to entertain customers. Furthermore, the music used rhythmic patterns that were associated with African American musical traditions. During those years, racist perceptions of African American musical practices in many communities meant that

---

[1] Edward A. Berlin, *King of Ragtime: Scott Joplin and His Era* (New York: Oxford University Press, 1994), 87.

ragtime was seen as undermining the more genteel, socially appropriate, and proper (i.e., white) cultural forms. Finally, ragtime was dance music, and dance music invoked sexual interpretations that again threatened the social decorum of the era. Although older generations mostly disapproved of the music, ragtime became immensely popular with the young people. Its rhythms, melodies, and performance traditions provided one of the foundations of jazz, and it became known as a quintessentially American musical style.

 ## Rhythmic Syncopation

The piece is in duple meter, and one can easily count "one-and-two-and-one-and-two-and" along with the music. Notice that every other high note in the opening few measures falls between those counted moments.

While it is easy to hear the beat in *Maple Leaf Rag* and tap along with it, many of the rhythmic accents, such as those high notes in the first few measures, do not fall on the beat. Instead, they occur at regularly spaced intervals that oppose the underlying beat. This rhythmic technique is called **syncopation**. It occurs in Western classical music as well as in many other traditions around the world, but its pervasive use in ragtime makes it a primary identifier of the style.

The syncopation in *Maple Leaf Rag* occurs because the music's accompaniment consists of notes that are evenly spaced two rhythmic pulses apart, while the melody uses patterns that are three rhythmic pulses long. (In music notation, these rhythmic pulses are sixteenth notes; see the following example.)

The rhythmic relationship between the melody and accompaniment creates the following pattern, where "x" represents rhythmic accents. To hear this pattern of syncopation, tap your foot in a steady beat of one tap for every "x" or "o" in the chart. Have one person clap on the "x's" in the accompaniment pattern, while a classmate claps on the "x's" in the melody pattern.

Melody:	x o o x o o x o o x o o…
Accompaniment:	x o x o x o x o x o x o…

This particular type of syncopation, where patterns of "2s" occur at the same time as patterns of "3s," is identified as **hemiola**. Hemiola is a more complex type of syncopation than what is found in many other ragtime compositions. Its use in *Maple Leaf Rag* helps the piece stand out from the hundreds of other ragtime publications from the same time period.

Another type of syncopation in the piece occurs when the melody sounds like it jumps in "early" in relation to the accompaniment. Listen to the repeated notes in the melody at 0:16–0:18. The first and the last of the melody's repeated notes come in before the metric downbeat, and sooner than the steady pulse of the pattern would indicate.

Joplin also writes rhythmically straight passages so that the syncopated patterns sound fresh in contrast. Like most effective rhythmic techniques, if syncopation were used continuously, it would lose its magic.

Hidden Melodies and Stride Bass

Listen to the melody that begins at 0:44. If you focus on all the notes that the pianist is playing in the higher register, the melody sounds jumpy and disjointed.

The red line on this score excerpt shows the jagged up-and-down contour of the melody.

However, the notes that form the peaks of this contour are all close in pitch. This passage uses a technique known as "compound melody," in which a single melody has additional pitches from other melodies woven between its notes. We can hear the main melodic line by focusing only on the notes that move down by half steps. The performer's task is to differentiate these notes from those of the other melody lines.

The connected melodic line is marked with circles and a red line:

At 1:48, we can identify three distinct registers in the music: a high melody, a low bass line that is played in octaves, and some chords in the middle register. There is a significant distance between the lowest notes and the chords in the middle of the piano. If we could watch the pianist play this passage, we would see his left hand jump from the bottom section of the piano keyboard for the bass notes to the middle section for the chords, and back again in rapid motion. This physical movement of the hand "striding" up and down the keyboard led to the term "stride bass." The stride bass pattern occurs throughout most of *Maple Leaf Rag* and was extremely common in ragtime piano compositions.

Here is the stride bass:

The stride bass pattern from ragtime became the foundation for an entirely new style of music known as stride piano. Stride piano developed in Harlem after World War I, and combined a stride bass pattern with an increasingly virtuosic and blues-influenced set of melodies and flourishes for the pianist's right hand. It was one of the ways in which ragtime contributed significantly to later jazz styles.

Sectional Form

There are four distinct musical sections in *Maple Leaf Rag*. The juxtaposition of discrete units of music to create the complete piece is known as **sectional form**, and in this book we have also encountered it in William Byrd's "Sing Joyfully" (see Chapter 9). Every section in *Maple Leaf Rag* is 16 measures long, which is standard for ragtime compositions, and every section is composed of phrases and subphrases in two-, four-, or eight-measure lengths.

TIME:	0:00	0:44	1:26	1:48	2:31
	0:21 (repeat)	1:06 (repeat)		2:09 (repeat)	2:52 (repeat)
FORM:	‖: **A**	:‖: **B** :‖	**A**	‖: **C** :‖	: **D** :‖
KEY:	A♭			D♭	A♭

The complete form is represented graphically above. The third section ("C") is known as the "Trio," an idea borrowed from ternary forms in the Western classical tradition (see Chapter 25). It features a change of key and a change of texture.

Now listen to this piece again, using the Listening Guide.

PERFORMANCE   How Did Joplin Play This Piece?

The recording used for the Listening Guide is the only evidence we have of how Joplin himself might have played *Maple Leaf Rag*. In 1916 the composer recorded it on a piano roll (a long strip of paper) designed to be played on a player piano (see the image). In the years before record players were commonly available, families purchased player pianos as a means of hearing the latest hits. The piano roll had holes punched in it to represent each note in the performance. The paper was placed in the player piano, where a mechanized device translated the holes in the paper back into sounds. The keys moved, the hammers struck strings, and it looked as though the piano was playing itself. On the piano roll he cut for *Maple Leaf Rag*, Joplin adds extra bass, arpeggios, and flourishes throughout the piece that are not in the notated score. He also plays the melody in some sections an octave higher than it is written in the score. These types of alterations are typical for a musician who is used to improvising and is not concerned with strict adherence to the score.

Whether Joplin actually played all the notes on the piano roll is subject to debate. Many piano rolls were edited after they were recorded, and additional embellishments were added simply by punching holes in the correct places on the paper. By this technique, elaborate performances were created, sometimes with so many additional notes that it would have been physically impossible for a live pianist to play them all.

Still, the existence of Joplin's piano-roll performance of *Maple Leaf Rag* hints that indeed the ragtime pianists of his day did not adhere strictly to the score. Furthermore, many of the most famous ragtime pianists from Joplin's era could not read music and learned the tunes by ear before recreating them in personalized versions. One of the traditions during that time was "cutting" contests, in which two ragtime pianists attempted to outplay each other by adding virtuosic

embellishments. Furthermore, in the 1920s and 1930s, jazz musicians frequently used ragtime melodies as the starting point for entirely new, improvised performances (such as Jelly Roll Morton's and Marcus Roberts's versions of *Maple Leaf Rag*—see "Expand Your Playlist"). In subsequent decades, attitudes toward the importance of the score in ragtime have varied. Thus, a performer today might stick to the score or embellish it in any number of ways, and either approach is historically justified.

An Aeolian player piano, c. 1925. The piano roll (with the holes cut out for each note in the piece) sits in the front panel area, and the "performer" pumps the pedals to power the pneumatic mechanisms in the instrument.

Scott Joplin Composed: 1899
Maple Leaf Rag (3:12)

Time	🏛 Form	🥁 Rhythm	🎵 Melody
0:00	**A**	Syncopation, with the hemiola pattern at the beginning.	Static, with emphasis on the same pitches and attention focused more on rhythm than on melody.
0:21	**A** repeats.		
0:44	**B**	Syncopation continues.	Compound melody, with a chromatic descending line.
1:04	**B** repeats.		
1:26	**A** returns again.		
1:46	**C**, in a new key. Also known as the Trio section.		High melody uses more chords (a different texture) than the previous sections. Clear stride bass in the accompaniment.
2:06	**C** repeats.		
2:28	**D**, in the original key.	Straight (nonsyncopated) rhythms at the beginning of this section.	Complex interactions between inner voice melodies and bass-line melodies at the end of this section.
2:52	**D** repeats.		

🔍 Student FAQs

Why does this piece remind me of Charlie Chaplin?

During the era of silent films, theater orchestras, organists, or pianists performed live music to accompany movies, an old-fashioned version of today's soundtracks. Ragtime was frequently used, partly because theater pianists knew the songs and audiences liked them. *Maple Leaf Rag* was certainly one of the most popular. Chaplin chose to include it in the music to accompany his 1928 film *The Circus*.

Is there anything in the music that connects the A, B, C, and D sections?

No, the melodies are different—that's what makes it sectional form.

PROFILE   Scott Joplin (1868–1917)

The King of Ragtime

Scott Joplin is widely known as the King of Ragtime, but he always wanted to be respected as a classical composer. During his lifetime there was a wide gulf between the two musical worlds, and in spite of his best efforts, Joplin never succeeded in obtaining recognition for his classical works.

Little is known for sure about the first decades of Joplin's life. He learned to play the piano, violin, guitar, and mandolin in his early teens. Shortly thereafter, he left his family's home in Texarkana, Arkansas, for St. Louis to pursue a musical career. In 1894, he moved to Sedalia, Missouri, and built a career as a pianist at local social clubs. These performances gave Joplin ample opportunity to hone his ragtime skills. Five years later, he began a long-term business association with John Stark, an ambitious businessman who agreed to publish *Maple Leaf Rag* in spite of his reservations that the piece was too difficult for amateur pianists. Sales were slow at first, but after a decade, the piece was selling approximately 15,000 copies a year, turning a healthy profit for both Stark and Joplin.

Joplin and Stark called his pieces "classic rags" in an attempt to make them sound more sophisticated, refined, and cultured than other ragtime pieces. While he made most of his money from ragtime hits, Joplin spent much of his life seeking critical acceptance as a composer of art music. He published a theater tableau piece for narrator and dancers, "The Ragtime Dance," and an opera, *Tremonisha*. Joplin spent his last years in New York composing prolifically and trying desperately to get a full production of *Tremonisha* staged.

Scott Joplin.

Sadly, he never succeeded in getting the opera produced during his lifetime, and modern audiences still know him best for his ragtime compositions.

EXPAND YOUR PLAYLIST: JOPLIN

Over the span of his career, Joplin published approximately 80 pieces. His best-known ragtime works include four that were featured (in instrumental arrangements by Marvin Hamlisch) in the 1973 movie *The Sting*, starring Paul Newman and Robert Redford (all for piano solo):

- *The Easy Winners*
- *The Entertainer*
- *Pine Apple Rag*
- *Solace*

HISTORICAL CONTEXT   Making Money on a Hit

John Stark, publisher of *Maple Leaf Rag*, was continually looking for new pieces. Sheet music was one of the most lucrative parts of the music business at the end of the nineteenth century. Long before most households owned a record player, live musical performance was the primary way most Americans enjoyed their entertainment. Touring musicians and theater performers presented new songs to their audiences, and amateur enthusiasts then purchased the sheet music, usually for a few cents, to perform those songs at home.

Songwriters and composers of popular music often sold their music to publishing firms for a flat fee of $25 or $50. The publisher registered the copyright for the piece and then retained all the profits on the sales. A popular song might sell several thousand copies a year, netting a handsome sum for the publisher. The composer, on the other hand, not only received no royalties but might not even have his or her name appear on the published sheet music.

Joplin signed a very different contract when he agreed to publish *Maple Leaf Rag* with Stark's firm. Their contract specified that Joplin's name would appear as the composer. It also guaranteed the minimum retail price for the music ($.25) and assigned to Joplin a royalty of $.01 per copy sold—a reasonable rate for 1899. A decade after the piece's initial publication, those royalties had netted Joplin approximately $600 per year, according to biographer Edward Berlin, which was enough to easily cover most of Joplin's basic living expenses.

With the rise of recordings and the popularity of new styles of music that were not as easily notated, sheet music sales plummeted after World War II. Songwriters and composers today still sign contracts with publishing firms, however, and they receive royalties required by copyright law. The contract between the songwriter and publisher determines how much of that money goes to the songwriter and how much to the publisher. Another source of royalties is the fee that businesses pay for the right to play recorded music in their establishments. Performance rights organizations collect these fees and distribute them to the publishers. The two major performance rights organizations are the American Society of Composers, Authors, and Publishers (ASCAP, founded in 1914) and Broadcast Music Incorporated (BMI, founded in 1939). When you go to a restaurant or nightclub, or listen to a radio station that plays recorded music, look at the business's window: You will likely see stickers confirming that the business has licenses with both ASCAP and BMI.

The cover for the first edition of Joplin's *Maple Leaf Rag*, published by John Stark in Sedalia, a small city in central Missouri.

 EXPAND YOUR PLAYLIST

Rooted in Ragtime

These pieces illustrate various piano styles that had their roots in ragtime.

James P. Johnson
- "Carolina Shout" (1921). Johnson's recording transformed basic musical ideas from ragtime into the style known as Harlem Stride Piano.

Zez Confrey
- "Kitten on the Keys" (1921). Confrey's composition was one of the most successful "Novelty Piano Pieces," which followed after ragtime faded from popularity. Novelty pieces were showy bits of entertainment that featured stride bass patterns under lengthy scalar passages and glitzy arpeggios.

Jelly Roll Morton
- "Maple Leaf Rag" (1938). Morton played the piece at the Library of Congress for collector Alan Lomax, and his version was heavily improvised and differed from the published version of the piece.

Meade "Lux" Lewis
- "Honky Tonk Train Blues" (1938). One of the next virtuosic styles of piano jazz to emerge was the boogie woogie style of Lewis, best demonstrated on his biggest hit.

Marcus Roberts
- *Maple Leaf Rag* (1998). This is a contemporary jazz pianist's improvisation derived from Joplin's classic and shows the incredible diversity of musical styles the piece can support.

50 Robert Johnson

"Terraplane Blues"

Composed: 1936

Early blues recordings captured an oral tradition with deep roots in the Mississippi Delta region. The characteristic "blue note" and the 12-bar blues form would go on to have influence in music of many different kinds.

Mississippi blues musician Robert Johnson made this chapter's recording in 1936, only a few years before his death at the age of 27.

Listen to This First

♪ Melody	⩙ Timbre	▦ Form	☺ Word–Music Relationships
Listen for notes that are indistinct and slide from one pitch to another. ■	Listen for the variety of sounds and syllables the singer utters. Listen also for the extra sound effects made on the guitar. ■	Within each separate text verse, what pattern of repetition, variation, and contrast do you hear? Do any of the verses follow a different pattern? ■	How might this text, which is nominally about a car ("Terraplane" is a brand name), be interpreted metaphorically? Can you understand all the words? Are the expressions familiar to you? ■

LEARNING OBJECTIVES

50.1 Explain the origins of "the blues" in the early twentieth century.

50.2 Identify "bent" or "blue" tones in the diatonic scale.

50.3 Characterize the vocal timbre of the blues.

50.4 Listen for and define the use of 12-bar blues form in Robert Johnson's "Terraplane Blues."

50.5 Discuss the idea of the composer and ownership in the blues.

50.6 Discuss Robert Johnson's life and legend as a "downhome blues" performer.

Derived from African American performance traditions, the blues is a musical genre that uses "blue notes" in its melodies and tells first-person stories of hard knocks and love gone wrong. It was originally transmitted orally, without any formal notation. The earliest recordings of **blues** were made in 1920, when record companies began sending producers and recording teams to different cities to capture folk traditions and local styles that they had previously ignored. These "city blues" or "vaudeville blues" usually featured a female singer with a small instrumental ensemble including a piano and sometimes a trumpet, cornet, clarinet, or saxophone. The first female singer to have a major hit was Gertrude "Ma" Rainey, but the most popular of these singers was Bessie Smith, who recorded prolifically through the 1920s.

About three years later, record companies began to send producers and small teams of sound engineers with portable equipment to more rural regions. Many of the most successful trips were to the Deep South, where a very different style of blues record was made. These recordings, often called "country blues," "delta blues," or "downhome blues," featured solo male singers accompanying themselves on guitar. Throughout the 1920s and 1930s, the Mississippi Delta and Texas in particular produced many of the most famous blues musicians. Robert Johnson recorded 29 blues tunes including "Terraplane Blues" in the 1930s. His recordings include some of the most influential examples of early "downhome blues" recordings ever made. "Terraplane Blues" was Johnson's only hit during his lifetime.

A Blue-Note Melody

One of the most significant musical features of downhome blues recordings is the use of **blue notes**, particularly in the melody. Blue notes are pitches that are performed flatter (lower) than the standard major scale; usually these notes occur as substitutes for the third and seventh (and occasionally the fifth) notes of the scale. These blue notes are not necessarily exactly a half step lower. Instead, a singer or instrumentalist lowers the note as much as the mood and emotional inflection indicates. An extension of this style is the incorporation of notes that are indistinct or slide between several different pitches. In the first line of "Terraplane Blues," the text is "When I feel so lonesome you hear me when I moan." Johnson uses exaggerated blue notes for the words "when," "so," "hear," and "moan." At 0:42, the word "flash" is sung over a wavering and changing pitch, another use of this blue-note technique.

 ## Historic Blues Timbre

What may strike you first about this recording is that it sounds old. There is continuous hiss and white noise in the background, and the recording is monophonic, which means that the left and right speakers play the same thing. Some contemporary listeners value blues recordings more if they sound old because the recording's timbre—raw, authentic, and noisy—invokes a sense of time and place before the music became fully commercial. Other listeners are bothered by the scratchy sounds. Consider for a moment how your response is affected by the timbre.

Many of the words Johnson sings are difficult to understand, sometimes because they are no longer common vocabulary or phrases, sometimes because his Mississippi accent blurs the syllables, and sometimes because of the poor quality of the recording. For instance, at 0:57, Johnson sings "I'm going to hoist your hood, mama . . . ," but many of the individual syllables are missing, merged together, or altered with different vowel sounds. Johnson's vocal style encompasses a variety of techniques that convey the song's emotional meaning even when the individual words are hard to understand: He sings some words in his regular voice, but he also speaks some words; sings other words in a high, hollow falsetto tone; adds a growl to his voice at times; and occasionally utters generic syllables instead of words. Note, for instance, the spoken interjection at 0:37, "Somebody's been running my batteries down on this machine." Here, Johnson takes on the role of commenting on his own song. The falsetto high notes, such as those heard when Johnson is "crying" at 1:30–1:32, convey the emotion of the text. At 1:46, he adds a vocal growl to the word "Highway" that evokes the gritty realism of the blues. When Johnson half-sings and half-speaks "and I'm booked and I got to go" at 2:05, the change in vocal timbre conveys both the casual nature of the performance and the sense that the singer is revealing his most sincere thoughts to the listener.

His guitar also offers a range of timbres that are as varied and expressive as those Johnson provides with his voice. At key moments, Johnson presses a short bar against the strings on the instrument to produce a wavering tone (a technique known as slide guitar), always on a long note in the middle of the guitar's pitch register. Listen for this at 0:26, 0:51, 1:14, 1:40, and several times later in the song.

Most early blues players came from and performed in southern states such as Texas, Louisiana, and Mississippi.

12-Bar Blues Form

Each verse of "Terraplane Blues" contains three vocal phrases:

- The first line of text.
- The first line repeated, sometimes with slight variation or additional commentary.
- The second line of text, often a response or reaction to the situation described in the first line.

The first verse begins at 0:06 and ends at 0:31, with the following text in the three-line pattern:

> And I feel so lonesome, you hear me when I moan.
> When I feel so lonesome, you hear me when I moan.
> Who been drivin' my Terraplane for you since I been gone?*

This text pattern is typical of verses in the **12-bar blues**, the best-known and most commonly used model for blues songs. The model is not strict; instead, it describes the underlying patterns from which individual songs and performers frequently deviate. Each three-line unit forms one verse of the song, and the overall form of the 12-bar blues is **strophic**, which means that it consists of a series of verses (strophes), each set to essentially the same music.

Although there are some typical text patterns, the 12-bar blues is first and foremost a musical form, not a textual one. Each verse consists of just that: 12 bars (measures) of music—although in many instances, musicians either stretch or compress the basic pattern a bit. The three lines of text each receive four measures of music. The singer typically finishes singing the words in the beginning of the third measure, leaving time for the guitar or other accompaniment to add a **fill**, or short, instrumental response that occupies the time between the singer's phrases. Each musical phrase has a predetermined chord progression, or pattern of harmonies, although musicians frequently add variations or substitutions. The three chords used in the 12-bar blues pattern are built on the first, fourth, and fifth scale degrees, represented in the following chart as roman numerals (I, IV, and V).

	vocal phrase		
First line of text.		(instrumental response)	
I	I	I	I
measure: 1	2	3	4

	vocal phrase		
First line of text repeats.		(instrumental response)	
IV	IV	I	I
measure: 5	6	7	8

	vocal phrase		
Verbal response.		(instrumental response)	
V	V*	I	I
measure: 9	10	11	12

*Some blues songs substitute a IV chord here.

Like most downhome blues artists, Robert Johnson seldom sings a verse that follows the 12-bar blues pattern exactly. His most common variation is to shorten the third phrase to less than four full measures of music. In the first verse, for instance, "Who's been drivin' my Terraplane since I been gone?" is three beats shorter than the 12-bar blues model predicts.

In the fourth verse, Johnson uses a different text pattern that became important to later generations of musicians. Instead of the usual three lines of text, he sings four lines, or a quatrain consisting of a pair of rhymed couplets:

> Now, you know the coils ain't even buzzin', little generator won't get that spark;
> Motor's in a bad condition, you gotta have these batteries charged;
> But I'm cryin', plee-ease, plee-ease don't do me wrong.
> Who been drivin' my Terraplane now for you since I been gone?*

The musical pattern of chords (harmonies) and musical phrases remains the same as in the other verses. Two of the lines of text are sung rapidly during the first four-measure musical phrase, with the other two lines of text placed over the second and third musical phrases as follows:

This four-line text pattern is only one of many used with the 12-bar blues. It also is a common pattern in the blues-based recordings from the 1950s that were made by rockabilly artists in Memphis.

Word–Music Relationships: Metaphors and the Vernacular

"Terraplane Blues" is ostensibly about a car—the Terraplane was an affordable automobile built by the Hudson Motor Company in the 1930s—but in the vernacular tradition of the blues, the car is merely a risqué metaphor for sexual troubles and an unfaithful woman.

Blues performances, particularly in the types of road houses and bars where Johnson played, were often lively events where audiences responded to the singer's tales of romantic woe not with depressed sympathy but with a humor-filled empathy. Blues lyrics occasionally relate to social protest, personal misery, depression, or discrimination; the vast majority of downhome blues songs, however, address romantic relationships, almost always with some sexual undertones and usually where love has gone wrong. Listeners familiar with the blues anticipated these topics and had no trouble hearing the wry humor and double meanings in these lyrics.

Now listen to this song again, using the Listening Guide.

CONNECT YOUR PLAYLIST

The Blues

Find a song written in the blues style.

Example: The White Stripes, "Ball and Biscuit" (2003)
This song from the rock duo The White Stripes features a traditional 12-bar blues pattern.

Listening Guide 🔊

Robert Johnson Composed: 1936
"Terraplane Blues" (2:59)

Time	Text	🎹 Form	🎵 Melody
0:00		Introduction	
0:06	And I feel so lonesome . . . . . . since I been gone?	Verse 1: three lines of text in a 12-bar blues form, with the length of the last phrase altered.	Basic melody for the blues tune is introduced. Blue notes on "when," "so," and "hear."
0:32	I'd said I flash your lights, mama . . . . . . it's way down below.	Verse 2	Melody is similar to the one used in Verse 1, but slightly varied. Wavering blue-note tone on "flash."
0:57	I'm gon' h'ist your hood, mama . . . . . . down in Arkansas.	Verse 3: the metaphoric interpretation of the text becomes more explicit.	
1:20	Now, you know the coils ain't even buzzin . . . . . . since I been gone?	Verse 4: the form of the text changes to a four-line (quatrain) structure. This verse is a point of contrast in the middle of the recording.	Vocal melody changes to a very repetitive pattern that emphasizes just two notes.
1:45	Mr. Highway Man . . . . . . I'm booked and I got to go.	Verse 5: the form of the text returns to the standard three-line pattern.	Vocal melody is a new variation on the first melody.
2:11	Mmm . . . . . . since I been gone?	Verse 6	Vocal melody is quite similar to Verse 1.
2:35	I'm gon' get deep down in this connection . . . . . . your spark plug will give me fire.	Verse 7	Vocal melody is quite similar to Verse 3.

Robert Johnson had unusually large fingers, which helped him play more complex guitar parts.

Timbre

Solo guitar, playing in a Delta, Mississippi, downhome blues style.

Johnson's voice slides between several notes, matching the sound of the slide used on the guitar (at 0:26).

At 0:37, spoken comment interjected. Johnson introduces a brief falsetto exclamation at 0:52, and there is a guitar slide.

Johnson uses the wooden body of the guitar to add percussive sounds. At 1:14, there is a guitar slide.

Johnson's falsetto expression on "Plea—, please" matches the meaning of the words. Guitar slide at 1:40.

At the end of this verse, Johnson adopts a speechlike pattern for the last few words.

Student FAQs

Were all blues singers black?

There were plenty of white blues musicians during Johnson's time. Record companies, however, kept two separate catalogs of recordings, sorted by the race of the performer, because the white musicians' recordings were not marketed the same way. Many early country musicians, including Jimmie Rodgers (shown here), recorded lots of blues tunes.

Did the blues musicians know about the 12-bar blues model?

They learned the style from other performers. Although they intuitively knew what patterns did and did not work in the style, they were not consciously trying to use a particular formal model, nor were they concerned with how many measures each phrase lasted. We use models like the 12-bar blues as analytical tools to help understand musical developments and styles.

What are the percussive noises at 1:08?

Johnson is tapping the wooden body of his guitar to add rhythmic energy to the performance.

PROFILE   Robert Johnson (1911–1938)

A Deal with the Devil

For many modern listeners, the legend of Robert Johnson making a deal with the devil is the most famous aspect of Johnson's entire career. According to the story, Johnson traveled at midnight to a deserted crossroads, where he met with the devil and traded his soul for the ability to play blues guitar. One of Johnson's blues recordings was titled "Cross Road Blues," and became associated with the legend.

The story first appeared in print in 1966 (nearly three decades after Johnson's death), based on a vague recollection from one of Johnson's contemporaries. The same year, a southern preacher gave an interview in which he described a bluesman's fateful deal with the devil, but this interview was about a musician named Tommy Johnson, not Robert. In subsequent years, the story gained credence merely through the telling, and in 1986, it appeared in a popular movie called *Crossroads*. By the 1990s, when Johnson's complete recordings were reissued on CD, the legend was inextricably linked to him in spite of the tale's sketchy sources. Part of its appeal is the story's similarities to the tale of Faust, a character in German legend who made a deal with the devil in exchange for knowledge, power, or happiness (in various versions of the tale). Faust has been a popular theme for many literary, musical, and artistic works.

Relatively little is known about Robert Johnson. He was born in Hazlehurst, Mississippi, and became interested in music at a young age. He traveled throughout Arkansas, Mississippi, and Tennessee, learning from and playing with the best blues musicians he could find. In 1936, Johnson started working with Don Law, a well-known producer, who arranged two recording sessions for him in San Antonio and Dallas. Several of his recordings including "Terraplane Blues" were released, but only "Terraplane Blues" was a hit.

Robert Johnson.

In 1938, Johnson booked two performances in Greenwood, Mississippi, at a jook joint, a roadside tavern that featured rowdy carousing and dancing (the term *jukebox* derives from the fact that coin-operated phonographs were installed in jook joints). He took up with a local woman, who—as misfortune would have it—was married to the owner of the joint. How exactly Johnson died has never been conclusively determined, but most evidence indicates that he was poisoned at his second performance, possibly by a bottle of tainted whiskey supplied by the cuckolded owner. Johnson died a few days later.

 EXPAND YOUR PLAYLIST: JOHNSON

Johnson made most of his recordings in the last three years of his short life. "Terraplane Blues" was Johnson's only real hit during his lifetime. It took decades for his other recordings to become popular.

- "Cross Road Blues"
- "I Believe I'll Dust My Broom"
- "Sweet Home Chicago"
- "Hellhound on My Trail"
- "Love in Vain"

PERFORMANCE   Who Wrote the Blues?

With "Terraplane Blues," we regard Robert Johnson as both composer and performer. As a composer he created the words, melody, and chords. As a performer, he also created a unique way to perform them. When other musicians played "Terraplane Blues" they used much of Johnson's original piece, and then in the downhome blues tradition they added their own nuances. This practice was not always welcome. Robert Johnson sometimes refused to play facing his audience, not due to shyness but because he didn't want other guitarists to figure out the fingerings for his signature motives and styles. Even in songs as unique in their use of images and metaphors as "Terraplane Blues," stock phrases appear that are common to many downhome blues songs. For instance, one can find variations on the phrases "since I been gone" and "I got a woman" in countless other blues songs. These common phrases tie together the many different songs and performers into a single tradition.

The blues tradition was one in which music was both shared broadly and occasionally protected as personal. Thus, while we talk about Robert Johnson as both composer and performer—and he certainly put his own signature on his songs—it is essential to bear in mind that blues, and, indeed, most oral musical traditions, are also the product of many different musicians.

Son House, (1902–1988), a blues performer who knew Robert Johnson, in 1960.

 EXPAND YOUR PLAYLIST

The Blues in Different Styles

Once you learn to recognize the 12-bar blues form, it is easy to spot it in many different recordings.

Bessie Smith
- "St. Louis Blues" (1925). This classic blues written by W. C. Handy in 1912 is one of the most popular of all blues styles and illustrates the 12-bar blues form. Smith's recording is considered the classic version. During the 1920s and early 1930s, female blues singers like Bessie Smith and "Ma" Rainey were far more popular than country blues singers like Johnson.

Since the 1960s, many British and American rock musicians have drawn inspiration from Robert Johnson's recordings and covered his songs. Listen to some of the cover versions to see how his blues tunes sound in different musical styles:

Cream
- "Crossroads" (1968). This live performance features Eric Clapton.

Rolling Stones
- "Love in Vain" (1969).

Fleetwood Mac
- "Hellhound on My Trail" (1971).

John Mayer
- "Crossroads" (2009).

51

Duke Ellington
"Cotton Tail"
Composed: 1940

Swing was a highly danceable style of jazz that emerged in the early 1930s. It featured large ensembles known as big bands. Duke Ellington recorded "Cotton Tail" in 1940 with a band of 15 stellar players on trumpets, cornet, trombones, saxophones, clarinet, guitar, bass, and drums, with the composer leading from the piano.

Listen to This First

Harmony	Texture	Rhythm	Form
Listen for patterns of chords (harmonies) that repeat frequently in the piece. ■	Notice how the different instrumental groups fill different roles of melody and accompaniment as the piece unfolds. Listen, too, for sections where groups of instruments engage in musical dialogue with each other. ■	What is it that gives this piece its momentum, or "swing" quality? ■	Try to identify the beginning of each new section. How does the ending of the piece relate to the opening? ■

LEARNING OBJECTIVES

51.1 Listen for the call-and-response pattern in Duke Ellington's "Cotton Tail."

51.2 Define rhythm changes.

51.3 Describe "swing" rhythms.

51.4 Define and recognize 32-bar standard song form.

51.5 Describe what is meant by "the head" in jazz.

51.6 Outline Duke Ellington's career as a performer and composer.

Jazz is a musical genre that evolved out of many styles of music, including ragtime and the blues. Its earliest practitioners were mostly black, and its earliest forms did not rely on musical notation. **Jazz** made heavy use of rhythmic features like **syncopation** (accents off the downbeat, a major characteristic of ragtime) and **swing** rhythms, which are discussed later in this chapter. **Improvisation**, in which a performer makes up the melody while playing it, is another key feature of most styles of jazz. Improvisation also alters the concept of the "composer." In the case of "Cotton Tail," Ellington wrote the main melody and many of the detailed instrumental sections, but the bulk of this recording is a solo improvised by saxophonist Ben Webster. Thus, while we talk about Ellington as the composer, in a certain way the soloist "composed" many of the notes we hear on this recording.

Harmony: Rhythm Changes

The harmonic progression used in "Cotton Tail" was written by American composer George Gershwin for his song "I Got Rhythm," which he used in his 1930 Broadway musical *Girl Crazy*. "Cotton Tail" is only one of dozens of jazz numbers that have borrowed Gershwin's pattern.

The pattern is so common, in fact, that it has come to be known by the term *rhythm changes*. There are three characteristic features of rhythm changes:

- A "circle-of-fifths" progression, a series of chords whose roots are all five notes below the previous chord. This chord progression is one of the most common chord patterns in **big band** jazz. The progression moves at a quick speed, with only two beats per chord. We hear the pattern twice in the first four seconds (0:00–0:02 and 0:03–0:04), then again at 0:08–0:10 and 0:10–0:12.

- A bass line that steps down chromatically (by half steps) from the first degree of the scale. You can hear this beginning at 0:04.

- A **sequence**, a short musical motif that repeats at successively higher or lower pitches. The sequential pattern occurs several times in the recording but is particularly clear at 2:20. Listen to the musical pattern when the saxophones ascend, then descend (2:20–2:23). That same musical material is then repeated (2:24–2:27), but it all starts one note lower.

Unlike classical music, in which the harmony is based mainly on three-note chords, jazz often uses "stacked" chords of many more than three pitches. Listen, for example, to the dense harmonies in the brass section at 1:32. Ellington makes frequent use of multinote chords like these, and in this arrangement he uses what are known as close, tight **voicings**. The term *voicing* refers to the spacing of the individual notes in a chord, and a close voicing is one in which as many individual notes of a chord as possible are played within the same octave. The result of a close, or "tight," voicing is a dense, colorful, and bright sound, which is heard again at 2:04 in the saxophone section and at 2:50 from the whole band.

Contrasting Textures

A big band is a jazz ensemble of 10 or more musicians that typically features some combination of brass instruments (usually trumpets and trombones), woodwinds (usually clarinets and saxophones), and a rhythm section that usually consists of drums, piano, and some sort of bass instrument such as a double bass or electric bass. When we refer to a **section** of any ensemble, we are referring to a group of instruments or voices with similar timbres or the same role within the ensemble (such as brass, woodwinds, rhythm section).

Ellington generates variety and excitement throughout the recording by using the different sections of his band to create striking contrasts in texture, in part by letting them trade roles in melody and accompaniment. At 0:45, the trumpets and tenor saxophone set up a **call-and-response** texture, in which the brass instruments offer a short musical motif and the saxophone improvises an answer. Within big band arrangements, call-and-response textures act as a form of musical conversation, moving the focal point of the music back and forth. The call-and-response at 2:35 is known as a "shout" chorus because the trumpets are playing long, attention-getting harmonies in an extremely high register. In many jazz pieces, the last section is a shout chorus because that brings the piece to an exciting conclusion.

Swing Rhythms

The fast notes throughout the recording alternate between slightly longer and slightly shorter durations, creating a rhythmic **groove** known as swing. Swing rhythms generate internal momentum because the shorter notes continually propel the music toward the longer ones. Musicians resist attempts to define the rhythmic pattern according to any fixed ratio; however, in most instances it approximates 2:1. Notated jazz music uses regular "straight," or even, notes on the page, and musicians intuitively know how to alter them to produce the effect of swing.

Another major component of the swing groove is bass player Jimmy Blanton's "**walking bass**," a steadily moving line that connects one chord to the next smoothly by moving stepwise, one note per beat. Ellington uses contrast between heavily syncopated rhythms played by some instruments, and "square" rhythms played on the beat by other instruments (including the bass line), to give his arrangement of "Cotton Tail" its energized, swing character.

 ## 32-Bar Standard Song Form

Composers of Broadway show tunes and popular songs from the 1920s and 1930s wrote many of their songs in the same musical form: a short verse that set up the characters and the scene, followed by a 32-measure "chorus" that followed a predictable form. The 32 measures were divided into four phrases as follows:

Section	Duration	Melody
A	Eight measures	First melody
A′	Eight measures	First melody, with slight variation
B	Eight measures	New melody that used a musical sequence
A″	Eight measures	Return of the first melody, with slight variation

This pattern of **AABA** (with or without variations to the "A" section) is known as s**tandard song form** because it was so pervasive among the "standards" or popular hits of the 1920s and 1930s. When jazz musicians borrowed the harmonic progressions (or sometimes even the melodies themselves) from these songs, they discarded the comparatively forgettable opening verse and simply repeated the more memorable 32-bar chorus several times. In "I Got Rhythm," the chorus is the part most people have heard, beginning with the title of the song, whereas the verse is seldom performed today at all.

"Cotton Tail" uses six iterations of the chorus, and the first chorus presents the main tune, which is called the **head**. However, Ellington subtly manipulates this structure. In the opening chorus, we expect to hear 32 measures that follow the form **AABA**. However, the fourth unit (starting at 0:25) is shortened to only half its expected length, and instead of the opening melody, we hear a bold passage played by the trumpets. The sixth chorus (2:35) begins as a bold shout chorus, and we expect it to finish with the same high-energy, high-volume style with which it begins. However, its final **A** section reverts to the opening texture and timbre and presents the first melody exactly as we had anticipated at 0:25. Ellington delays the sense of closure through the recording by moving the first chorus's expected conclusion to the very end of the whole piece!

Now listen to this song again, using the Listening Guide.

Listening Guide

Duke Ellington Composed: 1940

"Cotton Tail" (3:10)

Time	🏛 Form	👤 Harmony	🌐 Texture
0:00	First Chorus: **A** section (head)	Characteristic descent of the rhythm changes is audible at 0:04 in the upright bass.	The head (main melody) is introduced by trumpet and tenor saxophone, accompanied by the rhythm section.
0:08	**A** section		Opening melody repeats, accompanied by both rhythm section and trombones.
0:17	**B** section		Improvised trumpet solo over thick saxophone accompaniment.
0:25	**A** section (shortened to half its typical length.)		Full ensemble plays the melody.
0:29	Second Chorus: **A** section (improvised solo begins)	Harmonies are *implied*, with only occasional chords from guitar and piano supporting them.	Thin texture of solo (tenor saxophone) with occasional piano and guitar chords added.
0:37	**A** section		
0:45	**B** section	Solo incorporates a bit of the Gershwin song "I Got Rhythm."	High trumpets create a call-and-response texture with the tenor saxophone solo.
0:53	**A** section		Solo accompanied by rhythm section.
1:01	Third Chorus: **A** section	The piano interrupts the expected harmonic progression and plays a single chord as a means of building dramatic tension.	
1:09	**A** section	Expected chord progression returns.	
1:16	**B** section	Chord sequence is punctuated by band.	
1:24	**A** section		

🎵 Rhythm

Swing groove is established at the beginning of the tune. The "walking bass" line is present throughout.

Contrast between melody's rhythms (heavily syncopated) and trombone chords (on the beat).

Long, sustained chords in the saxophone.

Exaggerated syncopations in trumpets.

Staccato trumpets at 0:58 punctuate the end of this chorus.

Trumpets' chords on the downbeats contrast with the syncopated (off-beat) solo.

(Continues)

🔍 Student FAQs

Why does the trumpet have a strange timbre in its solo at 0:17?

Cootie Williams played this trumpet solo with a plunger mute—literally the rubber end of a bathroom plunger—which he held near the bell opening of the trumpet. By adjusting the angle and the distance between the mute and the trumpet, he was able to add "wah-wah" effects that imitate speech.

What instrument is playing the opening melody?

The head is played by both a trumpet and tenor saxophone at the same time, and this combination of instruments creates a unique timbre. Ellington enjoyed a well-deserved reputation for his innovative jazz orchestrations.

Cootie Williams playing trumpet with Duke Ellington's band.

Time	🏛 Form	👤 Harmony	🌐 Texture
1:32	Fourth Chorus: **A** section (new melodic material features the brass instruments)	Tight, close voicings in the trumpets emphasize jazz harmonies.	Homophonic section with brass instruments playing a new melody in close harmony.
1:41	**A** section		
1:48	**B** section	Baritone saxophone solo, accompanied by prominent, sustained piano chords.	
1:56	**A** section		Piano solo, accompanied by the rhythm section.
2:04	Fifth Chorus: **A** section (new melodic material features the saxophones)	Tight, close voicings in the saxophone chords.	Homophonic section with saxophones playing a new melody.
2:11	**A** section		
2:20	**B** section	Sequence is clearly audible.	
2:27	**A** section		
2:35	Sixth Chorus: **A** section (shout chorus)		Call-and-response between "shout" trumpets and saxophone section.
2:43	**A** section	Horn harmonies	
2:50	**B** section	Close jazz voicings create a harmonic climax for the tune.	Homophonic brass section creates a thick texture.
2:59	**A** section (return of the head)		Tenor saxophone plus trumpet play the opening melody again.

Rhythm

Piano solo emphasizes the downbeats.

Long, sustained trumpet chords contrast rhythmically with the active melody from the saxophones.

EXPAND YOUR PLAYLIST

Rhythm Changes in Jazz

Jodi Benson
- "I Got Rhythm" (1992). This track from the original Broadway cast recording of *Crazy for You* features a lively version of Gershwin's song in a contemporary recording. *Crazy for You* was a reworked revival of Gershwin's original musical, *Girl Crazy* (1930), and Benson performs it in a traditional Broadway style.

Count Basie
- "Lester Leaps In" (1939). Saxophonist Lester Young played with the famous, hard-swinging Count Basie Orchestra from 1936 until 1940. This recording, which is set to the rhythm changes, features one of his most famous solos.

Dizzy Gillespie Sextet
- "Dizzy Atmosphere" (1945). Gillespie's group (including saxophonist Charlie Parker) was a significant force in the birth of bebop, audible in the style of the solos here. This tune uses rhythm changes at a slightly faster tempo than "Cotton Tail."

Miles Davis Quintet
- "Oleo" (1956). This tune, by saxophone legend Sonny Rollins, follows rhythm changes with understated, cool-jazz soloing from trumpeter Miles Davis.

Ella Fitzgerald
- "Cotton Tail" (1957). Fitzgerald recorded this version with Duke Ellington's band. It features vocal scat (nonsense syllables) on the melody, as well as memorable improvised jazz solos on violin and guitar.

PROFILE Duke Ellington (1899–1974)

Composing Jazz and Beyond

Edward Kennedy "Duke" Ellington is widely revered as the greatest American jazz composer, but his musical ambitions reached far beyond any one genre. He was a major bandleader in the **swing music** era of the 1930s and the big band era of the 1940s, and he wrote hundreds of tunes that have become jazz standards. Yet he also wrote film scores for Hollywood, concertos and concert pieces, and works for theater, which influenced the development of many young jazz artists. His greatest compositional innovations include his use of unusual combinations of instruments and careful control of timbre in his orchestrations. He was also intimately aware of the strengths and styles of his individual band members and exploited those personal abilities to great effect.

Born and raised in Washington, D.C., Ellington found his big break as house bandleader at New York City's Cotton Club, an upscale nightclub in Harlem where celebrities, tourists, and New York's high society went to hear the hottest music and see a spectacular stage show (see "Historical Context: The Swing Revival"). Working with stage performers, he gained crucial experience that served him well when he began to compose for film.

Ellington never left behind his love of jazz, but he appropriated musical forms of Baroque suites, classical concertos, and other larger concert works for his own compositions. Public reception of these works never rivaled that of his shorter big band tunes, but those compositions challenged the idea that jazz and classical music should be perceived and treated as two different types of art.

Duke Ellington.

EXPAND YOUR PLAYLIST: ELLINGTON

- "It Don't Mean a Thing (If It Ain't Got That Swing)"
- "Satin Doll"
- "Take the 'A' Train"

- "Mood Indigo"
- *Black, Brown, and Beige*

CLOSER LK   Duke Ellington's Band

Duke Ellington was an extremely influential and prolific composer and arranger, as well as a gifted soloist and pianist, whose creative life spanned five decades. Even though the main traits of swing era dance music are present in his work, there is great variety and depth in his music. He went beyond the confines of Swing style by exploring innovative orchestration and extended compositional forms. This photo shows Ellington's band in the mid-to-late 1930s. Many of his musicians worked with him for two or three decades, and he made a point of showcasing their unique talents in his compositions.

Juan Tizol, Joe Nanton, Lawrence Brown (l. to r.) – Trombones The trombone section of swing era big bands contained usually two to three musicians. Trombone and trumpet players formed the brass section. Typical big band arrangements used the sax and brass sections as the two main melodic voices. These two groups were used prominently in call-and-response sections.

Sonny Greer – Drums Drums in swing era big bands were mostly timekeepers so that the beat could be better communicated to dancers. The use of high-hat cymbals was introduced during this period. Drummer Sonny Greer worked with Duke Ellington for 32 years!

Johnny Hodges, Ben Webster, Otto Hardwick, Harry Carney (l. to r.) – Alto, Baritone, Tenor Saxes The sax section contained three to five reed players, some often doubling on clarinet. Individual players would also be featured soloists.

Wallace Jones, Cootie Williams – Trumpets The trumpet section of swing era big bands contained two to five musicians, usually three.

Barney Bigard – Clarinet One of Ellington's best-known long-time collaborators, Barney Bigard also doubled on sax, the instrument he's holding here. However, his best solo work was as a clarinetist.

Duke Ellington – Piano Pianists in swing era big bands were not limited to playing chords and embellishments, but could also play melody. The rhythmic style of accompaniment included stride and occasionally "comping," a way of playing chords in improvised, flexible syncopated rhythms that complement and interact with the soloist. Ellington used stride-style in his early years, but thereafter developed his own, sometimes percussive, original style.

Fred Guy, Jimmy Blanton – Guitar, Bass Guitarists and bassists in this era were primarily timekeepers. They mostly played a "two-feel" (playing on the first and third beat of bar) or a "walking" bass line (playing on all four beats).

Rex Stewart – Cornet The cornet, an instrument that was losing its popularity during the swing era, is pretty much indistinguishable to the ear when compared to a trumpet.

HISTORICAL CONTEXT   The Swing Revival

In the 1920s and 1930s, New York's Harlem was home to a new movement in art, literature, and music, known as the Harlem Renaissance. New Yorkers, both white and black, were captivated by the new jazz sounds emanating from New York's nightclubs. The Cotton Club featured some of the greatest bands of the swing era, and the Savoy Ballroom hosted the best dancing.

Unlike the Cotton Club, which only allowed whites as customers (the musicians and waiters were black), the Savoy Ballroom opened its doors in the 1930s to white and black patrons alike, who came to hear hot swing bands engage in battles of musicianship and showmanship. On the floor, a group of young black dancers began to improvise a new social dance that borrowed from the Charleston, and other popular dances of the day. The new dance, called the Lindy hop in celebration of Charles Lindbergh's heroic solo flight or "hop" over the Atlantic, matched the high-energy swing rhythms of the bands with its footwork, including "breakaways," in which one partner flings the other out for a few solo steps, along with acrobatic jumps, throws, and kicks.

Herbert "Whitey" White, who worked as a bouncer at the Savoy, recognized the commercial potential in the new dance and assembled a performance troupe of the best Lindy hoppers. White's group, known as Whitey's Lindy Hoppers, was hired to dance not only in stage shows but in Hollywood films. African American and white dancers alike took up the Lindy hop during the 1940s, with new variations evolving on the West Coast. By the end of the decade, the Lindy hop began to fade from popularity.

In the 1980s, a new generation discovered the Lindy hop. Several of Whitey's Lindy Hoppers were still alive, and they began to teach their old footwork to young fans. In 1992, director Spike Lee featured an extensive Lindy hop scene in his biographical film *Malcolm X*. By the mid-1990s, the dance fad had grown into a full revival, which renewed interest not only in the dancers but also in the old bands, clothes, styles, and slang expressions from the 1930s and 1940s.

Dancers from "Burn the Floor," a dance extravaganza. This group of 44 of the world's most talented dancers from 11 countries performs a mix of styles, including the Lindy hop.

Charlie Parker

"Ornithology"

Composed: 1946

Saxophonist Charlie Parker's recording of "Ornithology" captures the jazz style known as bebop, which emerged in the years just after World War II. Smaller ensembles, more emphasis on virtuosic improvisation, and a serious attitude toward the music characterized the style.

Listen to This First

⊶ Timbre	♫ Melody	🌐 Texture	▦ Form
Listen as the instruments blend to play the opening melody and then introduce themselves separately with short solos. Notice the different sounds the drums make in different sections of the piece. ■	Listen for melodies that rise and fall rapidly, for sustained dissonant pitches, and for short motifs that repeat. ■	Notice the clear melodic line throughout, and its rhythmic accompaniment. ■	Listen for timbre changes that mark the beginning of new sections. Listen also for repeating chord progressions. ■

The instrumentalists who created bebop wanted jazz to be treated as serious music for listening. Unlike swing, **bebop** was too rhythmically and formally irregular to lend itself to dance. It emerged from the work of a group of young jazz musicians working in New York nightclubs in the period just after the end of World War II. They played in small groups that typically consisted of five to seven players, called "jazz combos." This, too, was a major move away from the big band ensembles that had been so popular in the 1930s and that still played the big dance halls. Bebop was considered the new, modern jazz, and the attitude of its proponents matched the serious, postwar developments in other arts as well.

The main emphasis of bebop was **improvisation**, spontaneously created solos. While improvisation had played a role in swing jazz, bebop called for a style that was even more free, individualized, and extravagant. Improvisation, the musicians believed, was the ultimate means of self-expression that reflected an individual's experience in the moment. The musicians devised a new approach to improvisation that emphasized fast, virtuosic playing. Bebop soloists used more **dissonant** notes, more extreme highs and lows, and a tone quality that was more intense and less sweet than their swing predecessors. They also developed a simple approach to musical form: They composed new melodies that were angular, dissonant, and challenging to the performer. These melodies, or "**heads**," were the core of a piece. The lead instruments (usually trumpet and saxophone) played the head through once and then took turns soloing. The piece ended with another rendition of the head. All of these features are evident in this 1946 recording by saxophonist Charlie Parker, trumpet player Miles Davis, and a group of backup musicians.

LEARNING OBJECTIVES

52.1 Discuss features of bebop style.

52.2 Listen for the timbres and texture of a jazz combo as represented in Charlie Parker's "Ornithology."

52.3 Discuss the role of improvisation in jazz.

52.4 Listen for three different melodic segments or "heads" in this work.

52.5 Describe the instrumentation of the different segments of Parker's "Ornithology."

52.6 Outline Charlie Parker's career as a musician.

Fans who were accustomed to big band swing music found bebop difficult to listen to. The music was strikingly dissonant, favored very fast tempos, and used radical new harmonies that added more notes to each chord. Drummers frequently played with irregularly spaced accents, while pianists inserted chords in rhythmically sporadic patterns.

Jazz Combo Timbre

The recording opens with an attention-grabbing drum solo. The lead instruments then fuse into a single timbre to play the head—much as the tenor saxophone and the trumpet had joined their sounds in Ellington's "Cotton Tail" (see Chapter 51). In this case, we hear the alto saxophone and trumpet play a unison line while the tenor saxophone plays the same notes an octave lower.

After the head, the instruments take turns introducing themselves with a short triplet motif, while the drums and bass remain in a supporting role. At the end of the song (2:50–2:57), each instrument plays the triplet motif alone once again, in a parting musical comment.

The extended solos feature some unique timbres that give the recording personality and intimacy:

- At 1:13–1:46, the trumpet plays with more buzz than a typical trumpet. Davis used a mute, which changed the timbre of his instrument.
- At 2:10–2:14, the tenor sax concludes its solo by moving into its upper register; it is possible to hear a faint whistling-wind sound above the notes.

Timbral changes, particularly in the drums, also mark new sections of the piece. In choruses 2 and 4 (0:39–1:12 and 1:47–2:20), we hear a high-frequency shimmer. The drummer is using his ride cymbal extensively. In chorus 3 (1:13–1:46), we hear a distinct change. The drummer has switched to more hi-hat and less cymbal.

From Improvisation to Melody

The head for "Ornithology" has three different melodic segments, each with different basic contours:

- The first segment (0:04–0:09) alternates rising and falling lines and presents the basic melodic idea for the tune.
- The second segment (0:10–0:13) is a short, descending fragment that is then **sequenced**, or repeated, starting on a different note.
- The third segment (0:14–0:17) is an ending or cadential motif, followed by a triplet motif that repeats the same notes over and over (0:15–0:17).

All three of these segments then repeat for the second half of the head (0:21–0:38), with only slight variations in the exact pitches.

The head of "Ornithology" comes from a famous solo that Parker had improvised four years earlier on a recording called "The Jumpin' Blues." For the harmony, Parker borrowed the chord progression from a popular song called "How High the Moon." Borrowing the chord progressions,

---

CONNECT YOUR PLAYLIST

Improvisation

Find a recording that incorporates improvisation.

Example: "Empire State of Mind," Jay-Z and Alicia Keys (2009) Jay-Z improvises his rapped lyrics, varying the number of syllables he chants against the unchanging accompaniment. He repeats words (like "Yankees" in the second verse) but varies where he places them against the beat.

or "changes," from popular songs was common practice in bebop and other styles of jazz (see also Chapter 51). "How High the Moon" shares not only its chord progression but also its opening melodic motif with the new composition.

Each new instrumental solo begins with a melodic fragment that loosely echoes the music preceding it. In this way, the soloists more easily transfer the focus of the song from one player to the next. The solos reveal some signature features of the bebop style:

- Angular melodic lines, from high to low and with jagged motion
- A squeezed, forced sound as players reach the highest ranges of their instruments
- Prolonged dissonant notes (notes outside the prevailing harmony)

Texture: Rhythm Section Plus Soloist

The rhythm section, comprising bass, drums, and piano, creates a steady foundation and groove for the tune. Together, the piano and bass articulate the chords of the song, over which the other instruments solo. The texture features a single-line melody even at the beginning when all the instruments are playing. The only instrument that moves between the roles of soloist and accompanist is the piano, which emerges briefly to provide **fills**, or very brief solos that occupy musical gaps between sections (2:35–2:38, for instance).

Sectional Form

In "Ornithology," the lead instrument changes with each of the five major sections, or choruses (0:04, 0:39, 1:13, 1:47, 2:21). Each is different except the last, which is a repetition of the opening chorus. Bebop compositions typically use this **sectional form**, with the head providing the first and last chorus and the number of iterations dependent on the number of soloists and how many choruses each soloist wishes to play.

Each chorus is 32 measures long—the typical length for early twentieth-century popular songs. The head divides each time into three sections. The five choruses of this recording are vaguely similar in concept to a theme and variations movement (see Chapters 23 and 24). However, because a different individual shapes each improvised solo, there is no large-scale plan or progression of the "variations." Furthermore, in the bebop performance practice, unlike in classical themes and variations, the last section revisits the opening melody in its original form.

Now listen to this piece again, using the Listening Guide.

Listening Guide

Charlie Parker Composed: 1946
"Ornithology" (2:59)

Time	🏛 Form	〰 Timbre	🎵 Melody
0:00	Introduction	Drum solo	
0:04	First Chorus (Head): **A** section	Trumpet and alto sax playing in unison, with the tenor sax one octave below.	First segment of the head
0:10			Second segment of the head
0:15			Third segment of the head. During the piano's fill (0:17–0:21), the pianist alternates ascending and descending runs.
0:21	First Chorus: **A'** section		First segment
0:27			Second segment
0:33			Third segment
0:39	Second Chorus	The drummer uses lots of ride cymbal, which adds a high-frequency shimmer to this section.	The first three notes of the alto sax solo are the same triplet figure that ended the previous section. Note the emphasized dissonance (0:53). The contour of his improvised melody spans extreme highs and lows in almost every measure (especially 1:08–1:13).
1:13	Third Chorus	Trumpet player uses a mute, which adds additional complexity to the timbre of the trumpet. Drummer shifts to more hi-hat.	This solo emphasizes repeated notes and pairs of notes (e.g., 1:32–1:33, 1:35–1:37). The climax of the solo is one section in a high register (1:38).
1:47	Fourth Chorus	Drummer switches back to heavy use of the ride cymbal.	Tenor sax uses his highest register, allowing the melody to become pinched (2:01, 2:03, 2:06). At the end of the solo, the sax player outlines the chords, playing their notes as alternating ascending and descending lines (2:16–2:19).
2:21	Fifth Chorus (repeats the head): **A** section		
2:38	**A'** section	All instruments except bass and drums play the final triplet motif in turn (trumpet, alto, tenor, guitar, and piano).	

🌐 Texture

Melody plus accompaniment (homophony), separating the rhythm section from the lead instruments.

Each lead instrument repeats the same triplet motif: trumpet, then alto sax, then tenor sax, then guitar, with a piano fill afterward.

Alto sax solo. Notice the piano plays chords in a free and asymmetric rhythmic pattern in the rhythm section.

Trumpet solo

Tenor sax solo

The head is played in unison. At 2:33–2:34, the trumpet plays the triplet motif as a solo, and the pianist fills the remainder of that phrase (2:35–2:38) with a short solo.

Piano becomes more active within the rhythm section (2:46–2:50).

Alto saxophone (left) and tenor saxophone (right).

🔍 Student FAQs ⚙

Where did the term* bebop *come from?

The term *bebop* came from the nonsense syllables that jazz vocalists used in their solos. The singers strung together syllables in interesting phonetic patterns that helped them sing the elaborate, improvised melodies.

What is the difference between a tenor and an alto saxophone?

A tenor saxophone is larger and plays lower notes than an alto sax. The mouthpieces and reeds are also slightly different, and the techniques for blowing into the reed differ somewhat, but the same basic principles of performance apply to both instruments.

I found another recording of "Ornithology" by Charlie Parker, but it sounds completely different. Is it still the same piece?

Jazz musicians play a piece differently almost every time they perform it, sometimes transforming even the head itself. Every recorded version of the piece captures a specific time, place, and moment in musical history, and jazz fans frequently talk not about a song (i.e., "Ornithology"), but instead about a specific recording, simply because they're all so different.

PROFILE Charlie Parker (1920–1955)

The Self-Destructive Artist

Charlie "Yardbird" Parker left behind a legacy as a jazz innovator of profound musical genius troubled by a lifetime of drug addiction, a series of failed relationships, and a frustrating inability to control his professional life. He was raised in Kansas City, Missouri, when that city's nightlife was hopping with innovative jazz musicians who gathered in open jam sessions. Parker honed his craft by sitting in with those local bands and practicing obsessively. In 1939 he moved to New York City and sought out the best jam sessions in Harlem. In the jazz clubs there, Parker developed a style of virtuosic soloing that used complex harmonies, lightning-fast technique, and dissonance. With those innovations, bebop was born.

At the same time he was crafting new styles of jazz, Parker was sinking deeper into his drug addiction and either failing to turn up at performances or showing up in such a state that he could barely play. As Parker's career progressed, it was pockmarked with arrests, emotional breakdowns, the failure of four relationships, and declining health. He lost his license to perform in New York City nightclubs because of his arrest record and, by 1955, was in a state of physical collapse and entertained thoughts of suicide. He passed away a recluse, living alone at the apartment of a jazz patron. Unlike his collaborator Miles Davis, Parker never shook off the demons of his addiction. But the music he created astounded listeners. Parker's name, his solos, his compositions, and his recordings are revered among jazz fans, who sometimes wonder if they came to fruition only through the same destructive yet mind-altering forces that ultimately cost him his life.

How he acquired his nickname of "Yardbird" is hotly debated. The Birdland jazz club in New York opened in 1949 as a tribute to him, and even the title "Ornithology" paid homage.

Parker in 1947.

EXPAND YOUR PLAYLIST: PARKER

- "Shaw 'Nuff"
- "Ko Ko"
- "Scrapple from the Apple"
- "Night in Tunisia"
- "Embraceable You"

PERFORMANCE Improvisation

When Charlie Parker improvised, his musical decisions were informed both by the chord progression of the song and by an extensive catalog of musical formulas he spent a lifetime collecting. In some styles of improvisation, the solo is essentially a variation on the song's main melody. In bebop, however, only occasionally did the musicians quote from the original melody. Instead, they devised a system in which certain scales were determined to match certain chords. When those chords appeared in the song, the musicians used notes from those chords to build a new melody. The musicians also spent hours working on short motifs that they could play rapidly starting on successive pitches to create a melodic sequence. They even borrowed short motifs from books on technique for violinists, pianists, and clarinetists.

Once the musicians had a catalog of motifs, scales, and arpeggios that they could play fluently in any key, they used this musical vocabulary to construct their new improvised solos. Thus, one can find the same motifs and musical fragments in many different Charlie Parker tunes.

In the decade after Parker's best known bebop recordings, jazz musicians pushed the concept of improvisation to the point where it became the very structure of the music itself. This style came to be known as free jazz.

Tommy Potter, Charlie Parker, Dizzy Gillespie, and John Coltrane in 1951 at the New York City club Birdland, which was named for Parker.

 EXPAND YOUR PLAYLIST

From Bebop to Free Jazz

Sonny Rollins
- "Strode Rode" (1956). This bebop recording mixes variety in the rhythm section's playing with Rollins's tenor saxophone solo. Note the extended section where the saxophone plays just with the bass.

Miles Davis
- "So What" (1959). Davis's solo is an example of modal jazz, in which melodic development becomes more important than adhering to tonal chord changes.

Ella Fitzgerald
- "How High the Moon" (1960). Fitzgerald uses vocal "scat" in one of her most memorable solos. Notice that she quotes Parker's "Ornithology" in her solo.

John Coltrane
- "Giant Steps" (1960). Coltrane's famous tune demonstrates the furthest reaches of bebop.

Ornette Coleman
- "Free Jazz" (1960). Coleman's recording is nearly 40 minutes long and illustrates simultaneous improvisation in the absence of a predetermined form or chord progression.

53

Ruth Crawford
Piano Study in Mixed Accents
Composed: 1930

Writing in a new style means avoiding old styles, and in her *Piano Study in Mixed Accents*, Ruth Crawford made a conscious effort to avoid using some of the most basic elements of music in any conventional sort of way. Instead, she used a new idiom that was freed from the conventional constraints of harmony, melody, and rhythm.

Listen to This First

🎁 Rhythm	🌐 Texture	👤 Harmony	🎵 Melody	🎹 Form
What is the meter of this piece? Can you tap the beats? Are some notes long and some short, or are they all even?	Do you hear one melodic line played at a time, or more than one? Do you hear a melody plus accompaniment?	Can you hear a tonal center?	How would you describe the contours of the melody?	How is this piece divided into sections? Can you identify what makes sections similar or different? Can you identify an overall shape to the piece?

LEARNING OBJECTIVES

53.1 Explain what Ruth Crawford means by "mixed accents" in her *Piano Study in Mixed Accents*.

53.2 Describe the texture of Crawford's *Piano Study in Mixed Accents*.

53.3 Discuss the absence of harmony in Crawford's *Piano Study in Mixed Accents*.

53.4 Listen for the way in which register functions as a structural element in *Piano Study in Mixed Accents*.

53.5 Describe the basic principles of 12-tone music and their partial application in *Piano Study in Mixed Accents*.

53.6 Outline Crawford's career as a composer, author, and collector of folk music.

Ruth Crawford blazed new ground for American women composers in the first half of the twentieth century. In 1930 she became the first woman ever to be awarded a prestigious Guggenheim Fellowship in composition. She used the funds to travel to Europe, where she spent most of her time in Berlin, a hotbed of modernism in all the arts. For a brief period in the 1920s and early 1930s, there was an "anything goes" mentality in all the arts there: Painters, playwrights, poets, and musicians were all exploring new ways of expressing themselves. Crawford did not study with Arnold Schoenberg or any of the other modernist composers while in Berlin; instead, she forged her own brand of modernism by working under a series of self-imposed limitations that helped her avoid such basic elements as meter, tonality, and patterned rhythms. The result is like no work of music ever heard before; its forward drive is relentless, and the absence of a tonal center has the effect of liberating the entire spectrum of notes.

Mixed Rhythms

These notes go by very fast, so it may be hard to tell at first, but they are all of equal value. Is the meter duple or triple? The answer is neither. The music establishes absolutely no sense of meter or fixed pattern of rhythms. Instead, we hear a series of small units. The music is organized into groupings of anywhere between two and eight notes, with the first note of each unit accented. The very opening of the work, for example, consists of a series of units made up of 6, 5, 5, 5, 3, 6, and 4 notes:

These irregular groupings create a series of what Crawford called "mixed accents." As you listen, there is no way of knowing in advance how many notes will be in any given unit. This unpredictability of rhythmic organization helps distance this work from the fixed metrical and rhythmic patterns that characterize more conventional music.

Monophonic Texture

Again, it may be difficult to tell at first because of the rapidity of the notes, which linger in our ear and mind even as the next ones are being played, but there is in fact only one melodic line. Texture is thus another way in which Crawford succeeded in separating this work from more conventional approaches to music: We haven't heard much **monophony** since the Middle Ages. Here, the pianist plays the same melodic line simultaneously in the right and left hands, only the register differs. The first three notes of the work in the right hand, for example, are D-F-E. The first three notes in the left hand are also D-F-E, played at exactly the same time and in the same rhythm, but an octave lower on the keyboard. (An octave is the distance between two different notes with the same name, like D and D, one higher than the other.) There is no accompaniment (as in homophony), and there is no interplay of equal melodic lines (as in polyphony).

👤 An Absence of Harmony

The monophonic nature of the music means that there is, by definition, no harmony. But even a melody alone can imply a harmony because a conventional melodic line implies a tonal center. We can usually sense when a melody has landed on the note that is central to its key area—in other words, its tonic. When we hear "brave" at the very end of "The Star-Spangled Banner" (in the phrase "home of the brave"), for example, we have a sense that the melody has concluded not simply because we know from experience that this is the end of the melody, but because we hear the note for "brave" as the tonic note. One reason we hear it this way is because of the position of half and whole steps in the scale on which the melody is based (see The Elements of Music and Chapters 45 and 47). Another reason we hear this particular note as the central one is that we have heard it early and often: "Oh, **say** . . . " "twilight's last gleam-**ing**" "Whose broad **stripes** . . . " "gallantly stream-**ing**" "O'er the **land** of the free **and** the home of the **brave**."

The melodic line in Crawford's *Piano Study in Mixed Accents*, by contrast, projects no sense of any such tonal center. In other words, it is **atonal**. Notes do not play specific roles based on a particular scale, and no one note returns more often than any other. Crawford avoids repeating any one note until 9, 10, or 11 other different notes have sounded. By avoiding repetition or repeated returns to any particular note, Crawford reinforces the essential equality of all notes in this work. In this way, she creates a very modern sound.

Let's look once again at the very opening of the *Piano Study in Mixed Accents*: We can see that although "D" is the first pitch we hear, we do not hear it again until we have heard 11 other pitches—every other pitch, in fact, except one (G#). (*Martellato* is Italian for "hammered"—that is, to be played in a very percussive style.)

🎵 Registers of Melody

Without certain notes being more important than others or having roles to play based on a tonal scale, it is difficult to create a melody that is easy for a listener to follow, remember, or understand in the usual ways. Crawford creates interest and variety by giving unusual prominence to the melodic element of **register**, the range in which the music is presented. The melodic line never makes very large leaps, but it does move gradually from its opening low range to a very high register in the middle of the work and then back down again at the end, finishing very close to where it had begun. This attention to register helps give the work a strong sense of shape, with a beginning, a middle, and an end. It also draws attention to the differing sounds of the piano in its low, middle, and high ranges. The growling rumble of the low bass gives way to the more delicate sounds of the upper range in the middle of the work, but the journey ends back where it began, in the bass.

Sectional Form

Piano Studies in Mixed Accents is in **sectional form**. The music is punctuated by a few brief but important moments of silence—musical rests—that help divide the work into five large-scale sections. The proportions of these sections combine with the rise and fall of the melodic register to create a strong sense of symmetry. The following musical timeline represents visually what you heard. Notice how the work begins by setting out two relatively short sections of eight and nine seconds each, then expands into a large section in the middle (which is almost as long as the other four combined), then shrinks back down into two very brief sections (nine and six seconds) on the other side. There is a kind of rough formal symmetry to the architecture of this work.

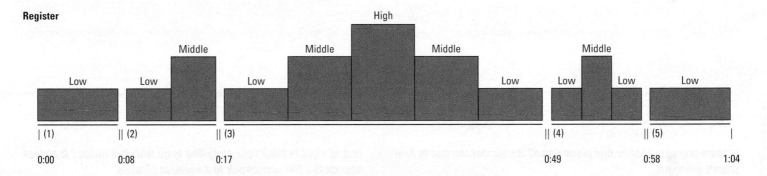

With these points in mind, listen to the work once again, using the Listening Guide.

Listening Guide

Ruth Crawford Composed: 1930
Piano Study in Mixed Accents (1:07)

Time	Form: Section	Melody: Register	Texture
0:00	1	Low	Monophonic
0:08	2	Low → Middle	
0:17	3	Low → High → Low	
0:49	4	Low → Middle → Low	
0:58	5	Low	

Q Student FAQs ⚙

Is there any way to slow this piece down? It's almost too fast to hear what's going on.

The speed is part of what makes this piece so challenging and exciting. Don't fight it: Accept it on its own terms and let it carry you along. It might help to think of this work as a piece that travels through the dimension of space, starting low, moving upward, and returning back to where it started. Multiple listenings will help, too.

Is it all right to think up a story line to go with this music? It almost sounds like the soundtrack to a scene in a movie.

Absolutely. You're free to associate whatever you hear with whatever you wish at any time, keeping in mind that the associations will be more meaningful if they relate in some concrete way with the musical elements of the work itself.

HISTORICAL CONTEXT Twelve-Tone Composition

Ruth Crawford's efforts to avoid giving prominence to any one particular note in a melodic line is typical of those modernist composers determined to cut all ties to conventional notions of tonality. The most widely used means for avoiding such repetition was developed in the 1920s by Arnold Schoenberg (see Chapter 47). He called this system **12-tone composition** because its fundamental basis is a series ("row") of the 12 notes in the chromatic scale (A-A#-B-C-C#-D, etc., up through G#). Here is the row for one of Schoenberg's early 12-tone works, the Suite for Piano, op. 25:

Row starting on E

Same row transposed, starting on B♭

E F G D♭ G♭ E♭ A♭ D B C A B♭

Rows could be written forward or backward, or even inverted (a sort of "mirror" image of the row) or inverted *and* backward. Rows could also be transposed to start on different pitches. All these variables allowed the composer considerable freedom but helped ensure that the music written in this system would not unintentionally imply a tonal center.

Twelve-tone composition (or serial composition, as it is sometimes called) was at the cutting edge of Western art music for the middle decades of the twentieth century. Even composers who did not write in this system experimented with it at times. By the 1970s, however, the system had begun to lose its grip on compositional thought, though all student composers continue to learn it as one of many different approaches to writing music.

 EXPAND YOUR PLAYLIST

Women Composers of the Twentieth Century

The opportunities for women composers expanded enormously over the course of the twentieth century. In addition to Ruth Crawford, Germaine Tailleferre (Chapter 54), and Tania León (Chapter 63), these women composers achieved renown:

- **Thea Musgrave** (b. 1928), born in Scotland, has lived in the United States since the 1970s. Some of her best-known works are the operas *Mary, Queen of Scots* and *Pontalba*.

- **Pauline Oliveros** (b. 1932), a native of Houston, has been at the forefront of American experimental music. Her *Sound Patterns*, for *a cappella* chorus, uses phonetic sounds rather than words.

- **Joan Tower** (b. 1938) teaches composition at Bard College in her native New York. Her *Fanfares for the Uncommon Woman* is a response to Aaron Copland's *Fanfare for the Common Man*.

- **Ellen Taaffe Zwilich** (b. 1939), born in Miami, was the first woman composer to win the Pulitzer Prize in music (in 1983), which she received for her *Three Movements for Orchestra* (*Symphony No. 1*).

- **Libby Larsen** (b. 1950) was the first woman to serve as resident composer with a major orchestra (the Minnesota Orchestra). She has written in many genres, including opera (*Frankenstein*) and song (*Songs from Letters: Calamity Jane to Her Daughter Jamey*).

- **Jennifer Higdon** (b. 1962) teaches composition at the Curtis Institute of Music, in Philadelphia. Her *Blue Cathedral*, a one-movement work for orchestra, has won wide praise from critics.

PROFILE   Ruth Crawford (1901–1953)

Modernist Composer and Folk Song Arranger

Ruth Crawford is known today in two fields of music that might at first seem wholly incompatible. She was an uncompromisingly modernist composer (as is evident in her *Piano Study in Mixed Accents*), and she was also an important collector and arranger of American folksongs. Her early career focused on composition. Born in Ohio (East Liverpool) and raised in Indiana (Muncie) and Florida (Jacksonville), she studied composition with Charles Seeger, whom she married in 1932. From that point onward she published her work under the name Ruth Crawford Seeger. While studying musical modernism in Europe, she continued her search for a new idiom different from that of the musical past.

After her return to the United States, Crawford continued to compose, but she began to devote more and more of her attention to collecting, editing, and arranging American folksongs. Part of the drive behind this was musical: Folksongs have captured the imagination of composers and music lovers in many countries for generations. But another element behind her interest in this repertory was social and political. Folk music, as she observed in 1948, "knows and tells what people have thought about the ways of living. It bears many fingermarks. It has been handled roughly and gently. It has been used. . . . It is not 'finished' or crystallized—it invites improvisation and creative aliveness. . . . It invites participation." Her children, Mike Seeger and Peggy Seeger, along with her stepson Pete Seeger, would later become major recording artists of folksong.

Source: Judith Tick, *Ruth Crawford Seeger: A Composer's Search for American Music* (New York: Oxford University Press, 1997), p. 320. By permission of Oxford University Press, USA.

Ruth Crawford, ca. 1930.

 EXPAND YOUR PLAYLIST: CRAWFORD

- *Five Songs to Poems by Carl Sandburg.* Settings of verse by one of America's most beloved poets.

- *String Quartet.* A modernist work based in part on the principles of 12-tone composition.

- *Rissolty Rossolty.* An "American Fantasia" for orchestra, based on folk tunes.

Germaine Tailleferre
Concertino for Harp and Orchestra, finale
Composed: 1927

Not all new music in the early twentieth century rejected the past. Germaine Tailleferre's Concertino for Harp and Orchestra was one of many new works in a Neoclassical style that sought to synthesize traditional applications of harmony, melody, and form with an idiom that was distinctively modern. This chapter presents the last of the work's three movements.

Listen to This First

♪ Melody

How would you characterize the opening melody? Does it seem balanced or unbalanced? Is it regular or irregular in its meter and the length of its phrases? Do the melodies in this piece seem to express intense emotion? ■

🙂 Harmony

Do you feel points of musical arrival and resolution? Does this piece have a harmonic center? In other words, is it tonal or atonal? ■

〰 Timbre

Listen carefully to the variety of timbres throughout the piece. Consider how the differing timbres emerge clearly even when groups of instruments are playing together. ■

▦ Form

Listen for the repeated return of the opening idea in this movement, which is structured as a rondo. ■

Modernism had barely established itself in the early twentieth century before it inspired a counter-reaction. While many composers wanted to write in a new and contemporary style, they were reluctant to discard traditional applications of the elements of music altogether. In the years after World War I, these composers began to develop a style of writing that, although distinctly modern, drew on older uses of melody, harmony, rhythm, and form. They incorporated more traditional ("classical") approaches to their music even while maintaining a modern edge. Rather than look to the nineteenth century for their inspiration—a century that had only recently passed—they turned back to the eighteenth century. This style is known as **Neoclassicism**. The "classic" in "Neoclassical" refers not to the music of the Classical Era specifically, but rather to the eighteenth century in general, including Bach and Handel as well as Haydn and Mozart. Neoclassical composers were not attempting to recreate or imitate past styles, but to incorporate past styles into a contemporary idiom, hence "*neo* (new)" classicism.

Germaine Tailleferre's Concertino for Harp and Orchestra, commissioned and premiered by the Boston Symphony Orchestra in 1927, reflects this new–old style quite well. Its finale reveals the basic characteristics of musical Neoclassicism. While clearly a work of the twentieth century, it draws on older conventions of melody built on the basis of periodic phrase structure (antecedent

LEARNING OBJECTIVES

54.1 Define Neoclassicism.

54.2 Explain how the finale of Tailleferre's Concertino for Harp and Orchestra reflects Neoclassicism in music.

54.3 Describe how the harmony in this finale sounds different from that of the Classical period.

54.4 Listen for the rondo form in the finale of Germaine Tailleferre's Concertino for Harp and Orchestra.

54.5 Discuss the relationship between the solo harp and the orchestra.

54.6 Outline Tailleferre's career as a composer.

54.7 Discuss why artists sometimes refer back to idioms of the past in their works.

and consequent phrases working together; see Chapter 19), tonal harmony, and a clearly audible conventional form. It even includes a fugue (in the contrasting **C** section of the Listening Guide), but in keeping with Neoclassical principles, it is a witty, almost light-hearted fugue, not heavy or particularly serious.

Melody: A Return to Tradition

The structure of the principal melody is quite traditional. It feels very balanced, with clear antecedent and consequent phrases, and it focuses on a clear tonal center.

For the sake of contrast, the second melody (**B**) is less symmetrical in its structure, yet we can still hear how it divides into distinct phrases. The third melody (**C**) does not divide into distinct subunits, but that is because it is the subject of a fugue (see the "Clarity of Form" section), a decidedly traditional way of writing. Even though this work was written in the 1920s, Haydn or Mozart would have felt quite at home with the general shape of all these themes, even if some of the notes would have sounded slightly "off" to them. The **dissonance**, compared to modernist works of the early twentieth century, is minimal. What stands out here is the structural clarity of the melodies and their goal-oriented sense of direction toward a tonal center. These characteristics are basic to Neoclassical melodies.

Tonal Harmony with Modern Inflections

While Haydn or Mozart would have recognized the shape and tonal grounding of Tailleferre's melodies, they would not have written them in exactly the same way. We can hear that this is a twentieth-century piece by its slightly dissonant inflections. The ending of the main melody (1), for example (see the previous notated example), flows into a wind fanfare (0:21–0:24) that sounds tonal but ever so slightly "off." The dissonant harmonies at 0:44–0:55, in turn, sound decidedly "modern," even while remaining within the bounds of tonality. These are small but telling moments: In both instances we hear the tonic, and there is never any real doubt about where we are tonally. But the tonic is inflected. It's a little like hearing someone speak a language with an accent: We understand perfectly well what the person is saying, but we also hear that this is not the standard, "classical" way of speaking. This kind of subtle harmonic inflection helps give the piece its twentieth-century sound, even while keeping it grounded in tradition.

Transparent Timbre

Neoclassical music strives for lightness and clarity, words that aptly describe the timbre of this movement. The harp itself is an unusually bright instrument; it seizes our attention from the very start with a long upward **glissando**, a scale that goes by so fast we almost cannot hear the individual notes. It is a blur, but a very pleasant and bright blur. The opening melody (Theme 1 in the Listening Guide) stands out over minimal accompaniment in the strings; when the strings take over the melody (at 0:24), the harp begins to strum a rapid accompaniment. Thus when the orchestra steps to the forefront, the harp recedes into the background; the two instruments share the music's sonic space and do not compete for it.

Tailleferre also creates a sense of transparency by giving prominent roles to the trumpet (0:34, 0:48, 0:56, 1:19) and flute (1:09, 2:24, 3:39), two instruments that stand out above or cut through the sound of the orchestra as a whole. She also tends to let the individual wind instruments—clarinet, horns, trombones—play individually rather than as a block. The snare drum is the only percussion instrument in the orchestra, and it appears only occasionally. All of this creates the kind of bright, transparent timbre typical of Neoclassicism.

Clarity of Form

The distinctive opening theme returns at regular intervals throughout the movement, separated by a series of contrasting musical ideas. The **rondo form** of the movement is easy to hear, and it evokes a type of finale common to concertos of the late eighteenth century. The themes of the contrasting sections (**B** and **C** in the Listening Guide) are markedly different from each other and from the principal opening idea, making the rondo structure particularly transparent.

With these points in mind, listen to the finale of this work once again, using the Listening Guide.

CONNECT YOUR PLAYLIST

Return to the Past

Find a song that uses elements of older musical styles.

Example: Mark Ronson, featuring Bruno Mars, "Uptown Funk" (2014) This catchy song pays homage to funk and soul styles of the late 1970s and early 1980s.

Germaine Tailleferre Composed: 1927

Concertino for Harp and Orchestra, finale (5:03)

Time	Form: Rondo Section	Melody	Timbre	Harmony
0:00	A	1 = conjunct, moving down and then up; clear antecedent–consequent structure	Harp solo at first with minimal orchestral accompaniment; full orchestra joins in at 0:21.	Strongly tonal, slightly inflected at cadences (0:10) and in wind fanfares.
0:44	B	2 = fragmented, slightly more agitated theme	Harp solo, trumpets interject.	Trumpet interjections are harmonically "off."
1:00	A′	1 returns	Harp carries the main theme.	
1:50	C	3 = fugue theme, disjunct, moves upward	Theme enters in the low strings, other instruments join in gradually from bottom to top.	Harmonies in entering voices do not always match perfectly with each other, though we never lose a sense of the tonic.
3:15	A″	1 returns	Harp takes the lead, then the orchestra carries the theme.	
3:57	B′	2 returns	Harp predominates; trumpets interject.	
4:12	A‴	1 returns	Flutes reintroduce the theme; harp and other instruments follow.	Strong tonic ending

---

🔍 Student FAQs ⚙

Does a soloist always memorize his or her part and perform in public without music?

Usually, but not always. At a professional level, every soloist has internalized the work he or she is playing, but some musicians prefer to have the notated part in front of them, even if they are playing essentially from memory.

Why aren't there more harp concertos?

There should be, but there aren't nearly as many harpists as there are pianists, violinist, clarinetists, or performers of other instruments in the standard orchestra, and so composers have traditionally been less inclined to write for harp and orchestra. The harp is an ancient instrument—it appears repeatedly in the Bible—but it has never figured prominently in the concerto repertory. However, the harp concerto by Alberto Ginastera (a twentieth-century Argentinian composer) is well worth exploring, as is Mozart's Concerto for Flute and Harp, K. 299.

PROFILE   Germaine Tailleferre (1895–1978)

One of Six

Germaine Tailleferre was the only woman in a group of young French composers of the 1920s who called themselves *Les six* ("The Six"). The six knew each other personally—Tailleferre, Georges Auric, Arthur Honegger, and Darius Milhaud had all studied counterpoint in the same class at the Paris Conservatory in 1917—but the music they wrote differed widely in style. What united them was their youth and their devotion to the idea of continuing a tradition of writing music that was distinctively French. This was particularly important in the wake of World War I, when French composers were anxious to establish a style free from German influence. In the case of "The Six," this meant writing music that was, among other things, lighter, more transparent, and less emotionally charged. For Tailleferre and others of the group, works like Schoenberg's *Pierrot lunaire* stood for everything music should not be.

Tailleferre first came to promise as a pianist, and her music (including the Concertino for Harp) reflects her understanding of the illustrious tradition of French composers who had written for the harpsichord in

"The Six" plus one. Jean Cocteau, the celebrated poet, novelist, and playwright, is seated at the piano: He was not a member of the group but helped publicize their cause. Standing are (from left to right) Darius Milhaud, Georges Auric, Arthur Honegger, Germaine Tailleferre, Francis Poulenc, and Louis Durey.

the seventeenth and eighteenth centuries. Much of Tailleferre's music from the 1920s incorporates the same sense of clarity and playfulness so typical of this earlier repertory. She later went on to write operas, ballets, incidental music to plays, film scores, choral music, songs, and a large quantity of music for solo piano.

EXPAND YOUR PLAYLIST: TAILLEFERRE

- **Harp Sonata.** For solo harp, also in a Neoclassical style.
- ***Partita.*** A three-movement work for chamber ensemble, a haunting mixture of Baroque and modern styles.
- ***Chansons populaires françaises.*** "French Popular Songs" for voice and chamber ensemble.

- **Piano Concerto no. 1.** A Neoclassical concerto for orchestra and piano.
- **Concerto Grosso for two pianos, female vocal quartet, male vocal quartet, saxophone quartet, and orchestra.** A work with a Baroque-sounding title for an unusual combination of forces.

Art is almost always a mixture of old and new. Few works of art ignore the past entirely, and few are entirely novel. But some works rely more openly on past traditions than others, and often for a reason. The Supreme Court building in Washington, D.C., for example, openly evokes the architectural style of ancient Greece because the style of the architecture is meant to create an implicit link to ancient Athens, the first great democracy in the Western world. Yet the building was not completed until 1935. Architects at the time could just as easily have designed something in a more contemporary style. The Empire State Building, a sleek, thoroughly modernist building, had opened its doors for business four years earlier. But this is not the message the government wanted to send. The law is based on principles of consistency, and the government wanted a building that would convey these ideals. A modernist Supreme Court might have conveyed the impression that the institution was heading in a new direction. So the Supreme Court today works in a building that from the outside, at least, looks like it might have been built some 2,500 years ago.

Music operates along much the same lines. What message would a modernist national anthem send? Could a large public

The U.S. Supreme Court building. Its Neoclassical architecture evokes the democratic ideals of ancient Greece.

gathering be expected to sing an atonal melody? Why are national anthems invariably tonal and metrically regular? The same questions could be asked about college fight songs and alma maters, hymns, or love songs.

 EXPAND YOUR PLAYLIST

Neoclassicism

Germaine Tailleferre belonged to a generation of composers who came of age during and after World War I, a war of unprecedented horror that included chemical warfare and widespread destruction. Many artists and audiences alike sought a return to what they called a more "civilized" kind of art, one that did not turn its back on the best traditions of the past. Some composers, like Stravinsky, could write in both modernist and Neoclassical styles. Indeed, Stravinsky is widely considered the key figure in the emergence of Neoclassicism in music.

Igor Stravinsky

- *L'Histoire du soldat.* "The Soldier's Tale" is a theater piece for three characters (who recite but do not sing), a small instrumental ensemble, and a dancer. It tells the story of a soldier returning from war and trading his violin with the devil for a magic book.

Sergei Prokofiev

- *Classical Symphony.* Openly indebted to the style of Haydn and Mozart, even in its title, this is a symphony that follows the standard pattern of four movements. It is squarely tonal yet at the same time decidedly a work of the early twentieth century.

Maurice Ravel

- *Le tombeau de Couperin.* "The Tomb of Couperin" is a piano suite in homage to—and somewhat in the style of—François Couperin, a French composer of keyboard music in the early eighteenth century.

Darius Milhaud

- *Scaramouche.* This suite for two pianos exemplifies Milhaud's own estimation of his musical style as one of "clarity, soberness, lightness . . . [a] sense for the proportions of the outlines, and aspiration to express oneself clearly, simply, and succinctly."

Paul Hindemith

- *Kleine Kammermusik.* German composer Paul Hindemith's "Little Chamber Music" is a concerto for small wind ensemble that uses the melodic and rhythmic structures of Baroque music, but with twentieth-century harmonies.

William Grant Still

"A Black Pierrot" from *Songs of Separation*

Composed: 1949

The text of this song takes up the same imagery Arnold Schoenberg used in *Pierrot lunaire* (see Chapter 47), but with a twist. In this text by African American poet Langston Hughes (1902–1967), the quintessentially pale-white figure of Pierrot is black. As in Schoenberg's "Columbine," Pierrot has again been rejected, but instead of seeking more whiteness, he creeps away into the night ("and the night was black, too") to "seek a new brown love."

Listen to This First))

👤 Harmony	🎵 Melody	🏛 Form
Does the music sound tonal, atonal, or somewhere in between? ■	Listen for the changes in register throughout. Where is the highest note of the vocal line? What passages in the song suggest the style of the blues? ■	Does the same music appear with each strophe, or is there new music for each strophe? ■

Like Schoenberg's Pierrot, Still's lovelorn clown is never successful in his amorous pursuits. But Still's Pierrot conveys the same profound sense of insecurity and quiet desperation in a very different musical style: The musical language is tonal, with melodic inflections borrowed from the blues. This "Black Pierrot" expresses himself in an idiom that at once mixes traditions of the **art song** used by composers such as Schubert and Schumann (see Chapter 31 and Chapter 35) with traditions more closely associated with African American music (for example, Robert Johnson—see Chapter 50).

Chromatic Harmony

From the very first puzzling, unsettled chord in the piano, we suspect this piece won't offer much comfort in the way of a home key. The octave notes that follow do little more to establish a tonic. When the voice enters, it starts in a low register with a simple statement ("I am a black Pierrot"), but it moves in wholly unpredictable directions. It wavers between major and minor and seems to change its mood constantly. And yet interspersed throughout this first, searching strophe we do hear sounds that we recognize and chords that give us moments of harmonic stability, even if they are only brief ones.

LEARNING OBJECTIVES

55.1 Identify William Grant Still's "A Black Pierrot" from *Songs of Separation* as an art song in the tradition of the German Lied, but with a poem from the Harlem Renaissance.

55.2 Listen for the blues elements and chromatic harmony in "A Black Pierrot."

55.3 Define through-composed.

55.4 Listen for the through-composed form of Still's "A Black Pierrot."

55.5 Outline Still's career as a composer and his "firsts" in the field.

55.6 Discuss the Harlem Renaissance.

The style of harmony Still employs here is called **chromatic**; it is tonal, but it has strong inflections that make the tonic less powerful. A chromatic scale consists entirely of half steps.

It therefore implies no tonal center. (In the same way, a scale consisting entirely of whole steps implies no tonal center—see Chapter 45.) To create a tonic sound, a scale must contain mostly whole steps and a few strategically placed half steps—as, for example, the familiar major and minor scales do. But additional half steps have the effect of obscuring the tonic. In this song, Still uses a melody based on a standard major scale, but he uses many additional half steps to make the tonic seem less clear, less "solid."

When we do hear the tonic in this song, it stands out quite clearly. It appears most strongly in the middle of the second stanza and again at the end (see the Listening Guide). Listen to the contrasting sense of tonal stability in these passages compared with the chromatic instability of the others. The harmonizations at the end of the very end of the song are particularly intense. While the voice stays in the tonic, the piano harmonizes in a highly chromatic fashion, using lots of half steps to pointedly avoid the tonic. Even the very last harmony of the work—normally a tonic—never really resolves. The effect is strangely haunting.

Melody: A Touch of Blue

The melody, always in the voice, is chromatic throughout, wandering and weaving around the notes of the chromatic scale. Like the harmony, it rarely establishes a firm sense of arrival, and when it does land on a point of stability, it does not stay there very long. Only at the end of the song do we hear an extended point of arrival.

The melody also shows certain affinities at points to the blues; this is, after all, the song of a rejected lover. When the music finally lands squarely on the tonic for the first time, for example (on the word "black" in "black Pierrot" at 0:40), we hear what sounds rather like a "blue note," a note that is slightly lower than its given pitch in a standard scale. The **walking bass** (the steady stepwise line in the bass) and the off-beat chords in the piano also help to evoke the spirit of the blues.

Still also uses changes of register in the vocal line to emphasize important moments in the text. The first strophe moves gradually from a low to a high register, the second occupies a middle range, and the third moves from high to low and back to high again, hitting the highest note of the entire song at the very end—the emotional climax of the song.

Through-Composed Form

In spite of a good deal of textual repetition between strophes—each strophe begins with the same two lines, and the first word of the third line ("So") is also the same—there is very little repetition or even variation of musical ideas in this song. Instead, each strophe receives its own musical setting. This type of form is called **through-composed**, in which the composer uses distinctly new music from beginning to end. Through-composed form differs from strophic form (same music for each strophe) and modified strophic form (a variation of the same music for each strophe).

Through-composed form was not new in the twentieth century; composers had been using this approach to setting texts for centuries. But it is one of the devices that tends to distinguish the art song repertory from that of popular song, which tends to use strophic or modified strophic form.

With these points in mind, listen to this song once again, using the Listening Guide.

CONNECT YOUR PLAYLIST

Through-Composed Form

Find a work in through-composed form.

Example: Queen, "Bohemian Rhapsody" (1975)
This song by Queen does not use a typical verse-chorus format, but instead has very different sections of music that proceed one after another.

Listening Guide

William Grant Still Composed: 1949

"A Black Pierrot" from *Songs of Separation* (2:26)

Because of copyright issues, the text of this song cannot be reproduced here.

Time	Form	Harmony	Melody
0:00	Strophe 1	Avoids landing on the tonic clearly.	Voice line moves from a low to high register.
0:37	Strophe 2	Establishes tonic clearly finally at 0:48, but then starts moving away from it again after 0:58.	The voice line stays in the middle register.
1:16	Strophe 3	The last two lines are repeated three times, with the voice and piano both in the tonic the first two times, but only the voice in the tonic the third time (from 2:00 onward), with the piano harmonizing against and not with the tonic key.	Moves from high to low and back to high again, reaching the highest note of the entire song at the very end.

🔍 Student FAQs ⚙

Schoenberg's Pierrot is sung by a female, Still's by a male. Why is that?

Still's setting preserves the male persona of Pierrot. Schoenberg's creates an even greater sense of distance between the character (Pierrot, a male) and the singer (a female). Which approach is more effective in setting texts like these? That is a matter of debate.

Did Langston Hughes and William Grant Still collaborate on these settings?

No. While the two were acquainted, Still set a text that Hughes had written more than 20 years before. It is also worth remembering that Still had to pay royalties to Hughes for using his texts in these new songs.

Langston Hughes.

PROFILE   William Grant Still (1895–1978)

A Career of Firsts

In an age when the world of the American concert hall was still largely closed to African American composers and musicians, William Grant Still compiled a remarkable record of "firsts." He was the first African American composer to have a symphony performed by a major orchestra (*Afro-American Symphony*, Rochester Philharmonic, 1931), the first to conduct a major American orchestra (the Los Angeles Philharmonic, in 1936), and the first to have an opera performed by a major American opera company (*Troubled Island*, New York City Opera, 1949).

Born in Woodville, Mississippi, Still was raised in Little Rock, Arkansas. After attending Wilberforce University, he studied composition at Oberlin Conservatory and the New England Conservatory of Music. (This was not a first: These schools, and others like them north of the Mason-Dixon line, had been accepting African American students for many decades, even if not in great numbers.) Still worked in New York City throughout the 1920s, arranging music for jazz bands and dance orchestra while launching his career as a composer. He moved to Los Angeles in the early 1930s and spent the rest of his life there, composing and arranging music for films and writing works for the stage and concert hall. In many of his works he sought to create an idiom that blended such African American idioms as spirituals or the blues into more traditionally European genres like the symphony, the opera, and the ballet.

William Grant Still, ca. 1930.

EXPAND YOUR PLAYLIST: STILL

- **Songs of Separation.** The complete cycle of songs for voice and piano.
- **Africa.** For piano.
- **Symphony no. 1 (*Afro-American Symphony*).** Uses blues progressions.

- **Troubled Island.** An opera.
- **And They Lynched Him on a Tree.** For chorus.

HISTORICAL CONTEXT The Harlem Renaissance

William Grant Still and poet Langston Hughes are only two of the many African American artists associated with a movement known as the "Harlem Renaissance." During the 1920s, Harlem—in upper Manhattan, in New York City—emerged as a kind of cultural capital of African American arts, including literature, painting, and music. Other artists associated with the Harlem Renaissance include writers Zora Neale Hurston and Wallace Thurman, entertainers Josephine Baker and Paul Robeson, and composer-musician Duke Ellington (see Chapter 51). Many works by these artists, including Langston Hughes's poem "A Black Pierrot," openly celebrated African American identity. In many ways, the Harlem Renaissance brought African American art into the American mainstream.

Culture and politics, never too distant from one another, were closely allied in the Harlem Renaissance. Artists and the public alike recognized that the production of art by African American artists could help promote the struggle for racial equality. Poet James Weldon Johnson (author of the lyrics to "Lift Ev'ry Voice and Sing") was a longtime activist in the National Association for the Advancement of Colored People (NAACP); singer Paul Robeson would later become an important leader in the civil rights movement.

Poet Langston Hughes in front of his home in Harlem, New York City.

 EXPAND YOUR PLAYLIST

Twentieth-Century African American Composers in the Western Classical Tradition

In addition to William Grant Still, Scott Joplin (see Chapter 49), Duke Ellington (see Chapter 51), and Tania León (see Chapter 63), many African American composers have established their place in the concert hall, writing in genres and idioms associated with the Western classical tradition.

Florence Beatrice Price (1887–1953)
• Price was born in Little Rock, Arkansas, and studied at the New England Conservatory. A number of her works incorporate Negro spirituals, including her *Mississippi River Suite*.

Henry T. Burleigh (1866–1949)
• Burleigh was born in Erie, Pennsylvania. He taught Czech composer Antonín Dvořák about the music of African Americans during Dvořák's years in the United States (see Chapter 44). He wrote many art songs that use melodies from Negro spirituals, including *Deep River*.

Margaret Bonds (1913–1972)
• Although she was born in Chicago, she spent most of her life in New York City. She was a friend of Langston Hughes and set many of his texts to music, including *Three Dream Portraits*.

George Walker (b. 1922)
• Born in Washington, D.C., Walker studied composition at Oberlin College and the Eastman School of Music. He was the first African American composer to win the Pulitzer Prize in music (in 1996) for his *Lilacs*, a work for voice and orchestra.

Keith Jarrett (b. 1945)
• Born in Allentown, Pennsylvania, he performs and composes in many different styles, including jazz, gospel, and classical. His *Elegy for Violin and Strings*, written for his Hungarian grandmother, uses idioms often associated with gypsy music.

Aaron Copland

"Hoe-Down" from *Rodeo*
Composed: 1942

How do you create the sense of a place through music alone, without words or images? Aaron Copland did just that in his *Rodeo* (pronounced "ro-DAY-oh") when he captured the sound of the American West in a ballet. "Hoe-Down" is a scene from that ballet.

Listen to This First

🎵 Melody

How long before you hear something in this work that actually sounds like a real melody? And when it finally arrives, what is it like? Is it conjunct or disjunct—that is, does it move by steps or by leaps? What about other melodies that come in later on? ■

〰 Timbre

This work is for a large orchestra, but how often do you actually hear all the instruments playing? Listen for long passages with smaller groupings of instruments within the orchestra. ■

🎲 Rhythm

Listen to the way the meter is simple at times, complex at others. Some sections are in straightforward duple meter, while others are full of syncopation (off-beat accents). ■

🎹 Form

Listen for the repeated return of the opening section's main idea and the contrast with sections based on other melodies. This movement is a rondo. ■

Copland composed *Rodeo* at the request of the dancer Agnes de Mille, who choreographed the work and danced the lead role. The story takes place somewhere in the American West and centers on the Cowgirl, who is determined to win the heart of the Head Wrangler. The Head Wrangler is unimpressed with the Cowgirl's prowess with ropes and horses. Not until the concluding Hoe-down—the big Saturday night dance—does she succeed in catching his eye (and his heart), having traded her cowboy outfit for a dress. De Mille once jokingly described the scenario as "The Taming of the Shrew—cowboy style." Shortly after completing the ballet, Copland extracted four scenes to be played in concert settings, of which "Hoe-Down" is the last.

Copland creates an identifiably American sound in this movement by using actual folk tunes that are rhythmically vigorous and cover a wide range. He also orchestrates his music in an extremely open fashion—that is, he uses the full range of registers from highest to lowest and leaves as much space as possible between groups of instruments. This "open scoring," as musicians refer to it, creates a kind of sonic counterpart to the open spaces of the American West.

LEARNING OBJECTIVES

56.1 Describe the connection between the ballet *Rodeo* and the American West.

56.2 Identify the main theme of Aaron Copland's "Hoe-Down" from *Rodeo* as one derived from American folk music.

56.3 Describe Copland's distinctive orchestration in "Hoe-Down."

56.4 Listen for Copland's use of rondo form in *Rodeo*.

56.5 Explain how later composers have reworked the fiddle tune Copland used in "Hoe-Down."

56.6 Discuss Copland's career in light of the political currents of his time.

HISTORICAL CONTEXT   Using "Hoe-Down"

Copland's reworking of a traditional fiddle tune in "Hoe-Down" has been used in a number of very different ways, from movie soundtracks to TV ads to the Olympics:

1. The British rock group Emerson, Lake, and Palmer recorded their version of the tune, called "Hoedown," on the 1972 album *Trilogy*. The album reached number 5 on Billboard's chart at one point.

2. In the early 1990s, the National Cattlemen's Beef Association and Beef Board began using Copland's version of the tune as the musical backdrop for a series of television commercials with the tagline "Beef: It's What's for Dinner."

3. The director Spike Lee used Copland's version in the soundtrack to the 1998 film *He Got Game*. Actually,

Lee used several of Copland's works in the soundtrack. "When I listen to Copland's music," Lee explained, "I hear America, and basketball is America. It's like he wrote the score for this film."

4. In 2000, the bluegrass-jazz group Béla Fleck and the Flecktones recorded their own version of the tune on *Outbound*.

5. The opening ceremony of the 2002 Winter Olympics, in Salt Lake City, used Copland's version from *Rodeo* as a backdrop to an enormous hoe-down with hundreds of dancers.

6. In 2006, Bob Dylan used a recording of Copland's "Hoe-Down" for his stage entrance at live performances.

CONNECT YOUR PLAYLIST

Folk Music

Find a piece that reworks a folk song or folk tune.

Example: Shirley Manson, "If I Had My Way" (2008)
Manson updated the traditional gospel song "Samson and Delilah" popularized by the Rev. Gary Davis in a brooding rock arrangement for the film *Terminator: The Sarah Connor Chronicles*.

 ## Folk Melodies

The opening melody—and the one that keeps returning in this movement—is a traditional fiddle tune called "Bonaparte's Retreat." Alan Lomax, a folklorist, recorded a version of it by "Fiddler Bill" Stepp (1875–1957) in eastern Kentucky in 1937. Ruth Crawford Seeger (see Chapter 53) transcribed the recording for Alan and John Lomax's anthology *Our Singing Country* (1941). Copland found the melody in this collection (called "Bonyparte" there), orchestrated it, and incorporated it into the larger movement he called "Hoe-Down." He introduces the theme gradually by first presenting only a small portion of it at the very beginning, followed by the sounds of a square-dance band tuning up. Only later do we hear the main melody in its full form. The music stays squarely in the tonic in this opening section, in keeping with the mood of a folk dance.

The jaunty, disjunct (leaping) melody in the middle of the movement (**C** in the Listening Guide) is also based on a traditional fiddling tune. Copland found this melody, called "McLeod's Reel," in another published anthology of American folk tunes. Like "Bonaparte's Retreat," it contributes to the identifiably American sound of "Hoe-Down."

 ## Timbre: Smaller Ensembles within the Orchestra

Copland creates variety within this movement by varying the orchestration throughout. At times we hear the full ensemble—a big orchestra, with a large percussion section of timpani, piano, xylophone, snare drum, bass drum, cymbal, and wood block—and at other times we hear a reduced ensemble of only a few instruments. The piano is a relative newcomer to the orchestra; Copland uses it sparingly but to good effect by imitating the sound of a piano one would typically hear in a Western dance-hall.

The timbres are noticeably bright and transparent. Even though Copland is writing for a large orchestra, he allows the individual instruments or groups of instruments to come through clearly because he writes in what might be called sonic layers, with each instrumental grouping projecting its own identity. Listen to the groups of sounds at the very opening: The strings are clearly divided into low and high groupings that are distinct from each other and distinct yet again from the brass instruments, which themselves are clearly divided into high and low groupings. This kind of writing helps reinforce the contrast of sound between these layers. And, like many twentieth-century composers writing for orchestra, Copland also gives unusual prominence to the percussion instruments. The notion of giving a fiddle tune to a xylophone (at 0:34, for example) creates a particularly penetrating sound.

Agnes de Mille as the Cowgirl and Frederic Franklin as the Head Wrangler in the original production of Copland's *Rodeo*, New York, 1942.

 ## Dance Rhythms

A hoe-down is an energetic, duple-meter dance that has come to be associated particularly with the tradition of Western square dancing, and Copland maintains duple meter throughout. But he varies the beat by presenting some sections in clearly demarcated duple meter while introducing a high degree of **syncopation** into other sections. Consider the opening melody ("Bonaparte's Retreat"): Copland accents the highest notes of the tune whenever it leaps upward. Or listen to the main melody when first presented by the full orchestra: The brass instruments come in consistently off the beat, and this creates a sense of forward momentum that would otherwise be lacking.

 ## Rondo Form

Copland constructs this dance in the form of a **rondo**. The main theme (**A**), or at least parts of it, alternates with contrasting melodic ideas. The opening is particularly clever: Copland captures the spirit and even the sequence of events in a Western-style dance by having the orchestra "tune up" early on, and by presenting accompanimental patterns but no real melodies until about half a minute into the piece: The ensemble is getting ready, but it takes a little while for it to get into the full swing of things. Only with the first return of the **A** section do we hear the main theme in its entirety for the first time. We've been anticipating it, and the orchestra has been hinting at it, but only now do we actually hear it.

Now listen to this music again, using the Listening Guide.

Aaron Copland Composed: 1942

"Hoe-Down" from *Rodeo* (3:05)

Time	Form: Section	🎵 Melody	〰 Timbre	🥁 Rhythm
0:00	**A**	Fanfare-like figure in the brass, swirling figures in the strings; then (0:04) an imitation of instruments being tuned in the strings, but no real melody yet.	Full orchestra	No clear sense of meter, much syncopation.
0:15	**B**	Dance-like accompaniment, but still no clear melody.	Piano bass line, wood blocks, imitation of a dance-hall double bass in the lower strings.	Clear duple meter
0:34	**A′**	Same swirling figure as in **A**, but now it continues to present the main melody of the movement, a rapid, energetic theme that swoops down and then up.	Violins play the melody as if it were being played on a country fiddle (0:42). Prominent parts for oboe (0:58) and xylophone (throughout).	Duple meter, but with syncopation in some voices.
1:25	**C**	Jaunty, disjunct melody with large upward leap.	Solo trumpet (1:25), solo oboe (1:33), solo violin (1:36), then the full orchestra (1:40).	Duple meter, no syncopation at first; then increasing syncopation as brass enter (1:47) and grow stronger.
2:07	**B′**	Dance-like accompaniment, again without any clear melody.	Piano bass line, wood blocks (2:09); trombone (2:15); strings and celesta (2:30).	Duple meter, no syncopation. Tempo gradually slows down, as if the music is running out of energy.
2:32	**A′**	Main melody returns	Full orchestra	Tempo returns to its original fast pace. Duple meter with much syncopation.

🔍 **Student FAQs** ⚙

What was Agnes de Mille's choreography of *Rodeo* **like?**

From still pictures, her notes, and eyewitness accounts, we know that de Mille's choreography combined the free movements of modern dance with more traditional elements of folk dancing and square dancing. Unfortunately, we have no film version of how she and her troupe performed this ballet.

This music is used so often and in so many places (see "Historical Context: Using 'Hoe-Down'"). Who gets the royalties today?

The royalties go to Aaron Copland's estate, which funds a program that allows individual composers to spend six weeks in residence at the house in which Copland lived for the last 30 years of his life, in Cortlandt, New York, in Westchester County, just north of New York City.

PROFILE   Aaron Copland (1900–1990)

Populist Modernist

Born in Brooklyn, Aaron Copland came of age in the 1920s and 1930s. He was consumed with the idea of writing "American music." Like so many of his contemporaries, he was trained in the European tradition, and he could write in the style of cutting-edge modernists when he wanted to. Yet he was politically and emotionally a populist at heart. He never lost touch with his American roots, using actual folk tunes in such works as *Rodeo* and *Appalachian Spring*. He also wrote music for a number of Hollywood films, including *Our Town*, *Of Mice and Men*, and *The Heiress*, for which he won an Oscar.

In addition to his work as a composer, Copland was also a superb lecturer and writer on music. His *What to Listen for in Music* remains a model of its kind.

Aaron Copland in 1945, shortly after completing the ballet *Rodeo*.

EXPAND YOUR PLAYLIST: COPLAND

- **Fanfare for the Common Man.** A short but memorable work, often used (like "Hoe-Down") in commercials.
- **Appalachian Spring.** A ballet written for Martha Graham, celebrating the virtues of frontier life.
- **Lincoln Portrait.** For narrator and orchestra, using Lincoln's own words as a spoken text.
- **Twelve Poems of Emily Dickinson.** For solo voice and piano.

HISTORICAL CONTEXT   The Politics of Culture

It is ironic that Aaron Copland, whose music has been so strongly identified with America, was the most prominent composer brought before Congress to testify in the McCarthy hearings of the early 1950s. Senator Joseph McCarthy was convinced that Communists and Communist sympathizers had infiltrated the U.S. government. The arts of all kinds, including music, were part of the Cold War effort to fight the influence of the Soviet Union, and Copland was an ideal ambassador for American culture. But he had also belonged to several musical groups that fostered contacts between American and Soviet composers, and this brought him—and many other artists—under the suspicion of being a "Communist sympathizer."

Copland protested strenuously that participation in such groups was based entirely on his concern with cultural and musical affairs. But the taint of association lingered, and Copland had trouble securing a passport to travel abroad for several years. When his *Lincoln Portrait* was performed on television's *Ed Sullivan Show* in 1956, Ed Sullivan pointedly did not identify the composer of the work. With time, however, Copland regained his status as an iconic American composer. In 1986, the same Congress that had investigated him 30 years earlier awarded him the Congressional Gold Medal, its highest civilian honor.

This photo of Copland was taken at the Cultural and Scientific Conference for World Peace held in New York in 1949. Congress would later grill Copland about his participation in this event, which sought to build cultural bridges between East and West.

 EXPAND YOUR PLAYLIST

The Sound of the American West

Rodeo was one of several works by Copland to evoke the American West, and other composers were quick to follow his lead in using sonic layers to create an open sound reflecting the open spaces of the region.

Aaron Copland
- *Billy the Kid*. A ballet commissioned by choreographer Lincoln Kirsten in 1938.
- *The Red Pony*. A film score to the 1949 movie, starring Robert Mitchum and Myrna Loy, based on the short story by John Steinbeck.

Ferde Grofé
- *Grand Canyon Suite*. A suite for orchestra, composed in 1931. Each of the five movements paints in sound a scene from the Grand Canyon.

Dmitri Tiomkin
- *High Noon*. The film score won an Academy Award both for best song ("Do Not Forsake Me, Oh My Darlin'") and for best soundtrack. Tiomkin was a Ukrainian who did not arrive in the United States until the age of 31.

Elmer Bernstein
- *The Magnificent Seven*. The main title theme has been used in innumerable commercials and is instantly recognizable as a sonic icon of the Old West.

Enrico Morricone
- *The Good, the Bad, and the Ugly*. One of the Italian composer's many scores for "spaghetti Westerns," so called because the films were produced and often directed by Italian artists (in this case, Sergio Leone). Morricone received a Lifetime Achievement Award at the 2007 Oscars ceremony for his film scores.

Béla Bartók

Concerto for Orchestra, second movement ("Game of Pairs")

Composed: 1943

Most concertos showcase the abilities of a soloist or small group of soloists, but in his *Concerto for Orchestra*, Béla Bartók created a work that allows all the instruments of the orchestra to come to the fore at different times. The style of the music reflects his lifelong interest in folk music not only from his native Hungary, but from other regions of Europe and the world as well.

Listen to This First 🔊

〰 Timbre

Listen for the variety of instrumental sounds, beginning with a succession of prominent passages by the woodwinds (first bassoons, then oboes, clarinets, and flutes), and then brass instruments (trumpets, trombones, horns, tuba). A small side drum introduces and ends the movement. ∎

🎵 Melody

Listen for phrases and cadences within each melody. Also listen for a tonal center in each: do these melodies have a tonal center, or are they atonal? ∎

🏛 Form

Listen for the large-scale A-B-A′ form: the opening section with the woodwinds returns in varied form about two-thirds of the way through the movement. Where does the "B" section begin? How is A′ different from the original A? ∎

Bartók's *Concerto for Orchestra* is one the most frequently performed of all twentieth-century orchestral works. Popular with audiences and performers alike, it gives every instrument a chance to shine. Bartók's style of writing reflects his fascination with the melodies and rhythms characteristic of eastern European folk music idioms.

〰 Wind Timbres

The second movement, titled *Giuoco delle coppie* ("Game of Pairs") features a series of statements by woodwind and brass instruments introduced mostly in pairs. The "game" element stems from the playful nature of the music; there is a loose, almost carefree feeling to the way each pair of instruments steps up to the spotlight and then gives way to the next pair. One might almost imagine this movement as a series of paired dancers who emerge out of a crowd to take center stage for a brief time and then recede back into the crowd.

LEARNING OBJECTIVES

57.1 Identify the instruments that come to the fore in each section of the second movement of Béla Bartók's *Concerto for Orchestra*.

57.2 Listen for the broadly symmetrical form of the movement.

57.3 Identify the form based on instrumental timbre in this movement.

57.4 Describe the work of ethnomusicologists and explain how Bartók's work was influenced by folk music of various kinds.

57.5 Outline Bartók's career as a scholar-composer-performer.

Listen for the contrast of timbres among these instruments:

- **Bassoons**   (0:12). A double-reed instrument in the lower register, with a gruff, slightly raspy sound.

- **Oboes**   (0:36). Another double-reed instrument, in a higher range, with a somewhat more piercing, nasal sound.

- **Clarinets**   (1:05). A single-reed instrument with a wide range and a resonant timbre.

- **Flutes**   (1:27). A woodwind instrument (though nowadays mostly made of metal) without a reed. The flute features a delicate, "breathy" sound in a relatively high register.

- **Trumpets**   (2:12). A brass instrument with a high register and a sharp sound. At first, each trumpet here plays with a mute, a "stopper" placed in the bell of the instrument, which creates a softer, more subdued timbre. At (3:12) the trumpets remove the mutes.

- **Trombones and Tuba**   (3:12). These low brass instruments join the trumpets and play quietly here, producing a rounded, mellow tone.

- **Horns**   (3:48). Also a member of the brass family, the horns (also known as "French horns") playing in the background here, quietly.

Source: Score of "A Game of Pairs" from Bela Bartok, *Concerto for Orchestra*, SZ116. Copyright © 1946 Hawkes & Son (London) Ltd. Reproduced by permission of Boosey & Hawkes Music Publishers Ltd.

From 4:18 onward, the same instruments return in varied form but now in groups of three (three bassoons) or in combination with one another (two oboes and two clarinets together at 4:42; then two flutes and two clarinets together at 5:17). Listen for the combinations of timbres throughout. Two harps join in for the first time, discreetly, at 5:53.

Folk-Inflected Melodies

Throughout his life, Bartók collected and sometimes used in his works melodies played and sung by folk musicians from his native Hungary, eastern Europe, and even as far away as northern Africa and the Middle East. Although the *Concerto for Orchestra* does not use any specific melodies collected by the composer, its thematic ideas, rhythmic patterns, and harmonies are shaped by sounds that clearly derive from sources outside the tradition of Western art music. The opening theme on the bassoons (0:12), according to one scholar familiar with this repertory of folk music, imitates a round dance melody popular in the Balkans. The slightly menacing-sounding melody played by the muted trumpets (2:12) is harmonized largely in seconds (think of the opening of "Chopsticks") rather than the more conventional thirds (think of the first change in harmony just after the opening of "Chopsticks"). This kind of harmonization in seconds is common among certain ethnic repertories of eastern Europe. The resulting idiom is tonal, but not in a conventional way: While there is a tonal center, the melodies and the associated harmonies do not follow the practices of "standard" repertory by composers like Beethoven, Schumann, or Brahms.

Asymmetrical–Symmetrical Form

The second movement is in **ternary form** (ABA′) and in many respects resembles a minuet from a classical symphony (see, for example, Haydn's Symphony no. 102; see Chapter 24), with a sharply contrasting middle section. But here, the return of the "A" section is far from literal: While the themes are recognizably the same as those heard before, they are altered in subtle ways and presented with new combinations of instruments.

The resulting form is basically symmetrical. Bartók held a lifelong fascination with the idea of musical symmetry at many levels; he liked melodies that balanced on a central axis, moving toward and away from a central point. He also frequently constructed entire movements—including this one—around a central point, with a beginning and ending that "mirror" each other. The solo side drum opens and closes the movement, and the woodwind sections (A and A′) surround the central brass section (B):

Introduction	A	B	A′	Coda
Side drum	Woodwinds	Brass	Woodwinds	Side drum
0:00	0:12	3:12	4:18	6:42

Within this basic framework of symmetry, Bartók varies the return of the A′ by changing both the instrumentation and the manipulation of the thematic ideas heard earlier in the movement. The result is a movement that is both symmetrical and asymmetrical at one and the same time.

Now listen to this music again, using the Listening Guide.

CONNECT YOUR PLAYLIST

Symmetrical Form

Find a work whose ending is either very similar or identical to its beginning.

Example: Muse, "Bliss" (2010)
The soft section that opens "Bliss" returns at the end of the song.

Listening Guide

Béla Bartók Composed: 1943

Concerto for Orchestra, second movement ("Game of Pairs") (6:47)

Time	🎵 Melody	〰 Timbre: Solo Instruments	〰 Timbre: Supporting Instruments	🏛 Form
0:00		Side drum	None	Introduction
0:12	1	Bassoons (2)	Strings, pizzicato (plucked)	A
0:36	2	Oboes (2)	Strings, both pizzicato and bowed	
1:05	3	Clarinets (2)		
1:27	4	Flutes (2)		
2:12	5	Trumpets (2)		
2:57		Side drum		Transition
3:02	6	Brass choir: Trumpets with mutes (2), trombones (2), tuba	Side drum	B
3:48		Brass choir: Horns (4), tuba		
4:09	1	Woodwinds return one by one		Transition
4:18	1	Bassoons (3)	Strings, pizzicato (plucked)	A'
4:42	3	Oboes (2), clarinets (2)	Strings, both pizzicato and bowed	
5:07	4	Flutes (2), clarinets (2), bassoons (2)		
5:53	5	Trumpets (2), clarinets (2)	Strings (with mutes) and harps (2)	
6:42		Side drum	None	Coda

🔍 **Student FAQs**

Don't the harps enter in the first section of the movement, when the trumpets come in?

Bartók creates a harp-like sound at this point (2:12) by asking some of the violins to play a series of glissandi or "gliding" figures in which the player moves a finger up and down the fingerboard continuously, creating a kind of sound similar to what harps produce. But the harps themselves enter the movement only at 5:53. This is a good example of Bartók's ability to create asymmetrical symmetry through timbre.

Is the side drum the same as a snare drum?

The "snares" on a drum are heavy strings or wires that, when engaged, vibrate against the drum-head, creating a sort of "rattling" sound. In this movement, Bartók calls for a side drum, which is, in effect, a drum without snares, or with the snares disengaged.

PROFILE   Béla Bartók (1881–1945)

Scholar-Composer-Performer

Although remembered today primarily as a composer, Bartók was active throughout his life as a scholar and performer as well. He devoted much of his early career to collecting, recording, and transcribing the music of various ethnic groups throughout central and eastern Europe (see "Historical Context: Bartók the Ethnomusicologist"). He also concertized widely as a pianist, performing his own works as well as those by other composers. In 1940 he emigrated from Hungary to the United States, where he worked for a time at Columbia University in New York City, editing collections of eastern European folk music. Aside from a devoted but relatively small group of enthusiasts, however, his music did not generate much interest in the United States. Yet his *Concerto for Orchestra* (1943), commissioned by Serge Koussevitsky, the conductor of the Boston Symphony Orchestra, soon attracted a wide following and established itself as one of the most popular of all twentieth-century orchestral works. Already ill, the composer died of leukemia less than a year after its premiere.

Béla Bartók.

EXPAND YOUR PLAYLIST: BARTÓK

- *Music for Strings, Percussion, and Celesta*. A work that features an orchestra without winds, and with the addition of a celesta, a keyboard instrument that creates a bell-like sound.

- **Piano Concerto No. 3.** The most popular of the composer's solo concertos, this work reflects Bartók's talents as a pianist.

- **String Quartet No. 4.** One of six Bartók wrote in this genre.

- *Mikrokosmos,* **for piano.** A large collection of mostly short works for piano, many of them inflected with folk-inspired elements.

HISTORICAL CONTEXT   Bartók the Ethnomusicologist

Ethnomusicology is a subfield of **musicology**—the scholarly study of music in general—that focuses on the social dimension of the art and the ways in which music is used within and between cultures. Although ethnomusicologists today study music of all kinds from all times and places, the origins of the discipline began in the late nineteenth century with the study of non-Western and vernacular ("folk") repertories, many of which had been transmitted by **oral tradition** from one generation to the next, without the use of musical notation.

Béla Bartók was among the first generation of scholars who did ethnomusicological fieldwork, traveling not only across his native Hungary but throughout eastern Europe and as far afield as the Middle East and northern Africa to record the music of communities whose music had never been documented. Like many other early ethnomusicologists, Bartók used a combination of musical notation and mechanical recording devices (including early phonographs) to capture and preserve a repertory that might otherwise have been lost in the coming advance of radio, television, and other mass media. At the time Bartók was doing his fieldwork, many of these communities were largely isolated and self-contained. When he visited an area of Transylvania (in a region that is now part of Romania) in 1909, he observed that "for miles on end, in these parts, there are entire villages with illiterate inhabitants, communities which are not linked by any railways or roads. . . . When one comes into such a region one has the feeling of a return to the Middle Ages."[1] Such isolation meant that the melodies of the people were (to use Bartók's own terms) "pure" and "uncontaminated" by the outside elements.

Bartók (fourth from left) records folksongs in a village located in what is now the Czech Republic. Before the advent of microphones and tape recorders, early recordings were made directly onto a disc or wire cylinder. In this photograph from 1908, Bartók assists a villager who is singing directly into the recording device.

In this "uncontaminated" music, Bartók found inspiration for his own compositions destined for the concert hall, a fresh source of material that was at once both very old and very new.

[1] Bartók, Béla. *Essays*, ed. Benjamin Suchoff (London: Faber & Faber, 1976), 119–120.

 EXPAND YOUR PLAYLIST

Orchestral Music of the Twentieth Century

Debussy, Ives, Schoenberg, Stravinsky, Copland, and Bartók are only a few of the twentieth-century composers who wrote works in many genres for the orchestra. Some others include the following:

Dmitri Shostakovich
- Symphony No. 7 (1942). Inspired by the Siege of Leningrad (St. Petersburg) during World War II.

Krzysztof Penderecki
- *Threnody for the Victims of Hiroshima* (1960). A work for large string orchestra that calls for performers to play their instruments in unusual ways. A "threnody" is a lament for the dead, in this case the victims of the first atomic bomb dropped on Japan in 1945.

Ellen Taaffe Zwilich
- *Three Movements for Orchestra (Symphony No. 1)*. Winner of the Pulitzer Prize for Music in 1983.

Leonard Bernstein

"Tonight" from *West Side Story*
Composed: 1957

The Broadway musical is a direct descendant of European operetta, a spoken play with ample quantities of sung music. While often lighter in tone than standard opera, many musicals, including Bernstein's *West Side Story*, have carried with them messages of social significance. The ensemble "Tonight" is particularly elaborate in its formal structure.

Listen to This First

🎵 Melody

Listen for the two contrasting melodies in this scene. How are they different? Who sings which? ◼

🌐 Texture

Listen for the growing complexity of texture, from the homophonic beginning (one singer with accompaniment) to the polyphonic ending (five different vocal lines). ◼

🏛 Form

Listen for the way in which the scene grows from a series of sections sung by individual singers (solos) to a trio (three singers) to a quintet. Also listen for the way in which the two main themes are varied and eventually combined. ◼

☺ Word–Music Relationships

The key word in this scene is "tonight." Listen for the way in which it is sung consistently (but very differently) in each of the two melodies. Notice, too, how all the singers arrive at this one word together from different routes at the very end of the scene. ◼

Unlike opera, which is sung from beginning to end, the **musical** is a spoken drama with substantial amounts of singing. The idea of working songs into spoken plays goes back to Shakespeare and even before. During the eighteenth century, however, the music in some of these plays became more extensive and important than the spoken parts. Mozart even wrote a few works like this (the German term is *Singspiel*, or "song-play"), and this new genre of **operetta**—literally "small opera"—flourished in the nineteenth century, particularly in the works of Johann Strauss (*Die Fledermaus*) and Gilbert and Sullivan (*Pirates of Penzance*, *H.M.S. Pinafore*, *The Mikado*). These works were typically comic and lighthearted, often sentimental. They were also enormously popular and profitable. Transplanted to the United States, the operetta reached new heights, becoming known as the musical or the "Broadway musical," in honor of the street in New York City with the greatest concentration of musical theaters. In the hands of such American composers as Jerome Kern (*Show Boat*), Richard Rodgers (*Oklahoma!*), and Alan Jay Lerner (*My Fair Lady*), the Broadway musical soon developed into an institution that would be exported throughout the world.

The musical *West Side Story* was an instant hit when it premiered in 1957. It is a modern-day retelling of the story of Romeo and Juliet. The feuding "families" in this case are urban gangs: the Jets (whites) and Sharks (Puerto Ricans). When Tony, a Jet, falls in love with Maria, whose brother Bernardo is leader of the Sharks, the stage is set for a tragic ending. Bernstein's music

LEARNING OBJECTIVES

58.1 Explain the distinction between opera and operetta.

58.2 Recognize Leonard Bernstein's *West Side Story* as a modern-day *Romeo and Juliet*, belonging to the genre of the musical.

58.3 Listen for the ways in which the contrasting melodic themes of "Tonight" reflect the feelings of the various characters who are singing.

58.4 Identify the process by which Bernstein structures the scene to build from beginning to end.

58.5 Explain why Bernstein's career has been described as "four lives in one."

uses strong elements of jazz, including heavily syncopated rhythms and jazz-like **orchestration**. The characters in the scene here are as follows:

- Riff, leader of the Jets, a gang of whites
- Bernardo, leader of the Sharks, a gang of Puerto Ricans
- Chorus of Jets
- Chorus of Sharks
- Anita, a Puerto Rican, the girlfriend of Bernardo
- Tony, a Jet in love with Maria
- Maria, the sister of Bernardo, in love with Tony

All of them have big plans for "tonight." The Jets and Sharks are planning a rumble (fight). Anita readies herself for a night of passion with Bernardo. And Tony and Maria plan to see each other when it is dark, for they cannot carry on their romance in the light of day.

Representative Melodies

There are two opposing emotions in this scene: hate (between the Jets and the Sharks) and love (between Tony and Maria). Bernstein gives each a representative melody. The opening of the scene sets out a choppy, fast-paced melody over an **ostinato** bass (marked as "1" in the Listening Guide) with strong syncopations. Though they are rival gangs, the Jets and Sharks both want the same thing, a fight, and we hear this in their music: Their words are different, but both gangs sing the same melody. Tony and Maria also want the same thing—to be together—and we hear this in the very different music the two of them sing ("2," in the Listening Guide), a soaring, lyrical melody. This melody ("Tonight") is one they had sung earlier in the show in the "balcony scene." (The balcony in this urban setting was a fire escape.)

Anita occupies an interesting position here. She is more worldly than Maria, and her interest in Bernardo seems largely physical ("Anita's gonna get her kicks tonight"). She sings words of passion ("Don't matter if he's tired, As long as he's here") to the same melody sung by the Jets and Sharks in anticipation of their rumble.

Additive Form

The scene introduces the characters one by one and brings them all together (musically, at least) in the following order. The principal themes (1 and 2) are shown in parentheses.

1. Chorus: The Jets (led by Riff) and Sharks (led by Bernardo) each lay out their grievances with the other group. The two gangs occupy opposite ends of the stage and do not interact, even though they are singing the same music together and at times even the same words (1).
2. Solo (Anita): Anita sings the same melody in anticipation of her evening with Bernardo, after the fight (1).
3. Solo (Tony): Tony sings a new melody in anticipation of his evening with Maria (2).
4. Solo (Maria): Maria sings the same melody as Tony, anticipating her evening with him (2).
5. Chorus (Jets): The Jets approach Tony (1).

6. Trio (Maria, Tony, Riff): Maria continues Tony's lyrical melody (2). But instead of echoing her, Tony agrees to Riff's demands (1). We hear both themes simultaneously.

7. Quintet (Maria, Tony, Anita, Jets, Sharks): All the characters sing at once: Tony and Maria sing their melody (2) while all the others sing theirs (1). Everyone lands on the same word—"tonight"—at the very end.

By using just two basic melodies and distributing them among different characters, Bernstein is able to create a kind of **additive form** in which nothing disappears, but new layers are constantly added. This is a technique Bernstein had learned from the world of opera, in which the music in a given scene often becomes more layered—and the stage more populated—as the action progresses.

Bernardo (George Charkiris) leads two of his Sharks down the street. Jerome Robbins's choreography, both for the 1957 Broadway production and for the 1961 film, won wide critical acclaim.

 ## Increasingly Complex Textures

Closely related to the scene's additive form are its increasingly complex textures, which move from a solo at the beginning, to a trio (three voices), to a quintet (five voices). What we hear at the end is, in effect, five monologues performed simultaneously. This reveals one of the great advantages of sung drama over spoken drama. If these same characters were merely speaking their parts, we would comprehend none of them, and it would all sound like mere babble. Because we hear the characters singing their parts, we can differentiate among the contrasting melodies and emotions and experience them simultaneously.

 ## Word–Music Relationships: "Tonight," Two Ways

The contrasts in the setting of this one word capture the basic conflict between the world of Tony and Maria and the world of the Jets and Sharks. Those anticipating the physical side of things—Riff and the Jets, Bernardo and the Sharks, and Anita—sing the word to a menacing-sounding figure that sounds impatient and pressed (Theme 1), while Tony and Maria sing the same word very differently, leaping up or down to a long, sustained note (Theme 2).

We would, of course, expect lovers to be singing the same melody to each other: In opera, this is one sure-fire indication that a couple is really in love, and it often marks a major moment in an onstage relationship. Bernstein plays off this convention by having the two lovers sing separately, in simultaneous monologues. He applies the same device to the two warring gangs; they are not singing to each other, either, and the fact that they share a common melody makes the whole situation that much more ironic, for in the end, the two gangs are not really all that different on a personal, human level. It is only their ethnicity that separates them.

With these points in mind, listen to this scene again, using the Listening Guide.

CONNECT YOUR PLAYLIST

Additive Form

Find a work in additive form.

Example: Adele, "Rolling in the Deep" (2010)
This song gradually introduces new musical layers during the first verse.

Leonard Bernstein Composed: 1957

"Tonight" from *West Side Story*

Time	🏛 Form	🎵 Character(s)	👤 Text
0:00	Orchestral Introduction		
0:07	Chorus	**Riff** **Bernardo** **Riff**	The Jets are gonna have their day—Tonight. The Sharks are gonna have their way—Tonight. The Puerto Ricans grumble: "Fair fight." But if they start a rumble, We'll rumble 'em right.
0:24		**Bernardo** **Riff and Jets** **Bernardo and Sharks**	We're gonna hand 'em a surprise—Tonight. We're gonna cut 'em down to size—Tonight We said, "O.K., no rumpus, No tricks." But just in case they jump us, we're ready to mix—Tonight.
0:43		**All**	We're gonna rock it tonight, We're gonna jazz it up and have us a ball!
0:50			They're gonna get it tonight; The more they turn it on the harder they'll fall!
0:56		**Bernardo and Sharks** **All**	Well, they began it! And we're the ones to stop 'em once and for all—Tonight!
1:03	Orchestral Interlude		
1:07	Solo	**Anita**	Anita's gonna get her kicks—Tonight. We'll have our private little mix—Tonight. He'll walk in hot and tired, so what? Don't matter if he's tired, as long as he's hot—Tonight!
1:25	Solo	**Tony**	Tonight, tonight, won't be just any night, Tonight there will be no morning star. Tonight, tonight, I'll see my love tonight. And for us, stars will stop where they are. Today, the minutes seem like hours, the hours go so slowly, And still the sky is light . . . Oh moon, grow bright, And make this endless day endless night!
2:15	Orchestral Interlude		

♫ Melody	🌐 Texture	🗨 Word–Music Relationships
Agitated fanfare	Prominent brass with accompanying strings	
1 = choppy melody with ostinato bass	Homophonic	The word "tonight" stands out because it is sung smoothly to the same upward-moving figure each time. The Jets and Sharks are leaders of opposing gangs, but they have the same ideas (and music) about what will happen "tonight."
		Both gangs sing in unison; they have agreed that there will be a fight tonight.
As in Intro	As in Intro, with added clarinet figure	
1 = variant of same melody		Anita is also singing of her (very different) plans for what will happen "tonight," using a variant of the same melody sung by the gangs.
2= a new lyrical melody	Homophonic	The ostinato bass gives way to a flowing accompaniment. This is the return of a melody sung by Tony and Maria earlier in the show in their "balcony scene."
Repeated fanfare	Full orchestra	

(Continued)

Time	🎵 Form	🎵 Character(s)	👤 Text
2:23	Group	**Riff**	I'm counting on you to be there—Tonight. When Diesel wins it fair and square—Tonight. That Puerto Rican punk'll go down. And when he's hollered "Uncle," we'll tear up the town!
2:40	Trio	**Riff** **Tony** **Riff** **Tony** **Riff** (spoken) **Tony** (spoken) **Riff** **Tony** **Maria**	So I can count on you, boy? All right. We're gonna have us a ball. All right. Womb to tomb! Sperm to worm! I'll see you there about eight. Tonight . . . Tonight, tonight, won't be just any night, Tonight there will be no morning star . . .
2:53	Quintet	**Sharks**	We're gonna rock it tonight! They're gonna get it tonight. They began it, they began it, they began it. We'll stop 'em once and for all. The Sharks are gonna have their way, the Sharks are gonna have their day, We're gonna rock it tonight. Tonight!
		Jets	We're gonna jazz it tonight! Tonight! They began it, and we're the ones to stop 'em once and for all! The Jets are gonna have their way, the Jets are gonna have their day. We're gonna rock it tonight. Tonight!
		Anita	Tonight, tonight, late tonight We're gonna mix it tonight. Anita's gonna have her day, Anita's gonna have her day, Bernardo's gonna have his way, tonight, tonight, tonight this very night. We're gonna rock it tonight!
		Maria and Tony	Today the minutes seem like hours. The hours go so slowly, And still the sky is light. Oh moon, grow bright, And make this endless day endless night,
		Maria	Tonight, tonight, I'll see my love tonight. And for us, stars will stop where they are.
3:29		**All**	Tonight!

Melody   Texture   Word–Music Relationships

Melody	Texture	Word–Music Relationships
1 = choppy melody	Homophonic	
1 2	Polyphonic: both (1) and (2) at the same time	Maria sings Tony's melody (2) while Riff reminds Tony that he has to be at the fight tonight (1); Tony agrees (1).
1 2 2	Polyphonic Maria and Tony sing the same music together for the first time in this scene	The climax of the scene, presenting the emotions of all the characters at once.

Q Student FAQs

What's the difference between music that is sung in an opera and music that is sung in a musical?

The two styles of writing overlap considerably—both genres have their arias, ensembles, choruses—so it's impossible to make hard-and-fast distinctions between the styles of the two. In general, the vocal parts in musicals tend to be somewhat less demanding from a technical point of view, though there are plenty of musically challenging roles on Broadway. There is perhaps more of a difference in styles of singing. Singers with a "Broadway voice" often project with a bigger, brassier kind of voice and in a manner that is more declamatory; they certainly have to be better actors than singers in a standard operatic production.

Why are the lyrics in the stage version slightly different?

The 1961 movie version "cleaned up" the lyrics at several points to conform to the standards for Hollywood productions of the time. In the movie version, for example, Anita sings: "He'll walk in hot and tired / Poor dear / Don't matter if he's tired / As long as he's here."

What happens in the fight?

That would be a plot-spoiler. The movie version of *West Side Story* won many Academy Awards and is well worth seeing in its entirety.

PROFILE   Leonard Bernstein (1918–1990)

Four Lives in One

Shortly after Leonard Bernstein died in 1990, the composer Ned Rorem observed that he had not died at the age of 72, but 288. Why? Because "Lenny led four lives in one." And indeed, Bernstein achieved what for many musicians would amount to four lifetimes' worth of accomplishments:

- As a conductor, he was the first American-born musician to lead a major symphony orchestra, the New York Philharmonic. He made his debut with the group in 1943 and served as its music director from 1958 to 1969. He was chosen to conduct the performance of Beethoven's Ninth Symphony in Berlin in 1989 that celebrated the fall of the Berlin Wall.

- As a composer, Bernstein wrote for the stage (*West Side Story*, *Candide*), the concert hall (three symphonies), the screen (*On the Waterfront*), and the ballet (*Fancy Free*).

- As a pianist, he collaborated with such prestigious groups as the Juilliard String Quartet, the Vienna Philharmonic, and the New York Philharmonic.

- As an educator, Bernstein worked tirelessly to expand audiences for classical music. His "Young People's Concerts," televised nationwide between 1958 and 1972, exposed millions to a repertory they might otherwise never have heard.

Bernstein in rehearsal in 1947 with American soprano Marian Anderson (1897–1993).

EXPAND YOUR PLAYLIST: BERNSTEIN

- *On the Town.* Bernstein's first Broadway hit (1944).
- *Candide.* Another musical, based on Voltaire's satirical novel.
- *Chichester Psalms.* A setting of Psalms for chorus and orchestra, commissioned by the dean of Chichester Cathedral, England.

- *Mass.* A "theater piece" for dancers, singers, and orchestra, commissioned to inaugurate the opening of the Kennedy Center, Washington, D.C. (1971).

The costumes have been updated but the music and the story endure. This scene from the high school dance in *West Side Story* is taken from the recent Broadway revival, whose soundtrack won a Grammy award.

 EXPAND YOUR PLAYLIST

Broadway's Social Conscience

West Side Story stands in a long tradition of musicals that combine entertainment with social commentary.

Show Boat
- (1927, music by Jerome Kern, lyrics by Oscar Hammerstein II.) The first major musical to tackle the issue of racial bigotry.

South Pacific
- (1948, music by Richard Rodgers, lyrics by Oscar Hammerstein II.) One of the plot strands deals with prevailing prejudices against interracial love; the story is set against the backdrop of World War II.

My Fair Lady
- (1956, music by Frederick Loewe, lyrics by Alan Jay Lerner.) Based on George Bernard Shaw's play *Pygmalion*, this musical tackles serious issues—poverty and social mobility—in a humorous but moving manner, focusing on language and speech as weapons of class warfare.

Les Misérables
- (1980, music by Claude-Michel Schönberg, lyrics by Alain Boublil.) An adaptation of Victor Hugo's novel of the same name, this French musical (translated into English in 1982) explores the nature of poverty.

Miss Saigon
- (1989, music by Claude-Michel Schönberg, lyrics by Richard Maltby, Jr. and Alain Boublil.) Based loosely on Puccini's *Madame Butterfly*, this musical considers the aftermath of the U.S. military involvement in Vietnam.

Rent
- (1996, music and lyrics by Jonathan Larson.) A reinterpretation of Puccini's opera *La Bohème* (1897), *Rent* confronts issues of sexual orientation, drug addiction, and AIDS.

59

John Cage
Sonata II from *Sonatas and Interludes*
Composed: 1946–1948

John Cage produced new sounds out of an old instrument by inserting everyday objects—screws, bolts, nuts, etc.—between the strings of the piano, altering the sound of the instrument in startling ways.

Listen to This First

Timbre	Rhythm	Form
How would you describe the sound of what you hear compared to that of a normal piano? ∎	Listen for brief rhythmic patterns that repeat many times. ∎	Listen for large-scale repetition over the course of the work, with whole sections repeated. ∎

LEARNING OBJECTIVES

59.1 Describe what is meant by prepared piano.

59.2 Listen for and describe the difference in sound between a prepared piano and a normal piano.

59.3 Explain how John Cage uses melodic phrase structure in *Sonatas and Interludes*.

59.4 Listen for the binary form of this work.

59.5 Discuss Cage's career as a composer, with emphasis on his ideas about the nature of music.

John Cage was not the first to alter the sound of the piano by attaching objects to its strings, but he was the first to make such systematic use of the technique. His *Sonatas and Interludes*, a cycle of 20 pieces (16 sonatas and 4 interludes) for "prepared piano," blend conventional and unconventional sounds in ways that make us hear an instrument we think we know in entirely new ways.

Timbre: The Prepared Piano

Pressing down a single key on a piano causes a felt-covered hammer to strike a set of either two or three identical strings, all tuned to the same pitch. (Only the lowest pitches on the piano have only two strings; most have three.) The fact that there are multiple strings for each note helps give the piano its characteristic resonance. Multiple stringing serves another purpose as well. When a performer depresses the "soft" pedal—the pedal on the far left—the hammers all shift sideways a fraction of an inch and strike only two of the three (or one of the two) strings for any given note, creating a softer sound. This is why Cage was so specific about exactly where each object should be placed, whether between the first and second string, or between the second and third, or both. With the "soft" pedal depressed, the sound of any "prepared" set of strings is very different from the sound of it without the pedal depressed. One key can thus produce very different kinds of sound, depending on the use (or nonuse) of the "soft" pedal.

The objects Cage calls for in his *Sonatas and Interludes* are as follows:

- Screws
- Bolts (small, medium, large, long, and "furniture bolt")
- Metal nuts
- Strips of plastic woven above and below specific strings
- Small pieces of rubber
- One rectangular pencil eraser ("American Pencil Co. #346")

Cage also gives measurements for the distance of these objects from the damper, the felt-covered block that falls down on the strings after the hammer has struck them. (When the damper pedal—the pedal on the right—is depressed, the

Cage's "prepared piano."

dampers disengage, allowing the notes to resonate longer and "blend" with one another.) The composer's directions are excruciatingly precise: He calls for one particular screw to be placed 1 and 13/16ths of an inch from the damper, another 2 and 15/16ths of an inch away, and so on.

The sound that results from all this "preparation" has been compared to that of the Indonesian gamelan (see Chapter 60), a percussion ensemble whose timbre Cage knew well from recordings. Cage was fascinated with Asian philosophy and music in general, and so it is no surprise that he would seek to blend the two worlds musically.

The Rhythm of Melody

Percussion instruments divide into two categories: those that can produce specific pitches (such as the piano or xylophone) and those that cannot (such as the gong or cymbal). The prepared piano can produce both, depending on the way in which any given set of strings has been prepared (or not prepared). The effect of this dense mixture of pitched and unpitched sounds is to give special prominence to the role of rhythm. Consider the very opening theme of Sonata II: Although notated in score, it would be impossible to sing it or whistle it as it actually sounds because at least some of its "notes" are unpitched.

The themes of Sonata II are in fact most readily recognizable not through their pitches but through their rhythms. Each of the two main themes has its own distinct rhythmic pattern. The rhythmic organization of Theme 1 is surprisingly straightforward, even old-fashioned. The melody conveys a strong sense of **periodic phrase structure**, with an opening antecedent phrase in the higher register "answered" by a consequent phrase in a lower register (0:00– 0:06). This antecedent–consequent rhythm then repeats with different pitches and unpitched sounds (0:07–0:15)

Theme 1:

Theme 2, in turn, is based on a contrasting rhythm base that opens with the distinctive LONG-short-short pattern. The phrasing here is more continuous, without any division into antecedent and consequent phrases.

Theme 2:

Theme 3 appears for the first time in the second section, and its most striking characteristic is its rapid rhythms. Up to this point, the music has been moving along at a fairly steady pace of eighth notes (short) and quarter notes (LONGs). Suddenly, at 1:01, the notes more than double in speed, and the piece ends with a dramatic upward flourish.

Theme 3 ending:

Excerpts of score from John Cage, Sonata II, *Sonatas and Interludes*. Copyright © 1960, 1988 by Henmar Press Inc., C. F. Peters Corporation, sole selling agent. Used by permission. All rights reserved.

Binary Form

For all its radical features, the form of Sonata II is quite conventional. It is in **binary form**, and its two sections are each repeated in performance.

SECTION 1   SECTION 2

‖ : Theme 1   Theme 2 : ‖ : Theme 2   Theme 3 : ‖
    0:00   0:16   0:47   1:09
    (0:24)   (0:39)   (1:24)   (1:46)

But this is no rounded binary form, for the opening theme does not reappear in the second section. To the contrary, this section closes with an entirely new theme (3), which, as noted above, introduces a sudden burst of speed into the piece. The form is thus at once both familiar and unfamiliar—rather like the sound of the prepared piano.

Now listen to this music again, using the Listening Guide.

CONNECT YOUR PLAYLIST

Old Instruments, New Sounds

Find a piece of music that gets unconventional sounds out of a conventional instrument (including the voice).

Example: Peter Frampton, "Do You Feel Like We Do" (1976)
In this recording, Frampton uses a device called the Talk Box, which combines his voice with the guitar, making it sound as if the instrument were speaking.

    EXPAND YOUR PLAYLIST

Experimental Composers of the Twentieth Century

A number of important twentieth-century composers confronted audiences with basic questions about the nature of music. John Cage is the most famous, but he was by no means alone.

Henry Cowell (1897–1965), a native of California, was one of John Cage's teachers. *The Banshee* calls for the performer to manipulate the strings inside the piano with the hands, creating an eerie, otherworldly sound.

Harry Partch (1901–1974), a native Californian who sometimes wrote under the name "Paul Pirate," designed and constructed his own new instruments capable of playing music based on unusual tuning systems, with as many as 55 notes in the span of a conventional octave. *O Frabjous Day!* is a setting of the poem from Lewis Carroll's *Alice in Wonderland* for voice and an ensemble of original instruments.

Moondog was the pseudonym of **Louis Thomas Hardin** (1916–1999), a blind American composer and musician who by his own choice lived on the streets of New York City for almost 20 years. *Bird's Lament*, written in memory of saxophonist Charlie Parker, was later sampled by the deejay Mr. Scruff for "Get a Move On" and eventually reused in a television commercial for the Lincoln Navigator SUV.

Lejaren Hiller (1924–1994) taught at the University of Illinois, where he wrote the *Illiac Suite* in 1957, the first work of music composed by means of a programmed computer.

Listening Guide

John Cage Composed: 1946–1948
Sonata II from *Sonatas and Interludes*

Time	Form	Melody/Rhythm
0:00	Section 1	Theme 1 (s-s-s-s-L)
0:15		Theme 2 (L-s-s)
0:23	Section 1 repeated	Theme 1 (s-s-s-L)
0:38		Theme 2 (L-s-s)
0:46	Section 2	Theme 2 varied
1:08		Theme 3 (very rapid upper voice, slower descending bass)
1:24	Section 2 repeated	Theme 2 varied
1:46		Theme 3 (very rapid upper voice, slower descending bass)

Q Student FAQs

How long does it take to "prepare" a piano?

Usually about two to three hours, assuming one has already made a trip to the hardware store. When Cage's *Sonatas and Interludes* are performed on a program with other works for "standard" piano, the performer will have two pianos on stage from the very beginning and switch instruments as appropriate.

Are there other works for prepared piano?

Yes. Cage's *Sonatas and Interludes* is by far the most famous work written for the instrument, but others have composed for it as well, including Volker Bertelmann (a.k.a. Hauschka), rock band Velvet Underground, and singer Tori Amos (in her 1994 song "Bells for Her"). Each work calls for a different specification of how the piano is to be prepared.

Why did Cage call these "Sonatas"?

Some of the earliest sonatas for keyboard are in binary form in a single movement, and it could be that Cage was referring to sonatas by composers like Domenico Scarlatti (1685–1757).

PROFILE   John Cage (1912–1992)

What Is a Composer?

"Everything we do is music," Cage once declared. He did not see himself as a high priest of art but rather as a facilitator between listeners and sounds. Profoundly influenced by Zen Buddhism and its renunciation of striving and the will, Cage maintained that his "purpose is to eliminate purpose," and many of his works from the late 1940s on seem to avoid or challenge the traditional stance of the composer as an omnipotent creator of a small musical world.

Born in Los Angeles, Cage studied composition with Arnold Schoenberg but soon moved on to composing in a manner even more radically modern than that of his teacher. In the 1950s, he became interested in the possibilities of electronic music and multimedia art that combined word, music, and movement and often mixed live and recorded sounds and images.

Cage and his music consistently polarized listeners. Most of the audience at New York's Lincoln Center walked out of his *Atlas eclipticalis* (whose notated score superimposes transparent staff paper on star charts to determine pitches) when it was first presented by the New York Philharmonic in 1964; even members of the orchestra hissed the composer. But Cage's provocative music and writings remained fresh over time, and toward the end of his life he was showered with honors. He delivered the prestigious Charles Eliot Norton lectures at Harvard University in 1988, continuing in the tradition of other composers before him, including Igor Stravinsky, Aaron Copland, and Leonard Bernstein. Some saw genius in his works, others charlatanism, but all were provoked by them to rethink the nature of music and its relationship to the world around us.

John Cage performs his *Suite for Toy Piano* (1948), a series of five short movements that requires a keyboard consisting of only nine keys. Like many of Cage's works, the music is at once both whimsical and serious.

EXPAND YOUR PLAYLIST: CAGE

- *Imaginary Landscape no. 4.* For 24 musicians working in pairs on 12 radios, one controlling the tuning, the other the volume. The instructions to the performers are quite specific, but the content depends on what is being broadcast at any given moment.

- *Fontana Mix.* A work for magnetic tape.

- *Roaratorio: An Irish Circus on Finnegans Wake.* For magnetic tape and live performers, based on James Joyce's novel.

- *0' 00".* The performer is instructed to perform "a disciplined action," sonically amplified to the greatest possible degree.

PERFORMANCE   *4'33"*: The Music (?) Of Silence (?)

Perhaps the most controversial work in the entire history of music, John Cage's *4'33"* has polarized listeners ever since its first performance in 1952. Its admirers find it endlessly fascinating, while its detractors dismiss it as a mere gimmick. Cage's score calls for the piece to "be performed by any instrumentalist or combination of instrumentalists and last any length of time," and it consists of three movements, each of which is marked "Tacet," the traditional indication for a musician not to play his or her instrument at all over a specified length of time.

4'33" is often said to consist of four minutes and thirty-three seconds of silence. This is not quite true. Neither the length of the work nor the "silence" is quite so straightforward. Cage's score contains the comment that when it was premiered by the pianist John Tudor on August 29, 1952, the performance on that occasion lasted for four minutes and thirty-three seconds. The real title of the work, Cage notes in his score, "is the total length in minutes and seconds of its performance," which can vary from performance to performance. The "silence,"

moreover, is an illusion. Even when musicians are not playing, we hear sounds. Cage's personal experience in a completely soundproof chamber, in which he describes how he could hear the sound of his own breathing and his heartbeat, reminds us that there is no such thing as true silence.

According to Cage, *4'33"* was inspired by the "white paintings" created by one of his friends, artist Robert Rauschenberg (1925–2008). These "blank" canvases are never truly blank: Each one has its own unique color and textures even before any paint is applied, and each canvas is constantly changing because of the way it reflects the light of its surroundings. But as viewers, we have been conditioned not to notice such details and to mentally compensate for them. In much the same way, Cage's *4'33"* challenges the idea that music can exist in sonic isolation, that some sounds are music while others are not. Sounds, as Cage reminds us, are always present. Whether we choose to hear them or not and treat them as part of the music is up to us.

Robert Rauschenberg (1925–2008) in front of one of his "White Paintings," blank panels of canvas he began producing in 1951. Rauschenberg and Cage were close associates, and Cage later said that these "empty" paintings gave him the courage to create a correspondingly "silent" work of music.

Gamelan Gong Kebyar of Belaluan, Bali

Kebyar Ding III, "Oncang-oncangan"
Recorded: 1928

GLOBAL CONNECTION
TIMBRE

Gamelan means "musical ensemble." It is played in Indonesia and consists of a number of instruments, typically a variety of bells, gongs, drums, and xylophone-like instruments. The shimmering percussive timbre and floating, nondirectional structure of Gamelan music have had a deep influence on other twentieth-century composers in the Western classical tradition as well, including Claude Debussy, John Cage, and Philip Glass.

Listen to This First))

⚡ Timbre	🎵 Melody	🎚 Dynamics	🎹 Form
How would you describe the sound of the individual instruments you hear? ■	How would you describe the melodies you hear? ■	Listen for the gradual changes in volume. ■	Listen for changes in the speed of the music and the way in which each section of the piece has its own tempo. ■

The gamelan consists of melody and rhythm instruments and originated at the courts on the islands of Java and Bali, in what is now Indonesia. The primary melody instruments of the **gamelan** are the *gender* (bronze-keyed **vibraphones**, similar to xylophones) and the *trompong*, which are horizontally mounted, bowl-shaped gongs. These instruments are played in pairs, with one set tuned slightly apart from the other, creating a shimmering sound. The rhythm section consists of vertically hung gongs, which are struck to mark off fixed beats within the metric structure of the piece. Each section of the performance has its own specific rhythmic pattern played by these gongs. They are joined by a number of drums and smaller percussion instruments (see "Closer Look: The Gamelan").

Gamelan music traditionally was not notated, and the players learned their parts by rote. Today, the music is taught using a

LEARNING OBJECTIVES

60.1 Describe the gamelan as an ensemble of instruments.

60.2 Explain what is meant by "kebyar" in reference to a gamelan.

60.3 Listen for the textured melody of *Kebyar Ding III*, "Oncang-oncangan" as performed by the Gamelan Gong Kebyar of Belaluan (Bali).

60.4 Describe the dynamics and tempo of "Oncang-oncangan."

60.5 Explain the concept of form in a *gamelan gong kebyar*.

60.6 Listen for the interlocking melodic patterns and ostinatos in this work.

INDONESIA
BALI
JAVA
Denpasar

Gamelan music comes from the Indonesian islands of Bali and Java.

numerical notation, with each number representing a corresponding scale step. Gamelans of all types are found in several music departments in many American, Canadian, and British universities.

Gamelan gong kebyar is easily distinguished from the older Javanese gamelan, which was sedate, elegant, and performed for princes. The Balinese style is energetic, with many abrupt changes of tempo and dynamics. The word *kebyar* means "explosive." Compositions are built of a series of **ostinatos**—repeated musical patterns—and each has a different length and is set in a different tempo. This recording of *gamelan gong kebyar* comes from the first historic set of Balinese music recordings made in 1928. It is the third part of a longer composition, so it is called *Kebyar Ding III,* "Oncang-oncangan". We already know that the term *kebyar* means "explosive"; *ding* means "first tone," referring to the tone that forms the central focus of the piece. The term *oncang-oncangan* imitates the sound of the pounding of rice mortars as grain is husked; in the section from approximately 1:22 and 1:38 you will hear a rhythm that is meant to evoke the sound of this physical activity.

Gamelan music has had a deep influence on twentieth-century composers in the Western classical tradition. Claude Debussy was one of the first to encounter this repertory at the famous Paris International Exposition in 1889, and the timbre of some of his piano pieces, like *Voiles* (see Chapter 45) may well owe something to the shimmering, floating quality of the gamelan's sound. John Cage, who knew the gamelan from recordings like the one presented here, was also influenced by the gamelan; this is particularly evident in his works for prepared piano (see Chapter 59). The music of minimalists like Philip Glass (see Chapter 61) creates an almost hypnotic quality in its repeated melodic fragments and interlocking patterns, devices that are basic to gamelan music.

Shimmering Timbre

The shimmering sound of gamelan music is often the first thing listeners notice about this music. This effect is produced by the paired melody instruments being intentionally tuned to tones very slightly apart. One instrument might be pitched slightly higher than the other; when they are played in unison, this creates a shimmering effect.

A Textured Melody

The melody is played on a group of high-pitched *gender* (bronze-keyed vibraphones). You may notice that the melody is often played at breathtaking speeds. How do the musicians do this? Instead of all of the gender playing every note, each pair of musicians plays a single note. Imagine a melody consisting of three notes, C-D-E; in the gamelan, C might be played by one pair of gender players, D played by another, and E by a third set. (Eventually you would return to the first pair of players, as there is in any one ensemble a finite number of lead instruments.) Each pair only has to play one note, in rapid succession. This speed would be impossible to

The *gender*, a metal-keyed xylophone, is one of the instruments in a gamelan.

achieve if all three notes were played by a single pair of instruments. In this way, the parts are said to "interlock" to form the melody. These melodies are then repeated to form an ostinato. *Trompong* (the bowl-shaped gongs) enter at points with their own repeated melodic patterns that run counter to the gender melodies. Drumming and gongs marking pulsations add to the textural coloration.

 ## Dynamics and Tempo

Dynamics vary widely in *gamelan gong kebyar* pieces, and they change along with tempo to create different sections. More abrupt changes in tempo occur to mark the end of a section and the start of a new one. This involves loud *kebyar*: striking of all the instruments in the ensemble together. Sometimes the loud *kebyar* is just one struck sound, and sometimes the *kebyar* proceeds briefly in an ensemble interlude in which all the instruments are playing in the same rhythm. Listen for these distinctive sections while you study this piece.

 ## Form

The *gamelan gong kebyar* is structured in different sections with varied tempo and dynamics. In this example there are six sections. The fifth section—occurring between 1:22 and 1:38—features two distinctive rhythmic patterns played in succession that are meant to imitate the sound of rice being pounded in a mortar-and-pestle. *Kebyar* explosions and sections where the ensemble plays in a unified rhythm mark off the sections, and a new section may be recognized by its tempo change.

Unlike traditional Western classical music, the piece seems to have no "direction." The sections simply follow one after the other. The overall effect is not a dramatic story, with melodies moving forward toward a stunning climax, but rather a static, almost meditative sound. This was highly influential on Western composers of the turn of the twentieth century like Debussy, whose *Voiles*, which we studied in Chapter 45, has a similar directionless feeling.

Now listen to this piece again, using the Listening Guide.

CONNECT YOUR PLAYLIST

Ostinato

Find a piece that contains a repeated melodic part.

Example: The Beatles, "Hey Jude" (1968) The extended coda to the Beatles' "Hey Jude" consists of a (seemingly) endless repetition of a simple melody sung as "lah-lah-lah/lah-lah-lah-lah/lah-lah-lah-lah/Hey Jude."

Listening Guide 🔊

Gamelan Gong Kebyar of Belaluan Recorded: 1928
Kebyar Ding III, "Oncang-oncangan" (2:56)

Time	🏛 Form	🎵 Melodic Texture
0:00	Introduction.	The *gender* state an introductory melodic figure.
0:03	Kebyar, or "explosion."	The entire *gamelan* strikes simultaneously.
0:05	First section. The lowest gong marks the beat, while a higher set of gongs mark other, more rapid pulses.	*Gender* play high-pitched rapid melody.
0:20	Second section. The sound of a higher gong marks the rhythmic structure.	New section with a slower ostinato.
0:32		*Trompong* gongs are struck.
0:40		Drumming begins and accelerates.
0:42		Higher gongs on the *trompong* enter in an interlocking ostinato.
0:44	Lull in activity.	A short rhythmic break.
0:46	Third section.	Continued *gender* interlock now with *trompong* part added.
1:07		Drumming again begins and accelerates.
1:10	Kebyar.	Another unison break of the ensemble.
1:12	Fourth section.	Continuation of interlocking melodic ostinato at a much faster tempo.
1:22	Fifth section.	Ensemble begins a prolonged unison passage; rhythm becomes grouped around three quick pulses.

Rhythm (Tempo)	Dynamics
Moderate	Soft
	Very loud
	Medium
Slow	Soft
	Medium
	Soft
Resumption of tempo	
	Very loud
Fast	Loud

(Continued)

(Continued)

Q Student FAQs ⚙

How hard is it to play this music?

While the overall piece is complex, each individual part is not that hard to learn. Each player, like the young girl pictured here, has to play a short pattern that is usually repeated many times through a composition. Most Balinese gamelan musicians are not professional and perform in this kind of ensemble only on specific holidays.

Who organizes a gamelan?

Originally, gamelans were sponsored by the Javanese courts and were heard only by the nobility. However, in this century, local villages and clubs have taken over the sponsorship of these ensembles.

Time	▥ Form	♫ Melodic Texture	
1:34		A counter rhythm (LONG-short-short) begins, set against the main rhythm of three quick pulses.	
1:38	Lull in activity.	Drum roll	
1:40	Sixth section.	The *gender* start a new, slow melody over a slow drum accompaniment.	
1:58		*Trompong* enter in interlocked ostinato.	
2:02		*Trompong* stop. *Gender* continue the slow melody.	
2:18		*Trompong* again enter in ostinato.	
2:21		*Trompong* stop. *Gender* continue the slow melody.	
2:31		*Gender* begin to accelerate the melody.	
2:38		Low gong begins to strike more regularly.	
2:41		Trompong join the low gongs to emphasize basic rhythmic structure.	
2:43		Drumming enters and accelerates. The *gender* accelerate to the end.	
2:53		Ensemble marks the end of the piece in a *kebyar* unison rhythm.	
2:54		Final drum strike marks the end.	

Rhythm (Tempo)   Dynamics

Rhythm (Tempo)	Dynamics
	Soft
Slow	Soft
Beginning to get quicker	Beginning to get louder
Getting faster	Getting louder
Faster to the end	Louder to the end

◄◄ **EXPAND YOUR PLAYLIST** ►►

Gamelan Music

Golden Rain: Balinese Gamelan Music, Nonesuch Explorer 72028.

- First released in the early 1970s, this was one of the first recordings of Balinese gamelan to be readily available in the United States. The group works in the same *kebyar* style in playing both traditional and recent compositions.

Gamelan Semar Pegulingan, Nonesuch Explorer 79720.

- In *Semar Pegulingan* the rhythmic changes are less abrupt than in the *kebyar* style, with more lyrical melodies although equally complex rhythms.

Javanese Court Gamelan, Nonesuch Explorer 72044.

- This offers an opportunity to compare the Javanese gamelan with the Balinese style. Note the use of the *rebab* (a bowed string instrument), along with zithers, flutes, and vocalists, as well as the xylophones and gongs heard in the Balinese ensemble.

Lou Harrison: *Gamelan Music,* Music Masters 67091.

- Contemporary classical compositions using the gamelan, written by one of the twentieth century's most innovative composers.

Philip Glass: *Koyaanisqatsi,* Elektra 79506.

- An edited version of the soundtrack for the influential film. The film is also available on DVD.

CLOSER LK   The Gamelan

Gamelan music originated in Indonesia in South East Asia. Centuries old, gamelan was largely a ceremonial type of music used in rituals and religious gatherings. The gamelan, like the Western orchestra, includes a variety of instruments: drums and other percussion instruments, gender (a kind of vibraphone), and trompong which are gongs.

Small percussion instruments: Depending on the individual gamelan, smaller percussion instruments may "fill out" the rhythmic part. Also, some gamelan feature flutes or stringed instruments to augment the melody line.

Double-headed drums: A pair of double-headed drums, one characterized as "male" and the other as "female," establish the rhythmic underpinning for the gamelan. Because the drummers also signal transitions from one section of the composition to another, they have sometimes been compared to Western orchestra conductors.

NOT SHOWN: Large suspended gongs. Large gongs suspended in wooden frames are typically included in the Balinese gamelan. These are used to mark off longer rhythmic units.

Trompong: These bowl-shaped brass gongs play one of the lead melody parts. In this ensemble, there is a single musician assigned to playing this part.

Gender: Along with the trompong, the gender—metal-keyed xylophones— are the primary lead instruments in the gamelan. The instruments are paired, with one tuned slightly higher than the other, which gives the characteristic "shimmering" sound to gamelan music.

Philip Glass

"Knee Play 1" from *Einstein on the Beach*

Composed: 1976

61

Minimalism is a style based on multiple repetitions and subtle variations of a few brief ideas. Philip Glass's *Einstein on the Beach*, an opera without a plot, captures the essence of the style. Minimalist techniques have been applied in many different kinds of music, including techno, minimal techno, and microhouse.

Listen to This First

🎵 Timbre

Listen for three layers of sound: (1) the bass line (the organ), (2) the chorus of voices that sing above it, and (3) the two speaking parts that operate seemingly independently of the music. ■

👤 Harmony

Listen for the simple and strongly tonal harmonic progression that is repeated over and over in this scene. ■

🎹 Form

Listen for the repeated pattern in the bass line (the organ) that continues from beginning to end. Try to identify variations in the basic rhythmic and melodic patterns of the voices. Finally, be aware of the added elements (new voices, both singing and speaking) that emerge over the course of the scene as a whole. ■

Glass's opera has no plot in the conventional sense. Instead, it is built around a series of recurring images: a train, a trial, a spaceship in a field. A character resembling Einstein appears at several points playing the violin (the real Einstein was in fact an amateur violinist). The four acts, performed without intermission, are introduced and connected by a series of "Knee Plays," a term Glass adapted from the joining function of the human knee. This chapter's selection, "Knee Play 1," is the opening number of the opera. Only small portions of the text are sung: Most of it is recited, and the text that is sung is limited to the counting of numbers ("One, two, three," etc.) or solfège syllables (do-re-mi-fa-so-la-ti).

Glass worked closely with director and playwright Robert Wilson (b. 1941) to develop this radical new form of opera. With the exception of Einstein—who never sings—there are no real characters, only a 16-voice chorus and four nameless actors in speaking roles. The idea, as Glass has since explained in interviews, was to let audiences read their own meaning into the work's various scenes. *Einstein on the Beach* premiered in France in July 1976 and has since been revived many times.

Glass's music is written in a style known as **minimalism**, in which a brief musical idea or group of ideas is repeated and varied incrementally over a long span of time, with a relatively slow rate of change. Minimalist music, in spite of its name, tends to unfold across long periods and relies on the passage of time to create an almost trance-like state in the mind of the listener. Indeed, there is so much repetition that as listeners, our scale of perception changes, so that even a slight variation in the rhythm becomes a major event. "Knee Play 1" is typical of minimalist music in its use of fairly simple melodic, harmonic, and rhythmic building blocks.

LEARNING OBJECTIVES

61.1 Identify the unconventional aspects of Philip Glass's *Einstein on the Beach* as a theater piece.

61.2 Define and recognize minimalism in all the arts, including music.

61.3 Discuss how Glass layers timbres in "Knee Play 1" from *Einstein on the Beach*.

61.4 Describe the harmony in "Knee Play 1."

61.5 Listen for the ostinato in this excerpt.

61.6 Listen for the timbre of the electronic organ, the vocal ensemble, and the female speaker.

61.7 Outline Glass's career as a composer.

Layered Timbres

The musical forces performing in this opening scene are quite modest: an electronic organ, a small chorus of mixed voices (soprano, alto, tenor, bass), and two speakers (both women). The organ and chorus move in close coordination, while the spoken voices enter and drop out in a manner that seems to be random. Glass allows for considerable latitude in the score, leaving it up to performers how many times they will repeat a certain section or exactly when the spoken texts will be recited and at what speed.

 Simple Harmony

The organ and chorus outline a standard harmonic progression, one often heard in cadences in tonal music. The chords used are those built on the fourth, fifth, and first scale degrees (IV, V, and then I, in musical terms). The 12-bar blues chord progression, for example, makes exclusive use of these three chords (see Chapter 50), and these are the same three chords that, according to some learn-how-to-play-music advertisements, will allow you to perform a thousand songs. By making the harmony so simple and by repeating it so often, Glass is able to draw our attention toward other elements of change, such as the varied rhythms of the melody and the gradual addition of new performing forces.

 Variation Form

The form of this scene is actually quite simple: It is a series of variations on a series of short melodic fragments, with the music unfolding over a constantly repeated bass, an **ostinato**. The rhythm of the theme and each of its variations remains essentially constant from beginning to end, with the singers counting the beats they sing out loud to some variation of this basic pattern:

1 2 3 4 | 1 2 3 4 5 6 | 1 2 3 4 5 6 7 8 |

Glass repeats this basic unit, with its three subunits of four, six, and eight beats, many times, but often with subtle variations. He creates variety in three ways:

1. **Altered rhythms.**   Certain beats at the beginning of each subunit drop out in no predictable pattern. For example, at 1:03 we hear

1 2 3 4 | [pause] 2 3 4 5 6 | 1 2 3 4 5 6 7 8 |

and at 1:45 we hear

[pause] 2 3 4 | 1 2 3 4 5 6 | [pause] 2 3 4 5 6 7 8 |

Glass uses these and other rhythmic permutations throughout, eliminating the "1" beat in one or more of the three subunits of four, six, and eight that make up the basic rhythmic unit.

2. **Divided voices.**   At 2:06, the two vocal lines we have heard up to this point—sopranos and altos singing the upper line together, tenors and basses singing the lower line—split into four parts. Sopranos now sing "do-re-mi" to the same notes as the altos, who continue to sing as before, but the sopranos sing these syllables at a much slower rhythm. The tenors do the same (on the syllables "la-so-do") with the basses underneath.

CONNECT YOUR PLAYLIST

Minimalism

Find a work whose formal structure is based on the principles of minimalism.

Example: Phoenix, "Bankrupt!" (2013) The short repeating patterns of this song (particularly the central section) evoke aspects of minimalist compositional styles.

The "Spaceship" scene from Philip Glass' *Einstein on the Beach*, as produced by the Los Angeles Opera in 2013.

3. **Added spoken voices.**   Glass makes no distinction between speech or song: All become a part of the sonic landscape. At 1:03, we hear the first of two women's voices recite (in speech) some of the numbers being sung by the chorus. At 1:24, these voices begin to recite their own independent texts. This text (by poet Christopher Knowles) is itself full of internal repetitions and is not meant to make sense syntactically. Here, for example, is the opening (beginning at 1:03):

> Will it get some wind for the sailboat. And it could get for it is.
> It could get the railroad for these workers. And it could be were it is.
> It could Franky it could be Franky it could be very fresh and clean.
> It could be a balloon.
> Oh these are the days my friends and these are the days my friends.
> It could get some wind for the sailboat. And it could get for it is.
> It could get the railroad for these workers. It could get for it is were.
> It could be a balloon. It could be Franky. It could be very fresh and clean.
> All these are the days my friends and these are the days my friends.
> It could be those ways.[1]

With these points in mind, listen to the scene once again, using the Listening Guide.

---

[1]Excerpt from *Einstein on the Beach*. Spoken text: Christopher Knowles/Samuel M. Johnson/Lucinda Childs. Copyright © 1976 Dunvagen Music Publishers, Inc. Used by permission.

Listening Guide 🔊

Philip Glass Composed: 1976
"Knee Play 1" from *Einstein on the Beach* (3:52)

Time	🏛 Form: Section (each section is stated twice)	〰 Timbre	📖 Rhythm
0:00	1	Organ only	Ostinato figure: long, slow notes
0:21	2	Sopranos and altos sing the upper line; tenors and basses sing the lower line.	1 2 3 4 1 2 3 4 5 6 1 2 3 4 5 6 7 8
0:42	3		1 2 3 4 1 2 3 4 5 6 [pause] 2 3 4 5 6 7 8
1:03	4		1 2 3 4 [pause] 2 3 4 5 6 1 2 3 4 5 6 7 8
1:24	5		[pause] 2 3 4 1 2 3 4 5 6 1 2 3 4 5 6 7 8
1:45	6		[pause] 2 3 4 1 2 3 4 5 6 [pause] 2 3 4 5 6 7 8
2:06	7	Two lines in chorus divide to become four. The sopranos now sing the same pitches in longer notes to "do-re-mi," and the tenors sing the same pitches in longer notes to "la-so-do."	1 2 3 4 1 2 3 4 5 6 [pause] 2 3 4 5 6 7 8
2:27	8		1 2 3 4 [pause] 2 3 4 5 6 [pause] 2 3 4 5 6 7 8
2:48	9		[pause] 2 3 4 [pause] 2 3 4 5 6 [pause] 2 3 4 5 6 7 8
3:09	10		1 2 3 4 [pause] 2 3 4 5 6 1 2 3 4 5 6 7 8
3:30	11		[pause] 2 3 4 1 2 3 4 5 6 [pause] 2 3 4 5 6 7 8

Spoken Text

First voice enters, speaking numbers with the sung chorus, seemingly at random.

First voice begins to recite the text ("Will it get some wind for the sailboat," etc.).

Second voice enters to join in reciting the text.

Student FAQs

Don't people get tired of so much repetition?

Some do, but to call this music repetitious reminds us that the term is relative. Like John Cage before him (see Chapter 59), Glass challenges listeners to reconsider the basic premises of how they listen. Listening to a minimalist work is a little like looking at something under a microscope: We begin to see (hear) things that we sometimes take for granted.

The spoken text makes no sense. What does it add?

As Glass suggests (see his comments earlier), the point is not so much what the opera "means" as what listeners hear in it. The text means whatever listeners think it means.

PROFILE Philip Glass (b. 1937)

Prolific Minimalist

Philip Glass stands out among contemporary composers for having become so famous that he is mentioned in no fewer than three episodes of *The Simpsons* and is satirized in an episode of *South Park*. He was born and raised in Baltimore, where he studied flute at the Peabody Conservatory of Music. He went on to study composition at the Juilliard School of Music in New York City, after which he worked in Paris with Nadia Boulanger, who 40 years before had been Aaron Copland's teacher. He traveled widely in Asia as well, studying Indian music with legendary sitar player Ravi Shankar. Glass returned to New York in the mid-1960s, convinced that modern music needed to reach out to audiences more directly, and so he established the Philip Glass Ensemble, a group of musicians who still tour the country on a regular basis and draw consistently large audiences to concerts of new music.

Glass is an astonishingly prolific composer. In addition to 10 operas, he has written large quantities of vocal and instrumental music, as well as soundtracks for a number of mainstream films, including *The Illusionist, The Secret Garden, The Truman Show*, and *Candyman*.

Philip Glass at the electronic organ, ca. 1985.

EXPAND YOUR PLAYLIST: GLASS

- *Etudes.* A series of technical studies for piano.
- *Violin Concerto.* A work written for violin and orchestra, in three movements.
- *The Hours.* Film score, one of three for which Glass was nominated for an Academy Award, along with his music for *Notes on a Scandal* and *Kundun*.
- *A Descent into the Maelstrom.* A dance theater piece inspired by Edgar Allen's Poe short story of the same name.
- *Akhnaten.* An opera set in ancient Egypt.

EXPAND YOUR PLAYLIST

Minimalism

Terry Riley

- *In C.* A series of 53 brief thematic fragments that can be played "by any number of instruments of any kind. "Each performer plays all 53 fragments but may repeat each as often as he or she likes, so the length of the work can vary enormously in performance. One recent recording runs for 43 minutes, another for 76 minutes.

Steve Reich

- *Three Tales.* A video opera made in collaboration with Beryl Korot, the composer's wife. The first of the three scenes revolves around the crash of the dirigible *Hindenburg* in Lakehurst, New Jersey, in 1937; the second centers on the testing of an atomic bomb in the South Pacific in 1946; and the third focuses on the sheep named Dolly, who in 1996 became the world's first successfully cloned mammal.

John Adams

- *Short Ride in a Fast Machine.* A brief work for orchestra that has proven extremely popular with concert audiences. The piece starts fast and becomes increasingly intense.

The Beatles

- "Tomorrow Never Knows." A drone-based composition influenced by Indian raga. The backdrop changes only minimally through the piece.

Peter Gabriel

- "This Is the Picture." A synthesized backdrop repeats a simple melodic figure, very much in the style of African traditional music, as Gabriel sings the lyric above it.

62

Mahalia Jackson
"It Don't Cost Very Much"
Recorded: 1958

Gospel music fuses such diverse musical traditions as hymnody, song, African American spirituals, jazz, and the blues. The vocal techniques in Mahalia Jackson's performance of "It Don't Cost Very Much" reinforce the spiritual dimension of this music.

Listen to This First

Form
Notice how the chords at the end of certain sections sound complete, while others sound unfinished. Listen for a long section that repeats. ■

Timbre
Listen to the combination of the organ and piano playing together. Listen also for the singer's vibrato and vocal power. ■

Rhythm
Pay attention to the slow, steady rhythms in the piano and bass that generate a sense of forward momentum. Notice how the singer's phrases sometimes anticipate and sometimes lag behind the accompanying musicians. ■

Harmony
Listen for chord progressions that propel the music toward cadences. ■

LEARNING OBJECTIVES

62.1 Explain the origins of gospel music.

62.2 Listen for and identify the verse-chorus form of "It Don't Cost Very Much."

62.3 Describe the various timbres typical of black gospel music.

62.4 Define "shuffle groove."

62.5 Explain the use of rhythm in classic gospel style.

62.6 Listen for and identify gospel harmonies in "It Don't Cost Very Much."

62.7 Discuss the careers of Thomas A. Dorsey and Mahalia Jackson.

62.8 Explain the black and white gospel music traditions.

On Sunday morning, July 6, 1958, the emcee at the Newport (Rhode Island) Jazz Festival took the microphone and announced, "Ladies and gentlemen, it is Sunday and it is time for the world's greatest gospel singer, Miss Mahalia Jackson." Jackson, accompanied by her longtime collaborator Mildred Falls on piano, Lilton Mitchell on organ, and Tom Bryant on bass, sang for 45 minutes to an adoring crowd. The live recording of this concert captures not only the music she sang but also the crowd calling out requests, Jackson's affectionate comments back to them, and the musical signals passed among her accompanists. "It Don't Cost Very Much," one of three compositions by Thomas A. Dorsey on the program, was the fourth song, sung as the energy level of the concert began to build toward a jubilant celebration of rhythm and sound.

Gospel music began in the 1920s and 1930s as musicians began to perform new songs with sacred, Protestant texts in popular musical styles. Gospel's vocal style combined aspects of blues with the expressive freedom and fervor found in the congregational singing of what were known as Sanctified churches. Sanctified churches encouraged their congregations to express themselves with loud, lively musical outbursts as moved by the spirit. Early gospel was typically performed by vocal quartets, with soloists slowly gaining popularity. The music was accompanied by piano, with later additions of organ, drums, bass, and, eventually, full choirs plus small orchestras.

The 1940s and 1950s are known as the "classic age" of gospel. During this era, gospel became a powerful force within popular music. Gospel artists sang newly composed works, but they also drew on hymns and inspirational songs from different worship traditions, including African American spirituals, which were songs with Christian texts that had been sung by slaves.

Simple Verse-Chorus Form

The title phrase, "It don't cost very much," occurs five times. In addition to reinforcing the song's message, this phrase helps delineate the form, which consists of a single verse followed by two iterations of the chorus:

FORM:	Introduction	Verse	Chorus	Chorus
	0:02	0:14	1:13	2:12

The first appearance of "It don't cost very much" is in the last line of the verse, a standard songwriting technique to foreshadow the entrance of the chorus. The chorus immediately repeats the phrase as its first line, and then uses it as a textual "bookend" to conclude. The chorus repeats, again framed by the title phrase.

The entire song is framed by two series of ascending chords on the keyboard. The opening gesture establishes the key, indicates to the audience that they should quiet down, and effectively announces to the other musicians that the next song is about to begin. The same pianistic gesture concludes the song and draws out the music while the audience begins to clap.

 ## Black Gospel's Timbre

Gospel singing styles vary widely, for each soloist attempts to create a sound that is distinctive and personal. Gospel singers often use a technique known as belting that is more closely related in its physical use of the voice to shouting or speaking. This timbre is different from the cultivated tone used by singers of classical art song (such as *Lieder* by Schubert or Schumann; see Chapters 31 and 35). Gospel singers are also expected to embellish a melody and linger over individual words for emphasis as they see fit, often improvising new phrases and short melodies as they respond to the emotional content of their own performance in the moment. The best gospel singers establish a strong on-stage connection with their audiences to convey a song's message as directly as possible.

The organ in this recording is one of the strongest signifiers of the gospel genre. Hammond organs, first built in 1934, are electric instruments with a unique, warble-like tone. During the subsequent decades, they were affordable enough for small churches to acquire, and portable enough to install on concert stages where no pipe organ existed. In "It Don't Cost Very Much," the organ enters with a sustained chord at 0:10, then adopts a supporting role to the piano for the rest of the recording. It provides melodic fills between almost all the vocal phrases.

The piano is also essential to classic gospel; from the beginning of this recording, the piano controls the harmonies, the groove, and the style of the song. The wide range of pitches available on the piano enable it to take four different musical roles:

- *Low bass notes.* These establish the foundation for the harmony and set the basic groove.
- *Rhythmic chords in the higher pitches.* These fill in colorful harmonies and provide the body of sound for the recording.

- *Fills*. These are short melodies and motives that maintain the musical intensity between the singer's phrases. At 1:22, the pianist's fill behind the word "place" uses a dissonant "slip-note" technique, in which she plays a note that is one pitch away from a note in the chord, then releases it quickly and slides immediately to the note in the chord.

- *Special sound effects*. A **glissando**, in which the pianist plays a rapid flourish up or down the keyboard, usually by sliding one or two fingers or the thumb across the keys, is a crowd-pleasing, showy gesture characteristic of gospel performances. Another effect is the use of the damper pedal, which lifts the felt pads (dampers) from the piano's strings and enables them to ring.

An upright bass completes the gospel instrumentation, reinforcing the low-note harmonies played by the pianist's left hand.

Slow Shuffle Groove with Free Rhythmic Phrasing

The slow shuffle groove in this recording is characteristic of classic gospel. In a shuffle groove, each beat in a four-beat measure is divided into three evenly spaced pulses. The rhythms in the performance tend to emphasize the first and third pulse of each beat, creating a LONG-short-LONG-short pattern:

```
Beats:    1      2      3      4
Pulses:   X x X  X x X  X x X  X x X
Rhythms:  —  -   —  -   —  -   —  -
```

The low notes in the piano at 0:14 produce a pattern that rocks back and forth in the shuffle rhythm. This particular rocking-pitch pattern is used in many classic gospel recordings.

When the singer enters at 0:14, she slows the tempo down and the instruments adjust to match her. With the second vocal phrase, the singer slows down the tempo even further, and the instrumentalists again make the adjustment. By about 0:25, the tempo is finally set. This audible change in tempo, one of the most intriguing aspects of the recording, is an artifact of the live concert. The previous song on the program was a livelier and faster number, and it takes a few moments for the ensemble to settle into the slower pace of this song.

In the classic gospel style, once the steady groove is established, the musicians stick to it. This creates a stable rhythmic foundation on top of which Jackson can take rhythmic liberties with the vocal phrases—speeding some up, slowing others down, sometimes entering earlier or later, rather like the kind of rubato Chopin strove for between the two hands on the piano (see Chapter 37). In gospel music, this technique allows the singer to be moved by spiritual inspiration in the middle of the song, intensifying the religious nature of the performance.

Gospel Harmonies

One feature of gospel music is its heavy reliance on stock, formulaic harmonic progressions. These patterns allow amateur musicians to more easily participate in music-making, and they make even new compositions seem familiar. Gospel pianists are so well versed in these progressions that they embellish them easily, and their hands fall into the patterns comfortably.

A typical progression starts at 0:58. The bass line moves chromatically, one pitch at a time, up the piano. When the singer arrives on the word "way" (at 1:04), the progression has traveled to the harmonic launch-point for a strong cadence.

The next few notes (accompanying "it don't . . . ," at 1:06) rise again up a scale, this time heading toward the fifth scale degree, which, in the harmonic language of this song, demands that the chord progression return to tonic (musical home base).

The Hammond organ, named after its inventor, Laurens Hammond (1895–1973), became associated with the sound of gospel music soon after its introduction in the 1930s. It is small, portable, and much less expensive than a full-sized pipe organ.

Now listen to this song again, using the Listening Guide.

Listening Guide

Mahalia Jackson Composed: 1958

"It Don't Cost Very Much"

Time	Text	Form	Timbre
0:00		Introduction	The sound of a foot tapping out the beat is audible on the recording.
0:12	Lyric describes the benefit of kindness to others.	Verse (first half)	The voice quivers on the word "smile," and enters with a dark, smoky tone.
0:41	Lyric encourages others to forgive.	Verse, continued (second half)	Bass is more audible here, playing on the downbeats.
1:11	It don't cost very much	Chorus (first half)	Organ moves into a higher register.
1:41	Lyric explains that even those who are not perfect can benefit from showing kindness; the song title is repeated.	Chorus, continued (second half)	The pianist echoes the singer's phrase at 1:46
2:09	It don't cost very much . . .	Chorus (first half)	Organ and piano become more active. At 2:29, piano's ascending fill builds toward climax.
2:39	Lyric explains that even those who are not perfect can benefit from showing kindness; the song title is repeated.	Chorus, continued (second half)	Pianist uses the damper pedal more and more, culminating in a very open, ringing sound at 3:05.

Rhythm

Rhythm	Harmony
Piano introduction establishes the shuffle groove.	Only two harmonies are used in the introduction. The two chords alternate and then repeat.
The tempo slows down substantially when the soloist enters.	The 16-bar chord-progression begins.
Rhythmic freedom in the vocal phrases.	
	Harmonic progression matches the first half of the verse.
	Harmonic progression matches the second half of the verse, with the one slight variation.
	Same harmonic progression as first chorus.
At the very end, the rhythmic groove is abandoned and the tempo slows substantially.	The pianist plays a series of ascending chords while the audience claps.

 Harmony

Student FAQs

How does Jackson tell her musicians to slow down the tempo while she is singing?

Jackson sings the rhythms of her melody just a little bit later than the band. We can't see the performers communicating on stage, but we can hear how the singer adjusts the tempo to her liking with the slightest rhythmic nuances, and the accompanying musicians respond almost instantaneously. The process requires the musicians to pay close attention to the singer.

Why is it difficult to understand Jackson's lyrics?

Jackson's pronunciation of individual words (for instance, the pulses she adds to "smile," at 0:21, or "mad," at 0:40), the wide vibrato ("pleasin'," at 0:30), and the occasional shift in the standard accentuation are all indicative of the vocal timbres in classic gospel that borrowed from earlier secular styles, particularly the blues. Her regional accent (New Orleans) radically changes some pronunciations as well, such as "church" (2:52). Vocal

nuances such as these conveyed the personal convictions, emotional investment, and biographical origins of the performer because audiences expected gospel singers to be living the messages contained in the songs.

PROFILE   Mahalia Jackson (1911–1972) and Thomas A. Dorsey (1899–1993)

A Divine Collaboration

Thomas A. Dorsey and Mahalia Jackson did not always get along, but for nearly a decade and a half, their collaboration as composer and performer resulted in some of the best classic gospel music of all time. Dorsey was always skeptical of the liberties Jackson took in changing the melodies, improvising embellishments, and pulling the song into her own gospel style. But although Dorsey composed many of the best-known songs in the gospel genre, it was Jackson's finishing touches that created the sound that gospel audiences loved. Working together, they helped transform gospel music into a widely accepted commercial style that sold millions of records.

Mahalia Jackson.

Born near Atlanta, Georgia, Dorsey spent his early years as a highly regarded blues pianist. He played for several of the most famous blues acts of the 1920s, including Ma Rainey. Dorsey's interest in gospel music extended beyond performance: He opened a publishing firm to sell new gospel compositions and helped organize the National Convention of Gospel Choirs and Choruses. He recognized that he could best promote his compositions by having them widely performed, so he hired singers to put on concerts of his songs. In 1928, he met young Mahalia Jackson, and by the early 1930s, she was singing his songs on tour.

Jackson grew up in New Orleans, listening to the powerful, expressive singing in the Sanctified church next door to her home (although Jackson attended a Baptist church herself) and to blues singers, including Bessie Smith and Ma Rainey. Jackson borrowed the vocal techniques and melodic embellishments from blues, and then she combined them with the vocal shouts and exuberance of Sanctified congregational singing to create her own style. She moved to Chicago in 1927, where she launched her career singing with church choirs and touring with a local gospel group. After little success with her early recordings, in 1948 she released a major hit, "Move on Up a Little Higher," which introduced the sound of the Hammond organ as a key component in gospel. With astounding sales of both records and concert tickets, Jackson became a bona fide superstar in the 1950s and 1960s, with performances on the *Ed Sullivan Show*, at the inauguration of John F. Kennedy, and at the funeral for Dr. Martin Luther King, Jr. in 1968 (where she sang Dorsey's "Take My Hand, Precious Lord").

Thomas A. Dorsey.

EXPAND YOUR PLAYLIST: JACKSON

- **"Move On Up a Little Higher"** (1948), by W. Herbert Brewster
- **"Take My Hand, Precious Lord"** (1956), by Thomas A. Dorsey
- **"He's Got the Whole World in His Hands"** (1958), spiritual
- **"Walk Over God's Heaven"** (1958), by Thomas A. Dorsey
- **"Were You There?"** (1967), spiritual

HISTORICAL CONTEXT   Gospel in Black and White

White gospel, which is generally known as "southern gospel," and black gospel emerged as two essentially separate traditions, although they share many characteristics. Southern gospel grew out of the religious revival and traveling camp meetings that blanketed the South and Midwest in the nineteenth century. By the early twentieth century, Baptist, Pentecostal, and Holiness (a Sanctified denomination) congregations had taken root in almost every community, and they sought rousing songs in popular styles to fan the flames of spiritual revival. Black gospel got its start when students at historically black colleges and universities assembled vocal quartets to revive traditional spirituals in concert settings. The quartets traveled widely, and some turned professional after the members graduated. These quartets later began to adopt the exuberant, free vocal styles and newly composed songs heard in Sanctified, Holiness, and Baptist churches, combined with the popular sounds of jazz and rhythm-and-blues.

Black and white artists sometimes shared songs and influenced each other's performance styles. For instance, the black Golden Gate Quartet and white Blackwood Brothers (see Expand Your Playlist) toured together on a few occasions in the late 1940s. Those collaborations were particularly difficult in the South, where segregation laws prevented the musicians even from dining together in public spaces.

The issue of what their audiences felt was and was not acceptable behavior for a gospel singer plagued both black and white gospel singers. In the 1930s and 1940s, gospel audiences demanded that their artists not only perform the music convincingly but also live in accordance with the gospel song's lyrics and eschew all secular music of questionable moral stature. This attitude led to trouble for many gospel musicians who wanted to perform secular music or sing in nightclubs occasionally. It also brought criticism to jazz and country musicians who performed gospel songs outside a gospel context. Trumpeter Louis Armstrong was openly chastised for his swinging version of "When the Saints Go Marching In." Similarly, gospel singers who ventured to perform in nightclubs faced intense criticism: Sister Rosetta Tharpe, one of the best-known female soloists in black gospel, sang with Cab Calloway at New York City's Cotton Club in 1938, and, later in her career, tried to pay off some debts by singing in nightclubs. Her audience never forgave her this perceived betrayal of gospel music's high moral standards, and her career sank as a result.

 EXPAND YOUR PLAYLIST

Southern and Black Gospel

These recordings provide a sample of gospel music, both white and black, from its earliest recorded days through the height of the classic gospel era.

The Stamps Quartet
- "Give the World a Smile" (1927). This white quartet was hired to publicize the Stamps publishing company's music. The way the quartet echoes the lead singer in several sections of the song is a technique known as "after-beat harmonies."

The Golden Gate Quartet
- "Swing Down, Chariot" (1946). This popular black quartet's recording presents a lively arrangement of a traditional spiritual. Both the Blackwood Brothers and Elvis Presley later recorded this song.

Red Foley
- "Peace in the Valley" (1951). Foley, like many other country music stars, included gospel music in his repertory, although he was not part of the gospel music scene. This recording of a Thomas A. Dorsey composition illustrates a white musician performing a black composer's gospel song for a country music audience.

The Dixie Hummingbirds
- "Let's Go Out to the Program" (1953). The Dixie Hummingbirds were one of the most successful black gospel quartets of this era. This song includes excerpts that imitate other famous black quartets, providing a sampling of several gospel songs.

The Blackwood Brothers
- "The Man Upstairs" (1954). One of the most famous southern gospel (white) quartets, the Blackwood Brothers, won first place on Arthur Godfrey's "Talent Scouts" TV show with this song. Notice how different members of the ensemble take turns singing lead.

63

Tania León
A la Par, second movement ("Guaguancó")
Composed: 1986

What happens when modernism confronts popular music in the same work? León's *A la Par* offers one possible scenario, for this playful postmodern work mixes the rhythms of a Cuban popular dance with atonal harmonies.

Listen to This First

〰 Timbre

Listen for the contrast between those percussion instruments that play specific pitches (like the piano, the vibraphone, and the bongo drums) and those that make only percussive sounds that cannot be tied to any specific pitch (like the cowbell, the cymbals, and the snare drum). ■

📖 Rhythm

Listen for the repeated melodic and rhythmic figure in the lower register of the piano. This kind of figure is typical of the Afro-Cuban dance known as the *guaguancó*. ■

🎭 Harmony

Listen for the mixture of tonal and atonal harmonies in this work. ■

🏛 Form

The movement divides into two very different sections. Where does the change occur? ■

LEARNING OBJECTIVES

63.1 Define postmodernism in the arts in general.

63.2 Define postmodernism in music specifically and explain the ways in which Tania León's "Guaguancó" from *A la Par* exemplifies musical postmodernism.

63.3 Listen for the differences between tonal and atonal passages in this work.

63.4 Listen for the different rhythmic patterns in "Guaguancó."

63.5 Outline León's career as a conductor and composer.

The Spanish title *A la par* translates loosely as "at the same time as" or "on the same level as," and it is a fitting description of the relationship between popular and modernist styles. The repeated rhythm in the bass line derives from a traditional Cuban dance, while the other instrumental lines reflect the principles of European modernism. Even though they are often quite distinct—each goes its own way—they nevertheless complement one another to create a whole larger than the sum of its parts. Every instrument seems to occupy its own space, yet in the end everything is indeed *a la par*. The composer herself has said that this work reflects her own attempt "to express the dichotomy between the folk-music traditions of my native Cuba and the Classical European training I received at the Havana Conservatory."[1]

This musical style in which modern and traditional elements are combined is often called **postmodernism**. Postmodernism is a late twentieth-century style of modernism—no one would think of León's music as old-fashioned—but it embraces tonality as well as atonality, rhythmic predictability as well as unpredictability. Postmodern works are often playful in spirit, a reaction against the unrelenting seriousness of much modernist art. As a work of postmodernism, León's *A la Par* is both tonal and atonal, rhythmically regular and irregular, serious and playful.

[1] Reprinted by permission of Tania León.

Percussion Timbres

A percussion instrument is one that produces sound by being struck or shaken, and all the instruments in this work belong to the percussion family, including even the piano (a finger strikes the key, which activates a hammer, which strikes a string). Some percussion instruments (like the piano or certain kinds of drums) produce specific pitches, while others do not. In the second movement of *A la Par*, León uses both kinds of instruments. The timings in the following list indicate examples of when you can hear these individual instruments. Notice that not all the instruments are played the same way all the time. The player striking the timbales (a pair of small drums), for example, sometimes hits the side of the instrument with a stick and sometimes hits the membrane surface on the top. The conga player sometimes uses the hand, sometimes a stick.

Pitched Instruments

• **Piano:** 0:00 and throughout.

• **Timbales** (a small drum): 0:06 and throughout. In this particular movement, the player most often uses a stick to strike the side of the instrument, but at other times strikes the membrane on top of the drum (as at 0:28–0:30), which is the more standard way of playing the instrument.

• **Tom-toms** (a pair of large drums): 0:35–0:40.

• **Bongos** (a pair of very small hand drums): 0:50–0:52.

• **Snare drum** (a medium-sized drum): 0:23–0:25.

• **Marimba** (a xylophone-like instrument with tubular resonators under each bar): 1:55–end.

• **Vibraphone** (an electrified marimba with motorized controls that can produce different degrees of vibrato, a wavering-like sound, for each pitch): 1:50–end.

Nonpitched Instruments

• **Conga** (a long, narrow drum): 0:05, very briefly, then again at 0:12–0:15, played first with the hand and then with a stick

• **Cowbell** (struck with a stick): 0:43–0:45.

• **Suspended cymbal** (a single cymbal, struck with a stick): 0:34.

• **Cachiche** (a maraca-like "shaker"): 1:02–1:08.

 Male and Female Rhythmic Lines

In the lower register of the piano, we hear a syncopated figure over and over, the kind of rhythmic pattern to which Cuban dancers could dance the *guaguancó*. The central element of this rumba-style dance is the *vacuno*, a pelvic thrust by the man toward the woman, who both encourages and avoids these thrusts. Listen to the way in which the repeated figure in the bass suggests a physical

CONNECT YOUR PLAYLIST

Repeated Melodic-Rhythmic Figure

Find an example of a piece that contains a repeated melodic-rhythmic figure.

Example: Michael Jackson, "Bad" (1987)
The prominent repeated bass line in this song establishes both a melodic pattern and rhythmic support for the vocal line.

thrust and how the voices around it—all the other percussion instruments, including the piano in its middle and upper ranges—seem to both encourage and resist this repeated thrusting figure.

Parallel (Non-) Harmonies

The repeated figure in the lower register of the piano is chromatically inflected but squarely tonal: It keeps landing over and over on the same note, so we feel that the music—or at least this portion of the music—has a tonal center. It has some notes that sound slightly dissonant, but the repeated note is so prominent that our ear hears this note as a harmonic foundation. Everything else—including even the higher notes on the piano—is insistently atonal. (The nonpitched percussion instruments cannot play a role in the harmony: They function in a purely rhythmic fashion.) This movement thus combines elements of both tonality (the repeated *guanguacó* figure in the bass) and atonality.

A couple in Havana dances the *guaguancó*; drummers are visible in the background.

Sectional Form

The contrast between the last third of the movement and all that has gone before is sudden and obvious: The steady rhythmic figure disappears; the tempo shifts suddenly from fast to slow; almost all the percussion instruments drop out; and two new instruments, the marimba and the vibraphone, enter for the first time. On closer listening, we realize that the first quarter or so of this movement is an introduction of sorts, for while it presents the basic *guanguacó* figure, it does so only sporadically. Only after a short break in the music (at 0:39) does this figure become an ostinato. The movement thus divides into three sections: an introduction, the central *guanguacó*, and a coda. The first two sections are closely related, while the third is quite different.

With these points in mind, listen to the second movement of this work again, using the Listening Guide.

Tania León Composed: 1986

A la Par, second movement ("Guaguancó") (2:27)

Time	🏛 Form: Section	🥁 Rhythm	〰 Timbre	☁ Harmony
0:00	(1) Introduction (fast)	*Guaguancó* rhythm in lower register of piano, but not continuously. The upper register of the piano and all the other instruments weave around this recurring figure.	Piano, percussion instruments	No sense of tonality at first, but the melodic figure in the bass (starting at 0:11) establishes its lowest note as the central tone.
0:39	(2) Ostinato (fast)	The rhythmic figure now becomes an ostinato in the bass, repeated without a pause.		Nonostinato pitches are atonal; ostinato figure centers on its lowest note.
1:33	(2) Coda (slow)	*Guaguancó* rhythm drops out for the first time. Piano plays a disjunct, atonal line in its place.	Reduced instrumentation and new instruments: Piano, cowbell (briefly), then the vibraphone and marimba enter for the first time.	Wholly atonal; no sense of a tonal center at all.

A marimba.

🔍 Student FAQs

How many musicians does it take to perform this work?

In a percussion ensemble, one player usually covers multiple instruments, switching from, say, marimba to vibraphone to claves (wooden sticks) as the score demands. The number of performers is optional, but the score determines how many are needed at a minimum. The excerpt given here would require at least four percussionists.

What's the difference between postmodernism and neoclassicism?

The two are related but not the same. Both make reference to earlier idioms, though neoclassicism is generally associated with the 1920s and 1930s, whereas postmodernism is a phenomenon of the late twentieth century. Postmodern music, unlike neoclassicism, embraces modernism as one of many legitimate approaches to artistic expressions, whereas neoclassicism rejects the extremes of modernism. In the end, the terms are labels whose applicability to any given work or artist can be debated.

PROFILE   Tania León (b. 1943)

Synthesizing Traditions

As a composer, Tania León defies easy categorization: Her music synthesizes a great many traditions, from Cuban dance to atonality and many other styles in between. In this respect, it reflects León's exposure to multiple musical styles and idioms, not only in her native Cuba, where she studied to become a pianist, but also in the United States, where she turned her attention more and more toward composing and conducting. Shortly after immigrating to the United States in 1967, she became the first music director of the Dance Theater of Harlem in 1969 and has taught composition at Brooklyn College since 1985. She has received commissions from throughout the world for works in a variety of genres, including operas and several works for orchestra. As a conductor, she has performed with such prestigious ensembles as the Gewandhaus Orchestra of Leipzig and the New York Philharmonic.

Tania León has received numerous awards and honors not only for her compositions but also for her work as a conductor and music educator.

 EXPAND YOUR PLAYLIST: LEÓN

- *Rituál.* A modernist work for piano.
- *Pueblo mulato.* Three songs to texts by Cuban poet Nicolás Guillén, for soprano, oboe, guitar, double bass, percussion, and piano.
- *Indigena.* A work for chamber orchestra that draws on the composer's Cuban roots.
- *Scourge of Hyacinths.* An opera based on a radio play by Nobel Prize–winning Nigerian author Wole Soyinka.
- *Momentum.* A work for piano, with an energetic rhythm, as its title suggests.

Postmodern Architecture

The spirit of postmodernism is perhaps most readily apparent in the field of architecture. For many decades in the middle of the twentieth century, modernist architecture dominated the scene. The typical modernist building favored clean, straight lines with little or no hint of ornamentation.

Advocates of modernist architecture praised its emphasis on functionality and its break with traditions of the past. But in

the second half of the twentieth century, more and more critics came to see this style as cold and impersonal. Postmodern architects began adding elements to building that were not driven entirely by function. The curved walls of the Walt Disney Theater in Los Angeles (2004) capture the more playful spirit of postmodernism.

With its symmetrical design and clean, straight lines, the John F. Kennedy Center for the Performing Arts in Washington, D.C. (1971), exemplifies modernist architecture.

The fanciful, irregular shape of the Walt Disney Concert Hall in Los Angeles (2004) reflects the more recent style of postmodern architecture.

 EXPAND YOUR PLAYLIST

Postmodern Music

The postmodern idiom has attracted a number of leading composers in recent decades, including the following:

Rochberg (1918–2005)
• String Quartet no. 6. A postmodern work by a composer who was an avowed modernist in his early career. The slow movement is a set of variations on Pachelbel's celebrated Canon.

William Bolcom (b. 1938)
• *Songs of Innocence and Experience*. A setting of texts by William Blake, this cycle of songs juxtaposes a wide range of musical idioms, including atonal and tonal, jazz, gospel, blues, ragtime, and rock.

Luciano Berio (1925–2003)
• *Sinfonia*. The second movement of this work for orchestra and eight amplified voices uses the second movement of Gustav

Mahler's Second Symphony as its basis, with samplings from works by many other composers superimposed on it, along with a text by Samuel Beckett.

Rodion Shchedrin (b. 1932)
• *Carmen Suite*. This is a reworking of themes from Georges Bizet's well-known *Carmen* (1875), rewritten and reorchestrated in such a way as to create an arresting mixture of nineteenth- and twentieth-century idioms.

John Zorn (b. 1953)
• *The Big Gundown: John Zorn Plays the Music of Ennio Morricone*. This album, released in 1985, superimposes idioms of jazz, soul, and other genres on the film scores of a composer who specialized in creating soundtracks for films set in the American West (*A Fistful of Dollars, Once Upon a Time in the West*).

64

Corey Dargel
"On This Date Every Year"
Composed: 2010

Corey Dargel's "On This Date Every Year," a song for baritone, violin, and digital looping, straddles the conventional divisions between "art" and "popular" music in ways that make such distinctions seem pointless. It also offers an example of the way in which many current composers work across identifiable styles and genres to create their own blend of music. This particular number is part of a larger set called *Every Day Is the Same Day: A Song Cycle about Clinical Depression*.

Listen to This First 🔊

Timbre	🌐 Texture	🎵 Rhythm	🔄 Word–Music Relationships
What instruments do you hear? How many? How many voices are singing? ■	What is the predominant texture here? ■	Does the rhythm follow a fixed meter or beat? ■	Does the music match the meaning of the words? Why? Why not? ■

LEARNING OBJECTIVES

64.1 Define postmodernism in music.

64.2 Describe what is meant by a digital loop.

64.3 Discuss how digital looping creates a series of different textures throughout the piece.

64.4 Explain how digital looping reinforces the ideas behind the text.

64.5 Listen for the use of 5/4 meter in this song.

64.6 Describe the career of Corey Dargel.

The distinction between "classical" and "popular" music is sometimes quite meaningless. More and more composers nowadays avoid working within easily identifiable styles or genres and create their own blend of music. Corey Dargel straddles the worlds of classical and popular in works like his "On This Date Every Year," a haunting song in which the singer recalls the anniversary of the death of his significant other.

Like Tania León's *A la par* (Chapter 63), "On This Date Every Year" is a good example of musical **postmodernism**. Its idiom is clearly recent—modern—but it is not afraid to draw on more conventional means as well. With its references to plane crashes and e-mail, the text is edgy and up to date, and digital looping is a relatively recent technology. At the same time, Dargel uses a basically tonal (if at times slightly dissonant) harmonic language and combines it with the kind of dense polyphony that was standard in much Renaissance music (see Chapter 9, William Byrd's "Sing Joyfully," for six voices).

Looped, Overdubbed

This song is performed by only two musicians: a singer and one violinist. With a microphone attached to the instrument, the violinist uses a specially constructed pedal to send short phrases of what he or she is playing into a computer that records and immediately plays back (through on-stage loudspeakers) until switched off. The recorded phrases are all the same length and all the same tempo and are called "**loops**" because they keep repeating themselves. The successive digital loops play back through loudspeakers on the stage even as the live violinist continues to play (and as the singer continues to sing). The violinist can control almost all variables using foot pedals, telling the computer when to record, when to repeat, when to stop recording, and when to stop repeating.

The singer's voice, in turn, is overdubbed—digitally modified in a way to make it sound richer and more resonant, almost as if there is more than one singer actually singing, though this of course is not actually the case. Overdubbing is a common recording technique that has been used in many kinds of music since the middle of the twentieth century.

Source: Excerpt of score from Corey Dargel, "On This Date Every Year." Words and music by Corey Dargel. Copyright © 2011 Automatic Heartbreak (ASCAP). Used by permission.

Texture: One to Eight Voices

Digital looping allows the violinist to play simultaneously against the sound of recorded music he has played only moments before. For most of the song, we hear a texture of five voices:

1. The voice singing the text
2. The live violin line
3. Violin loop 1
4. Violin loop 2
5. Violin loop 3

Each violin loop is a different melodic figure exactly 15 beats long (three measures, each with five beats). The successive layering of these loops creates a dense polyphonic texture among the violin lines, and these all run simultaneously against the independent voice line. Toward the end of the song, the violinist adds three additional loops to create a texture of eight distinct voices.

Form: On Again, Off Again

The text of the song is a series of irregular units with no consistent pattern of meter or rhyme. The first unit has four lines, the second has five, the third has four, and the fifth has six. In between the third and fifth unit is a refrain-like repeat of two lines heard earlier ("Will I observe the anniversary of your death / On this date ev'ry year").

Foot pedals can send looping sequences from any number of instruments, including the electric guitar as well as the violin. The multiple foot pedals on the equipment shown here can accommodate many sequenced loops.

The music maps one loop cycle onto each of these five units of text. Each of the five loop cycles begins with the live violin by itself. The violinist "sends" the first three measures into the looping software, and those three measures (15 beats) repeat multiple times through the loudspeaker, even

This screen shot from the laptop used in a performance of Dargel's "On This Date Every Year" shows the various loops repeating and layering on top of one another at the beginning of the piece.

as the live violinist continues on with different music. This process continues until we reach the full texture of that particular loop cycle. At that point, the violinist (using a foot pedal) stops all the loops and starts the process over again. Once again we hear only the live violinist, and once again, the violinist proceeds to add one, two, three, or more loops that continue until the end of *that* cycle. And so on. In the final cycle, as noted, the violinist adds six loops to create a total of seven violin lines (six loops plus one live).

 ## Rhythm: Five Is an Odd Number

The meter of this song is 5/4: five beats per measure (5/), with the quarter-note (/4) the basic unit of the beat. In music, five is an odd number in ways that three is not. Five beats are a little too long to establish a regular pattern the way we can with only three beats to a bar (as we do all the time, including, for example, the *Star-Spangled Banner*): **1**-2-3 \| **1**-2-3 \| **1**-2-3. Five poses another problem in that unlike six (**1**-2-3-**4**-5-6 \| **1**-2-3-**4**-5-6 \| **1**-2-3-**4**-5-6) we can't divide it into smaller groupings of an equal number of beats. With five, the basic choices for subdivision are 3 + 2 (or 2 + 3) or 4 + 1 (or 1 + 4). Neither is a conventional grouping.

The metrical pattern of this song, especially in the violin looping, is mostly 3 + 2 (**1**-2-3-**4**-5 \| **1**-2-3-**4**-5 \| etc.). This gives a slightly hesitant, jerky feeling to things, a little like a car or motorcycle that sputters, speeds up, then slows down over and over. The voice generally moves in a freer rhythm, which sets up another contrast between voice and violin.

 ## Word–Music Relationships

The text is about an anniversary, and thinking about the events of an anniversary can make us go back in time in our imaginations: We relive events over and over. What better way, then, to bring out the idea of recurrence than through a series of musical figures that loop around and repeat, over and over, almost in the way certain episodes of some dreams do at times? Yet the repetition is never entirely literal and can take on a life of its own. The voice, in contrast to the violin looping, seems to be moving forward, or at least trying to move forward, to get on with things. The vocal melody repeats certain figures from time to time ("On this date every year," for example), but not nearly as often as the figures we hear in the violin.

The seemingly relentless pace of the song slows down for the final strophe (marked "Wistfully" in the score). This loop cycle lasts twice as long as each of the ones before, fitting with the unexpected turn in the meaning of the words. The number of voices grows steadily from five to eight. The music becomes more tranquil, ethereal, less agitated, even if the final cadence does not sound like a conclusive ending. Life goes on. But it is not the same as the way it seemed at the beginning of the song. "Different is all that's desired," as Dargel himself has noted. "'Better' doesn't matter."

With these points in mind, now listen to this song again, using the Listening Guide.

CONNECT YOUR PLAYLIST

Live/Recorded Music

Find a work that combines acoustic and electric sounds.

Example: The Beatles, "Sgt. Pepper's Lonely Hearts Club Band" (1967) The electric rock sound is briefly interrupted by the sound of a traditional brass band on the opening track of the album.

Corey Dargel Composed: 2010

"On This Date Every Year"

Time	Form: Loop Cycle	Text	Texture: Number of Voices	Word–Music Relationships
0:00	1	I imagine your plane crashing All the exit lights flashing Your oxygen mask does not inflate I look at today's date And worry	5	Disjointed declamation; the vocal line seems unconnected to the violin loops.
0:31	2	Will I observe the anniversary of your death On this date every year The day you take your last breath The day you disappear On this date every year	5	
1:00	3	Will I make phone calls in distress To all your family and friends Will I log in to your e-mail address And send the last e-mails you'll ever send	5	Longer than usual solo violin introduction to this loop cycle.
1:35	4	Will I observe the anniversary of your death On this date every year The day you take your last breath The day you disappear On this date every year	5	
2:03	5	Strangely it's not entirely devastating To imagine such a catastrophe Everyone will be so accommodating And when someone else makes a pass at me I can stop equivocating The way I had to when we were dating	5 6 7 8	The tempo slows and the note values become longer to match the unexpected turn of the text's content.

Source: Lyrics from Corey Dargel, "On This Date Every Year." Words and music by Corey Dargel. Copyright © 2011 Automatic Heartbreak (ASCAP). Used by permission.

🔍 Student FAQs ⚙

Is this song autobiographical?

This is a good question that raises even better questions: Does it matter if the composer actually experienced the events described in the lyrics? Could he not have imagined them? How would that change the way we hear the song? And can we—should we—understand the words literally? Isn't it possible that "plane crash" is a metaphor for something else? (We sometimes say that a certain situation is a "train wreck" even when we don't mean that literally.)

Pedals?

Pedals allow musicians to keep their hands free to play their instruments. Electric guitarists have been using pedals ("stompboxes") for years to create special effects like distortion or reverberation. The development of computer technology has expanded the range of possible sonic effects even more.

PROFILE   Corey Dargel (b. 1977)

Born in 1977 in McAllen, Texas, composer, poet, and singer Corey Dargel studied composition at Oberlin College with Pauline Oliveros and John Luther Adams. He now lives in New York City. "I've always been sympathetic to people who won't (or can't) conform to society's expectations," Dargel says. "This is undoubtedly because I grew up as a closeted gay kid in a very conservative part of Texas."

In his music, Dargel likes to "begin with a challenge to myself, a challenge to tackle a subject that I can't easily relate to (like hypochondria, voluntary amputation, religious cults). I research the subject in conventional and unconventional ways. I try to take a sideways look at characters and behaviors in difficult situations, and I try to do it with a sense of humor and compassion. My hope is that, throughout a performance of my work, the audience goes through a similar process: Someone or something they can't initially relate to becomes more and more relatable as the songs go on. This process, for me, is about empathy. I believe that cultivating our ability to empathize with others makes it easier for us to relate to the world around us in more fulfilling and creative ways."

Corey Dargel in performance, New York City, 2012.

EXPAND YOUR PLAYLIST: Dargel

- **"Last Words from Texas."** Last statements of Texas prisoners on death row, set to music. A free download is available at *www.-automaticheartbreak.com/2011/12/last-words-from-texas-free-ep-download*.

- **"Someone Will Take Care of Me."** An album of Dargel's theatrical song cycles, "Thirteen Near-Death Experiences" (about hypochondria) and "Removable Parts" (about voluntary amputation) on New Amsterdam Records, 2010.

- **"Other People's Love Songs."** Custom-made love songs commissioned from one significant other to the, uh, other, on New Amsterdam Records, 2008.

- **"Con Dolcezza (with Sweetness)."** A musical setting of various speeches by former Secretary of State Condoleezza Rice. Listen online at *www.condisongs.com*.

EXPAND YOUR PLAYLIST

Crossover Music

Crossover artists are not a new phenomenon: George Gershwin (1899–1937) and Duke Ellington (1899–1974; see Chapter 51) moved easily between the worlds of jazz and classical music. Some more recent musicians whose style resists easy classification include:

- **Brian Eno (b. 1948).** Eno began his career as a rock synthesizer player before becoming more interested in crossover styles and new musical forms. His music emphasizes ambient sounds and the effects of chance. He has collaborated with many well-known musicians, including David Bowie, Paul Simon, U2, Coldplay, and Philip Glass. His single most famous "work" at one time was "The Microsoft Sound," heard at the Windows 95 startup screen.

- **Björk (b. 1965).** The Icelandic singer and composer Björk released her first album at age 12, beginning a multifaceted career in many genres, including classical, electronic, rock, jazz, world, and folk. Her recent collaborations have included musicians from across the world as well as British composer John Tavener, and she composed the score for the award-winning film *Dancer in the Dark* (2000), in which she also starred.

- **Yann Tiersen (b. 1970).** Tiersen, a French musician, has a background in both classical and rock styles. Outside France he is best known for his score to the film *Amélie* (2001), which is made of music from his previous studio albums. His work is heavily influenced by minimalist music (particularly Philip Glass and Michael Nyman) and is notable for its combinations of instruments, ranging from the fairly traditional (accordion, toy piano, ukulele, banjo, etc.) to the unorthodox (typewriter, bicycle wheel, chains, etc.).

Austin Wintory
"Nascence," from *Journey*
Composed: 2012

The award-winning music for the 2012 video game *Journey* evokes a fantastic landscape and creates a memorable and emotional experience for its players.

Listen to This First

🎧 Word–Music Relationships

This game is a story about one character on a journey, traversing long distances and overcoming obstacles along the way. How does this piece of music reflect that idea? ■

〽 Timbre

Listen to the diversity of instruments: solo cello, harp, and bass flute, as well as a full string orchestra. This variety helps to keep the piece exciting, and allows the melody to stand out from the accompaniment. ■

🎵 Melody

"Nascence" begins with a melody played by the cello. Listen for how this melody changes each time it is repeated. ■

🌐 Texture

Listen to the way the music moves through three textures in a short period of time: a monophonic opening, a homophonic central section, and finally a polyphonic dialogue between the cello and the orchestra. ■

***Journey* is a video game** created by the small independent group thatgamecompany and released as a downloadable game for Sony's Playstation 3 video game console. In many ways, it is not a typical video game. The "journey" in the title is less about testing players' reflexes than about making them reflect on the game's meaning. There are no complicated puzzles, fights, or dialogue, and completing the game is not terribly challenging. *Journey* also only takes a few hours to complete, so players can experience it in one sitting rather than spread over several days or weeks. The simple plot follows the player's character on a trek across the desert to a mountain far in the distance, but the real meaning of the game is experiencing the journey itself.

There are no words in "Nascence," and there is no particular story to go along with it, such as a poem or narrative. But the music is still to some extent responsible for creating the game's plot, much like a piece of program music. Music has many roles in media like film and games. It can set a particular mood, for example, reflecting the overall tone of the game. Music can also give us information about the world we're watching—giving us clues as to where and when we are. And most importantly, music helps us know how to feel about events and characters we see. All those functions are at work in the musical elements of "Nascence," as we can see by looking at its timbre, melody, and texture.

The game's music, by film and game composer Austin Wintory, plays a hugely important role in immersing players in *Journey*'s atmosphere. The soundtrack has won numerous awards, and it

LEARNING OBJECTIVES

65.1 Discuss the role of music in video games.

65.2 Explain why Austin Wintory used "Nascence" as the title for this part of *Journey*.

65.3 Listen for and identify the different instrumental timbres in "Nascence."

65.4 Discuss how changes in melody and texture evoke drama and meaning in "Nascence."

65.5 Listen for and identify the different sections of "Nascence" based on the use of melody, timbre, and texture.

65.6 Discuss how changes in technology have resulted in new compositional techniques.

65.7 Describe the career of Austin Wintory.

is the first video game soundtrack nominated for a prestigious Grammy Award, suggesting that video games are beginning to gain widespread acknowledgment for their artistic merit.

Word–Music Relationships: Beginnings

This piece is called "Nascence," meaning "birth" or "coming into existence." ("Renaissance," you will recall, means "rebirth.") This title has many meanings in the context of *Journey*, all of which suggest that this music represents a beginning of some kind. It is both the first music Wintory wrote for the game—on the first day he was hired, according to the composer—and the basis for much of the game's music in general. It introduces the solo instruments that will recur throughout *Journey*, and the melodies and harmonies we hear in this piece set the tone for the rest of the player's experience. We hear parts of "Nascence" near the beginning of *Journey*; the cello melody is one of the first sounds players hear after leaving the title screen and starting a new game. This is another kind of "coming into being" associated with this music: the beginning of the game, and of the player's own journey through it. The music we first hear in "Nascence" develops and sometimes transforms during *Journey*, paralleling—and enhancing—how players and their characters change over the course of the experience.

Timbre: Between Familiar and Exotic

Along with standard Western string instruments, "Nascence" includes some that may be less familiar to many listeners. The first sound we hear in "Nascence" is the solo cello, which Wintory uses throughout the soundtrack to *Journey*. The cello has been a fairly common solo instrument in Western classical music since the Baroque period, but other timbres we hear are less common: bass flute, finger cymbals, and folk-style harp.

The second section of the piece in particular (starting at 0:27) uses an atypical combination of instruments to achieve an effective combination of timbres. We hear a concert harp play a repeating pattern, imitating the smaller folk version of the harp common in many countries (Ireland, for example), often used to accompany singing. We also hear a ringing percussion sound accenting the first beat of every measure. This sound is the zill (also called finger-cymbals), a traditional Turkish instrument common throughout the Middle East. These two instruments give the music an international, exotic sound that matches the unfamiliar desert landscape of *Journey*.

Wintory also switches timbres of the solo instrument dramatically in this section. Instead of the solo cello we expect, we hear a wind instrument. Its round, breathy tone sounds somewhat like the wood flutes found in many cultures around the world, but it is actually a European concert instrument. The standard Western flute we think of in orchestras is actually just one part of a larger flute family—you may already know the piccolo, a type of flute with a higher range. In "Nascence" we hear the bass flute, which as its name suggests has a lower range and a different tone from the standard flute. This combination of familiar and unfamiliar timbres helps create a mood unique to *Journey*, and gives players important information about the game's world while immersing them in the experience.

Bass flute.

Melody: A Journey in Sound

The melody to "Nascence" appears three times: first in the solo cello, then in the bass flute (after 0:27), and finally in the cello again, this time combined with an orchestra (starting at 1:10). The second and third times we hear it, the melody is varied—it never sounds the exact same way twice. It always has the same basic phrase shape, and many of the same notes and rhythms, but some of the details differ each time. The final time the melody appears, for example, it is played in a much higher range on the cello than before. Such variations make the piece less predictable, and they also reinforce the story of the game. As we travel through this journey, we (and our character in the game) remain the same person, but we are changed by the events we experience; they shape the way we understand the world around us.

Texture: Layers of Meaning

Although "Nascence" is not a long piece of music, it has a sense of drama that increases from beginning to end. Part of that rising tension comes from the gradual embellishments to the melody, but another part comes from the addition of new layers throughout the piece, creating expanding textures. This textural growth, combined with the evolving melody, creates a sense of constant development.

The piece begins monophonically, with the solo cello playing only the melody. This solo cello suggests a sense of solitude in the game, symbolizing the character's isolation in a vast desert. The second section begins as the cello fades out, when it is replaced by the harp, finger cymbals, and eventually the bass flute melody. This adds accompaniment to the melody, producing another musical layer, incorporating the element of harmony, and creating a homophonic texture. In the final section, the harp, cymbals, and flute disappear, but the cello returns, this time with the full string orchestra. The violins in the orchestra play a contrapuntal countermelody, giving this section a polyphonic texture. The gradual shift from monophony to homophony and finally polyphony gives "Nascence" a sense of direction, building up from least to most complex.

With these points in mind, listen to the work again, using the Listening Guide.

CONNECT YOUR PLAYLIST

Multicultural Timbres

Find a piece that uses instruments from more than one culture.

Example: Metallica, "Wherever I May Roam" (1992)
The beginning of this song features the sitar, a plucked instrument from India (see Chapter 34).

Listening Guide

Austin Wintory Composed: 2012
"Nascence," from *Journey*

Time	♫ Melody	∿ Timbre	🌐 Texture
0:00	Basic statement	Solo cello playing only melody	Monophonic (solo cello)
0:27		Harp and zill (finger cymbals)	Homophonic
0:35	More complex	Bass flute enters with melody	Homophonic
1:02	Most complex, high range	Full orchestra enters; counterpoint with solo cello melody	Polyphonic

🔍 Student FAQs ⚙

Are these live instruments, or generated by a computer?

All of these instruments are acoustic instruments being played by live musicians. Many games, however, use either entirely synthesized strings or a combination of live and synthesized instruments.

Is all of "Nascence" in the game?

Like many recordings released for film and game soundtracks, "Nascence" never appears in its complete form in the game. More often, especially in games (see "Performance: Interactivity") longer compositions are broken up into smaller excerpts, called "cues."

Is this music ever performed in concerts?

Yes. Music from *Journey* has been included in a number of orchestral concerts since the game's release, and Wintory has composed a "mini-concerto" for cello and orchestra called "Woven Variations," which is adapted from the *Journey* soundtrack.

Although games share many similarities to film and television, they present unique challenges and opportunities to composers. Today, when technological limitations present few obstacles (see Historical Context), the main difference between composing for games and other media is the interactivity inherent to games. Films are a fixed art form, like painting or sculpture. No matter how many times you watch them, they stay the same. That means that composers who are writing for film can create music that corresponds exactly to what's happening on-screen from moment to moment. Games, however, are much less fixed. Although some moments are always the same, the experience can be very different each time players interact with the game. Think of it as a piece of music: Composers write the notes down, but musicians determine how to play them, meaning that performances of any work will always be somewhat different.

This variability means that game composers can't write music the way film composers do, which would limit a player's ability to enjoy the game differently each time. Game composers have had to find new ways to write more adaptable music, capable of matching what players are experiencing. For example, many composers now use a technique called "layering." They write parts for many different instruments all in the same key, meter, and tempo, so that any combination can be played at the same time. In quieter moments when nothing particularly exciting is happening only a few layers might play, with others added as the circumstances in the game change. Layers might be triggered

Virtual reality is the newest innovation in video gaming. Will video game music change in some way as a result?

by actions, location, danger, or other criteria. Another common technique is "branching," which is when a composer writes music with multiple possible options depending on the choices players make. These branches are like musical forks in the road: The music goes down a different path depending on which direction the player chooses. Layering and branching can even be combined; each branch might have its own layers. As games continue to get more complicated, composers are constantly developing new and exciting ways to ensure players get the best possible experience.

HISTORICAL CONTEXT Changing Technologies

Like many recent video games, *Journey*'s soundtrack includes a variety of instruments, including a live string orchestra. Game composers today have almost no technical limitations on what they can write—an enormous change from the situation only 25 years ago. As one example, the sound technology of the Nintendo Entertainment System, the most successful gaming system of the 1980s, only allowed for three notes to sound at once (just enough to form a triad), and those pitches sounded nothing like traditional instruments. Restrictions on memory also limited the amount of music that could be included with the game. Composers quickly innovated solutions to these problems, resulting in many of the traits of video game music that are familiar decades later. To save memory, composers began writing music in endlessly repeating patterns called "**loops**," and the "blips" and "bloops" of synthesized audio became a part of the gaming experience.

Advancing technology quickly erased many of these limitations: In the early 1990s a new generation of home game systems increased memory and improved sound production. Many pitches could sound simultaneously, and specific

instruments could more realistically be synthesized. On personal computers and home gaming systems of this era composers could write full orchestral scores, for example, or more popular styled soundtracks. By the end of the decade technology advanced to CD-based games, meaning that for the first time games could include prerecorded musical tracks rather than relying entirely on audio hardware to synthesize sounds. In recent years games have mostly migrated to DVDs or Blu-Ray discs, allowing for many hours of prerecorded music.

For a variety of reasons, however, many composers and game designers choose to include synthesized rather than entirely prerecorded music. For one thing, not all game companies can afford to hire orchestras or license enough popular music to fill an entire game. Synthesized music also allows for much greater interactivity with the player (see "Performance: Interactivity"), since prerecorded music cannot effectively adapt to player input. Many game composers now choose to create "blended scores," which combine prerecorded music and synthesized sounds.

PROFILE Austin Wintory (b. 1984)

A native of Denver, Colorado, Wintory showed an interest in film music as a child. Even before he began piano lessons at age 10, he taught himself to play melodies from his favorite soundtracks by ear. He quickly became interested in composition, writing works for his high school ensembles to perform. By the time he was 18, he had already been invited to conduct the Utah Symphony in a performance of one of his works.

Wintory went on to study music at New York University and then at the University of Southern California, where he composed the music for an innovative thesis project in game design. This project became *flOw*, thatgamecompany's first game, which has since been put on display in the Smithsonian American Art Museum in Washington, D.C. This collaborative effort paved the way for *Journey*, for which Wintory has won a number of awards, including several from the Game Audio Network Guild, the Spike TV Video Game Awards, and the British Academy.

Because the techniques video-game composers use are unique, many choose to specialize in that medium. Wintory, however, remains active in three different areas: games, film, and concert music. He has composed music for dozens of films, including the Sundance Award–winning *Captain Abu Raed* (2007), which earned Wintory a Hollywood Music Award for "Best New Film Composer." He has also continued to write concert music, and has recently been a composer in residence for the Boulder Symphony.

Austin Wintory at the 2013 Grammy Awards. His music for *Journey* was nominated in the category of "Best Score Soundtrack for Visual Media."

EXPAND YOUR PLAYLIST

Video Game Music

A number of video game soundtracks are available for purchase, both in their original form and in versions arranged for other ensembles.

The Legend of Zelda: Skyward Sword (Koji Kondo et al., 2011)

- Kondo is the composer of many of the best-known video game soundtracks, including most of the *Legend of Zelda* series. There are many recordings of his music for these games in both its original form as well as versions for live orchestras. *Skyward Sword* is a good representative of a blended musical score, featuring both live and synthesized music.

Final Fantasy VI (Nobuo Uematsu, 1994)

- Uematsu is a prolific composer of video-game music, but he is best known for his music for the *Final Fantasy* series. This music is frequently performed live in concert by ensembles ranging from orchestras to rock bands—including Uematsu's own rock band, The Black Mages. *Final Fantasy VI*, released for the Super Nintendo system, is an excellent example of how composers created musically rich scores with synthesized sounds. The game features an almost operatic musical structure, complete with a system of Wagnerian leitmotifs.

Bastion (Darren Korb, 2011)

- Like *Journey*, *Bastion* is another successful independent game with a thoughtful perspective. *Bastion*'s soundtrack illustrates the inclusion of popular music styles in games, blending folk-rock elements such as steel guitar and percussion with orchestral strings.

Bioshock (Gary Schyman, 2007)

- The soundtrack to the philosophical action game *Bioshock* includes two separate but equally important styles of music: a film-like orchestral score from Schyman, and a collection of popular songs from the 1940s and 1950s, the era when the game takes place. This game highlights the thoughtful inclusion of preexisting popular music into video games, as well as how cinematic game music has become since its early days.

Chiptopia (8 Bit Weapon and ComputeHer, 2013)

- *Chiptopia* is not a video game, but rather a greatest-hits album released by two musicians, 8 Bit Weapon and ComputeHer. Both artists are well known in the chiptune music subculture. Chiptune music is a style of popular music created by using the hardware from older video game systems (predominantly Nintendo Game Boys). This album is a good introduction to the variety of styles in this genre, and it illustrates the aesthetic appeal of the "blips" and "bloops" of early video game music.

PART 6 Summary

	Nineteenth Century	Since 1900
Texture	Full spectrum between homophonic and polyphonic	Same
Melody	Longer, more complex melodies, often with wider range, often quite technically demanding	Both tonal and atonal, with or without metrical structure
Rhythm	Wider range of extremes, from balanced to irregular; use of folk rhythms occasionally	Full range of possibilities, from regular to irregular, predictable to unpredictable
Timbre	Emergence of the modern orchestra with large brass and percussion sections	Even greater possibilities of sound from new techniques for playing old instruments, increased use of percussion instruments, and audio technology
Harmony	Increasingly chromatic, undermining a sense of a tonal center	Tonal and atonal, both with and without a sense of a harmonic center
Form	Earlier forms, plus new emphasis on cyclic form (in instrumental music) and larger basic units of construction (in opera)	All earlier forms continue; emergence of aleatory music based on chance
Word–Music Relationships	Greater use of program music; intense cultivation of the song as a genre	Continued use of program music; new techniques of singing (*Sprechstimme*)

IN REVIEW: Since 1900

Genres

Ballet A staged work that presents a drama through dance.
- Stravinsky, *The Rite of Spring* (Chapter 48)
- Copland, *Rodeo* (Chapter 56)

Song A relatively short work for a singer and accompanying instruments.
- Still, "A Black Pierrot" from *Songs of Separation* (Chapter 55)
- Johnson, "Terraplane Blues" (Chapter 50)
- Jackson, "It Don't Cost Very Much" (Chapter 62)
- Dargel, "On This Date Every Year" (Chapter 64)

Minimalist music Music based on the frequent repetition (with slight variations) of a small musical idea.
- Glass, *Einstein on the Beach* (Chapter 61)

Musical A spoken play with ample sung numbers (arias, ensembles, choruses).
- Bernstein, *West Side Story* (Chapter 58)

Film music Music written expressly for a film.
- Williams, *Star Wars* (Chapter 69)

Jazz Popular music style that weds African American rhythms with European influences.
- Ellington, "Cotton Tail" (Chapter 51)
- Parker, "Ornithology" (Chapter 52)

Rock Dominant popular music of the second half of the twentieth century.
- Berry, "School Day" (Chapter 66)
- Sex Pistols, "God Save the Queen" (Chapter 67)

Rap African American popular music style, combining rhymed recitations with complex recorded accompaniments.
- Public Enemy, "Fight the Power" (Chapter 68)

Stylistic Developments

Impressionism Music that emphasizes timbre (color) at the expense of line (melody).
- Debussy, *Voiles* (Chapter 45)

Atonality A style of writing without a tonal center.
- Ives, *The Unanswered Question* (Chapter 46)
- Schoenberg, "Columbine" from *Pierrot lunaire* (Chapter 47)
- Crawford, *Piano Study in Mixed Accents* (Chapter 53)
- Cage, Sonata II from *Sonatas and Interludes* (Chapter 59)

Polytonality The simultaneous sounding of two different harmonies.
- Stravinsky, *The Rite of Spring* (Chapter 48)

Neoclassicism A style of writing that embraces the harmonic, rhythmic, and formal styles of the past (specifically, those of the eighteenth century), with limited modernist inflections.
- Tailleferre, Concertino for Harp and Orchestra, finale (Chapter 54)

Postmodernism A style of writing that integrates modernism with more traditional idioms.
- León, *A la Par* (Chapter 63)
- Dargel, "On This Date Every Year" (Chapter 64)

Syncopation A rhythmic style that emphasizes the off-beat.
- Joplin, *Maple Leaf Rag* (Chapter 49)

Analyze This: Create a Listening Guide for Your Own Music

An ideal way to apply the listening skills you have developed in this course is to create your own Listening Guide for a musical work of your choice.

Step 1: Choose Your Work

Choose a work of music you like or you'd like to know more about (or better still, both). Your instructor may have specific guidelines about such things as when your work of music was written or how long it lasts. He or she will probably also have specific instructions about the format in which to turn in your recording (burned CD, mp3, etc.). Follow your instructor's guidelines as you complete this section.

Step 2: Listen

You will have almost certainly listened to your chosen work before, but this time, hear the elements: melody, rhythm, harmony, texture, timbre, dynamics, form, and word–music relationships. It will help to focus on only one or two elements at a time. Listen once, for example, for changes in timbre, listen another time for changes in rhythm, and so on.

Step 3: Identify the Central Elements

Decide which three or four elements are central to this work. If an element does not change at any point—for example, if your work is loud from beginning to end—this will not be a particularly meaningful basis on which to break down the music. If, on the other hand, the dynamics keep moving between loud and soft, that may well be a useful parameter to explain how the work is constructed. Make special note of the timing of important changes in the music. When the words begin a new section, does the music change as well? Do you hear a modulation at some point? Does the timbre shift at some point? Does the texture change markedly anywhere?

Step 4: Construct a Grid

Following the pattern of the Listening Guides in this book, construct a grid with the timings of key points in the work in the far left column and the three or four central elements you have identified to the right. If there is a text that is sung, reproduce the text within the grid in a way that reflects its musical setting. Gradually fill in the grid. Apply the terminology and concepts used in the Listening Guides throughout this book.

Step 5: Review Your Work

Have you identified the key elements in your work? Have you charted their progression through the work thoroughly and accurately? Listen again, following your own grid, and imagine that you have never heard the work before. Does your grid show its essential features? Are the timings accurate? Have you followed your professor's instructions? Remember to proofread your work. You might also ask a friend to follow your Listening Guide as a further way to proof your work.

If you have carried out this assignment carefully, you will almost certainly gain added appreciation of how music works. What might seem like a "simple" song is often far more intricate than it appears on the surface. Most important of all, you will have learned valuable skills that will help you listen to any kind of music, from any time or place, with greater understanding.

Happy listening!

Glossary

A cappella   Sung without instrumental accompaniment of any kind.

Accompanied recitative   Recitative accompanied by the orchestra, as opposed to by basso continuo alone.

Additive form   A compositional technique in which nothing disappears, but new layers are constantly added.

Aleatory music   Music composed using elements of chance.

Alto   A voice range between soprano (the highest) and tenor; the lower range of the female voice.

Anacrusis   A starting note that falls on a beat before the downbeat. Also called a pickup beat or an upbeat.

Antecedent phrase   In periodic phrase structure, an opening phrase, which sets up the consequent phrase to follow.

Anthem   An English sacred choral work.

Aria   Italian for "air" or "melody"; any lyrical movement or piece for solo voice, usually with some kind of instrumental accompaniment.

Art song   A song set to serious poetry, usually for solo voice and piano, in the tradition of the German Lied.

Atonal   A style of writing that establishes no harmonic or melodic center of gravity; without a tonic, all notes are of equal weight and significance.

Ballad   A poem or song that tells a story.

Ballet   A story told through music and dance; essentially an opera without words.

Bar form   A melodic form in which the opening phrase is sung twice and a contrasting phrase follows (**AAB**). Also called song form.

Baritone   A voice range between bass (the lowest) and tenor.

Baroque   The historical period in music extending from approximately 1600 to 1750.

Bass   The lowest of the voice ranges.

Basso continuo   "Continuous bass"; a small ensemble, widely used in music of the Baroque, that plays throughout a work and provides an underlying bass line and harmonies. It consists of two instruments: one that can sustain long notes (such as a bass viol, a cello, or a bassoon), and one that can play chords (such as a lute or a harpsichord).

Bebop   New jazz style of the late 1940s/early 1950s that developed in response to the popularity of big band music. Bebop is characterized by fast tempos, short bursts of melodic phrases, heavy and unexpected rhythmic accents, and virtuosic soloing.

Big band music   A style of jazz popular in the 1930s and 1940s in which instruments were grouped into sections by function, with carefully constructed arrangements. Many of these arrangements featured call-and-response between the sections, often based on repeated, short melodic riffs.

Binary form   A musical structure consisting of two repeated halves (**AABB**).

Binary song form   A form common in popular song in the early twentieth century. The basic pattern (**AABB**) is 32 bars long, with each of the four sections occupying 8 bars of music.

Blue note   A pitch performed flatter (lower) than the standard major scale would indicate; usually blue notes occur as substitutes for the third and seventh (and occasionally the fifth) notes of the standard major scale.

Blues   A musical genre derived from African American performance traditions that uses blue notes (flattened pitches) in its melodies and tells first-person stories of hard knocks and love gone wrong.

Brass instruments   A family of wind instrument made of brass that produces sound by the vibration of the player's lips in a cup-like metal mouthpiece. Brass instruments include the horn, trumpet, trombone, and tuba.

Cadence   A point of arrival signaling the end of a musical unit.

Cadenza   In a concerto, an elaborate improvisation by the soloist on themes heard earlier in the movement, with no accompaniment from the orchestra. It occurs near the end of the recapitulation.

Call-and-response   A technique in which one musician or group sings or plays an opening motive, and another musician or group sings or plays an answer.

Cantata   A type of vocal genre typically sung during a service of worship. In Italian, "that which is sung," as opposed to *sonata,* "that which is played."

Chamber music   Instrumental music for a small ensemble, with only one player to each part.

Character piece   A relatively short work, usually for piano solo, that captures a particular mood ("character").

Choral music   Vocal music with more than one singer to a part.

Chorale   A hymn tune.

Chord   Three or more notes played or sung at the same moment.

Choreographer   The individual responsible for devising the dancers' movements in a ballet.

Chorus   An ensemble with multiple singers to a part; "chorus" is also the name for the musical number or movement sung by this ensemble. In Baroque opera, the chorus comments on the action and emotions unfolding onstage.

Chromatic   A type of harmony or melody that incorporates many more notes than occur naturally in the scale or key area on which a work is based. A chromatic scale is produced by playing all half steps. On the piano, this would mean all adjacent keys—black or white.

Classical era   The period from approximately 1750 to 1800 in which the ideals of balance, clarity, and naturalness were highly valued in the arts.

Coda   Italian for "tail." A section at the end of a musical work or movement that stands outside any formal structure and brings the whole to a close.

Comic opera   In Italian, *opera buffa.* A genre that uses many of the same conventions as serious opera—arias, recitatives, ensembles, choruses—but with plots revolving around believable, everyday characters rather than mythical or historical figures.

Concerto   An instrumental genre for a soloist (or sometimes more than one soloist) and a larger ensemble.

Concerto grosso   Italian for "big concerto"; a concerto with multiple soloists.

Conductor   The director of any musical ensemble; responsible for keeping the musicians together in time and for shaping the interpretation of the music being performed.

Conjunct motion   Melodic motion of pitches by step.

Consequent phrase   In periodic phrase structure, a closing phrase that follows an antecedent phrase and creates a sense of musical completion.

Consonance   The sound of notes together that our ear finds naturally right. Like dissonance, consonance is a relative concept that can change over long periods of time.

Contrafactum   A work setting new words to an established melody.

Counterpoint   A style of writing in which every voice is a melody and all voices work together; from the Latin word *contrapunctum,* or "note-against-note." Counterpoint is basic to polyphonic texture.

Contour   The general shape of a melody: up, down, up-and-down, down-and-up, etc.

Courtly love   A code of behavior in medieval courts in which the knight worshipped a lady from afar.

Cyclic form   A form in which individual movements are linked in some tangible and distinctive way, usually through the use of a common musical idea.

Da capo   Italian for "from the head"; a direction to go back and play from the very beginning of the piece.

Da capo aria   An aria that opens with two contrasting sections, **A** and **B**; at the end of the **B** section, the singer and orchestra return to the beginning of the **A** section, following the direction in the score of "da capo"—literally, "from the head." When the singer performs this **A** section a second time, he or she embellishes it heavily.

Development   The section within a sonata-form movement that thematically and harmonically manipulates ("develops") the movement's themes most intensively.

Diatonic scale   A scale consisting of whole and half steps.

Diegetic music   Music in a film that originates from the scene in the film itself, as in a character listening to the radio or playing the violin; the opposite of non-diegetic music.

Disjunct motion   Melodic motion of pitches by leap.

Dissonance   The sound of notes that clash, either harmonically or melodically, and do not seem to belong together. Dissonance is a relative concept: what was dissonant in one era is later perceived as consonant.

Dotted rhythm   Consistent alternation between long and short notes.

Double   To play or sing the same musical line in multiple voices or on multiple instruments; most often used to describe an instrument playing the same line being sung by a voice.

Double-exposition concerto form   A structure based on sonata form but with two expositions, one for the orchestra alone and one for the soloist and orchestra together. It also includes, near the end of the recapitulation, a cadenza for the soloist.

Double variations   A type of theme and variations form featuring two themes, each of which is varied in alternation (A B A' B' A'' B'' etc.).

Downbeat   The first note of a measure, which is usually emphasized in relation to the notes on other beats of the measure.

Drone bass   A single long note held underneath the melodic line.

Drone harmony   A texture in which a melodic instrument plays over a constant repeated pattern of only a few tones.

Duple meter   An underlying pattern of rhythm in which each unit (measure) consists of one accented (strong) beat followed by one unaccented (weak) beat (1 2 | 1 2 | 1 2 | etc.) or some multiple of two (such as four or eight). A unit of four beats per measure, for example, in which the first is the strongest and the third is the next-strongest (**1**-2-**3**-4 | **1**-2-**3**-4 | **1**-2-**3**-4 | etc.), is a type of duple meter.

Dynamics   The volume of sound, determined by the size (amplitude) of each sound wave.

Electronic music   Music using sounds generated (and not merely amplified) either in whole or in part by electronic means.

Elided cadence   In a polyphonic texture, a cadence between two or more voices that overlaps with the entry of another voice or voices. An elided cadence is often used to begin a new line of text and music before the previous one has come to a complete stop.

Enlightenment   An intellectual movement of the late seventeenth and eighteenth centuries that advocated critical thinking, empirical science, and reasoned discussion as means to advancing humankind.

Episode   In a fugue, a passage in which the subject is not present.

Ethnomusicology   A sub-field of **musicology**—the scholarly study of music in general—that focuses on the social dimension of the art and the ways in which music is used within and between cultures.

Exposition   The section within a sonata-form movement that introduces ("exposes") all of the movement's themes.

Expressionism   A broad artistic movement that flourished in music, painting, and literature in the early decades of the twentieth century, in which psychological truth took precedence over beauty, and inner emotion took precedence over any sense of external reality.

Extramusical   Referring to an idea outside the sound. This term is used by ethnomusicologists to describe the equivalent of program music, in Western music.

Falsetto   A technique for singing in a very high range by which a singer causes the voice to bypass the larynx, which is the part of the throat that otherwise gives men's voices a deeper register.

Fill   In jazz and popular styles, a short, instrumental response between a singer's phrases, or a brief solo occupying a musical gap between sections of a piece.

Finale   A last movement of a multimovement work.

Folk music   Any music passed down from generation to generation by a living tradition.

Folk dance   A type of dance passed down from generation to generation by a living tradition; each folk dance is typically associated with a particular rhythm and dance step.

Form   The structure of a musical work; the way in which its individual units are put together.

Forte   The commonly used Italian term for "loud."

French overture   An overture common in French Baroque opera, usually consisting of a slow introduction with dotted rhythms, followed by a fast section frequently employing imitation.

Fugal exposition   The opening section of a fugue, in which all the voices enter with the main subject.

Fugue   A polyphonic work based on a central theme and employing imitation.

Full cadence   A musical point of arrival that creates a strong sense of closure.

Gamelan   An Indonesian musical ensemble consisting primarily of a variety of pitched gongs and xylophones. The conductor or leader of the ensemble often plays a double-headed drum.

Genre   The category of a work, determined by a combination of its performance medium and its social function.

Glissando   A continuous ("gliding") melodic motion up or down that goes by so fast we almost cannot hear the individual notes.

Gospel music   Religious-themed music that borrows from R&B, blues, and other popular styles in its vocal and instrumental styles.

Gregorian chant   Monophonic vocal music in the medieval church, designed to project religious texts. So called because it was alleged to have been written mostly by Pope Gregory I, in the late sixth century. Also known as **plainchant**.

Groove   In popular and jazz styles, the underlying rhythmic pattern of a song.

Ground   See ground bass.

Ground bass   A short pattern of notes repeated over and over; another name for an ostinato in the bass part.

Half cadence   A point of musical arrival that is not yet closure. If thought of as punctuation, a half cadence is like a comma, whereas a full cadence is like a period.

Half step   The smallest distance between two adjacent notes on a piano (white or black), such as C-C#.

Harmony   The sound created by multiple voices playing or singing together.

Head   In jazz, the main melody of the song.

Hemiola   A type of syncopation in which patterns of twos occur at the same time as patterns of threes.

Heterophonic texture (heterophony)   The simultaneous playing or singing of two or more slightly different versions of a melody.

Hip hop   A cultural movement of the late 1970s through the turn of the century that included fashion, dance (break dancing), art (graffiti), and music (rap). Hip hop music is characterized by semispoken lyrics that are recited against an accompaniment often consisting of short, repeated melodic fragments set against a heavily rhythmic beat.

Hocket   A form of polyphony consisting of two or more rhythmically interlocking voices.

Homophonic texture (homophony)   A musical texture in which a melody is performed with a supporting accompaniment.

Hook   A short, catchy motive that forms the memorable core of the song.

Humanism   An early-Renaissance intellectual and cultural movement that explored human interests and values through the pursuit of science, philosophy, literature, painting, sculpture, and music, particularly vocal music.

Hymn   A sacred poem or song, often sung by a large group of worshippers.

Idée fixe   In psychology, a "fixed" or unchanging idea, an obsession; in music, the term used by Hector Berlioz in his *Symphonie fantastique* to indicate the melody associated with the artist's beloved.

Imitation   A shortened form of the term "imitative counterpoint": the same theme introduced by different instruments or voices in succession.

Imitative counterpoint   A particular type of counterpoint in which one voice introduces a new theme and is answered ("imitated") by other voices that enter in succession shortly afterward, even as the first voice continues to sing or play.

Impressionism   An artistic movement focused more on sensations, perceptions, and light than on the direct representation of objects. In music, the term was used by critics of the early twentieth century to describe harmonies, melodies, and forms they considered indistinct.

Improvisation   The technique of embellishing or elaborating on a melody on the spot, spontaneously and unrehearsed.

Interlocking voices   Voices that complement one another by one of them filling in the spaces left by another's rests to complete a single, continuous melodic unit.

Interval   The distance between two pitches.

Intonation   In Bahamian rhyme singing, as well as in other African-influenced musical cultures: a melody line consisting of words spoken in tones.

Jazz   A broad category of music that features many different styles, often including syncopation, swing rhythms, and improvisation.

Jingju   In Chinese, "capital theater." The principal form of opera in China today. Characters are stock types distinguished by singing style, costume, makeup, and role. On stage, there is no scenery, and the action usually takes place in front of a curtain.

Key   The central note and mode on which a melody or piece is based.

Koto   A plucked stringed instrument from Japan.

Leitmotif   A brief musical phrase or idea connected dramatically to some person, event, or idea in the drama.

Libretto   The text (words) of an opera.

Lied (*plural* **Lieder**)   German for "song." A genre for voice and piano, popular from the late eighteenth century onward, particularly in Germany but in many other countries as well.

Looping   A technique by which a unit of music is sent to a synthesizer and repeated as many times as desired.

Madrigal   A musical setting of a text in a single strophe (stanza).

Major mode   A type of scale produced by singing "do-re-mi-fa-so-la-ti-do," or by playing the white keys of the piano between C and C, in which half steps occur between notes 3 and 4 and notes 7 and 8. The sound of the major mode is often described as "bright" or "happy," in contrast to the minor mode.

Manual   The keyboard of an organ or harpsichord. These instruments often have more than one manual.

Mazurka   A polish folk dance in triple meter, often with a heavy accent on the second or third beat of each measure.

Measure   A rhythmic unit, indicated by bar lines in notated music, that presents one complete statement of the meter.

Melisma   A syllable of text sung to many notes.

Melismatic   A style of setting a text to music so that there is more than one note per syllable.

Melodic motion   The movement of pitches within a melody up or down, either by step (conjunct motion) or by leap (disjunct motion).

Melody   A single line of notes heard in succession as a coherent unit.

Meter (of music)   An underlying pattern of beats that maintains itself consistently throughout a work. See also "duple meter"; "triple meter."

Meter (of poetry)   A poem's basic rhythmic unit.

Mezzo-soprano   A voice range between soprano (the highest) and alto.

Middle Ages   The historical period in music extending from approximately 500 to 1420.

Middle entries   In a fugue, later entries of the subject, after the exposition.

Minimalism   In music, a style in which a brief musical idea or group of ideas is repeated and varied incrementally over a long span of time, with a relatively slow rate of change.

Minor mode   A type of scale produced by playing the white keys on the piano between A and A, in which half steps occur between notes 2 and 3 and notes 5 and 6, but often with the seventh note raised so that a half step also occurs between notes 7 and 8. The sound of the minor mode is often described as "dark" or "sad," in contrast to the major mode.

Minuet form   A ternary form (**ABA**) in which the opening section, known as the minuet proper (**A**), is followed by a contrasting trio (**B**), which is followed by a repeat of the minuet proper. The minuet is always in triple meter and its individual units—the minuet proper and the trio—are each in binary form.

Mode   A type of scale on which a melody is based. Since the Baroque era (1600 onward), the term is used to distinguish between major and minor modes.

Modernism   A spirit that took hold in all the arts, in the early twentieth century, representing a quest for novelty that far exceeded any such drive in the past.

Modified strophic form   A form in which each strophe is modified musically to fit the text in a particular way.

Modulate (*noun* **modulation**)   To move to a different key area.

Monophonic texture (monophony)   A musical texture consisting of a single melodic line.

Motet   In the music of the Renaissance and Baroque, a sacred choral work used in both Catholic and Protestant services.

Musical   A spoken drama with a substantial amount of singing.

Musical appropriation   The use or adaptation of a work to serve something other than its original purpose.

Musicology   The scholarly study of music.

Musique concrète   French for "concrete music." Music using sounds generated by everyday, real ("concrete") objects not normally thought of as musical instruments and then manipulated electronically.

Nationalism   In music, the use of melodies, rhythms, harmonies, or instruments that reflect the musical practices of a particular nation.

Neoclassicism   A style of composition in the years after World War I that, although distinctly modern, drew on older (particularly eighteenth-century) uses of melody, harmony, rhythm, and form.

Nocturne   "Night piece." Originally a vocal serenade from lover to beloved. Later, an instrumental work that imitates, through its homophonic texture, such a song.

Non-diegetic music   Film music that is added to the scene from the outside for purposes of heightening the mood or feeling of a scene; the opposite of diegetic music.

Note   The smallest unit of musical notation, indicating a specific pitch and duration, or the sounded pitch itself.

Octave   The interval between two pitches of the same name (C to C, G to G, etc.). The frequency of the higher pitch is twice that of the lower pitch.

Opera   A drama sung from beginning to end.

Opera buffa   Italian for "comic opera"; a genre that uses many of the same conventions as serious opera—arias, recitatives, ensembles, choruses—but with plots revolving around believable, everyday characters rather than mythical or historical figures.

Opera seria   Italian for "serious opera"; Italian Baroque opera on a serious subject, typically consisting of alternating recitatives and da capo arias.

Operetta   Italian for "small opera." A nineteenth-century stage work that incorporated both singing and spoken dialogue, typically on a comic, lighthearted, or sentimental subject. A precursor to the American musical.

Oral tradition   One passed down without the aid of written words or notated music.

Oratorio   A work musically similar to an opera but not staged, and usually on a sacred topic.

Orchestra   A large ensemble that consists of several different kinds of instruments, usually of different families (strings, woodwinds, brass, percussion).

Orchestration   The manner in which various instruments are assigned to the musical lines.

Ostinato   A short pattern of notes repeated over and over.

Overture   A purely instrumental opening movement that introduces a longer work, often for voices (as an opera).

Pentatonic scale   A scale consisting of five tones.

Percussion instruments   A family of instruments that produce sound when struck. Percussion instruments include timpani, snare drum, cymbals, gong, and the piano.

Periodic phrase structure   A musical structure in which antecedent and consequent phrase units make up a larger whole.

Phrase   A brief musical statement.

Piano trio   A work written for an ensemble of piano, violin, and cello. The term is also used for the ensemble itself.

Pitch   The position of a sound on a range from very low to very high, determined by the frequency of its sound waves.

Plainchant   Monophonic vocal music in the medieval church designed to project religious texts.

Polyphonic texture (polyphony)   A musical texture consisting of multiple lines of equal importance.

Polytonal   See polytonality.

Polytonality   The juxtaposition of two conventional harmonies in a way that creates a new dissonance.

Postmodernism   A style in music and the other arts, beginning in the mid-twentieth century, in which modern and traditional elements are combined.

Powwow   An intertribal gathering where Native Americans of mixed tribes express their mutual bond and identity.

Program music   An instrumental work that is in some way associated with a story, event, or idea.

Punk   Popular music of the mid-1970s that originally arose in reaction to the increasingly commercial and corporate rock of the era. Punk emphasized a do-it-yourself (DIY) attitude. Musical or vocal skills were downplayed; lyrics expressed anger at the failings of the economic and social systems. Fashions included torn T-shirts, body piercings, brightly dyed hair, and other "anti-fashion" looks.

Raga   In the music of India, a mood, color, or musical scale that forms the basis of a musical composition.

Ragtime   A style of music from the early twentieth century that emphasizes rhythmic syncopation while continuing many of the characteristics of marches, cakewalks, two-steps, and popular songs from the late nineteenth century.

Recapitulation   The third and final section within a sonata-form movement, in which all the themes presented in the exposition return, all in the tonic key.

Recitative   A style of singing that lies somewhere between lyrical song and speech; also, the operatic number that is sung in this style.

Refrain   The same words with the same basic melody recurring at regular intervals over the course of a work.

Register   The range of a pitch or series of pitches, usually described as high, middle, or low.

Renaissance   The historical period in music extending from approximately 1420 to 1600.

Responsorial chant   A type of plainchant in which a soloist's passage is followed by a response from the chorus.

Rhyme singer   In a Bahamian rhyme singing group, the lead singer.

Rhythm   The ordering of music through time.

Rhythm changes   A harmonic progression common in jazz that features specific changes of harmony and the bass line.

Ritornello   Italian for "little return"; name for the statement and return of the full ensemble, in a work alternating between the orchestra and soloist or soloists.

Ritornello principle   The formal design of alternating ritornello and solo sections.

Rock 'n' roll   A style of music that evolved in the mid-1950s out of R&B and country styles. Rock 'n' roll is teenage music, expressing the concerns of mid-century young people (romance, cars, dancing). The typical rock group consisted of electric guitar, bass, and drums, with the occasional addition of piano or saxophone.

Romanticism   An artistic movement of the nineteenth century that emphasized imagination and freedom from structural conventions.

Rondo form   A form in which an opening theme (**A**) returns repeatedly over the course of the movement, interspersed with contrasting ideas (**B**, **C**, etc.). An example of the resulting pattern would be **ABACA**.

Rounded binary form   A binary form in which the opening idea returns in the tonic key about halfway through the second section, "rounding out" the form.

Rubato   See tempo rubato.

Sample   To record music or sound from an existing album.

Scale   A series of notes that provide the essential pitch building blocks of a melody.

Scenario   The story line of a ballet.

Scherzo   In Italian, "joke." A musical scherzo is a lighthearted movement in a fast tempo and in triple meter, similar in form to the minuet.

Section   In a musical ensemble, a group of instruments or voices with similar timbres or roles.

Sectional form   A form in which each verse or half-verse receives its own material (for example, **ABCD**).

Sequence   A short musical motive that repeats at successively higher or lower pitches.

Serialism   A style of writing in which notes are drawn not from a scale, but from a predetermined series of notes. Serial composition flourished between ca. 1920 and 1980. See also "twelve-tone composition."

Shawm A double-reed wind instrument common in the Middle Ages and Renaissance but later replaced by the oboe.

Shuffle groove (or, **shuffle rhythm**) A mid-tempo rhythmic pattern, typically in quadruple meter, in which each beat is subdivided into three pulses.

Sitar A plucked stringed instrument widely used on the Indian subcontinent.

Sonata A type of instrumental genre, usually for one or two instruments; literally, a work that is played, as opposed to sung ("cantata").

Sonata form A musical structure consisting of an exposition, development, and recapitulation, allowing for the presentation, development, and resolution of multiple themes within a single movement. Sonata form was widely used throughout the Classical Era and the nineteenth century.

Soprano The highest of the voice ranges.

Sprechstimme In German, "speech-voice." A style of singing halfway between speech and lyrical song, in which the singer hits precise pitches and then allows them to tail off, rather than sustaining them, as in lyrical singing.

Standard song form A common form for the choruses of "standards" or popular hits of the 1920s, 1930s, and 1940s. It consists of 32 measures divided into four phrases in the pattern **AABA**.

Stanza A verse of poetry, or the music corresponding to that verse (see also "strophe").

Stop time A kind of musical punctuation between sections, in which the instruments that provide the basic accompaniment strike a single note on a downbeat of a measure together, then remain silent for the rest of the measure.

String instruments A family of instruments that produces sound when a taut string is plucked or stroked with a bow. String (or stringed) instruments include the violin, viola, cello, and double bass.

Strophe A verse of poetry, or the music corresponding to that verse (see also "stanza").

Strophic A type of form in which every verse (strophe) of text is sung to exactly the same music.

Subject The central theme of a fugue.

Suite A series of individual dance movements, typically in a variety of types such as minuets, gavottes, and gigues, and a variety of characters such as fast versus slow, lively versus stately, duple versus triple.

Swing A rhythmic pattern of long and short notes approximating a two-to-one ratio, but varying from piece to piece and performer to performer.

Swing music The name given generally to the popular jazz of the 1930s and 1940s that prominently featured a swing rhythm.

Syllabic A style of setting a text to music so that there is one note per syllable.

Symphony A large-scale work for orchestra, most commonly consisting of four movements.

Syncopated rhythm (syncopation) A type of rhythm in which the notes run against the regular pulse of the musical meter, with accents on beats other than the ones usually accented.

Syncretism The combination of different forms of belief and practice.

Tabla A set of two drums, struck with the fingertips, widely used in music of the Indian subcontinent.

Tag In popular styles, a closing section that relies on extensive repetition of a short motive.

Tala Fixed, repeated cycles of pulses widely used in music of the Indian subcontinent.

Tambura A plucked stringed instrument similar to the sitar, used only to provide a drone in music of the Indian subcontinent.

Tempo The speed at which a piece of music is performed.

Tempo rubato In Italian, "robbed time." Subtle changes of tempo (speeding up and slowing down) applied by the performer, with expressive intent.

Tenor A voice range between bass (the lowest) and alto; the higher range of the male voice.

Ternary form A form consisting of three parts, labeled **ABA or ABA'** (that is, with the return of "A" varied).

Terraced contour The motion of a melody that moves up or down through a series of stages, remaining in one general area a while before moving up or down to the next.

Texture The number and general relationship of musical lines or voices to one another.

Theme and variations form A form in which a theme is presented and then altered in some way—through harmony, melody, texture, dynamics, or some combination of these—in a succession of individual variations.

Through-composed form A form in which each section has its own music, with very little or no repetition between sections.

Timbre The character or quality of a sound.

Tonal A style of writing that establishes a central note (the tonic) as a harmonic and melodic center of gravity, which in turn creates the potential for a strong sense of resolution and closure.

Tonality A system of organizing pitches (both melodies and harmonies) around a central note, as opposed to atonality, a system with no tonal center. See also "tonal" and "atonal."

Tonic The note that establishes a key, based on its distinctive relationship with a particular set of harmonies or other notes in the underlying scale. Also, the chord based on the first scale degree.

Tremolo A rapid back-and-forth repetition of one or two notes that gives a sensation of trembling.

Trio sonata A work for two high-ranged instruments (such as two violins, or two oboes, or two flutes) and basso continuo.

Trio-sonata texture A texture consisting of three main voices: two in the soprano range and one in the bass (the basso continuo).

Triple meter An underlying pattern of rhythm in which each unit (measure) consists of one accented (strong) beat followed by two unaccented (weak) beats (**1**-2-3, **1**-2-3, **1**-2-3, etc.).

Tutti Italian for "all": the full ensemble (as opposed to a soloist).

Twelve-bar blues A common model for blues songs, in which each verse consists of three lines of text over twelve measures of music. Each line receives four measures in a predetermined harmonic pattern using chords built on the first, fourth, and fifth scale degrees.

Twelve-tone composition A type of serial composition in which twentieth-century composers manipulated a series ("row") consisting of all twelve notes of the chromatic scale, not repeating any one of these notes until all other eleven had been sounded, thereby effectively avoiding any sense of tonality.

Unison More than one performer playing or singing the same pitch or pitches at the same time.

Variation An altered restatement of musical idea; also used to designate a form consisting of multiple variations in succession.

Verse-chorus form One of the simplest models in popular music. The chorus contains the main idea of the song, usually incorporating the title as well. When the chorus returns, it keeps the same text and music. Verses advance the plot, using the same music each time but different texts. Verse-chorus form can use any combination of verses and choruses, although the last unit will always be a chorus.

Vibraphone   A percussion instrument similar to the xylophone, with resonators that cause the pitches to vibrate.

Virtuoso   A performer capable of playing music that is technically extremely demanding; also used as the adjective to describe such music.

Vocables   Meaningless sung syllables that take the place of song lyrics.

Voicing   The spacing of the individual notes in a chord.

Walking bass   bass line that moves at a steady pace and in largely conjunct motion.

Whole step   Two half steps. On the piano, a whole step skips exactly one key, white or black.

Whole-tone scale   A scale with only whole steps, no half steps; this eliminates any sense of a tonal center.

Wind instruments   Any instrument that produces sound by means of a player blowing air into it. Wind instruments include both woodwind and brass instruments.

Woodwind instruments   A family of wind instruments played by blowing either directly into the instrument (as with a flute) or into a single or double reed (as with an oboe, clarinet, bassoon, or saxophone).

Word painting   Music that imitates, describes, or conjures images of the text being sung.

Word-music relationships   The way a text influences our hearing of the music, and the way music affects our perception of the words.

Text Credits

CHAPTER 00
pp. 4 John Stafford Smith, "The Star-Spangled Banner", Francis Scott Key, 1814; p. 6, 8, 15 Francis Scott Key, "The Star-Spangled Banner", 1814.

CHAPTER 01
p. 27, 30 *Nine Medieval Latin Plays*, translated and edited by Peter Dronke. Copyright © 1994 Cambridge University Press. Used by permission of Cambridge University Press; p. 32 Epistle 47: To the Prelate of Mainz. From Strunk's *Source Readings in Music History*, Leo Treitler, General Editor. Copyright by Leo Treitler. Used by permission of Leo Treitler.

CHAPTER 03
p. 41 *The Daily Mail*, May 2, 2008, Dr. Alan Watkins © 2008.

CHAPTER 04
p. 45 *The Works of Francesco Landini*, edited by Leonard Ellinwood, © 1939. Translated by Mark Evan Bonds.

CHAPTER 05
p. 50 Guillaume de Machaut; p. 50 *The Art of Repetition: Machaut's Ballade 33, Nes qu'on porroit*, Guillaume de Machaut. Copyright (C) 2003 by Oxford University Press. Used by permission of Oxford University Press.

CHAPTER 06
p. 57 King James Version, Psalm 150: 3-4, *The Holy Bible*, 1665.

CHAPTER 07
p. 67 "The Cricket" by Josquin des Prez, ca. 1500. Translated by Mark Evan Bonds.

CHAPTER 08
p. 73 Thomas Weelkes, *Since Robin Hood*, 1608.

CHAPTER 09
pp. 77, 78 William Byrd, "Sing Joyfully", 1590; pp. 77–79 King James Version, Psalm 81: 3-4, *The Holy Bible*, 1665.

CHAPTER 10
p. 85 Giovanni Pierluigi da Palestrina, Pope Marcellus Mass, "Gloria", 1555; p. 86 Pope Marcellus Mass, "Gloria" by Giovanni Pierluigi da Palestrina, ca. 1555. Translated by Mark Evan Bonds.

CHAPTER 12
p. 94 Orchesography by Thoinot Arbeau, 1589, translated by Mary Stewart Evans. Copyright © 1967 by Dover Publications.

CHAPTER 13
p. 111 Act II of "Orpheus" by Claudio Monteverdi, 1607. Translated by Mark Evan Bonds.

CHAPTER 14
pp. 118, 119 Henry Purcell, "Dido and Aeneas", 1689.

CHAPTER 16
pp. 128, 130 "Revenge" by Barbara Strozzi, 1654. Modified by Mark Evan Bonds; p. 131 From "Il primo libro di madrigal", per 2–5 voci e basso continuo, op. 1 by Barbara Strozzi. Copyright © 1644 by A-R Editions.

CHAPTER 17
pp. 136, 138 Dover Miniature Music Scores: The Four Seasons, Opus 8, Nos. 1-4. "Winter", Antonio Vivaldi. Copyright © 1999 by Dover Publications, Inc. Used by permission by Dover Publications, Inc.

CHAPTER 18
p. 142 Johann Sebastian Bach, "Melody", ca., 1700.

CHAPTER 20
p. 157 The Chorale: Movement 7 from "Awake, a Voice Calls To Us" (Wachet auf, rufe uns die Stimme) by Johann Sebastian Bach; p. 158 "Awake, a Voice Calls To Us" by Johann Sebastian Bach. Translated by Mark Evan Bonds; p. 159 Letter to Georg Erdmann by Johann Sebastian Bach, 1730. Translated by Mark Evan Bonds; p. 160 Johann Sebastian Bach, "Awake, a Voice Calls To Us" (Wachet auf, rufe uns dle Stimme).

CHAPTER 21
p. 163 "Messiah" by George Frideric Handel. Modified by Mark Evan Bonds; p. 163 King James Version, Psalm 2:9, *The Holy Bible*, 1665; pp. 164, 165 King James Version, Revelation 19:6, *The Holy Bible*, 1665; p. 165 King James Version, Revelation 11:15, *The Holy Bible*, 1665; pp. 165–166 George Frideric Handel, Hallelujah chorus of Messiah; p. 167 King James Version, Psalm 2:4, *The Holy Bible*, 1665; p. 167 King James Version, Psalm 2:9, *The Holy Bible*, 1665; p. 168 King James Version, Revelation 19:6, *The Holy Bible*, 1665; p. 171 Charles Burney, An Account of the Musical Performances in Westminster-Abbey, Commemoration of Handel, 1785.

CHAPTER 22
p. 182 Jens Peter Larsen, The New Grove Haydn by Joseph Haydn. Copyright © 1982, by W. W. Norton and Co.

CHAPTER 24
p. 196 Letter to Maria Anna von Genzinger by Joseph Haydn, 1791. Translated by Mark Evan Bonds.

CHAPTER 27
pp. 224-226 "The Marriage of Figaro", Act I, Cosa sento by Wolfgang Amadeus Mozart, 1786. Translated by Mark Evan Bonds.

CHAPTER 29
pp. 235–236, 238 William Billings, "The New-England Psalm Singer", 1770; p. 240 William Billings, Wolfgang Amadeus Mozart, The Marriage of Figaro, Act I, Cosa sento, 1786.

CHAPTER 30
p. 250 Symphony no. 5 in C Minor, op. 67 by Ludwig van Beethoven, 1810.

CHAPTER 31
pp. 260, 262 Johann Wolfgang Goethe, Erlkönig in German.

CHAPTER 32
p. 270 Overture to A Midsummer Night's Dream by Felix Mendelssohn-Bartholdy, collected and edited by Rudolf Elvers, ©1968. Translated by Mark Evan Bonds.

CHAPTER 33
pp. 272-274 "Symphonie Fantastique": The symphony's programme by Hector Berlioz, 1845. Translation by Mark Evan Bonds; p. 273 The program for "Dream of a Witches' Sabbath" movement by Hector Berlioz. Copyright 1830, by Hector Berlioz. Translated by Mark Evan Bonds.

CHAPTER 34
p. 278 Henry Wadsworth Longfellow, "Song of Hiawatha", 1855.

CHAPTER 35
pp. 284-286 "Dedication" by Robert Schumann, 1840; p. 286 "Dedication" by Robert Schumann, © 1840. Translated by Mark Evan Bonds.

CHAPTER 36
p. 292 Clara Wieck Schumann, Forward, 1848; p. 292 "Forward" by Clara Wieck Schumann, 1848. Translated by Mark Evan Bonds.

CHAPTER 37
p. 297 Pianoforte-Werke, vol. 4: Balladen by Carl Mikuli, 1879. Translated by Mark Evan Bonds.

CHAPTER 38
p. 303 Louis Moreau Gottschalk, edited by Clara Gottschalk, translated by Robert E. Peterson, "Notes of a Pianist", Williams Lippincott & Wilkins, 1881; p. 304 Richard Shuckburg, "Yankee Doodle", 1780; p. 304 Daniel Decatur Emmett, Dixie, 1861; p. 307 Louis Moreau Gottschalk, edited by Clara Gottschalk, translated by Robert E. Peterson, "Notes of a Pianist", Williams Lippincott & Wilkins, 1881.

CHAPTER 40
p. 320 Giuseppe Verdi, "La Traviata", Act I. Libretto by Francesco Maria Piave. 1853; p. 320 "La Traviata", Act I. Libretto by Francesco Maria Piave, 1853. Translated by Mark Evan Bonds.

CHAPTER 41
p. 326 From "The Letters of J.R.R. Tolkien", by J.R.R. Tolkien, edited by Humphrey Carpenter and Christopher Tolkien. Copyright © 2000 by Houghton Mifflin; p. 328-330 Richard Wagner, "The Valkyrie", Act III, sc. 3, 1870.

CHAPTER 44
p. 355 Michael Beckerman, "New Worlds of Dvořák: Searching in America, Inner Life" by Antonín Dvořák. Copyright © 2003 by W. W. Norton and Co; p. 356 Antonín Dvořák, "Music in America". Harper's New Monthly Magazine. Vol. 90, no. 537, 1895.

CHAPTER 45
p. 373 Anonymous, Musical Courier (NY), HathiTrust Digital Library; p. 373 Hugo Schlemuller, Signale, Princeton University Press, 1907.

CHAPTER 46
p. 374 "Ives Studies", Published by Cambridge University Press; pp. 376, 379 "Mavericks and Other Traditions in American Music" by Charles Ives. Copyright by Yale University Press.

CHAPTER 47
p. 383 Arnold Schoenberg, "Pierrot Lunaire", Op. 21, "Columbine", 1912.

CHAPTER 48
p. 390 "Montjoie!" p. 13. by Igor Stravinsky, 1913. Translated by Mark Evan Bonds; p. 386 Igor Stravinsky, "The rite of spring", Published by Imagem.

CHAPTER 49
p. 398 "King of Ragtime: Scott Joplin and His Era" by Edward A. Berlin. Published by Oxford University Press, © 1994; p. 400 Scott Joplin, Maple Leaf Rag.

CHAPTER 50
pp. 407, 409, 410 "Terraplane Blues". Words and Music by Robert Johnson. Copyright © (1978), 1990, 1991 MPCA King of Spades (SESAC) and Claud L. Johnson (SESAC). Administered by MPCA Music, LLC. All Rights Reserved. Reprinted by permission of Hal Leonard Corporation.

CHAPTER 53
p. 434 Francis Scott Key, "The Star-Spangled Banner", 1814; p. 438 "A Composer's Search for American Music" by Judith Tick., Ruth Crawford Seeger. Published by Oxford University Press, © 1997.

CHAPTER 57
p. 458 Concerto for Orchestra, SZ 116 by Béla Bartók © Copyright 1946 by Hawkes & Son (London) Ltd. International Copyright Secured. All Rights Reserved.; p. 462 "Essays by Béla Bartók", edited by Benjamin Suchoff. Published by Faber & Faber, © 1976.

CHAPTER 58
pp. 466-468 Tonight (from West Side Story) by Leonard Bernstein and Stephen Sondheim © Copyright 1956, 1957, 1958, 1959 by Amberson Holdings LLC. Copyright Renewed. Leonard Bernstein Music Publishing Company LLC, Publisher. Boosey & Hawkes, Agent For Rental. International Copyright Secured. All Rights Reserved; p. 470 Other Entertainment: Collected Pieces by Ned Rorem. Published by by Ned Rorem, © 1996.

CHAPTER 59
p.474 Sonatas and Interludes by John Cage, Copyright © 1960, 1988 by Henmar Press Inc., C. F. Peters Corporation. Sole selling agent. Used by permission. All rights reserved; p. 477 "Conversing with Cage", 2nd edition, by John Cage, Richard Kostelanetz. Published by Routledge Publishers © 2003; p. 478 Score of the work, John Cage, 4'33". Published by C.F. Peters, © 1960.

CHAPTER 61
p. 490 Excerpt from Einstein on the Beach Spoken Text: Christopher Knowles / Samuel M. Johnson/ Lucinda Childs ©1976 Dunvagen Music Publishers Inc. Used by Permission.

CHAPTER 62
p. 494, "Jazz On A Summer's Day" by Willis Conover, Directed by Bert Stern. Documentary film of the 1958 Newport (Rhode Island) Jazz Festival, © 1959.

CHAPTER 63
p. 502, Tania León Indígena by Tania León. Copyright © 1986 New World Records. Used by permission of New World Records.

CHAPTER 64
pp. 509, 512, Corey Dargel, "On This Date Every Year.", from Words and music by Corey Dargel. Copyright © 2011 Automatic Heartbreak (ASCAP). Used by permission of Automatic Heartbreak (ASCAP).

Image Credits

CHAPTER COVER
Cover: Andy Harmer/Alamy Stock Photo; Cover: Ipopba/Fotolia

CHAPTER 00 ELEMENT
8: LGI Stock/Corbis; 9: Jan Persson/JazzSign/ Lebrecht Music & Arts Photo Library; 10: Kentucky\Cengage Learning; 18: Keystone Pictures USA/Alamy Stock Photo

CHAPTER PART 1
20: Gianni Dagli Orti/Corbis; 20: Los Angeles/The J. Paul Getty Museum; 21: AKG Images; 21: Georgios Kollidas/Alamy Stock Photo; 21: Johny007pan/ Fotolia; 22: Claudio Giovanni Colombo/Shutterstock; 22: Danielle Gali/AWL Images/Getty Images; 23: British Library/AKG Images; 23: The British Library/Bridgeman Art Library; 24: Los Angeles/The J. Paul Getty Museum

CHAPTER 1
25: Pictorial Press Ltd/Alamy Stock Photo; 25: Lucasfilm/20th Century fox/Album/SuperStock; 27: AKG Images; 29: Pictorial Press Ltd/Alamy Stock Photo; 30: Pictorial Press Ltd/Alamy Stock Photo; 31: PH College/Pearson Education, Inc.

CHAPTER 2
34: Chuck Place/Alamy Stock Photo

CHAPTER 3
38: Bibliotheque Mazarine, Paris/Archives Charmet/ Bridgeman Art Library; 39: Bibliotheque Mazarine, Paris/Archives Charmet/Bridgeman Art Library; 40: Bibliotheque Mazarine, Paris/Archives Charmet/ Bridgeman Art Library; 40: Vincenzo Pinto/AFP/ Getty Images; 41: Ed Kashi/VII/Corbis

CHAPTER 4
42: Scala/White Images/Art Resource, NY; 45: Lebrecht Music & Arts Photo Library; 45: Scala/ White Images/Art Resource, NY; 46: Scala/White Images/Art Resource, NY; 47: Scala/White Images/ Art Resource, NY

CHAPTER 5
48: AKG Images; 50: AKG Images; 51: AKG Images

CHAPTER 6
52: Oronoz/Newscom; 53: Magdalena Rehova/ Alamy Stock Photo; 54: Chris Stock/Lebrecht Music & Arts Photo Library; 54: Pavel Sazonov/ Fotolia; 55: Geoff Dann/Dorling Kindersley, Ltd.; 55: Oronoz/Newscom; 55: Philip Dowell/Dorling Kindersley, Ltd.; 56: Oronoz/Newscom; 57: Scala/ Art Resource, NY

CHAPTER PART 2
60: Abigail Lebrecht/Lebrecht Music & Arts Photo Library; 60: Photos.com/Thinkstock; 61: Abigail Lebrecht/Lebrecht Music & Arts Photo Library; 61: Akg-images/Newscom; 61: Moviestore Collection Ltd/Alamy Stock Photo; 61: National Portrait Gallery, London/SuperStock; 62: British Library/AKG Images; 62: National Gallery, London/Art Resource, NY; 63: AKG Images

CHAPTER 7
64: Abigail Lebrecht/Lebrecht Music & Arts Photo Library; 65: British Library, London, UK/Prismatic Pictures/Bridgeman Art Library; 67: Abigail Lebrecht/Lebrecht Music & Arts Photo Library; 69: Private Collection/Bridgeman Art Library

CHAPTER 8
70: Dorling Kindersley, Ltd.; 73: Central Press/ Hulton Archive/Getty Images; 73: Dorling Kindersley, Ltd.; 73: Philip Dowell/Dorling Kindersley, Ltd.; 74: CW Images/Alamy Stock Photo; 75: Musee des Beaux-Arts, Rennes, France/ Giraudon/Bridgeman Art Library

CHAPTER 9
76: Abigail Lebrecht/Lebrecht Music & Arts Photo Library; 79: Abigail Lebrecht/Lebrecht Music & Arts Photo Library; 80: Abigail Lebrecht/ Lebrecht Music & Arts Photo Library; 80: Stapleton Collection/Bridgeman Art Library; 81: Erich Auerbach/Hulton Archive/Getty Images

CHAPTER 10
82: Bettmann/Corbis; 83: Godong/Alamy Stock Photo; 86: Bettmann/Corbis; 86: Wiskerke/Alamy Stock Photo; 87: Bettmann/Corbis; 88: Gustavo tomsich/Marka/Alamy Stock Photo

CHAPTER 11
91: Michael Ochs Archives/Corbis; 93: David Gahr/ Premium Archive/Getty Images

CHAPTER 12
94: Interfoto/AKG Images; 95: Piffaro the renaissance band; 97: Interfoto/AKG Images; 98: Interfoto/AKG Images; 99: New York Public Library Digital Collection

CHAPTER PART 3
103: Christie's Images/Bridgeman Art Library; 104: Dorling Kindersley, Ltd.; 104: Lebrecht Music & Arts Photo Library; 104: VPC Travel Photo/Alamy Stock Photo; 105: Jonathan Smith/ Dorling Kindersley, Ltd.; 105: Lebrecht Music & Arts Photo Library; 106: Imagebroker/Alamy Stock Photo; 106: Jean Marie Leroy/Sygma/ Corbis; 107: Museo Civico, Turin, Italy/Bridgeman Art Library

CHAPTER 13
108: Akg-images/Newscom; 111: Akg-images/ Newscom; 112: Akg-images/Newscom; 113: Clive Barda/ArenaPAL/The Image Works

CHAPTER 14
114: Henry Purcell, c.1695 (oil on canvas), Johann Closterman (1660–1711) (after)/National Portrait Gallery, London, UK/De Agostini Picture Library/ Bridgeman Art Library; 115: Robbie Jack/Corbis; 117: Henry Purcell, c.1695 (oil on canvas), Johann Closterman (1660–1711) (after)/National Portrait Gallery, London, UK/De Agostini Picture Library/ Bridgeman Art Library; 118: Henry Purcell, c.1695 (oil on canvas), Johann Closterman (1660–1711) (after)/National Portrait Gallery, London, UK/De Agostini Picture Library/Bridgeman Art Library

CHAPTER 15
122: Nick Greaves/Alamy Stock Photo; 126: Michael Ochs Archives/Getty Images

CHAPTER 16
127: Akg-images/Newscom; 129: Clive Barda/ ArenaPal/The Image Works; 130: Akg-images/ Newscom; 131: Akg-images/Newscom; 132: RMN-Grand Palais/Art Resource, NY

CHAPTER 17
134: Lebrecht Music & Arts Photo Library; 137: Lebrecht Music & Arts Photo Library; 138: Lebrecht Music & Arts Photo Library; 139: Portal Painters/ Bridgeman Art Library; 140: Peter Chadwick/ Dorling Kindersley, Ltd.

CHAPTER 18
141: Lebrecht Music & Arts Photo Library; 143: Imagno/Hulton Archive/Getty Images; 144: Bettmann/Corbis; 145: Lebrecht Music & Arts Photo Library; 146: Lebrecht Music & Arts Photo Library; 147: Lebrecht Music & Arts Photo Library

CHAPTER 19
149: Lebrecht Music & Arts Photo Library; 150: Dea Picture Library/Getty Images; 152: Lebrecht Music & Arts Photo Library; 153: Geoff Dann/ Dorling Kindersley, Ltd.; 153: Graham Salter/ Lebrecht Music & Arts Photo Library

CHAPTER 20
155: Lebrecht Music & Arts Photo Library; 158: AKG Images; 160: Lebrecht Music & Arts Photo Library; 161: Ken Walsh/Bridgeman Art Library

CHAPTER 21
162: Album/Newscom; 167: Album/Newscom; 168: Album/Newscom; 169: Boston Globe/Getty Images; 170: Lebrecht Music & Arts Photo Library; 171: Album/Newscom

Arts Photo Library; 392–393: Jacques Sarrat/Sygma/Corbis; 394: Berko/Pix Inc./The LIFE Images Collection/Getty Images; 396: Bettmann/Corbis

CHAPTER 49

398: MPI/Archive Photos/Getty Images; 402: Richard Booth/Lebrecht Music & Arts Photo Library; 403: Dave King/Dorling Kindersley, Ltd.; 403: MPI/Archive Photos/Getty Images; 404: MPI/Archive Photos/Getty Images; 405: Library of Congress

CHAPTER 50

406: Robert Johnson Estate/Hulton Archive/Getty Images; 410: Robert Johnson Estate/Hulton Archive/Getty Images; 411: Michael Ochs Archives/Getty Images; 412: Robert Johnson Estate/Hulton Archive/Getty Images; 413: Tom Copi/Michael Ochs Archives/Getty Images

CHAPTER 51

414: Bettmann/Corbis; 418: Bettmann/Corbis; 419: AS400 DB/Corbis; 419: Dorling Kindersley, Ltd.; 422: Bettmann/Corbis; 423: Michael Ochs Archives/Getty Images; 424: Gerry Penny/Agence France Presse/Getty Images

CHAPTER 52

425: Metronome/Archive Photos/Getty Images; 428: Metronome/Archive Photos/Getty Images; 429: Geoff Dann/Dorling Kindersley, Ltd.; 429: John D. Kisch/Separate Cinema Archive/Moviepix/Getty Images; 429: Odile Noel/Lebrecht Music & Arts Photo Library; 430: Metronome/Archive Photos/Getty Images; 431: Michael Ochs Archives/Getty Images

CHAPTER 53

432: Family of Ruth Crawford Seeger; 436: Family of Ruth Crawford Seeger; 438: Family of Ruth Crawford Seeger

CHAPTER 54

439: Bettmann/Corbis; 442: Altrendo images/Getty Images; 442: Bettmann/Corbis; 443: Bettmann/Corbis; 444: James H. Pickerell/Fotolia; 445: Lebrecht Music & Arts Photo Library

CHAPTER 55

448: Hulton Archive/Getty Images; 448: Lebrecht Music & Arts Photo Library; 449: Lebrecht Music & Arts Photo Library; 450: Robert W. Kelley/Time & Life Pictures/Getty Images

CHAPTER 56

451: Pictorial Press Ltd/Alamy Stock Photo; 453: Constance Bannister Corp/Hultan Archive/Getty Images; 454: Pictorial Press Ltd/Alamy Stock Photo; 454: Rodgers & Hammerstein Organization/Lebrecht Music & Arts Photo Library; 455: Pictorial Press Ltd/Alamy Stock Photo; 456: Leonard Mccombe/The LIFE Images Collection/Getty Images

CHAPTER 57

457: Akg-images/Newscom; 460: Akg-images/Newscom; 460: Geoff Dann/Dorling Kindersley, Ltd.; 461: Akg-images/Newscom; 462: Dea/A. Dagli Orti/Getty Images

CHAPTER 58

463: Ruth Orkin/Premium Archive/Getty Images; 465: AF archive/Alamy Stock Photo; 466: Ruth Orkin/Premium Archive/Getty Images; 469: Ernst Hass/Getty Images; 469: Sputnik/Alamy Stock Photo; 470: Ruth Orkin/Premium Archive/Getty Images; 471: Andrew H. Walker/Getty Images

CHAPTER 59

472: Betty Freeman/Lebrecht Music & Arts Photo Library; 473: Sisi Burn/ArenaPal/Topham/The Image Works; 476: Betty Freeman/Lebrecht Music & Arts Photo Library; 477: Ben Martin/The LIFE Images Collection/Getty Images; 478: Allan Grant/Time Life Pictures/Getty Images

CHAPTER 60

480: Sylvain Grandadam/The Image Bank/Getty Images; 483: Kate Mount/Lebrecht Music & Arts Photo Library; 486: Haga Library/Lebrecht Music & Arts Photo Library

CHAPTER 61

487: Lynda Stone/Hulton Archive/Getty Images; 489: Lawrence K. Ho/Los Angeles Times/Getty Images; 490: Lynda Stone/Hulton Archive/Getty Images; 492: Lynda Stone/Hulton Archive/Getty Images

CHAPTER 62

494: Keystone/Hulton Archive/Getty Images; 497: Geoff Dann/Dorling Kindersley, Ltd.; 498: Keystone/Hulton Archive/Getty Images; 499: Bettmann/Corbis; 499: Don Cravens/Time Life Pictures/Getty Images; 500: Keystone/Hulton Archive/Getty Images; 500: Pictorial Press Ltd/Alamy Stock Photo

CHAPTER 63

502: Jordan Strauss/Invision/AP Images; 504: Günter Nindl/Moment/Getty Images; 505: Geoff Dann/Dorling Kindersley, Ltd.; 505: Jordan Strauss/Invision/AP Images; 506: Jordan Strauss/Invision/AP Images; 507: Bill Helsel/Alamy Stock Photo; 507: UIG/Getty Images

CHAPTER 64

508: Hiroyuki Ito/Hulton Archive/Getty Images; 509: Corey Dargel; 509: Russell Watkins/Alamy Stock Photo; 512: Hiroyuki Ito/Hulton Archive/Getty Images; 513: Hiroyuki Ito/Hulton Archive/Getty Images

CHAPTER 65

515: Steve Granitz/Wireimages/Getty Images; 516: Fotolia; 518: Steve Granitz/Wireimages/Getty Images; 519: Leungchopan/Fotolla; 520: Steve Granitz/Wireimages/Getty Images

Index